D1094463

PROTEST!

Student Activism in America

PROTEST!

Student Activism
in America

Edited by Julian Foster and Durward Long

 William Morrow & Company, Inc. New York

To Our Wives

Printed in the United States of America
by The Colonial Press Inc., Clinton, Mass.

Library of Congress Catalog Card Number 75–93053

Foreword

It is only a few years since discussions of university aims and structures were carried on virtually without reference to student power or student protest. Prior to the eruption at Berkeley in 1964, "student demonstration" conjured up pictures of post-game celebrations, or else alien happenings on some Latin American campus. But now such demonstrations are recognized as posing perhaps the most urgent and difficult of the problems facing higher education in America, and in many other parts of the world. In terming this a "problem," we do not mean to imply that protest should be seen only as a difficulty, something to be resolved, out-maneuvered or suppressed. Activist students have become the single most potent force for changing colleges and universities, and changing such complex and tradition-bound structures naturally presents problems as well as opportunities. Academic administration has never been an easy art to master, and the new incidence of protest has increased the difficulty of it immeasurably. This is largely because major protests are a new phenomenon in this society, unpredictable and little analyzed or understood.

These observations justify, we hope, the existence of this book. Much has already been written about student protest, but most of it is purely anecdotal, or speculative, or simply *ad hominem* argument and the venting of unsupported opinions. As of this writing, no one

book has appeared on student protest in America, and no broad effort
has been made to collect descriptions and analyses of protests on a
major scale. We hope that putting together such a collection has been
a useful enterprise. We are acutely aware of many shortcomings and
many aspects of the subject which we would have liked to cover, yet
could not, and we are sensitive to the risks involved in attempting to
pin down a volatile subject during a period of its rapid development
and change.

Student protest can be studied and described in almost endless
ways. In Part I, we have included various overviews of activism, including reports of the results of the only three inclusive surveys of the
incidence of protest yet undertaken. In Part II, the focus is on the
activists themselves: their backgrounds and personalities, their views
of the world and the organizations they have formed to express those
views. Part III consists of seven case studies. What happened at
Berkeley and Columbia has been described exhaustively elsewhere, so
we have selected accounts of the action at other campuses to demonstrate the variety of form and style which protest can exemplify. Part
IV represents a pulling together of particular events in some attempts
at generalization. To draw strategic lessons while the battle is still at
its height may be dangerous, but it may also be more functional than
delaying until hostilities are over. Finally, Part V consists of a variety
of interpretations and commentaries on student activism. Part VI, had
there been one, might have included some "solutions" to activism or
some solemn pronouncements on its moral character; some may expect conclusions of this kind, but we have preferred to restrict the
book to explaining how things are, leaving to others the question of
how they ought to be. The editors themselves disagree on such questions as whether obstructive or illegal actions can be legitimate within
the context of the American system, or whether the changes brought
about by activism will prove to be healthily progressive or ill-con-
sidered and wasteful. Since we cannot convince each other, we hesitate to impose opinions on the reader.

In selecting and structuring the material, we have been motivated
by several convictions, the most significant being that student activism
offers the most serious immediate challenge to higher education in
America, and perhaps the most serious challenge of this century.
Critical changes in college and university governance, in curriculum
structures, in the training, practice and evaluation of the "professariat"
and in the role of students in the teaching-learning experience—all

these have begun to develop in response to student protest, and no end to them is presently in sight. The old, reliable authority structures are collapsing, and much creative energy and humane involvement will be needed if the new order is to be an improvement on the old. If we can provoke further studies and reassessments of the crisis, or even have some impact on the ways in which the participants behave in protest situations, we shall have succeeded in some measure; if the changes are such that our book becomes outdated and obsolete, we shall be gratified.

Our most major debt is obvious, since it is to those authors whose names appear in the table of contents; almost all the contributions were written specifically for this volume. We have perhaps some stronger feelings of gratitude, mixed with remorse and guilt, toward eight other authors who cooperated with us but whose names do not appear in the table of contents, and had best not appear here. We acknowledge with appreciation our debts to a number of faculty and student colleagues who encouraged and assisted in the preparation of the volume. A special word of gratitude to Professor Robert Gutchen, Chairman of the History Department at the University of Rhode Island, who not only contributed much assistance in the early stages of planning the project, but also worked as a fellow editor until the press of administrative duties forced him to withdraw. We are heavily indebted to the American Council on Education for supporting us in 1967–68 as Fellows in Academic Administration, and thus enabling us to undertake this book. E. Joseph Shoben provided invaluable help by permitting us to mail our questionnaire under A.C.E. sponsorship. William H. Sewell and James W. Cleary (University of Wisconsin – Madison), Charles G. Bell (California State College, Fullerton), Dennis Gray (Princeton University) and Robert Phillips (Oregon State University) also aided us at various stages of the project. Special thanks are extended to Mrs. Margaret Lilly, Mrs. Marybeth Kantner, Miss Kay Davis and Miss Emily Peterson (all of the University of Wisconsin) and to Mrs. Beatrice Wiltsie, Mrs. Marianne Kreter and Mrs. Ella Mae Burke (all of the California State College, Fullerton) who patiently typed and retyped what appeared to be endless drafts of the manuscript. We are also grateful to our respective institutions for a variety of help, and to our wives, Nina Long and Beatrice Foster, for support on an even more permanent basis. Dan Johnson, of William Morrow & Company, kept the faith when it seemed to us pure madness.

Convention requires that we take responsibility for any mistakes herein, so we shall do so. But frankly, we think they are more likely to be the fault of someone else.

JULIAN FOSTER
DURWARD LONG

Contents

II. THE ACTIVISTS

III. SCENES OF CONFLICT: SEVEN CASE STUDIES

IV. NEW PATTERNS OF POWER

V. PERSPECTIVES ON PROTEST

ONE

The Conflict

1

STUDENT DISSENT
AND CONFRONTATION POLITICS

*by Clark Kerr**

FOR THE first time in American history, student dissent and the prospect of student power have become a source of nationwide interest and concern, and even, in some quarters, of fear. This is a phenomenon unique to the decade of the 1960's.

This new student orientation contrasts sharply with that of the 1950's, when the general complaint was about the silent or apathetic generation, the generation of pre-organization men. The 1930's was the only prior decade to foreshadow the shape of things to come. But then students were campus auxiliaries to the off-campus dissidents—trade unionists, socialists, communists of the Old Left, isolationists, pacifists. Today, significant numbers of university students have developed their own centers and modes of activity, their own positions of dissent on major issues and their own leadership in an effort to exert an impact on the whole society.

Students are not, of course, a class apart. Youth both reflects and responds to the society in which it grows, often in an exaggerated

* Dr. Clark Kerr, formerly President of the University of California, is presently Chairman of the Carnegie Foundation Commission on the Future of Higher Education. This chapter originally appeared in the April, 1968, issue of *Impact Magazine,* Copyright 1968 by Impact: Vanderbilt University's Weekend Symposium on Topics of National Significance, and appears here with permission.

fashion. It ostentatiously imitates, rejects, and even distorts current characteristics of American society. It is often more sensitive to new developments, and thus the new developments may first be seen dramatically through the actions of youth. As goes youth, so may the nation go—only more slowly and less completely.

In the United States in the 1930's, when the nation was concerned with depression and the threat of fascism and war, so also was youth —only more so. When the nation went to war, so did youth—only more so. When the nation returned to "normalcy" and concentrated on personal material welfare, so did youth—only more so. When "extremism" of the Right and of the Left became more prevalent in the 1960's, it did so with youth also—only more so. Each time the movement of youth was in a direction which the nation, or some influential part of it, was going. Youth has no single permanent ideological orientation. It moves with the tides of national life, and is often in the vanguard.

During the past few years in the United States, students have participated in the central concerns of national life—as illustrated particularly by the Civil Rights movement and the debate over American involvement in the war in Vietnam—more dramatically than at any other time in American history. It is this involvement of American students at the center, rather than on the periphery, of social issues that has aroused the current interest, the concern, and the fear. Many observers feel that a new force may have entered our history; that students may play a more influential political role for good or for ill than ever before.

Among the conditions which have led to increased student participation in American political life are these:

1. Mass higher education: Fifty percent of college-age students now enter college. It was more nearly five percent a half-century ago. Students are now drawn from nearly all segments of the population, not just the middle and upper classes. Altogether, almost seven million students are in colleges and universities in the United States today.

2. Concentration in the mass university: The large and often quite impersonal campus has become the standard habitat for many of these students. There is little sense of a united community of scholars. The recent neglect of the undergraduate in favor of graduate students, research, and external service intensifies the impact of greater size.

3. The permissive environment: The family has become more permissive and so has the church. The college no longer stands so much *in loco parentis*. The law gives wider latitude for freedom of action. All in all, there are fewer restrictive or explicit authorities, and the student relies more on himself or his peer group for standards of morality and behavior.

4. The student culture: By now students have been associated long enough in large, cohesive, relatively autonomous groups so that an independent student "culture" can develop with its own style of dress and behavior, its own ethics and orientation. Such a culture may be particularly strong on a large campus where there is little student contact with faculty or family. It reinforces and protects itself and may attract some non-student and faculty adherents.

Today's student culture is less concerned with internal collegiate activity and more with external political affairs, less with material advancement and more with the meaning of life. The "affluent society" finds a "countervailing power" in students who place political reform above vocational advancement, and existential experience ahead of affluence itself.

5. The explosive issues: The 1960's have seen the United States torn by some explosive issues—particularly Civil Rights and the Vietnam War. Internal justice and worldwide peace are especially compelling issues for idealistic youth, and coming together, they have abetted each other. Beyond these lie other issues of great concern: the quality of education, control of the bomb, adjustment to the computer, the quality of work and leisure in an age of automation, mass corporations, government bureaucracies, and spectator sports.

6. The anomalous dependence of students: Students are better educated than ever before; they are encouraged to question established beliefs, to seek meaningful occupations, to make fresh contributions. Yet society, through the operation of seniority in large-scale organizations, postpones longer than ever before their chance really to participate. Lacking financial independence, and with little influence at the ballot box or in the existing centers of power, they seek other means to assert their positions on the crucial issues that so deeply concern them.

It is from these conditions that the new student political tone has emerged. It is interesting to note that, although the same conditions affect most American students, only a relatively small minority has responded politically. But this small minority can set the tone of a campus and even of the national student body, just as small numbers in other generations of students have established other tones. In the 1920's it was set by the collegiate group—the athletes, the fraternity men, the Big Men On Campus. In the 1930's, the political activists challenged this collegiate culture, but on most campuses the collegiate group continued to dominate the scene. After World War II the returning GI's set the tone, and the emphasis was on the "vocational" and the "academic" cultures, to use the terminology of Berkeley sociologist Martin Trow. The new tone of "aggressive political activism" began to emerge in the late 1950's and then burst into national prominence in the 1960's.

It is always remarkable how so few can set the tone for so many. The present dominance of this group tends to mask two other relatively new and partially related segments of student life: the Bohemians who are few in number on campus because they tend to "drop out"; and the Peace Corps public-service types, who are the most neglected of all in terms of public attention but who, I believe, are potentially the most significant in the long run. The current tone of political activism is set by few students on few campuses as compared with the collegiate and GI tones of earlier years. Perhaps on only ten percent of the campuses has there been sustained political activity, and, on these campuses, the leadership group would seldom exceed one percent, the regular followers ten percent, and the occasional followers thirty percent. Nevertheless, the life of an institution and the public reaction to it are greatly affected by the tone of the dominant student minority.

The student political movement of the 1960's is unique in American history. No single element of its approach is entirely new, but the combination of these elements is new. To speak of a "movement" at all is to overstate the situation, for there are changing localities of action and vehicles of expression and tactics, and no developed ideology. But the essence of this fluid and diverse student movement is "confrontation politics"—confrontation with the power structure on Main Street, on the campus, in Washington. Civil Rights tactics have been the great source of inspiration. The general approach is to pick an issue and confront the power structure with it as dramatically as possible. The phrase "New Left" has been used to describe this whole development, but this term implies a greater connection with the "Old Left" than actually exists. Confrontation politics deserves to be looked at in its own right. The Left has joined the "popular front" rather than created it.

Among the leading characteristics of confrontation politics are the following:

1. A concern for power: The constant refrain is the acquisition of power. It is assumed that, with power, evil can be eradicated; without it, nothing can be accomplished. There is a determination to combine the new morality of the students with the old power now held by other people. The role of persuasion in getting results is discounted.

2. The university as a power base: The campus is the chosen focal point for activity. It is the place to arouse interest, recruit members, raise money, and organize action, and from which to launch attacks on chosen targets. The trade union, the political, and established voluntary organizations are no longer viewed as generally useful vehicles. Politics, in particular, takes too long and involves too much compromise.

3. Distaste for the "establishment": There is almost total rejection of the organizations that administer the status quo, which is viewed as under the domination of the "military-industrial complex." The university is seen as a handmaiden to this complex, doing its research and training its servants. Most intellectuals are regarded as having "sold out" to this establishment. Consensus politics is abhorred and so are the liberals, who are considered the worst hypocrites of all since they know what is right but do too little about it.

4. Orientation to specific issues: Ideology is suspect, and, given the variety of viewpoints among participants, potentially divisive. The choice, rather, is for individual issues, especially those with a high moral content involving equality, freedom, and peace.

5. Participatory democracy: All bureaucracies are distasteful, including their own. The ideal is the Town Meeting, or the Quaker committee meeting. Maximum opportunity should be given for a sense of participation, even if it is only by a vote at a mass meeting. Legitimacy depends on group participation and ratification—not on passive acquiescence to the decisions of a central body.

6. Tactics for the short run: Students of earlier generations have used the petition, the picket line, and the strike to call public attention to their views. The new student generation has added new weapons: the sit-in, the teach-in, the mill-in, the mass demonstration

or march covered by the press and TV. Students can communicate with each other quickly across the nation. They can travel readily. They can develop and use a loose network of friendships and contacts. Thus they can concentrate their talents and their attention at selected pressure points. The methods are all aimed at quick results or quick impact. The preparation of big programs, the conduct of prolonged negotiations, the organization of an extensive educational program, the establishment of an organization to exert constant pressure—all these are avoided. The emphasis is on the event and not the process.

7. The importance of style: The new reformation starts by nailing bold theses to the classroom door—with flash bulbs and cameras ready to record the scene. Demands are made suddenly, dramatically, publicly. The appeal is directly to the mass public, and so it is necessary to get the attention of the press and TV. Violation of rules and the law is one quick way of doing this. The student activist is the new PR expert.

8. Allies and allied enemies: The new activists can look for support within the campus from the few Bohemians and often from the Peace Corps and academic types as well; and outside the campus, from the Old and New Left, the New Theologists, and the remaining minorities. Essentially, however, they stand by themselves, asking for little help, as the slogan "don't trust anyone over 30" implies. But "student power" may be used by others. The Left embraces it as evidence that the revolution might really yet come. The Right takes it as a target to energize support.

These characteristics of confrontation politics are exhibited in varying degrees by the diverse groups that make up the aggregate of student political activism today. The activists might be divided very roughly into three groups:

1. The issue-by-issue protesters: These students accept the existing system but seek to correct its deficiencies of operation at specific points, sometimes through orderly protest, sometimes through stronger confrontation tactics.

2. The liberal-radicals: These students feel that the only answer to specific problems is a restructuring of the entire society along different lines, but they work toward this goal mainly through the traditional "liberal" techniques of organization, discussion, and persuasion rather than via more violent tactics. They are radical as to ends but mostly liberal as to means.

3. The radical-radicals: These students comprise the most dissident group on the student scene today. They believe they can eradicate current evils only by restructuring the entire society, and they are willing to use violent tactics if necessary to reach this goal. Thus they are radical as to both ends and means.

Confrontation politics has been the particular method of the first and third of these groups—the issue-by-issue protesters and the radical-radicals—with support from the second group often reluctantly given because of doubts about the effectiveness of the technique.

These groups have met with some limited success in the short run and in specific areas. The ultimate test of confrontation politics, however, is effectiveness in the long run and across broad areas of society. What are the future directions and prospects for the student as dissenter and activist?

Two conclusions appear inescapable. First, student power in some form is here to stay. The sheer numbers of students today and their concentration in large masses on huge campuses inevitably make them a new power group to be reckoned with by the rest of society. They are better educated and more politically sophisticated than ever before; they have many real concerns; and they can make some valuable contributions to society as a whole.

My second conclusion, however, is that students cannot be permanently effective as a power group until and unless they adopt new tactics, build lasting organizations, accept the framework of the law, and work themselves into the mechanisms of decision-making that mark our pluralistic society. Confrontation may be effective in some areas, and in the short run. But it is a specifically, not a universally, useful weapon. It works better with the easily accessible local merchant or campus administrator than with a state legislature or with Congress. It can eliminate a particular practice or rule, but it cannot end poverty or a war. It builds up such massive opposition that it becomes less and less effective. For the accomplishment of long-term goals, continuing organization and negotiation and accumulation of support and allies are required. Like the nation's labor unions, the students will become most effective when they become a recognized part of the decision-making process.

Student activism has now reached a major divide. It can move directly toward more constructive and, in the end, more effective levels. On the other hand, it can move, and may now be moving, toward a period of greater disruption which will delay considerably the eventually more effective stage of student power. The chief lever moving student dissent toward more violent tactics is frustration. Students want action now. They are apt to feel that solutions to urgent problems have been already far too long delayed, and that delay, in accord with Parkinson's new law, is the most deadly form of denial. If they meet constantly with frustration, the answer for some of them is to escalate the tactics. If these ultimately involve the use of force, then force is excused on the grounds that the higher values of the goals override the normal limitations on the means. To frustration is added the design of the ideologically motivated; and intellectual absolutism is often closely associated with physical authoritarianism.

This escalation is occurring in some quarters, and may even accelerate as the moderating influences drop away from the struggle. The dependence upon force separates the moderates and liberals and even the liberal-radicals from the radical-radicals, and most of the faculty from the most activist student groups. Thus it appears possible that student activism may go through an even more violent stage before it becomes so counter-productive that the majority of student dissenters will seek new and more constructive leadership that turns its back always on force and usually on confrontation but never on dissent.

Faculty members and university administrators—and, indeed, all of society—can ease this difficult stage by listening to what the students have to say, by moving promptly to take corrective actions and make adjustments in the face of legitimate student demands, by undertaking in good faith the academic and other reforms that deeply concern the students—in short, by doing whatever is reasonably possible to break the cycle of frustration and escalation of tactics. But consultation with students is not enough. More importantly, the students deserve a fair chance to participate appropriately in the making of rules and decisions, rather than being relegated to the position of dissenting to rules already enacted and decisions already proclaimed.

The new students have a role to play, for better or for worse, in the new age in the United States. This is one of the new realities that neither the campus nor society can escape.

2

STUDENT ACTIVISM IN THE SIXTIES

by Frederick W. Obear*

IT IS important to consider the historical development of student activism during the sixties which produced the conditions of life, the patterns of protest, and the various groups of activists described by Dr. Kerr in the preceding chapter. Indeed, selected quotations may seem to indicate that the condition is not new.

Indulged, petted, and uncontrolled at home, allowed to trample upon all laws, human and divine, at the preparatory school . . . [the American student] comes to college, but too often with an undisciplined mind, and an uncultivated heart, yet with exalted ideas of personal dignity, and a scowling contempt for lawful authority and wholesome restraint. How is he to be controlled? [1]

Although these reflections and the closing question have a decidedly modern ring, they were made by a professor at Davidson College over one hundred years ago. A similar ageless passage referring to young people comes from Aristotle:

* Dr. Frederick W. Obear received his doctorate in Chemistry and is Provost of Oakland University at Rochester, Michigan. This paper was written in the spring of 1968 and, with the author's approval, was updated by the editors prior to going to press.

They are high-minded, for they have not yet been humbled by life nor have they experienced the force of necessity; further, there is high-mindedness in thinking oneself worthy of great things, a feeling which belongs to one who is full of hope.

In their actions, they prefer the noble to the useful; their life is guided by their character rather than by calculation, for the latter aims at the useful, virtue at the noble. . . . All their errors are due to excess and vehemence . . . for they do everything to excess, love, hate, and everything else.[2]

Idealism is no more a new characteristic of youth than student activism is a new phenomenon on the American campus scene. When viewed, however, against the immediate backdrop of the so-called Silent Generation, mass student activism and marked changes in tactics in the sixties do represent a startling change of pace. These dramatic differences were unique developments of the sixties.

Prior to the twentieth century, isolated events ranging from the Saint Scholastica's Day riot at Oxford in 1354 to the sacking of Princeton in 1817 can be cited as examples of mass student activities. The earliest revolt at Harvard was recorded in 1766. John Brubacher and Willis Rudy have noted that

anyone who studies the history of American undergraduate life from the first colonial colleges to the Civil War will find ample evidence . . . [that] this was a period when constant warfare raged between faculty and students, when college government at best was nothing but a paternal despotism, when the most outrageous pranks and disturbances were provoked by undisciplined and incredibly bold young men. It was pre-eminently a period of rowdies, riots, and rebellions.[3]

They further observed that

the most dramatic response of the pre-Civil War college student to the disciplinary system which ruled him was violent and open rebellion. Nearly every college experienced student rebellions or riots, some more serious than others. In certain cases, they eventuated in broken windows or cracked furniture; in others, they resulted in deaths. All involved some kind of collective action, either of a class or of a whole student body. These outbursts could be found in all sections of the country, at state universities and denominational colleges, at "godless" Harvard and Virginia and at pious Yale and Princeton. Everywhere the atmosphere was like that of a revolutionary brawl, or a violent modern strike.[4]

It was not until 1930, however, that student activism began to be linked with national politics. The Depression introduced a measure of seriousness into student disorders, and this was soon reenforced by the worsening international situation. The City College of New York became the center of student protest. Strikes were called to oppose the breakdown of disarmament and the approach of war.[5] At the end of World War II, however, the returning veterans brought a new and businesslike atmosphere to American campuses. Older than the normal college student, they were interested in obtaining their educational credentials, and neither political protest nor traditional revelry had much appeal. Throughout the fifties, college students remained quiet—too quiet for many observers. In 1957, one writer deplored the "dull conformity" among students and lamented "the day of student action, of petitions, eager discussions and picket lines is long gone." [6] In that same year, Philip Jacob characterized American students as being "gloriously contented" and "unabashedly self-centered" and stated that they "do not intend to crusade for non-discrimination, merely to accept it as it comes. . . ." He observed further that students are

dutifully responsive towards government. They expect to obey its laws, pay its taxes, serve in its armed forces—without complaint but without enthusiasm. They will discharge the obligations demanded of them though they will not voluntarily contribute to the public welfare. Nor do they particularly desire an influential voice in public policy. Except for the ritual of voting, they are content to abdicate the citizen's role in the political process and to leave to others the effective power of governmental decision. They are politically irresponsible, and often politically illiterate as well.[7]

In 1959, Louis E. Reik suggested that "Students . . . have too much to lose to run the risk of open rebellion during their college days," [8] while Clark Kerr wrote that "The employers will love this generation, they are not going to press many grievances. . . . They are going to be easy to handle. There aren't going to be any riots."

Meanwhile, the college population in other parts of the world was deeply involved in politics. Latin American students, following a long tradition of political activism, played significant roles in bringing down such dictators as Perón (Argentina, 1955) and Pérez Jiménez (Venezuela, 1958). Students were prominent in the abortive uprisings against the Communist puppet regimes in Hungary, Poland and East Germany. In 1960, Japanese students brought down the government with their massive riots against the Security Treaty with the U.S., and students had a considerable part in overthrowing the dictatorships of Rhee (Korea) and Mendes (Turkey). In the United States, one frustrated activist complained that

. . . to attain self-discovery, we must dissent, disaffiliate ourselves from all the clichéd and stereotyped burdens the educated and the non-educated would impose; dissent from the dogma of the politician, the business man, the critic and the truck driver. If our "revolt" appears mild, it is because we have not found anything to promote. . . .9

In 1960 this vacuum was suddenly filled. On February 1, four black students from North Carolina Agricultural and Technical College sat in at a segregated lunch counter in Greensboro, and were arrested for trespassing. Within a month, their lead had been followed by students from predominantly black colleges and high schools in the upper South and even in Alabama; the sit-in, accompanied by marches, picketing and boycotts of various kinds, became the characteristic tactic of the new movement for integration. More than 300 students were arrested at Southern sit-ins the first month of the new movement. In the North, picket lines appeared in front of department stores which practiced segregation in the South. The struggle for civil rights became the first focus of activism in the sixties. It remained the most significant protest issue for the next four years, but events at Greensboro seemed to galvanize a variety of other protests into being.

In February, a hundred students marched to San Quentin to protest (unsuccessfully) the execution of Caryl Chessman. In May, thousands of protesters, mainly from Berkeley and San Francisco State, picketed the HUAC hearings in San Francisco. Sixty-eight were arrested, and many more got their first taste of physical combat with authority when police cleared the steps of City Hall with the aid of fire hoses. At Harvard, a protest walk against this country's nuclear arms policy was staged by a thousand students favoring unilateral disarmament. Late in the summer, the National Student Association articulated what action had demonstrated the previous spring, insisting that a student "must be willing to confront crucial issues of public policy that affect him beyond the classroom and that determine the source of his society." The decades of non-involvement were over; the election of John Kennedy brought fresh youth and vigor to the Presidency, and much of his rhetoric and some of his actions seemed to reflect the new mood.

During 1960–61, radical political parties appeared on a variety of campuses: VOICE at Michigan and PILOT at Chicago joined the pioneering SLATE at Berkeley. *Time* reported that 315 new political groups were formed on 353 campuses in 1961. On the national scene, Students for a Democratic Society, the Du Bois Clubs and the Young Americans for Freedom were formed, but were overshadowed by the Student Nonviolent Coordinating Committee, which almost immediately assumed a leading role in the South. New radical magazines began publication on various campuses: *New University Thought* (Chicago), *Studies on the Left* (Wisconsin), *Advance* (Harvard), *The Activist* (Oberlin), *Alternatives* (Illinois) and *New Freedom* (Cornell). By 1962, 27 radical journals had appeared, originating on 17 different campuses; their existence was in some cases fleeting or erratic, but the surge of interest in the "new politics" was very clear. An anti-war "teach-in" was planned by Cornell faculty members, though their efforts eventually subsided into a lecture series. Yet in spite of this variety of activities and issues, 1961 must be seen primarily as the year during which students became deeply involved in positive action on behalf of the Negro. The Southern Regional Council reported that

The movement, first begun as a protest against segregated lunchcounter facilities, has, in the year and a half, embraced parks, swimming pools, theatres, restaurants, churches, interstate transportation, libraries, museums, art galleries, laundromats, employment, beaches, and courtrooms.

In 1961, *The Nation* had given its survey of campus thought the title "Rebels with a Hundred Causes." The following year, however, it was able to call a similar survey "Integration and Survival." With the February march on the Pentagon in which about 5,000 students participated, "peace" became firmly established alongside civil rights as a major issue in student protest. The year 1962 saw the first major demonstration on a campus in the Deep South when 250 Negro students were arrested at Southern University. More than a thousand blacks and whites were arrested in Albany, Georgia, while a demonstration of another kind failed to prevent the enrollment of James

Meredith at the University of Mississippi. A sit-in at the University of Chicago raised an issue which was to become of increasing importance when it challenged the propriety of certain of the university's auxiliary activities; the specific demand was for integration of apartment buildings owned by the university.

During the early sixties, campus conservatism also enjoyed a brief boom. The Young Americans for Freedom achieved some initial successes, and the candidacy of Barry Goldwater later brought temporary strength and fleeting encouragement to their ranks. However, David Riesman could remark in 1963 that "campus conservatives must now be much more vocal and better organized to expound their views because they are increasingly in a minority." [10] Lipset and Altbach have concluded that

The conservative student organizations, despite their impressive financial and organizational backing, have not been notably successful in building a movement which has much commitment from its membership, nor have they made any real impact on the campus.[11]

During the Berkeley fracas, some conservative groups joined the Free Speech Movement to press their demands, but by 1968–69 YAF was offered a different appeal, as a rallying-point for the anti-protester.

The early part of the sixties was thus sharply distinguished from the fifties in the degree of activism; it was no longer possible to speak of the Silent Generation. Yet the activists, while conspicuous, were a very small proportion of the total population, and on the vast majority of campuses, they were barely in evidence. In 1963, Edward Eddy could still voice a complaint reminiscent of the fifties. Suggesting that youth was beginning to retreat behind excellence, he observed that "on too many campuses, intellectualism emerges as an insidious form of a new vogue in collegiate conformity. The result, on the part of students, is a steady diet of gruel and grades." [12] According to *U.S. News & World Report* "College officials who used to worry because students didn't study hard enough now worry that they may be studying too hard." [13] David B. Truman, then Dean of Columbia College, expressed the sentiments of many of his colleagues: ". . . students today are more studious and more serious about intellectual interests." [14] *Time* described the campus atmosphere as one of "utter classroom sobriety relieved by after-hours explosion." [15]

This sweeping categorization of the campus scene may well have been an exaggeration but some relief was very much in evidence during the "Intercollegiate Spring Riot Season" in 1963 on the campuses of Princeton, Yale and Brown Universities. To many faculty and administrators, the new activism was entirely admirable, even if it was an occasional source of embarrassment when dealing with conservative donors or trustees. Protest was aimed at integration, an ideal close to the hearts of Northern academic liberals, and to a lesser extent at peace, a barely less acceptable goal. More important, perhaps, protest during this time was generally staged off-campus, primarily in the Southern states. The only governments challenged were Southern segregationist ones; these regimes, in the minds of most Northern liberals, deserved no support. In the North, during 1963 and early 1964, students became involved on a growing scale in such community projects as the tutoring of culturally disadvantaged children, while many of the churches increasingly joined in similar projects. Throughout Kennedy's presidency and the first year of the Johnson era, there was little of the violent criticism of established institutions or the hostility towards the federal government which later came to characterize many protest movements. *Life* reflected the general liberal satisfaction with developments when it concluded a survey of protest by observing: "Given the choice we'll take noisy wrong-headedness before gray-flannel silence, any day."

Yet there were those who saw that eventually the students who were crusading for such worthy liberal causes would turn their attentions to conditions on the campuses themselves. In 1963, Clark Kerr observed in his Godkin Lectures that "the undergraduate students are restless. Recent changes in the American university have done them little good . . . lack of faculty concern for teaching, endless rules and requirements, and impersonality are the inciting causes." Ironically, it was during the same lectures that Kerr coined the term "multiversity," which came to symbolize the bigness which some students found so repellent. The next year, Mario Savio was to refer to Kerr's multiversity as "a knowledge factory" where "nobody knows my name," and to conclude that "the operation of the machine becomes so odious, you've got to make it stop."

The Free Speech Movement (FSM) started at Berkeley as a protest against new directives designed to prohibit the use of a 26-foot strip of university property for "on-campus solicitation of funds and planning and recruitment of off-campus social and political action." [16]

Within three months, the protest movement which succeeded in promoting boycotts of classes and a sit-in at the university's administration building, gradually expanded its demands to insist on "the elimination of all university restrictions of political activity on campus." [17]
The sit-in at Sproul Hall tied up that building for 15 hours and resulted
in the arrest of about eight hundred students; the subsequent strike
almost crippled the university with the controversy centering on
free speech. The basic policy at issue was stated in a Dean of Students
publication: "University facilities may not be used to support or advocate off-campus political or social action." The policy was interpreted
by the activists to mean a ban on free speech, and they maintained
that the implications of the ban clearly opposed the accepted purpose
of educational institutions.

An analysis by Philip Selznick is particularly helpful in understanding the circumstances.

Although the general ban on advocacy was swiftly eroded, a sticky
problem remained. On November 20 the Regents officially accepted the
idea that political activity, including recruitment and fund-raising, could
be conducted on campus. However, they included the proviso that such
activity must be "for lawful off-campus action, not for unlawful off-
campus action." Thus free speech was still at issue, for the university apparently reserved the right to regulate speech or organization that in its
judgment was directed to illegal off-campus action. Under ordinary circumstances, this might not have been a fighting issue. But civil rights-
conscious students saw a direct threat to the possibility of organizing on
the campus "direct action" in the community. At the same time, the energy and commitment that had already won large gains against the policy
of September were still available for the achievement of unabridged freedom of speech.[18]

On December 8, the Berkeley Academic Senate passed resolutions
supporting much of the FSM position. The Regents voted to accept
some of these demands while Chancellor Strong resigned under the
pressure. By the end of 1964, the students at Berkeley had proved
that they had the power to initiate change, and that their direct action
techniques would work outside the South. To some, the possibilities
seemed limitless.

Meanwhile, the war in Vietnam was taking more and more U.S.
servicemen, and protest against it mounted proportionately. In 1964,
students at Haverford College organized the first drive to collect medi-

cal supplies for the Vietcong. The following year 16 draft-deferred University of Michigan students took part in a sit-in at the Ann Arbor draft board. Also at the University of Michigan, a faculty protest was converted from the threatened strike in opposition to the war in Vietnam into the country's first teach-in. On May 15 of that year, there was another teach-in lasting more than 15 hours in Washington which thrust scholars from all over the nation into the political arena to discuss the Vietnam issue. Televised in part by the three major networks and carried completely by one educational TV channel, the debate generated additional student support for involvement. On October 15 and 16, a march on Washington was joined by approximately 50,000 students protesting American intervention in Vietnam. Another march sponsored by SANE drew 40,000 people in December. Protests on such a scale were unprecedented.

Another element was added to the situation when protests concerning on-campus grievances multiplied. At Tufts University, students carrying signs proclaiming that "Education Comes First" picketed to support reinstatement of a discharged philosophy professor and to oppose the policy of "publish or perish." Similar cases were fought by students at Yale, Brooklyn College, and elsewhere. A major confrontation over free speech occurred at Ohio State University. Outside the chancellor's office at the University of Kansas, students joined a sit-in protesting segregation in that university's fraternities and sororities. Students at the University of Washington demonstrated against compulsory membership in the student association. Curfew hours for women's dormitories occupied activists at the University of Chicago. At the St. John's University in Jamaica, New York, mass demonstrations were held by students who supported faculty striking for salary increases and greater academic freedom. A survey of the year's activities found that while civil rights issues still outdistanced all others as a cause of campus protest, such mundane matters as dormitory regulations, food services and dress regulations were becoming popular issues on many campuses. College administrators were replacing Southern sheriffs as the targets of student wrath.

While in many places, protest concerning on-campus issues simply sought remedies for grievances, an increasing number of confrontations were based on the principle that students should govern their own affairs, and should participate in making the policies of the institution. The demand for student power was greeted with mixed feelings by many in the academic community. Kingman Brewster, President of

Yale, probably spoke for many of the more liberal administrators when he commented that

> There are some who think that it is a question of almost having the students take over the management of educational enterprises, which is absurd. But it is just as absurd to say the students should be ignored.

Beginning in 1964, a great number of colleges and universities moved to place students on faculty and administrative committees.

Yet, not only on-campus issues were protested on campus. More and more, university administrators found themselves held responsible for complicity with the hated war in Vietnam. Sit-in protests over draft deferment testing procedures and university involvement with Selective Service were held at CCNY, Wisconsin, Stanford among others. Four hundred students at the University of Chicago demonstrated their dissatisfaction with the use of class rankings to determine deferment by occupying the administration building for 36 hours. At Columbia, about a thousand students engaged in civil war when protesters blocked an ROTC review. A new form of protest, the walk-out, also became popular in 1966. Approximately 300 Berkeley students walked out of a convocation at which Arthur Goldberg, then U.S. Ambassador to the United Nations, received an honorary degree. Similar walk-outs protested appearances of Secretary of Defense Robert McNamara at Amherst and NYU. In March, Selective Service Director Lewis Hershey was jeered off a stage at Howard University. These and other such activities led most cabinet officers to eschew campus appearances for the future.

Meanwhile, recruiters were with increasing frequency coming to be regarded as symbols of the war. Demonstrations focused on representatives of the armed services, the CIA and Dow Chemical Company, the latter corporation being held responsible for its production of napalm. Physical obstruction of recruiters occurred at Brown, Williams, Stanford, Brooklyn, Harvard, Pennsylvania and Oberlin, and at the state universities of Wisconsin, Colorado and Illinois during 1967–68; less violent demonstrations erupted in many other places. Involvement in war-related research became another focus of attack; the Institute of Defense Analyses, a consortium of twelve major universities which handled much classified work, was attacked with skill and persistence at Chicago, Princeton and Columbia, and as a result was forced to divorce itself from its institutional sponsors. These developments, it was argued, made it increasingly difficult for colleges and universities to retain the traditional political neutrality which most of them seek.

In November, 1967, the National Students Association sponsored a conference on student power and announced plans to establish a "nationwide legal network to supply attorneys and advice to students who battle with college administrators." [19] Ed Schwartz, the president of that previously less than radical organization, told 350 delegates to the meeting, "Test your rights in the courts. The climate is receptive." Early in December, court action, sought by the NSA against the Selective Service System for reclassifying college students demonstrating against military recruiters or local draft boards, was announced. By 1968, there was a definite increase in the number of students taking to the civil courts to sue universities over rules and disciplinary actions. Cornell President James Perkins viewed "with some alarm the . . . rash of court cases challenging decisions in areas that were once considered the educational world's peculiar province." "The student," he observed further, ". . . is moving away from the general protection of the academic community into the general domain of civil law." [20]

Perkins' concerns about the consequences of activism were, by the late sixties, coming to be widely shared. By 1965, Fred Hechinger remarked that "the current commencement speaker's concern is no longer how to arouse [students] from their lethargy, but rather how to prevent their new enthusiasms from getting out of hand." Such a contrast was exemplified by Princeton's president, Robert Goheen. In 1960 he had advised the in-coming freshmen to cultivate "a substantial discontent" in order that they might "seek a possible better instead of being content with an actual worse." [21] Seven years later, his emphasis was very different:

What of the role of students? Over against the claims of the university as a place for enquiry, reflection, and the long view, there sound insistent calls for immediate action, for involvement, for participation. Some argue that the problems facing the nation are so pressing that the young man's obligation to engage himself in their solution overrides his obligation to his university studies—or any good these studies can help him do later on. Well, the premise—that urgent and massive problems confront us— cannot be denied. . . . But from this premise it does not necessarily follow that you, or other students, should divert a *major* part of your limited time and energy from study to action at this stage of your lives. There is sense behind the old adage about there being appropriate times and seasons.[22]

Such administrative caution was strongly reenforced by events at Columbia in the spring of 1968. What started as a peaceful protest over the construction of a controversial gym and the institution's affiliation with the Institute of Defense Analyses ended in the suspension of classes for two weeks, the arrest of more than 600 persons, damage to five student-seized buildings, and the resignation of some of the university's top administrators. Underlying the protest was a hostility towards two long-standing traits of Columbia's administration: an apparent lack of concern with student or faculty wishes, and disinterest in the fate of the surrounding community. Students occupied the office of President Kirk for more than a week and held Dean Coleman in his office for twenty-four hours. After several days of unrest, however, Columbia's tenured faculty, by a vote of 466 to 40, condemned the students' occupation of the buildings and the accompanying disruption of the campus, and urged that the issues be resolved by a tripartite committee of students, faculty, and administrators. After the sit-in had lasted for a week, President Kirk called city police onto the campus to clear out the protesters. Numerous injuries and arrests resulted from the violent clashes between the students and the police. The "Big Bust" did not, however, put an end to the disturbances on the campus, and many courses had to be abandoned and final examinations canceled. In the aftermath, Grayson Kirk resigned and David Truman, his vice president and probable successor, went with him.

The escalation of student unrest in the late sixties was not confined to American campuses. The near assassination of a radical student leader in Germany brought widespread disorders there. Strikes in Italy closed down several campuses. A student uprising in Paris during the spring of 1968 threatened the government of President De Gaulle. Student disturbances in Mexico City resulted in several casualties, while the University of Tokyo was closed for much of 1968–69 by a massive student sit-in, eventually routed by the army. A modest form of student radicalism appeared in authoritarian Spain, while in Czechoslovakia students played a leading role in offering resistance to the Russian reoccupation of their country.

Explanation of such a worldwide phenomenon is not easy. However, one common factor rather generally assumed by those not unfriendly to student protest was that the quality of administration in the institutions hit by the severest protest was traditional and unresponsive. University education in Europe is characterized by extreme remoteness of faculty from students; in no country is the demand for a "relevant" education taken even with the seriousness which it commands in the United States. The administrations of Chancellor Strong at Berkeley and President Kirk at Columbia were not considered to be in close touch with student sentiments, and many alleged that neither displayed much agility when his respective crisis began to develop. Thus in mid-1968 it was still possible to hold that while minor conflicts could take place on any campus, a sympathetic and responsive administration could always head off a major and prolonged confrontation; those administrators who met the full blast of student discontent were, so this theory held, those who had in some way invited trouble.

This theory had sustained some damage when, in 1967, William Sewell, Chancellor of the University of Wisconsin and reputedly a sympathizer with the "New Left," found himself held responsible for a bloody battle between students occupying the placement offices and the Madison police, who had been called to eject them. In the California State College system, administrators of what were generally regarded as the most liberal campuses encountered the most trouble. President Robert Clark at San Jose managed to ride out a year which included cancellation of a football game in face of a threat to burn the stadium, and numerous other near-violent confrontations. At San Francisco, however, the conciliatory posture of President John Summerskill proved insufficient to pacify aggressive black and third world militants, and his equally liberal successor, Robert Smith, caught between the demands of the trustees on the one hand and striking activists on the other, resigned after a few months. These and many other troubles of liberal responsive institutions and administrators brought a reappraisal of the theory that rigid and unresponsive stances are more likely to prompt forceful, obstructive protest.

Black protest dominated the 1968–69 campus scene. The creation of departments of ethnic studies became the principal demand, and attitudes to this educational experiment became the touchstone of racism. Opposition, regardless of the reasons for it, tended to be met with uncompromising militancy. A student strike lasted four and a half months at San Francisco State; less prolonged disturbances disrupted the operation of other campuses. Bombings became routine at San Francisco and at Berkeley, presidents encountered physical violence or the threat of it at San Fernando State and the College of San Mateo, and considerable and deliberate damage was done by sitters-in at Berkeley, Wisconsin State at Oshkosh, and elsewhere. Two Black Panthers were killed on the UCLA campus by political rivals, and the President of Swarthmore died of a heart attack while black students were occupying the administration building to press their demands. In many instances, white radicals matched or outdid black and brown ones in their violence and their denunciation of compromise. Colleges and universities thus became the place where a new and less submissive generation of ethnic minorities vented its rage at white-dominated society. While this rage might certainly be justified in general terms, by 1969, it was becoming unclear whether there was any constructive course which could be followed which would meet black complaints. Increasingly, the tendency was to counter force with force: the Tac Squad at San Francisco State, the highway patrol at U.C. Berkeley, and the National Guard at the University of Wisconsin and at Duke.

Thus evolution of student protest during the decade of the sixties was extremely rapid. Beginning with an inheritance of quietism, students came awake politically to fight segregation and racial injustice in the South. The escalation of the war in Vietnam had the effect of broadening their concern; the resultant draft calls added self-interested motives for political action to the existing idealism. Events at Berkeley showed how activist techniques could be applied to campus reform. The three strands, race relations, peace and educational reform, became gradually fused together in a movement based largely on the campuses: a movement which has come to be called the New Left.

When Martin Luther King claimed that peace must also be a concern of civil rights workers, he was criticized by many who thought that the cause of liberalized race relations would be hurt by such an ideological broadening. Such criticism seems already outdated. Radicalism, which in 1960 connoted only fringe groups on the margins of American political life, has become a real force. While the New Left is certainly not in a majority among the students at any college or university, its members have been able to mobilize broad support on certain issues.

Attempts at employing normal political processes have attained some successes for the radical movement. Yet the war on poverty can hardly be regarded as a triumph, civil rights bills and the implementation of *Brown v. Board of Education* hardly seem to have touched the core of black problems, and the McCarthy movement has failed to end the war in Vietnam. The development of "Black Power" and "resistance" ideologies has further worked against such efforts. More militant tactics have at least made colleges and universities reform-minded, although the dimensions of the changes involved are still uncertain. For those hostile to "the Establishment," the campus has thus emerged as the one place where real progress seems possible. It therefore appears unlikely that the pressure on institutions of higher learning will abate in the near future.

[1] Frederick Rudolph, *The American College and University: A History* (New York: Alfred A. Knopf, 1962), p. 105.

[2] Aristotle, *The "Art" of Rhetoric,* trans. J. H. Freese (London: William Heinemann Ltd., 1959), pp. 249–250.

[3] John S. Brubacher and Willis Rudy, *Higher Education in Transition* (New York: Harper & Row, 1958), p. 50.

[4] *Ibid.*, p. 53.

[5] Max Heirich and Sam Kaplan, "Yesterday's Discord," in Seymour M. Lipset and Sheldon S. Wolin (eds.), *The Berkeley Student Revolt* (New York: Doubleday and Company, Inc., 1965), pp. 10–11.

[6] Charles Shapiro, "The Careful Young Men," *The Nation,* March 9, 1957, p. 212.

[7] Philip E. Jacob, *Changing Values in College* (New York: Harper and Brothers, 1957), pp. 1–3.

[8] Louis E. Reik, "War of the Generations," *The Nation,* May 16, 1959, p. 451.

[9] Stanley Kunitz, "The Careful Young Men: Queens College," *The Nation,* March 9, 1957, p. 201.

[10] Dave McNeely, " 'A Wide Variety,' " *The New York Times Magazine,* November 17, 1963, p. 128.

[11] Seymour M. Lipset and Philip G. Altbach, "Student Politics and Higher Education in the United States," in Seymour M. Lipset (ed.), *Student Politics* (New York: Basic Books, 1967), p. 207.

[12] Edward D. Eddy, "Distortions in the Pursuit of Excellence," an address, May 2, 1963.

[13] *U.S. News & World Report,* February 17, 1964, p. 66.

[14] *Ibid.*, p. 67.

[15] *Time,* November 22, 1963, p. 44.

[16] Seymour M. Lipset and Sheldon S. Wolin (eds.), *op. cit.,* p. 109.

[17] *Ibid.*, p. 341.

[18] Philip Selznick, "Berkeley," *Commentary,* March, 1965, pp. 80–81.

[19] *The Chronicle of Higher Education,* Vol. 11, No. 6 (November 22, 1967), p. 1.

[20] *The Wall Street Journal,* March 7, 1968, p. 10.

[21] Robert F. Goheen, "A Substantial Discontent," *Vital Speeches,* October 15, 1960, pp. 6–8.

[22] Robert F. Goheen, "Study, Action, and the Long View," an address, September 17, 1967.

3

STUDENT PROTEST:
WHAT IS KNOWN, WHAT IS SAID

by Julian Foster

ONE CANNOT know "the truth" about student protest—or, indeed, about any other complex subject. As in the fable of the blind men and the elephant, each of us is limited to that part of the whole which he has experienced. The sum of human knowledge on any topic is generally the sum of what has been written about it, since only what is written is generally available. In this chapter, an attempt is made to outline what is known so far about student protest in America, and thus to provide some sort of conceptual framework for the chapters which follow.

Bibliographic chapters which contain a mass of authors and titles, publishers and dates, *ibid.*'s and *op. cit.*'s are seldom distinguished for their charm. We have tried to confine these details to the bibliography at the end of this chapter, and to focus instead on the variety of methodological approaches which have been used and on the uneven and sometimes chaotic way in which knowledge is accumulated. Each reference letter relates to works of a particular kind which are grouped together in the bibliography. In that listing, we have attempted to include most of the significant work which has been done on student protest in America, at the cost of excluding related material on such subjects as protest in general, student behavior in general, and the problems of higher education which may lead to protest. We have also excluded materials which are unlikely to be available, such as dissertations, mimeographed publications, and the more ephemeral periodicals of the New Left. For readers who seek a more comprehensive coverage, Philip Altbach's bibliographic monograph (1a)* is recommended.

Descriptions and Analyses

Student protest is a subject of peculiar difficulty; almost everyone knows what he thinks about it and the description of certain protest events is a matter of simple journalism, yet pinning down such a vast and rapidly changing phenomenon so that generalizations about it can be made seems almost impossible. The series of protest actions which began with the Berkeley revolt of 1964 are sufficiently unlike anything which has occurred before to deserve separate treatment. In each year since, the character of protest has changed in some way, the most observable trends being in the direction of increasing frequency and increasing violence. There has been little time yet for scholars to assess what is happening, or to grasp the variety of action which is possible. Further, the study of activism does not fit neatly into any of the disciplines as traditionally understood; it has interest for the sociologist, the psychologist, the political scientist, the historian and those who teach "education," and each of these can employ his professional tools upon it. But equally, each can leave the matter to others with a confidence that he is not neglecting any special responsibility of his own field. These uncertainties are reflected in teaching about protest; what courses there are (and there are few on a subject of most pressing interest to many students) are offered in a variety of departments or under interdisciplinary programs. An inspection of the background of those who write about protest in a book such as this offers another illustration of the disciplinary confusion and overlap which obtains. It is therefore not surprising to find that the literature is widely scattered.

The development of knowledge about student activism illustrates the chaotic way in which scholars undertake inquiry. The beginning of the movement happened to be at Berkeley, so Berkeley has dominated the academic scene. Four anthologies contain a reference to Berkeley in their titles (1e, 1h, 1i, 1m), even though each contains much

---

* See bibliography of this chapter for all parenthetical references.

which has more general application. Seymour Martin Lipset, a professor of sociology at the University of California campus during the heyday of the Free Speech Movement, was so intrigued by the experience that he has edited three books (1i, 1k, 1l) and a special issue of a scholarly journal on protest, in addition to contributing numerous articles and chapters to other publications. Edward Sampson, a psychologist at UCB, has edited another symposium (1n). Another collection of readings is dominated by an account of the action at Berkeley (1g). When the *American Behavioral Scientist* put together a special issue on the after-effects of protest, the focus was on Berkeley, and all the authors either were teaching or had taught there (1b). Lewis Feuer, whose book *The Conflict of Generations* (1f) is certainly the most massive contemporary treatment of student politics by a single author, was a professor of philosophy at Berkeley in 1964, and he includes a lengthy chapter on events there. Even before the free speech controversy, radical student culture at Berkeley was attracting attention; David Horowitz, himself an activist, described various happenings at UCB in 1962 in *Student* (2d). Of the places where a variety of good materials on student protests are gathered together, only two (1p, 1q) are not under the Berkeley influence.* In any listing of scholars who have written about protest, the proportion of those who are or were at Berkeley will be substantial.

Student protest has become widespread in America, but only a few incidents have received the bulk of scholarly attention. Altbach lists 12 books and 84 articles on Berkeley, one book and 16 articles on Columbia, 2 books and 6 articles on San Francisco State, and only one monograph and 6 articles dealing with events on various other campuses. Our own listings (2a–y) perforce reflect this imbalance. We have attempted to compensate for it by selecting the case studies in Part II from elsewhere. In part, the situation may be due to the fact that there is no institution which has yet rivaled these three in the scope and violence of its protests. In part it may be that campuses which have less talented and creative social scientists in residence are doomed to scholarly neglect regardless of how dramatic their confrontations may be. Clearly there are risks involved in any attempt at describing events at an institution other than one's own, for such trespassing invites retorts such as Nathan Glazer's "I under-

---

* Naturally, this statement may become dated; the output of books and articles on student protest is increasing rapidly, and any bibliography soon becomes incomplete.

stand Paul Goodman's difficulty in writing about Berkeley from a
distance, but there are things in his brief article that are really odd,
when read on the scene. . . ." (9c). But for whatever reasons,
scholarly accounts of other campuses are rare.

Combining, compressing and generalizing such information to make
some general picture of protest can be very easy or very difficult, depending on the standards of the writer involved. Popular magazines
are replete with surveys of protest constructed simply by culling examples of this and that and stringing them together. The total picture
which emerges more often reflects whatever has happened to catch the
author's attention than it does the pattern of protest. A different kind
of introduction is that written by the scholar who is familiar with the
detailed research which has been done, and has used it in arriving at
what may look at first glance like unsupported speculations. Articles
of this kind tend to compress as much as possible into minimal space.
They are usually highly informative in the sense that the obvious is
omitted, nor is there any room for clichés and the padding and vagueness which are too often present in discussions of the subject. They
tend also to be very stimulating, for they combine the best of what has
been done with some original hypotheses suggested by the data.
Seymour Martin Lipset has become the foremost practitioner of this
school (3e–h). Block *et al.* have provided what may be the best summary of work done (3c). Edward Sampson's article contains perhaps
more original insights than the others (3k); Philip Altbach is the most
ready to take the risks of prediction (3a). Mallery's *Ferment on
Campus* (3j) gives a sense of immediate participation by the device
of "fictionalizing" conversations and events at the expense (too high,
in this reviewer's opinion) of keeping even the identity of the campus visited a secret. Woodring's treatment of protest typifies what can
be expected from texts on higher education (3n). We have included
chapters of this kind by Richard Flacks and E. Joseph Shoben, Jr.

The inspiration for much of this work comes from painstaking
empirical studies of activists. Most of these were done by psychologists
and sociologists, intent on determining the nature of the activist's
background, his attitudes and his personality. Always the control
group, with which the radicals can be compared and against which
their distinctiveness can be illuminated, is a sample of "ordinary"
students, usually chosen in some random fashion.

Identifying the activists presents the first problem. Flacks initially
selected names from the mailing lists of various radical organizations

at the University of Chicago, but reported that "some were found to have little involvement in the student movement" (4a). In a second study, he obtained questionnaire and interview data from 65 students who had sat in at the University, and 35 others who had signed a petition critical of the sit-in (4a). Westby and Braungart also studied students of opposite persuasions at Pennsylvania State University by questioning small samples of Young Americans for Freedom and a radical peace group (4l). In later work, they have expanded both the number of universities from which the sample is drawn, and the groups involved. Soloman and Fishman administered questionnaires to a large sample of the 1962 Peace March on Washington, interviewed a smaller segment of the same group, and also interviewed some counter-protesters (4g).

Berkeley has, once again, provided the bulk of the data on activists. Both Heist (4b) and Katz (4c) drew their samples from the long lists of those arrested in the course of the Free Speech Movement's activities. Lyonns (4e) distributed his questionnaires from the FSM's recruitment table. Somers (4h) used his undergraduate sociology course as a means of obtaining interviews with 285 students representative of the Berkeley population as a whole. Watts and Whittaker were perhaps the most resourceful gatherers of data. Their questionnaires to activists were completed by students while they sat in Sproul Hall, a few hours before massive arrests began (4i). In a companion study of the professional non-students, the same researchers paid five dollars a head to those of the itinerant population who collaborated with them (4j). The findings of these studies have been summarized (3c, 3g, 5i). We have included probably the most all-embracing comparison of activists and non-activists, by Leonard Baird, and an experimental investigation in activists' visions of the future by David Westby and Richard Braungart.

Quantitative methods are not the only ones by which social scientists can gather information about activists. The presence of some hard statistical data does offer a rule of thumb by which those who have made some attempt at an objective search for facts can be distinguished from those who "know" that protest is the result of long hair, dirty morals and the Communist Conspiracy. However, there are also social scientists who pursue non-statistical approaches. Undoubtedly the most successful of these so far has been Kenneth Keniston, a Yale psychologist, whose method is to interview a quite small number of students in depth and over a considerable period. His book *The Un-*

committed (5c) offered deeper insights into the mind of "the silent majority" than most quantitative studies could claim, and *Young Radicals* (5d) does the same for the activists. Keniston's method, less dependent on the gathering and interpretation of hard data, has more in common with literature; the findings it can offer can be broader and more complex than those derivable from quantitative studies, but they are also more dependent on the special skills of the observer, and more in the realm of the hypothetical than of the demonstrated.

The findings of both quantitative and non-quantitative studies of activists tend to be remarkably congruent. Militants come from upper-middle-class backgrounds, or from families with higher incomes on the average than those of non-militants. While one early study reported that "Those who disagreed with their parents . . . are more likely to have 'rebelled' on campus also. . . ." (4h), the more general conclusion is that activists are *not* usually in revolt against domestic authority. Their parents tend to be markedly liberal, and their parents' values tend to be close to those of the activists themselves, but the latter act on the values in a way that the older generation hesitated to do. That activists are further to the left politically may now seem obvious, but it is characteristic of social science to assume the obvious needs proving—so often it isn't so.

Activists tend to have less attachment to any formal religion; many are agnostics or atheists. They also tend to be more intellectual than non-activists—they have higher IQs, get better grades, possess wider intellectual horizons and generally a greater measure of cultural sophistication. These traits tend to parallel those of their parents, who are above average in both formal education and intellectual interests. Activists usually major in the humanities, social sciences or natural sciences; students in engineering, business administration or vocational studies are seldom involved in protest. As might be expected, protesters do not conform to the "Joe College" stereotype, and rarely join fraternities and sororities. They are open-minded and flexible, rather than dogmatic or rigid; they are sensitive, and have more than the average concern for humanity.

This picture is sharply different from that which many critics of student activists have formed of them. It is charged that protesters are anti-intellectual, careless of others' feelings and intolerant of all disagreement, violent, self-righteous and destructive. In interpreting the data it should be borne in mind that all such studies are limited in terms of time and place, and that almost all the studies were done at highly selective and prestigious universities. Changes in the character of protest may produce a different kind of protester; it may be, for example, that where protest at Berkeley was something so original, so fraught with unknown potential and uncertain risks that only students possessed of some strong commitment and a strain of originality would become involved in it, later protests have become much more imitative, and may even take on some of the mindlessness of the panty raid or the fraternity riot.

In California and, to some extent, other parts of the country, Black Students Unions played a leading role in protest activities during 1968–69. In many cases the students involved had entered college under special academic dispensations for the culturally deprived, and often they were dependent on special funds for financial support. It seems highly unlikely that such students would fit the picture of the protester outlined above. Harry Edwards, the black sociologist who led the movement to boycott the Olympics, has suggested that the violence of the black protests in California was the violence of the ghetto, a way of life in which the way to get what one wants is to fight for it, and that it was directed at authority which, in the ghetto, is wont to impose its will by force and so invites forceful resistance.* Such an interpretation has little to do with white affluent liberalism. The limitations of studies of protesters carried out only at elite institutions like Berkeley, Yale and the University of Chicago are becoming apparent.

Studies of particular campuses can give information which will be of general interest, but in order to assess the scope, incidence and volume of protest, and to chart the variations in it from one kind of institution to another, a broad survey is essential. Three such studies have been reported to this point; each is described in later chapters.

When Richard E. Peterson conducted his survey *The Scope of Student Protest in 1964–65* (4n), he chose the same sample of colleges and universities as that used by Williamson and Cowan in their massive study of *The Student's Freedom of Expression*. Questionnaires were sent to all four-year institutions, asking deans of students for assessments of the incidence of protest on a variety of issues. The study was replicated for 1967–68 (4o); an account of the later study, with some comparisons to the earlier one, forms the next chapter. Previously, Peterson had joined a team which correlated the data he had obtained in 1965 with the performance on College and University

---

* Conversation with the author.

Environment Scales (CUES) taken on 109 campuses. The CUES tests, which require students to describe their collegiate environment by responding to 150 true-false statements, yield scores on five collegiate characteristics. It was found that CUES scores were good predictors of protest on race and foreign policy issues, but not local ones. Campuses identified by students as "Aware" or "Scholarly" tended to be the scene of protests; campuses rated high on "Practicality," "Community," and "Propriety" did not (4p).

The second major survey was undertaken by the editors, working with Robert M. Gutchen. This instrument dealt, like Peterson's, with protest in 1967–68; unlike his, it was addressed to two-year as well as four-year institutions, and where Peterson had sought information mainly of members of protests and numbers of students involved on each of several issues, our questionnaire attempted to bring out the sequence of events involved in the year's major protest action. The Foster-Long-Gutchen questionnaire was distributed by the American Council on Education, though that organization had no responsibility for its content.

The A.C.E.'s own research, conducted by Alexander Astin, was on a more massive scale. Sixty thousand questionnaires were sent to entering freshmen, of which 35,000 were returned. A great number of topics were covered, and student protest was only one among many interests. However, Astin has done considerable analysis designed to isolate those variables which constitute good predictors of protest. His findings give some reasons for questioning the emphasis on different types of institution suggested by the work of Peterson; it may be that students are "protest-prone" or not, and that incidence of protest at some institutions is greater than at others only because these institutions somehow attract the kinds of students who will become activists.

John M. Orbell (4m) has reported on a survey of 264 students attending black colleges in the South, taken in 1962—before student protest became a commonplace in the North, but about two years after militant activities had begun in the South. He finds participation in freedom rides, sit-ins, etc., to be more frequent among students at private than at public colleges; students in the latter institutions perceived their administrators as considerably more sympathetic to black militant action. Colleges of good academic quality, situated in heavily urban counties in areas with a comparatively low proportion of Negroes, were found more likely to house militants than those in the opposite categories. But in light of Astin's findings, one should be hesitant to ascribe these variations to institutional characteristics, rather than to characteristics of those who choose to attend one or other type of institution.

Correlation is not necessarily explanation, nor does it prove causation. All that the demonstration that characteristic "A" is associated with characteristic "B" proves is that where there is an "A" there is often a "B," and vice versa. "A" may cause "B," "B" may cause "A," or both may be caused by a so far unobserved factor, "C." But one who would interpret society cannot afford not to speculate on causal relationships. Bay has suggested some explanations for the facts unearthed in the empirical studies of activists (5a). Peterson (5f) and Trent and Craise (5p) have used data about students in general as a basis for more speculative treatments of activists. Other writers have offered some direct causal explanations of activism (5g–5l), a topic discussed later by Seymour Halleck.

A somewhat different type of theoretical study focuses on the protest action rather than the protester. Work in this area is extremely fragmentary. Boulding (6c) and Brzezinski (6d) have looked at protest in light of strategic theory, somewhat in the value-free (and therefore apparently cynical) spirit of Machiavelli. Lipsky has written of "Protest As a Political Resource" (6e). Altbach (6a) and Moore (6f) have taken different routes in attempting to assess what protest can and cannot accomplish. Ben-David and Collins (6b) have attempted a theoretical treatment of academic freedom and student protest, with more attention to the former than the latter. In Part IV, we have tried to compensate for the neglect of this area which has been the general rule. Two chapters by the editors examine strategies, developments and outcomes of protest from the viewpoint of the participants and of the institution. Edward Schwartz, former President of the National Student Association, offers an analysis of the dynamics of protest. Daniel Kornstein and Peter Weissenberg have applied social exchange theory to student protest, with special attention to events at Columbia.

An easier approach to the study of student protest is through the organizations which express it. Most organizations have structures, officers, membership figures, programs, ideologies, and internal rifts, some of them public and some not so public, but all usually accessible eventually to the enterprising inquirer. The trouble with New Left organizations is that so few of them conform to this model. The SDS, which has come to overshadow most others in the realm of student protest, appears to take its strictures about participatory democracy so seriously that it is indeed very difficult to pinpoint any cohesive structure or nationally influential leadership. On most campuses, its membership is uncertain, its constitution non-existent, and its leadership shifting. The Black Students Unions are more cohesive, but they can be frustrating to an observer in another way; their membership being exclusively reserved to blacks, their meetings closed, and their communication with other black groups secret, it is abnormally difficult to discover how they operate.

Most treatments of student left groups, therefore, tend to be journalistic; they are essentially subjective pictures of what the author has been able to see of a certain movement from his particular vantage point. Newfield (7e) focuses on various aspects of the revival of the radical left, placing its beginning in the South in 1960; he includes chapters on SDS and SNCC. Jacobs and Landau's *The New Radicals* (7b), which selects SDS and SNCC from the "formal" organizations for chapter-length attention, is mainly devoted to readings from and about the New Left. Cohen and Hale's (7a) book of readings on the New Left, published in 1962, devotes less attention to SDS, and more to community work, especially in the South; any work done on this subject dates very quickly. Zinn has done a book on SNCC (7k), and Douglass (1d) has focused one on the Student Christian Movement. There is as yet no authoritative book on SDS.

Much of this kind of literature is more of historical than of contemporary interest. An article called "Is There a Student Movement?" (7g) published in 1961 is useful today only in that it gives a perspective which was valid enough at that time; another piece which appeared the same year called "The Right at NSA" (7m) tells of some conspiratorial politics which have nothing whatever to do with the NSA as it is today. Phillip Abbott Luce's *The New Left* (7c) is of more recent date, but its atmosphere is further from the contemporary scene—straight early fifties stuff about "the conspiracy" which supposedly lies behind the chaotic activities of the New Left. Mr. Luce spent some years as a "member" of the New Left, specifically of the Progressive Labor Party, and his book is a denunciation "from the inside." Equipped with long hair, boots, jeans, and a selection of radical obscenities (but all, please note, quotations from other sources), Mr. Luce now lives on the lecture circuit; like so many who have departed from the far left with a maximum of noise, he has gravitated to the far right—the Young Americans for Freedom. The student right has not played the influential role on the campuses which some forecast for it a few years ago, but it has received some scholarly and journalistic attention (7l–7p). Our chapter on activist organizations is a hybrid in terms of authorship; Philip Werdell did the basic research on SDS and SNCC, and Joseph Shoben refined and recast his ideas when both worked at the American Council on Education; Durward Long added information on other organizations to this foundation.

The focus of this book is on student protest in the United States. However, in limiting the study of any phenomenon geographically one runs some danger of provincialism, of failing to appreciate the whole spectrum of possibilities, and of applying standards formed without a proper awareness of the total picture. Limitations of space have prevented the inclusion of material on protest in other countries in the present volume, but some of the work available in English is listed in the bibliography, Section VIII.

Evaluations

We turn now to materials which, while they may include a measure of description or analysis, have evaluation as their primary thrust or intent. So long as student protest remains in the news, there are likely to be frequent treatments of it in the popular magazines. Most of these reflect a strong bias, and the reader who knows what he wants to hear should have no difficulty in finding something to his taste. For articles which identify with radical protesters, there are *New Left Notes, Liberation, Ramparts* (one of whose editors is Eldridge Cleaver, a cause célèbre of protest himself) and other more transitory journals put out by activist organizations. Moving to the right, liberal journals like *Dissent,* the *New Republic,* and *The Nation* generally take a position sympathetic to the students, but become critical of violent, irrational or intolerant tactics. On the conservative side, *U.S. News & World Report* generally holds that students attend college in order to learn, a process which takes place in the classroom and only there. *National Review* tends to be more outraged and more condemnatory; the pessimism of Russell Kirk's articles "From the Academy" make it difficult to remember that in his book *Academic Freedom* he once denounced tyrannical university administrators with all the bitterness of a Rudd or a Savio, albeit in more genteel style. Finally, the manic right position, in which no protest contains the slightest justice and all are manifestations of the Communist Conspiracy is represented by such extremist journals as *Human Events* and *American Opinion.*

The commentary in popular journals is usually embodied in the choice and telling of incidents, and in references to such evocative matters as napalm and police brutality, obscene slogans and damaged property. More interesting kinds of evaluation focus on the issues which underlie student activism, and on its overall impact on American society in general and higher education in particular. Articles of this kind are scattered in a number of intellectual magazines; the only significant collection of them yet in book form is George F. Kennan's *Democracy and the Student Left* (9a), in which America's former ambassador to Russia delivers an attack on protest, receives a number of critical responses by both students and "the older generation," and finally gives his rebuttal.

Kennan's approach represents one major school of anti-protest thought, other distinguished spokesmen for which include Jacques Barzun, Lewis Feuer and Sidney Hook. This school may be described as authoritarian, in that its objections to recent events on the campuses are rooted in a traditional concept of the place of the student. Barzun made clear some years ago his benevolently paternal view of the student when he entitled a chapter about him "The Human Boy." In the course of that he comments that "friendship between an instructor and a student is impossible. . . . For friendship has strict prerequisites, freedom of choice and equality of status. Neither of these can exist in the teacher-student relation (9o)." Hook insists that students neither can nor should enjoy academic freedom in the same sense as faculty:

. . . the faculty always retains the right of intervention in school affairs whenever they adversely affect the integrity of the educational process. The faculty possess enough expertise to know not only what an education is good for, but what a good education is. (9u)

Kennan remarks that student objections against practices *in loco parentis* are now directed against rules so lax that "a thousand forms of self-indulgence are now permitted which in an earlier day would not have been tolerated" (p. 154). He recalls nostalgically the pleasure in breaking the old-fashioned rules, the lack of bitterness when one was caught, the lack of apparent student desire to change the structure.

The starting point for the authoritarian critics is thus the traditional view of the student as apprentice, without rights in the system, and certainly without any legitimate claim to power over it. Their view of the university, too, is a traditional one. Kennan opens with a description of the learning process as ideally characterized by "a certain detachment and seclusion, a certain voluntary withdrawal and renunciation of participation in contemporary life. . . ." (p. 3). Barzun, while Dean at Columbia, was prominently associated with policies which were designed so far as possible to insulate the University from the slums at its back door and the other pressing realities of urban life, policies which themselves became a major target for student protesters. Hook is slightly more tolerant of student involvements in contemporary political and social questions, but he insists that "No service is done to students by flattering them or giving them the impression they can acquire an education in any other way than the hard intellectual disciplines of the logic of ideas and events . . . good works off the campus cannot substitute for good work on the campus" (9u).

Within such a framework, the student activist, impatient with classroom learning as "irrelevant," and anxious to play an immediate role in both the running of the university and of the larger world, is plainly an anachronism. Barzun tends rather to dismiss him with elegant sarcasms; he is willing to admit that certain shortcomings in higher education may justify complaint, but his underlying view of protest is clinical:

Cheating, civil disobedience, sex and drugs ad lib, the campus as soapbox, the cry for a voice in university administration, and the declaration of war against the institution as such, belongs not to academic theory and practice but to the tortured conscience of man; and although the conflict breaks out again and again at the universities, it is not to be finally judged or cured there . . . they are rebels without a cause. The cause is simply to ruin the going scheme. (9o, p. 74)

Hook is more outspoken—"callow and immature adolescents"—and Kennan writes of "screaming tantrums and brawling in the streets . . . eyes glazed with anger and passion, too often dimmed as well by artificial abuse . . . like a flock of truculent village geese. . . ."

(9a, pp. 4, 120). Hook draws the inevitable conclusion when he identifies "The Trojan Horse in American Higher Education" (9u). This is not the radicals, for they are openly the enemy, but soft-minded faculty and administrators who, misled by their "false view of liberalism," misapply the notion of academic freedom in permitting militance and disruptive activism.

The most thorough and carefully documented statement of the conservative critique of protest is Lewis Feuer's *The Conflict of Generations* (1f). Feuer, in 1964 a professor of philosophy at Berkeley and now one of sociology at Toronto, uses an encyclopedic knowledge of history to illustrate his theme: that student protest is essentially a protest of youth against age, sons against fathers, and as such devoid of worthy content, sound judgment or political responsibility. The author detects recurring patterns of terrorism, suicide proneness, rejection of father and authority, intellectual elit-ism, intolerance and other undesirable qualities in a number of student movements. Plainly irritated by any tendency to romanticize the student radical, Feuer finds student interventions generally dis-astrous and sometimes—for example, in a chapter entitled "The Bosnian Student Movement Blindly Provokes the First World War" —catastrophic. The author's wide-ranging style allows him fairly controversial interpretations, as when he cites Julius and Ethel Rosen-berg as products of student radicalism at CCNY, or when he ac-counts for Paul Goodman's sympathy for student activism in terms of homosexuality. When he discusses events at Berkeley, his findings include that "The moral level of the University of California became the lowest in the history of American education" (p. 454), and that "A chairman of a department of science . . . became convinced that Mario Savio was a reincarnation of Jesus" (p. 463), and one section concludes with

the memory of their beautiful Pied Piper, Joan Baez, her long black hair waving in the wind, her olive face lit by the sun, as she sang with proud head thrown back and her guitar more summoning than any bugle call— singing of love, as the children marched into Sproul Hall in defense of the right of Mario Savio to bite a policeman in the left thigh. (p. 470)

Whether such flamboyances cast doubt on the value of the work as serious history, whether sarcasm can successfully be interwoven with objective reporting, readers may decide for themselves. But it is clear that Feuer is among the most totally condemnatory of the critics of student protest, and it is also clear that while he can marshal much historical evidence for his views, he also finds it emotionally congenial, for he sees student radicals to be crude, irrational, self-righteous and indeed to possess, perhaps, almost all those human traits which he most dislikes.

The aristocratic disdain of the elite for the unwashed masses, of the intellectual for the over-simplifier, of the restrained for the demonstrative characterizes the authoritarian critique of student activism. Such views of protest see it as an educational problem; the content is almost irrelevant. These critics may fairly be termed conservative, in that they imply that society, while far from perfect, is the best we have and certainly not to be tampered with by enthusiastic youth; that respect for law and order is essential; and that in a well-ordered universe all should recognize the primacies of knowledge, experience and wisdom, or, in a word, of authority.

The basis of this authority has been challenged by those more sympathetic to protest. The revolt at Berkeley occurred shortly after UC President Clark Kerr had introduced the concept of "the multiversity" into the language, and the confrontation dramatized the extent to which the student was remote from the professor who, in turn, could know little about the impact of the education which he was helping to impart. Many sympathetic faculty became aware of the shortcomings of mass education, often with a sense of guilt for their past acquiescence in it. According to Philip Selznick

If we still have something to teach our students about the relation of means to ends (and I believe we have), it is also true that they have had much to teach us. Their mode of instruction has been passionate and in part irresponsible, but it has not been such as to justify a shrinking back in horror. Much of what the students did was clearly necessary if we were to be made to *really listen*. (9d)

The protests at Berkeley and elsewhere brought about considerable rethinking of educational practices, especially those which condemned the student to a purely passive role. Insofar as they also marked a definitive change from "the silent generation" of students, they could be defended as an attribute of a new and higher commitment. Hal Draper voiced the sense that perhaps academia had sold out to just those materialistic values which it is supposed to hold in contempt when he said

You can decide whether you will act—for justice and for your social and moral imperatives as you see them—or whether you're going to be simply another misguided Organization Man, with your eyes very firmly fixed on the gleaming goal of some day having your own, very own, Research Center, with a heartwarming flow of grant money: you know, that heaven to which all good professors go when they die. . . . (9b)

Thus to the liberal, the conservative view of protest may be both presumptuous and blind. Martin Duberman (9f) dismisses Hook's "gray-bearded arrogance" and tears ruthlessly into Barzun, for what he considers the latter's patronizing and myopic view of contemporary student concerns. His main wrath, however, is directed at his Princeton colleague George Kennan, whose comments he characterizes as ". . . appalling. There is barely a sentence in the article free of false accusation, self-enclosed argument, misplaced indignation." He remarks that evidently the young are "regarded with considerable hatred in our country," and suggests that this may be because the older generation, irritated at the unmistakable physical superiority of youth, have long been consoling themselves with the notion that they are at least morally, intellectually and emotionally superior to their juniors. Duberman himself sees the activists as intelligent, idealistic and highly committed, and as applying the values which their parents may have held but seldom acted on. "It is," he concludes, "a generation for which we should be immensely grateful and immensely proud."

The argument between the conservative critics of protest and those who would refute them is thus to some extent an argument about reform: whether it is needed and whether the activists have contributed constructively to it. There can be little doubt that student protest has unleashed a considerable amount of experiment in higher education, has brought about at least a theoretical reemphasis of the teaching function, and has made the need for education to be "relevant" so clear that the phrase has become a cliché. Assessment of protest must in part depend on the assessment made of the post-protest state of higher education. But where the conservatives tend to see protest as strictly a campus matter, the protesters themselves have viewed their activities in a wider context:

In our free speech fight against the University of California, we have come up against what may emerge as the greatest problem of our nation—depersonalized, unresponsive bureaucracy. We have encountered the organized status quo in Mississippi, but it is the same in Berkeley. (9n)

Mario Savio went on to picture a society confronted by automation and by racial injustice, and run by a bureaucracy fundamentally unable to control either. In his view, student protest should be weighed in terms of its total societal import. It is concern with this import which forms the major focus of what may be called the liberal criticism of protest.

Unlike the conservative critics, the liberals have considerable sympathy with the radicals' general aims and with some of their actions, yet deplore some of the excesses and implications of student protest. Nathan Glazer, a Berkeley sociologist, can conclude that radicalism is "a great reservoir of energy which moves the establishment to pay attention to the most serious and urgent problems, and tells it when it has failed . . ." (9t). Yet the burden of his argument is that New Left analysis of the flaws in American society itself contains crucial weaknesses. He argues that in attributing all current problems to self-interested misuses of power, the New Left has grossly oversimplified matters, especially in view of the inevitability of fresh difficulties which are necessarily associated with rapid technological progress. He finds the New Left disdain for institutions anarchic and naïve—"there can be no substitute for institutions, even though they may become tired, bureaucratic and corrupt." Participatory democracy, proffered by the radicals as a substitute and a cure-all for what we now have, "inevitably means depending on that part of the people which is willing, for one reason or another, to stay permanently in session." Such democracy seems to Glazer little more than a disguise for a philosophy which disdains majority rule, a fairly traditional assessment, precedents for which can be found in much liberal anti-Marxist literature, most notably in George Orwell's *Animal Farm*.

Irving Howe, whose progressive credentials are extensive and impeccable, has commented on the new radicals' "extreme, sometimes unwarranted, hostility towards liberalism" (9v). He clearly suspects that this hostility may stem from a difference in style which leads the radicals to be careless of democratic rights and freedoms, and he condemns them for "A vicarious indulgence in violence, often merely theoretic and therefore all the more irresponsible." Lewis Feuer states the same concerns in stronger language (9g):

Beyond all the phraseology of dialogue there is the simple fact that the ideology of the New Left is one of imposing the will of a small elite, a band of activists, on national policy . . .

Like Lenin . . .

The participatory democrat . . . has no use for elections, votes, parliamentary procedures; he founds himself on the notion that since the masses are non-participant, the elite activists will act on their behalf.

On a less theoretical level, Irving Kristol argues the same sort of case. He stresses the unconstructive nature of much contemporary student radicalism—"their 'platform' is literally without one legislative plank" (9x). While according some not overly generous praise to the white students who went to the South in the early part of this decade, he points out that the civil rights crusade in fact had the backing of much of that organized American society which radicals now excoriate. He speculates that the real motives may too often be boredom, leading to a desire for confrontation. He too views participatory democracy with considerable suspicion, and is highly critical of radical willingness to denigrate America so sweepingly while apparently failing to see anything amiss with Communist regimes in Cuba and China.

Three other prominent liberal critics of protest should be mentioned. Daniel Bell, author of *The End of Ideology,* a title which has goaded the New Left into considerable argumentation, has retaliated by pointing out inherent weaknesses in contemporary radicalism which may prevent it from making a constructive contribution:

The SDS will be destroyed by its style. It lives on turbulence, but it is incapable of transforming its chaotic impulses into a systematic, responsible behavior that is necessary to effect broad sociological change.

Seymour Martin Lipset has written in *Political Man* that "democracy is not only or even primarily a means through which different groups can attain their ends or seek the good society; it is the good society itself in operation" (p. 439). It is in the light of this attachment to democracy that his conclusions on protest are drawn:

The indifference to legality shown by serious students can threaten the foundations of democratic order if it becomes a model for student political action. Extremism in the pursuit of liberty was quite recently a favorite slogan of the radical right. Berkeley has shown that anyone can play this game. (9y)

Elsewhere (3g) he has dismissed the philosophers of protest as "intellectual Poujadists" for their preoccupation with grievances at the expense of coherent thought about solutions.

Charles Frankel has elaborated his ideas about protest in *Education and the Barricades* (9r). His main concern is whether violence "works" in higher education, as has been alleged by some protesters; his fear is that it destroys the delicate fabric of the academy, and enables the minority to dominate the majority. Yet, like many of the liberal critics, his final assessment of student protest is by no means entirely negative:

Our colleges and universities, damaged though they have been by recent events, have the chance to produce new forms of education and self-government. Those who disapprove of the tactics of some students cannot let their anger and shock leave them rigid in the face of this opportunity to bring new coherence and excitement to higher education.

Several contrasts between the conservative and the liberal critics of protest may be mentioned. While the conservatives come primarily from the tradition of the humanities, the liberals tend to be behavioral scientists; this difference in professional concern may in part explain why the conservatives tend more to evaluation than explanation of protest, why the liberals see protest more as part of the total political system, and why the conservatives seem to focus on the style of protest while the behaviorists are more concerned with its possible impact. Further, the conservative posture tends to be one of incomprehension: why are these people behaving so badly? The liberals, on the other hand, understand the imperatives of dissent and social reform, and ask instead why so often the activists seem to neglect these goals or to adopt means which tend to undermine the very precepts of freedom and democracy which are supposedly at the heart of the radical movement. The liberals, because protest against existing conditions has long been a part of their own philosophy, automatically distinguish different types of protest, and tend to use the absence of coercive elements as a touchstone for approval; the conservatives are more all-embracing in their rejection of student activism.

Response to the liberal critique is not easy. This was demonstrated when the SDS, in a moment of unusually candid self-criticism, declared in calling its December, 1965, Conference:

We have slogans which take the place of thought: "There's a change gonna come" is our substitute for social theory, "Let the people decide" has been an escape from our own indecision; we scream "No leaders," "No structures" and seem to come up with implicit structures which are far less democratic than the most explicit elitism.

It is not immediately evident that this challenge has borne fruit; SDS has become a more strident critic of the existing order since 1965, but remains silent on specific alternatives.

One kind of response is to admit or ignore much of the liberal critique, but then to offer countervailing considerations which may outweigh it. This kind of argument can be offered either by radicals or by temporarily radicalized liberals. One of the latter, Dwight MacDonald, appealed in a letter to the *New York Review of Books* for funds for SDS during their battles at Columbia; while admitting their shortcomings, he insisted that on Vietnam, race and poverty, the "Establishment" was so totally bankrupt that "extra-legal pressures" were justified and necessary.

This form of defense is essentially attack. Participatory democracy, however vague its machinery, gains in attraction if it can be shown that representative democracy is a dismal fraud. The apparent conflicts between the stress on freedom and self-determination on the one hand and the enthusiasm for Castro and Mao on the other become obscured if one can insist that anything would be more free than the present tyranny. Indeed, if present horrors can be illustrated with sufficient conviction, a request that aims be clarified before the revolution is begun can seem like pure prevarication. Once the enemy has been identified, further discussion can only spell disunity in his presence; one does not start arguing about peace terms at the height of the battle.

To the extent that student protest aims at practical reforms, the liberal critique does not apply, for liberals too are reformers. What the liberals object to is the unfocused or impractical protest, the "non-negotiable demands" for the impossible, the disruptive tactics when other avenues are open. But these strategies make sense if destruction rather than reform is the aim. Tom Hayden has written of "Two, Three, Many Columbias" (9g) echoing Ché Guevarra's call for more Vietnams; what to liberals appeared a tragic escalation in face of administrative obduracy to Hayden apparently seems a state of affairs preferable to orderly change. Carl Davidson of SDS has explained the nature of the university:

Our educational institutions *are* corporations and knowledge factories. What we have failed to see in the past is how absolutely vital these factories are to the corporate liberal state. . . . What would happen to a manipulative society if its means of creating *manipulable* people were done away with? . . . Our universities are already chief agents for social change in the direction of 1984. . . . (9e)

Thus the university as we know it is beyond redemption, so essentially anti-social that its destruction must have first priority. If such a view is accepted, it is clear that the liberal critique would have no force.

A more moderate variant of this argument has been put forward by Paul Potter, a President of SDS in the days when that organization was centralized to the extent of having a president. Potter rejects the politics of reform and of the regular democratic process, yet claims credit for reforms already enacted; students, he suggests, are not well suited to play a role in regular democratic politics, but by remaining outside the system, they can make the system itself more responsive:

The point is that the students forget what's made them effective if they start making deep commitments to these reforms. They begin to lose their political independence, I suspect, if they believe that the only way they can get reforms is to concede other points they have been making. . . . So in that sense there needs to be an uncompromising quality to what the "movement" is doing. At the same time, I think we can effect compromises. (9l)

Michael Rossman exemplifies another radical approach which circumvents the need for conventional means or goals. Asked to review three books about Berkeley (1e, 1i, 1m), the former FSM leader remarked on "the indelible sense of unreality, of irrelevance they leave me with" (9m). These compilations of description, analysis and evaluative debate are inadequate, he maintains, because they lack humor and poetry and so miss the whole point of the protest. He talks of the "Police Car Episode": "Understand it and you understand the FSM; for FSM was forged around that car, *not* at the later convention, and those two days were a miniature of the entire conflict. They furnished the emotional impetus for our fight, they were our signature on a promissory note of the heart. . . ." The value of protest thus lies in commitment and in the sense of community which it engenders. Measured against such standards, programs and tactics become as arid and irrelevant as the intellectualism of the liberal analysts.

Thus the radical rebuttal of the liberal critique is not really a rebuttal, but rather an assertion that the criticisms, whether valid or not, are relatively unimportant. Dialogue is not a part of the contemporary radical style; it has never been congenial to extremists of either the far left or the far right. The conservative and authoritarian critics of protest are answered by the liberals, but when the liberals formulate their own attack on radicalism, they generally encounter *ad hominem* responses, attacks on the integrity of the critic, or counter-assertions of globally moralistic scope. In consequence, the radicals themselves have strangely little to contribute to the debate about their own activities; perhaps this is inevitably the fate of any group which adopts a frame of reference very different from that of the majority, and then makes little effort at the intellectual conversion of that majority.

BIBLIOGRAPHY

I. GENERAL READINGS ON STUDENT PROTEST

1a. Altbach, P., *Student Politics and Higher Education in the United States: a Select Bibliography*. St. Louis, Mo., and Cambridge, Mass., United Ministries in Higher Education and Center for International Affairs, Harvard University, 1968.

1b. "Authority and the University," a special issue of *The American Behavioral Scientist,* Vol. II (May–June, 1968).

1c. Brown, Michael, *The Politics and Anti-Politics of the Young.* Beverly Hills, Calif., Glencoe Press, 1969.

1d. Douglass, Bruce, *Reflections on Protest*. Richmond, Va., John Knox Press, 1967.

1e. Draper, Hal, *Berkeley: The New Student Revolt.* New York, Grove Press, 1965.

1f. Feuer, Lewis S., *The Conflict of Generations.* New York, Basic Books, 1969.

1g. Howe, Irving, *Student Activism.* Indianapolis, Ind., Bobbs-Merrill Co., 1967.

1h.   Katope, Christopher G., and Zolbrod, Paul G., *Beyond Berkeley.* Cleveland, World Publishing Co., 1966.

1i.   Lipset, Seymour Martin, and Wolin, Sheldon, *The Berkeley Student Revolt.* Garden City, N.Y., Anchor Books, 1965.

1j.   Lipset, Seymour Martin (ed.), Special Issue on Student Politics, *Comparative Education Review,* Vol. 10, No. 2 (June, 1966).

1k.   ———, *Student Politics.* New York, Basic Books, 1967.

1l.   ———, and Altbach, Philip (eds.), *Students and Politics.* Boston, Houghton Mifflin, 1969.

1m.   Miller, Michael V., and Gilmore, Susan, *Revolution at Berkeley.* New York, Dial Press, 1965.

1n.   Sampson, Edward T. (ed.), "Stirrings Out of Apathy: Student Activism and the Decade of Protest," *The Journal of Social Issues,* Vol. 23, No. 3 (July, 1967).

1o.   Schwartz, Edward (ed.), *Student Power: Philosophy, Program, Tactics.* Washington, D.C., National Student Association, 1968.

1p.   Special Issue on the Universities, *The Public Interest,* No. 13 (Fall, 1968).

1q.   "Students and Politics," *Daedalus,* Vol. 97, No. 1 (Winter, 1968).

1r.   "Youth 1967: The Challenge of Change," *The American Scholar,* Vol. 36, No. 4 (Autumn, 1967).

Very recent additions:

1s.   Axelrod, Joseph, *et al., Search for Relevance: the Campus in Crisis.* San Francisco, Jossey-Bass, Inc., 1969.

1t.   Bell, Daniel, and Kristol, Irving, *Confrontation: the Student Rebellion and the Universities.* New York, Basic Books, 1969.

1u.   McEvoy, James, and Miller, Abraham, *Black Power and Student Rebellion.* Belmont, Wadsworth, 1969.

1v.   Schwab, Joseph J., *College Curriculum and Student Protest.* Chicago, University of Chicago Press, 1969.

1w.   Spender, Stephen, *The Year of the Young Rebels.* New York, Vintage Books, 1969.

1x.   Taylor, Harold, *Students Without Teachers: the Crisis in the University.* New York, McGraw-Hill Book Co., 1969.

II. EVENTS ON PARTICULAR AMERICAN CAMPUSES

On Berkeley. See *1e, 1h, 1i, 1m,* also:

2a.   Feuer, Lewis, "Rebellion at Berkeley," *New Leader,* 47 (December 21, 1964), pp. 3–12.

2b.   Glazer, Nathan, " 'Student Power' at Berkeley," in *1p,* pp. 3–21.

2c.   Hook, Sidney, "Second Thoughts on Berkeley," *Teachers College Record,* 2 (1965), pp. 32–63.

2d.   Horowitz, David, *Student.* New York, Ballantine Books, 1962.

On Columbia:

2e.   Avorn, Jerry L., *et al., Up Against the Ivy Wall: A History of the Columbia Crisis.* New York, Atheneum, 1968.

2f.   Barton, Allen H., "The Columbia Crisis: Campus, Vietnam, and the Ghetto," *Public Opinion Quarterly*, Vol. 22, No. 3 (Fall, 1968), pp. 333–351.

2g.   Bell, Daniel, "Columbia and the New Left," in *1p*, pp. 61–101; *1t*, pp. 67–107, and *1w*, pp. 31–74.

2h.   Cox, A., *Crisis at Columbia*. New York, Vintage, 1968.

2i.   Donadio, Stephen, "Black Power at Columbia," *Commentary*, September, 1968.

2j.   ———, "Columbia: Seven Interviews," *Partisan Review* (Summer, 1968).

2k.   Kunen, James Simon, *The Strawberry Statement*. New York, Random House, 1969.

2l.   Spender, Stephen, "The Columbia Happenings," in *1w*.

2m.   Starr, Roger, "The Case of the Columbia Gym," in *1p*, pp. 102–121.

On San Francisco State College:

2n.   Axen, Richard, Pentony, Vere, and Smith, Robert, *In the Jaws of the Vice*. Forthcoming.

2o.   Bunzel, John H., "Black Studies at San Francisco State," in *1p*, pp. 22–38; *1t*, pp. 22–42.

2p.   ———, "Costs of the Politicized College," *Educational Record*, Vol. 50, No. 2 (Spring, 1969), pp. 131–137.

2q.   Daniels, Arlene, *et al.*, *Academicians on the Line*. Forthcoming.

2r.   Duerr, Edwin C., "Police on the Campus: Crisis at SFSC," *Educational Record*, Vol. 50, No. 2 (Spring, 1969), pp. 126–130.

2s.   Goldman, Ralph, "Confrontation at San Francisco State," *Dissent*, Vol. 16 (March–April, 1969), pp. 167–179. A later version of this article forms a chapter in Part III of the present volume.

2t.   Halperin, Irving, "San Francisco State College Diary," *Educational Record*, Vol. 50, No. 2 (Spring, 1969), pp. 121–125.

2u.   McEvoy, James, and Miller, Abraham, "San Francisco State: 'On Strike . . . Shut It Down'," in *1u*, pp. 12–31.

On other campuses, see *1u* for studies of events at the University of Chicago, Duke and Stanford; also:

2v.   Hilberry, Conrad, "Civil Disobedience at Oberlin," *Educational Record*, Vol. 49, No. 2 (Spring, 1968), pp. 133–138.

2w.   Redford, Edward H., "Profiting from Activism," *The Junior College Journal*, Vol. 38, No. 3 (1967). (On Merritt College)

2x.   Scimecca, Joseph, and Dauriano, Roland, *Crisis at St. Johns: Strike and Revolution on the Catholic Campus*. New York, Random House, 1967.

2y.   Tarcov, Nathan, "The Last Four Years at Cornell," in *1p*, pp. 122–138.

III. GENERAL AND SURVEY ARTICLES
ABOUT STUDENT PROTEST IN AMERICA

3a.   Altbach, Philip G., "The Future of the American Student Movement," *Liberal Education*, 52 (October, 1966), pp. 313–324.

3b.   ———, "Students and International Affairs," in *1d*, pp. 71–82.

3c.   Block, Jeanne H., Haan, Norma, and Smith, M. B., "Activism and Apathy in Contemporary Adolescents," in J. F. Adams (ed.), *Contributions to the Understanding of Adolescence*. Boston, Allyn and Bacon, 1968, pp. 198–231.

3d.   Glazer, Penina, "The New Left," *Journal of Higher Education*, 38 (March, 1967), pp. 119–130.

3e.   Lipset, Seymour Martin, "Students and Politics in Comparative Perspective," in *1q*, pp. 1–20.

3f.   ———, and Altbach, Philip G., "Student Politics and Higher Education in the United States," in *1j*, pp. 320–349, and *1k*, pp. 199–252.

3g.   ———, "The Activists: a Profile," in *1p*, pp. 39–51, and *1t*, pp. 45–57.

3h.   ———, "Student Opposition in the United States," *Government and Opposition*, 1 (April, 1966), pp. 351–374.

3i.   Lynch, James J., "Disorder, Power, and the Students," *Virginia Quarterly Review*, 43 (Winter, 1967), pp. 36–52.

3j.   Mallery, David, *Ferment on the Campus*. New York, Harper & Row, 1966.

3k.   Sampson, Edward E., "Student Activism and the Decade of Protest," in *1n*, pp. 1–33.

3l.   Shoben, Edward J., "Towards Remedies for Restlessness: Issues in Student Unrest," *Liberal Education*, 51 (May, 1968), pp. 221–230.

3m.   Ways, Max, "On the Campus: A Troubled Reflection of the United States," *Fortune*, 72 (September, 1965, and October, 1965), pp. 130–135 and pp. 140–147.

3n.   Woodring, Paul, *The Higher Learning in America: A Reassessment*. New York, McGraw-Hill Book Co., 1968, pp. 58–105.

IV. ACTIVISTS AND ACTIVISM: QUANTITATIVE STUDIES

Activists Compared with Non-Activists: Questionnaire and Interview Studies.

4a.   Flacks, Richard, "The Liberated Generation: An Exploration of the Roots of Student Protest," in *1n*, pp. 52–75, and *1v*, pp. 354–378.

4b.   Heist, P., "Intellect and Commitment: The Faces of Discontent," in O. W. Knorr and W. J. Minter (eds.), *Order and Freedom on the Campus: The Rights and Responsibilities of Faculty and Students*. Boulder, Colo., Western Interstate Commission for Higher Education, 1965, pp. 61–69.

4c.   Katz, Joseph, "The Activist Revolution of 1964," in Katz (ed.), *No Time for Youth*. San Francisco, Jossey-Bass Inc., 1968.

4d.   Kerpelman, L. C., "Student Political Activism and Ideology: Comparative Characteristics of Activists and Non-activists," *Journal of Counseling Psychology*, in press.

4e.   Lyonns, Glen, "The Police Car Demonstration: A Survey of Participation," in *1i*, pp. 519–529.

4f.   Olsen, Marvin E., "Perceived Legitimacy of Social Protest Actions," *Social Problems*, 15 (Winter, 1968), pp. 297–310.

4g.   Solomon, F., and Fishman, J. R., "Youth and Peace: A Psychosocial

Study of Student Peace Demonstrators in Washington, D.C.," *The Journal of Social Issues,* Vol. 20 (1964), pp. 54–73.

4h.   Somers, Robert H., "The Mainsprings of the Rebellion: A Survey of Berkeley Students in November 1964," in *1i*, pp. 530–557.

4i.   Watts, William A., and Whittaker, David, "Free Speech Advocates at Berkeley," *Journal of Applied Behavioral Science,* Vol. 2 (1966), pp. 41–62.

4j.   ———, "Profile of a Non-Conformist Youth Culture: A Study of the Berkeley Non-Students," *Sociology of Education,* Vol. 41 (Spring, 1968), pp. 178–200.

4k.   ———, "Some Sociological Differences Between Highly Committed Members of the Free Speech Movement and the Student Population at Berkeley," *Journal of Applied Behavioral Science,* Vol. 1 (January–March, 1965).

4l.   Westby, D. L., and Braungart, R. G., "Class and Politics in the Family Backgrounds of Student Political Activists," *American Sociological Review,* Vol. 31 (1966), pp. 690–692.

Questionnaire surveys of institutions:

4m.   Orbell, John, "Protest Participation Among Southern Negro College Students," *American Political Science Review,* Vol. 61 (June, 1967), pp. 446–456.

4n.   Peterson, Richard E., "The Scope of Organized Student Protest in 1964–1965," Princeton, N.J., Educational Testing Service, 1966.

4o.   ———, "The Scope of Organized Student Protest in 1967–1968," Princeton, N.J., Educational Testing Service, 1968.

4p.   ———, Sasajima, Masu, and Davis, J. A., "Organized Student Protest and Institutional Climate," *American Educational Research Journal,* Vol. 5 (1968), pp. 291–304.

V. ACTIVISTS AND ACTIVISM: IMPRESSIONISTIC, NON-QUANTITATIVE OR THEORETICAL STUDIES

5a.   Bay, Christian, "Political and Apolitical Students: Facts in Search of Theory," in *1n*, pp. 76–91.

5b.   Coles, Robert, "Psychiatric Observations on Students Demonstrating for Peace," *American Journal of Orthopsychiatry,* Vol. 37 (January, 1967), pp. 107–111.

5c.   Keniston, Kenneth, *The Uncommitted.* New York, Harcourt, Brace & World, 1965.

5d.   ———, *Young Radicals.* New York, Harcourt, Brace & World, 1968.

5e.   May, Henry, "The Student Movement at Berkeley: Some Impressions," in *1i*, pp. 453–463.

5f.   Peterson, Richard E., "The Student Left in American Higher Education," in *1q*, pp. 293–317.

Focusing on causal hypotheses about activism:

5g. Bakke, E. W., "Roots and Soil of Student Activism," in *1k*, pp. 54–73, and *1j*, pp. 64–67.

5h. Brown, Donald R., "Student Stress and the Institutional Environment," in *1n*, pp. 92–107.

5i. Keniston, Kenneth, "The Sources of Student Dissent," in *1n*, pp. 108–135, and *1v*, pp. 309–340:

5j. Katz, J., and Sanford, N., "Causes of the Student Revolt," *Saturday Review*, 48 (December, 1965), pp. 64–67.

5k. Wilson, Everett K., "Our Privileged Pariahs," *Antioch Review*, Fall, 1966, pp. 318–331.

5l. Zinberg, Norman E., "A Return to Commitment," *Antioch Review*, Fall, 1966, pp. 332–344.

Focusing on students, with some attention to activism:

5m. Gordon, David M., "Rebellion in Context: A Student's View of Students," in Robert Morrison (ed.), *The Contemporary University: USA*. Boston, Houghton Mifflin, 1966, pp. 292–314.

5n. Keniston, Kenneth, "The Faces in the Lecture Room," *ibid.*, pp. 315–349.

5o. Meyerson, Martin, "The Ethos of the American College Student: Beyond the Protests," *ibid.*, pp. 266–291.

5p. Trent, James W., and Craise, Judith L., "Commitment and Conformity in the American College," in *1j*, pp. 34–51.

VI. STUDIES OF PROTEST ACTION: STRATEGIC, THEORETICAL AND PREDICTIVE

6a. Altbach, Philip G., "Students and Politics," in *1j*, pp. 175–187, and *1k*, pp. 74–93.

6b. Ben-David, Joseph, and Collins, Randall, "A Comparative Study of Academic Freedom and Student Politics," in *1j*, pp. 220–249, and *1k*, pp. 148–195.

6c. Boulding, Kenneth E., "Reflections on Protest," in *1d*, pp. 61–70.

6d. Brzezinski, Zbigniew, "Revolution and Counter-revolution (Not Necessarily at Columbia)," *New Republic*, Vol. 158, No. 22 (June 1, 1968), pp. 23–25. For a not unfriendly critique of this by Daniel Bell, see *2g*.

6e. Lipsky, Michael, "Protest as a Political Resource," *American Political Science Review*, Vol. 62, No. 4 (December, 1968), pp. 1144–1158.

6f. Moore, R. S., "Protest and Beyond," in *1d*, pp. 51–60.

VII. ACTIVIST GROUPS AND ORGANIZATIONS

Books about the New Left.

7a. Cohen, Mitchell, and Hale, Dennis, *The New Student Left*. Boston, Beacon Press, 1966.

7b.   Jacobs, Paul, and Landau, Saul, *The New Radicals*. New York, Random House, 1966.
7c.   Luce, Phillip Abbott, *The New Left*. New York, David McKay Co., 1966.
7d.   Menashe, Louis, and Radosh, Ronald, *Teach-ins: U.S.A.* New York, Praeger, 1967.
7e.   Newfield, Jack, *A Prophetic Minority*. New York, New American Library, 1966.
Matthews, Donald, and Prothero, James, "Negro Students and the Protest Movement," in *1u*, pp. 379–419.

On leftist student movements:

7f.   Douglass, Bruce, "The Student Christian Movement and Student Politics," in *1d*, pp. 13–41.
7g.   Feinstein, Otto, "Is There a Student Movement?", *New University Thought*, 1 (Summer, 1961), pp. 23–28.
7h.   SDS, "The Port Huron Statement," in *7b*, pp. 150–162; extracts in *7a*, pp. 220–223.
7i.   Jacobs, James, "SDS: Between Reform and Revolution," *The Nation*, Vol. 206 (June 10, 1968), pp. 753–756.
7j.   Kelman, Steven, "SDS: Troubled Voice of the New Left," *New Leader*, 47 (September 27, 1965), pp. 8–14.
7k.   Zinn, Howard, *The New Abolitionists*. Boston, Beacon Press, 1964.

On rightist student movements:

7l.   Cain, Edward, *They'd Rather Be Right: Youth and Conservatism*. New York, Macmillan, 1963.
7m.   Dorfman, Ron, Levy, Paul, and Merbaum, Richard, "The Right at NSA," *New University Thought*, Vol. 2 (Autumn, 1961), pp. 25–32.
7n.   Opinion Research Corporation, "Conservatism on the Campus." Princeton, N.J., Opinion Research Corporation, 1962.
7o.   Schiff, Lawrence, "Dynamic Young Fogies: Rebels on the Right," *Transaction*, November, 1966, pp. 30–36.
7p.   ——, "The Obedient Rebels: A Study of College Conversions to Conservatism," *Journal of Social Issues*, 20 (October, 1964), pp. 74–96.

VIII. ON STUDENT POLITICS AND PROTEST IN OTHER COUNTRIES

General:

Bereday, George Z. F., "Student Unrest on Four Continents: Montreal, Ibadan, Warsaw, and Rangoon," in *1j*, pp. 184–204, and *1k*, pp. 97–123.
Brammer, Lawrence M., "The Student Rebel in the University," *Journal of Higher Education*, 38 (May, 1957), pp. 257–262.
Koplin, Roberta E., "A Model of Student Politicization in the Developing Nations," *Comparative Political Studies*, Vol. 1, No. 3 (October, 1968).

Lipset, Seymour M., "University Students and Politics in Underdeveloped Countries," in *1j*, pp. 132–162, and *1k*, pp. 3–53.

Roucek, Joseph, "The Political Role of Students in Underdeveloped Countries," *Comparative Education*, 3 (March, 1967), pp. 115–121.

Soares, Glaucio A. D., "The Active Few: Student Ideology and Participation in Developing Countries," in *1j*, pp. 205–219, and *1k*, pp. 124–137.

On the West:

Allardt, Erik, and Tomasson, Richard F., "Stability and Strains in Scandinavian Student Politics," in *1g*, pp. 156–165.

Cockburn, Alexander, and Blackburn, Robin (eds.), *Student Power*. London, Penguin Books, 1969.

Cornell, Richard, "Students and Politics in the Communist Countries of Eastern Europe," in *1g*, pp. 166–183.

Halsey, A. H., and Marks, Stephen, "British Student Politics," in *1g*, pp. 116–136.

McGuigan, Gerald F., *et al., Student Protest*. London, Methuen, 1969. Mainly about Canada.

Martin, David, *Anarchy and Culture*. London, Routledge & Kegan Paul, 1969.

Pinner, Frank A., "Tradition and Transgression: Western European Students in the Postwar World," in *1g*, pp. 137–155.

Seabury, Paul, "Student Freedom and the Republic of Scholars: Berlin and Berkeley," in *1j*, pp. 350–358, and *1k*, pp. 253–266.

Spender, Stephen, "Notes on the Sorbonne Revolution," "Czechoslovakia and Western Students," and "The Berlin Youth Model," in *1w*, pp. 37–95.

Worms, Jean-Pierre, "The French Student Movement," in *1j*, pp. 359–366, and *1k*, pp. 267–282.

On Asia and Africa:

Altbach, Philip G. (ed.), *Turmoil and Transition: Higher Education and Student Politics in India*. New York, Basic Books, in press.

———, "Student Politics and Higher Education in India," in *1g*, pp. 254–273.

DiBona, Joseph, "Indiscipline and Student Leadership in an Indian University," in *1j*, pp. 306–319, and *1k*, pp. 372–394.

Finlay, David J., "Students and Politics in Ghana," in *1h*, pp. 51–69.

Israel, John, "Reflections on the Modern Chinese Student Movement," in *1g*, pp. 229–253.

Moore, Clement H., and Hochschild, Arlie R., "Student Unions in North African Politics," in *1g*, pp. 21–50.

Roos, Leslie L., Roos, Noralou P., and Field, Gary R., "Students and Politics in Turkey," in *1g*, pp. 184–203.

Shimbori, Michiya, "The Sociology of a Student Movement—A Japanese Case Study," in *1g*, pp. 204–228.

Silverstein, Josef, "Burmese Student Politics in a Changing Society," in *1g*, pp. 274–292.

Spencer, Metta, "Professional, Scientific, and Intellectual Students in India," in *1j*, pp. 296–305, and *1k*, pp. 357–371.

On Latin America:

Albornoz, Orlando, "Academic Freedom and Higher Education in Latin America," in *1j*, pp. 250–256, and *1k*, pp. 283–292.

Bonilla, Frank, and Glazer, Myron, *Student Activism in Chile.* New York, Basic Books, in press.

Glazer, Myron, "Student Politics in a Chilean University," in *1g*, pp. 99–115.

———, "The Professional and Political Attitudes of Chilean University Students," in *1j*, pp. 282–295, and *1k*, pp. 332–356.

Nasatir, David, "University Experience and Political Unrest of Students in Buenos Aires," in *1j*, pp. 273–281, and *1k*, pp. 318–331.

Scott, Robert E., "Student Political Activism in Latin America," in *1h*, pp. 70–98.

Walker, Kenneth N., "A Comparison of University Reform Movements in Argentina and Columbia," in *1j*, pp. 257–272, and *1k*, pp. 293–317.

Walter, Richard, *Students and Politics in Argentina.* New York, Basic Books, 1968.

IX. THE EVALUATION OF STUDENT PROTEST

Debates about student protest and its merits. See 1v, also:

9a. Kennan, G. F., *Democracy and the Student Left.* Boston, Little, Brown, 1968.

9b. Draper, Hal, "FSM: Freedom Fighters or Misguided Rebels?" in *1c*, pp. 324–332.

Glazer, Nathan, "FSM: Freedom Fighters or Misguided Rebels?" in *1c*, pp. 333–339.

9c. Goodman, Paul, "Thoughts on Berkeley," in *1b*, pp. 77–82, *1c*, pp. 316–320, and *1d*, pp. 27–31.

Glazer, Nathan, "Reply to Goodman," in *1c*, pp. 320–322, and *1d*, pp. 198–200.

Goodman, Paul, "Reply to Glazer," in *1c*, pp. 322–324, and *1d*, pp. 200–203.

9d. Glazer, Nathan, "What Happened at Berkeley," in *1b*, pp. 43–66, *1c*, pp. 285–303, *1d*, pp. 160–181, and *1e*, pp. 15–23.

Selznick, Philip, "Reply to Glazer," in *1c*, pp. 303–312, *1d*, pp. 182–192, and *1e*, pp. 24–29.

Glazer, Nathan, "Reply to Selznick," in *1c*, pp. 312–315, and *1d*, pp. 192–197.

Some defenses of student protest include 1x, 2k, also:

9e. Davidson, Carl, "University Reform Revisited," *Educational Record,* 48 (Winter, 1967), pp. 5–10.

9f. Duberman, Martin, "On Misunderstanding Student Rebels," *Atlantic Monthly,* Vol. 222, No. 5 (November, 1968), pp. 63–70.

9g. Hayden, Tom, "Two, Three, Many Columbias," *Ramparts,* June 15, 1968, p. 40.

9h. Lynd, Staughton, "The New Radicals and Participatory Democracy," *Dissent,* Vol. 12 (Summer, 1965), pp. 324–333.

9i. Neff, Charles B., "The Administrative Challenge of the New Student Activism," *Journal of Higher Education,* Vol. 39 (February, 1968), pp. 69–76.

9j. New Republic, *Thoughts of the Young Radicals.* New Jersey, Harrison-Blaine, Inc., 1966.

9k. Oglesby, Carl, "Let Us Shape the Future," *Liberation,* Vol. 10 (January, 1966), pp. 11–14.

9l. Potter, P., "Student Discontent and Campus Reform," in O. A. Knorr and W. J. Minter (eds.), *Order and Freedom on the Campus.* Boulder, Colo., Western Interstate Commission for Higher Education, 1965, pp. 71–78.

9m. Rossman, Michael, "Barefoot in a Marshmallow World," in *7b,* pp. 208–212, and in *Ramparts,* 4 (January, 1966).

9m. ———, "The Movement and Education Reform," *The American Scholar,* 36 (Autumn, 1967), pp. 594–600.

9n. Savio, Mario, *et al.,* "The 'New Radicals': An Exchange," *New Politics,* 4 (Fall, 1965), pp. 13–31.

9n. Savio, Mario, "An End to History," in *1e,* pp. 179–182, and *7b,* pp. 230–234.

Some critiques of student protest. See *1f, 2g,* also:

9o. Barzun, Jacques, *The American University.* New York, Harper & Row, 1968, especially Chapter 3. See his *Teacher in America* also.

9p. Crane, Robert M., "Unrest on Campus—Revolution or Evolution," *College and University,* 42 (Winter, 1967), pp. 209–217.

9q. Feuer, Lewis, "The Student Left in the USA," *Survey,* 62 (January, 1967), pp. 90–103.

9q. ———, "Rebellion at Berkeley," *New Leader,* Vol. 47 (December 21, 1964), pp. 3–12.

9r. Frankel, Charles, *Education and the Barricades.* New York, W. W. Norton & Co., Inc., 1968.

9s. Gallagher, Buell, "Student Unrest," in Esther Lloyd-Jones and Herman A. Estrin (eds.), *The American Student and His College.* Boston, Houghton Mifflin, 1967, pp. 291–298.

9t. Glazer, Nathan, "The New Left and Its Limits," *Commentary,* 46 (July, 1968), pp. 31–39.

9t. ———, "Student Politics in a Democratic Society," in *1r,* pp. 202–217.

9u. Hook, Sidney, "Academic Freedom and the Rights of Students," in *1i,* pp. 432–442.

9u. ———, "The Prospects of Academe," *Encounter,* August, 1969, pp. 60–66.

9u. ———, "The Trojan Horse in American Higher Education," *Educational Record,* Vol. 50 (Winter, 1968), pp. 21–29.

9v. Howe, Irving, "New Styles in Leftism," *Dissent,* 12 (Summer, 1965), pp. 293–323; also in Howe (ed.), *The Radical Imagination.* New York, New American Library, 1967, pp. 64–89.

9w. Kahn, Tom, "The Problem of the New Left," *Commentary,* Vol. 42 (July, 1966), pp. 30–38.

9x. Kristol, Irving, "What's Bugging the Students," in *Atlantic Monthly,* Vol. 216, No. 5 (November, 1965); also in the Editors of Atlantic, *The Troubled Campus.* Boston, Little, Brown, 1965, pp. 3–12.

9y. Lipset, Seymour Martin, and Seabury, Paul, "The Lesson of Berkeley," in *1i,* pp. 340–349.

4

THE SCOPE OF
ORGANIZED STUDENT PROTEST*

by Richard E. Peterson

COLLEGE STUDENT unrest has escalated to the point where perhaps most officials responsible for the higher learning in America would now consider it their number one problem. Ordinary people outside the university, in a year when law and order are much on their minds, are outraged at the prospect of affluent youth openly in opposition to all manner of institutionalized practice and authority. The significance of the student activist movement can hardly be minimized.

This study has two general purposes. The first is to describe the dimensions of organized student protest during the year 1967–1968, to delineate some of the realities of the "student movement" of the 1960's at this particular point in its evolution.

The second broad purpose is to assemble information that could be compared to the findings of a similar study conducted in 1965 and reported in a monograph entitled "The Scope of Organized Student Protest in 1964–1965" (Princeton, N.J.: Educational Testing

* Dr. Richard E. Peterson is Research Psychologist for the Educational Testing Service, Princeton, N.J., and author of "The Scope of Organized Student Protest in 1964–1965," Copyright © 1965 by Educational Testing Service. This chapter is an adaptation of "The Scope of Organized Student Protest in 1967–1968," Copyright © 1968 by Educational Testing Service, and appears here with permission.

Service, 1966), thus enabling statements about trends in organized student protest during the three-year period. Assertions about trends will be somewhat tentative, however, since the results of the two surveys are not based on exactly identical samples.

In that the present survey was intended to provide data maximally comparable to the findings of the 1965 study, the method followed in the two surveys is nearly identical. Questionnaire format, the population of colleges polled, and statistical procedures are all identical with the earlier study. The only important difference on the questionnaire is that five new issue statements were substituted for issues that were judged not to be relevant in 1967–68.

The survey instrument consisted of 27 issue statements organized into five categories: instruction, faculty, freedom of expression, student-administration, and off-campus issues. The statements are listed in Table 1. In each category, space was provided for writing in additional issues and for providing a summary estimate of the proportion of students involved in any and all protests in that category.

For each issue, the respondent indicated either that there had been no organized protest or the frequency of protest, the proportion of the student body involved, and the extent of active faculty involvement. In addition, the respondent provided information on some six institutional characteristics: type of institution, total enrollment, approximate proportion of faculty with doctorates, region, approximate proportion of students living on campus, and approximate proportion of student body belonging to organizations comprising the student Left.

The population consisted of all the regionally accredited, four-year degree-granting institutions in the United States, the same population surveyed in the earlier study.[1] Questionnaires were addressed to the ranking student personnel administrator, in most cases the dean of students. By July 5, 1968, when data processing commenced, 859 or 86 percent of the questionnaires had been returned.

In addition to the questionnaire, the survey package included a cover letter and a sheet entitled "Notes on Defining 'Organized Protest.'" Within the cover letter were the sentences:

Organized protest may of course take many forms. In completing the questionnaire, it is suggested that the basic idea be the existence of a *group* of reasonably like-minded students which sought in some collective manner to make its opposition to some existing situation known to the appropriate authorities.

On the "Notes" page, a distinction was drawn between private, essentially passive discontent on the one hand, and public, active protest on the other hand. Respondents were advised that the survey was concerned only with the latter, that is, with

. . . planned, public expressions of disapproval on the part of *groups* of students and . . . what issues have given rise to such active protest. The assumption is that overt actions of groups of students on campus or of individual students participating with off-campus groups are generally known to the respective deans of students, and that these organized protest activities can be reported on a survey questionnaire.

A list of examples of forms that organized protest activities might take (picketing, sit-in, and the like) was also given.

The "definition" of "organized protest" provided was deliberately in general terms in order to allow respondents to report what each one perceived as an organized protest incident in whatever form it might have taken. While so broad a definition may render a given questionnaire somewhat invalid for that institution (assuming some kind of objective criterion), the variation in definition of organized protest from one respondent to another is likely to be generally random and hence to cancel out when fairly large numbers of institutions are combined and described in summary fashion (which is the practice throughout this report).

Perhaps the most important limitation on the results to be presented is that they represent only the perceptions of deans of students.[2] While reality is seldom known except as it is viewed by someone, it is unlikely that the reality of student protest at College X is the same in the eyes of its dean of students as it is for its president, or the editor of the school newspaper, or the chairman of the sociology department.[3] The results, then, provide a picture of student protest as it is drawn by deans of students. The criticism that "Dean So and So never gets out of his office and has no idea what's going on" can probably be answered by assuming that there are also deans who overestimate the situation, and that this sort of random variation also tends to cancel out in summary statistics.

An inevitable limitation on the validity of results in mail survey research stems from the possible differences between respondents and nonrespondents. An 86 percent rate of return is quite good in view of the general experience in survey research; our judgment is that results based on the total pool of 859 need not be seriously questioned. Return rates differed to some extent for various subgroups of colleges. The category of Teachers Colleges, with a return rate of 71 percent, however, is probably the only subsample that calls for caution in interpreting results. For all other categories—enrollment, region or type and control—responses ranged from 82 percent to 95 percent.

The survey instrument asked for information about student protest during the period September 1967 to June 1968; these survey results, then, serve to describe the protest-by-issues situation only as of the academic year 1967–68. Reference will be made to the results of the earlier study when it is patently evident that some change has occurred or trend is underway.

The Protest-by-Issue Picture Nationally, and in 50 Large Public Universities

In Table 1, figures are presented which show the proportions of the 859 institutions (deans) reporting organized protest during 1967–68 for each of the 27 issues listed on the questionnaire. Similar data for the 849 institutions responding to the 1964–65 survey are also shown. Results for the 50 largest universities in 1967–68 are also included, as are analogous data from the 1965 study; the two sets of data, however, are not strictly comparable in that the samples of 50 universities in either survey are not identical.

Taking first the five issues comprising the instruction category, one can see that the first two, the "classes too large—instruction too impersonal" and the "senior faculty insufficiently involved in teaching" issues loom very small in the overall picture. One rather obvious reason is that only a fairly small fraction of American institutions of higher education can be regarded either as very large or as having instructors that are truly "senior," that is, senior in ways other than gross seniority (time in service at the institution—or simply age). However, even students at the universities seem not to be notably discontented with impersonal instruction as such.

Some 13 percent of the 859 colleges reported organized student dissatisfaction with the quality of some aspect of instruction other

TABLE 1

PERCENTAGES OF ALL INSTITUTIONS AND OF 50 LARGE PUBLIC UNIVERSITIES REPORTING SOME DEGREE OF ORGANIZED STUDENT PROTEST IN RELATION TO 27 ISSUES, FOR 1967–68 AND 1964–65

		All Institutions 849 in 1965, 859 in 1968		50 Large Public Universities	
		1967–68	1964–65	1967–68	1964–65
Instruction	Undergraduate classes typically too large, instruction too impersonal	03	04	10	10
	Senior faculty not sufficiently involved in undergraduate instruction	02	03	08	16
	Poor quality of instruction—in general or specific instances	13	12	18	10
	Generally prevailing system(s) of testing and/or grading	12	09	20	12
	Curriculum inflexibility	15	08	18	14
Fac-ulty	Academic freedom for faculty—in principle	04	04	08	16
	Faculty tenure policies, e.g., "publish or perish"	04	04	06	08
	Controversy surrounding a particular faculty member	20	16	26	26
Freedom of Ex-pression	"Censorship" of certain publications, e.g., student newspaper	10	14	20	18
	Campus rules regarding speeches, appearances by "controversial" persons	08	09	06	24
	Actual appearance by a particular person of leftist persuasion	05	05	08	22
	Actual appearance by a particular person of rightist persuasion	04	05	06	18
Student-administration	Dormitory and other living-group regulations, e.g., women's hours	34	28	30	22
	Food service	25	29	18	28
	Dress regulations	20	20	06	20
	Policies, regulations regarding student drinking	11	11	08	10
	Policies, regulations regarding student use of drugs	05	**	08	**
	Disciplinary action against particular student(s)	16	18	16	18
	Alleged racial discrimination: in admissions, nonaction on frat. discrim., etc.	18	24	48	24
	Student-administration communication; students unable to voice grievances	19	24	28	24
	Insufficient student participation in establishing campus policies	27	26	36	26
Off-campus Issues	Civil rights: local area (off-campus)—protest and/or work	29	38	46	56
	The draft	25	**	46	**
	On-campus recruiting by one or another of the armed services	25	**	56	**
	On-campus recruiting by any other firm or agency, e.g., Dow, CIA, etc.	20	**	68	**
	U.S. policies regarding Vietnam	38	21	64	68
	Classified defense and related research on campus	04	**	16	**

** No comparable data.

than class size and absence of senior professors. Systems of testing and grading were an issue for protest at 12 percent of the colleges; curriculum inflexibility was at issue in 15 percent of the reporting institutions. In sum, it appears that the general nature of undergraduate teaching is not being widely disputed by the students affected, although there is evidence of increasing student dissatisfaction with curricular rigidities.

Within the faculty issue category, it was controversies surrounding particular faculty members (a firing or resignation or some published radical idea) that enlisted the widest active student concern. Academic freedom for faculty was seldom at issue insofar as the students were concerned. Faculty tenure policies were likewise rarely an issue for students; "publish or perish" type policies, of course, only prevail at the more prestigious institutions, or at colleges struggling to be so regarded.

Alleged "censorship" of student publications by a slight margin was the most frequently cited freedom of expression issue; it gave rise to organized protest on one in ten campuses in the nation. Regulations governing appearances by controversial persons (e.g., speaker bans) were actively contested by the students at 8 percent of the colleges (there was substantial variation by type of institution, however, as will be touched upon later). While appearances by particular persons of known "off-center" political views were seldom causes for student demonstration (most colleges never invite such personages), it is of some interest that appearances by rightists and leftists provoked protest in about equal number (no apparent change from the earlier survey).

The student-administration issue category was something of a mixed bag. There is little reason to believe that protests over food service, for example, would be related to protests about most of the other issues in the category. At any rate, food service reportedly upset students on one in four campuses, with little variation across types of colleges. Quite possibly the nature of institutional cooking, menus, etc., provides an easy target for frustration-induced hostilities on a more or less continuing basis, independent of earth-shaking historical events. In 1965, food service stood second in the field of 27 as an issue for campus protest; in 1968 it was surpassed by at least four kinds of issues.

One in three deans reported organized protest about living-group regulations, such as rules governing women's hours. Such regulations, which generally impinge in some degree or other on the personal lives of students, probably constituted the most significant *on-campus* issue for organized student protest. Cutting across all the institutional types, there can be little doubt that college students continue to be very widely in opposition to *in loco parentis* controls over personal conduct (28 percent of the colleges in 1965; 34 percent in 1968).

Drinking (alcohol, on or near the campus) and the nature of campus dress are other aspects of personal behavior that many colleges have traditionally tried to regulate. Of the two, dress regulations were twice as often reported to have evoked protests. While there have not been new fashions in drinking, there continue to be noticeable shifts in clothing preferences among students—to the new, different, shorter, etc.—that authorities on some campuses no doubt find intolerable; more importantly, many colleges (mainly women's) still require their students to wear a kind of uniform. (The 1965 and 1968 data are identical for both the drinking and dress issues.)

Use of drugs (including chiefly marijuana but also other more potent agents) is undeniably on the rise among college students. Most colleges have probably not yet decided what their stand will be. It is conceivable that a confrontation over narcotics could usher in an era of total freedom for students (in all but the most fundamentalist of colleges). In the past year, however, student protest over campus drug-use policies was reported at only 5 percent of the colleges.

Alleged racial discrimination was an important "new" issue in 1968. Eighteen percent of the deans reported incidents. The problem in the past year, of course, has been less one of discrimination than of institutional recognition of the higher education needs of an emerging black consciousness. In the spring of 1968 black student groups, mainly at the public and independent universities, were notably successful in pressing for admission of more Negro students, hiring of black faculty, establishment of programs of black studies (at Negro as well as white colleges), and so forth.

Close to one in five colleges reported organized discontent over unsatisfactory "student-administration communication." Better than one in four deans reported protest aimed at larger student roles in campus governance. These "student power" issues are much on the minds of the more sophisticated and aggressive of "legitimate" (elected) student leaders across the country (generally excepting those at the many small, parochial, usually sectarian colleges that do not belong to NSA).

Among the off-campus issues, civil rights, the paramount issue in 1965, has declined in significance during the past three years in terms both of absolute numbers of colleges reporting incidents (29 percent versus 38 percent in 1965) as well as importance in relation to other issues. A large number, perhaps as many as half, of all the reported student-generated civil rights demonstrations were in response to the assassination of Martin Luther King. The era of mass student direct involvement in civil rights work has passed (possibly temporarily, however). White student activists, at the behest of blacks, have largely withdrawn to other matters, leaving conduct of the on-going civil rights revolution almost exclusively to black activists.

Interference with recruiting activities of military and war-related agencies by student radicals was much in the news in the fall of 1967. Demonstrations were staged against armed services recruiters on one in four campuses, and against recruiting from other agencies and firms (such as Dow Chemical and the CIA) on one in five campuses. Opposition to war-effort recruiters took place mainly at the public and independent universities. In large part these demonstrations were organized by local chapters of Students for a Democratic Society, in pursuance of a "direction" approved at their national meeting the previous summer, and may be taken as a gauge of SDS's ability to override its cherished localism and mount a coordinated "program" on a national scale.

The draft was protested by students at 25 percent of the colleges across the country. The Vietnam war came under attack at 38 percent of the campuses (compared to 21 percent in 1965). The war, then, was the predominant issue for student activists during the academic year 1967–1968.

It would be well, at this point, to take special note of the overriding significance of the factor of institutional size. It is not, though this may be important, the size-induced feeling of impersonality, alienation, and being lost that have been so widely discussed that is of concern here. Rather it is the simple notion of a critical mass, that a relatively large number of individuals on a given campus constitutes a relatively greater potential for protest activities (and many other kinds of activities); the likelihood of almost any imaginable activity being instigated is rather greater if there are, say, 10,000 unique personalities (students, faculty, administrators) on hand than if there are only 1,000 individuals present. Thus in the section immediately following, for example, where data are given indicating protest activities to be more often reported in public universities than in other types of institutions, the factor of gross size is implicit in many of the explanatory comments that are offered.

Differences in the "protest rates" between the 50 large public universities and the total sample (which includes the 50 PU's) are generally not large in the first three issue categories (instruction, faculty, and freedom of expression). The largest difference came on the "censorship" issue, with twice as many of the large universities reporting organized protests. Viewed against the earlier findings, the differentials between the large PU's and the "norm" are not only generally smaller, but the absolute rates of protest over these issues (the first 12 on the questionnaire) tend to be lower than in 1965 (six lower, two the same, and four higher). The decreased rates are most noticeable for three of the four issues in the freedom of expression category. Apparently campus rules about controversial speakers in the large universities have either been relaxed or they were less often put to the test in 1967–1968. Visits by political "extremists" to the large universities were either less frequent as compared to three years ago, or else such visitors were greeted by their student ideological opponents with greater tolerance, courtesy or resignation than was the case three years ago.

With the exception of drug policies, issues bearing on institutional control of personal conduct (women's hours, drinking regulations, etc.) were generally less often contested on the large campuses than elsewhere. In view of the many students at most large universities who live off-campus free from institutional controls, establishment of such rules is likely to represent a kind of token homage to institutional authority and traditional morality; real, continuing enforcement of these regulations is usually seen as an exercise in futility.

Almost half of the 50 large public universities (compared to 18 percent in the total sample) indicated outbreaks prompted by racial circumstances. Most of the public universities outside the South now have black student organizations on campus; as noted earlier, many of these groups in the past year took strong action toward introducing black studies and recruiting large numbers of Negro students and faculty. Additionally, most of the largest (and oldest) public university campuses still come equipped with national Greek-letter fraternities and sororities, and their persisting "social selectivity" continues to be a "good" issue for protest-prone students.

The issues of student-administration communication and insufficient participation in establishing campus policies led to somewhat more frequent protest among the 50 large universities than in the total sample. Thirty-six percent of the 50 PU's reported activism on behalf of a larger student role in campus governance (as opposed to 20 percent in 1965). Student leaders on these campuses are likely to be relatively sophisticated in the sense of being abreast of the most advanced thinking (e.g., from NSA) on what it should mean to be a student leader. In addition, student power has become an important concern for student Left groups, such as SDS, which were reported to exist on 46 (92 percent) of the 50 campuses.

On this note, we move finally to the off-campus issues, for which the numbers of large public universities reporting organized student protest were large indeed in contrast to the total sample. Most of the reasons for the differentials have already been touched on: critical masses of morally sensitized, convention-rejecting, protest-prone students; presence of SDS chapters for whose members the war and the university's "complicity" in it are *the* key issues; support from radical faculty; support from radicalized townspeople (including the renowned "nonstudent"); and so forth.

Variation by Type of Institution

In Table 2 one can read, issue by issue, the variation in incidence of organized protest according to type of institution. The figures are percentages of institutions in each of eight breakdowns reporting protest activities in relation to each of the 27 issues listed on the questionnaire.[4]

Differences by type of institution were generally small for the issues comprising the instruction category. On the very first item—large classes and impersonal instruction—as one would expect, the public universities differed somewhat from the other subsamples. Protests about insufficient undergraduate teaching on the part of senior faculty was also largely confined to the universities—where there are, in fact, significant numbers of faculty that can be regarded as senior. Active protest concerning (poor) quality of instruction and testing and grading policies was fairly uniform across the institutional subsamples. Whereas three years ago Catholic institutions and public

TABLE 2

PERCENTAGES OF DIFFERENT TYPES OF INSTITUTIONS REPORTING SOME INCIDENCE OF ORGANIZED STUDENT PROTEST IN RELATION TO 27 ISSUES (1967–68)

	All	Public Lib. Assts. Coll.	Public Univ.	Indep. Lib. Assts. Coll.	Indep. Univ.	Cath. Inst.	Prot. Inst.	Teachers Coll.	Tech. Inst.
	n = 859	n = 97	n = 144	n = 146	n = 58	n = 143	n = 191	n = 53	n = 27
Instruction									
Undergraduate classes typically too large, instruction too impersonal	03	04	09	03	05	01	01	02	00
Senior faculty not sufficiently involved in undergraduate instruction	02	00	06	01	03	01	01	00	00
Poor quality of instruction—in general or specific instances	13	14	15	14	10	15	12	08	11
Generally prevailing system(s) of testing and/or grading	12	13	17	12	12	13	10	08	15
Curriculum inflexibility	15	12	18	14	19	17	11	11	19
Faculty									
Academic freedom for faculty—in principle	04	05	09	02	03	03	03	04	04
Faculty tenure policies, e.g., "publish or perish"	04	05	07	02	05	02	04	04	04
Controversy surrounding a particular faculty member	20	21	28	18	29	14	18	25	07
Freedom of Expression									
"Censorship" of certain publications, e.g., student newspaper	10	08	16	03	09	12	11	06	11
Campus rules regarding speeches, appearances by "controversial" persons	08	04	18	03	09	10	07	02	00
Actual appearance by a particular person of leftist persuasion	05	03	08	01	03	07	04	04	04
Actual appearance by a particular person of rightist persuasion	04	02	09	03	03	03	03	02	04
Student-administration									
Dormitory and other living-group regulations, e.g., women's hours	34	26	35	39	36	27	36	28	41
Food service	25	26	21	21	29	29	31	15	33
Dress regulations	20	15	12	19	10	31	24	13	19
Policies, regulations regarding student drinking	11	05	10	10	09	10	17	06	11
Policies, regulations regarding student use of drugs	05	04	08	07	07	02	05	02	04
Disciplinary action against particular student(s)	16	11	17	14	20	17	21	08	04
Alleged racial discrimination: in admissions, nonaction on frat. discrim., etc.	18	13	35	17	41	04	14	15	07
Student-administration communication; students unable to voice grievances	19	15	20	20	26	25	17	08	07
Insufficient student participation in establishing campus policies	27	26	31	25	41	28	24	19	19
Off-campus Issues									
Civil rights: local area (off-campus)—protest and/or work	29	19	35	34	40	31	24	21	22
The draft	25	22	36	27	55	15	20	06	19
On-campus recruiting by one or another of the armed services	25	27	42	32	48	13	16	06	15
On-campus recruiting by any other firm or agency, e.g., Dow, CIA, etc.	20	19	50	13	60	10	04	02	26
U.S. policies regarding Vietnam	38	31	53	44	68	28	30	21	33
Classified defense and related research on campus	04	02	11	01	16	03	02	02	00

69

universities were most often protested for their curriculum inflexibility, active student interest in this matter has expanded throughout the spectrum of higher education, most notably in the independent universities and technical institutions (one in five deans in both categories reporting protest).

Moving on to the faculty issues, one notes the slightly higher incidence of active student concern over academic freedom for faculty in the public institutions (excepting teachers colleges). While partly a function of size—that is, more teachers (and students) on hand potentially to create an academic freedom issue—the public institutions, more importantly, are subject to closer scrutiny by and greater accountability to political and various other citizen interests. Variation on the "controversial professor" issue also seems related to the critical mass notion (the more professors on hand, the greater the likelihood of a controversial one). The shifts between 1965 and 1968 on this issue were substantial for both teachers colleges (25 percent versus 13 percent in 1965) and technical institutions (19 percent versus 7 percent in 1965); reasons for these trends are not immediately apparent.

Institutional variation on the issues in the freedom of expression category also tended to be fairly small. On the issue of alleged censorship of student publications, the range was from 16 percent in the public universities and 12 percent in the Catholic institutions down to 3 percent in the independent liberal arts colleges. Protests over campus regulations on appearances by controversial persons were reported most often at public universities (18 percent) and least often at teachers colleges (2 percent) and technical institutions (0 percent). Differences among the types of institutions in regard to protests over appearances of both right-wing and left-wing personages were negligible.

Several of the issues in the student-administration category elicited substantial differences in organized protest among the eight institutional subsamples. On the issue of living-group regulations, the range was from 41 and 39 percent in the technical schools and independent liberal arts colleges down to 27 and 26 percent in the Catholic institutions and public liberal arts colleges respectively. It also appears that in the three-year interval between the two surveys, the kinds of students attending Protestant and technical institutions in particular have increasingly come to espouse the burgeoning ethic of personal freedom and indifference to traditional moral restraints. On the matter of dress regulations, the most noteworthy result was the relative frequency of protests over this issue at the Catholic institutions, suggesting that it is chiefly the Catholic (and to a lesser extent the Protestant) institutions that are trying to hold the line on this manifestation of the "cultural revolution." With regard to student drinking (alcoholic beverages) it is the Protestant colleges that are now most concerned to hold the line. College drug-use policies, generally not yet at issue, were protested slightly more often at the public universities and independent institutions, places to which hippies and other uninhibited, experience-seeking drug-prone youths tend to be attracted.[5]

As noted earlier, agitation on behalf of black educational interests occurred primarily at the public and independent universities. At these places there would be relatively large pools of Negroes on campus out of which to generate confrontations. In contrast to the other subgroups, the universities would also tend to attract the most articulate and intellectually able of Negro youths (which seems to imply, parenthetically, that the Negro youth-intelligentsia is the main component of the black power-pride-identity movement).

Are the Negroes at the four-year colleges, then, more conventionally gentle, pursuing, for example, vocational interests, as at the teachers and technical colleges? [6] Or are there simply too few Negroes on most of these campuses to form critical masses? [7] Of particular interest is the near absence of black agitation at Catholic institutions. What does one make of this apparent fact? Are Catholic colleges, contrary to the general trend, not going out of their way to increase the numbers of Negroes (of any religion) in their student bodies? Can Catholic Negroes, the few that there are, be the most docile of *all* Negroes?

Problems of "student-administration communication," a somewhat vague and catch-all theme at best, were less often reported at the teachers colleges and technical institutions. On these campuses where the work of the college is more narrowly focused, the range of matters over which "communication" could conceivably break down is rather obviously reduced. Perhaps more important, the kinds of students attracted to teachers and technical colleges are probably by interest and temperament less inclined toward conflict with institutional authorities whose modus operandi (especially at teachers colleges) are typically more authoritarian or paternalistic than at other types of colleges.[8] This same interpretation could apply to the as yet relative disinterest in student participation in campus governance at the teachers colleges and technical institutions (one in five respondents reporting organized concern). By contrast, student power vis-à-vis faculty, administration and trustees is an expanding point of contention, especially at the (other) public and independent institutions.[9] Student demands for a meaningful role in campus governance will continue to have an important impact on the conduct of higher education.

The largest variation in incidence of organized student protest according to type of institution was in relation to the several off-campus issues listed on the questionnaire. With regard to civil rights, the range was from 40 percent in the independent universities to 22 and 21 percent in the technical institutions and teachers colleges respectively.

The draft is an issue that could presumably engage students throughout the spectrum of colleges, save perhaps at the places that are all or heavily female. Differences among the institutional sub-samples, however, are quite striking, ranging from the independent universities where 55 percent reported draft protests, down to the Catholic and teachers colleges, with 15 and 6 percent respectively indicating protest (a good number of these colleges are entirely or heavily women). The same general pattern held also for protests over the Vietnam war as such: greater incidence of protest in the public and independent institutions (except teachers colleges) than at the sectarian colleges (which account for roughly a third of all the colleges, though not nearly this proportion of students).

While recruiters from the Armed Services systematically cover nearly all campuses in the country—save perhaps the women's colleges, although there are women's auxiliaries to the various military services—the variation across types of colleges was substantial: the public and independent institutions stood above the national norm (25 percent); the sectarian and vocationally oriented colleges fell below. Recruiters from businesses and governmental agencies whose activities are war-related (e.g., Dow Chemical, the CIA) would generally concentrate their efforts at the universities and technical schools, where the scientific and professional manpower sought after tends to be "produced." This state of affairs in large part explains the institutional differences, which range from 60 and 50 percent in the independent and public university subsamples down to 4 and 2 percent in the Protestant colleges and T.C.'s respectively.

Protest of institutional involvement in war-related research was generally limited to the public and independent universities, where the bulk of such "defense" research within the academic world is conducted. The institutions associated with the Institute for Defense Analyses are all prestigious public or independent universities. The 0 percent figure (rounded) for the technical institutions may represent a sampling anomaly. Maybe not, however; it may be that these generally very intelligent future scientists and engineers tend to be somewhat indifferent to the moral implications of the work they represent.

Variation among the types of institutions on the off-campus issues, then, is quite marked, and substantially larger than for the on-campus issues. Some of the variation is easily explained by the different structure and function of the various types of colleges; Dow recruiters and classified research are found only at the large universities, for example. Sheer size of student body increases the likelihood of organized protest. Many of the Catholic institutions are small women's colleges. And so forth. But this is not the total explanation. Why the variation on issues that are potentially relevant on the great majority of campuses—civil rights, the draft, military recruiters, the war itself? Most certainly part of the explanation lies in the differing background and value patterns—different "input characteristics," as the jargon has it—of students attracted to different types of colleges.[10] There are differences in tested intelligence or academic aptitude, a personal trait known to be related to political activism; protesters have been shown generally to be noncareerist; various studies have shown "protest proneness" to be related to parental political, child-rearing, and religious values.[11] Of particular interest in view of the differing rates of protest between sectarian and nonsectarian campuses is the matter of commitment to an established religion on the part of the individual student. Religious preference, or lack thereof, is known to be associated with a variety of social attitudes.[12] Very recently, Alexander Astin has reported that *absence* of a religious preference is the single personal characteristic most predictive of protest behavior in college freshmen.[13] In short, the so-called "new" college students, the "post-modern youth" in Keniston's words[14] who aggressively reject the conventional middle-class ethos, are unevenly distributed across the spectrum of American colleges;

at the very least, they are over-represented in the independent and public universities and liberal arts colleges, and under-represented in the sectarian and career-oriented institutions.[15]

Other Factors Related to Protest

Responding institutions were further classified according to (1) Regional accreditation: New England and Middle States, Southern, North Central, and Western and Northwest, (2) Proportion of faculty holding the doctorate, (3) Estimated (by the dean) percentage of students in leftist organizations, and (4) Proportions of students living on campus. Of these, the last yielded no findings of significance.

Generally speaking, geographical variation in organized student protest in 1967–68, while not notably large, was somewhat more pronounced than in 1964–65. The major regional difference was for the off-campus issues (civil rights, the draft, Vietnam, etc.): colleges in the South reported substantially less organized protest than did institutions in other parts of the country.

Proportion of faculty holding doctorates was taken as a rough index of institutional quality. While the correlations with protest, issue by issue, are generally positive—that is, student activism almost regardless of issue is related to institutional quality[16]—only the correlation with Vietnam war protest is strong enough to have any real significance. This is a finding to be reckoned with, however, if the Vietnam action continues to grind along; students from these "good" colleges are likely to be the opinion leaders of the under-30 generation.

Three years ago the student Left, typified by SNCC and SDS which had emerged out of the civil rights movement, was usually viewed as a temporary aberration actuated by romantic and idealistic kids who would soon outgrow it all. It hasn't turned out this way, as the popular media love to remind us.[17] College administrators, for one, don't need to be reminded. In 1965, 26 percent of the colleges reported having student Left groups; by 1968 the figure had risen to 46 percent.[18] (SDS was founded in 1962.)

The proportion of the student body estimated by the dean as belonging to Left organizations correlated positively with incidence of protest on all but one issue (dress regulations). (The reader is reminded that statistical correlation means association not causation.) For on-campus issues the degree of association was not large. On the two student power issues, the correlations were slightly larger than in the earlier study, suggesting an increasing interest in this area on the part of, say, SDS. Once pessimistic about the possibility of instigating university reforms,[19] student radicals after successes at Columbia and elsewhere are fast shedding their pessimism.

The relationships involving regulations impinging on personal freedoms (dress, drinking, etc.) tended to be negligible. One reason is that colleges that are liberal enough to allow student Left groups to exist would probably also tend to place relatively few restrictions on other aspects of student personal conduct.[20] In contrast to the campus issues, the correlations with the off-campus issues are more substantial, ranging from .18 for defense research to .37 for Dow, etc., and the Vietnam war per se. As we've reiterated, the war, the draft, and university "cooperation" (as with defense recruiters) have been the principal targets of the student Left in the past year.[21]

Proportions of Student Bodies Involved in Organized Protest

For each issue on which a dean indicated that there had been organized student protest, he also provided an estimate of the proportion of the student body involved. Estimates were made on a fourpoint scale, ranging from "5 percent or fewer" to "25 percent or more." In Table 3, the percentages of all institutions at which deans reported the varying levels of protest participation are presented. For each issue, a mean level of involvement was computed. Because of the grossness of the four-point scale, the actual means are not reported here; instead the issues were ordered in Table 3 according to the proportion of students involved. Those issues appearing at the top of the table tended to involve large proportions of the student bodies, while those at the bottom involved the smallest proportions of students on the campuses where such protests occurred.[22]

For the issues in the student-administration category, while there was considerable variation by issue in the numbers of colleges "afflicted," the proportions of student bodies involved were *at or above* the average on all but one issue.[23] Three issues that bear on the personal conduct of students—dorm, etc., rules, dress and drinking regulations—galvanized especially large proportions of students on campuses where these questions led to protest. The matter of dress regulations was *the* paramount issue in terms of proportions of stu-

TABLE 3

PROPORTIONS OF STUDENT BODIES REPORTED INVOLVED IN PROTESTS OVER EACH OF 27 ISSUES (1967–68)

	Institutions Reporting Protest		Extent of Student Body Involvement in Protest 1967–68				
	1967–68 n = 859	1964–65 n = 849	No. Reported Protest	1–5%	5–10%	10–25%	25% or more
High level of involvement:							
1. Dress regulations	169	170	81.1	6.7	5.9	3.0	3.3
2. Dormitory and other living-group regulations, e.g., women's hours	289	238	66.8	13.0	8.3	7.2	4.7
3. Policies, regulations regarding student drinking	92	93	90.2	3.8	2.5	2.2	1.3
4. Food service	218	246	75.2	9.4	6.6	5.5	3.3
Above average involvement:							
5. Insufficient student participation in establishing campus policies	231	161	74.5	13.0	7.3	3.2	2.0
6. Curriculum inflexibility	125	68	87.1	6.4	3.7	1.9	0.9
7. Civil rights: local area (off-campus) protest and/or work	249	323	71.7	14.6	8.2	4.0	1.7
8. Policies, regulations re student use of drugs	44	*	95.4	2.4	1.6	0.3	0.3
9. Generally prevailing system(s) of testing and/or grading	107	76	88.2	7.0	2.6	1.1	1.1
Average involvement:							
10. U.S. policies regarding Vietnam	327	178	62.6	21.0	11.1	3.7	1.6
11. Disciplinary action against particular student(s)	138	118	84.4	8.7	5.1	0.9	0.9
12. Senior faculty not sufficiently involved in undergraduate instruction	14	25	98.6	0.9	0.3	0.1	0.1
13. Alleged racial discrimination: in admissions, nonaction on frat. discrimination, etc.	155	42	82.7	11.2	4.8	1.2	0.1
Below average involvement:							
14. Poor quality of instruction—in general or specific instances	113	102	87.3	7.9	3.4	1.2	0.2
15. Faculty tenure policies, e.g., "publish or perish"	34	34	96.8	2.3	0.5	0.2	0.2
16. Undergraduate classes typically too large, instruction too impersonal	28	35	96.9	1.8	1.0	0.2	0.1
17. "Censorship" of certain publications, e.g., student newspaper	84	119	90.6	6.6	1.6	0.9	0.3
18. The draft	213	*	75.5	15.8	6.7	1.0	1.0
19. Student-administration communication; students unable to voice grievances	163	127	81.7	8.3	6.5	2.3	1.2
20. Campus rules regarding speeches, appearances by "controversial" persons	69	77	92.2	5.1	1.6	0.8	0.3
21. Actual appearance by a particular person of leftist persuasion	39	43	96.1	2.8	0.7	0.3	0.1
22. Academic freedom for faculty in principle	36	34	96.7	2.4	0.6 ᵃ	0.1	0.2
23. Controversy surrounding a particular faculty member	174	136	80.1	13.8	4.5	1.3	0.3
24. On-campus recruiting by one or another of the armed services	215	*	75.5	16.8	6.5	1.0	0.2
Low level of involvement:							
25. On-campus recruiting by any other firm or agency, e.g., Dow, CIA, etc.	174	*	80.0	14.2	5.2	0.5	0.1
26. Classified defense and related research on campus	38	*	97.0	2.0	1.0	0.0	0.0
27. Actual appearance by a particular person of rightist persuasion	35	42	96.5	2.8	0.5	0.2	0.0

* No comparable data.

dent bodies activated. College officials still seeing fit to regulate this aspect of their students' lives appear to be rather heavily outnumbered. And increasingly so: of the 27 issues considered in the survey, the issue of correct dress was marked by the greatest *increase* in the numbers of protesting students between the 1965 and 1968 surveys.

The faculty-related issues, and those concerning freedom of expression tended not only to generate protests on relatively few campuses, but also tended to enlist the active support of relatively small proportions of those student bodies. Among the off-campus issues, only civil rights called forth above average proportions of student bodies. Proportions of students involved in interferences with war-related recruiters and research were comparatively speaking very small, and in most instances were probably limited to members of student Left groups.

Using the four-point scale of student involvement, the mean for 1967–68 was 1.62. The corresponding figure for 1964–65 was almost identical—1.64—indicating that the proportions of protesting students at colleges around the country have not grown in the past three years (according to the deans). This does not mean, however, that there are not more student activists in absolute numbers in 1968 than in 1965, for two reasons. First, more colleges around the country experienced organized protest in 1968 than in 1965. Second, many, perhaps most, colleges in the country have increased their enrollments substantially in the past three years; the same proportion (in 1968 as in 1965) therefore means a somewhat larger absolute number of students (activists). There most certainly *are* more student activists now than there were three years ago. Nonetheless the fact of no change in proportion of protesting students should be of some interest to people on a given campus, particularly if the college has not grown appreciably in the three-year interval. That is, if it is a "plain fact" to President X of Y College that there are more student activists on his campus now than three years ago (and the school is no larger now), Y College is an exception to the "norm" in this respect.

Conclusions

Conclusions about trends in the student movement based on the results of this and the earlier study must be tentative, the reason being the samples of institutions in the two studies are not identical (though they are quite similar in that 85 percent of the population is included in both surveys). Nonetheless, the following assertions seem warranted:

(1) Campuses experiencing organized student protest of the Vietnam war almost doubled in the interval between 1965 and 1968.

(2) Activism toward a larger student role in campus governance (including curriculum development) has increased substantially.

(3) Civil rights activism among college students (some 94 percent of whom are white) has declined significantly. White student activists are leaving prosecution of the on-going civil rights revolution to black activists.

(4) From no such insistence in 1965, black college students are now insisting that their college provide educational experiences consistent with their new self-conception.

(5) Proportions of activists within student bodies on campuses around the country have not increased (according to deans of students). Substantially larger proportions of protesting students were reported only in relation to the dress regulations issue. This is not to say that the absolute number of activist students has not increased, for reasons that were outlined earlier.

(6) The number of colleges reporting student Left groups (these would mainly be SDS chapters) has almost doubled, from 26 percent in 1965 to 46 percent in 1968.

The student movement is still a minority phenomenon. "Members" of the student Left amount to something on the order of 2 percent of the national student population. An additional 8 to 10 percent are strongly sympathetic with the "movement for social change" and are capable of temporary activation depending on the issues. And the numbers of activist students, while not increasing spectacularly, are nevertheless rising steadily.

Despite its minority status, however, the radical student movement is having a very substantial impact—most importantly in recent months on the nature of campus governance. Perhaps a majority of college and university officials around the country have come to acknowledge the legitimacy of most of the students' demands.

Citizens outside the academic world tend to be hostile, abhorring particularly the students' occasional recourse to violence and destruction. Given the present mood of the country, a tactics of violence most certainly risks an overpowering backlash. On the other hand, a tactics of relentless pressure on many fronts to expose, modify or eliminate unjust social patterns—politicizing people in the process— holds for this observer great promise. If the Movement can be sustained, and if ethical responsibility can prevail along with the great freedom sought by the students, the potential of the Movement in time for the renewal of American life fairly staggers the imagination.

NOTES

[1] This is also the same population used in the E. G. Williamson-John L. Cowan study (commissioned by the National Association of Student Personnel Administrators) published under the title, *The American Student's Freedom of Expression: A Research Appraisal* (Minneapolis: University of Minnesota Press, 1966).

[2] Approximately 90 percent of the respondents were deans of students or other student personnel officials; the balance had primarily academic responsibilities.

[3] Data in the Williamson-Cowan study indicated considerable variation in responses (perceptions) among deans of students, presidents, student newspaper editors, and student body presidents. On a question asking for an estimate of the percentage of students "participating in activities designed to express their viewpoints on 'controversial' issues," the deans generally indicated fewer student participants than did the other reporters. Also for this question, compared to the other respondents, fewer deans of students checked the "cannot estimate" category; presumably they more often considered themselves qualified to provide an estimate.

[4] The number of institutions in each subpopulation is given below each type designation, e.g., the percentages given under "Public L.A. Coll." are based on responses of 97 such colleges.

[5] See K. Keniston, "Heads and Seekers: Student Drug Use, Counter Cultures and American Society," *The American Scholar*, Winter, 1969, in press.

[6] Obviously not at San Francisco State.

[7] Some 5 to 7 percent of the college population nationally is Negro.

[8] See Williamson and Cowan, *op. cit.*, pp. 162–163.

[9] For the independent universities category, student agitation almost doubled between the two surveys—from 22 percent to 41 percent.

[10] See A. W. Astin, R. J. Panos, and J. A. Creager, "National Norms for Entering College Freshmen—Fall, 1966," *Ace Research Reports* (Washington: American Council on Education, 1967).

[11] For a review of this literature, see K. Keniston, *Young Radicals* (New York: Harcourt, Brace & World, 1968). Also, R. E. Peterson, "The Student Left in American Higher Education," *Daedalus*, 97 (Winter, 1968), pp. 293–317.

[12] R. T. Hartnett and R. E. Peterson, "Religious Preference as a Factor in

Attitudinal and Background Differences Among College Freshmen," *Sociology of Education,* 41 (Spring, 1968), pp. 227–237.

[13] A. Astin, "Personal and Environmental Determinants of Student Activism," *op. cit.* James Trent has commented on the attitudinal opposition to Communism on the part of the Catholic Church and Catholic students; see J. W. Trent with Jenette Golds, *Catholics in College* (Chicago: The University of Chicago Press, 1967). Attitudes of avowedly Protestant students toward broad political and social issues are not likely to be greatly dissimilar from their Catholic peers. (Cf. Hartnett and Peterson, *op cit.*)

[14] K. Keniston, "Youth, Change and Violence," *The American Scholar,* 37 (Spring, 1968), pp. 227–245.

[15] A respondent from one such school volunteered the following: "I am most happy to report my belief that, because the self-disciplined type of student studying an engineering curriculum is basically a clear-thinking, highly responsible and hard-working individual and is treated as such, we have no problems of student protest and uprising at ——— Tech."

[16] The issues of alleged censorship and proper dress are apparent exceptions.

[17] See, for example, E. Dunbar, "Vanguard of Campus Revolt," *Look* magazine, October 1, 1968.

[18] Only eleven of the 859 deans, however, reported *more than 5 percent* of their student bodies belonging to student Left groups.

[19] Several years ago, Paul Potter, a past president of SDS, spoke of campus life as a kind of "gumpot." See P. Potter, "Student Discontent and Campus Reform," in O. A. Knorr and W. J. Minter (eds.), *Order and Freedom on the Campus* (Boulder, Colo., Western Interstate Commission for Higher Education, 1965).

[20] Many colleges would (or do) outrightly prohibit radical student groups. Of some relevance is the following rank order of the eight types of institutions according to the proportion of each where the deans reported the presence of students belonging to student Left organizations (in parentheses are the figures three years ago): independent universities, 93 percent (63 percent); public universities, 76 percent (48 percent); independent liberal arts colleges, 52 percent (30 percent); public liberal arts colleges, 44 percent (26 percent); Protestant institutions, 35 percent (18 percent); technical institutions, 30 percent (14 percent); Catholic institutions, 27 percent (9 percent); teachers colleges, 15 percent (13 percent).

[21] It is of incidental interest that there is a correlation of .32 between the presence of student Left groups and proportion of faculty with doctorates.

[22] The scale mean for all 27 issues was 1.62, and the standard deviation was 0.26. The issues designated as high or low level of involvement in Table 3 are those which are more than one standard deviation from the mean. Those designated as "average involvement" are within 0.1 of the mean.

[23] The issue was "student-administration communication." One cannot help wondering if the deans may have either overestimated on the issues in this category, or perhaps underestimated on the issues not in the student-administration category (on account of less information).

5

LEVELS OF PROTEST

by Durward Long and Julian Foster

STUDENT PROTEST can be perceived in a variety of ways and, the questionnaire survey being a flexible research instrument, it can be made to reflect these varied perspectives. Richard Peterson's survey emphasized the issues and scope of protest, and his method of analysis stressed institutional categories and variations. Alexander Astin approached the problem primarily through the student; he collected massive data on characteristics of individuals at the time of their admission to college, and was able to follow up a substantial number of them, and to discover, among other things, which engaged in protest. In a later section, Leonard Baird describes another student-centered study, in which characteristics of activists and others are compared. The present chapter deals with yet another survey, but one having quite a different emphasis. Where Peterson, Astin and Baird were all focused on incidence of protest and the characteristics of those populations which engage in it, the concern here was rather with protest as a political phenomenon, and our questionnaire was designed to find out what the patterns of protest development were, how institutions responded, and what the overall effects of activism appeared to be at each institution.

This questionnaire, constructed by Julian Foster, Robert Gutchen and Durward Long and hereinafter referred to as the Protest Survey, was mailed to the presidents of all colleges and universities in the United States during May, 1968. Since any account of protest must have subjective elements, total reliance on the president's view of things naturally has its limitations; on the one hand, we attempted to make our questionnaire items unambiguous and factual, while on the other we resigned ourselves (as have Peterson and others) to the necessity of depending on someone's view of events, and selected the president in the hope that his view was more comprehensive than most. Both Williamson and Cowan[1] and Morgan (see Part IV, Chapter 1) chose instead to send their surveys to a number of people on each campus—people whose perspectives might be expected to differ. This procedure has some obvious advantages, but also difficulties when applied to a search for mainly factual data; where accounts conflicted we would again have been reduced to some subjective method of reconciling them, of choosing among rival truths. Rather than invite responses from persons likely to have less information available to them than would the president, we decided to depend on him alone. The reader may make allowances for possible bias as he wishes.

Respondents supplied the names of their institutions, but were guaranteed that the information given would not be identified with a particular institution; this permitted analysis by types of institution, region, etc. The person completing the questionnaire was not asked to sign it; letters accompanying returns made it clear that the president often handled the matter himself, but there can be little doubt that some delegated this chore to subordinates, of whom the dean of students seems the most probable choice. The American Council on Education kindly agreed to mail the Protest Survey, and to serve as the return addressee.

A total of 1,251 colleges and universities, or 47% of those institutions on the A.C.E.'s list of colleges and universities, completed the questionnaire. The response rate was highest in liberal arts colleges (61%), followed by teachers colleges (59%), universities (40%), junior colleges (39%) and miscellaneous theological, professional, technical and fine arts schools (30%). Measured by region, the level of participation varied little: returns from Northeast, Midwest, South and West were all between 46 and 49%. Response rates increased

[1] Cowan, John L., and Williamson, E. G., *The American Student's Freedom of Expression: A Research Appraisal,* Minneapolis, University of Minnesota Press, 1967.

with size; 42% of those institutions enrolling less than 2,500 students replied, while 71% of colleges and universities with larger enrollments did so. A spot check against newspaper accounts of protest suggests that it was the relatively quiet institutions which did not respond, while more of those experiencing activism told their stories of it. While the rate of return was considerably lower than that obtained by Peterson (perhaps because our questionnaire was considerably longer than his and contained some open-ended questions), it is believed that the results provide a useful amount of data and a sufficient basis for some generalizations about the course and form of student protests.

Slightly less than 43% of the institutions responding to the Survey reported having experienced protest in 1967–68. Universities had the highest incidence of protest (76%), followed by four-year colleges (48%), fine arts schools (41%) and junior colleges (37%). Junior colleges were excluded from Peterson's survey, and there has been little publicity given to activities on such campuses except for incidents in which blacks have been involved; the relatively high figure for them may therefore indicate that protest is more general among institutions of higher education than has been realized. Private secular schools had somewhat more protest than public institutions, and—possibly another surprise—protest was about as frequent in Catholic colleges and universities as it was in public or in Protestant but nonfundamentalist institutions. The incidence of protest did not fluctuate dramatically by region; the South, as might be expected in view of its greater social conservatism, had the least protest (36%), while the Northeast (49%) had the most, and the Midwest (44%) and West (40%) were nearer the mean. Predominantly Negro institutions had more protest (57%) than predominantly white ones (42%). All-male and coeducational institutions reported protest on 44% of campuses, while all-female institutions had 34% in this category.

However, the feature most impressively associated with incidence of protest was size of enrollment, as is shown in Table 1. One plausible explanation of this suggests that factors associated with large enrollment, such as impersonality and alienation, give grounds for protest. Another hypothesis is that size tends to be associated with quality, and that that in turn attracts more protest-prone students. Perhaps the most plausible explanation is the direct one: that a large enrollment increases the possibilities that the campus contains a sufficient number of that small minority of militants to mount a

TABLE 1

INCIDENCE OF PROTEST INCREASES
WITH SIZE OF ENROLLMENT

Enrollment	Number of Institutions	Percent Reporting Protest
Less than 500	247	21
500–999	327	34
1,000–2,499	350	45
2,500–4,999	156	48
5,000–7,499	75	63
7,500–9,999	33	76
10,000–14,999	34	79
15,000–19,999	18	78
20,000 or more	11	100

demonstration. If it is assumed that militants are distributed fairly equally among American campuses (which, of course, it should not be, save for the sake of argument) and assumed further that fifty militants equal one demonstration, then the association of demonstrations with enrollment size is simply explained.

Respondents were asked to indicate not only whether their institution had experienced protest, but what was the highest level it had reached, selecting one of the following alternatives:

> *Violent protest* (eg., students resisted arrest passively or actively, persons were attacked, property damaged).
>
> *Physically obstructive but non-violent protest* (e.g., officials were held "captive," buildings sealed, strikes hampered normal operations, etc.).
>
> *Physical but non-obstructive protest* (e.g., peaceful picketing, marches, rallies, mass protest meetings, etc.).
>
> *Diplomatic protest* (e.g., petitions were circulated, demands were issued by student government or other groups, etc.).

Of the 535 colleges and universities reporting protest, 3% stated that it was violent, 9% that it was obstructive, 33% that it was physical but non-obstructive, while the remaining 55% of institutions encountered diplomatic protest only. It is apparent that the scenes of battle so eagerly recorded by the television cameras are not "typical" of student protest, or of American campuses in 1967–68. When the levels of protest are examined by types of institution, the patterns resemble those for incidence of protest, particularly in respect to enrollment, which again appears to be the determining factor; see Table 2.

TABLE 2

LEVEL OF PROTEST IS ASSOCIATED WITH SIZE OF ENROLLMENT

		Size of Enrollment:		
Level of Protest:	N	*Under* 2,500	2,500–10,000	10,000 *or more*
Violent	17	12%	35%	53%
Obstructive	48	27	44	29
Physical	174	43	46	11
Diplomatic	296	79	17	4
		100%	100%	100%

Protest takes place on a variety of issues. Since our data focused only on the major protest event of the year, they provide a far less reliable guide to the incidence of protest on each issue than does Peterson's analysis. It is possible, however, to relate the issue with the level of protest, as is done in Table 3. As can be seen, protests

TABLE 3

NATIONAL ISSUES STIRRED MORE VIOLENT PROTESTS
THAN ON-CAMPUS ONES

		Issues:				
Level of Protest:	N	Recruit- ment	Race	Vietnam & Draft	Educa- tional Policies	*In Loco Parentis*
Violent	17	8%	10%	0	1%	1%
Obstructive	48	27	12	13	6	3
Physical	174	49	38	55	28	25
Diplomatic	296	16	40	32	65	71
		100%	100%	100%	100%	100%

against recruiters, a temptingly obstructable or capturable target, were the most violent, with racial issues, Vietnam and the draft also occasioning more militant styles of action, while agitation about on-campus issues was comparatively peaceful. The Students for a Democratic Society and the black students' organizations, which have acquired widespread reputation for the militance of their tactics, have both concerned themselves largely with national rather than local grievances. Students may protest more frequently about institutional conditions than about national affairs, as Peterson has shown, but the militance of the protest on the latter contributes to the general impression that students today are more motivated by radical ideology than by concerns over food, visiting hours, dress codes and other such issues.

The choice of protest issues also has much to do with the level of faculty involvement. Table 4 indicates that on all issues, activists

TABLE 4

PERCENTAGE OF FACULTY INVOLVED AS RELATED
TO THE PROTEST ISSUE

| | | Faculty Role: | |
| | | Participants in a | |
Issues:	Leaders	Violation	Supporters
Censorship	43%	14%	64%
Vietnam & the Draft	23	9	63
Educational Policies	19	4	63
Recruitment	26	14	51
Race-related	8	2	51
In Loco Parentis	4	1	42
Other Issues	8	0	8

received a substantial degree of support from at least some of the faculty. Issues of on-campus censorship, with their implications for academic freedom, and of educational policy, stirred the faculty into action; protests against in loco parentis policies did not, though they often commanded some faculty sympathy. It is less easy to see why faculty were more active in recruiting and anti-war demonstrations than in ones concerning race, but the most probable explanation appears to be that the latter were often developed and led by black students, and were perceived by sympathetic professors to be an exclusively black concern. The data does suggest that black students are less prone than white radicals to look to faculty for leadership in activism, perhaps because of the scarcity of black faculty, and also perhaps because the few black faculty members are seldom prone to militant action.

The proportion of faculty participation varied somewhat by type of institution. At universities, faculty were involved in some capacity in 70% of the protests which took place; in four-year colleges, the corresponding figure was 60%, and at junior colleges, 48%. These differentials may well reflect contrasts in institutional tradition: at universities, it has long been accepted that faculty play a role in setting institutional policies, whereas at the other extreme, junior college faculty have been far more prone to perceive themselves as employees, rather than management.

It is sometimes thought that professors, being intellectuals rather than men of violent action, may approve legitimate or peaceful protests, but will not tolerate more violent or obstructive exercises. If this were generally true, one might expect the presence of faculty among the protest leadership to produce some softening of tactics, and might also expect that the proportion of protests with faculty support would decline as the level of violence increased. Neither expectation is fulfilled. Of those protests which eventuated in violence, 29% had some faculty leadership, compared with 20% of obstructive non-violent ones, 19% of non-violent physical protests, and only 10% in the diplomatic category. Where 46% of the diplomatic protests enjoyed some faculty support, 60% of the physical but nonobstructive protests, 76% of the obstructive and 59% of the violent ones did so. It is possible that the latter figure indicates the tendency of violence to turn off the enthusiasms of militant faculty, but if so, this is the only piece of the data to reflect the image of the professor as a man of peace. It should be stressed, of course, that all that is involved here is the presence of some faculty, playing various roles in the protest; none of the figures given refers to the proportion of faculty involved. The conclusion might be that many campuses possess faculty members who are as militant as the most militant students, and no less prone than they to attack the institution at which they work.

The main focus of the questionnaire was, as indicated, on the development of protests. It was intended to function as a quantitative supplement to case studies of other accounts of events on particular campuses, to show how more or less general particular patterns of events were. It seems appropriate, then, to defer consideration of the major part of the findings until these subjects have been more fully dealt with. Further information from the Protest Survey will be presented in Part IV, Chapter 5, and Part V, Chapters 1 and 2.

6

DETERMINANTS OF STUDENT ACTIVISM

by Alexander Astin*

THIS RESEARCH is based on an analysis of longitudinal data collected from students who enrolled as freshmen in a national sample of 246 colleges in the fall of 1966. Basically, the study is concerned with the old question of individual differences, both among students and among institutions. Why do some students participate in demonstrations and others not? What characteristics of the student as he enters college predict his participation in various types of protest activity? How accurately can the potential protester be identified at the time of matriculation?

With respect to differences among institutions, we are concerned with why some institutions experience severe and frequent student activism and others experience virtually no such behavior. What role do administrative policies play in occurrence of student protest activity? Is it likely that protest activity could be modified by modifying certain administrative practices? What role is played by the peer group? How important are structural factors, such as size, type of

* Dr. Alexander Astin is Director of the American Council on Education's Office of Research. This chapter was written while he was a Fellow at the Center for Advanced Study in the Behavioral Sciences at Stanford. A modified version of it appeared in *Measurement and Evaluation in Guidance,* Vol. 1, No. 3 (Fall, 1968), Copyright © 1968 by American Personnel and Guidance Association, and is used with permission.

community, and living arrangements? Are there institutional characteristics which interact with particular student characteristics?

The three principal informational components of our research data bank are shown schematically in Figure 1. The box on the right—Stu-

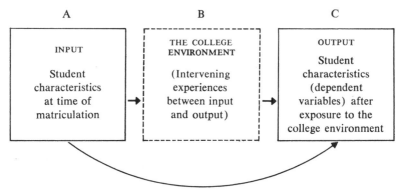

Figure 1. Schematic diagram showing three basic informational components of the ACE Cooperative Institutional Research Program.

dent Output Information—refers to the skills, attitudes, and social behavior of students that the higher educational institution does influence or attempts to influence. These output or dependent variables consisted of the student's participation in each of three types of protest activity. The box on the left—Student Inputs—includes the talents, skills, aspirations, and other potentials for growth and learning that the student brings with him to the college. In a sense, these inputs represent the raw materials with which the institution has to work. In our study of student activism, we were particularly interested in identifying student input variables which predicted later participation in protest activity.

The college environment—the box in the middle—includes anything about the college that is capable of affecting the student's output behavior. These environmental characteristics would include administrative policies and practices, curriculum, the physical plant and facilities, peer groups, teaching practices, and so forth. Although the great diversity among college environments has been construed by some critics as evidence of chaos in American higher education, it is this very diversity which makes our research studies possible. For example, the fact that there are colleges of such greatly varying sizes enables us to estimate the impact of institutional size on the student's development. Although it is not possible to assign students at random to colleges of different sizes, the fact that there is extensive overlap in the input characteristics of student bodies entering large and small institutions makes it possible to estimate the impact of size by means of controlled longitudinal studies. Since there is always some hazard in making causal inferences from such nonexperimental data, we believe that it is essential to study *changes* in the students as they progress through the different educational environments. This requirement clearly necessitates the use of input and output information collected from the same students over time, and precludes the "one-shot" cross-sectional studies of educational influence that characterize so much of the current educational research. Some of my experimentally minded colleagues may still cringe at the idea of drawing causal inferences from the results of such research, even with elaborate longitudinal data such as ours and elegant statistical controls. My only answer is that if one insists upon randomization or experimental manipulation of treatments, then he had better abandon any idea of studying the real world. This is not to imply that we can ever expect to have an ironclad guarantee that our causal inferences are valid in the absence of adequate randomization; all we can hope to do is to design our research so as to minimize the possibility that our inferences will be wrong.

In selecting a sample, we settled on the arbitrary figure of 300 institutions, which we considered small enough to be economically feasible and large enough to permit us to compute reasonably stable correlations using the institution as the unit of analysis. We rejected the idea of simple random sampling from the population, since this procedure would have yielded a very large number of small, private colleges and very few large universities or highly selective institutions. Fortunately, enough was already known about the entire population of institutions to permit us to develop a sophisticated stratification procedure that would yield a better sample and would also control a substantial amount of sampling error. Institutions were first sorted into four broad strata: universities, 4-year colleges, 2-year colleges, and predominantly Negro colleges. The 4-year colleges were then subdivided into public, private-nonsectarian, Catholic and Protestant. Within each of these administrative types, institutions were further stratified into terms of a variable called "selectivity" which represents an estimate of the average academic ability of the entering students.

Since this estimate was not available on many of the 2-year institutions, some of these were subdivided on the basis of another measure of institutional quality: the per-student expenditures for educational and general purposes, which we have called "affluence." The sample of 246 institutions was somewhat smaller than the total sample of participants (307 institutions), since we had to exclude several institutions that were not able to obtain data from all (or a representative subsample) of their students.

Our study of student protests involves data collected from the entering freshmen classes at these 246 institutions in the fall of 1966, and followup data collected one year later in the late summer of 1967. The freshmen input data were obtained from a 150-item questionnaire administered to each student during the fall of 1966 freshmen orientation and registration periods. The data included standard biographical and demographic information, as well as data on student's career plans, life goals, self-concept, and daily activities. The student was asked to indicate whether he had performed each activity "frequently," "occasionally," or "not at all" during his senior year in high school. We assumed that one of these high school activity items, "participated in organized demonstrations," would be an especially important item of student input information.

Output information was collected by means of a questionnaire mailed to the student's home in the late summer of 1967 (after completion of the freshman year). Since it was not necessary to study the entire student body at the large institutions, we collected random samples of approximately 300 students from each institution enrolling more than 300 students in the previous fall. All students from the smaller institutions were followed up. Thus, questionnaires were mailed to a subsample of approximately 60,000 selected from the initial entering freshman sample of approximately 200,000 students. The initial mailing and one followup of nonrespondents yielded a return of approximately 35,000 usable questionnaires, which represents a rate of return of approximately 60 percent.

The followup questionnaire repeated many of the items from the initial input questionnaire, and included several items concerning the student's activities during his freshman year. The three followup items which served as our dependent variables were

1. Participated in a demonstration against racial discrimination.

2. Participated in a demonstration against the war in Vietnam.
3. Participated in a demonstration against some administrative policy of the college.

The student was asked to indicate, for each of these items, whether he had participated frequently, occasionally, or not at all during the past year in college. For the purposes of our study, the categories of "frequently" and "occasionally" were combined. Thus, we were concerned with participation versus non-participation, rather than with frequency of participation as such.*

Table 1 shows the distribution of the population of institutions in terms of the percentages of students who reported participating in the different types of protests during the 1966–67 academic year. All three distributions are skewed in a positive direction, with the bulk of the institutions piled up near the low end. In fact, more than one-fourth of the institutions in the population had virtually no students participating in demonstrations against racial discrimination, and more than one-third of the institutions had no students participating in demonstrations against the war in Vietnam. Nevertheless, the range among colleges in the extent of student involvement in these two types of protests is considerable: more than fifty institutions had at least one-fourth of their students participating in demonstrations against racial discrimination, and a comparable number of institutions had a fourth or more of their student body participating in demonstrations against the war in Vietnam. These findings indicate that although student participation in demonstrations against racial discrimination and against the war in Vietnam are the exception rather than the rule, a substantial proportion of the student body at some institutions participated in such demonstrations.

* In order to compensate for biases in the sample of students who responded to our followup questionnaire, we carried out a series of multiple regression analyses to identify input variables that predicted responding vs. nonresponding to the followup questionnaire. The results of these analyses were used to compute a set of weights to be applied to the respondents' data. Since the rate of response was lowest among students who had relatively poor academic records in high school, who were male, and whose educational aspirations were relatively low at the time of entrance to college, these students received the largest weights. An additional set of weights was computed to adjust the weighted total number of respondents in each college to the actual number of questionnaires mailed out to students from the college. Although these weighting procedures do not insure that all biases in the respondents' data have been corrected, evidence from some of our earlier questionnaire studies indicates that many of the biases are compensated for by this kind of procedure.

TABLE 1

DISTRIBUTION OF THE POPULATION OF INSTITUTIONS WITH RESPECT
TO PERCENTAGES OF STUDENTS PARTICIPATING IN EACH
OF THREE DIFFERENT TYPES OF PROTESTS

Percentage of Student Body Participating in Protest	Type of Protest		
	Racial Discrimination	*Vietnam*	*Administrative Policy of the College*
0	555	767	129
1–5	1,076	802	683
6–10	146	230	317
11–15	112	94	326
16–20	46	42	153
21–25	23	13	59
26–30	29	9	66
31–35	1	16	58
36–40	0	3	27
41–45	0	6	38
46–50	0	3	23
51–55	0	3	0
56–60	0	0	37
60+	0	0	72
(range)	(0%–31%)	(0%–55%)	(0%–85%)
(median)	(2.1%)	(1.7%)	(8.2%)

The distribution of student participation in demonstrations against administrative policies of the college showed a somewhat different pattern. Some proportion of the student body at more than 90 percent of the institutions participated in such demonstrations, and more than 100 institutions experienced demonstrations involving more than half of the student body.

In short, these findings indicate that the typical institution can expect to experience some degree of protest activity concerning administrative policies, but that only a few institutions are likely to experience protests against either racial discrimination or the war in Vietnam involving more than a very small fraction of the student body. Although a few institutions experienced student protests against the Vietnam war involving nearly half of the student body, at no institution did that high a proportion of the students participate in demonstrations against racial discrimination.

The various student input characteristics were matched with the three protest items to determine if information provided at the time of matriculation makes it possible to predict whether a student will engage in protest activity during his freshman year in college. The results suggest that such prediction cannot be made very accurately. Participating in protests against the Vietnam war, however, can be predicted about twice as accurately as protesting against either racial discrimination or the administrative policies of the college. This finding would suggest that protesting against the Vietnam war tends to be more an expression of values, attitudes, and other personality characteristics which the student brings to college than do the other two types of protests. The fact that protesting against administrative policies of the college was the least predictable of the three types suggests that such protests may typically be in response to local conditions at the institution and therefore less dependent upon the individual characteristics of the student himself. As we shall see shortly, this interpretation is strongly supported by the results of the analyses in which the institution was used as the unit of sampling.

Because of the very large number of student input variables considered, only the results of analyses of those variables which were most clearly predictive will be discussed. These variables are listed in Table 2, which indicates that students who participate in different types of protest activities have many traits in common. The three input variables which were predictive for all three types of protest were having a current religious preference of "none," a high self-rating on political liberalism, and having participated in organized demonstrations in high school. The importance of having no religious preference at the time of matriculation is illustrated by the fact that this item received the largest weight in the final analysis for two of the protest items and the second largest weight in the final solution of the other. The fact that protesting is positively related to political liberalism, artistic interests, and wanting to join the Peace Corps or VISTA, and negatively related to political conservatism and wanting to be successful in business, suggests that engaging in protest activities during college is to some extent an expression of political attitudes and values. This conclusion applies more to protests against the Vietnam war and against racial discrimination than it does to protests against administrative policies of the college.

TABLE 2

PREDICTING PARTICIPATION IN THREE TYPES OF PROTEST ACTIVITY
FROM FRESHMAN INPUT CHARACTERISTICS: SUMMARY
OF STEPWISE REGRESSION ANALYSES
(n = 4,336 Freshmen)

Freshman Input Characteristic	Rank Order of Importance for Predicting Protests		
	Racial Discrimination	Vietnam War	Administrative Policies
Present religious preference "None" . .	1	2	1
Negro	2	*	10
Participated in organized demonstrations in high school	3	1	11
Political liberalism (self-rating) . . .	4	19	5
Mother is a lawyer.	5	8	*
Join the Peace Corps or VISTA (life goal)	6	3	*
Attended a public recital or concert . .	7	12	*
Participated in informal group singing .	8	*	9
Mother is a research scientist. . . .	9	6	*
Parents' religion Jewish	*	9	6
Originality (self-rating)	*	11	2
Argued with other students	*	18	4
Drank wine.	*	4	*
Political conservatism (self-rating) . .	*	−5	*
Creating artistic work (life goal) . . .	*	7	*
Being successful in my own business (life goal)	*	−10	*
National Merit recognition	*	13	*
Male.	*	14	*
Father is an artist or performer . . .	*	15	*
Father is a clergyman	*	16	*
Prayed	*	−17	*
Home is in a large city	*	*	−3
Become an outstanding athlete (life goal)	*	*	7
Smoked cigarettes	*	*	8
Popularity with opposite sex (self-rating)	*	*	12

* Of little or no consequence in predicting protest activity.
− Variable is associated negatively with protest activity.

The pattern of association involving being a Negro is of special interest. As expected, Negroes are more likely than non-Negroes to participate in protests against racial discrimination, but it was somewhat surprising to find that they are no more likely than others to participate in protests against the Vietnam war. These results indicate that Negro college students have not, as some writers have suggested, associated their concerns about racial equality with the Vietnam war.

The next step in our analyses was to explore the influence of college environmental variables on student protest activity. The initial step in these analyses was to examine the relative contribution of student input and environmental variables using the institution as the unit of analysis. We first computed mean scores for each institution on the three protest items and on the 197 student input variables. These means were then intercorrelated, and stepwise multiple regression analyses performed. At the point where input variables could no longer account for variance in the protest item, a number of environmental variables were permitted to enter the equation. These 58 environmental variables included 33 measures of the college environment from the Inventory of College Activities, and 25 variables based on the type of control, sex, race, type of college town, and geographic region of the institution. In this second stage, college environmental variables were permitted to enter the regression equation until no additional variable was capable of significantly reducing variance in the protest item.

The most striking feature of the results of these analyses were (a) the very high correlations between student input characteristics and each of the three protest items, and (b) the absence of any pronounced environmental effects. This latter finding was especially surprising in view of the fact that several of the correlations between environmental characteristics and frequency of protest activity were quite high prior to the control of input variables. The analysis showed that protests are most likely to occur in liberal arts colleges located in the Northeast, and least likely to occur in junior colleges. The environments of these protest-prone institutions are characterized by a good deal of informal dating among the students, a high degree of verbal aggressiveness in the classroom, irregular sleeping habits, and little use of automobiles. Their administrative policies against student drinking, aggression, and heterosexual activity all tend to be relatively permissive. However, virtually all of these relationships disappear when student input characteristics are controlled. In fact, some of the relationships, such as the one between protests against racial discrimination and use of automobiles, are actually reversed by the control for differential student inputs.

Not surprisingly, the percentage of Negroes in the student body carries the largest weight in predicting the percentage of students who will participate in such protests. In fact, a highly accurate prediction of the percentage of students at the college who will participate in protests against racial discrimination can be obtained with only ten student input variables. Only two college characteristics—public control and verbal aggressiveness in the class—showed significant correlations with protests against racial discrimination after the control of the input variables, and these relationships were of borderline significance.

Next we analyzed protests against the war in Vietnam. An even better estimate of the percentage of students who engage in such protests (about 70 percent of the variation among institutions) can be obtained from only nine student input characteristics. Although only one environmental characteristic, Musical and Artistic Activity, contributed significantly to the prediction, this variable may have special significance. Since we found in our earlier analyses that artistically inclined students are relatively likely to indulge in protest activity, it seems probable that the expression of protests would be encouraged in an environment where a relatively high proportion of students are artistically inclined. Note that such an environment would also be likely to include a relatively large number of faculty members who are also artistically inclined.

Finally we analyzed the environmental effects on the proportion of students participating in demonstrations against the administrative policies of the college. Here, as in the analysis using the student as the unit, the prediction is considerably less reliable than the prediction for the other two types of protest activities. Moreover, several environmental characteristics appear to be significant. The likelihood of student participation in protests against the administration seems to be increased by a low degree of organization in the class, a low degree of student-faculty involvement in the class, and a high degree of snobbishness.

Perhaps the most interesting of these environmental effects concerns the variable "Organization in the Class." Organization is defined primarily in terms of having assigned seats, taking attendance, and

TABLE 3

PREDICTING THE PERCENTAGE OF PARTICIPANTS IN DEMONSTRATIONS, USING THE INSTITUTION AS THE UNIT OF ANALYSIS
(n = 246 Institutions)

Independent Variable:	Rank Order of Importance in Predicting Protest on:		
	Racial Discrimination	Vietnam War	Administrative Policies
% Negroes	1		
Mean self-rating on political liberalism	2		
% whose fathers are lawyers	3		
% choosing "none" as religious preference	4	1	
% whose home is in a large city	5		
Mean value placed on "succeeding in own business"	−6		
Mean level of fathers' education	7		
Mean self-rating on academic ability	−8		
Mean self-rating on intellectual self-confidence	9		
% whose mothers are elementary school teachers	10		1
% National Merit Award winners		2	
Mean value placed on "achieving in a performing art"		3	
% whose parents are Jewish		4	
% choosing "Jewish" as religious preference		−5	
% Orientals		6	
Mean self-rating on political conservatism		−7	−4
% whose mothers are physicians		8	
% whose fathers are high school teachers		9	
% whose home is in the suburbs			2
Mean value placed on "becoming an outstanding athlete"			3
% majoring in a technical field (excluding engineering)			5
Mean score on "listened to Dixieland music"			6

− Variable is associated negatively with protest activity.

holding the class only at a regularly scheduled time and place. That institutions scoring low on this factor should experience more protests against the administration than would be expected from their student inputs suggests that the absence of such organizational variables may create a sort of "hang loose" atmosphere in the institution which encourages the students to express their dissatisfactions with administrative policies. This interpretation is supported in part by the negative effect of the other classroom variable, "Involvement in the Class." Institutions low on involvement tend to have large classes, instructors who do not know the student's name and who do not encourage class discussion, and a high proportion of students who oversleep and miss classes.

There was a strong association between "Snobbishness" and protesting. Colleges with high scores on snobbishness are perceived by their students as both snobbish and sophisticated. The atmosphere of the college is inclined to emphasize the intellectual and theoretical rather than the practical aspects of college education, and there tend to be a high proportion of "avant-garde" students on campus. Of particular interest is the fact that the students attending snobbish institutions are likely to feel "out of place" at the institution. It seems plausible that such a complex of environmental characteristics would encourage the expression of dissatisfaction with institutional administrative policies.

It should be recognized that our failure to find many environmental characteristics which affect student protest behavior may be due in part to the methodology employed: the use of the institution as the unit of analysis for controlling differential student input characteristics will tend to obscure peer group effects, since the nature of the student peer group is to some extent reflected in the mean characteristics of the entering class. Currently under way at ACE are several analyses which will attempt to control student input characteristics using the student as the unit of analysis rather than the institution. If significant peer group effects exist, these alternative analyses should reveal them.

Summary

Our longitudinal study of student activism in 246 institutions indicates that activists differ from non-activists in several respects that are consistent with the findings of earlier studies conducted at individual institutions. The activist student is more likely to have no religious preference, to be politically liberal rather than conservative, to express an interest in artistic pursuits, to rate himself high on originality and to come from relatively well-educated and affluent parents. Although Negroes are more likely than whites to participate in demonstrations against racial discrimination and administrative policies of the institution, they are no more likely to participate in demonstrations against the war in Vietnam. Demonstrating against the war in Vietnam appears to be more dependent upon the student's personal attitudes and values than does demonstrating against either racial discrimination or administrative policies. Although the bulk of the institutions in the United States experience little or no student protest activity with respect to the war in Vietnam or to racial discrimination, there are a few dozen institutions where a substantial proportion of the students participate in such demonstrations.

Demonstrations against administrative policies of the institution, on the other hand, are more the rule than the exception, although the proportion of students participating in such demonstrations tends to be relatively small. Nevertheless, a few institutions experience protests of this type which involve a majority of their students.

The proportion of students who participate in demonstrations against either the war in Vietnam or racial discrimination can be predicted with substantial accuracy solely from a knowledge of the characteristics of the students who enter the institution. Environmental characteristics of the institution seem to play almost no part in the emergence of such protest activity. Environmental factors seem to be somewhat more important with respect to protests against the administrative policies of the college, although student input characteristics still appear to carry much more weight than environmental characteristics in determining whether or not such protests will occur.

TWO

The Activists

1

HYPOTHESES OF STUDENT UNREST

by Seymour L. Halleck*

STUDENTS CAN no longer be taken for granted. It does not matter that a great majority of students remain largely content, conservative and apathetic. A determined minority of college students have forced us to examine and sometimes change institutions, rules and values which were once considered inviolate.

Some students reject the political and economic status quo and are making vigorous attempts to change the structure of our society. These are the student activists. Other restless students reject the values of their society as well as the values of their own past and are developing a style of life which is contradictory to the Western ethics of hard work, self-denial, success and responsibility. These students sometimes participate in efforts to change the society but for the most part they are withdrawn and passive. They can be described as alienated.

Both activist and alienated students tend to come from affluent, upper-middle- or upper-class homes. They are sensitive and perceptive individuals. They are also highly intelligent. Such students have difficulty in relating to the adult generation. They are articulate, irreverent,

* Dr. Halleck is Professor of Psychiatry, University of Wisconsin Medical School. This paper was originally presented at the American Association for Higher Education in March, 1967, and is used by permission.

humorless and relentless in their contempt for what they view as adult hypocrisy. Highly peer-oriented, they turn to one another rather than to their parents when shaping their belief system or when seeking emotional support.

Alienated students and, to a lesser extent, activist students find it difficult to sustain goal-directed activity. Their capacity to organize for any kind of action is limited. Consequently, they often fail at work or school; even their political efforts seem highly disorganized. They live at the edge of despair. Although they seem at times to be enjoying life, there is always a sense of foreboding about them. Often they become depressed and suicidal. Activist students are more emotionally stable but are also prone to deep feelings of hopelessness and self-pity.[1]

There is no dearth of explanations of the above phenomena. Some explanations seem to be based on opinions which support the prejudices of differing political viewpoints; others are presented with greater analytic objectivity. But no hypothesis thus far advanced can be considered a sufficient explanation of student unrest. At best, each is only a partial explanation which sheds only a small light upon a highly complex phenomenon.

Certain propositions often made about students are not hypotheses but are value judgments. The unsupported statement that the behavior of our restless youth represents a healthy and sensible response to the corruptions of our world is exhortative rather than explanatory. Such a belief is embraced by those who are discontented with the status quo, and wish to emphasize and exploit student restlessness as a phenomenon that justifies their own grievances. Similarly, unsupported statements that students are more emotionally disturbed than they used to be have no explanatory value. Implying that students act as they do because they are mentally ill serves to demean their behavior by casting doubts upon the validity of the messages which that behavior is designed to communicate.

A more interesting proposition concerning student unrest is that it is neither new nor exceptional. Precedents can be cited which suggest that there were times in our history when students were even more restless than they are now. Periods of unrest do seem to run in cycles and it is conceivable that we happen to be in an active phase of a predictable cycle. This proposition is reassuring to those who look forward to a quiet future. Its weakness, however, is that it assumes that those forces which make for cyclical behavior will remain relatively constant. The author's opinion is that the world is changing so rapidly that using historical precedents to predict future behavior is a risky business. We can deplore student unrest or we can welcome it, but we cannot ignore it or simply wait for it to go away.

This brief chapter considers the various hypotheses of student unrest under one of three categories: critical hypotheses, sympathetic hypotheses, or neutral hypotheses. No attempt will be made to consider every explanation of student unrest that has been put forth. The rejection of certain hypotheses such as the influence of earlier biological maturity, the mass university, the irrelevance of much of modern education, the alienation engendered by drug use or the assassination of President Kennedy is based in part upon the writer's belief that they are not as critically influential as the following hypotheses.

Critical Hypotheses

Those who are critical of student activism and alienation are most likely to seek its causes in factors which they believe have created a moral weakness in our youth. They believe students are restless because they lack discipline, values or purpose. These deficiencies are believed to originate within the disturbed family, particularly that family which has been influenced by affluence, liberal thinking and modern psychological notions of child rearing. While these hypotheses may also appeal to those who are sympathetic toward students they are primarily critical in the sense that they imply that something is wrong with those students who protest or withdraw.

The Permissiveness Hypothesis

The commonest explanation of student unrest is that it is the result of too much permissiveness in rearing children.[2] The proponents of this view argue that those students whose behavior is most disquieting were raised by parents who believe that children should almost never be disciplined, frustrated or deprived of freedom. This new permissiveness is angrily blamed on the influence of Freudian and other psychological theories. It is argued that some parents have, through painstaking efforts to avoid creating neuroses in their children, abdicated their responsibility to teach and discipline their children. In so doing, they have reared a generation of spoiled, greedy youth who are unable to tolerate the slightest frustration without showing an angry or infantile response.

Although the permissiveness hypothesis has been used in the most crude manner to berate and deplore the behavior of youth, it cannot be lightly dismissed. There is considerable evidence that activist and alienated students come from well-educated families, deeply committed to liberal doctrines.[3] In such homes children are given freedom to criticize, debate and question. Restless students also have frequently attended primary and secondary schools dedicated to the ideal of progressive education, schools which in their efforts to maximize freedom and creativity seek to minimize discipline and frustration.

It can, of course, be argued that children raised in permissive homes will be better citizens than those raised in stricter homes. Restless students do seem to be more open to ideas, more involved with social issues and more flexible than their peers. The critics, however, can point to other characteristics of restless students which seem to be related to their permissive upbringing and which are not so salutary. The response of such students to discipline, for example, is in no useful sense adaptive. Arbitrary regulations enrage them; even rational forms of discipline, such as the need to master basic concepts before moving on to more abstract ideas, bother them. Restless students also react inappropriately when their demands are not immediately accepted. They are prone at such moments to protest violently, to give up and withdraw or to wrap themselves in a cloak of despair. Much of their abrasiveness and much of their ineffectiveness can be explained by their uncompromising demands for immediate gratification. This inability to tolerate frustration or delay must be considered a weakness or defect.

The Responsibility Hypothesis

Many who are concerned about the dangers of permissiveness also believe that our culture has been "psychologized" to an extent that youth have become unwilling to assume responsibility for their own behavior. The expansion of the social and psychological sciences has confronted the public with elaborate deterministic explanations of behavior. When a behavior is totally explained, there is a tendency for people to act as though they are no longer responsible for that behavior. They confuse the theoretical issue of scientific determinism with the society's practical needs to have its citizens remain accountable for their own actions.[4]

When the sociologist documents the impact of poverty and discrimination upon Negro youth, he is conducting a logical and scientific exercise. The subjects of his research, however, are tempted to utilize his findings to support an individual and collective feeling of responsibility. The Negro adolescent who participates in a riot for example might say, "How could I do otherwise? I am moved by forces over which I have no control." Psychological explanations are also utilized to avoid accountability. It is becoming more common to hear criminals say, "It is not I who should be held responsible for what I have done because I am neurotic or mentally ill."

Psychiatry, particularly Freudian psychiatry, has been maligned as a critical agent in producing a climate of non-responsibility. While there is nothing in the theoretical doctrines of psychoanalysis which favors abdicating personal responsibility, it does seem that the psychiatrist's ability to expand and legitimize the mental illness role has had an impact on the manner in which people view the question of responsibility. Behavior once considered bad is now considered sick. Sickness implies that one cannot help himself or that one is not responsible for his actions. The proponents of the non-responsibility hypothesis would argue that by expanding the sick role to include forms of behavior that were once considered in terms of good or bad the healing professions have helped create a social climate in which more people manage to avoid accountability for their actions. Youth growing up in such a society are tempted to behave in a pleasure-seeking, anti-social and irresponsible manner. Many feel that this is exactly what restless students are doing.

The evidence that activist and alienated youth are deeply influenced by a climate of irresponsibility is inconclusive. Some activist students are often impressively willing to hold themselves accountable for their actions. On the other hand, most alienated students are not. They tend to seek medical or psychiatric excuses from their obligations at the first sign of stress. They also have a discouraging tendency to break laws and to insist that their own personal needs and problems are such that they should not be held accountable for these actions.* It is almost as if they say, "Because the world is so bad and because it has

* The situation with regard to use of marijuana is a case in point. Thousands of students use this drug illegally yet it is practically impossible to organize students to do anything to legalize the sale of marijuana. When students are occasionally arrested for smoking marijuana they almost always avoid punishment by becoming informants and thus not only avoid legal accountability but seem unable to adhere to their perceived obligations towards their deviant subcultures.

treated me so badly I cannot be blamed for my actions. There is no point in holding me accountable for things which I cannot help doing anyway."

The Affluence Hypothesis

A third hypothesis which appeals to critics of student unrest is based on the alleged hazards of growing up in an affluent society. It is sometimes argued that affluence which is unearned and which is unaccompanied by a tradition of service and commitment creates a sense of restlessness, boredom and meaninglessness in our youth. The child raised in an affluent society has difficulty finding useful goals. He does not learn to use work or creativity as a means of mastering some aspect of the world. He, therefore, according to this argument, is trapped in a never-ending search for new diversions and new freedoms which sooner or later begin to feel sterile and ungratifying.[5]

It does seem likely that man is less likely to be troubled if he is distracted by some monumental task which dominates his life goals. In a relatively poor society, the very need for survival creates a structured and seemingly purposeful life. In an affluent society, man has the time and freedom to contemplate the meaning of his existence. Many restless students do come from affluent homes and many have decided that their lives are devoid of meaning. Sometimes it seems that their provocative behavior is designed primarily to invent new struggles and even imaginary hardships which will free them from their lethargy and help them atone for their guilt over "having it so good."

The affluence hypothesis has certain undertones of criticism directed towards the parents of restless students. Affluence, after all, does not always produce protest or indolence. Traditionally, many of our most useful public servants have been products of wealthy homes. The critics of student unrest would reserve their harshest barbs for those newly affluent parents who have themselves become so caught up in materialistic pleasure-seeking life that they have failed to meet their responsibility of teaching children the kinds of values which would lend meaning to a young person's existence.

Family Pathology Hypotheses

A number of explanations of student unrest focus upon the disturbed family. According to these hypotheses, activist and alienated students behave as they do because they are responding to an unresolved conflict within the family unit. It is usually suggested that the restless student has been subjected to too much pressure by his parents or is "acting out" a need of his parents. A more general approach to the problem focuses upon a family structure in which the father is a weak or shadowy figure. This approach emphasizes the breakdown in authority of the paternal figure, the confusion of sexual roles in our society and the break with tradition which such confusion produces.[6]

The evidence for the existence of a high degree of pathology in the families of restless students is inconclusive. Sociological studies of students and their families do not support any family pathology hypothesis. In fact, such studies suggest that activist students, at least, come from rather stable families.[7] Psychiatrists, on the other hand, find some evidence of serious familial conflict in most of the families of restless students they treat. It must be emphasized, however, that the psychiatrist deals with only a small proportion of such students.

If family disorganization is an important cause of student unrest, the manner in which it exerts its influence must be complex and subtle. Sociological techniques are simply too superficial to get at the complexities of the problem. The findings of psychiatrists are based on depth explorations which may be valid for some families but which cannot be generalized. Neither sociologists nor psychiatrists can provide valid answers. The most we can say is that some aspects of student restlessness are directly related to family pathology. Certainly, it is conceivable that in today's highly charged social climate even minimal family disturbance may be translated into highly provocative behavior.

Sympathetic Hypotheses

The next group of hypotheses puts the student in a favorable light. They view him as a victim of man-made circumstances and maintain that student unrest is a legitimate and rational effort to change these circumstances. The student is viewed as either a helpless victim of a world he never created, or as a hero seeking to cleanse the world of the evils of previous generations. To be useful these hypotheses must not simply define what is wrong with the world, but must suggest how various factors have made students more capable of perceiving and acting upon the injustices and irrationalities of our world.

The Two Armed Camps Hypothesis

This generation of students has grown in an age when the world has been divided into two large camps which compete with each other ideologically, politically and sometimes militarily. Since the Russians launched their first satellite, the competition has also been educational. Students are trained in a school system which emphasizes the competitive acquisition of knowledge as a source of power and stability. By the time they arrive at our universities they are better educated than any previous generation of students but they are also more overworked.

All of this emphasis on education and competition is not easily sustained after the student arrives at the university. By this time, he is at least partially "burned out." The personal benefits of intensive studying and searching for a profitable career begin to appear less attractive in an affluent world and particularly in a world which seems to be making it increasingly difficult for a young person to become an integral part of the economic system. As the student comes to view objectively the implications of our competitiveness with Communism as a never-ending phenomenon, he also begins to question the social value of his efforts. Even if he maintains his enthusiasm for academic work through the undergraduate years, by the time the student reaches graduate school, he increasingly asks himself whether the competitive search for knowledge is worth it. At this point he begins to view our competition with the Communist world (and sometimes competitiveness itself) as a form of mass paranoia and he views the university as an agent of the government which contributes towards the perpetuation of the paranoid system.[8] He reacts by protest or withdrawal.

The War in Vietnam Hypothesis

Although student unrest began long before the war in Vietnam ever escalated to massive proportions, there can be little doubt that in the past few years this conflict has been a major factor influencing the behavior of students. The war is particularly unpopular on major campuses. A large proportion of students, perhaps the majority, see it as a misguided effort while a significant minority see it as wholly immoral. Much of the restless behavior of students can be directly related to their efforts to do something to stop the war or to their sense of total frustration when they feel powerless to stop it. The draft and the inequities engendered by the 2S deferment also contribute to unrest. The major issue is fear. The average male student on campus is plagued with fears that he will fail in school, will be drafted and will run the risks of being killed in a conflict he may not consider vital to the interests of his country. The second issue is guilt. The university student knows that he is spared from military service only because he is richer or smarter than someone else. While he may believe that the war is immoral, he also knows that his privileged status is immoral. When he accepts the 2S status he suffers guilt. Much of the activism on our campuses is a means of atoning for that guilt. Much of the alienation on our campuses is a means of denying the relevance of the society that created such guilt.

Students also feel some shame in not participating in those aspects of military service that might make them feel more masculine. It is rare for anyone even in peacetime to eagerly embrace military service and a normal late adolescent has justifiable concern with interrupting his career to face the harshness of life in the service. The unpopularity of this war gives the student a cogent reason for avoiding military service but it does not resolve his nagging fears that he is somehow or other being cowardly or less masculine by being treated specially.[9]

It is also true that the anti-war climate on many campuses makes the student progressively more disinclined to serve in this war the longer he remains on campus. Education breeds a dislike of violence. Furthermore, whatever romantic thoughts a young man may have about war at 18 are somewhat attenuated with a year or two of maturation. Students spend many many hours arguing about the war, the draft, and means of avoiding the draft. This preoccupation creates a highly tense situation in which the student feels supported only by his peer group. He begins to relate to subcultures which become progressively more separated from the rest of the nation and particularly from the adult generation.

The Deterioration in the Quality of Life Hypothesis

There are many who believe that student unrest is an appropriate response to the deterioration of the quality of life in America. Overpopulation which results in crowds, traffic jams and businesses run on the basis of mass production has taken much of the joy out of

life in our towns and cities. Personal care or service is hard to find
in any shop, restaurant, or hotel. People begin to feel faceless and
insignificant.

Students, it can be argued, are among the first to sense the painful
anonymity associated with bigness. This is a particularly serious problem on overcrowded campuses where students are painfully isolated
from their teachers and other adults. A sense of student-faculty intimacy or a sense of scholarly community are hard to find on any
large campus. Students find it difficult to develop a sense of identification or loyalty towards a university that they perceive as monolithic and impersonal. In their complaints that they are treated like
numbers or IBM cards they strike a poignant note for all of us.[10]

Overcrowding is only a relative thing and would not be so destructive if it were not for the manner in which we have incredibly
neglected the planning and development of town and country. Our
cities grow with no respect for the land. Beauty and wilderness are
easy prey for the builder and contractor. Clean air and clear streams
are almost a thing of the past. An adolescent who grows up in a world
in which he must sit back and watch beauty fade and pollution gain
must come to despair of the future. One way of looking at student
unrest is as a massive reaction to the destruction of that kind of
world and way of life which their forebears enjoyed but which will
be denied to them. It is not uncommon to hear a student say to an
adult, "In your world life had some hope and meaning, but in the
world you have left for me, these qualities are gone."

The Political Hopelessness Hypothesis

Many individuals see our mass society as immutable to change.
It has been argued that our society is so complex, our systems of
checks and balances so intricate and our interplay of pressure groups
so self-equalizing that really effective change is no longer possible.
Our business-oriented economy has so indoctrinated us into the role
of credit-bound consumers that we are all beholden to a way of life
which may not be in our best interests. An increasing number of
radical students are convinced that the forces of government, industry and education are totally interdependent and allied to one
another for the purpose of warding off any reasonable attempts to
change the society. They believe that a system of life has developed
in our country which simply absorbs legal efforts to change our

society, even protest, in a manner which ultimately preserves the status quo.*

Guided by the philosophy of Herbert Marcuse many students are convinced that constructive change within our society is not possible by working through the system.[11] They do not have any sort of vision as to what will replace the old order, but they are convinced that our society is fundamentally irrational and must be destroyed. They do not reject illegal acts or even violence as agents of destruction. While one may disagree with their solutions, the source of their desperation is understandable.

The Civil Rights Hypothesis

The civil rights movement not only made youth aware of a historical injustice which made it difficult for them to be proud of this country, but also served as a training ground for future radicals. The new campus protest began at Berkeley when students demanded the right to work freely on their own campuses on behalf of oppressed Negroes. Many campus radicals shaped their images of "the Establishment" and of unreasonable authority on the basis of their early work in the civil rights movement. Students throughout the country have developed an amazing empathy and identification with Negroes. Their commitment to the Negro cause has taught them the psychological meaning of oppression and has encouraged them to seek out and attack sources of oppression in their own lives.

Neutral Hypotheses

Some explanations of student unrest focus upon impersonal processes. The causes of unrest according to these hypotheses are not to be found in the actions or philosophies of other men, but are believed to reside in changes in our highly complex society which seem to create the need for new modes of psychological adaptation.

The Technology Hypothesis

Man has always lived with hope, particularly with the hope that his efforts in the present will be rewarded with gratification in the

---

* In this regard it is somewhat distressing to note the manner in which hippies and protesters have not only been institutionalized as part of our folklore and humor but have been exploited by the advertising industry, an institution which they initially intended to destroy.

future. A certain degree of predictability in the future enables one to make commitments to goals and to other people. To the extent that we live in a society in which past, present and future lose their inter-relatedness, the power of hope to shape man's behavior is diminished. New means of adapting to the world must then be found and the manner in which people relate to one another must be profoundly altered.

Post-war America has been characterized by a massive and continuous growth of technology. Our society is one in which the conditions of everyday life are constantly changing. Moreover, the rate at which technology changes our lives is itself increasing. No one can predict what life will be like in 20 years, 10 years, or even 5 years. Today's knowledge, today's work skills and today's values may be totally irrelevant to tomorrow's world. Kenneth Keniston has described the manner in which some youth, who, when exposed to an ever-increasing rate of technological growth, come to perceive that the values of the past will be totally inappropriate for the world in which they will be adults. Moreover, they feel powerless to anticipate or direct the future. In this environment, hope no longer sustains. It is adaptive to be cool, to learn to live in the present.[12]

What are the advantages and disadvantages of living in the present? The advantages are more or less obvious. One is more flexible and superficially at least more comfortable. It is not necessary to delay gratification nor need one allow himself to be tortured by the mistakes of the past or be deluded by unrealistic hopes for the future. The disadvantages of life in the present are more subtle, yet more powerful. To live in the present one must narrow his commitments. He must travel lightly and be ready for anything. More intimate relationships are unlikely since they cannot be sustained by reference to past experience or to promises of a better future. Passion and romantic longing must be avoided because they may breed pain or impair one's flexibility. In short, if carried to extremes, life in the present is a selfish life which is incompatible with the growth of that intimacy and passion which man has always found to be essential to a fulfilled life.

Distrust of the future and a determination to live in the present seem to be characteristic of both activist and alienated students. The student activist seeks immediate change and has difficulty in developing the patience or optimism for long-term planning. The alienated student adopts the philosophy of the "hippie." Believing that the only certainty in life is change, or uncertainty itself, he adapts by "doing his own thing" and behaves as though he is responsible only to himself.

The Media Hypotheses

There are several hypotheses that attempt to relate the growth of new media, particularly television, to the troubling behavior of students. It can be argued, for example, that simply by being available to publicize student activists and hippies the media exaggerate the importance of these groups. The television camera forces all of us to take seriously forms of behavior that might have been dismissed lightly in earlier decades. Conceivably, the media may be creating a "climate of expectation" in which youth are subtly seduced into dissenting roles which may not represent their actual interests. It is also true that many television commercials, radio ads and most modern music are directed towards the youth market. The self-consciousness of youth is thereby heightened. They are made more aware of their potentialities and sometimes develop an exaggerated sense of their own power.

Another attempt to relate changing media to student unrest has been implied in the writings of Marshall McLuhan.[13] McLuhan believes that electronic media are bringing us all closer together in a more truly communal and shared society than ever existed. Our youth who have grown up with the new media are ready for such a society. Elders who are committed to sustain the institutions of the past are not. Much of youthful rebellion can then be visualized as an effort to make older people see that the world has changed and that many of the values of the past are now irrelevant.

While McLuhan's hypothesis is intriguing, it does not focus upon the context of media. I would like to suggest a new hypothesis of student interest based on the manner in which the media influence the character structure of youth by prematurely confronting them with the harsh truths and realities of life.

As an animal whose growth and development requires him to be dependent upon others for a long period of time, man learns to rely on others for an optimal amount of structure and order in his life. It is obvious that authority is not always benevolent or just and yet it is true that no man can be at ease if he does not commit a part of himself to some authority, whether it be his church, his family, his government or an ideology. Nor can one come to develop a firm sense of who he is without making such commitments. It is at least partly through experiencing limitations which are imposed by others, by respecting others, and by emulating those who are respected that one finds his own identity. The process by which one comes to terms with authority is not always deliberate or rational. Sometimes even benevolent authority relies on faith, mystique or untruth to retain its control.

This is especially relevant to the situation of young people. The most well meaning parents must on occasion deceive their children because they know that children would find many of the hard and cynical facts of life to be unbearable. Until recently it was possible for young people to begin to experience the world as adults know it only after they have reached adolescence. Most of the time the adolescent absorbed this new knowledge gradually and painlessly. Even when he did feel that his parents had been hypocritical or had deceived him, his awareness of their dishonesty came so gradually that his resentment and rebelliousness were restrained. Today it is different. One of the significant developments in post-war America has been the influence of mass-communication media, particularly television, which are capable of disseminating information to all age groups immediately.

Even before adolescence, television acquaints youth with the cynical facts of life at a time when such truths may be indigestible. Other media communicate knowledge so quickly now that there is little opportunity for anyone to live comfortably with myth or self-delusion. Beliefs which were once casually accepted are vigorously scrutinized. The belief that there is equality for all Americans can hardly be sustained when one has a front row seat from which he can observe the Negro's unsuccessful struggle to maintain a decent life in this country. Blind faith in the veracity of leaders in the nations is quickly lost when one can watch the proceedings of an organization such as the United Nations in his own living room. I have no doubt that diplomats have always lied to one another but what is new about this world is that children can now watch them lie in living color.

The hypocrisies of older generations have always been with us. What is new today is that it is ridiculously easy to expose them. The effect on our youth of premature emergence of truth has been to create a deep skepticism as to the validity of authority. Neither the family, the church, the law nor any institution demands the automatic respect it once did. There may be other factors contributing to this decline in respect for authority but in my opinion it is best understood in terms of the psychological impact of our new media.

The Overreliance on Scientism Hypothesis

Today's restless youth have grown up in a world which has not been dominated by religious faith but which has sought many of the answers to the questions of life in science, particularly social science. In my work with students, I am often impressed to find how easily they believe or once believed in the perfectibility of man. Hostility is not seen as an innate quality of man but rather as a response to frustration. The teachings of the social psychologist that aggression is a learned phenomenon have gained prominence over Freud's more ominous warnings that aggression is innate.

This generation of students seems to have grown up with the belief that original sin in the religious sense or Thanatos in the psychoanalytic sense do not exist. (Much of this belief has been reinforced by the mode of their existence. Many are affluent and have grown up in suburban communities where, except for what they see on television, they are shielded from the tragedies of life. The realities of their own lives convince them that whatever calamities are imposed upon others are not inevitable.) Statements such as "life is a vale of tears," or "the mass of men lead lives of quiet desperation" seem absurd to them. In their adherence to scientific rationality they also cannot comprehend guilt. They are convinced that in a perfectible world man should be joyful and guiltless.

When a person raised with such beliefs begins to encounter the harsh realities of life, he has little to fall back upon. If he begins to perceive his own aggressive tendencies, he is frightened by them and attempts to deny them. He may project his anger upon those who he feels are frustrating him or he may simply deny that such anger exists. When he perceives the evil of others he is mortified. In this conviction that there are rational solutions to any problem, he cannot help but be intolerant of the irrationalities of those who prevent progress. He finds himself frustrated and impotent. In his belief that life and especially the sexual aspects of life can be enjoyed without guilt, he becomes highly disturbed when he discovers that he cannot escape his past and that a certain amount of guilt is inevitable. He even becomes plagued with additional guilt over the realization that he is guilty.

The restless student is one who has taken the message of science, rationality and perfection too literally. He is not equipped to understand, to deal with the depth of that irrationality in man which resists change and seeks his own destruction. Too often such a student finds it necessary to construct "devil" theories of history in which the existence of evil is attributed to only a few who block the progress of the many. He has sacrificed the comfort and patience which comes with the idea of accepting "original" sin.*

Conclusions

Hopefully this review has been more than an exercise in cataloguing. By emphasizing the diversity of explanations of student unrest, I have attempted to demonstrate the intellectual futility of searching for simple explanations of a highly complex phenomenon. As citizens we may wish either to support or attack the causes which restless students have dramatized. But as scholars concerned with educating and understanding and helping students we must take a more objective approach and recognize that there is some truth to the most critical as well as the most sympathetic hypotheses.

Some of the hypotheses suggest guidelines for action. The critical hypotheses remind us that youth are not always as wise or powerful as we might suspect. Like adults, their actions are as much determined by personal weaknesses and selfishness as by sensitivity or idealism. While youth certainly do not need more paternalism and coddling, they can still learn much from adults who are committed to the pursuit of ideals in a climate of tolerance, compassion and responsibility. The critical hypotheses need not be used to berate students but can be helpful in freeing adults from that unreasonable guilt which impairs an honest confrontation with the issues which students have raised.

The sympathetic hypotheses emphasize the unusual degree of stress this generation of students has experienced. Those hypotheses which invoke the war, overpopulation and pollution as sources of stress

---

* Sometimes the student becomes totally overwhelmed with the irrational aspects of the world and reacts by totally abandoning his earlier beliefs. In their disillusionment some alienated students seem to be turning away from the promises of scientism and searching for solace in the most dubious forms of mysticism, magic and astrology.

forcefully remind us that student unrest is not entirely inappropriate. Other hypotheses raise many questions for those entrusted with the management of our universities. Does the emphasis on education as a means rather than an end have any meaning in an affluent society? Should youth be encouraged to remain in a passive role as students throughout the first third of their lives? Are there means of bringing young people into important roles in the power structure of our universities and social system before they reach the age of 25 or 30? Is the 2S classification anything more than a bribe which weakens the moral position of dissenting students and creates havoc upon our campuses? Should it be abolished? To what extent can we continue to centralize and enlarge our campuses without creating a generation of alienated youth who feel no sense of identity, no sense that they have a voice in what is done to them and no sense of commitment to anything but their own interests?

The neutral hypotheses may be the most valid explanations of student unrest but at the same time they are the most difficult to live with optimistically. If progress itself, in the form of technology, science or new media, is the most severe stress in the lives of our young people, then we are faced with a seemingly impossible task, namely how to control the rate of progress, make it possible for people to live in a world which guarantees hope, comfort and stability in the future.

Students have demonstrated to anyone who is willing to read their message that a complacent drifting into the future, an unchecked growth of technology, science and media cannot take place without profoundly altering the nature of human existence and the character of man. We can no longer sit back and rely on man's supposedly unlimited ability to adjust. In this regard it is important to note that the most severely alienated students have in a sense adequately adjusted themselves to a society that already exists or is about to exist. Yet they are miserable and ineffective. We must not only deal with the questions of man's survival in the society of the future, but must also ask, "If he survives will he still be man?" We need to define those conditions of life which make for the most compassionate, responsible, committed and happy existence. We need to work towards creating a society in which such an existence is possible. If we cannot accomplish these goals, man's tenure on earth has been meaningless.

NOTES

[1] Seymour L. Halleck, "Psychiatric Treatment of the Alienated College Student," *American Journal of Psychiatry,* November, 1967, pp. 96–104; and Seymour L. Halleck, "Why Students Protest; A Psychiatrist's View," *Think* magazine, November–December, 1967, pp. 3–7.

[2] The arguments for permissiveness and the responsibility hypotheses are rarely found in scholarly literature. One of the least exhortative is George F. Kennan, "Rebels Without a Program," *New York Times Magazine,* January 4, 1968, subsequently published as *Democracy and the Student Left* (New York, Bantam Books, Inc., 1968). A popular description of the permissiveness view is given by Christopher Jencks, "Is It All Dr. Spock's Fault?" *New York Times Magazine,* March 3, 1968. There has been an abundance of statements by politicians, law enforcement officers, and theologians decrying permissiveness and non-responsibility. One of the most typical is J. Edgar Hoover's recent testimony before the President's Commission on Violence which received nationwide television coverage in the communications-press media.

[3] E. E. Sampson, "Student Activism and the Decade of Protest," *Journal of Social Issues,* 23 (1967), (3) pp. 1–33.

[4] For more on this point, see Thomas S. Szasz, *Law, Liberty & Psychiatry* (New York, Macmillan, 1963).

[5] Graham Blaine, *Youth and the Hazards of Affluence* (New York, Harper & Row, 1966); E. E. Sampson, *op. cit.,* and Irving Kristol, "What's Bugging the Students," in *Atlantic Monthly,* November, 1965; also in the Editors of Atlantic, *The Troubled Campus* (Boston, Little, Brown and Company, 1965), pp. 3–12.

[6] Seymour L. Halleck, *op. cit.*

[7] E. E. Sampson, *op. cit.*

[8] J. R. Seeley, "Plantation Politics," *Psychiatry and Social Science Review,* July, 1968, pp. 16–18.

[9] Seymour L. Halleck, "Students and the Draft," *Progressive* magazine, February, 1968.

[10] See the publication *Students & Society,* Center Occasional Paper, Vol. 1, No. 1 (Santa Barbara, Calif., Center for the Study of Democratic Institutions, 1968).

[11] Herbert Marcuse, "Repressive Tolerance," in Robert Wolff, *Critique of Pure Tolerance* (New York, Beacon Press, 1965).

[12] Kenneth Keniston, *The Uncommitted* (New York, Harcourt, Brace & World, 1964).

[13] Herbert Marshall McLuhan, *Understanding Media* (New York, McGraw-Hill, 1964).

2

WHO PROTESTS:
A STUDY OF STUDENT ACTIVISTS

*by Leonard L. Baird**

STUDENT ACTIVISM has become a topic of debate and controversy, as this and other books attest. Much has been written about student activists, both pro and con. However, the careful reader of this material, whether he is an interested citizen, or a social scientist, will soon notice a peculiar lack of *facts* in most discussions. Too much of the work is anecdotal and journalistic. Even the few factual studies by social scientists offer conclusions which may be questioned. Many of them are confined to a single campus, and focus only on the students involved in a single event, thus causing one to doubt their generality. Furthermore, many studies have used only one measurement instrument, and thus have lacked comprehensiveness. Often the data was gathered after the protest event rather than before it, with the possibility that participation in the event caused some students to change their responses.

The present study was designed to deal with these limitations. It involved a large sample of students in diverse colleges, on whom comprehensive data were gathered during their freshmen and sophomore years. The data included information on students' interests,

* Dr. Leonard L. Baird is Research Psychologist with The American College Testing Program, Iowa City, Iowa, under whose auspices the study here described was undertaken.

achievements, goals, competencies, self-concepts, and personalities. We also used a scale of "activism" which allowed us to group the sample according to the *degree* of activism. The American College Survey was administered to 12,432 college freshmen in 31 institutions during April and May of 1964.[1] The sample for the present study was the 5,129 students in 29 colleges who participated in this, and also in a follow-up study carried out in the spring of 1965 at the end of their sophomore year.[2] Complete follow-up data were obtained for 2,295 men and 2,834 women, or 43 percent of the original sample. Some had left college, and others still enrolled did not complete the follow-up questionnaire. When students who participated in this study were compared with those who did not as to achievements and ability, there were few consistent differences; thus, we think the sample was reasonably representative.[3]

The Student Activism Scale was presented to students when they were sophomores.[4] They were asked whether they had

> Organized a college political group or campaign.
> Worked actively in an off-campus political organization.
> Worked actively in a student movement to change institutional rules, procedures, or policies.
> Initiated or organized a student movement to change institutional rules, procedures, or policies.
> Participated in one or more demonstrations for some political or social goal, such as civil rights, free speech for students, states' rights, etc.

We characterized any student who checked three or more of these items as an "activist"; those who checked one or two were termed "moderate activists," while others were "non-activists." Very few students in our sample were "activists": only 2.7 percent of the men and 2.5 percent of the women. About a quarter (21.6 percent of the men and 24.5 percent of the women) displayed moderate activism; 75.7 percent of the men and 73.0 percent of the women had not engaged in *any* of the activities of the activism scale. Simple one-way analysis of variance was used to test for differences between these three groups of students. The means of the groups are reported to show trends in the data. Because of the large sample size, a significance level of .001 was used.

All students rated themselves on twenty-one common traits—writing ability, aggressiveness, understanding of others, etc.—on a four-point scale ("Below Average," "Average," "Above Average," and "Top Ten Percent"). These ratings, made in the freshman year, provided simple measures of the self-concepts of the students.[5]

Compared to other students, both men and women who were to become activists described themselves as socially ascendant and capable (higher on Leadership, Popularity, Aggressiveness, Speaking Ability), socially sensitive and gregarious (higher on Understanding of Others, Sensitivity to the Needs of Others, Sociability), aesthetically talented and expressive (higher on Originality, Writing Ability, Expressiveness, Acting Ability), and independent (higher on Independence, Intellectual Self-Confidence).[6] Women activists described themselves as having a high drive to achieve, artistic ability, and perseverance. Men activists also described themselves as socially self-confident. Thus, students who later became activists thought of themselves as confident, interpersonally capable, sensitive, driving and talented.

All students rated themselves on twenty-three items pertaining to their goals and aspirations, such as "making a theoretical contribution to science," "helping others who are in difficulty," and "following a formal religious code." Each of the life goal items was rated by the subject on a four-point scale ("of little or no importance," "somewhat important for you to achieve," "very important for you to achieve, but not essential," and "essential to you, something you must achieve").[7]

Social ascendancy and desire for a central role in political affairs again appears among activists-to-be. Men and women activists gave higher values to becoming a community leader, being influential in public affairs, keeping up to date politically, having executive responsibility for the work of others, and to obtaining rewards and recognition. However, they also gave a higher rating to "helping others in difficulty." Their serious concerns are reflected in the goals of being well read and of developing a meaningful philosophy of life. This last must be distinguished from "finding a real purpose in life." The activist students seem confident of their purpose and did not give a high rating to this goal. The activist students did not give significantly lower ratings to life goals we might expect them to reject: be well off financially, make my parents proud of me, follow a formal religious code, be successful in my own business.

Student activists are sometimes described as affluent youth in revolt. To examine this description, we used three measures of family background. To give an indication of social class, students were asked to estimate their family's income on a seven-point scale.[8] Second, students checked from a list of 76 items those places they had visited or those events they had experienced, such as visits to museums, factories, mental hospitals, and sports car races. Third, they checked those things they had in their homes from a list of 39 items, such as an encyclopedia set, sculpturing tools, and power tools. Analyses of these scales showed that student activists did *not* come from wealthier families, but that their homes did provide many intellectual resources, and that they have had a wide range of experiences.

Checklists of extracurricular achievement for the high school years were used and included the following areas: art, music, writing, leadership, dramatic art, and science.[9] Some examples of the items in these scales: "built a piece of laboratory apparatus on my own (not as part of a course)," "was elected president of my class (any year)," "had leads in high school or church sponsored plays," "exhibited a work of art (painting, sculpture, etc.) in a city or county art show," and "had poems, stories, essays or articles published in a school publication." Students also reported their average high school grades. Analysis revealed that activists had significantly more nonacademic high school achievements in every area with the exception of music for women. They had notably greater achievements in leadership, speech, and writing. In contrast, their academic achievement as measured by high school grades was not significantly different from that of other students.

We also wished to study activists' vocational interests, potentials for achievement and special competencies. The *Vocational Preference Inventory* is composed of occupational titles, which a student indicates that he likes or dislikes.[10] It was scored for 7 scales: Realistic, Intellectual, Social, Conventional, Enterprising, Artistic, and Aggressive. The mean scores of students on these scales are shown in Table 1. Student activists are characterized by interests in aggressive, social, enterprising and artistic occupations. High scorers on these scales have been described as sensitive, critical, aggressive, dominating, leading, sociable, having verbal skills, interested in others, imaginative, and self-sufficient. Males low in activism seem to prefer realistic occupations (technical and skilled trades). Women activists prefer intellectual or scientific occupations.

The *Potential Achievement Scales* are revised versions of those used by Nichols and Holland.[11] They were empirically constructed for men and women separately to predict extracurricular achievement by comparing the preferences of achievers and non-achievers for 275 daily activities, hobbies, reading habits, school subjects, and sports. Typical items included working on guns, playing chess, giving talks, collecting rocks, and drawing cartoons. In several studies they have been shown to predict later achievement in the areas of the scales. The findings in Table 1 indicate that both men and women activists prefer activities, reading, hobbies, etc., which would suggest high po-

TABLE 1

MEANS ON INTEREST, POTENTIAL, PERSONALITY,
AND COMPETENCY SCALES BY LEVEL
OF STUDENT ACTIVISM

	Men				Women			
	Low	Mod	High	F	Low	Mod	High	F
Vocational Preference Inventory								
Realistic	4.57	3.85	4.13	7.75*	1.54	1.76	2.01	3.86
Intellectual	5.72	5.83	5.39	0.32	3.90	4.53	5.03	8.51*
Social	4.18	5.41	6.53	33.48*	8.08	9.01	8.50	16.54*
Conventional	3.04	3.33	4.47	5.74	2.74	2.91	2.71	0.74*
Enterprising	4.01	5.16	5.77	26.18*	3.63	4.29	4.99	18.73
Artistic	3.38	4.30	4.90	16.17*	5.56	6.80	6.49	22.69*
Aggressive	4.99	6.67	7.44	47.91*	4.79	6.16	7.10	48.55*
Potentials for Achievement								
Leadership potential	23.27	27.15	30.32	56.47*	18.66	20.82	23.51	63.58*
Literary potential	14.99	17.63	20.27	54.58*	13.94	16.29	19.19	78.13*
Art potential	10.10	11.92	14.23	36.82*	10.39	11.74	14.21	21.7̄*
Science potential	17.78	18.14	19.95	3.26	13.31	14.57	16.82	19.57*
Drama potential	11.45	13.85	16.11	67.47*	17.27	19.87	22.86	67.88*
Competency Scales								
Total competency	49.24	57.51	63.86	50.26*	55.04	62.94	68.51	71.28*
Governmental	0.68	0.90	1.19	25.29*	0.57	0.80	1.01	32.55*
Social	5.23	6.44	7.34	44.58*	7.45	8.21	8.88	30.99*
Arts	6.60	8.88	10.16	41.63*	10.05	12.54	13.78	56.75*
Leadership	3.95	5.53	6.18	67.75*	4.59	5.83	6.81	56.44*
Personality and Value Scales								
Preconscious activity	16.50	17.40	19.39	13.46*	18.64	19.89	20.99	22.74*
Dogmatism	17.36	17.44	17.53	0.06	16.93	16.81	16.97	0.13
Academic type	4.41	4.89	5.36	17.01*	4.52	5.14	5.69	37.04*
Vocational type	4.92	4.64	4.65	5.45	4.32	4.27	4.25	0.27
Interpersonal comp	10.61	11.84	12.36	32.46*	11.18	12.19	12 50	28.58*
N	1737	496	62		2062	689	72	

* Indicates significant beyond .001 level.

tential for achievement in leadership, literary work, art, and speech and drama. In addition, women activists show potential for achievement in science.

Students were also asked to check from a list of 143 activities those which they could do competently or well. Items included: "I can make jewelry," "I can read Greek," and "I can use logarithm tables." The number of activities checked equals a student's total range of competencies. Subscales developed for several subareas of competence included governmental, social and educational, arts, and leadership scales. As shown in Table 1, the results for the Competency scales are similar to the results for the Potential scales. The largest F-value is associated with the total of all competencies claimed, an indication of general capacity and effectiveness. The activist students also score higher on every competency subscale.

Students' personalities and value orientations were assessed by several measures. According to Kubie, ideas and concepts are freed from their usual associations in the preconscious, the region of the mind which lies between complete awareness and the unconscious. Presumably, the original person can make effective use of his preconscious processes, and can thereby produce novel solutions to problems. The *Preconscious Activity Scale* attempts to assess this originality by such items as "I often daydream about unsolved problems," and "I am regarded as a person of many ideas." [12] The activists had high scores on this scale.

We also included a revised version of a widely used *"Dogmatism" Scale* developed by Rokeach to measure dogmatic and rigid thinking, characterized by intolerance of ambiguity and inflexibility. Interestingly, activists were neither more nor less dogmatic than other students. Two scales were used to measure students' general approaches to education: The *Academic Orientation Scale,* which reflects an "identification with the intellectual concerns of the faculty," and the *Vocational Orientation Scale,* which reflects a valuing of college as a preparation for the world of work. As shown in Table 1, activists scored higher on the former but were not different from other students on the latter. Thus, the activists in our sample seemed to support rather than to reject the values of the faculty. Finally, we attempted to assess students' effectiveness in dealing with other people by the use of an *Interpersonal Competency Scale.* [13] Scale items simply poll the subject for those factors believed to be conducive to, or typical of, interpersonal competency, such as social experience and skills, positive self-regard and good health. As shown in Table 1, activists also scored higher on this scale.

In short, the analyses reported in Table 1 suggest that student activists are talented in many areas, interested in people and positions of leadership, are artistic and original, and can work effectively with other people.

Variables from the Follow-Up Survey

In addition to the measures we have described so far, which were obtained while students were freshmen, data were also obtained about the college experiences of the students near the end of their sophomore year. First, we assessed students' college experiences. On a simple checklist, students indicated whether they had been members of fraternities or sororities, participated in intercollegiate athletics, worked for pay 15 hours or more a week, dropped out of college, or had had psychotherapy or counseling. Surprisingly, men who were moderate or high in student activism were somewhat more likely to be members of fraternities. Women activists were not more likely to be sorority members, but were slightly more likely to have participated in athletics. Activists were *not* likely to have dropped out of college, worked, or to have had psychotherapy or counseling.

In addition, students were asked to agree or disagree with various opinion items about their college. Activists were found less likely to think that "the classroom or the lab is the place one is most likely to encounter ideas" but were *more* likely to report that "there is at least one faculty member with whom I like to discuss my ideas." They were also more likely to hold that "a major drawback of this college is that there are too many rules and regulations." Thus, while activists seemed to communicate with faculty members and, as we saw in the last section, shared the faculty's intellectual concerns, they looked outside the classroom situation for ideas.

The College *Nonacademic Achievement Scales* are lists of extracurricular accomplishments which range from common to rare and more important ones.[14] The student checks those accomplishments he has attained. Examples of the items include: "Elected as one of the *officers* of a class (freshman, sophomore, etc.) in any year of college," "Had drawings, photographs, or other art work published in a public newspaper or magazine," and "Received a prize or award for a scientific paper or project." Students were also asked to report their average letter grades in their last term. (Several studies have shown that such self-reported grades are highly correlated with grades taken from transcripts.)[15]

TABLE 2

COLLEGE ACADEMIC AND NONACADEMIC ACHIEVEMENT
BY LEVEL OF STUDENT ACTIVISM

Achievement Area	Men				Women			
	Low	Mod	High	F	Low	Mod	High	F
Leadership	0.66	1.59	3.57	179.02*	0.95	1.96	2.68	122.05*
Art	0.43	0.87	1.61	57.35*	0.74	1.23	2.00	57.09*
Social service	0.53	1.28	2.44	145.80*	0.91	1.66	2.57	133.44*
Science	0.26	0.39	0.87	19.75*	0.08	0.12	0.35	19.32*
Business	0.60	0.96	1.66	55.88*	0.30	0.47	0.61	21.37*
Humanities	0.90	1.53	2.61	88.61*	1.28	1.99	2.68	91.78*
Religious service	1.17	1.58	2.15	12.23*	1.72	2.28	2.40	17.31*
Music	0.21	0.32	0.66	12.48*	0.21	0.36	0.39	14.57*
Writing	0.24	0.56	1.11	63.94*	0.38	0.78	1.04	62.18*
Social science	0.29	0.54	1.39	95.95*	0.26	0.51	0.97	78.89*
Speech & drama	0.22	0.60	1.26	68.52*	0.27	0.55	0.81	36.25*
Special educational experiences	0.30	0.36	0.69	12.14*	0.34	0.45	0.50	7.47*
College GPA†	4.02	4.06	4.42	2.58	4.24	4.33	4.27	1.34
N	1737	496	62		2062	689	72	

* Indicates significant beyond .001 level.
† College GPA's are based on seven-point scale.

The results of these achievement measures are shown in Table 2. As in high school, the activists had significantly more achievements in every nonacademic area but did not obtain higher grades. They also had more special educational experiences, such as honors programs, independent study, etc. (which are generally moderately related to grades), and had notably greater achievements in leadership, social service, humanities, and social science. The activists apparently did not reject traditional forms of student government, and were more likely to hold student offices. They also were more frequently involved in serving as foreign student advisers, in voluntary on-campus and civic improvement projects, as volunteer aides in hospitals or clinics, and in other such services. The significant difference on business achievement may be due to items which refer to managing the affairs of a student group and of a student publication. The activist's artistic talent and potential we noted earlier is expressed in achievement in art, writing, and speech and drama.

Conclusions

In agreement with most other studies, the activists in our sample were found to be more independent, service-oriented, artistic, and expressive than other students. Their home life was stimulating and included a wide variety of educationally useful experiences, but their parents were not wealthy. As Keniston[16] also found, they were leaders in high school and were talented before they became activists.

However, some of the present results are in disagreement with some other studies and with the popular conception of activists. The activists in our sample seemed practical rather than "romantic." They were neither more nor less dogmatic than other students, and they did not seem to be less religious than other students.[17]

These last points suggest an important general finding: that the student activists in our sample did not appear to be alienated. Indeed, one must recognize their normality and similarity to other students, in that they did not rate themselves lower in self-control, conservatism, or practical mindedness, nor did they give lower ratings to the life goals of "be well off financially," "invent a useful product," "make my parents proud of me," "be successful in one's own business," and "follow a formal religious code." In religious service and business achievement, they scored above average. Their college experiences resembled those of other students; in contrast to stereotypes, they did not more frequently drop out or seek counseling or psychotherapy. In brief, they were not ideologues and were, on the whole, well balanced and well liked persons.

One result is in disagreement with the impressions of many writers: activists were not outstanding students. They were, however, talented in many other areas we have called nonacademic. The student activists seemed to accept the goals of liberal education, but to perceive the classroom and grades as unrelated or tangential to the attainment of those goals. They gave high ratings to the goals of developing a meaningful philosophy of life and of being well read, and they scored highest on a scale designed to measure "academic" values; but they did not obtain better high school grades. They rated themselves high in originality, independence, writing ability, and intellectual self-confidence, but not in scholarship; nor were their college grades above average. Classroom experiences apparently had not encouraged the activists to put forth the same effort that they seemed willing to give to extracurricular matters. They seemed, then, to be intellectual, but not academic.

Finally, the present results suggest that activists are concerned with personal prominence as well as public morality. They differed most from other students in their potential and accomplishment in leadership, and on measures reflecting a desire to influence events and other people. In addition to their desire to serve, they appear strongly power-oriented. They seem to be aggressive, self-confident, purposive, and well organized.[18] The activists in this sample very probably were not motivated solely by an altruistic concern for particular issues or injustices; they are seeking a sense of community, they also seem to think of themselves as the community leaders.

In summary, the student activists in this sample were distinguished by their talent rather than their alienation, by their intellectuality rather than their academic performance, and by their leadership rather than their anomie.

NOTES

[1] D. Abe, J. L. Holland, S. W. Lutz, and J. M. Richards, Jr., *A Description of American College Freshmen,* ACT Research Report No. 1 (Iowa City: American College Testing Program, 1965). This includes detailed information about the content, reliability, etc., of the instruments described below.

[2] The sample is described in more detail in J. M. Richards, Jr., J. L. Holland, and S. W. Lutz, "The Assessment of Student Accomplishment in College," *Journal of College Student Personnel,* 8 (1967), 360–365.

[3] J. M. Richards, Jr., J. L. Holland, and S. W. Lutz, "The Prediction of Student Accomplishment in College," *Journal of Educational Psychology,* 58 (1967), 343–355.

[4] These items were not presented to the students as a scale, but were distributed among many items dealing with extracurricular participation and achievements.

[5] J. M. Richards, Jr., "A Factor Analytic Study of the Self-ratings of College Freshmen," *Educational and Psychological Measurement,* 26 (1966), 861–870.

[6] Although these figures are not shown here, to conserve space, all the differences reported were significant beyond the .001 level.

[7] J. M. Richards, Jr., "Life Goals of American College Freshmen," *Journal of Counseling Psychology,* 13 (1966), 12–20.

[8] Alternatives were provided for students who considered this information confidential or who could not provide an estimate of their family's income.

[9] For a report of an earlier use of these scales, see J. L. Holland, and J. M. Richards, Jr., "Academic and Nonacademic Accomplishment: Correlated or Uncorrelated?" *Journal of Educational Psychology,* 56 (4) (1965), 165–174.

[10] J. L. Holland, "A Personality Inventory Employing Occupational Titles," *Journal of Applied Psychology,* 42 (1958), 336–342.

[11] *"Prediction of the First Year College Performance of High Aptitude Students."* Psychological Monographs, 1963, 77 (7, Whole No. 570). See also: L. L. Baird, "The Prediction of Accomplishment in College: An Exploration of the Process of Achievement," *Journal of Counseling Psychology,* in press.

[12] J. L. Holland and L. L. Baird, "The Preconscious Activity Scale: The Development and Validation of an Originality Measure," *Journal of Creative Behavior,* 2 (1968), 217–225.

[13] J. L. Holland and L. L. Baird, "An Interpersonal Competency Scale," *Educational and Psychological Measurement,* 28 (1968), 503–510.

[14] Richards, Holland, Lutz, *op. cit.*

[15] J. M. Richards, Jr., and S. W. Lutz, "Predicting Student Accomplishment in College from the ACT Assessment," *Journal of Educational Measurement,* 5 (1968), 17–29.

[16] K. Keniston, *Young Radicals* (New York, Harcourt, Brace & World, 1968).

[17] It is illuminating to recall that *Ramparts* magazine, a widely read journal among activists, began as a lay Catholic opinion magazine.

[18] However, the trait of dominance is compatible with other attitudes; see R. B. Cattell, *The Scientific Analysis of Personality* (Baltimore, Penguin Books, 1965). Activists may very well expect a high level of individual independence from everyone. Further, their need to break with convention may be supported by their "toughness."

3

WHO PROTESTS: THE SOCIAL BASES
OF THE STUDENT MOVEMENT

by Richard Flacks*

Personal Characteristics and Family
Backgrounds of Student Activists

POPULAR DISCUSSION of student protest tends to depict protesters in a number of ways indicated in preceding chapters. These ways may be generally organized into two broad views. On the one hand, there are those who attribute rebelliousness and alienation to the whole of the younger generation, who declare that it is natural for youth to be idealistic and self-assertive, and who see the current campus protests as an aspect of a "generation gap" or generational conflict. On the other hand, there are some who believe that student protesters represent a pathological fringe of the student population, a group which is incapable of adapting to academic life because of their personal insufficiencies; this view tends to see protest as somehow imported into an otherwise healthy student population whose more intelligent and serious members reject the influence of the protesters. Neither view is supported by the several careful empirical studies of student protesters which now exist. There is a remarkable

* Dr. Richard Flacks, long active in the movement himself as a student and faculty member, has made important contributions to understanding the phenomenon by several empirical studies of student protesters and their parents. He is presently assistant professor of sociology at the University of Chicago.

convergence in the findings of these studies concerning the characteristics of white students who participate in protest activity. This chapter represents an effort to review briefly such findings, and to sketch out a way of interpreting them.

1. *Movement participants tend to be recruited from the most selective universities and colleges; the highest incidence of off-campus and on-campus protest activity has occurred at major state and private universities and prestigious liberal arts colleges.*[1] There are a number of ways of demonstrating the relationship between protest and the quality of the institution. For example, the higher the percentage of PhD's on a faculty, the more likely it is that the campus in question will have had organized protest concerning the Vietnam war, civil rights and other public issues. The largest SDS chapters, and the most continuously active ones, exist at the major universities and colleges. For the most part, prolonged, intense on-campus rebellions have tended to occur at the prestigious institutions—e.g. Berkeley, Columbia, Michigan, Wisconsin, Stanford, Chicago, Oberlin. On the other hand, there are some important instances of intense protest at less selective institutions—for example, San Francisco State College, Catholic University, Texas Christian University, Long Island University. For the most part, however, the latter confrontations have been generated either by black students' grievances, or by strong faculty-administration conflict, and consequently have somewhat different sources from those which underlie the white student revolt. Black protest is sufficiently different to deserve a separate study and is not treated in this chapter. The most precise generalization concerning the distribution of white student protest is that there is a strong correlation between student involvement in national and social off-campus issues and the selectivity and quality of the institution. This relationship tends to break down with respect to student protest concerning local, on-campus issues and as the spread and change in the composition of the student movement continue, this and other generalizations of this chapter may be weakened. Protest seems to have originated at the elite schools, but is having increasing impact across the full range of institutions.

The basic reason for this pattern is unclear. It may be that student self-selection is operating to influence "protest-prone" students, described in Dr. Astin's chapter, to choose institutions in which liberal attitudes and emphases actually encourage protest and dissent. Furthermore, prestigious institutions are more likely to encourage student

independence and participation in national political and social issues.
2. *Student protesters are rarely recruited from among those with below average grades; there is some tendency for those with high grades
to be disproportionately represented in protest activity.* Some studies
suggest that student protesters do better academically than the rest
of the student body; others indicate that the distribution of grades
among protesters resembles that of the student body as a whole. Most
studies show substantial under-representation of academically deficient students in the movement.[2] Dr. Baird's recent study, however,
reported in the previous chapter, indicates a difference between intellectual ability and academic performance. But there is no support
for the hypothesis that student protest is related to academic failure or
is an expression of the frustration of those students who cannot hold
their own in academic competition. There is some evidence that
academic failure is associated with participation in conservative student organizations, however.[3]

3. *In terms of aptitudes and interests, activists tend to be more
"academic" than non-activists.* One study indicates that activists score
higher in verbal aptitude (but not mathematical aptitude) on the
Scholastic Aptitude Test.[4] In another study, activists scored higher
on a variety of standardized scales measuring interest in intellectual
and aesthetic matters.[5] In surveys, they report themselves as having
been influenced by courses and teachers more often than do non-
activists. A recent study of entering freshmen at various California
institutions indicates that those who support student protest differ
from those who oppose protest in being "interested in increasing their
understanding of people with different backgrounds and values, in
having the opportunity to be exposed to the best thinking of the
ages, and of being challenged to critically reexamine their basic beliefs." These potential activists among the freshmen indicated a preference for education based on independent research and reading, and
small group discussions and seminars; the anti-protest freshmen said
they preferred a system based on lectures, standardized assignments
and examinations. The latter group was more interested in parties and
athletics than the former, who placed more importance on intellectual
work and discussion with friends as central aspects of the college
experience.[6]

In defining their long-term goals activists tend to rank intellectual
and aesthetic pursuits ahead of conventional career and family activities, while non-activists are much more likely to reverse these

priorities. Again, Baird's study raises questions about changes in this generalization. Activists typically indicate that they read more widely and extensively than non-activists, and they tend to be better informed about political and social events.[7] They are overwhelmingly recruited from among the more intellectual and academically serious students and the data show that they tend to be highly concentrated in the social sciences and humanities. Students majoring in the sciences, or in pre-professional or vocationally oriented programs are substantially under-represented in protest activity, as are students who are active in fraternities, sororities and other expressions of the non-academic, collegiate student subcultures. Vocationally, there is a general tendency for activists to be more undecided than other students; however, the most prevalent career choice among activists is academic—more are interested in college teaching, in scholarship and intellectual work than any other career.[8]

4. *Activists are disproportionately recruited from a particular social background: they are the sons and daughters of high income families, in which both parents have at least four years of college and tend to be employed in occupations for which advanced educational attainment is a primary requisite.*[9] Virtually all studies of protesters indicate that the average family income of activists is higher than that characteristic of their non-activist classmates. But the source of this high income is special—it derives from occupations that are intellectual or professional in character. Not only are the children of blue-collar and lower white-collar workers under-represented in the movement, but so are the offspring of business executives and entrepreneurs. A particularly striking fact about activists is that they tend to have mothers with unusually high educational attainment, and, for the most part, these are mothers who are employed at high skill levels, rather than housewives. Movement participants come from urban and suburban environments rather than small towns; they tend to come from the East and West coasts rather than the Midwest or the South. They are seldom the first in their family to attend college; in fact, a large proportion tend to come from families in which college education has been characteristic over several generations. In this sense, they tend to be less upwardly mobile than many of their non-activist classmates.

This picture of student activists has been confirmed repeatedly in studies undertaken in many parts of the country. But it is important to stress that, although this background is the *modal* one for student activists, there are certainly a wide variety of other backgrounds represented in the movement. Indeed, some of the most prominent leaders of the movement have come from working-class origins, or from small towns, or from families with little previous contact with higher education. Furthermore, there is some evidence indicating that the more recent recruits to protest activity tend to represent more heterogeneous backgrounds than those active at an earlier time or over a longer period.[10]

5. *The typical activist family is quite secular; however, a significant minority of activists come from families with a strong religious orientation.*[11] The great majority of activists have parents who have little or no active involvement in religious activity; in fact, a considerable number of parents profess no religious preference. On the other hand, a disproportionate number of activists are children of ministers, or have been highly active in religious denominations or groups which stress social concern—e.g. Quakers, Unitarians. In other words, the parents of activists are typically secular, but if they are involved with religion such involvement is often integrated with strong social and humanitarian orientations.

Obviously the religious composition of student protest groups on a particular campus is affected by the distribution of religious preferences among the student body as a whole; in general, however, one finds that Protestants are represented in the movement in expected proportions and are in the majority, that Jews are highly over-represented (though rarely, of course, a majority) and that Catholics are under-represented (except, of course, on Catholic campuses). There have been suggestions that student radicalism can in large part be explained as a protest by Jewish students deriving from the inconsistency between their social class position (which is high) and their social status (which is relatively low due to the lingering effects of anti-Semitism).[12] Such "status inconsistency" hypotheses, however, are contradicted by the finding that Jewish participation in protest tends to be uncorrelated with the income and educational levels of parents, while Protestant and Catholic participation is very strongly associated with high income and education. The high rates of Jewish participation in protest may be more simply attributed to the long tradition of Jewish support for civil rights, social justice and liberal programs.[13]

6. *The typical activist's parents are politically liberal; the proportion of activists who have "converted" from a background of conservatism*

is quite small, as is the proportion who have parents who are themselves left-wing or liberal activists.[14] In general, studies of the political socialization of college students suggest that the majority of students come from homes which may be described as moderately conservative and Republican. Moreover, the higher the family income and educational levels, the more likely it is that the student will have Republican and conservative parents. All studies of student activists indicate that most of them are recruited from students whose parents are Democrats. Studies based on students' reports of their parents' political views suggest, moreover, that the parents of activists tend to be more liberal than the parents of non-activists.

These findings are strongly reinforced by a study involving interviews with parents themselves. These interviews revealed substantial continuity between the views of student activists and the views of their parents on such matters as the war in Vietnam, civil rights and other foci of student protest. Parents of activists range politically from moderate liberalism to radicalism; in most studies, not more than 15 percent are reported to be Republicans, and even these often turn out to be liberal on many issues. Another 15–20 percent of activists' parents are reported to be socialists or otherwise radical. This is, of course, a far higher percentage than one would find in a random sample of college students, but it suggests, on the other hand, that most student activists have moved away from the liberalism of their parents to more radical positions. Thus, although there is broad agreement between most movement participants and their parents on political direction (especially with respect to foreign policy, disarmament, support for civil rights, support for freedom of speech, acceptance of increased public spending for social welfare purposes, and a generally unfavorable attitude toward "hard-line" anti-communism), it is obvious that students are typically more radical than their parents. For the most part, the greater radicalism of the students is expressed in terms of a pessimistic and alienated attitude toward American life, a considerably greater support for civil disobedience and other forms of direct action, a more skeptical or hostile attitude toward traditional liberal leaders and symbols, and, on the part of a minority of student activists, a stronger identification with socialist or other ideological forms of radicalism. But the most obvious difference between parents and students is that the latter have *acted* on their beliefs, while the parents, on the whole, have not been unusually active in political affairs (though they are as a group un-

usually *interested* in politics). It is safe to say that the great majority
of students in the movement are not "converts" to the positions they
now hold; their political development is better understood as an effort to express and fulfill certain broad values and perspectives which
they acquired, to a substantial extent, from their parents.

7. *The religious secularism and political liberalism characteristic of*
activist families are expressions of an underlying cluster of values
articulated by parents and shared by their activist offspring.[15] Our
own study of the parents of activist and non-activist students indicated
that these two groups of middle-class, middle-aged people were
markedly different with respect to central values, interests and aspirations. Parents of activists described their interests as primarily intellectual and aesthetic in content, whereas the leisure-time pursuits of
non-activist parents (even those with college degrees) were far more
likely to be conventionally recreational. Activist parents read extensively, attended concerts and art shows, traveled to culturally en-
riching places; non-activist parents were more interested in sports
and outdoor recreation, social clubs, vacation resorts, do-it-yourself
hobbies. These differences in intellectualism were, of course, reflected
in differing expectations concerning the activity of children—activist
parents quite consciously and systematically attempted to influence
their children's interests and tastes; non-activist parents tended to be
more permissive in this regard.

A second major difference between the two groups of parents related to the matter of conventional morality and self-control. Activist
parents placed considerable emphasis on fostering the capacity for
autonomy and self-expression on the part of their children and declared that they would be unwilling to discipline their children if
they transgressed some conventional norm, provided the transgression
contributed to the emotional growth of the child or was an expression
of his moral convictions. Thus, for example, activist parents accepted
the desirability of their children's involvement in social action which
might lead to trouble with the authorities. In response to a hypothetical question, they typically expressed a relaxed attitude toward
the possibility that their son or daughter might be living with a member of the opposite sex. In this respect, non-activist parents tended
to be much less permissive, generally claiming to uphold conventional
standards of morality with respect to pre-marital sex, or "trouble"
with the authorities resulting from political activities. In general, non-

activist parents valued self-discipline and respectability over self-expression and individuality; the reverse was true for activist parents.

A final major difference between the two groups of parents had to do with what might be called "social responsibility." Activists' parents expressed the hope that their children would be highly conscious of the need to help others or make a contribution to social betterment; for many, such goals took precedence over material success and status aspirations for their children. Non-activist parents, however, hoped primarily that their children could achieve stable, materially secure, and healthful lives, and a reasonable amount of success and satisfaction in their careers. They were much less likely to say that they encouraged humanitarian or socially useful activity for their children.

Both groups of parents agreed on the primary importance of stable vocational and familial roles for their children, but it should be clear from the above discussion that activist parents usually coupled such expectations with an equally strong emphasis on the importance of achieving genuine fulfillment in one's work and of serving others. Many activist fathers expressed some regret that they themselves had "compromised" their earlier values and aspirations in order to achieve material well-being; they hoped that their own children, having been born to material comfort, would realize that "other things in life were more important."

Both activist and non-activist students tended to reflect their parents' value-orientations in describing their own interests and aspirations. Activist students greatly resembled their parents in their intellectualism and their skepticism about conventional middle-class values. They were clearly attempting to fulfill their parents' expectations concerning personal autonomy and humanitarianism. They shared, and indeed were more explicit about, their parents' criticisms of themselves for failing to lead lives which were fully consistent with their values. In fact, the desire for a morally consistent and coherent life was an extremely important one for most student activists in our investigation—so much so that it clearly interfered with their ability to fix easily on clear-cut vocational objectives.

There is evidence from other studies concerning the orientation of activists toward principle and conscience rather than conformism. Smith, *et al.*, using Kohlberg's measure of moral development, found that students active in protest and social action were strongly characterized by moral reasoning based on self-accepted moral principles,

and were oriented either to a concern for justice and social welfare
or to their own conscience as a directing agent. Inactive students
tended, however, to be oriented to existing rules and legal structures.
Either they accepted without question the legitimacy of traditional
authority, or their moral choices were based on a desire to maintain
smooth relations between themselves and their peers or superiors.[16]

8. *Activists tend to come from homes in which a relatively democratic
and egalitarian child-rearing ideology was emphasized; there is little
evidence, however, for the popular view that student protest is related to parental over-permissiveness or indulgence.* There has been
much discussion in the media and during the recent election campaign about the effect of parental permissiveness on young people's
willingness to accept established authority. Increasingly it is being
argued that indulgent and overly tolerant attitudes on the part of
parents lie at the root of student protest. Some evidence exists, both
in our own studies and those of others, that activist parents are more
lenient and less punitive than more conventional parents. Indeed, the
humanist values of activist parents leads, as we have seen, toward an
emphasis on encouraging the autonomy of the child and a skepticism
about conventional moral standards. But such child-rearing practices
do not seem to be characterized by indulgence, or by a failure by the
parents to assert standards. As a matter of fact, activists' parents typically had high expectations and standards—for instance, as we have
seen, they strongly and directly influenced their children to maintain interest in intellectual and creative activity, in academic work, and
in socially useful activity.

Most observers of the personal backgrounds of activists have
tended to describe these parents as unusually principled and active
in the socialization of their children. Moreover, it is clear that differences with respect to punitiveness and restrictiveness between
the parents of activists and non-activists are not marked. In one
recent study, comparing 25 liberal parents active in civil rights, with
a similar number of conservative parents active in opposition to
open housing, few differences in the extent of "permissiveness" were
found. Nevertheless, nearly half of the college age children of the
liberals had become active in student protest, while only two of the
children of conservatives were politically active. This and other studies
have demonstrated rather clearly that *the political activity of young
people is strongly related to the political interests and attitudes of
their parents and shows no substantial relationship with "permissive-*

ness" as such.[17] Perhaps the best statement which can be made on this point would be this: activist students do tend to come from homes with a rather democratic, egalitarian and anti-authoritarian atmosphere. The traditional domination of the father is likely to be totally absent. The children are encouraged to speak their minds, to take initiative, to make decisions for themselves. The family as a whole may often decide questions of importance to all members. The parents are likely to encourage, explicitly or implicitly, a skeptical or relaxed attitude toward the traditional virtues of cleanliness, thrift, order, self-control, and the like. But they are also likely to be rather demanding in matters of intellectual and academic attainment, and to expect cooperative, unselfish behavior on the part of their children. Young people emerging from such families are likely, on the one hand, to take school and adult ideals seriously (and they have a history of high academic achievement and generally "good" behavior as teen-agers). On the other hand, they are likely to feel at odds with adult authority which is arbitrary, restrictive or Victorian, and also with peers who are anti-intellectual, unserious or "square." When authority can be seen as morally consistent, and based on democratic consent, such youth are likely to be acceptant of it.

In some respects, the families of activist youth represent one expression of a more general trend in the American family. In general, middle-class children are being raised in less authoritarian settings than those of an earlier era. It is still true that many middle-class families are highly regulating and conventional—and their offspring on the whole turn out to be non-rebellious and conventional. Many others, however, may express a rather confused mixture of tolerance, indulgence and non-punitiveness, but *without the emphasis on principle, humanitarianism and intellectualism characteristic of activists' families*. Instead these families combine permissiveness with a continuing, if ambivalent, adherence to conventional goals and values. It is clear that the traditional middle-class family is on the decline, and that the humanist family represents a small minority of the middle class, though probably a growing one. It is the ambivalent family—combining elements of conventionalism with indulgence—which is probably most typical of the American middle class. There is little evidence that *political* rebellion and activism is a likely outcome of this family situation; more evidence that identity diffusion expressed as both anxious conformism and *cultural* alienation are likely outcomes. In any case, the propensity of young people for disruption of institutions and defiance of authority is more clearly the result of their experience with those institutions and that authority than of their early treatment by their parents.[18]

The research we have been reviewing indicates that the behavior of student activists is *not* a projection of rebellion against parental authority; it does tend to show that humanist parents do foster character traits and attitudes which may dispose toward a questioning of tradition, convention, and authority. In the current atmosphere, it may be necessary to add that such traits and attitudes have always been ones which Americans have claimed to value. In short, the tendency for youth with "democratic" character structures and "humanist" values to become angry opponents of the political system derives from the failure of that system to fulfill its democratic claims.

9. *Although the prototypic background of student activists is the "educated humanist" family, factors other than family background are also important in determining recruitment to the movement, and forms of participation in it.* Significant numbers of highly active movement participants have working-class, or small town, or Catholic, or Southern backgrounds—indeed, some of the best known leaders and spokesmen for the movement have such origins. Furthermore, as the movement becomes increasingly visible, and as its activities on any given campus develop, new participants with heterogeneous personal histories are attracted to it. For instance, a study of participants in the University of Chicago sit-in of 1966 indicated that, while those in the sit-in with a prior history of activism tended to come from the "educated humanist" kind of family, the first-time participants more closely resembled the student body of the College as a whole in terms of background characteristics.

Once a student becomes involved in movement activity, it is not possible to predict his attitudes and behavior directly from the values and attitudes of his parents. The principal determinant of the degree of radicalism which an activist espouses, and the kinds of activity he is likely to join, tends to be the length of his exposure to the movement and his prior experience with it. Thus, for example, in the spring of 1968, among students who opposed the war in Vietnam, there was a tendency for those with little or no prior activism to participate in the presidential campaign of Senator Eugene McCarthy, while those who were "veterans" of anti-war protest were more likely to participate in draft resistance and direct action.[19]

A study of volunteers who worked in the "Vietnam Summer" project in 1967 showed that the youngest volunteers were on the whole less radical in their attitudes than those in their early twenties who had substantial experience in the movement.[20] The conclusion to be drawn from these studies is that "educated humanism" predisposes to participation in the movement but that the movement is broadening its constituency beyond the ranks of the "educated humanists": particular modes of activism and political attitudes are shaped by experiences in the movement rather than family socialization—i.e., regardless of one's family background, there is a tendency toward "radicalization" after one has become involved in protest activity.

Individual Backgrounds in an Historical Context

It is particularly important to try to understand why the student movement began among young people who were particularly advantaged in status and economic terms, and who were uniquely socialized to be oriented to the university and its values. The most obviously puzzling feature of the white student revolt is that it has been sparked by those youth who have had the best opportunity for experiencing the material benefits and privileges of this society. Why they should reject those privileges, and identify their fate with the most disadvantaged groups in the society, is a very important part of the story of the contemporary student movement.

The starting point for any understanding of the roots of the American student rebellion is the fact that the United States is an advanced industrial society with a capitalist economy. Such a society and such an economy require a culture and a value-system which produces types of persons who have the capacity to meet the system's needs for efficient performance of a vast number of specialized occupational and economic roles. In particular, our culture has emphasized that individual worth is primarily measured by one's success or achievement in a competitive occupational system; that such achievement is in turn measured by one's income and its appropriate use; and that such achievement is possible only if the individual learns to discipline his impulses and feelings in the service of personal advancement and efficient performance. The use of occupational achievement and material success as fundamental signs of personal worth is a necessary central value orientation of a culture suitable for a society based on a privately incorporated economy; an emphasis on mastery and self-discipline is necessarily going to be characteristic of any society which values rationalization in order to achieve industrialization, maximize productivity, and become technologically advanced.

During this century, there have been significant changes in the way these values have been interpreted by the members of the society although the basic themes of individual achievement and self-rationalization have remained constant. For instance, "success" is no longer defined in entrepreneurial terms; instead, occupational success increasingly means advancement in careers in large-scale organizations and in professions. Self-discipline no longer means the cultivation of guilt with respect to the experience of sensual pleasure—the Puritan is in the process of becoming a deviant. Self-discipline has come to mean the development of an ability to express impulses in one's private life, while maintaining a fully rational, impersonal perspective in one's work.[21]

Ever since Marx, sociologists have looked to the working class for the sources of opposition to the culture of capitalism. More recently, even many Marxists have come to the view that the proletariat, for a variety of reasons, has been more or less fully integrated into that culture, and is not likely to be a major source of counter-values. For several decades, sociologists of deviance have documented and sometimes celebrated the existence of such counter-values in various subcultures of the society; typically, however, such enclaves of the anti-bourgeois have been viewed as marginal or exotic, and functional for the maintenance of dominant values. In the case of lower-class subcultures, counter-values are usually seen as a symptom of disorganization requiring intervention and treatment. Until recently, the prevailing capitalist culture has been regarded as fundamentally stable and progressive, and as fully capable of absorbing the pockets of inarticulate opposition which emerge out of "deviant" or "deprived" subcultures.

The student revolt and the symptoms of cultural alienation among wider sectors of the youth, however, have led to considerable speculation about a possible erosion of the dominant culture. As the studies described earlier in this chapter indicate, the youth revolt includes a very explicit rejection of occupational success and self-rationalization as central values, and a quite definite search for a new, anti-bourgeois culture. For some, the youth revolt is a prophecy of the collapse of the prevailing value-system. Others, impressed by the apparent strength of the American social order, stress the generational quality

of the youth revolt, regarding it as an expression of a particular stage in the life-cycle which is given up as the individual moves toward maturity.

It is true that the most articulate and visible opposition to capitalist culture is presently being expressed by young people. But it is not necessarily true that such expression represents a portent of the future. On the other hand, the continuity in values between student protesters and their parents suggests that disaffection with the prevailing value-system may not be restricted to the young. Indeed, the existence of this continuity leads one to wonder about the historical origins of anti-capitalist values; the concentration of disaffection among the offspring of educated middle-class parents makes one ask why these youth in particular should be most disposed to be disaffected in this way.

There has been, for a considerable time, a tradition of antipathy toward capitalism and its culture, and a yearning for some alternative to it in parts of the middle class. The families of student protesters, and the protesters themselves, can be located within this tradition. Its primary roots lie in the revolt of European intellectuals against bourgeois culture in the 19th century. This revolt was expressed in a variety of quite divergent ideological forms, ranging from socialism on the left to romanticism on the right. It was acted out in a variety of ways, from direct participation in revolutionary movements to withdrawal into bohemias. But it seems clear that the writers and artists and members of the intelligentsia in Europe shared an increasingly profound hostility toward the bourgeoisie and the values represented by that class. This hostility was due in part to the difficulties experienced by artists and writers as they tried to maintain their identities when confronted by the commercialization of art and literature, and in part to a classic pattern of overproduction of educated young people in rapidly industrializing societies, resulting in widespread inability to obtain stable employment commensurate with their aspirations and educational attainment. It was further due to the rationalization of life associated with industrial development and the consequent problems this process creates for those who need leisure and value spontaneity in order to do creative work. Finally, it was due to the fact that the role of intellectuals requires that they be intensely conscious of the limitations of prevailing values, and of the discrepancies between official values and actual practice. In addition, of course, many intellectuals experienced censorship and other forms of punishment as a result of their critical stance—and this experience alienated them further from established authority. In short, just as capitalism in the 19th century created its own "antithesis" in the *working class,* its rise and its destruction of traditional culture created forms of opposition among ostensibly *middle-class* intellectuals.[22]

In the United States, it is certainly the case that many 19th century writers opposed the cultural and human consequences of industrial capitalism. But it was not until the early years of the 20th century that such opposition took collective forms, when bohemian communities with a European flavor became rooted in major American cities—most particularly in Greenwich Village. As in Europe, the alienation of American intellectuals took diverse forms—muck-raking journalism, little magazine literary and social criticism, realistic novels, avant-garde poetry and painting, salon conversation, scholarly radicalism, progressive politics, labor organizing, the socialist movement. But the American radical intellectuals added some unique components to anti-bourgeois sentiment.

First, American intellectuals tended to have a relatively optimistic and rationalist perspective, believing that social, political and personal reform were possible, especially if science and reason were brought to bear on pressing problems. Second, their own revolt coincided with the rise of the feminist movement; the emancipation of women was inextricably bound up with the broader aspirations of the emerging literary radicalism. One consequence of the impact of feminism on the perspective of intellectuals was the obliteration of boundaries between private and public issues—political reform in the larger society was seen as linked to reform of family life and individual character. In fact, what is most characteristic of intellectual radicalism as it developed in the early 20th century in the United States was the perception that *cultural* renaissance, *political* reconstruction, and *characterological* transformation were all part of the same process of progressive change which the intellectuals were hastening through their individual and collective work. This perception was of course strongly reinforced by the introduction of psychoanalytic perspectives into the intellectual community. And one derivation from this perspective was an emphasis by many intellectuals on conscious, deliberate and scientific reform of the socializing institutions —the family and the school—in order to create new values and character types and facilitate social change.[23]

The specific hopes of the early 20th century radical intellectuals were, of course, frustrated; by the end of World War I much of the cohesion which had been developing was shattered, to be only partly recreated during the Thirties. But the ferment of pre-war intellectuals was institutionalized in a variety of ways. In the first place, the intellectual and artistic products of the anti-bourgeois revolt of both Europe and the United States were imported into the universities and made an increasingly central part of the curriculum. Second, a host of new vocations emerged which embodied implicit or explicit criticism of the dominant culture and had their original impulse in the desire to cure or correct the effects of that culture—e.g., progressive education, social work, child psychology, psychotherapy, etc. Moreover, these values had an impact on the established, traditional professions—scientific perspectives influenced criminal law, social amelioration and psychoanalysis influenced medicine, progressivism and social welfare ideologies influenced public bureaucracies. Third, psychoanalysis, progressive education and behaviorist psychology generated new principles of child-rearing, while simultaneously college educated women became vulnerable to the notion that expert knowledge about child-rearing ought to shape their actual behavior as mothers. The combined result of these new ideas, plus feminism and the rising status of women, was, of course, to create a new middle-class family —less authoritarian, less hierarchical, more child-centered, more democratic, more self-conscious.[24]

In these ways, the criticism of capitalist culture by tiny groups of European and American intellectuals became rooted in American life and incorporated into the value-system of a sector of the American middle class. That sector participated in mass higher education, and entered occupations for which advanced, specialized education was a necessary prerequisite, especially the new vocations associated with reform, social service and the creation and distribution of culture. These vocations embody values which run counter to the competitive individualism and self-control valued in capitalist culture and they tend to be located structurally outside of the primary institutions of the capitalist economy. They are not directly connected to the pursuit of private profit; indeed, one is not supposed to enter them in order to achieve material gain.

Obviously, most of the people in this sector have not been politically radical or culturally unconventional. Rather, they have been optimistic about the direction of society, and wholeheartedly committed to the legitimacy of the national political system, while strongly hostile to those political and cultural elements they could identify as reactionary and regressive. Their faith in three inter-related instruments of change supported their optimism. First, they believed that the federal government could be molded into a force for social amelioration, economic progress and equality. Second, they believed that the new vocations—the service and "helping" professions, the educational professions, etc.—which they had entered, would be significant in curing and preventing social and psychological pathology, extending the possibilities for democracy and upward mobility, and raising the intellectual and cultural level of the people. Third, they tended to believe that the values they held were best implemented through self-conscious efforts to create families and personal-life-styles embodying democratic, humanistic, egalitarian principles (in contradistinction to the authoritarian, repressed, Victorian, anti-intellectual and acquisitive life-styles which they perceived as characteristic of the rest of the middle class).

Such orientations could be maintained during the New Deal period and the Forties, when it appeared that the welfare state would in fact be successfully realized. The horrors of fascism and Stalinism permitted many of the educated to feel that the United States, whatever its flaws, was the major defender of democratic values. Post-war prosperity greatly raised the living standards and cultural possibilities for this group, and also seemed to be creating the conditions for social equality. McCarthyism led educated liberals to withdraw from political engagement and pursue private goals of personal fulfillment. Thus, the parents of the present generation of student activists, despite their anti-capitalist values, maintained a generally complacent view of American society when they themselves were young, and in the years when their children were growing up.

It is probable, as Jerome Skolnick has suggested,[25] that this complacency began to break down as the decade of the Fifties drew to a close. Certainly the McCarthy period produced a more critical attitude on the part of many with respect to super-patriots and anti-communist ideology. The Eisenhower administration's inability to sustain prosperity and expand the welfare state also stimulated critical political attitudes. At a more fundamental level, there is evidence in our interviews that the fathers of student activists frequently conveyed to their children a sense of doubt about the moral worth of their own occupations and about the pursuit of status and material comfort for its own sake. As the present group of student activists reached adolescence they probably sensed a rising disillusionment on the part of their parents concerning the progressive possibilities of American society.

By 1960, then, the subculture of the educated humanists had come to this: demographically, it had grown over several decades from small pockets of isolated "free" intellectuals, to a substantial stratum of the population, including many in new white collar vocations. Culturally, it had begun to develop a family structure and value system which was at odds with the traditional, capitalist, Protestant Ethic middle-class culture. Politically, it had passed through a period of optimistic reformism and a second period of political disengagement. The newest and largest generation of this stratum was thronging the nation's colleges at just that point, historically, when the sustaining ideologies of industrial society—liberalism, socialism, communism—had reached exhaustion, also at the point when the Cold War and anti-communism had ceased to be a workable framework for American international policy, and when the colored population in the nation and around the world was breaking into active revolt.

This new generation of the educated middle class had been reared to take education seriously as a central means to personal fulfillment and as a goal which was intrinsically worthwhile. It had been raised in an atmosphere which encouraged autonomy and individuality. Implicitly and explicitly it had been taught to be skeptical about the intrinsic value of money-making and status, and also to be skeptical about authority imposed from above. It incorporated new definitions of sex roles: having seen their parents share authority and functions more or less equally, and having been taught to value aesthetic and intellectual activity, these were boys who did not understand masculinity to mean physical toughness and dominance, and girls who did not equate femininity with passivity and domesticity. They were, moreover, young people for whom the established means of social control were bound to be relatively ineffective: growing up with economic security in families of relatively high status, the normal incentives of the system—status and income—were of relatively little importance, and, as we indicated earlier in this chapter, they had been encouraged to feel that such incentives ought to be disdained. They were, finally, young people who anticipated a future of extraordinary promise for personal fulfillment, based on their own material security, on the apparently unlimited possibilities for expanding affluence, and on their capacity to make use of the vast educational and cultural opportunities which seemed to be available. It is inevitable that young people of this kind should come into some conflict with the established order. Because of their central values, they, like the earlier generations of intellectuals, would likely be social critics. Because of their material security, they, like other generations of high status youth, were likely to be experimental, risk-taking, open to immediate experience, unrepressed. Because of their character structure, they would be very likely to come into conflict with arbitrary authority in school and other situations of imposed restriction. Because of their values and sex-role identifications, they would find themselves out of harmony with the conventional youth culture, with its frivolity, anti-intellectualism, and stereotypic distinctions between the sexes. Because of the convergence of values, character structure and material security, they were likely to experience strong "identity conflicts." Their impulses to autonomy and individuality, their relative freedom from economic anxieties, and their own parents' ambivalence toward the occupational structure made it difficult for them to decide easily on a fixed vocational goal or life-style, made them aspire to construct a life outside of conventional career-lines (in many cases modeled after the 19th and 20th century free intellectual artist or bohemian), and made them deeply critical of the compromise, corruption and unfreedom inherent in the occupations of their fathers—the occupations for which they were being trained.

What was not inevitable was the transformation of these personal conflicts and discontents into a *social movement*. The culture had previously offered many opportunities for discontented middle-class intellectuals to work out private solutions to their problems, without resorting to political action. Among such adaptations were bohemian-ism, humanitarian and service occupations and avocations, and the "hipster" life-style involving public conformity and private unconventionalism (a common pattern among Fifties "organization men"). For many, the academic world, with its apparent commitment to intellectual activity and academic freedom, offered an appropriate solution. But a set of "triggering" experiences led previously privatized youth toward collective action and organization. The non-violent civil rights movement, especially the Negro student sit-ins beginning in 1960, had a triggering impact because it offered to white humanist students a way of directly acting on their values—a way previously unavailable—with a moral purity and personal commitment present nowhere else in society. To identify with this movement offered a way of crystallizing and focusing the values, impulses and aspirations which these youth incorporated but could find no satisfactory way to express.

As we have elsewhere tried to document,[26] the early stages of the student movement were relatively optimistic; movement participants tended to accept the legitimacy of the political system, even as they tried to challenge and reform its inhumane and undemocratic features. Furthermore, in its early stages, the student movement took seriously the official self-justifications of the university, and despite its criticisms of campus life, never frontally challenged university authority. During this period (1960–1964), the movement took root. More and more humanist youth were attracted to it, more and more established their identities as activists for social change and democracy through participation in the movement. New issues, beyond civil rights, became foci of action and organization by students; commitments deepened, intellectual rationales for the new movement were constructed, hopes for its political impact rose.

The combined effect of the Vietnam war, the racial crises in the cities, the Johnson administration, and the failure of universities to respond to the movement's thrust for citizenship for students in the universities, has been to frustrate the early hopefulness of the activists and transform much of the movement into an angry insurgency. The new phase is marked by a delegitimization of national and university authority, a search for revolutionary ideology, and a deep alienation from the "system" on the part of many students. Thus, the events of the Sixties have tended to shatter many of the expectations about the society which had developed within the educated humanist subculture; for the student members of that subculture particularly this period has had the effect of first politicizing and, more recently, radicalizing them. A similar politicization is evident among older generations in this subculture (the peace movement and the McCarthy campaign are good recent examples of this process) though, for obvious reasons, the over-thirty members have generally speaking not adopted the revolutionary outlook which has spread among the students.

During this period, as we have suggested, the movement has been able to expand its constituency beyond the ranks of the offspring of the educated middle class. It is possible to outline briefly some of the factors which make the student movement capable of mobilizing people who do not derive from the subculture which first provided the soil for its growth. First, there are large numbers of students of conventional middle- and working-class backgrounds who aspire to occupations which lead them toward middle-class humanism. These are, as we have suggested, occupations requiring high education, located outside of the corporate system, emphasizing collective, humanist values. Some research suggests that young people who plan to enter such fields as education, social work, public service, etc., are moving to the left politically, despite their parents' political and social values.[27] This may be due in part to "anticipatory socialization," and in part to the fact that these students are more likely to come into direct contact with student activists, and with critical perspectives in their courses.

Second, student movement criticism of the universities for their lack of responsiveness to students' demands, for paternalism, for impersonality, for personally and socially irrelevant educational content strikes responsive chords among very large segments of the student population. Student power is a very broadly appealing idea to students, as is the demand for reducing the regulation of students' personal and political lives. Campus confrontations led by radical students have repeatedly attracted wide support from non-radical, non-humanist students when the issues have involved the exercise of arbitrary authority by school administrators. Many who get involved with the movement initially over such local issues may remain involved as they get exposed to the life-style of the movement and to its social criticism.

Third, the movement's attack on Victorian morality and restrictive adult authority appeals to large numbers of youth still in high school or who are not in school at all. Millions of young people have been raised by parents who were themselves losing confidence in the repressive, self-denying practices of the traditional middle class; moreover, these practices are under continual attack in the mass media, and are, as many observers have pointed out, simply incompatible with an affluent and rapidly changing society. The movement has helped to crystallize the inarticulate and ambivalent attitudes of many young people about the "old morality." Furthermore, its impact on the young is greatly strengthened by the TV and magazine publicity, especially since the media tend to emphasize the culturally liberated qualities of the movement. The protest against traditional values has at this point become deeply rooted in the youth culture; the past five years has seen a total transformation of that culture, from bland conformism to overt rejection of conventional values. The new music, dress, films, and even advertising created by or directed at youth is quite explicitly rejecting the Protestant Ethic, Victorianism and related values and symbols. These developments in the youth culture, which were in part sparked by the student movement and in part paralleled its development, have made large numbers of youth more open to the political perspectives of the movement. At the same time, they have fed back into the movement itself, affecting the style, the jargon, the appearance and the attitudes of student activists. Alienated, rebellious youth of all classes and ages are now much more readily identifiable to each other, thus facilitating communication and a sense of common identity. The spread of the new youth culture has been, therefore, a very important medium for expanding the base of the student movement beyond the ranks of the children of educated middle class, urban, liberal professionals.

Fourth, the war in Vietnam has greatly expanded the movement's ranks and broadened its appeal. Movement arguments about the immorality and unwinnability of the war have repeatedly been confirmed by the media and by numerous public spokesmen. Moreover, the anti-war protest finds a response among many draft-age youths, especially as protest activity has increasingly involved support for draft resistance and counseling of youths to facilitate avoidance of the draft. More recently, the movement has attempted, with success, to reach members of the armed forces and ex-GI's.

Fifth, the racial crisis, the unwillingness of political leaders to undertake programs which can foster equality and end poverty, the increasingly dark and violent quality of American public life—all of these are factors which have turned many young people toward the New Left and radical change.

Finally, it is the case that youth generally are likely to find radical ideology and activism at least interesting. All youth experience a sense of subordination and deprivation due to the social position of adolescents in our society. All are likely to feel some revulsion at adult "hypocrisy." All experience a sense of dislocation due to rapid social change. Even had there been no Vietnam war, and no racial crisis, one would expect that, once a political movement favoring equality, the abolition of hierarchy, and a quest for community had

emerged, it would have a considerable impact on the rising generation. Militarism and racism have greatly accelerated and intensified
that impact. We can therefore expect a continuation of protest activity
among students even when the Vietnam war comes to an end. The
offspring of educated humanists continue to increase in proportion to
the student body as a whole, and their problems persist in a society
which values material success, which increasingly organizes careers
into large, impersonal and authoritarian bureaucracies, and which
fragments identity. Moreover, the life-styles and values which emanate
from the movement, however protean these may appear to be, are
likely to remain attractive to large numbers of youth of all strata. The
form and intensity of protest, the relative strengths of revolutionary or
reformist orientations within the movement, depend on events and
processes which cannot be predicted. One can say with some confidence, however, that the anti-capitalist, anti-authoritarian sentiments
which have their historical roots in the revolt of the intellectuals will
continue to exert a powerful influence on succeeding generations of
students. What began over a century ago as a protest among small
numbers of isolated individuals has now become a rooted presence on
campuses throughout the world, and in the United States, at least, has
become deeply influential for an important and rapidly growing sector of the adult population as well.

NOTES

[1] R. Peterson, *The Scope of Organized Student Protest in 1964–65* (Princeton, N.J.: Educational Testing Service, 1966).

[2] R. Flacks, "The Liberated Generation," *Journal of Social Issues,* 23 (1967),
52–75.

[3] L. Schiff, "The Obedient Rebels," *Journal of Social Issues,* 20 (1964), 74–
96.

[4] J. Katz, *The Student Activists* (Washington, D.C.: United States Office of
Education, 1967).

[5] P. Heist, *Intellect and Commitment: the Faces of Discontent* (Berkeley,
Calif.: Center for the Study of Higher Education, 1965).

[6] K. Mock, *The Potential Activist and His Perception of the University*
(Berkeley, Calif.: Center for the Study of Higher Education, 1968).

[7] Flacks, *op. cit.*

[8] Flacks, *op. cit.*; W. A. Watts and David Whittaker, "Free Speech Advocates
at Berkeley," *Journal of Applied Behavioral Science,* 2 (January–March, 1966).

[9] Flacks, *op. cit.*; D. Westby and R. G. Braungart, "Class and Politics in the

Family Backgrounds of Student Political Activists," *American Sociological Review,* 31 (1966), 690–692.

[10] C. Weissberg, "Students Against the Rank," unpublished MA paper, Department of Sociology, University of Chicago, 1968.

[11] Flacks, *op. cit.;* Watts and Whittaker, *op. cit.;* Westby and Braungart, *op. cit.*

[12] Westby and Braungart, *op. cit.*

[13] Based on unpublished data from the author's 1965 study.

[14] Flacks, *op. cit.;* K. Keniston, *Young Radicals* (New York: Harcourt, Brace & World, 1968); cf. also S. Lubell, "That Generation Gap," *The Public Interest,* Fall, 1968, 52–61.

[15] C. Derber and R. Flacks, "Values of Student Activists and Their Parents," mimeographed, University of Chicago, 1967; R. Flacks, "Student Activists— Result, Not Revolt," *Psychology Today,* October, 1967.

[16] N. Haan, M. B. Smith, and J. Block, "The Moral Reasoning of Young Adults" (Berkeley, Calif.: Institute for Human Development, 1967).

[17] Lamar Eugene Thomas, unpublished dissertation research, University of Chicago, Committee on Human Development, 1968.

[18] Cf. Keniston, *op. cit.*

[19] From unpublished data collected by the author.

[20] Based on published data collected by the author.

[21] Our discussion of dominant values in America is indebted to T. Parsons and W. White, "The Link Between Character and Society," in S. Lipset and L. Lowenthal, *Culture and Social Character* (New York, The Free Press, 1962).

[22] The anti-bourgeois orientations of 19th century writers and artists are systematically explored in C. Grana, *Modernity and Its Discontents* (New York: Harper & Row, 1967).

[23] Some of the historical sources of anti-capitalist attitudes among American intellectuals are sketched in R. Hofstadter, *Anti-intellectualism in American Life* (New York: Vintage Books, 1966). Two important recent works on 20th century literary radicalism in America are C. Lasch, *The New Radicalism in America* (New York: Knopf, 1965), and J. Gilbert, *Writers and Partisans* (New York: Wiley, 1968).

[24] On changing patterns of childrearing in America, cf. U. Bronfenbrenner, "Socialization and Social Class Through Time and Space," in E. Maccoby, T. Newcomb, and E. Hartley (eds.), *Readings in Social Psychology* (New York: Holt, Rinehart & Winston, 1958). Also D. R. Miller and G. Swanson, *The Changing American Parent* (New York: Wiley, 1958).

[25] Jerome Skolnick, personal communication.

[26] R. Flacks, "Student Power and the New Left: the Role of SDS," paper read at the American Psychological Association Meetings, San Francisco, September, 1968.

[27] Cf. D. Seligman, "A Special Kind of Rebellion," *Fortune,* January, 1969, 67 ff.

4

ACTIVISTS AND THE HISTORY
OF THE FUTURE

*by David Westby and Richard Braungart**

STUDENT POLITICAL organizations in the United States have in recent years projected themselves into national politics with a fervor and effect unknown in this country for years. The present chapter deals with one aspect of a larger study of four student political activist groups of national importance: the Students for a Democratic Society (SDS), the Young Americans for Freedom (YAF), the Young Democrats (YD), and Young Republicans (YR). While the first two groups are relatively new and radical, the latter are venerable and generally reformist. We shall be interested mainly in the SDS and YAF and references to the YD and YR will be for comparative purposes only. The reason for this is the focus of the chapter, which may be stated as the nature of the utopian conceptions of radical student political groups, and their distribution within such groups.

* David L. Westby, Associate Professor of Sociology and Anthropology at the Institute of Public Administration at The Pennsylvania State University, has conducted several research studies on the backgrounds and aspirations of student activists of which this chapter is a part. Richard A. Braungart, an Instructor in Sociology and Anthropology and a candidate for the doctorate in Sociology at The Pennsylvania State University, has collaborated with Dr. Westby in studies of student activists. The authors wish to thank former Vice President for Student Affairs Robert Bernreuter and Assistant Dean for Research Thomas Magner of the College of Liberal Arts, both of whom were instrumental in making available the funds on which the research for this chapter is based.

Radical student organizations such as YAF and SDS see themselves as potential agents of social change. Such groups represent both a critique of existing societal arrangement and a crystallization of conceptions of the future of society in terms of socially transcendent ideas —the "utopias" analyzed so incisively by Mannheim.[1] Mannheim's conception of utopian thought embraces two main characteristics: (1) it transcends the present and is oriented to the future in terms of actions that do away with present unbearable conditions; and (2) it distinguishes between the particular substantive programs or content of political ideas and the forms in which these are cast. For example, utopian socialist thought, as Mannheim describes it, is always a set of socially transcendent rationalizations for smashing the existing structure of economic and political power through revolution. Such utopias are, for Mannheim writing in his time, anchored in society's class structure, and provide the only available "perspectives" for viewing and interpreting reality.*

Distinct from the "official" utopias of such groups as SDS and YAF are the expectations their members actually hold concerning the possibility or probability of their beliefs actually becoming institutionalized as principles of social order—that is, of the nature of future history. While all or nearly all of the members of such groups may be true believers in the moral worth and necessity of their utopias, it does not follow that they actually expect them to come into being. Perhaps the utopias analyzed by Mannheim could be considered fully utopian, but today matters are more complex. In the 20th century most of the literature of utopia is negative; for instance, that of Orwell, Huxley and Zamiatin. Utopian thought takes on more and more the character of an eschatology rather than a heaven on earth. In our research we have broadened Mannheim's definition of utopia to include such conceptions, and we wish to understand the way the student utopians assimilate these trends of 20th century life.

In this chapter we shall see how these perspectives vary among different student political groups, particularly the left-wing Students for a Democratic Society and the ultra-conservative Young Americans for Freedom. First, we will briefly discuss the method used in the col-

* While the thrust of Mannheim's thought generally led him into a completely relativistic position, he nevertheless attempted to formulate the social conditions under which intellectuals might deal with politics in a relatively objective fashion. While most critics have been sympathetic to this attempt, they have almost universally rejected the result as inconsistent with the basic assumptions of his analysis. See the discussion of "relationism" in *Ideology and Utopia*.

lection of the data; second, a presentation and discussion of utopian projections of future history held by the groups will be given; and third, we will suggest the manner in which other research in the field relates to an understanding and explanation of the two dominant patterns occurring in SDS and YAF respectively.

Our primary data consist of responses to a request to: "Write the history of the U.S. from the present to the year 2000, indicating only the most important general developments or particular events in that period." [2] The sample included members of the four organizations at ten institutions in the eastern United States.[3] The YAF and SDS representatives attended their respective national conventions. All the

TABLE 1

INCIDENCE OF MAJOR THEMES IN ESSAYS FOR
FOUR ACTIVIST GROUPS (IN PERCENT)*

Theme	SDS	YD	YR	YAF
Nuclear War, World War III	35.7	11.4	36.6	22.9
Revolution, urban guerrilla warfare	29.9	15.2	7.3	9.7
Social justice, civil rights, humanitarianism	12.1	34.2	18.3	5.7
State socialism	15.9	20.3	25.6	30.9
Negative utopia, mass society	14.6	5.1	13.4	13.1
Conservatism, conservative ideals	7.6	5.1	20.7	54.9
Totalitarianism	27.4	3.8	18.3	9.7
Technology	10.8	29.1	30.5	7.4
Communist takeover	1.3	3.8	9.8	18.3
American colonialism, imperialism	35.0	2.5	1.2	0.6
U.S. on a world crusade for freedom	0.0	1.3	12.2	26.3
Decline in world tension due to U.S. actions	17.8	40.5	23.2	6.9
Decline in U.S. foreign involvement and influence	19.1	6.3	11.0	14.9
Series of elections	1.9	35.4	17.1	11.4

Usable Essays:

SDS: n = 157
YD: n = 79
YR: n = 82
YAF: n = 175

* Percent totals for each group sum to more than 100 percent, since many essays contained more than one theme.

essays were written between March and December, 1966, in an average writing time of slightly more than half an hour. A total of 689 essays were obtained, each with a short accompanying questionnaire. Of the total, 493 (71.4 percent) were usable; the usability rate ranged from 81.4 percent for YAF to 63.3 percent for SDS. The investigators, independent of each other, coded the essays and compared their categorization afterward. They were in complete agreement on 85 percent of the essays; differences on the remaining 15 percent were reconciled by discussion and the judgment of an independent third reader. Our procedure was to develop categories capable of encompassing all the important *concrete* themes found in the essays, as one act in constructing the formal utopian categories. Table 1 gives the incidence of mention of major concrete or substantive themes for each group. It should be emphasized that the mention of any of these themes does not imply that its espouser has anything particular in mind as to ultimate developments relative to group ideals or values. For instance, the mention of "State Socialism" by relatively few SDSers simply reflects the general absence of conviction that socialism will deepen before a return to the true values occurs.

Five utopian conceptions were developed inductively by intensive familiarization with the essay materials. Table 2 gives the utopian conceptions articulated by the four student activist groups. Criteria for classification were stated as follows:

(1) *Progressive Utopia:* A steady upward movement toward a state of affairs defined as desirable in the official pronouncements of the group.

(2) *Revolutionary Utopia:* Overthrow of existing structure of power and related institutions, and their radical transformation into a state defined as desirable in the official pronouncements of the group.

(3) *Conversionist Utopia:* Drift toward an extreme state or condition of society defined as disastrous by the group, then a dramatic or sudden reversal having the character of an "awakening" or rebirth with immediate or rapid institutionalization of the state of affairs defined as desirable in the official pronouncements of the group.

(4) *Linear Decline Dystopia:* Continuing drift or movement by society toward a state of affairs viewed as highly undesir-

TABLE 2

UTOPIAN CONCEPTIONS OF FOUR STUDENT GROUPS
(IN PERCENT)

	Groups			
	SDS	*YD*	*YR*	*YAF*
Utopian Conceptions				
1. Progressive	13 (21)	51 (40)	28 (23)	15 (27)
2. Revolutionary	10 (15)	0 (0)	1 (1)	1 (2)
3. Conversionist	4 (6)	4 (3)	5 (4)	36 (63)
	27 (42)	55 (43)	34 (28)	52 (92)
Dystopian Conceptions				
4. Linear Decline	34 (54)	10 (8)	29 (24)	29 (50)
5. Eschatological	15 (24)	5 (4)	6 (5)	4 (7)
	49 (78)	15 (12)	35 (29)	33 (57)
Mixed Conceptions				
	24 (37)	30 (24)	31 (25)	15 (26)
	100%(157)	100%(79)	100%(82)	100%(175)

able from the standpoint of the official pronouncements of the group.

(5) *Eschatological Dystopia:* Sudden cataclysmic event or events that, from the standpoint of the desired goals of the group, represents the total extinction of all hope, and removal of any possibility of achieving the goals of the group. A conception of "the end of history."

In order for an essay to be placed in any of these categories, it was required that it exhibit the defining property of the type *as a clearly organizing principle* of whatever themes were present. In other words, classification of an essay was a judgment on the total conception of future history informing whatever particular events were related. In cases of doubt, the essay was classified as mixed. Many of the mixed cases, especially among SDS, result from statements of alternative futures: either civilization will be destroyed by the bomb or there will be peace and socialism; either totalitarian dictatorship or democracy and freedom. In classifying essays in one or another utopian category it is important to note that there is no one-to-one correspondence with the concrete themes extracted from the essays.

The meaning of a particular theme within the total pattern of an essay may be radically different from essay to essay. For example, the theme of nuclear war or of World War III (defined in terms of hostilities between the major powers, United States, Russia and China on a global scale) occurs in 22.9 percent of YAF essays, but only occasionally as catastrophic. Indeed, only 4 percent of the YAF essays were classified as eschatological, and some of these did not involve nuclear war or World War III. When YAFers mentioned such wars it was more frequently in the context of a conversionist utopia, often as no more than an incident in a chain of events, and one that actually might have the salutary effect of vanquishing communism and bringing the American people to their senses.

Another example of this is the way in which "decline in U.S. foreign involvement and influence" fits into the total pattern. For YAF this is always a pattern of linear decline, or an early element of a conversionist utopia. For SDS and YD, on the other hand, it is usually, though not always, part of a progressive utopia.

Utopian and Dystopian Futures

We may characterize the utopias of the groups in question as follows: SDS envisions a democratic socialist order with widespread participation in all matters affecting the citizenry—this is the meaning of "participatory democracy." Ideally, there would be no large, monolithic organizations such as the federal government and giant corporations. Such organizations are objected to on the grounds they increasingly extend their control over people and resources in authoritarian fashion, and they are unfit environments for men to work in since they dehumanize the process of human productivity and creativity. SDS envisions an idyllic communal order where all are free to express their creative impulses in work, art, and love. In foreign relations, the United States should follow a policy of military disengagement from all its present commitments, especially Vietnam, and all armaments should be done away with.

YAF, while employing much of the same rhetoric ("freedom," "democracy," etc.), envisions a radically different future. This group wants a conservative order based on minimum government except that which is necessary for the defense of the Free World. In their utopia the hegemony of the "free enterprise system" is unquestioned. YAF mythologizes about an order of rugged individualists who remain outside the norms and laws of society in their devotion to principle. In foreign affairs, YAF wishes the United States to remain dominant throughout the world and basically supports the existing policies of economic superiority and military intervention in the underdeveloped world. Such policies are necessary to stop the spread of communism, which has world-wide designs of conquest, although it is no longer perceived to be totally monolithic. Thus, we may say that while SDS is socialistic, universalistic, egalitarian, pacifist and communal in its utopian conception, YAF is capitalistic, nationalistic, status-based, militaristic and societal in emphasis.

By far the largest mainstream political activist groups on American college campuses are the YD and YR. The overriding objective of both organizations is to support the adult party through campus recruitment, educational programs and campaign work. Members in each group are encouraged to participate in party affairs and to develop their knowledge and parliamentary talents which will one day provide party leadership at the local, state and national levels. Both groups are active on campuses throughout this country and operate within the legitimate framework of conventional American politics. Although local leadership may be taken over occasionally by the more radical right and left wing elements on campuses, the general normative thrust of the groups remains committed to the *status quo* political system. Many campus elections of local YD and YR officers rarely amount to more than popularity contests in which leadership positions become sources of personal status rather than bases of campus power.

Traditional groups such as the YD and the YR cannot be said to be strictly the bearers of utopias in Mannheim's or, perhaps, any other sense. For one thing, the range of their political identification is far broader than that of the SDS and YAF. The spectrum of political identity for YD comprises a range from Staughton Lynd to Nelson Rockefeller, for the YR from Hubert Humphrey to William Buckley.* Additionally, these groups on the whole are much more pragmatic and less rigid than those at the extremes. Like the parent parties, they are primarily concerned with the everyday matters of politics, such as the particulars of legislation and the general ability of the party to win elections. They operate within the two party system and are, in essentials, less utopian than the new radical groups. Therefore, our characterization of their future conceptions is sketchier, and

---

* Based on data collected during our study. All respondents were asked to pick from a list of national political figures, "The one you feel is closest to your own political philosophy."

should be thought of more as a "central tendency" within a broader spectrum of political and social ideas.

The four groups we are concerned with here have their intellectual roots in rather different styles of thought. This is especially true when we compare SDS and YD. The YD are heirs of indigenous American democratic rationalism: Jefferson, de Toqueville, and Dewey fairly represent the tradition to which they belong. SDS, on the other hand, look to the post-rationalist thinkers of Europe: Weber, Camus, Sartre, Fanon, Debray, and Marcuse. All of these, in contrast to the former, deal in themes of increasing nihilism, destruction of values, technologism and generally the growing power of irrational forces in modern society. While the lines are not as clear, YR and YAF can be similarly differentiated. YR and YAF alike seem to be predominantly within the tradition of social Darwinist conservatism (or classic liberalism), but YAF much more so. SDS, then, are socialists of the post-capitalist existentialist type. YD are contemporary liberals with roots in the indigenous democratic tradition. YAF are classic liberals (Spencer, Carnegie, Sumner) and YR are a softened offshoot of the latter exhibiting a much wider spectrum of political identification.

Using Table 2 as a reference point we will present material illustrative of the major orientations in each of the groups in the remainder of this section.

Young Democrats

Among YD, the progressive utopia is completely dominant. Excluding the mixed group from consideration, the progressives constitute about 75 percent of the group. Domestically, YD envision the gradual liberalization of government and extension of services for all sectors of society. All citizens will experience and benefit from free health care, free education, increasing social justice and extension of civil rights:

> The essential problem of this era will be the solution of the general malfunction in distribution of economic goods and services. The solution . . . will embody a general shift away from production capitalism to a social democratic distribution system based predominantly on K. Galbraith's "Affluent Society." The general pattern will be an evolving toward a greater bureaucratization of society and all social functions. . . .*

* With the exception of only a few grammatical corrections, which make the essay material comprehensible to the reader, all quotations are presented verbatim. All indented quoted material appearing hereafter, unless otherwise noted, is from the essays written by the students.

This liberal movement operates within the two party system. The end of poverty and civil strife, progress generally, comes about through a series of elections with Democratic candidates victorious:

Late in 1967, the Vietnam war is brought to the conference table. L.B.J. is elected in a close race with Romney in 1968. Robert Kennedy is elected President in 1972 over John Lindsay. He wins two terms. In 1980, Teddy Kennedy runs but he is given a close fight and just barely wins. He wins bigger in 1984. Then, in 1988 the G.O.P. takes over. They stay two terms but in 1996 the Democrats take over. ("John-John" Kennedy was suggested as the possible Democratic candidate in 2000.)

Social progress is closely connected to great advances in science and technology. YDs generally perceive technological developments as increasingly beneficent to man, a natural and important adjunct to his social progress.

In the field of foreign policy YDs see the end of the war in Vietnam followed by a *rapprochement* with Russia, and eventual accommodation with China. They see the U.N. playing an increasingly important role in world affairs.

The overwhelming tone of YD utopianism, despite a minority of dissenters, is optimistically progressive. However, those YDs who do depart from this projection of the future and embrace dystopian conceptions (15 percent) envisage extended cold war between world powers, continuing hostilities between the U.S. and nations of the underdeveloped world, the demise of U.S. prestige in the world along with increasing domestic crises involving continuing poverty and the decline in civil rights advances.

Young Republicans

Among the YRs, there appear two principal orientations: the utopian progressive theme (28 percent) and the dystopian belief in continuing downward drift, or linear decline (29 percent). In some respects the progressives seem similar to their YD counterparts. They project a solution to the Vietnam war in a Korean-like settlement and a general movement toward peace. The U.S. and Russia move closer together, and both further away from China. China is not allowed in the U.N.

Domestically, YRs foresee a conservative Republican trend as the party becomes dominant. Further, there is an increasing assumption of government responsibility at the local and state levels. This is typically seen, as with the YDs, as coming to pass through a series of elections in which the Republican party grows in strength and registers convincing victories:

Conservatism becomes dominant belief in politics. Communism collapses as an ideology. Republican Party is in majority. Democrats in minority.

With the advent of the 1970's a much greater effort was being made by state governments to take back and run responsibly much of the jobs that the federal government had taken by default. This was due to a depression in '68 which was a result of continuous inflation and the unfortunate economic effects of the conclusion of the Vietnam War. Republicans were in office, political scientists were pleased to see their cyclical theory of party change come true. The country as a whole has a greater technological base with computers even more important as a means of production. No major war and no race war took place.

Thus, most YR progressives* project a utopia stated in terms of party success and a retreat of federal power from state and local encroachment. Fewer YRs than YDs allude to such liberal-humanitarian developments as general improvements in the living conditions of the lower class, decline or end of poverty, more affluence, and generally "a bright world future." Again like the YD, a few see science and technology as the handmaiden of these developments.

On the other hand, the linear decline faction in YR presents us with a future projection very much in accordance with the conservative conception of the mass society.[4] Increasing apathy or "don't give a damn attitude" characterizes the future as the quality of life declines. Very important in this image is the great increase in population, the rise of the minorities and working classes generally, and the breakdown of the old distinctions of status and wealth. This leveling means further decline in the ethic of individualism. Many YRs would sum up the process as a vast societal decline in morality:

The United States in the last 34 years became the first truly mass society in the history of the world. After the negotiated neutralization settlement in Vietnam which later resulted in the conquest of Southeast Asia by

* We remind the reader that our definition of "progressive," like our definition of all the types, refers to the formal properties and not the substantive aspects of the style of thought in question.

China, the U.S. turned inwardly continuing the great society program until approximately 1972 with the election of Robert Kennedy to the Presidency, at this time because of the graduation from college of the young radicals and the apathy of the rest of the nation a law was passed prohibiting wills—meaning that after the death of individuals their property, dissolved by the state, could be distributed equally among all people. Arts and letters declined because the society became so mass that creativity was stifled because it was different. About 1985 or '95 a war between Russia and China wiped out the communist threat. The American mass society meanwhile entered the next century in complete mediocrity.

Along with the future demise of an individualistic morality, comes the ascendance of socialism, "welfare-statism," and governmental centralization as the hand of federal bureaucracy weighs ever heavier on the individual citizen.

In foreign affairs the YR linear declinists see a decline in the economic power of the U.S. abroad, relegation to second power status and an ultimate communist world takeover, as a result of the sell-out of American politicians and cooperation which permitted the Russians to rule the world after 1992. Generally, the YR linear declinists are concerned with the breakdown of the capitalist status system as we have known it historically and the imminent decline in world status of the United States. In contrast to the YD, they are not much concerned with humanitarian issues as presently defined.

Students for a Democratic Society

Among SDS, dystopian conceptions are dominant. If the mixed group is ignored, a considerable majority of SDS sample falls into this general category. Most dystopians have been classified as linear declinists (34 percent). This group see the demise of U.S. power abroad resulting from her imperialist foreign policy. Accompanying this is the growth of a fascist state within. Such dystopias, while overwhelmingly pessimistic, nevertheless lack the total nihilism of the essays we have classified as eschatological. SDSers see the loss of U.S. prestige and the increase in domestic problems as a direct result of the country's irrational commitment to Vietnam, and the related rise of anti-American sentiment throughout the world.

During the 1960's and 1970's, the gradual escalation of the war in Vietnam led inexorably to the erosion of civil liberties at home. By 1980 the United States was a democracy in name only; the outward forms of a federal republic had become a façade for the rule of a corporate-managerial power elite. Freedom of dissent was virtually nonexistent. In 1970 China entered the war directly, leading to a full-scale land war, which the United States won only by the use of tactical nuclear weapons which rendered the Indochinese Peninsula virtually uninhabitable. The Cold War then took a new direction: The United States and the Soviet Union (whose socio-politico-economic systems by that time were fairly similar) both assumed the role of reactionary, neo-colonial powers, opposed by China and much of the "Third World." This situation had reached an unbreakable stalemate by 1985. By 2000 the entire world had settled down to a more or less stable situation of world-wide authoritarianism, continuous "limited" warfare, nuclear stalemate, and widespread poverty and overpopulation. As of 2000 A.D., the ideal of democracy appears destined for oblivion.

Domestically, a high unemployment rate among Negroes, violence in the cities, and unrest among other groups plague the country. "But though this unrest grew in 2000, the increased technology of 'the military complex' had adequate control over the large numbers of American people and hence the unrest had not been translated into revolutionary demands."

SDSers characterize the main drift of American society, superficially at least, as similar to that of the YRs. They lament the projected loss of individual freedom, increasing bureaucratization, increasing alienation and suppression, but project the growth of a wide progressive movement as a result.

Eschatological dystopian conceptions (15 percent) among SDSers mostly involve the catastrophic theme of nuclear war. This is often seen as the direct product of Lyndon Johnson's foreign policies, either directly from the Vietnam involvement or because of world-wide rejection of American imperialism. Others see the holocaust as the historically imminent consequence of the more impersonal forces of automation, bureaucratization, and militarism:

In the middle of the 20th Century change seemed to come only slowly. It seemed as if the American Empire would continue to expand and crumble, Russia and America and China would grow closer together in outlook and interest, while continuing to control their populations by means of the "the other-guy-is-out-to-rule-the-world" crisis technique. And so it was. But some developments began to eat away at the *status quo*.
1. The economy of America changed radically under the impetus of automation.

2. The social life of America began to revolve around pseudo-mysticism and pseudo-psychedelic religion and other forms of escape.
3. Somewhere towards the end of the century the academic structure began to collapse under the weight of published material. The advance of science slowed down and things had to be discovered three and four times before they came to the attention of anyone who could make use of them. As we know, there is no longer any communication between the disciplines.
4. In order to channel the new muscle of the economy, the war effort had to be increased, with damage resulting to population and territory, thus maintaining the economic ecology.
5. Crisis followed crisis, and all was normal till somebody slipped. The siren is sou--.

Some SDSers evidently wishing to convey the idea that ordinary language was inadequate for the expression of their feelings, simply sketched mushroom clouds, mathematical equations or other intense or terse symbols of nuclear annihilation.

Utopian themes among SDSers, while in small minority, deserve some treatment. The progressives (13 percent) envisage a gradual decrease or end to neo-colonialism throughout the world and project a world-wide movement toward peace. This is accomplished by the neutralization of Vietnam, the rise of new world powers in both the East and West and the eventual unification of all countries under the United States.

Hopefully American neo-colonialism and imperialism defeated and a domestic revolution supplanting rule of power elite for democratic control.

Domestically, SDSers also perceive an end to laissez-faire capitalism, a movement toward domestic socialism and radicalized universities. Often these consequences are seen as the result of the New Left.

SDS revolutionaries (10 percent) typically see in the future an alliance between oppressed blacks, poor whites and radical intellectuals, born of the Vietnam war, poverty, unemployment, racism and increasing suppression at home. The goal to be achieved is a democratic socialist society of free men.

With the war in Vietnam continuing for a decade, the American people became very dissatisfied. While a million American soldiers were dying needlessly in Vietnam, revolutions also broke out all over Asia, Africa, and Latin America. The poor people were at last rising against oppression. The reactionary government of the U.S. spread its armed forces all over the globe. But the soldiers, seeing no reason to fight, refused to shoot defenseless peasants. Meanwhile, at home opposition grew to the imperialist policies of the capitalist government. As the economic crisis at home deepened hell broke loose in the black ghettos. The workers, black and white, struck all across the nation. They demanded nothing less than the complete and immediate capitulation of the capitalist ruling class. Now they were out to destroy the oppressor! Led by the Socialist Workers Party, the American workers successfully overthrew the bourgeois state, and joined the other nations in constructing a socialist society, without oppression, without exploitation. A society where man is invaluable, and where culture can really develop at an unprecedented pace. A truly free society, where all contribute as much as they are able to, and draw as much as they need.

Young Americans for Freedom

The YAF exhibit three principal future conceptions: the utopian conception we have called conversionist, dystopian linear decline, and to a lesser extent the progressive utopia. In a progressive theme:

The history of the United States from 1966–2000 was drastically changed because of the war in Vietnam. Despite all his efforts President Lyndon B. Johnson (1963–1968) was unable to end the war. The Republicans met and nominated Governor Ronald Reagan of California who won the Presidency. Reagan achieved a victory in a short period. Reagan started a Republican trend which dominated the period. The Republicans were mostly moderates or conservatives. Both the U.S. and Russia became allied in order to fight off the Chinese in Asia. The U.S. succeeded in liberalizing the communists by the use of economic pressures. This caused a lessening in the Cold War tension. Instead of a desperate fight for survival there was more cooperation and competition. With the help of the younger generation of Russian leaders the U.S. eliminated Castro. . . .

On the home front YAFers also see the end of collectivism with the liberal tide changed toward a free society. The federal principle is reasserted in stronger state and local government, and the "conservative" party draws new strength and assumes full control aided by private capitalism.

Those expressing a linear decline projection (29 percent) are quite similar to their counterparts in the YRs, except that the tone is more stringent, unyielding, and the events more desperate. Also YAFers do not measure future history in the pedestrian terms of national elections, although the election of a Goldwater, a Reagan or a Tower symbolizes massive changes.

Internationally, dystopian YAFers expect to see a communist world-wide movement takeover in Asia, Africa, Latin America and, in some cases, the United States. American "communists" such as Robert Kennedy and Hubert Humphrey will aid this development. One essayist indicated that by 1975 communist dictators would rule most of South America, Africa and Southeast Asia, "and by 1993 the communist movement in America was successful in disarming the U.S. to such an extent that preemptive surrender was the only road open to us."

Internally, the country drifts away from its historic ideals due to the phony concern with civil rights and foreign aid by the government:

The great decline of the U.S., formerly the greatest country in the world, was caused by the influence of those politicians who were more concerned with "civil rights and welfare benefits" at home and "foreign aid to underdeveloped countries" abroad.

The drift is toward tyrannical socialism: Communism takes over most of Asia by 1980–85; by 2000 the "U.S.A., for all intents and purposes, is 100% socialistic, and Russia has softened in economic policy so that the whole world is basically one big Socialist economy." Intermeshed throughout are the themes of the rejection of God, atheism, decline of morality and the submergence of the individual.

The most prominent projection among YAF is the one we have called conversionist,* defined as a conception of a continuing drift toward one extreme, then a dramatic or sudden reversal having the character of an "awakening," or rebirth, in which radically opposed ideas flood society in near-total fashion. The awakening is manifested in specific events such as national elections (Reagan wins). Conversionists see a continuing drift toward socialism, the welfare state or

---

* We should note that the figure of 36 percent for the YAF conversionist type in Table 2 probably underrepresents its true incidence in the group, since some of those classified as mixed, if more information were available, would probably be classified as conversionists. Also, since the internal pattern of the conversionist type is more complex than the progressive in particular, it is probable that simplification of the process in some essays of the students has led to our classifying some true conversionists as progressives.

weakness in international affairs, as well as general "moral decay," followed by a millennial awakening to the true values of conservatism. Sometimes the key event is an economic depression, sometimes the continuing expansion of communism. Sometimes there is no particular event mentioned, just a "realization."

The great majority of conversionists project conversion into the relatively distant future.

The United States led by hypocritical and unprincipled leaders becomes very bureaucratic and increasingly socialistic. The United States generally loses the battles (politically, etc.) in foreign affairs because it does not present its philosophy of free enterprise, libertarian beliefs, etc., as well as it should. Finally in the 1980's or thereabouts the American people realize that economic security is not necessarily freedom. They realize their freedoms are being abridged. They realize the economy is becoming too regimented and the government too bureaucratic. The people will then change the trend of events back to common sense, conservative principles of government.

The conversionist mentality, it should be understood, is not a revolutionary one. YAFers are not revolutionaries generally. The revolutionary theme is mentioned by only 9.7 percent of the entire group and by 10 percent of the conversionists. The term "obedient rebels" nicely captures their stance toward society, embodying the traditional conservative value of authority with their will to remake society.

Compared with their SDS counterparts on the left, YAFers seem to have a mountain of naïve faith. Taking the conversionists, revolutionists and progressives plus a minimal number from the mixed category, the percentage of "optimists" would be in the neighborhood of 60 percent compared with SDS's approximately 30 percent. In the final section of the chapter we will deal with this question by relating the modal or dominant type to the findings of other studies of the problem.

Creating Utopia: the YAF and SDS

In this section we intend to look more closely at the main types found in the two new radical groups: SDS dystopians (mainly linear declinists) and YAF conversionists. We will argue that the predominance of these types in the two groups is related to the process whereby their proponents came to be left-wing radicals and ultra-conservative rightists. Our argument will be an interpretive one, in that it applies ideas developed elsewhere *ex post facto* to the findings of our own research.

SDS Dystopians

First, let us consider the fact that, if mixed essays are excluded from consideration of utopian conceptions in Table 2, about two-thirds of our SDS sample would have to be considered dystopians. Many of these (30 percent) enunciate the primary theme of the imminent end of history and even of men through unprecedented catastrophe, nuclear war. Even the linear declinists' essays are full of accounts of limited or guerrilla wars, occurring in the United States as well as the underdeveloped world. In effect, violent conceptualizations of history are evidenced at a much higher incidence for SDS youth than for the other groups. (See Table 1) Nuclear war, revolution, urban guerrilla warfare, totalitarianism, and American imperialism pervade SDS essays.

The view of future history held by the great majority of SDSers in our sample is a grim one indeed. Yet, SDS (and the New Left in general) is increasingly in evidence—tenacious and persistent in its protest. The situation is a bit like Weber's classic Calvinist-turned-capitalist. It would have seemed that a religion that foreordained the religious fate of everyone before his birth would have occasioned a more fatalistic, passive response than it evidently did (assuming the argument survives the army of critics that have attempted to do it in). The New Left activist, often a Marxist of some sort, finds himself driven to oppose and to dissent, even in the face of his evident belief in the coming of the holocaust. And in 1968 the dissent quickened— Columbia probably represents a shift toward revolutionary dominance and from the standpoint of much of the New Left, greater acceptance of violence (mainly by the military industrial "establishment") as essential to the extension of radicalization by the movement in general. SDS embodies the twin themes of a belief in imminent disaster associated with violence and a tenacious commitment to action directed toward remaking the structure of society. The analysis by Kenneth Keniston provides us with some understanding of the genesis of the pattern whereby these two themes are held in tension.

In his recent study of 17 leaders of Vietnam Summer (an organization of college youth put together to oppose American involvement in Southeast Asia during the Summer of 1967), Keniston demonstrates that the themes of (1) violence, and (2) the sense of responsibility and belief in principle, stemming from childhood and enervating the life of the young radical, are crucial in understanding him.[5] The young leftist radical, as considerable independent research has shown, typically comes from an upper middle-class family of substantial affluence. Keniston's radicals had their roots in such families, but they were families of a rather special type, clearly not the status-oriented materialistic families in which so many critics of radical leftist dissenters have assumed such youth were reared. Rather their principal characteristic, at least insofar as it relates to the later radicalization of their progeny, was their parents' insistence on the very great importance of general ethical principles.[6]

The theme of personal responsibility for the actualization of ethical principles is, in Keniston's view, fundamental in the radicalization and, above all, to the intense style of commitment exhibited by such youth. Yet while these radical youth are products of principled homes, Keniston emphasizes that many are ambivalent toward their fathers who, while idealistic, sympathetic and honest, are relatively ineffectual in family matters and did not exhibit a personal commitment to radical activities consistent with their stated principles. The sense of moral responsibility inculcated as a youth became decisive in the development of the later radical commitment.[7]

Running parallel to, and perhaps even more important in developing a radical commitment among these youth, is the theme of violence. Keniston found that many of the earliest recollections of childhood were associated with violence in one form or another. Thus, one youth remembered at a very early age looking through an encyclopedia and finding a picture of an atomic bomb and a tank running over a field of rubble. He recalled, ". . . I became hysterical. I screamed and screamed and screamed. I do remember that." [8] Another remembered a riot in his home town and the terrifying events connected with it. A third lived through traumatic inner conflicts involving rage directed at his sadistic father and his mother.[9] Ordinarily, these experiences were connected to the larger social and historical scene. This early confrontation with violence, both inner and outer, is in Keniston's judgment crucial in the development of the radical commitment.

It is our suggestion that the violent dystopias of SDS youth are related to their life-long preoccupation with the problem of violence experienced by them. Yet this in itself scarcely sets them apart from others. All of "post-modern youth" have, "objectively" speaking, been subjected to the same conditions, and they have not become radicals. But it is probable that few have lived with the question of violence so intimately and intensively. Few have made it the principal modality of their capacity to relate personally to the world and to history. The meaning of violence in its relation to one's life is a complex question that cannot be dealt with adequately here. But it is clear that the way violence enters into a man's life is extraordinarily variable. To the military man, for instance, violence is reduced to an array of problems that must be dealt with by the application of available technology. This is a professionalized view and if such a man holds any other it is apt to intrude on his capacity to play his role. Similarly, for the black cornerman in the ghetto, as for the lower-class white generally, violence is an accepted and generally expected medium of social exchange, with a structure of norms to justify it under given conditions. It is, in fact, virtually endemic to lower-class culture, and is not at all viewed as a special problem, nor does it command the total life-preoccupation that characterizes contemporary radical youth. Again, the issue of violence may simply be ignored through dissociative techniques and the privatization of life. Or it may be banalized, as is seen among many ultra-conservative youth in this study and certainly a great many others, as long as it does not touch one directly. What evidently sets radical youth off from most others is the special way in which they have experienced violence, both directly and vicariously. In our interpretation, this special and intense preoccupation seems to be a necessary element in comprehending the predominance of violent dystopian futures among SDS youth.

At the same time, the great moral commitment to personal ethical responsibility, engendered during childhood, evidenced but generally latent during adolescence and renascent thereafter, seems to account for the persistence of dissent and activism generally. And this commitment is maintained despite the projected "end of history" view. This suggests that, despite their ethic of an integrated life, there does exist an important psychological dissociation among these youth that results in the most intense kind of concentration on the everyday, immediate matters of life as a radical, with a studied absence of concern for the long-term future. The preoccupation with matters of organization, the continuous discussion of tactics and the need for meaningful acts demonstrating personal commitment, such as getting arrested, are a part of this syndrome and have been noted by many observers, including Keniston and the present authors. The New Left has no program, no concrete plan of a future society, and the groups that make up and sustain it seem to be no nearer to this now than when they began to form 6 years ago. It is difficult to avoid the inference that their view of the future, as a consequence of the manner in which personal confrontation with violence has channeled their development, makes such considerations superfluous. If this is correct, it is perhaps their deepest tragedy.

Conversion as a Means to Utopia

Why is the conversionist utopia so attractive an orientation among YAF? And why does it appear so incidental a conception among other student political groups? On the face of it, there seems to be little in the *corpus* of conservative thought as such that would suggest this pattern of elements. In fact, certain conservative ideas would seem to imply quite different utopian conceptions; for example, the doctrine that change in general should be slow because any particular set of social institutions, by their very existence, must have something to recommend them.[10] A possible answer lies in the knowledge of the manner in which these youth have come to their commitment. The work of Lawrence Schiff is especially germane to this question.[11]

Schiff has argued that the characteristic experience of the YAF member is psychologically one of conversion. The youth, usually from a conservative socio-political background, experiences a dramatic change not just in the content of his beliefs, but in his perception of threats toward them and in his commitment to their defense. Evidently all, or the great majority of the youth he interviewed, were found to have a conversion experience, although there are distinctions to be made among different sub-groups of boys. Most members come from homes in which they have been subjected to very high achievement expectations with the consequence that later when they found themselves in situations of great personal threat, many rebelled because they could not live up to such pressure and many were not prepared to cope with "radicalism," "immorality," and personal hardship which confronted them on campus and in everyday life. Schiff argues that their reaction was a total rejection of their social environment and of the general trend of modern society, accompanied by a conversion to the values of conservatism not much different from what they had been taught at home.[12] In other words, conversion was not only a return to principles to which the youth already had been formally subjected, but a committed return, in which they experienced the acceptance of conservatism as a personal act of will and not superficially as a passive object.

Furthermore, the conversion experience was often mediated by a "hero," "who had great influence, both as recruiter and example." [13] Such a hero could be either a personal acquaintance or a celebrated person, such as William Buckley or Ayn Rand, and they were frequently instrumental in mediating the conversion through the convert's identification with them. One function of this identification is to effect "identity foreclosure" [14] as part of a security-attaining mechanism, after which, in Schiff's judgment, the conflictful process of true growth and maturation is avoided. So conversion does not effect genuine personality change but only a way out of the crisis, through total but rather unreflective commitment to conservatism. That is, commitment among these adolescents tends to be "all out." [15] Converts experience a total realignment of the personality—they feel like new men, and they hold to their identity-creating creed in its totality.

Most of those converted to YAF conservatism, according to Schiff's account (these being especially the late converts), embrace conservatism more in its formal qualities than its substantive precepts.

The late convert identified himself with the overall posture and prestige of the new conservatism, rather than with its detailed content. He was concerned mostly with status, with position, with social identification, with responsibility and role—not with passionate belief. As such he could accept its doctrine totally, without much quibble, since what counted was what it stood for, rather than what it was.[16]

What it stands for, in other words, is its *general* significance and not the details—it gains its meaning as an abstraction and in its instrumental significance.

The conversion to conservatism is a way of coping with personal maladjustment involving problems centering on high achievement goals. Their adjustment is directed toward and achieved by identification with a high-status philosophy. In other words, Schiff thinks that the appellation "conservative" as a prestigious identity is, for YAFers, a substitute for real achievement, or, if you will, a pseudo-achievement. This does not, of course, mean that such an identification or related activity is particularly honored or valued by others, particularly in academic milieux.

We argue here that the point-for-point correspondence between the conversionist utopian mentality and the conversionist experience is too close to be coincidental.[17] We are suggesting, although certainly not claiming to have proven, that a clear affinity exists between the two patterns:

(1) The direction or route of change, following general conservative theory, is a *return* to a former state of affairs idealized as a perfect or near-perfect condition. In the case of YAF youth, of course, this condition is allegedly found in pre-20th century times and involves myths of free enterprise and the self-reliant, risk-taking individualist making it on his own. Rather than the older conservatism of Burke and some of the founding fathers which looked to the past for a model of social order, it is the economic liberal, social Darwinist conservatism of the late 19th century that is expressed in the essays.

(2) The dynamics of change involve a sudden shift rather than a gradual movement or process. Contemporary society is perceived to be moving rapidly away from professed conservative principles by the vast majority of YAF. Evidently, under these conditions it makes little sense to espouse gradualism.

(3) Conversion is effected through the medium of a hero, the archetype of conservative ideals, who becomes the focus of collective identification of the people. YAF expectations of conservative rebirth are strongly linked to the role of the leader-hero. Images of Goldwater, or more currently Reagan, smashing the opposition (whether Democrats or liberal Republicans) function as catalytic agents essential to the conversion process. Reagan now, like Goldwater earlier, embodies in pure form the qualities of the conservative. In our study, 21 percent of YAF essayists mentioned well-known conservative politicians as against the 2.5 percent of SDS members who mentioned liberal or radical figures. In addition, culture heroes such as Ayn Rand are sometimes referred to among conversionist types, while the left has no counterparts to such figures. SDS members have much less of the faith in large-scale reform the YAF displays and none whatever in the ability of political supermen to pull it off.

(4) The conversionist shift is a total one, involving a complete societal transformation and embracing all conservative principles. Piecemeal efforts and partial reforms are out. Social Security will not

be modified but abolished. Federal regulatory agencies will not be considered individually and adjustments made, but will be collectively eliminated. Total conversion implies, in addition, the removal of conflict and organized dissent from society, for if everyone is converted to internally consistent sets of ideals conflict is automatically eliminated.

(5) The conservative principles instituted through conversion are more important as abstractions and for what they *stand against* and *replace* than for their detailed substantive content. A society converted back to conservatism is good as a totality not because this, that or the other change has presumed or observable effects, but because the society *in toto* embodies conservative truth and stands in the stead of the horror it replaced. A very important aspect of this is a deemphasis of events *as such.* Generally, events are considered important only in terms of what they lead up to or exemplify, that is, as abstractions. For instance, we mentioned earlier that some YAF members indicated the probability of nuclear war in their essays, but only as an incident in a larger chain of events. This is a form, and a very important one, of the dehumanizing of history and, potentially, of action.

(6) Finally, conversion results in a return to a higher place among nations whereby prestige is restored, and lost honor recovered. The conversion process is seen either as restoring status, or (in the minority type) as providing the condition under which status can be regained. Usually, this is linked to and articulated through themes of militancy. Only 6.9 percent of YAF see a decline in world tensions due to American action, much lower than the other groups, while 26.3 percent placed the country on a world crusade for freedom, often leading to total world dominance alone (or, in some cases with Russia), but always eliminating China in the process. In this, YAF supports the concept of sheer military power being the criterion of international prestige.

The type of analysis we have performed here, as we said earlier, fails to prove beyond doubt the relationship we think exists. The method of analogy is among the weakest of formal procedures for establishing truth. Fortunately, some of our data on YAFers can test further implications of the hypothesis. If, as Schiff argues, the anxiety over status and achievement among YAF youth is the source of their conversion to conservatism, and if indeed this is the source of the dominant conversionist utopia of the group, then it follows

(1) that YAFers, more than members of the other groups, should have low-status origins; and (2) that the conversionists in YAF should be overrepresented among youth from low-status origins. Indeed, this seems to be the case. When stratified by social class* the great majority of YAF members are drawn from lower-middle- and respectable working-class strata. Members of SDS and other groups come much more frequently from middle- and upper-middle-class strata. Further, YAF conversionist utopians are significantly over-represented in the lower stratum: they were found to constitute 48 percent of the lower-middle and respectable working class, but only 28 percent of the middle class and 26 percent in the upper-middle class respectively.† These data, we believe, strengthen our thesis of a relation between conversionist experience and conversionist utopian projections among YAF youth.

Conclusion

In this chapter we have tried to adapt Mannheim's conception of utopia to one sector of the contemporary political scene by adding a dystopian conception and a reality dimension of actual belief in the trend of future history. Second, we have suggested that, in the cases of two dominant utopias among SDS and YAF members, there is a relation between the characteristics of the utopia (or dystopia) and the process whereby the young activist came to his commitment. The arguments we have presented in support of this relationship are relatively weak in terms of what we would consider to be desirable scientific proof. The data from our study are, unfortunately, incapable of carrying us much further in this direction. However, the principle of the thing, that such relationships may in fact exist, is of consider-able importance in the understanding of social movements and per-

* The Hollingshead Index of Social Class was used for this purpose. The Index combines scores on (1) the Edwards 7-point occupational prestige scale, with (2) a 7-point educational scale.

† This is based on the Hollingshead scale in which Classes I and II closely ap-proximate the upper-middle class, Class III the lower-middle, and Classes IV and V the working class. For a full development of these ideas and for an anal-ysis of the relationship between student radicalism and class structure see our "The Alienation of Generations and Status Politics: Alternative Explanations of Student Political Activism," in Roberta Sigel (ed.), *Learning About Poli-tics: Studies in Political Socialization* (New York: Random House, Inc., 1968).

haps of politics in general. From Marx to Mannheim, it has been the fundamental tenet of the sociology of knowledge that ideological and utopian conceptions arise from the "existential base" of one's class position. In more recent times, theories of mass society have been brought forward to explain seeming discrepancies in this relationship, especially with respect to modern movements such as Nazism and McCarthyism, but they have not developed notably more explanatory power than class theory. Our data suggest that the issue is unlikely to be resolved clearly in one direction or the other. Mass society theory suggests that the massification of modern society isolates and alienates the individual from significant, meaningful and influential relationships, preparing him for radicalization as a "true believer" by some extremist mass movement. Class theory argues that political action arises from basic economic activity. Neither of these theories seems adequately to comprehend the dissenting youth we have studied. While there are class and more particularly status elements involved in the picture, their relevance for the development of utopian and dystopian conceptions of the future seem to be indirect and intertwined with other factors, such as achievement pressure, status concern, emphasis on principle, maternal dominance in the family, and the psychological processes developing out of these situations. We think that we have established some evidence and an argument that utopian (and perhaps ideological) conceptions may be related to the processes whereby individuals in different types of social situations involving class and family elements come to relate themselves to the nature of the social order. As the materials from the Schiff and Keniston studies show, this is a process of increasing awareness of the character of society and of one's relation to it. In the future we will need further study of this process and the complexities involved before we will be able to assert with confidence that we understand the role of the existential base in the germination of utopias and ideologies.

NOTES

[1] Karl Mannheim, *Ideology and Utopia,* trans. by Wirth and Shils (New York: Harcourt, Brace & World, 1936), p. 40.

[2] This follows the procedure of K. Danziger, to our knowledge the author of the only other study in the literature bearing a similarity to ours. See K. Danziger, "Ideology and Utopia in South Africa: A Methodological Contri-

bution to the Sociology of Knowledge," *The British Journal of Sociology,* Vol. XIV, No. 1 (March, 1963), pp. 59–76.

³ These institutions are the Pennsylvania State University, the University of Pennsylvania, the University of Pittsburgh, Carnegie-Mellon University, Temple University, Harpur College (now the State University of New York at Binghamton), the City University of New York, Brooklyn College, the University of Maryland, and Johns Hopkins University.

⁴ See William Kornhauser, *The Politics of Mass Society* (Chicago: The Free Press, 1959), Chapter 1.

⁵ Kenneth Keniston, *Young Radicals* (New York: Harcourt, Brace & World, 1968), pp. 66–67.

⁶ *Ibid.,* pp. 66–73.

⁷ *Ibid.,* pp. 133–135.

⁸ *Ibid.,* p. 48.

⁹ *Ibid.,* pp. 68–69.

¹⁰ For treatments of conservative thought in America see Clinton Rossiter, *American Conservatism* (New York: Vintage Books, 1962), and Richard Hofstadter, *Social Darwinism in American Thought* (New York: George Braziller, Inc., 1959).

¹¹ Lawrence Schiff, "Dynamic Young Fogies: Rebels on the Right," *Transaction* (November, 1966), pp. 31–36; and "The Obedient Rebels: A Study of College Conversions to Conservatism," *Journal of Social Issues,* Vol. 20, No. 4 (October, 1964), pp. 74–95. Schiff's sample (47 New Englanders) is too small and regionally biased to be used as a base for serious quantitative analysis. We have some doubts about the relative distinctiveness of the sub-groups he delineates, particularly since the distinctions made in his two published articles are quite different. In our use of his material we are therefore going to ignore these matters and proceed to select, as we see fit, from his generally excellent material.

¹² Schiff, "Dynamic Young Fogies: Rebels on the Right," *op. cit.,* p. 32.

¹³ *Ibid.,* p. 34.

¹⁴ See Erik Erikson, "The Problem of Ego Identity," in Maurice R. Stein, A. Vidich and D. Manning (eds.), *Identity and Anxiety* (Glencoe, Ill.: The Free Press, 1960), pp. 37–87. The issue also brings to mind the work of Piaget on the limitations of identification for the development of young children.

¹⁵ Schiff, "Dynamic Young Fogies: Rebels on the Right," *op. cit.,* p. 35.

¹⁶ *Ibid.,* p. 32.

¹⁷ For Schiff's treatment of the question of the attraction of conservatism for YAF youth see, "The Obedient Rebels: A Study of College Conversion to Conservatism," *op. cit.,* pp. 87–90.

5

THE IDEOLOGY OF THE NEW STUDENT LEFT

*by G. David Garson**

*

Changes in Ideology: the Fifties and the Sixties

WORLD WAR TWO left Americans with a new toughness of mind.
As neutralist and collectivist nations rejected American forms of
democracy and economy abroad, Americans abandoned older ideologies and found comfort in the new formulations of "social science"
with its vision of pluralism and consensus in domestic affairs and its
foreign policy of deterrence and containment. Sociologists like Raymond Aron and Daniel Bell proclaimed "an end to ideology" and an
"exhaustion of political ideas in the 1950's." [1] Seymour Martin Lipset
wrote that "The characteristic pattern of stable Western democracies
in the mid-twentieth century is that they are in a post-politics phase—
that is, there is relatively little difference between the democratic
left and right." [2] And in fact many Americans could see little difference between the party of Eisenhower and the party of Stevenson.

The 1960's were different. Within a decade, the young intellectuals

* G. David Garson was active in SDS activities at Princeton during his undergraduate days 1961–65. Completing the doctorate in the Department of Government at Harvard University in 1968, he accepted a position with Tufts University where he is presently an Assistant Professor of Political Science. His
doctoral dissertation at Harvard was "Collective Violence: On the History and
Theory of American Disturbances, 1863–1963."

of the 1950's had become part of the "old left" or "establishment." What had happened? In part, there was a realization that the decade of the 1950's had over-reacted against Depression ideological themes; and race, poverty, and even imperialism were "rediscovered" as important social problems. Encouraged by legitimization of social grievances by various authorities, social movements began to develop in these problem areas. But there was also a growing awareness of the inadequacy of the liberal theories of the 1950's: containment and deterrence had become too closely identified with the sterile ideology of "anti-communism," whereby America justified its worldwide reactionary alliances. Similarly, pluralism had developed into a rationale for the tolerance of defective institutions, for inaction, and for the anarchic fragmentation of power among public groups and private enterprise. The "politics of consensus" did not explain the sense of powerlessness and the deep cynicism toward government felt by large segments of the American people. On the academic side, the "scientific" pursuit of social studies had not produced its promised fruit in the "real world," but instead was leading its students into ever more labyrinthine scholasticism.

Moreover, a new generation had arisen which had never known the ideological factionalism of the 1930's or the McCarthyite intimidation of the early 1950's. These young people saw the increasing American abundance not as a reason for political quietism, but as a compelling justification of their demands for social goals too long deferred as "utopian." In turn, this attitude was related to the development of a distinctive material youth culture in the late 1950's and early 1960's.[3] America could now "afford" to be radical. Indeed, in the face of relative abundance, the lack of concerted action to fulfill the American promise of equality, opportunity, and democracy seemed hypocritical.

These attitudinal developments were given an organizational structure in the formation of the Students for a Democratic Society (SDS). The 1963 convention of the SDS adopted a document entitled "America and the New Era," which argued that the Cold War sloganeers were proponents of an increasingly implausible ideology. To the supporters of the SDS position, the toughminded, almost cynical "pragmatists" of the 1950's seemed to be passionate disciples of an increasingly outdated system of beliefs, spawning an opposition which came to be known as "the movement." The movement was composed of student organizations, certain magazines and reviews, and some unaffiliated individuals, but it centered around the largely black Student Non-violent Coordinating Committee (SNCC) in the South and the mainly white Students for a Democratic Society in the North and West. It was clear that with the new generation had come a beginning of change in ideology, setting the scene for a confrontation of beliefs.

The change reflected a dramatic difference from the views of the Fifties. Writers of youth in the 1950's emphasized the themes of conformism and apathy towards social issues, attitudes fostered by the all-is-well-and-improving ideology of that decade. Adherents of the liberal "establishment" line of explanation talked of "equilibrium," "consensus," and "pluralism." These men saw the new movements for social change as vehicles for the integration of "minority groups" into the "mainstream," ending "the culture of poverty." They believed that since the resources of power were widely dispersed, any group might "pyramid their resources" and gain a slice of the growing American pie.

This politics of pluralism implicitly blamed the powerless for their apathy. It could not explain why all interests of importance were not organized in the game of politics, or why a widespread sense of political impotence and cynicism existed. The liberals, accepting established channels of participation as basically adequate, could only arrive at a paternalistic position which sympathetically found the failure to gain power rooted in the characteristics of the powerless. The radicals (often synonymous with the "movement") rejected this view, tracing the failure to the structure of participation itself.

Radicals perceived that the liberal explanations of "the psychopathology of the poor" echoed earlier conservative formulations which throughout history had blamed the poor for their own condition. This liberal view was differentiated from a conservative position primarily by being phrased in sympathetic terms. In thrust, however, it was an analysis which undercut the possibilities of concerted social change. If the problem was perceived as "apathy," "psychopathology," and "family instability," then only two courses were open: mass psychotherapy (which was impossible) or awaiting changes wrought by economic advance over generations (the conservative view). By the 1960's both conservatives and liberals had explicitly or implicitly adopted this laissez-faire resignation to the problem, differentiating themselves primarily by the degree to which they favored or opposed various welfaristic maintenance operations.

The liberal-conservative view was misleading, radicals asserted, because it failed to recognize any strengths among the poor; it did not see any basis by which the poor could help themselves. The radicals sought to contradict this liberal-conservative view not by analysis, but by organizing previously unorganized constituencies of the poor. The radicals also opposed the same view because it failed to connect the many issues that concerned them: violence abroad *was* connected to violence at home, the defense budget *was* connected to the poverty budget, corporate power *was* connected to the maldistribution of income. In their view, Martin Luther King's much-criticized early connection of civil rights with opposition to the war in Vietnam was so obviously correct as almost to preclude discussion.

To men whose analyses traced back to notions of class conflict in the 1930's, the mild pluralistic interpretation of the contemporary scene seemed plausible. To the students who had not been involved in the factionalism of those bitter years, it did not. After many years of painfully slow or absent progress, these young people had spearheaded a successful drive to organize the power of tens of thousands of blacks, and a self-sustaining black movement had been achieved which no longer depended on a student base. An eclectic university system had been vastly liberalized and democratic concepts legitimized where they had previously been ignored. A hated war had not been stopped, but its high domestic costs had been made clear by a movement which again moved so far beyond its original university base that repetition was much less likely.

In the development of the ideology, the movement for the rights of black people was not merely one directed towards integration of a group of dispossessed Americans into the mainstream of American life—it was far more than that. It was a movement which forced millions of Americans to face the contradiction between their country's proclaimed ideals and her actions in practice. The movement served to educate innumerable students and supporters in a general radical view of society, not just on civil rights, but on a broad array of issues. What liberals saw as a *movement* for a social change, radicals understood to be a *period* of social change.

In contrast to the simplistic pluralism-consensus theory advanced by liberals, the radicals viewed conflict and confrontation as having social relevance. In this frame of reference, the view was considered valid, according to the number of people who perceived it to be descriptive of reality and hence a guide to action at the moment. To the radicals, pluralism-consensus was not wrong (it *was* descriptive of part of the 1950's); rather, as a self-fulfilling ideology, it was being superseded by another. The instruments of that change, radicals believed, were movements serving a broad socialization function, not merely seeking the remedy of specific grievances. In McLuhanite terms, the medium of change was the real message.

Where others saw only the integration demands of the civil rights movement, the new student left, born as a by-product of that movement, saw a broad social lesson being taught. If America had betrayed her promise on so fundamental a question as civil rights, might not other areas also be in need of reexamination and revision? The lesson involved the need for rededication to earlier ideals of democracy which, as Bachrach has described, had come to find themselves in new and threatening contexts.[4]

As the lessons of the black revolution confronted the older themes of abundance and pragmatism that were the legacy of the 1950's, two reactions seemed to emerge. The dominant reaction, ignoring that lesson, adopted an increasingly cynical and callous pragmatism which rationalized tokenism in civil rights, endorsed brutal warfare in Vietnam, denied the poor representation on the agencies which dominated their lives, and remained indifferent to students' own demands for a voice in their universities. To the Left and their host of qualified sympathizers, this view seemed born of inertia and despair, carried by men who had given up hope of real social change. An increasingly influential group of intellectuals and activists, in a minority reaction, adopted a truly American radical ideology.[5] In America, as elsewhere, an apathetic majority stood between the two, in crossfire. This essay is about the second reaction, and about the new student left which articulated its ideology.

Differentiation in Ideology: The New Left and Liberalism

1. The Explication of Values. The first task of the new left was to make their values explicit. This continuing task was begun formally with the framing of the "Port Huron Statement" by the 1962 convention of the Students for a Democratic Society. This statement focused on the need for maintaining an individualistic community in the face of an increasingly bureaucratized society marked by undemocratic, hierarchical authority and by the relentless, undiscriminating enforcement of rules for the sake of rule enforcement.

"We regard men," they wrote, "as infinitely precious and possessed of unfulfilled capacities for reason, freedom, and love." These values were seen threatened by the corruption of political terms by earlier ideologies—by the "establishment's" reference to their adherents as "the free world" or by the Marxists' use of the term "the people's democracies" to denote their followers. According to the movement's view, individualistic values were threatened by a widespread desire to be "toughminded" which, the radicals said, meant "to have no serious aspirations." They were threatened by the routinized use of military violence by liberal-conservative leaders and as significantly by the rise of giant, impersonal corporations and bureaucracies which brought "the depersonalization that reduces human beings to the status of things."

The first stage of differentiation from liberalism involved the assertion of values in tension with contemporary trends. In the context of these trends, the radicals asserted that "Human relationships should involve fraternity and honesty" and that "work should involve incentives worthier than money or survival." With this emphasis on the individual went an emphasis on fraternity and community. "Politics," the Port Huron Statement read, "has a function of bringing people out of isolation and into community." Moreover, "as a social system, we seek the establishment of a democracy of individual participation." They rejected the implication raised in voting studies that a decrease in apathy need mean an increase in political instability. On the contrary, radicals took the reverse view.

By themselves, these concerns were not new, and from a cynical point of view they might be considered naïve. Others, including many of the "old left," chose to dismiss them as a mere fashion or style. There was much in the way of flair to support this view. In the early period, for example, letters among members might be signed "Love . . ." Yet if style were all that the radical ideology implied, the new left would not have distinguished itself from other humanitarian ideologies.

2. On the Concept of Freedom. Ideology, of course, was not born full-blown, but rather emerged gradually. The new left clearly realized that it was rejecting the older ideologies of the "establishment" liberals and Marxists, but it was at first necessary to be vague about what was to be substituted. It seemed originally that a general radical orientation with love and commitment was enough, and that things could be "played by ear." Tom Hayden, a president of SDS and a

community organizer in Newark, New Jersey, wrote in 1961 that "The radical program is simply the radical style as it attempts to change the practical life." [6]

Already in 1962, however, the SDS Port Huron Statement insisted that "a new left must transform modern complexity into issues that can be understood and felt close-up by every human being." [7] "Vision" was the word chosen to describe this need, and "style" was de-emphasized. As the SDS chapter organizer's handbook noted, "values alone, though vitally important, are not sufficient. In order to build a political program a clear understanding and analysis of contemporary life is also required." [8] What, however, was to be the content of "vision"?

The most important aspect of "vision" was raised in the SDS constitution, which described the organization as one which

maintains a vision of a democratic society, where at all levels the people have control of the decisions which affect them and the resources on which they are dependent. It seeks a relevance through the continual focus on realities and on the programs necessary to effect change at the most basic levels of economic, political and social organization. It feels the urgency to put forward a radical, democratic program. . . .[9]

This linking of freedom and democracy, repeated in the "Port Huron Statement" and later documents, was used as a prime point differentiating the new left from liberalism.

Freedom has meant many things. To Grotius it had meant simply not being imprisoned.[10] To Hobbes it had consisted in the state of being uncoerced and unopposed.[11] To Rousseau it was acting in accord with one's "rational will." [12] The theory of liberal pluralism, in contrast, rejected the Rousseauan and other "internal" conceptions of freedom as not adequately facing the problem of coercion. Freedom for the pluralists was not delineated by acting as one thought right, or as acting unopposed, but was defined by the degree of choice the more or less coercive institutions of society allowed to the individual. Freedom was said to lie in the interstices of choice between undemocratic and coercive institutions. Freedom was the choice between factories, between products, between schools. Freedom was pluralism because pluralism was choice.

The "establishment" conception of freedom, even in its sophisticated forms, seemed deficient to the new radical community, as it had to certain sections of the "old left." They too rejected the internal concepts of freedom which suggested that one could be "free" by one's behavior and thoughts regardless of the coerciveness of the environment. In their view, freedom involved more than plurality of choice. It involved power. The choice between similar factories did not seem to be the essence of freedom, nor did students accept their supposed "right" to select universities as the most important aspect of their freedom.

Liberty was viewed by the radicals as the right to live under conditions one had helped to set. Democracy and freedom were seen as realistic ideals yet to be achieved, the substance of which involved far more than the forms of elections and suggestion boxes. To be free, students needed a real voice in their universities, workers in their factories, the poor in their neighborhoods, and even doctors in their medical associations. Here SDS was accepting its heritage as the offshoot of the League for Industrial Democracy, but the new ideology left its nominal parent behind as SDS became a formally independent association.

Thus new left ideology came to revolve around four components: freedom and democracy on the one hand, and the preciousness of the individual and of community on the other. Each component reinforces the others. It maintains that there is no real freedom without democracy in all of America's institutions and that there is no real community without a high value placed on the dignity of the individual. Asserting that no real democracy exists without community, the new left argues that community provides the basis for a consensus of discussion rather than one of manipulation.

3. On the Nature of Democratic Institutions. To the reliance on expertise by the "establishment" the new left countered:

We oppose, too, the doctrine of human incompetence. . . . We see little reason why men cannot meet with increasing skill the complexities and responsibilities of their situation, if society is organized not for minority participation but for majority participation in decision-making. . . . Personal links between man and man are needed, especially to go beyond the partial and fragmentary bonds of function that bind men only as worker to worker, employer to employee, teacher to student. . . .[13]

Levels of participation needed to be raised greatly. "The people," a 1965 paper held, "through democratic channels [and] community organizations can and must give guidance to and set priorities for the technocrat, the planner." [14] Such community organizations were not, of course, to be confined to official boards and councils. Another 1965 paper argued, "Today in the United States there does not exist a democracy in the sense that democracy implies freedom for the individual. . . . Today, increasingly our news, our ideology in general, is fed to us through impersonal media which allow us no chance for response, no means for intelligent interrogation." [15]

In spite of what sociologists taught about kinship associations and voluntary groups, the tremendous increase in scale that accompanied the rise of Keynesian government and corporate economy had injected an undeniable "mass" character into American life. This was a new development which eroded the reality and perhaps even the future possibility of "substantive democracy." The widespread feeling of inadequacy of community motivated men to search for new communion in churches, unions, suburbs, and all manner of voluntary associations. But these too were plainly inadequate substitutes. Radicals believed that the democratization of information by modern mass media tended to consolidate opinion behind decisions which had already been made. Isolated individuals and families listening to television in their own homes and apartments seemed incapable of coming to decisions based on discussion. The "democratic process" which was the foundation of freedom necessitated a confrontation of views, a personal interchange and discussion; in short, democracy necessitated participation in decision-making institutions in order to be "substantive." It is on this basis that the new left concern for counter-institutions such as community unions and free universities is to be interpreted.

"Democracy," "freedom," "individualism," and "community" were all words found in liberal ideology; in the radical interpretation, however, their connection was made apparent, giving them a new meaning and vitality. For radicals, a free society would democratize all institutions. Academic life, for example, was seen in these terms: "In the 'mass-producing' of men into machines, freedom is the loser. Although the student is usually free to choose between various course offerings, he has little freedom to determine what will be offered. . . . The student's recognition of his subordinate status stems not from a respect for his professor's intellect, but, simply stated, from an acquiescence to authority."

An extreme statement of this concern was articulated by Lee Webb and Paul Booth:

The America which we face denies democracy—it is a nation in which crucial economic decisions which affect us all are made by corporate managers and bankers, in which millions of people are dependent on the indulgence of public welfare systems over which they have no control, in which the decisions of war and peace are made by a clique of advisers and experts. Can this be a democracy? We understand democracy to be that system of rule in which the people make the decisions that affect their lives. . . . In America, community is practically non-existent. In its absence, the only result of an individual's recognition of the root of his problem is frustration born of isolation.[16]

In the tangled complexity of modern industrial society, where everything causes everything else, or so it seems, the first function of ideology is to break into the ring (sphere?) of causation and identify a place where analysis should begin. The economic factors of production had seemed the most pressing area of concern in the Depression years, and ideology of bread-and-butter unionism focused attention on this area by its very structure. In the incomplete but relative abundance of the 1960's, the point to begin analysis seemed to lie in the interrelationships among freedom and democracy, individualism and community institutions. Initial evaluations of social phenomena seemed most relevant if viewed in these terms rather than in terms of "equilibrium," "pluralism," or "consensus." The challenge was to build or point the way toward the kind of democratic institutions demanded by radical ideology but now lacking in American society.

4. The Connection Between Liberals and Corporate Managers. In various publications, the radicals argued that the widespread sense of powerlessness and isolation was itself strengthening the power of elites and undermining democracy. That is, the very alienation and apathy of most citizens magnified the power of existing decision-makers and in turn made participation seem even more futile. Moreover, the process of fragmentation which was at the heart of pluralist ideology (and which was accepted by the new left with serious qualifications) implied not only the break-up of pyramidal elite control of cities as political units grew more complex, but implied as well the breaking up of community solidarity and the disintegration of community itself. To the extent that citizens were apathetic, power was vested in the hands of more (local level) or less (national level) fragmented but nevertheless entrenched elites. The loss of a sense of community (or the failure to achieve it in the first place) meant

the absence of a sense of power and a will to participate. The abdication of popular power was the basis of elite power. The new radicals came to understand that elitism and pluralism were two sides to the same coin, a notion foreign to liberal ideologists.

"Liberal corporatism" was the name given to the form elitism took in America. In part, this was a renaming of the "establishment" ideologists as corporate liberals. In a November, 1965, speech at the second massive march on Washington to protest the war in Vietnam, SDS President Carl Oglesby discussed "Liberalism and the Corporate State." In that speech he said:

Seven months ago at the April March on Washington Paul Potter, the President of Students for a Democratic Society, stood in approximately this spot and said we must name the system that creates and sustains the war in Vietnam—name it, describe it, analyze it, understand it, and change it.

The original commitment in Vietnam was made by President Truman, a mainstream liberal. It was seconded by President Eisenhower, a moderate liberal. It was intensified by President Kennedy, a flaming liberal. Think of the men who now engineer that war . . . Bundy, McNamara, Rusk, Lodge, Goldberg, the President himself. They are not moral monsters. They are all liberals. . . .

. . . the anti-communist ideology . . . depicts our presence in other lands not as coercion, but as protection. It allows us to say that our napalm in Vietnam is only another aspect of our humanitarian love like those exorcisms of the Middle Ages that so often killed the patient. . . . This is the action of corporate liberalism. It performs for the corporate state a function quite like what the Church once performed for the feudal state. It seeks to justify its burdens and protect it from change.[17]

The dichotomy was posed: "corporatism or humanism, which? It has come to that." Were the "establishment" ideologists self-declared liberals? They were. Were they active in the movements for change —civil rights, power for the dispossessed, anti-imperialism, student representation? They were not. Did they defend governmental policy in these and other areas? They did. From the perspective of the new left, "corporate liberalism" seemed an undebatable description of these older ideologists.

For the new left, the corporate state was not free. It could not be because its institutions were undemocratic.

The fact is that a reasoned case may be made to suggest that modern industrial society faces problems so complex as to render our traditional democratic procedures no longer workable as they were in the past, and historic conceptions of civil and political liberty no longer viable. . . . It isn't enough to talk of changing human nature, nor is it particularly rewarding to concentrate on original sin. There must be an institutional change, for the problem is the problem of power. To be explicit, huge private collectives must be brought under effective control, i.e., rendered fully responsible to society. That there is no pat method for achieving this end does not eliminate its necessity.[18]

Similarly, Kim Moody argued that "The gigantic corporations that are the basis of our present system are authoritarian in essence. . . . The 'democratization of change,' which we are all agreed is a goal, is the most consistent with an economy that has its main units under democratic management." [19] Robb Burlage's "The American Planned Economy: A Critique" also called attention to the "private government" of business.[20] The decisions of businessmen no longer seemed private, and the liberal techniques of control did not seem effective, much less democratic.

Liberalism, in its defense of corporate America, argued that unions and government countervailed business. But as Burlage noted, "The federal government's powers are chiefly in a frozen tax system, marginal regulatory prerogatives as often regulated by the industries as by the commissions, and subsidy policies which all contribute to rather than countervail the corporation economy." [21] The elites that ruled private government in the pluralist system seemed to gain at least as much power through influence over government as they lost to it by regulation by government. Nothing less than the democratization of private government in some form could be consistent with the ideology of the new left and with their definition of freedom.

Differentiation in Tactics: The New Left and Liberalism

1. On Electoral Politics. Since the ideology of the new student left centered on a critique of existing channels of participation, it is hardly surprising that the tactics adopted by the movement tended to ignore the usual liberal strategy of working within the Democratic Party to influence "influentials." To be sure, there was a certain carry-over of strategy from the early civil rights movement, as evi-

denced by SNCC's efforts at voter registration or even SDS's 1964 anti-Goldwater activities under its Political Education Project—yet even these were seen more as vehicles for community organization than as direct quests for power. Indeed, the vigorous debate within SNCC during the summer of 1961 posed voter registration with community organization in contrast to continuing direct action such as sit-ins or freedom rides. Maturing somewhat later, SDS turned from initial concerns with university reforms and coalitions with student government and other groups to a concern with community organization. This was manifested as early as 1963 in Cambridge, Maryland, but it flowered with the undertaking of community organization projects in ten cities in the summer of 1964. Similarly, SNCC's Freedom Summer imported Northern white college students to augment their Mississippi Freedom Democratic Party and Summer Freedom Schools efforts.

In contrast to the coalition of labor, intellectual and political groups required by liberal strategy, the radicals envisioned a coalition of grass-roots organizations under indigenous leaders. The radicals rejected the liberal strategy because it was not sufficiently democratic. It ignored the constituencies most in need, constituencies which had to be organized, tactical considerations aside. Tom Hayden and Eugene Feingold, for example, stated:

Though usually dismissed as utopian, the commitment to democratic participation contains a basic practicality. First, no political program such as the war on poverty can be tailored to fit human needs unless the people, in action, demonstrate the true dimensions of the need and have the determining voice in solving their problems. Second, a public program if enacted in a climate of political indifference rather than participation is likely to be corrupted, ill used, or destroyed by the restraining hand of those who oppose the program, if not by the indifference or, indeed, the active hostility of those who are purported to be the beneficiaries.[22]

Democracy was seen to give dignity and community a sense of identity. These values, shared widely, gave the appeal of the new left great potential force.

Participation in the "normal democratic process," even as a mere tactic for organizing, however, soon came under scrutiny. Essential to this reevaluation was a series of disillusioning experiences from 1963 to 1965, the peak of what may now be considered the "classic" phase of the movement. For SNCC there were several crucial events: the censoring of Lewis' speech at Martin Luther King's 1963 March on Washington, which taught SNCC the dangers of liberal coalitions; and the offering of only two at-large seats to the Mississippi Freedom Democratic Party by the 1964 Democratic Convention and the seating of the disloyal regular delegation taught that the barest tokenism was the result of the hardest labors within the Democratic Party umbrella. Similarly, the continuing white violence, epitomized by the Birmingham Sunday bomb blast which killed four black girls, and the civil rights murder of SNCC workers Chaney, Goodwin and Schwerner, demonstrated convincingly to SNCC that the most powerful weapons of the other side were not democratic-rational ones at all.

For SDS the crucial disillusionment was two-fold. There was the frustration of the 1964 community organizing projects which, although able to mobilize community support, were unable to affect seriously the labyrinthine centers of responsibility for housing, employment and other major concerns (thus making them even more vividly aware that pluralism, the fragmentation of power, was a central obstacle to democracy). Perhaps more important was the lack of manifest effects on policy despite the organizing of the largest anti-war movement ever mobilized in this country during wartime.

2. On Counter-Organizations and Increased Militancy. There were two effects of this disillusionment. The first to appear was the impetus given to "counter-organizations" which turned their backs on the democratic process to construct desirable institutions directly. Such were the hundred-odd "free universities" formed in the summer and fall of 1966. In part, this was a shift in constituency organizing policy. The summer 1965 community organizing projects of SDS had attracted nearly 200 students, but the ascendancy of the war issue and the combination of frustrations and success in transferring leadership to indigenous activists led the 1966 Clear Lake convention to recommit the organization to campus organizing. This in turn led into draft and war organizing, culminating in the 1967 Spring Mobilization which brought 200,000 to New York and tens of thousands to San Francisco.

The second effect of disillusionment was a radicalization of tactics, especially pronounced in SNCC's "black power" rhetoric under the chairmanship of Stokely Carmichael after spring 1966. In SDS also, however, there was a radicalization of tactics relying less on changing public opinion than on forcing issues to the forefront by all means necessary. Such were the demonstrations against war-related recruiting agents on campuses in 1967–68. Although these much-reported new tactics (e.g., San Francisco State) often obscured the continuing commitment to constituency organization, it continued both within the university, in the community and in labor organizing, even if with constantly changing emphasis.

The increasing importance of the Vietnamese War as a moral issue provided the basis for essentially single-issue operations like Vietnam Summer in 1967 and the McCarthy campaign in 1968. These undertakings took some credit for the many moderate actions undertaken by some new left members (in contrast to 1964, when SDS mounted its own campaign operation). Nonetheless, the anti-electoral viewpoint dominated the new left by 1968. This, combined with the disillusionment mentioned above, led the new student left to reemphasize university issues, thus returning to SDS's initial concern with university reform, while continuing its many other organizing efforts.

The increasing militancy was also a direct consequence of the war. In the draft movement, for example, one may trace the progression from individual protests of the traditional pacifist sort, such as the early New York draft card burning, to the circulation of "We Won't Go" pledges and advertisements (spring 1967), to organizing to help others, including inductees, resist the draft (summer 1967), to larger-scale defiance of the selective service system by hundreds of draft card returners (1967–68). This was, of course, only one area of action by the new left movement, but it illustrates the tendency to escalate protest over issues which cannot be ignored after previous protests have not had the least effect on policy.

Although talk of urban guerrilla warfare has occasionally been heard for over a year now, violence cannot as yet be said to be a part of new left tactics. This is true in spite of the movement of Progressive Labor Party members into SDS after the dissolution of the May 2nd (anti-Vietnam War) Movement. Disruption, in contrast to violence, has received more attention as a means of forcing an issue to the center of the political stage when other means have failed, the Dow demonstrations being a case in point.

The new left has not yet made the tactical shift from confrontation to disruption however, especially if the realities of the actions by SDS chapters are taken as a guide rather than exaggerated rhetoric of some national meetings. Many of the excesses, such as the burning of a professor's papers at Columbia, are the results of individual frustrations acting in opposition to radical tactical interests. The case is rather that the level of militancy now believed to be necessary in some cases is sufficient to provoke occasional police aggression and violence. Only at the extreme fringes of the black movement, among persons who could hardly be considered "new left," is popular aggression against authorities seriously considered and practiced as a tactic.

Conclusion

The ideology of the new student left differs from that of liberalism primarily in its assertion of the immediate relevance of democratic practices for all institutions, and in its rejection of current modes of participation as inadequate. It is differentiated from liberalism in tactics primarily by its rejection of a strategy of working within the Democratic Party and in coalition with old-line liberal institutions, including trade unions. Thus in the New York City school strike, SDS was clearly in opposition to its erstwhile parent, the League for Industrial Democracy, and to the old left Socialist Party, which took the side of the United Federation of Teachers.

Although it has centered its activity on university and community organizing, the unifying theme has been a concern with the democratization of our institutions. The Vietnam War has gained a temporary ascendancy, but even here the new left is differentiated by its insistence that war protest be combined with more permanent community organizing. The war, in combination with the disillusioning experiences of trying to participate in the democratic process as it is now structured, has led to a firmer rejection of electoral activity and a convinced need for more forceful tactics. The choice has seemed to lie between the adoption of these tactics or the abandonment of the pursuit of change. Given the ideological goals of the new student left and their sincere sense of urgency, and given the sincere but token response of most authorities from the president on down to most university officials, the general shift in tactics seems inevitable.

If the original purpose of the new left was to revitalize discussion of domestic and foreign policy and to catalyze change in a thousand expected and unexpected places, it seems to have done that. If its purpose was to democratize the corporate state, we may understand

that what we have treated here as the history of the new left is but
a series of preliminary skirmishes in what may be a long period of
creative development.

NOTES

[1] See Daniel Bell, *The End of Ideology* (New York, The Free Press, 1960),
and Raymond Aron, *The Opium of the Intellectuals* (New York, W. W. Norton,
1958).

[2] For a discussion of this point, see Seymour Martin Lipset, *Political Man*
(Garden City, N.Y., Doubleday, 1960), Chapter 13, "An End of Ideology."

[3] G. David Garson, "Collective Violence: On the History and Theory of
American Disturbances, 1863–1963," unpublished doctoral dissertation, Department of Government, Harvard University, 1968. For an anthology of the
new student left, see Mitchell Cohen and Dennis Hale (eds.), *The New Student
Left* (Boston, Beacon Press, 1968).

[4] Peter Bachrach, *The Theory of Democratic Elitism: A Critique* (Boston,
Little, Brown, and Company, 1967), Chapter 7.

[5] See Staughton Lynd, *The Intellectual Origins of American Radicalism* (New
York, Pantheon Books, 1968).

[6] Tom Hayden, "Letter to the New Left," mimeographed letter, Ann Arbor,
Mich., SDS, 1961.

[7] The "Port Huron Statement," Cohen and Hale, *op. cit.*

[8] SDS Organizers Handbook, published by the Students for a Democratic
Society.

[9] *Constitution of the Students for a Democratic Society.*

[10] Hugo Grotius, *The Encyclopedia of Philosophy,* trans. by Gustov Emil
Miller (New York, Philosophical Library, 1955).

[11] Thomas Hobbes, *The Leviathan, or the Matter, Form and Power of a
Commonwealth, Ecclesiastical and Civil,* London, 1651.

[12] Jean Jacques Rousseau, "The Social Contract," in Alan P. Grimes and
Robert H. Horwitz (eds.), *Modern Political Ideologies* (New York, Oxford
University Press, 1959), pp. 20–33.

[13] From the "Port Huron Statement," published in Cohen and Hale, *op. cit.,*
pp. 12–13.

[14] Anonymous, "Reflection on a Radical Movement," mimeographed paper,
Ann Arbor, Mich., 1965.

[15] Anonymous, "S.D.S.: Present and Future," mimeographed paper, Ann
Arbor, Mich., 1965.

[16] Lee Webb and Paul Booth, "The Anti-War Movement: From Protest to
Radical Politics," mimeographed paper, Ann Arbor, Mich., SDS, n.d.

[17] Carl Oglesby, "Let us Shape the Future," published in Cohen and Hale,
op. cit., pp. 312–321.

[18] Anonymous, "A Letter to Young Democrats," mimeographed paper, SDS,
1964.

[19] Kimberly Moody, "American Capitalism," mimeographed paper, Ann Arbor, Mich., SDS, n.d.

[20] Robb Burlage, "The American Planned Economy: A Critique," mimeographed paper, SDS, n.d.

[21] *Ibid.*

[22] Tom Hayden and Eugene Feingold, "Politics 1964: Corporation and Crisis," mimeographed paper, Ann Arbor, Mich., SDS, 1964.

6

RADICAL STUDENT ORGANIZATIONS

*by E. Joseph Shoben, Jr., Philip Werdell
and Durward Long**

IN KEEPING with their loose ideologies of anarchism and participatory democracy, student militants affiliate with a variety of radical organizations. Paying little attention to the organizations themselves, they use first one and then another as devices by which, through focusing intensely on a particular issue, they work toward their eventual goal of radicalization. Although there is little evidence that significant numbers of college students actually affiliate with such anarchist organizations as the Industrial Workers of the World, the Anarchist Federation, the Libertarian League, or Resurgence Youth, there are definite signs that many are influenced by ideas which are emphasized by these groups. It is also significant that about half of the

* Dr. E. J. Shoben, Jr., a co-author of, and a contributor to, *Learning and the Professors* (Ohio University Press, 1968), was formerly with the American Council on Education. He is University Professor of Higher Education at the State University of New York at Buffalo, where he also serves as Director of the Center for Higher Education, Coordinator of Academic Planning and Chairman of the Council on Higher Education Studies.

Philip Werdell, formerly with the staff of the National Student Association and editor of *Moderator,* was an assistant to Dr. Shoben and the American Council on Education during 1967–68. Part of this chapter, although written originally for this volume, was published earlier in *School and Society,* October 26, 1968, and is produced herewith with their consent.

Wobblies' membership is under twenty-five years of age, and that Paul Spencer, a student from C.C.N.Y., is one of the founders of the Anarchist Federation. Spencer is assisted in Federation work by Charles T. Smith, an activist graduate from Harvard. The Resurgence Youth Movement, begun by teen-agers in New York in 1964 and with never more than 100 members, has probably influenced a number of students who became activists on the college campus.

In addition to the various small anarchist groups that emphasize intellectual disciples rather than organization, there are the socialist varieties that find doctrinal and passing support by activists. The Socialist Labor Party (SLP) maintains a small cadre of followers on campuses where socialist student organizations were strong in the thirties. At the University of Wisconsin, for example, spasmodically but frequently, student supporters of the SLP maintain propaganda tables in the Memorial Union at Madison and are found among regular participants in protests. Outnumbering the SLP on the Wisconsin campus, as at most other institutions, are the Trotskyite Socialist Workers Party (SWP) and its youth arm, the Young Socialist Alliance. Militant YSA members follow the tactic of infiltration, but because of their emphasis on destruction and obstruction, they are not always welcomed by other New Left groups.

Students who are members or merely supporters of the anarchist and socialist groups briefly described here often provide the radical know-how to organize campus groups for politically aggressive demonstrators. Many affiliate or cooperate with local chapters of Students for a Democratic Society (SDS) in order to form (either at their initiation or support) temporary *ad hoc* issue-oriented protests. In this strategy, the local student government organization, which may or may not be affiliated with the National Student Association, is often brought into the protest after the initial stages are past. On many occasions, a truly spontaneous protest is simply joined and redirected by the militant adherents of anarchist, socialist, or SDS thought.

New Left organizations which have recently enjoyed the most support on college campuses are SDS, a description of which follows below, the W. E. B. DuBois Clubs, begun in 1961, and the Progressive Labor Party (PLP), also formed in 1961 by a number of Communists who had been excluded from the Communist Party, U.S.A. The PLP is strictly Maoist, a revolutionary group that talks of violence and studiously cultivates college students. Most of its twelve hundred members are under twenty-five, and approximately one-fourth of its membership is Negro and Puerto Rican. The DuBois Clubs approximate the CPUSA line so closely that it has been listed by the United States Attorney General's Office as a Communist Front. Its members so successfully infiltrated the Students for a Democratic Society that by 1969 they evoked widespread fear that SDS might eventually be taken over by the PLP.*

The issues which the variety of New Left supporters in 1966–69 have found most effective for fielding active protest include the draft, the war in Vietnam, peace and disarmament, campaigns to end poverty, and rights and privileges for blacks. Other campus groups formed around these issues have found ready support from most of those identified with the various organizations discussed here. For example, there is the Vietnam Day Committee (VDC), which aspires to a radical restructuring of universities. Less campus-based, the pacifist Committee for Nonviolent Action, which advocates active civil disobedience, has organized national protests against nuclear testing, the construction of missile sites, the draft, and the Vietnam war. Its direct action efforts have been among the most intense in the country. Other peace groups—the War Resisters League, the Draft Resistance Union, and the National Committee for a Sane Nuclear Policy (SANE)—also cooperate with these two major anti-Vietnam war groups and draw support from the campus militants.

Militant organizations of black and other minority students have also emerged at the local level. Some of them began with alumni of SNCC, Black Panthers, CORE, or other groups which have bases of support outside the university as well as on campus. The Third World Liberation Front was organized on several California campuses (most notably at San Francisco State and Berkeley) and perhaps was successful only there in its attempt to unite Mexican Americans ("chicanos"), Indians, Orientals, and blacks. The United Mexican American Students (UMAS) and the Mexican American Students (MAS), both militant in their tactics and objectives, also pressed for minority control in some California institutions. Ron Karenga's US exerts influence and supports its members who attend California's colleges in their quest for cultural identity.

Within this setting on the campus, when militant leadership has

* The formal split in SDS in the summer of 1969 was in great part the result of increasingly apparent differences between the PLP members and other SDS supporters.

been strongly attracted to the various action groups referred to above, the role of the United States National Student Association (NSA) and its campus affiliates has been a trying one. Faced with intensifying threats from radical groups to assume control either of the organization or the campus, the NSA has itself been revolutionized in recent years.

Until recently, the NSA was not considered an activist organization although its political stance has been rather consistently liberal. Founded in 1947 at the University of Wisconsin as an organization of "affiliates" of a variety of local campus student governments, the national association has fluctuated from 300 to 400 institutional members. By the late fifties and early sixties, the organization was under fire from student conservatives because of its political stance. Particularly repugnant to the attackers was NSA's support of federal aid to education, of the general suspension of nuclear testing, and of international student movements. The association was also condemned by conservatives for its opposition to the House Un-American Activities Committee, loyalty oaths, and the disclaimer affidavit in the National Defense Education Act. In fact, internal opposition to the political views advanced by NSA leaders and to the structure of the organization led to the formation of a counter group called Students Committed to Accurate National Representation (SCANR) in 1960. The internal cleavage led a number of campus government groups to secede from the NSA in the early sixties.

When it was discovered in 1967 that NSA was subsidized in part by the Central Intelligence Agency, the organization was subjected to severe strains. Pressed to demonstrate their independence of government controls and their authenticity as student spokesmen, the liberal leaders intensified their "student power" campaign, actually begun in 1965–66, which urged that each of NSA's campus affiliates seek full control over matters of "solely student concern." Given significant shape under the presidency of Eugene Groves in 1966–67, this effort came to fruition the following year in the Statement of Student Rights and Freedoms, drafted by a group drawn from the NSA, the American Association of University Professors, the Association of American Colleges, and other bodies. When Edward Schwartz, the president that year, was succeeded by Robert Poweli, the student power theme was expanded to include the distinctive rights and special programs for black students, the elimination of grading, and increasing participation by students in the academic decisions of university departments like those affecting the promotion and tenure of faculty members.

During this period of increasing activism in NSA, its affiliates and national officers have been pushed from liberal and moderate positions toward the left by competing organizations like SDS and radical individuals occupying posts in particular student governments. In part because of this political pressure and in part because of campus student opinion, NSA and its affiliates have often cooperated with local *ad hoc* coalitions protesting the draft, the Vietnam war, university-imposed social regulations, and the absence of students in academic decision-making. The activist role of NSA may lead student government into more than a "sandbox" organization, but it has severe competitors: apathy and reaction on the right, and radical anarchists on the left. Whether a moderate activist organization can be successful, students will decide; but an organization which more than lurks in the wings—SDS—will influence the outcome significantly.

SDS

Beginning its active career, as has been the case with most relatively militant student organizations, during the civil rights drives of 1960–61, Students for a Democratic Society emerged from the youthful arm of the League for Industrial Democracy. Essentially an organizational vehicle for a wide variety of welfare-oriented liberals like Harold Taylor, Bayard Rustin, Michael Harrington, and Norman Thomas, the LID paid little attention to the Student League for Industrial Democracy until the youngsters broke away from it. The break apparently was animated largely by the model presented by the Student Nonviolent Coordinating Committee and its vigorous activity in the South.

With an articulate vision of a white, middle-class, northern counterpart to SNCC as their goal, Albert Haber of the University of Michigan and a handful of colleagues maneuvered themselves into control of the Student League for Industrial Democracy in the autumn of 1961. Based in New York (where Haber's salary as president was $50.00 per month), this group, comprising primarily people who had shared experiences in southern states in pursuit of civil rights, began to travel from campus to campus in the North, organizing students either for SLID or "a new organization which may emerge." A loose network of students rapidly formed, with small clusters of individuals in several colleges and universities. All tended to be strong and supportive admirers of SNCC, but they accepted the twin notions that a broader array of goals than those defined by civil rights were necessary and that the achievement of those wider aims required a more directly political involvement deriving from a more specifically political analysis of contemporary American culture. The consensus quickly evolved that a "New Left" was needed, and that students would have to build it themselves through their own efforts.

In June, 1962, some 150 students, the great majority of them undergraduates, gathered in Port Huron, Michigan. The major enterprise of the meeting was the discussion and revision of a long and analytical paper, the first draft of which was prepared by Tom Hayden, recently graduated from the editorship of the *Michigan Daily* at the University of Michigan. By the time the group adjourned on June 15, *The Port Huron Statement* had acquired substantially both the form and the content in which it was published shortly afterward. The first major pronouncement of the New Left, the *Statement* was the founding document on which Students for a Democratic Society was based. With Hayden elected as its first president, SDS announced its basic goals in this fashion:

We seek the establishment of a democracy of individual participation with two central aims: that the individual share in those social decisions determining the quality and direction of his life, and that society be organized to encourage independence in men and to provide the media for their common participation.

By the opening of the academic year of 1962–63, the new organization had established 11 chapters on various campuses and had enrolled about 300 members. Although friendly relations with the League for Industrial Democracy for the most part were preserved, all formal connections with the parent body very quickly were broken; and, in the early part of 1963, SDS had set up an independent national headquarters in Chicago from which it conducts its national business.

Structurally, SDS is an individual membership organization, but both its requirements and its bookkeeping are essentially casual. To belong, one need only pay annual dues of $2.00 and offer a "reaffirmation of one's belief in democracy." From the beginning, however, there consistently have been at least as many students who associate themselves with SDS activities and ideas without formally becoming affiliated as there have been dues-paying members. In a roughly similar fashion, there always have been regional and national offices in the organization, but the local chapters, granted an extremely high degree of autonomy, regularly have been perceived as the central source of strength. When national policies are formulated, they virtually always are phrased as "recommendations" to the membership, and they typically contain explicit statements like "local chapters must decide for themselves what is appropriate and effective action."

Even under these conditions, however, the regional and national patterns of leadership are kept under constant and stringent review in an attempt to make them "more democratic." Voting at quarterly regional meetings and at the annual national convention follows the one-member, one-vote principle, with an emphasis on direct participation in the meetings rather than on representation by chapter, by region, by college or university, or by some other basis. After some years of continuing debate, the offices of president and executive secretary were abolished in 1966 on the ground that such officers, willy-nilly, had an excess of authority and that it was impossible for two people to serve as spokesmen for so diverse a constituency. Three national secretaries and a National Interim Council were established to serve in lieu of officers of a more conventional kind. In 1967, the council was enlarged to 11, including the secretaries, to involve more people, to permit the interplay of more points of view, and to divide the responsibility for keeping in relatively close touch with local chapters. Members of the council are required to work actively with campus-based groups in order to maintain a loose, but personalized, liaison between the national office and the rank-and-file membership. The rapidity of structural and procedural changes within SDS makes its leadership rather amorphous to an outsider, but reflects its apparently deliberate struggles to avoid bureaucratization and to operate internally in as democratic a manner as it demands in its literature that the larger society observe.

Since its founding, SDS has gained annually in both chapters and individual members. Founded by fewer than 60 students from 11 institutions, by 1964 it had about 2,000 members on some 75 campuses. In 1966, the numbers had grown to almost 20,000 in nearly 200 institutions. Currently, chapters in 275–300 colleges and universities enroll nearly 30,000 individuals. These figures apply only to formal members; many more students can be rallied to participate in the discussions, programs, and demonstrations which SDS often catalyzes.

The dynamic quality of this sort of growth seems to stem from two principal factors in the group's appeal and its mode of operation. First, its ideological umbrella is a very wide one. Sharply critical of contemporary American society, SDS accommodates people whose views range from straightforward anarchy to ideas deriving from what is called the "Old Left." The great majority of members seem to fall between these two extremes, finding the organization a comfortable base from which to develop their own political style and stance. It is from this large middle range that the national leadership has been elected quite consistently. Second, the local leaders, schooled by those who participated in the civil rights movement, have been unusually successful in developing the strategy and (especially) the tactics by which students can take direct and immediate action with respect to issues on which their feelings run high. At the local level —which is the level that is looked upon as counting—the development of SDS can be understood as a function of the almost yearly generation of new programs and emphases, coupled with tactical innovations that have given them a considerable proportion of successes.

After a first year of reliance on involvement in civil rights activities, the organization moved into new arenas in 1963, with the launching of its Economic Research and Action Program (ERAP). Thus, its first independently formulated emphasis was on community organizing. One of its best known enterprises of this type is Tom Hayden's work in the slums of Newark. The essence of this mode of action entails the moving of a group of young people into a poor metropolitan area, where they themselves live and devote virtually all of their time to talking at length with the local residents about their problems, surveying major grievances, and presenting their findings to indigenous leaders in the community, whom they then assist in pressing these systematic formulations on the city's relevant "power structures." Out of these efforts have grown tenant unions, local *ad hoc* community action committees, neighborhood newsletters, and programs of adult education and tutorial services for school children. By 1966, 300 full-time field workers were representing SDS in over a dozen cities. Salaries rarely exceeded $15.00 per week; but the programs, though meagerly funded, all were financed independently, essentially through local donations, and ERAP had become something of a model for future efforts in SDS.

By the autumn of 1964, the war in Vietnam had become an increasingly serious object of criticism, and several chapters made it the focus of their energies. At the University of Michigan in particular, SDS members worked in close association with faculty members to organize the first teach-ins against the American posture in Southeast Asia. This anti-war emphasis spread rapidly across the country, and burst into full bloom in March, 1965, when the Ann Arbor teach-ins won considerable publicity in the national press, and in April, 1965, when 20,000 people, the majority of them students, converged on Washington to march against the war and to provide a platform for a wide variety of speakers critical of American policies in Vietnam. Reinforced by the success of this demonstration, the march or mass mobilization has continued as a major tactic in the anti-war movement and has spread to other issues as well. Having demonstrated its potency in organizing such affairs, SDS often has played a significant if not a key role in the development of new coalitions of national leadership and in the generating of student participation in relation to various problems, most of them associated with the war and the draft, which have evoked a strongly critical response from a significant segment of American youth and from a sizable proportion of liberal intellectuals.

Spurred by the model of the Free University of New York, SDS moved into a new realm of emphasis in 1965, this time on radical innovation in higher education. In 1965–66, nearly 100 Free Universities, most of them fragile and short-lived, were founded on U.S. campuses, about half of them coming to birth through SDS's local influences. As this experience cumulated, plans for a Radical Education Program (REP) were formulated nationally and came to fruition in an operation based in Ann Arbor, blessed by the Institute for Policy Studies, and devoted to stimulating and coordinating student investigations, ideas, and experiments with respect to college-level education. REP also collects "radical writing" from both the Old and the New Left on education, prepares annotated bibliographies of such items, and makes this kind of material available to SDS study groups on local campuses. The *Proposal*, published in 1966, out of which REP developed as an apparently viable though shoestring enterprise, is considered by many members of SDS as a fundamental document that ranks along with *The Port Huron Statement* in the literature of the organization.

Meanwhile, as the war in Vietnam and the draft, perceived as a mechanism for supplying young men to fight in battles of which they disapproved, became increasingly an object of criticism, some SDS chapters, recalling tactics of the civil rights movement, tried occasional sit-ins during the latter part of 1965 at local draft boards. Selective Service appeared unmoved, but the press paid a good bit of heed to these actions, and newspaper disenchantment with President Johnson's policies in Asia seemed to grow—if not because of, certainly concurrently with, stepped-up protest from college students. During the same period, SNCC, with apparent success, shifted to a much more militant set of postures; community organizing was legitimized by approval from the intellectuals and the welfare-oriented liberals; teach-ins still commanded impressive attention, both from within major colleges and universities and from outside the purely academic precincts; and Free Universities were taken up by a wide range of students, not infrequently including those involved with formal student governments. Thus encouraged, SDS quite deliberately took the step, in the words of the slogan donated by Arthur Waskow, "from dissent to resistance." In this new emphasis on institutional opposition, the organization began to initiate and to support individuals and groups in the public and ceremonial burning of draft cards, in the election of jail rather than military service, and in civil disobedience to obstruct the functioning of induction centers. In part at least, this move toward heightened activism grew out of the way in which military escalation and increased draft calls seemed to define the official response to speeches, publications, and a variety of public assemblies in opposition to the war. New tactics of a more drastic sort appeared necessary, and SDS was prepared to furnish them. Although Selective Service headquarters has reported that no more than 700 college students have burned or turned in their draft cards, SDS representatives are persuasive in arguing that this number is an underestimate for California alone and that the national estimate would be more accurate if it were 10 or even 20 times the size of General Hershey's comfortable number.

Most recently, the issue which SDS has emphasized has been that of university complicity in the Vietnamese war and in racial injustices. Charging that such complicity is more frequently a matter of how "the system" operates than it is one of some conspiracy of evil between government and higher education, students have been particularly sensitive to war-related research within the academy, to the recruitment of students by the CIA and representatives of the "industrial-military establishment," to perceived inadequacies in admissions policies with respect to Negro students or hiring policies with respect to Negro professors, and to a series of comparable matters. Civil disobedience and active resistance, not all of it nonviolent, have become more frequent in the SDS style of expression, rationalized on the ground that "the Establishment" fails to listen when protests are merely verbal.

The charge of academic complicity in war and social injustice and the alterations in style toward resistance as well as dissent have been reflected in the writings of such present officers as Carl Davidson, Robert Pardon, Gregory Calvert, and Michael Spiegal. In its insistence on the strategy and tactics of resistance, Davidson's *The Multiversity: Crucible of the New Working Class* is very different from *The Port Huron Statement* and the earlier work of such early SDS leaders as Hayden, Paul Potter, Paul Booth, and Carl Oglesby.

With—and perhaps in spite of—this hardening of line and approach, however, SDS continues to be a highly diversified and heterogeneous organization in both its membership and its activities. Community organizing programs, cut very much from the original ERAP cloth, continue to grow. "Radical education," taking its cue from REP, but not bound by its recommendations, is the central concern of a number of local chapters. In a variety of colleges and universities, the main investment of energy is in challenges to the *in loco parentis* doctrine and to parietal rules; on such issues, SDS rapidly forms alliances with representatives from the National Student Association, with the official personnel of formal student governments, and even with members of the highly conservative Young Americans for Freedom. Older SDS members, often calling themselves "alumni" of the organization, are busy in several institutions with efforts to build radical professional and professorial associations. In short, the evidence suggests that SDS has combined with reasonable effectiveness the business of generating new programs almost every year with the ability to retain old enterprises that appear particularly relevant and rewarding in special communities or on special campuses.

Financially, SDS clearly functions mainly because of a willingness among its leadership to participate in the affairs of the organization with little or no compensation. The annual budget nationally has never been more than $100,000; currently it is reported as between $80,000 and $90,000. Something over half, but under two-thirds, of this amount comes from dues and subscriptions; the balance comes from contributions, nearly all of which are reported as small, mostly under $10.00 in size, and virtually all of them under $25.00. "Alumni" are apparently the most reliable donors. For local programs or projects, money often is raised locally, typically from wealthier but sympathetic students. Such local fund drives seem to be too sporadic, unsystematic, and diffused for their results to be estimated with any accuracy.

About half of the expenditures at the national level are for staff salaries, which seem to average a little less than $20.00 per week, for the travel expenses of secretaries and members of the National Interim Council, and for similar costs. The balance of the budget is for the production and distribution of *New Left Notes* and other publications, the rent of the national office in Chicago, stationery and postage, telephone, and equipment items like duplicators and a mimeograph machine. Small amounts of money sometimes are contributed to local chapters to meet special needs. Legal costs are negligible; by means of closely maintained relationships with the American Civil Liberties Union, both through the ACLU's national headquarters in New York and its offices in a number of cities, the services of lawyers can be obtained for virtually nothing if, as is usually the case, an issue of civil liberties either is inherent in the situations that demand legal aid or can be injected into them.

Both by principle and as a result of its experience, SDS works with virually any individual or group with whom sympathies are shared in relation to any given issue. This point holds for both local and national activities. Indeed, there are many ways in which the potency of the organization lies in its capacity to develop constituencies outside of its own membership around the problems to which it chooses to address itself. One of its reasonably clear goals is that of "radicalizing" these constituencies, inducing a widening circle of young people to join it in its ambitions, as well as in its programs, through the personal relationships, the sense of belonging, and the experience of participation that collaboration with SDS tends to provide. Without contradiction, the organization also is quite willing to play a kind of bridging or linking role, holding more militant and more moderate factions in a particular situation in a working relationship. As more "alumni" become available to it, this kind of function becomes somewhat more apparent on campuses where student and faculty elements not infrequently are joined through the efforts of SDS into functional coalitions.

Increasingly, SDS members perceive no other political organization, either student or adult, as ahead of or above their own pattern of working together, and their aspirations have risen steadily as they have broadened. Sincere in their commitments to individualism, participatory democracy, and the primacy of conscience (often derived from the Nuremberg decisions) in an age of bureaucracy and institutionalized consensus, the leadership at least enjoys a rhetorical power that is broadly persuasive to many. Serious in their study of tactics and inventive in their application of them, they have achieved a degree of success that permits a feeling, significantly reinforcing whether or not it is accurate, that they played a major part in inducing President Johnson to decide against seeking another term in the White House. Thus exhilarated, SDS understandably has set its sights on the reforming of society at large, as well as on the reconstitution of the American university. So long as they need to lead only from the position of the negative critic, and are required neither to construct alternatives nor to administer them, they represent a force to conjure with in the increasing influence exercised by youth in the United States.

SNCC

The origins of the Student Nonviolent Coordinating Committee, like the origins of many such groups, are lost in the complexities of recent history. Perhaps the most obvious beginning can be attached to February, 1960, when four Negro students from the A. & T. College, Greensboro, North Carolina, after long and serious discussion among themselves, decided that direct action was required of *individuals* to achieve equal rights for black people. On February 1, they sat down at a lunch counter, requesting service which always had been reserved for whites. Within a week, learning of the action in the newspapers and by word of mouth, students on several other campuses in the South were organizing sit-ins of their own. With white and black students over the country joining the movement, over 100 sit-ins took place in the next two months. For the first time in America, young people—almost all of them college undergraduates—had seized political initiative with respect to a vital social issue.

By April 15, there already were over 60 centers of sit-in activity.

With a major role played by Ella Baker (formerly with the NAACP and the Urban League, and associated with the late Martin Luther King's Southern Christian Leadership Conference since 1957), a conference was called in 1961 at Shaw University, Raleigh, North Carolina, including 126 students and 58 adult delegates from different southern communities. Most of the participants already were experienced in direct-action techniques, and their meeting concentrated on questions of strategy and tactics and on how they might support one another most effectively as they continued to press for change through variations of the sit-in. The conference has been described as an *ad hoc* committee with mutual assistance and reinforcement as its major goal. To the dismay of some adults present, the students clearly voiced their disinterest in joining or becoming affiliated formally with established civil rights organizations. Although the students then developed no formal organization of their own, the conference foreshadowed the mood and behavior which would dominate SNCC meetings from its inception until 1966.

A month later, at Atlanta University, the Temporary Student Nonviolent Coordinating Committee was formed. Marion Barry, then a student at Fisk University, was elected chairman. The abolition of racial segregation was the central and explicit goal, and the sit-in mode of direct, nonviolent civil disobedience was identified as the most legitimate form of action. Despite the considerable diversity of the participants, agreement on a basic statement was not very difficult. Its essence was contained in the opening sentences:

We affirm the philosophical or religious ideal of nonviolence as the foundation of our purpose, the presupposition of our faith, and the manner of our action. Nonviolence as it grows from the Judaic-Christian tradition seeks a social order permeated by love. Integration represents the first step toward such a society. . . .

During the summer, SNCC set up temporary headquarters in a corner of the SCLC offices in Atlanta. Jane Stembridge dropped out of Union Theological Seminary to become the first office secretary. Julian Bond, then in student status, and Robert Moses, a Harvard graduate teaching high school in New York City, came to Atlanta for the summer. Together with SNCC officers and a growing number of part-time volunteers, they began to raise money, to plan nonviolent institutes for the summer, to print a newsletter called the *Student Voice,* and to attempt to coordinate student activities throughout the South. "Coordination" meant keeping abreast of plans for local action and, when possible, putting people in touch who might be able to help each other—e.g., protest leaders and sympathetic lawyers. This pattern set the norm and, with a few important exceptions, the limits of national organization throughout SNCC's history. By October, 1960, the number of sit-ins was increasing and winning attention in the national press; the Freedom Rides and other new thrusts were being planned; and the increased communication and travel of student activists nationally were making the vision of a "movement" seem, in student activists' minds, more and more capable of realization. Several hundred delegates met in Atlanta a little over a year later and put SNCC on a permanent basis.

SNCC was not at its beginnings and never has been a membership organization. "Members" are simply those people who share its sympathies and objectives, who by their own individual work and action define its activities, and who attend its meetings. Consequently, there is no structure of local chapters; and, until 1967, participation in SNCC's annual summer conference was entirely self-selective. (Even then, it possibly could be argued, whites did not attend out of respect for the blacks' decision to take responsibility for what they saw as a black problem, not out of explicit policies of exclusion.) Everyone attending these conferences was eligible to vote for national officers, for a 21-man executive committee, and on any statements presented for consideration.

Many student activists in other groups now point to SNCC as having pioneered a politically viable "staff organization," a critical concept in understanding contemporary student politics. Young people who take individual responsibility for direct action and community organizing are the self-selected staff, identifying themselves in terms of their commitments to issues or to the community in which they are organizing, rather than to a formal organization per se. To put this vital notion another way, responsibility is defined as much in terms of the responsiveness of SNCC "members" to the needs of the poor and the disenfranchised as in terms of the responsiveness of national officers to the mandates of members. A feeling of political, though emphatically non-ideological, fraternity and the mutual reinforcement of individual actions replace traditional organizational machinery in holding together these different levels of responsibility. SNCC always has been better understood as a movement than as an organization.

There have been three significantly different, though complexly overlapping and intertwined, phases in SNCC to date. Though not as clear as analytical categories make them seem, it is helpful to talk about the integrationist phase, the community-organizing phase, and the Black Power phase.

The first and *integrationist phase* focused upon equal rights under the Constitution, especially the Bill of Rights and the 13th, 14th, and 15th Amendments. In the rhetoric of liberalism and the Bible, SNCC emphasized a strategy of autonomous, sporadic acts, frequently direct-action civil disobedience. This included a wave of sit-ins, marches, and Freedom Rides to challenge local and state laws and customs which enforced public segregation, small and large symbolic marches on county seats, state capitals, and on Washington, D.C., in favor of stronger laws banning *de jure* and *de facto* discrimination, and the picketing of large corporations financially involved with segregated institutions. Twelve months after the first Greensboro sit-in, over 3,000 people spent time in jail (the NAACP Legal Defense Fund records defending 1,700 itself), a vast majority of them being young people in their twenties. Although the charges varied widely, almost all arrests were a result of civil disobedient acts. While other civil rights organizations moved steadily to follow SNCC's direct-action lead and, by the culmination of the integrationist phase in 1964–65, were the public leaders, it is probably meaningful, as often has been urged, to take the number of people (consistently a large majority of them students) actually arrested as a fair index measure of SNCC's special influence at the time. This figure appears to have exceeded 8,000 by 1966.

The *community-organizing phase* of SNCC began in August, 1961, when Robert Moses set off alone to begin a pilot voter-registration project in Amite County, Mississippi, perhaps the most segregated and lawless county in the South. Within three years, there were about 200 full-time volunteer "field workers" living and organizing in poor, usually rural, usually Negro communities. While chairman John Lewis and executive secretary James Forman represented SNCC in demonstrations and to the press, these field operatives built Freedom Schools to help adults gain the literacy necessary to pass voter-registration tests. They developed voter-registration campaigns, the best publicized, though not necessarily the most effective of which brought hundreds of students south in the summer of 1964; they served as the primary catalysts and early staff for such varied organizations as the Poor People's Corporation, the Mississippi Freedom Democratic Party, and the Black Panther Party in Lowndes County, Alabama. By 1966, the field workers clearly were the "hard core" of SNCC, the practitioners as well as the preachers of the New Left concept of "participatory democracy," which Moses probably coined for them. Dispersed all over the country, many worked with adult civil rights organizations; a few took field positions in the Community Action Projects of the War on Poverty; some went back to school or just rested for a while. Most—several hundred of them— have continued to live and work in the communities they first entered between 1961 and 1964.

The present *Black Power phase* of SNCC is difficult to comprehend. Its strongest roots seem to lie in the setbacks of 1964 and 1965: the increasing numbness of activist veterans from being beaten and jailed; the failure of the Mississippi Freedom Democratic Party to be seated at the 1964 Democratic Convention; the seeming impossibility of bringing the accused murderers of Goodman, Chaney, and Schwerner to trial; the increasing frustration of hard-core organizers with "moralistic" white, middle-class students who ventured south for as little as a weekend and at most a summer. All these factors seemed to create a sense of bitterness and a desire for more militant and effective forms of political power.

By 1966, figures showed that school integration was proceeding very slowly, and that the percentage of unemployed Negroes was increasing rather than decreasing. The federal government was perceived by activists as reluctant to enforce the 1965 Civil Rights Act; and, of greatest significance for them, Stokely Carmichael had been effective in organizing a countywide, all-black political party in Lowndes County. In May, 1966, the SNCC executive committee voted to endorse a close version of the Black Power statement drafted by the SNCC Vine Street Project in Atlanta almost a year before.

Thus, the focus of SNCC has shifted towards independent Black Power, fierce racial pride, and militant support of revolutionary forces in the Third World. Stokely Carmichael and then Rap Brown turned to making firebrand speeches against white "racism" in northern ghettos as well as in the South. New and old hard-core SNCC people began to organize student power fights on predominantly Negro campuses, to form Black Student Unions on predominantly white campuses, and, to a large degree, to go "underground." Many outsiders saw this as the death of SNCC, much as many had scoffed at the futility of SNCC's initial moves in both its integrationist and community-organizing phases. Recently, when Carmichael organized a Black United Front in Washington, D.C., the moderate Negro leadership joined in, as they put it, "to keep in touch with the grass roots." The ability to manage this kind of political feat, similar to the one which Martin Luther King failed to accomplish in Chicago a year and a half before, coupled with the growing acceptance of the rhetoric and strategy of "Black Power," both on college campuses and in metropolitan ghettos, suggests that SNCC may command, in a loose but effective fashion, the bulk of the Negro leadership in the United States.

If such is the case, then a number of expectations follow from it, some of them at least partially confirmed by the events of 1968. One is an increasing number of all-black political blocs and even political parties at local levels and within student movements. A second is sporadic, but increasing, numbers of rebellions in predominantly Negro colleges, many of which will be successful. Third, there is a possibility that a Black Student Union will spin off from the National Student Association, splitting that organization along racial lines, and reducing to some degree the probability and effectiveness of any coalition of the more moderate and typically liberal students of both ethnic groups. Fourth, there almost is sure to be a strongly encouraged, continuing, and militant demand by Negro students on white campuses for special housing arrangements, for special curricular offerings, and for black professors and administrators. Fifth, SNCC may officially reject its commitment to non-violence. Some of the workers in SNCC offices in Washington and in New York and the *SNCC Newsletter* (which continues to appear occasionally although the central headquarters in Atlanta has been closed) are given to the rhetoric of "by any means necessary," and imply that there is substance behind the talk of weapons being cached against a day when "the word is passed." One hardly knows what to make of responses to unofficial inquiries of police and the Department of Justice, but these sources deny any systematic efforts along these frightening lines. At the same time, the facilitation of riots and the practice of acts of technical sabotage by no means are unthinkable in this context.*

Without a central office, and with Stokely Carmichael under sur-

*In the summer of 1969, SNCC altered its name, substituting "National" for "Non-violent."—Eds.

veillance and Rap Brown under sentence, SNCC has been described recently as "merely a group of 150 wandering, homeless, hard-core militants." There is much that seems accurate in this characterization. But for all its shapelessness, this organization appears to enjoy a discipline, a flexibility, and a degree of sympathy and loyalty—among some white young people as well as Negroes—that make it a strong, serious force despite (or even because of) its lack of firm outlines. Some of those "wandering militants" show up on campuses that are ripe for trouble or after protest activities have broken out, and it is reported by student and faculty sources from some colleges that both the intensity and the discipline of black students can be accounted for significantly by this kind of outside leadership.

The funding of SNCC never has been easy to understand. Its decentralized and fragmentary organization is complicated by the fact that financial records, apparently seldom adequate at any point in SNCC's history, have been lost or destroyed. Three points seem relatively sure. One is that SNCC began with no money at all in any central organizational till, and that the local projects which it has emphasized consistently more often than not have returned to a state of no money at all. In these local enterprises, office space was borrowed, donations or loans of second-hand equipment were solicited, and field workers lived with families in the region in which they happened to be working. In many ways, it is the SNCC field workers' strong and articulate tradition of living on "subsistence or less" that has made both them as individuals and the organization itself beyond fiscal comprehension in the usual sense and beyond financial constraints when outside funds have not been available. Second, the peak annual budget was reached, it would seem, in 1963–64, when about $250,000 was raised by direct-mail appeals, benefit performances by Negro entertainers and artists, and occasional foundation grants. In this period, it must be remembered, SNCC was concerned much more with desegregation than with Black Power, and was inclined less toward the militancy that has marked its activities in more recent years. Estimates indicate that about a fourth of that top budget was spent for field staff salaries that averaged $10–$15 per week. Another quarter, roughly, went for supplies, printing, and postage—mainly in the service of publishing pamphlets, posters, newsletters, press releases, etc. The balance, possibly running as high as $150,000, went into local projects in Mississippi, Alabama, and Georgia. Third, since 1965, money for this kind of loosely conducted, informal, and overwhelmingly and almost exclusively Negro civil rights work has become increasingly hard to come by; and since 1966, when SNCC vociferously espoused the Black Power doctrine and stance, both Negro and white sources of funds virtually have dried up. Some field workers have taken jobs in order to support their community efforts; some have taken to panhandling as a way of acquiring the small amounts of money necessary to their continuing to function in some minimal fashion. Most of Carmichael's money—and it has obviously been a good deal—has come from speaking engagements, and a fair proportion of it is understood as having been reinvested in the purposes SNCC has represented, if not directly in SNCC itself. The same seems to be generally true of Rap Brown. Although there is some talk about money for SNCC through "sources at the United Nations" and through Communist sources, there seems to be no way to verify these notions, and there seems to be little evidence of money being spent that could not be explained as earned by SNCC people or as donated in small amounts. The amounts are far from large, and, insofar as one can determine from a confused and cloudy picture, finances are not central to SNCC's influence.

With respect to its relationships with other groups, SNCC has maintained an insistent independence. When they have joined coalitions or organizations, SNCC has been clear about its own stand on the particular issue, and regularly has tended to pull the other associations into more radical positions. As the integrationist phase of the civil rights movement has faded, however, it has withdrawn from national programs and shown much less interest in united fronts. Its stress has been on local communities, including some college campuses, where SNCC representatives have shown a good deal of talent in building alliances among highly diverse people, including some whites as well as blacks. As in the early sit-ins, the criterion of these alliances has been a matter of commitment to issues felt as important by local people, and this sensitivity to grass-roots frustration and discontent gives it a potency that seems to exceed by far its organizational resources, its financial capability, or its numbers of active workers. If SNCC has become more a psychological force than a national association, it is not without a shadowy but considerable power.

As is pointed out in the chapter "Black Protest," in 1968, a number of black leaders met at Shaw University, the birthplace of SNCC, to form an organization to replace SNCC on the college campus. Calling itself the Congress for the Unity of Black Students (CUBS), the group agreed to press for more black students on campus and to support demands for black studies and other programs exclusively for their race. Although the organization's name has been conspicuously absent from the news, its objectives and the views of Ron Karenga, LeRoi Jones, and James Cheek, all speakers at the organizational session, have clearly been accepted by a significant proportion of black college students.

Whether CUBS, SNCC, SDS, or NSA, activist student organizations have carefully developed the skill of exploiting the particular weaknesses of a campus to secure a wide range of support and the maximum of propaganda value. Further, the most radical groups have become expert at infiltrating other groups. One of the most effective tactics is the radical's and the radical organization's creation of temporary one-issue coalitions which draw "official" support from a variety of campus groups. A multiplicity of small groups (even with overlapping membership), all issuing statements of support for a demonstration on a particular issue, can be very effective in the propaganda battle. An additional tactic of warfare often practiced by radical groups is to formulate the issue in as "uncompromising" terms as possible. An *ad hoc* coalition sometimes accomplishes that purpose more effectively than can a group with a more familiar set of vested ideological interests.

It is clear that activist students are mastering the arts of tactical organization with which to confound their institutions and to win new cohorts to their ideologies. These arts are effective only where there is a widespread dissatisfaction among the great majority of students who are still not habitually activist, but this kind of discontent can be mobilized around a large number of concerns. Mere recognition or non-recognition by the university of the organization which foments revolutionary protest is in itself neither a defense nor a solution. Formal organizations and informal groups, developed to achieve a temporary specific objective or to express a particular sentiment, are only the carriers of student desires and student ideas. Activists do not invest their commitments in organizations *per se;* they regard them simply as the vehicles for deeper concerns. Only a considered and sustained response by universities to those concerns can preserve their integrity and insure their effectively continued operation as socially useful educational enterprises.

THREE

Scenes of Conflict: Seven Case Studies

AN INTRODUCTION TO THE CASE STUDIES

by Julian Foster and Durward Long

PROTEST ACTIVITIES, especially those which are violent or successful, or both, are news. To harassed administrators it may indeed seem that nothing else that happens on their campuses is so well reported. Years of patient work may be carried on in obscurity, only to have the public image of the institution formed during a few hours of chaos. Whatever the desirability of this, there is no doubt that one who desires information about a particular protest can find it in the files of the campus paper, the local press or—in cases of major disruption—in national news magazines.

A case study must be more than an hour by hour account of what happened, or a summary of the press coverage. We have selected the chapters which follow not only because they describe events at a particular campus, but because they do one or more of three additional things. The first of these is to place events in perspective, and to analyze the factors which underlie them. The second is to place the story of one campus in a general setting, and to draw from it hypotheses and conclusions which may be applicable elsewhere. The third is to illuminate the problem of evidence and truth. Few observers can be neutral towards a phenomenon like student protest, and it is doubtful that any should lay claim to complete objectivity. The most "factual" description of events is inevitably selective, for each reporter must choose whatever seems to him significant from the welter of raw data which face him. Thus when the police drove the students from Columbia's buildings, a violent process accompanied by hundreds of injuries and arrests, *The New York Times* gave its readers a lengthy and heartrending account of the condition of Grayson Kirk's office, with emphasis on the loss of his personal ashtrays. Less establishment periodicals like the *New Republic* stressed instead the happy and courageous spirit of the activists before "the big bust," and on the property damage done by the police. We believe that some of the chapters in this section reflect viewpoints on protest which are widespread, and which must be understood in context, since they are those of the participants themselves.

The first study—"Indiana: The Anatomy of Violence"—has a purview which is the most limited of any in this section, yet paradoxically the amount of evidence gathered exceeds that for any other chapter. In its effort to determine exactly what happened and why during a few minutes in the University's Placement Office, a Faculty Committee spent more than 30 hours interviewing 23 arrested students; read the transcripts of ten trials and the reports of two police departments; interviewed three deans, four policemen and eight other staff members; and inspected 311 photographs taken by four different reporters. The Committee comments that "throughout this investigation we have had to deal with conflicting testimony and with mistakes in the identification of people or recalling a sequence of actions. We have resolved these difficulties where we could, but . . ." The resultant report is a lesson in the search for and ultimate impossibility of objectivity.

Any protest action can be perceived in relative isolation, or as part of an on-going sequence of events. Durward Long, writing from a vantage point in but not of the administration at the University of Wisconsin, focuses on the development of protest and of administrative responses to it. When an attempt is made to evaluate what was done in response to protest, the key difficulty is that one cannot know how alternatives would have worked out. The University of Wisconsin underwent two radical changes in its style and strategy of response to protest during a relatively short time, enabling the observer to make better comparisons than are usually possible. Ralph Goldman's perspective as a faculty member at San Francisco State College is also somewhat detached from the battle which enveloped his campus. Exploited by student and faculty militants, faculty unions, conservative trustees and ambitious office seekers, events at San Francisco are a classic example of the academic community torn apart by largely external political pressures.

The next two chapters illustrate the effects of a firmly partisan perspective. Jerry Hoffman was a leading spokesman for SDS at Princeton during 1967–68, and his account of events there naturally reflects this. Billy Mac Jones worked in the Office of the Vice President for Student Affairs at the University of Colorado during the same period, and the subtitle he has chosen—"Sounds of Student Protest Deftly Muted"—reveals his approach.

The relativity of truth is illustrated by the reactions of members of the Princeton faculty and administration to the Hoffman account. They insist, for example, that Mr. Hoffman's picture of the University's students, clubs, faculty and trustees reveal more about radical perspectives than they do about Princeton. Mr. Hoffman looks at the legal structure of the University, and asserts that the faculty lacks power; others dismiss these as "corporate technicalities" and assert the contrary. Changing positions, Mr. Hoffman turns behavioral in interpreting the withdrawal of Princeton from the Institute of Defense Analyses as a repudiation of war-related research and a triumph for the values of SDS; his critics revert to a more legalistic style, pointing out that the faculty resolution recommending withdrawal from IDA explicitly denied such political import. Mr. Hoffman stresses the refusal of the trustees to meet with SDS; others suggest that the willingness of a trustee committee to hear SDS, and the latter's rejection of this invitation, was more significant. It is evident that in these and many other respects it would be impossible to reach a consensus on "the facts."

Such failures of communication are a vital feature of student protest. While to an administrator radical perceptions may seem simply erroneous, the reverse is also likely to be true. Dr. Jones' chapter originally provoked the more protest-minded of the editors to several pages of detailed and vitriolic criticism. But on reflection, it seemed more enlightening to let the accounts stand as they are, rather than to impose some impossible goal of neutrality or interpretive consistency upon them.

The next chapter is by an outsider rather than a participant. Lawrence B. de Graaf is a white historian who served as a visiting lecturer at Howard University during that institution's recent upheaval. From his vantage point as an outsider-participant, de Graaf sees present events at Howard as springing directly out of the past, and as intertwined with the larger history of the Negro people in the mid-twentieth century.

Finally, James Turner describes more than a decade of struggle against censorship at the Ohio State University. Himself a participant in some of the events he records, Mr. Turner was the only one of these writers able to draw on some scholarly work already completed. While most accounts are necessarily incomplete because they deal with events still continuing, this particular series of happenings at Columbus appears to be finished, the goals of the protesters having been attained. We felt that to demonstrate that protest could have an end might be an encouragement to some of our readers.

1

INDIANA: THE ANATOMY OF VIOLENCE

by The Faculty Committee to Investigate the Dow Incident of Indiana University*

ON OCTOBER 30, 1967, a group composed almost entirely of Indiana University students went to the Graduate School of Business Building to attempt to persuade a recruiter for the Dow Chemical Company to debate the morality of Dow's manufacture of napalm. The subsequent events of that day precipitated a crisis in the life of the University: the administration, the faculty, graduate and undergraduate students, and many outside of the University were drawn into a debate that was intense, often acrimonious, sometimes salutary, and always in need of more facts than could be obtained from the news media or administrative statements.

Since there had been demonstrations protesting the presence of Dow recruiters on many campuses prior to last October, there was good reason to expect one here. The first administrative action taken in anticipation of such a demonstration originated with Professor J. Douglas Snider of the Business Placement Bureau. He telephoned

---

* This chapter is based on the report of faculty committee at the University of Indiana, which undertook to clarify the events surrounding the Dow demonstration of October 30, 1967. Members of the committee were Albert Klassen (research sociologist), Frederick Stare (Psychology), Priscilla Zirker (English) and Charles Eckert (English). The report has been shortened somewhat, those sections of mainly local interest being deleted, and is used by permission.

Captain William G. Spannuth, I. U. Director of Safety, on the morning of Tuesday, October 24. He explained that the Dow Chemical Company would have several job interviewers at the Business Placement Bureau on the following Monday and Tuesday, October 30 and 31, and he requested that Captain Spannuth meet with him to consider what measures should be taken if a demonstration occurred.

That same afternoon, Captains Spannuth and Dillon met with Professor Snider at the Business Building to look at the area where interviews were held and to make plans in relation to it. Since they knew of no intended demonstration on this campus, they had to think in terms of the student demonstrations which had occurred elsewhere. Relying upon their familiarity with such incidents (Captain Spannuth told us that he had viewed movies of violent demonstrations), they anticipated the possibility of "fist fights," the need to carry out students who refused to leave, and so forth.

After this initial meeting a general plan was developed for controlling a demonstration if one materialized. Because the plans that were made determined many of the subsequent events, we have attempted to summarize them from explicit statements and from inferences we have drawn from actions taken prior to the demonstration of October 30.

First of all, two pairs of I. U. Safety Officers in plain clothes were to take turns patrolling the first-floor hallway in the Business Building —particularly in the vicinity of the Interview Room. This patrolling, which was to begin at 8:00 A.M. and continue throughout Monday, October 30, was to serve two purposes: to detect and report any signs of a developing demonstration, and to place officers where they might be needed. Some thought was given to moving the interviews to a new location, but because this would inconvenience everyone concerned, and as there were as yet no indications of a demonstration, this was decided against.

Second, Dean of Students Shaffer was to be informed immediately if a demonstration began. He would then arrange for the prompt representation of the University administration by someone from the Student Activities Office (the supervision of demonstrations is one of the duties of Dean Smith of this office).

Third, Captains Spannuth, Dillon and Cox and other officers of the Safety Division would come to the Business Building. All ranking officers of the I. U. Safety Division have been deputized by the Sheriff of Monroe County and carry official credentials. They could therefore back up administrative officials with the threat of arrest. They could also provide an even more important deterrent: in the past, any student disobedience in direct confrontation with a Safety Division Officer (such as the attempt to enter the door blocked by Captain Dillon which is described later in this report) has always led to severe disciplinary action.

Fourth, decisions were made concerning what student behavior would or would not be tolerated. We have been told that Dean Shaffer approved (and perhaps originated) the plan to permit protesting students to gather in the hallway outside the reception area of Room 131 in the Business Building, if they remained orderly and did not become a safety hazard. Demonstration within University buildings is, of course, prohibited by the Regulations Affecting Student Life, published by Dean Shaffer's office. However, the students were not to be permitted to enter Room 131, and the police were instructed to arrest those who did so.

Fifth, to provide for a large-scale and potentially violent demonstration, the Bloomington Police Department and the Indiana State Police were to be briefed and on the alert.

Sixth, an arrangement was made with the administrator of the I. U. Campus Bus Service to provide buses should they be needed for transporting arrested students to the Monroe County Jail.

Having developed this plan, Captains Spannuth and Dillon met with Bloomington Chief of Police James East and his subordinates and with members of the Indiana State Police. They briefed them concerning a possible demonstration and their plans for dealing with it. According to established procedures, off-campus police can come to aid Safety Division Officers only on calls received from Captains Spannuth, Dillon or Cox. At this time, it was their responsibility to determine at what point assistance was needed, and whatever the circumstances, it was understood that Captain Spannuth was in charge of all officers present on campus.

These preparations for the demonstration ignored two possible actions: Captain Spannuth did not see any need to inform the Office of the President, nor were concerned students asked about their plans. The only additional actions taken by University officials seem to have been a phone call made by Dean Shaffer about noon of Sunday, October 29, to brief Dean Smith on the plans that had been made, and a luncheon discussion between the two on Monday, during which they concluded that there probably would be no demonstration.

There was, indeed, no reason to expect a demonstration, even at that late hour. The earliest date for any discussion of a demonstration by students was apparently Thursday, October 26, when the *Herald-Telephone* carried an announcement of the Dow interviewers' forthcoming visit. A friend called this announcement to the attention of Russell Block, Chairman of the Student Committee to End the War in Vietnam (CEWV), and Block determined to discuss a possible demonstration at a meeting of the CEWV scheduled for Friday, October 27. At that meeting, however, all attention was turned to preparations for demonstrating against Dean Rusk, who was due to speak on campus on October 31. The hour was late before the subject of the Dow interviews came up. It was obvious that there was little time to prepare a second demonstration, that the Rusk demonstration could be jeopardized by one preceding it, and that everyone was too exhausted to debate the matter further.

Over the weekend, however, students continued to discuss the visit of the Dow recruiters, in casual conversations and as they prepared mimeographed "hand-out sheets" and picketing posters for the Rusk demonstration. It was generally felt that something should be done; but on the morning of Monday, October 30, there was still no consensus for a demonstration, few ideas as to the form one might take, and no information as to where or when the Dow interviews would be held.

By about 10:30, after several phone calls, the presence of the Dow interviewers was verified, and groups of students in hallways and in the coffee lounge passed the news along. Russell Block and Robin Hunter, confronted with queries about action, agreed to open the question again at an impromptu meeting to be held in Ballantine Plaza at 1:00 in the afternoon. Again this news was spread by word of mouth, and a few students began making signs on scratch paper for the occasion.

By 1:15 the meeting had attracted a small crowd; as it progressed, more people joined. Block and Mark Ritchey led the discussion about what action, if any, the group wanted to take in relation to Dow's presence. The students generally felt that they had a right to demand that the recruiters speak to them. Some talked of a sit-in if they were met with refusal. Others mentioned the University's war-complicity in providing space for Dow.

Classes were again in session in Ballantine after 1:30, and the talking in the plaza disturbed at least one teacher. He shouted his displeasure to the group, suggesting that they respect the rights of others. At the same time voices in the plaza were asking the speakers to talk louder. It was clear that deliberations could not be continued in that spot. Acting on what seemed a consensus, Block and Ritchey led the gathered students to the Business Building, discussing on the way what should be done when they arrived.

The number of students involved in the meeting and march varied from moment to moment, and estimates vary with witnesses. Robin Hunter reported that 25 had gathered in the plaza when he arrived at 1:20. The CEWV estimated that between 75 and 100 marched to the Business Building. The Shaffer-Snider-Smith report says that 45 to 50 students "appeared" at the building. It is certain that many students joined the demonstration at the 2:15 class break and therefore could not have been part of the march.

At about 2:00, the students arrived at a large reception office, Room 231, and talked amicably with the secretary there. She told them where the interviews were to be held, and while most of the students sat in Room 231, Block and Ritchey went downstairs to request a meeting with one of the Dow interviewers.

The secretary in Room 131, Joyce Bergman, was worried by the arrival of the two students. She called Frank Bianchi, a graduate student who was on duty in the office, to talk with the students. There were different versions of the conversations that ensued. Mr. Bianchi recognized Block and Ritchey as "typical protesters" with long hair and no ties—a type not often seen on those premises. When they said they wanted to talk with the Dow interviewer about his company's manufacture of napalm, Bianchi told them that they couldn't because they hadn't signed up for interviews by 11 A.M. the previous day. According to Block, when he and Ritchey made their request, they were told that their hair was too long, their shoes unshined, and that they had no appointment and had not turned in 50 copies of their résumés.

In the meantime, Mr. McHutchinson, one of the Dow recruiters, was informed that demonstrators had arrived. Asked if he wanted to talk with the students, McHutchinson said that he would see only those who had signed up for interviews; to do more would be against company policy in his view. This message was conveyed to Block and Ritchey. Since the students had read in newspapers that Dow representatives had previously met with groups and discussed their position, they did not take the refusal as final. When they insisted that they had fifty people waiting to speak with the Dow man, Bianchi asked where they were. Block replied that they were upstairs and that he would bring them down. While Ritchey waited, Block went to Room 231, told the students what had happened, and asked them to come down to Room 131.

Bianchi warned Ritchey, who stayed in the ante-room, that the students would not be permitted to enter there, that they would have to stay in the hallway outside. When Block returned with the students, Ritchey passed this information on to him and then left the group to make some phone calls. Down the hallway he noticed curious spectators gathering and conversing. After attempting to phone other students who could bring support to the demonstration, he left the building to go to Block's apartment for leaflets that would explain to gathering onlookers the presence and purpose of the students.

Soon after the students came downstairs, one of the officers patrolling the first floor hallway called the Safety Division officials to tell them of the arrival of the demonstrators. Captain Dillon telephoned Chief East "to inform him that a demonstration was in progress," then went with Captains Spannuth and Cox to Room 131, arriving about 2:15. Professor Snider called Dean Shaffer and he in turn asked Dean Smith to send someone from his office; Smith decided to go himself. A number of graduate assistants, job interviewers, and students awaiting interviews were also in the room at this time.

During the period between 2:15 and 2:45 the officials inside the room watched the students closely. Dean Smith was at first worried about the possibility of windows being broken because of the congestion in the hall, but he observed that the students were orderly and they seemed content to stay in the hallway. He also told this committee that he feared for the safety of the Dow interviewer should he come out to meet the group: "I felt that his life might be in danger." Randall Powell of the placement office thought that the student spokesman had the demonstration under control and that there was no reason for fear or apprehension.

His reaction was shared by most of those in the room; but one of the graduate assistants urged the Safety Division officials to remove the students from the hallways. When students taped signs to the outside of the windows, he took one down (it was against Business School regulations to post signs inside the building); but then he was told by Professor Snider to leave the signs where they were. About 2:30 Captain Dillon made a second call to Chief East to tell him of the progress of the demonstration. In the hall during this period, the protest leaders repeatedly asked the students to maintain an open passageway and to avoid gathering in groups. Photos show that their requests were complied with and that most of the students sat against the walls conversing or reading. A few passed out anti-war literature to bystanders or discussed the demonstration with them, and others made signs from notebook paper which they held or taped to the windows of Room 131. Typical signs read, "War is good business, but does it belong in the Business School?" and "Check your appearance. Are you responsible enough to be interviewed by the makers of jellied death?"

At the 2:15 class break more onlookers gathered at the edges of the demonstrating group to watch or to taunt them, and the hallway became more difficult to keep open. One of the demonstrators, because he was concerned about the congestion, telephoned a secretary in Room 131 and asked if the demonstration would interfere with an interview appointment he had made. The secretary said that everything was all right and that he should keep his appointment. Another student, Karen Nichols, entered Room 131 and sat down near the door. Frank Bianchi asked her to leave, but Dean Smith thought that she should be left alone. After a few minutes she rejoined those in the hall and told some of them that they could sit in the room if they wanted to. No others entered at this time, however.

During this same period (2:15–2:45), there were a number of conversations at the doorway between student spokesmen (principally Dan Kaplan and Robin Hunter) and Dean Smith and Professor Snider. In these conversations, Dan Kaplan repeated the students' request to see a Dow representative to discuss with him the morality of Dow's manufacture of napalm. He said that they would wait until current interviews were ended or meet with the Dow interviewer at another time. Dean Smith replied that the Dow interviewer would not meet with them, but that they could continue their demonstration in the hallway as long as no fire hazard was created. They could not, he said, enter the room and would be arrested if they did.

As the minutes passed and as it became clear that the Dow interviewer would not appear before them, the students began to doubt the effectiveness of their demonstration. When someone suggested at 2:40 that they enter the reception room, a general discussion followed. The leaders tried to impress on the group the implications of such an action. Russell Block insisted that no action should jeopardize the Rusk demonstration the following day. Dan Kaplan tried to impress on the group that entry almost certainly meant arrest and that if they entered the room they should be prepared to stay. Some students had the understanding that entry would be as simple a matter for them as it had been for Karen Nichols—that they had only to walk into Room 131 to confront the Dow representative or at the least to register their disapproval of the interviews; others, however, anticipated that there would be trouble. Only a small part of the group were affected enough by Block's and Kaplan's admonitions to vote against going in.

The question of when to enter was then discussed and many of those who had enthusiastically voted to go in were for immediate action. Others suggested that they enter at 3:00. Kaplan asked for a longer wait, but the students, tired of waiting already, would not approve. A vote was then taken by voice and show of hands. The decision, delivered by Kaplan to Dean Smith, took the form of a forceful ultimatum: if the Dow representative did not come out to talk by three o'clock, the students would enter Room 131.

Soon after the vote was taken, Captain Dillon made a third call to Chief East requesting immediate assistance. He then went to the door, held up his badge, informed the nearby students who he was, and told them that they would be arrested if they entered the room. In court Dillon testified that he spoke at a normal voice-level and that some of the students looked directly at him and laughed as he spoke, and that one student said, "That's Safety. We'll walk over them." A number of students said that they could not hear him, and others said that they did not see him at the door.

At an earlier time the door had been momentarily locked, but in the last few minutes before 3:00, in response to student statements that the door was locked, the door was opened to show students that it was not locked. Dean Smith felt that if it were kept locked and if the students attempted to force it open, they might break it down or break the windows and cause serious injuries. When the 3:00 deadline arrived, John D'Arcy tried the door, then told the group that it was locked (it may have seemed locked; we were told that occasionally someone inside held the doorknob). Several students who were tense with anticipation felt relieved when they heard that the door was locked. It seemed that the demonstration had gone as far as it could go. A few seconds later, however, a click was heard, and another student tried the door and found it open.

At this point, one student stuck a book between the opened door and the jamb, and Captain Cox took the book and threw it on a desk. What happened from this point on was recorded in a series of over 50 photos made by four cameramen from the local press, who were inside the room. Arranged in sequence, these photos provide an almost cinematic record of the entry into the room. The first eight show that Captain Dillon stood holding the door slightly ajar as several of the students spoke to him. The next nineteen photos record Captain Dillon's attempt to hold the door. As several students began to push at the door, Captain Dillon grabbed the edge of the door with his left hand and the outer door jamb with his right hand. Captain Spannuth placed his shoulder against the door itself. As the door was slowly forced open, the students in the vanguard of the group were pressed against the door and Captain Dillon's arms.

Dwight Worker testified in court that he told others several times to push against the door, but not against people. As he entered he got under Dillon's right arm, then placed his elbow against the door jamb applying strong pressure to Dillon's arm and body. Dillon alleges that Worker also kicked his ankles and legs and that he suffered bruises, including a severe one on his left ankle. Other students visible in the photos appear reluctant to push against Captain Dillon. There are occasional smiles—perhaps owing to the awkwardness of the situation. At some point, one of the girls scratched Dillon's arm with her fingernails and another student attempted to pry his fingernails from the door jamb. David Hunter asked Dillon to let the group through. The last of this long series of photos shows that added pressure from those in the hallway finally broke Captain Dillon's grip on the door jamb.

The next series of photos shows that the entering students attempted to get around the Safety Division officials, but that at least two of the students were grabbed by Captains Dillon and Spannuth and that, as a result, there was a vigorous struggle. One of the Business personnel saw both Captain Dillon and Captain Spannuth lose their footing; he thought that a rather slippery tile floor was partly responsible. The door was partly blocked again; but because the pressure of the group was too strong, officials allowed the last fifteen to twenty students to enter unopposed.

In court, Captain Dillon testified that James Wallihan struck Captain Spannuth in the ribs with his fist as he entered (a charge Wallihan denies), but this is the only allegation of assault by entering students that we have heard, except for the charges against Dwight Worker. Not all of the students pushed to gain entry; some of those we have interviewed emphasized that once the group began to move, there was nothing to do but go along with it: "Going in was like riding on a bubble."

Once inside, the students seated themselves on couches or on the floor in the center of the room. Some laughed, others gestured to those looking in to join them, and others told the group to link arms. After a few minutes of disorganized talking during which one or more of the students shouted emotionally at the officials in the room, the question of how they should proceed with the demonstration arose again. Marco Walshok stood up and told the group that they should explain what they were demonstrating against, and that they should do so in an orderly fashion, speaking one at a time.

The conversations of the next fifteen minutes were orderly with only occasional loudness or attempts by several to speak at once. Impressions of the debate vary considerably; some of the Business personnel found the student arguments respectable and rational; others thought them irrational and "truculent." The students generally thought that their questions were received with sarcasm or contempt.

Throughout this period, one of the Dow interviewers sat in Room 131Q, not ten feet from the students at the back of the room. One student who entered for an interview testified in court that he had to squeeze by and step over students in order to get in Room 131Q; the photos show, on the other hand, that the students attempted to maintain passageways by sitting closely together. No attempt was made to locate the Dow interviewers or to interrupt them. The students' intention remained the same: to sit-in until an interviewer agreed to meet with them.

Off-campus police began to arrive at the Business Building at 2:45, about the time the students were voting. Officer Branam testified in court that he was advised by Chief East to take riot equipment with him. This equipment is not normally carried in police cars. According to Chief East, a total of about 10 or 20 Bloomington police, some in plain clothes, others in riot helmets and uniforms, were present before 3:15. Deputies from the County Sheriff's Office also arrived. The State Police, some with full riot equipment including gas grenades, did not arrive until students were already being taken from the building, and did not, so far as we can discover, make arrests.

The police were advised of what was happening in the interview room by Captains Spannuth, Dillon, and Cox, and, at their direction, entered the Business Building about 3:15–3:20. Officer Branam testified that he heard Captain Dillon tell the students that they were under arrest for disorderly conduct, and that he himself repeated the statement. Lieutenant Simes added that they could leave peacefully or be taken out by force. This is a rough paraphrase of a statement that we have heard in many versions including "You can walk out or get hurt"; the statement was at least strong enough that one student asked Simes for his name and was given it.

These statements were apparently made at a normal voice-level and were heard by perhaps half of the students. Others, engaged in conversation or seated far from the door, say that they didn't hear what the police said and were not aware of their intentions until they saw the arrest and removal begin.

Captain Dillon and a plainclothesman then took Norman Krampetz, who was seated nearest the door, by the hands. Krampetz heard someone say, "If you don't walk out, we'll carry you out." He asked if he could walk out, and was allowed to get to his feet. At this point many conversations began, some students electing to leave because they were fearful of the riot-sticks, or because they felt that the demonstration had run its course, and others discussing the prospects of staying in the room. Most of the students stood up, gathered their books, and prepared to leave.

Apparently the police were unsystematic in their arrests; some students were taken by the arm or merely escorted individually to a bus in the parking lot, others walked out in small groups, and a few simply stepped into the crowd in the hall and avoided arrest. There were no serious incidents during these arrests, and about 22 students boarded the bus. Estimates of the length of time this action took range from one to twenty minutes. Certainly there was some lapse of time, since two officers who can be seen escorting students to the bus were involved in later actions in the room. Approximately 15 students remained in the room, most of them toward the back and most of them standing. Some were still discussing whether to leave or not, a few sitting on a couch had linked arms, and three had donned helmets which, according to their testimony, they carried with them because they had ridden motorbikes to school.

While some of the last students to leave voluntarily were walking out and while some of those remaining were trying to decide what to do, four policemen approached those seated on the couch. According to the courtroom testimony of Captain Dillon, Ann McNaughton screamed, "Police brutality," before the police touched anyone. In conversations with Safety Division and Administration personnel we were told that this screaming appeared to be planned. At any rate, it was believed to have added to the disorder and tension in the room, and Miss McNaughton was given a heavier sentence in court than others accused only of disorderly conduct. The students who remember the screaming say it began as the police pulled students from the couch, and none remember the phrase "police brutality." Officer Branam testified that he and Lieutenant Simes used their hands in seizing two students from the couch; however, student witnesses, Business personnel, and photos indicate that riot-sticks were used from the beginning of these forcible arrests.

William Lhamon, seated on the couch, was jabbed in the stomach with a stick, and slipped to the floor. There, he covered his head with his hands and drew his legs up against his body, receiving repeated jabs to head and body. He then rolled over and grabbed the stick of the officer who stood straddling him. According to Lhamon, the officer became furious, twisted the stick free, kicked him in the back and jabbed him with the stick. Lhamon got his head under the couch, heard the officer curse him and ask him if he was done now; he was then pinned to the floor by a stick against his temple. Finally he was carried or dragged out to the bus, hearing cries of "Hit them again" from bystanders.

Robert Johnson stood up as the police approached, intending to walk out and urging others to stand. After warding off a blow or two, he was forced first to his knees and then back to his feet by a stick under his chin. Johnson grabbed the stick and was then pushed so that he spun backwards towards the door and against Captain Dillon, protester Jane Dillencourt and others.

There is a total conflict of testimony about what happened next. Captain Dillon testified that he was struck on the left side of his jaw, then turned and saw Johnson and asked him if he had struck the blow. According to Dillon, Johnson cursed him, said that he had struck the blow, and would hit him again if he had the chance. Sergeant Wilson of the Bloomington Police testified that he saw the blow. According to Johnson, Captain Dillon grabbed Jane Dillencourt by the hair, and Johnson in turn grabbed Dillon's wrist and pulled his hand away, but did not strike him. Dillon denies that he grabbed "any girl" by the hair. Dillon next told officers to "Get that colored man and book him for assault," a phrase he felt was the logical way of identifying Johnson, the only Negro in the room. Business personnel and students both testify to shouts of "Get that colored boy" or "Get the nigger," both before and after the incident at the door.

Dwight Worker was pulled from the couch by a stick placed around the back of his neck, under the edge of his helmet. On the floor, the back of his helmet was pulled up and he was struck on the back of the neck. About this time, Officer Branam was tripped or fell over Worker's body; he and another officer dragged Worker to the east side of the room, where Branam got behind Worker, pulled his helmet up, and struck him on the back of the neck. Worker kicked at Branam and grabbed his stick; Branam dragged Worker across the floor, twisted his stick loose, pulled Worker's helmet up and (by his own and photographic testimony) struck him once or twice in the mouth with his fist. During this struggle, Worker kicked repeatedly at the officers. Worker was eventually dragged, semi-conscious, to the bus. From there he was taken to jail, and spent about three hours being booked, mugged, fingerprinted, and in the drunk tank before being transferred to the University Health Center. He remained there for two days and was examined for fractures, brain damage and scalp injury. The discharge diagnosis was contusion (bruise) with hematoma (a collection of hemorrhages).

George Walker did not enter the room with the others. Although Captain Dillon testified in court that he saw Walker enter at 3:00 and stand near the back of the room, and that he later saw him lying on the floor with an officer over him, there is positive evidence, including photos, that Dillon confused Walker with two or more other students. Walker stood in the hall talking to friends until after the first arrests were made, then followed several officers into the room and joined the group that had not left.

He carried a motorcycle helmet, which he did not put on, and a briefcase. After placing these against the wall near the alcove, he stood facing the front of the office as the police approached those on the couch. Officer Branam testified that Walker wore his helmet, was seated on the couch next to Worker, and attempted to kick him in the thighs and to take away his stick. Officer Shepard testified that Walker hit Branam and also kicked Branam in the ribs. All of the evidence indicates that these allegations are false.

Officer Shepard of the Safety Division approached Walker from his left and struck him high on the left side of the head with a two-handed overhead stroke of his stick, and Walker fell to the floor. A girl standing nearby cursed Shepard and according to one of the Business personnel, he raised his stick as if to threaten her. This may have been the moment when a student being interviewed by a Dow representative in an office not 10 feet away heard a girl shout, "You bastard, don't hit me. Don't hit me, you bastard." Walker was momentarily unconscious, but recovered enough to regain his helmet and briefcase and walk to the bus.

Walker, like Worker, had to wait three hours before being transferred to the University Health Center for medical attention. He complained of headache, impairment of hearing, and absence of feeling on the left side of his head. A blood clot was found along the edge of the inflamed left eardrum. Though the possibility of skull fracture or brain damage was investigated over a four day period, staff physicians and a specialist concluded that Walker had only a perforated left eardrum.

The rest of the students made their way to the bus with only minor incidents. Several were prodded with riot-sticks, and one, while being carried through the hall, felt a stick being swung upward between his legs several times. The following injuries to officers have been reported in interviews: Captain Spannuth—a large swollen bruise on the right upper thigh; Captain Dillon—a badly bruised jaw and left ankle, and minor bruises on both legs; Officer Donald Branam— bruises on both legs (reported by Captain Dillon). There were, in addition, many minor cuts and bruises suffered by both officers and students—a predictable consequence considering the amount of furniture in the room and the narrow and crowded hall through which everyone had to leave.

Critique

The students who went to the Business Building or joined the demonstration at a later time were all opposed to the war and use of

napalm; but they were in other respects a widely diverse group. Some were well-known campus activists (members of SDS or CEWV), others were committed or moderate pacifists with no interest in political activism, and a few were friends of demonstrators who felt compelled to go along or interested or sympathetic onlookers whose participation was nominal. The diversity of this group has been most clearly shown by the events of the past six months. The interrogations conducted by Dean Shaffer's office and the court trials have demonstrated that some students were dismayed at having become involved in an incident that has threatened their academic careers, caused them great emotional and financial strain, and consumed so much of their time. Some have "turned evidence" against others, sought separate lawyers, pleaded guilty in court, or privately expressed their resentment of those who acted as spokesmen or were most eager to enter the room.

The cohesion the group had when it entered Room 131 seems to have been produced by the experiences of that day as much as by any shared sense of identity. When Russell Block went to bring the group downstairs from Room 231, he repeated the insulting references to long hair and unshined shoes which one of the Business personnel had made. While still in the hallway the students were frequently heckled, often abusively, by spectators. The officials confronted the students with humorless assertions of their authority ("Now listen up, this is one of the bosses speaking"), with repeated warnings not to enter the room, and with indifference or disdain for their convictions and stated purposes. As the officials became more stern and the hecklers grew in numbers, the students drew together, covering their resentment and their sense of isolation in a strange and hostile building with a show of bravado. When they voted to enter the room, the desire to protest the presence of the Dow interviewers was still the major, but no longer the only, motive for supporting a strong action. In many subtle ways, a challenge had been issued and accepted.

Most of the students do not themselves question the University's legal right to arrest them for entering the room. It was the prospect of arrest or of disciplinary action that made entering an act of extreme commitment—to the group itself and against napalm, the war, and the University's complicity in the war. Since they were preoccupied with what they were risking, they did not think of the risks that officials would feel they posed to others. And since they knew what they intended to do after they entered, they felt that it was "silly" for officials to bar the door. The allegation that one of the students said, "Let's get the Dow man," which has been made by officials, strikes all of the students as ludicrous. But it is a measure of the fear that their forceful discussions and strongly worded ultimatum inspired. What the students did not properly assess were the adamant attitudes of officials, the potentialities for physical violence (and, therefore, injuries to themselves and others, criminal charges, and court trials), and the possibility that their motives would be obscured in later discussions of their actions. When, after the first arrests, some of the students linked arms or defensively donned helmets, they did not foresee that their actions would provoke police—and would count heavily against them in the court trials.

In addition, some students who were members of SDS ignored their own precepts in committing themselves to an action which had not been preceded by planning, educational programs, or other activities designed to make the action effective and its purpose clear. Some students, who immediately after the incident were pleased that their actions had aroused faculty debate and dramatized some issues, are now convinced that the price they had to pay was too high. All of these criticisms, with which many of the students agree, are easy to make now. They were difficult to anticipate in a confused and tense situation.

The chief officials of the I. U. Safety Division, who are professionals with over twenty years of police experience, showed restraint in a difficult situation. The local police and the Safety Division officers who were involved in the later violence varied widely in their reactions. Some officers exercised restraint in making arrests or held their tempers under the verbal abuse of angered students. A few became highly emotional, used excessive force, or were clearly hostile in making arrests. One of the Bloomington police referred to the students in his official report as "hippies." Witnesses, including Business personnel, observed at least two officers who were highly agitated and who handled the students with obvious anger and repugnance. Clearly, the sight of those students who had beards or long hair and the knowledge that this was a group of "protesters" whom officials wanted removed from the building were enough to incense some of the police.

If there was one cause that contributed more than any other to the violence, it was the previously laid plan to cope with a riot. Conceived on a tough line, inflexibly structured, and left to low-level officials to administer, this plan determined most of the events of October 30. The off-campus police were called when the possibilities for violence were difficult to assess. But once the students had entered the room and it became obvious that there would be no riot, there was no reason to bring off-campus police inside the Business Building. What authority Dean Smith and Professor Snider possessed was relinquished early, and the orders that Captain Spannuth gave had been previously determined when the plan was made.

The course of events could only have been altered by someone with enough judgment, authority, and knowledge of the students to assess the situation, improvise, and decide what to do about the specific kind of sit-in demonstration the students were conducting. Unfortunately for the students, the University, and the police, the plan was lacking this key piece.

2

WISCONSIN: CHANGING STYLES
OF ADMINISTRATIVE RESPONSE

by Durward Long

THE UNIVERSITY OF WISCONSIN is a first-class institution, and has been for almost a century. A critical element in forging its national reputation has been its uncompromising attachment to academic freedom, which has helped to attract an outstanding faculty and talented, independent students. Few periods in the University's history have been tranquil, but fewer still have presented challenges as difficult as those of the past two years. The University's administration has been struggling to contain some of the fiercest and most militant student protest found anywhere in the country, while at the same time preserving in full the right freely to express dissent.

Madison is not only the home of the University, but also the seat of the state government. The two elements coexist, sometimes with difficulty. The legislature, which, due largely to overrepresentation of rural areas and small towns, has been controlled by the Republican Party throughout most of this century, is usually strongly conservative. The Democrats, who absorbed the still more liberal Progressives, have been fairly successful in capturing statewide offices; the Governorship has been shared by the two parties almost equally over the years. The University must deal with both executive and legislative branches. The Governor appoints the Board of Regents, and proposes budgetary grants and other legislation; the legislature has the right to modify or reject his program, or to propose alternatives, and is seldom reluctant to use its powers. In a state where the political traditions of Joseph McCarthy and Robert LaFollette are both very much alive, it has not been easy for the state university to retain the political support it needs. The spectacular militance of student activities compounded the problem over the years 1966–68, and will probably continue to do so.

The faculty of the University have generally been far to the left of the legislature. When LaFollette was Governor, they provided much of the social and political theory which underlay his administration. The students, too, have been to the left, particularly those who were politically active enough to draw attention to their attitudes. The University has been under fairly continuous attack from the right since the end of World War I, the usual hostility between a center of learning and provincial anti-intellectualism being exacerbated by conservative perceptions of the Madison campus as a breeding ground for political enemies. The University has been fortunate in having a number of Regents who were willing to defend their institution from political attack, and a series of Presidents who refused to use academic freedom as a bargaining counter, exchangeable for higher budgets or other political favors.

Student militance is nothing new on the campus. In the thirties, for example, the Student League for Industrial Democracy (SLID), a socialist organization and ancestor of the Students for a Democratic Society (SDS), was quite active. In a climactic incident, conservative students attacked SLID members, and the brawl reached such proportions that a professor summoned the local police to break it up. President Frank responded by calling a convocation to discuss free speech, while the legislature appointed a committee to investigate "Communism, atheism and other perversions" [1] on the campus. No legislation came of this, but the President was pressured into resignation two years later. Relations between the students and the Madison police were cool; they are still cool today.

The University is poorly equipped to make agile political responses, control over policy being widely diffused. At the top of the formal structure is the President, who serves as chief administrator of the University system, which now contains campuses at Milwaukee, Parkside and Green Bay, seven two-year campuses, and an Extension Division, besides the original Madison campus, which still dominates the system in terms of size and prestige. At the head of the Madison campus is a Chancellor. His power, however, is circumscribed both by tradition and by practical wisdom, for the faculty expects to be consulted on major matters, and it would be difficult indeed for a Chancellor to do his job in face of strong opposition from them. The general faculty meeting, normally attended by no more than 10 percent of the more than 2,000 who are eligible to do so, discusses and votes upon all important educational policies and many administrative ones also. Faculty committees, of which the University Committee, functioning in an executive capacity, is the most important, do the detailed work of preparation which must precede faculty action. The Chancellor presides at faculty meetings, but his presence in the Chair clearly has no inhibiting effect; debate is free, and votes are seldom unanimous. Students, the press and the public may attend faculty meetings; the agendas, reports and actions of the faculty are public knowledge. The administrative style at Madison has tended strongly to openness, with ready access to information and a willingness to make controversies public.

The most recent wave of student protest began in May, 1966, and there have been few intervals in the uproar since. Robben Fleming was Chancellor of the Madison campus during the first part of this period, resigning in June, 1967, to become President of the University of Michigan. His successor, William Sewell, adopted a different style in dealing with his first major student demonstration; where Fleming followed a policy of flexibility and conciliation, Sewell insisted on a firm line: enforcement of policy despite obvious personal reservations about the wisdom of that policy. This led to a confrontation which in turn produced a rather bloody melee, and Sewell later adjusted his approach; rather than confrontation, he came to rely on careful preparation and on dealing carefully with the protesters, but from a position of strength. The outcomes of these three administrative styles cannot easily be weighed at this point in time, but we will hope to indicate at least some of the patterns of behavior which developed during each period.

Phase One: Tolerance and Flexibility

The first issue to arise in the period under discussion concerned the draft. Like almost all other colleges and universities, the University of Wisconsin supplied information about grades, etc., to local Selective Service Boards, this being done only on the request of the students concerned. It also administered Selective Service exams. The practice of basing draft deferment on academic standing has been widely criticized, particularly by faculty and by students themselves, and the University was acting as an instrument of a policy which some believed unwise or immoral. It was this involvement of the University which became the target of a protest in May, 1966, led by the SDS and a group calling itself the Ad Hoc Committee on the University and the Draft. In response to initial representations, the President of the University system, Fred Harrington, pointed out that failure of the University to work with the draft boards could deny deferments to students who were entitled to them; the University would not, therefore, yield to the protesters' demands. Chancellor Fleming was more conciliatory, and agreed to place the draft on the agenda of the next regular faculty meeting.

The protesters' next move was to occupy the corridors outside the Registrar's Office, the center of draft-related operations. There they remained for more than a week. Designed primarily to dramatize their cause to the campus and to the wider public who could watch the action on television, the sit-in was carefully controlled and disciplined by its leaders. No one was obstructed, and normal University business proceeded without interference. These tactics brought immediate support. A group of teaching assistants formed another *ad hoc* anti-draft committee. The student government called for a faculty-student committee to study the draft. U.S. Sen. Gaylord Nelson issued a supportive statement, terming the draft "ridiculous." Most important of all, many members of the faculty were impressed with the students' willingness to espouse a cause inimical to their own immediate interests, and moved towards support of student demands.

Chancellor Fleming's first problem was what should be done about a group of students in apparently permanent occupation of a part of the Administration Building. At the time there was no regulation limiting protest activities except a general guarantee of freedom of speech and the state disorderly conduct law. He announced that they would be permitted to stay there, so long as they did not "obstruct." On the third day of the sit-in, he made further conciliatory gestures. Speaking at the protesters' own rally, he congratulated them on "their disciplined behavior throughout the demonstration," and declared that they had proved that "the right to protest, which is essential in a democratic society, can be handled in a responsible manner at the University of Wisconsin." [2] He then announced that,

rather than wait for the next regular faculty meeting, he would summon a special one to discuss the draft issue. Further, he underscored
the Administration's readiness to discuss the matter with concerned
students.

The special faculty meeting on May 23 attracted approximately
1,000 members and required a move to the largest auditorium on
campus. In his opening remarks to the faculty, Fleming argued that
the issue was not so much Selective Service as the question whether
the "University's great reputation for protest without coercion" [3]
could be maintained. The Chancellor broke precedent by inviting
three students representing the Student Senate and protest groups to
address the faculty. After considerable debate, the faculty voted to
continue sending information on class standing, not to local boards
but to individual students who requested it, and who could then report it to their draft boards if they wished. It was also voted to establish a faculty-student committee to study the issue, as the Student
Senate had requested. Finally, the special meeting reaffirmed the
Administration's policy of allowing Selective Service exams on campus. Following the special meeting, Chancellor Fleming stated that
student demands had been considered and that the sit-in should be
ended.

Unhappy with the outcome of the faculty meeting, and charging
betrayal, the protesters returned to the Administration Building only
to find it locked, whereupon they staged a small sit-in in Bascom
Hall, where the offices of the President, the Chancellor, and the Dean
of Student Affairs were located. No action was taken by the Administration that night, but on the following day Chancellor Fleming
met with student leaders and warned that students would be subject
to disciplinary action if the sit-in continued. The students then voted
to end the eight-day protest. Both the Administration and the protesters had some reason to feel satisfaction with the outcome, and
neither appeared anxious for further action; meanwhile, those who
had demanded the clearing of the Administration Building by police
while the sit-in was in progress pressed unsuccessfully for disciplinary
proceedings against the students involved.

When the University resumed operation after the 1966 summer
vacation, it soon became clear that anti-war sentiment was still strong.
The initial target was not the University, but a Democratic Party
rally held on campus. The featured speaker was Sen. Edward Kennedy. Hecklers demanded that he abandon his prepared remarks,

and speak about Vietnam. The Senator did so, but was subjected to such continuous interruption that the audience was unable to hear most of his speech.

Reaction to this protest style contrasted sharply with that in the spring. The Student Senate adopted a resolution to place the Committee to End the War in Vietnam on probation. The Chancellor, however, explained that the University would not take any disciplinary action because the rally was a political meeting, neither chaired by a University representative nor sponsored by the University, and because a University requirement that a question session follow an address by a political speaker might not have been fulfilled. The Kennedy incident did, however, focus attention on the need for University regulations concerning protests and related disorders. A code provision stressing the need to respect the rights of others and the obligation not to obstruct University business was adopted shortly after; no provisions for penalizing violators were mentioned.

In February, 1967, Dow Chemical was due to send a recruiter to the campus. SDS and others decided to demonstrate against them, and to obstruct, rather than to picket peacefully. They argued that peaceful methods had failed to gain their objectives during the Selective Service controversy the previous May. Despite the public announcement of this strategy, the Chancellor and his staff met with protest leaders, in an attempt to induce them to abide by the spirit of the new code provision—not to obstruct. These discussions were not effective; protest leaders announced plans for a peaceful demonstration on February 21, to be followed by obstruction the following day.

However, even the 21st did not pass off peacefully. At midmorning three students were arrested by University police and charged with disorderly conduct when they carried picket signs into the Commerce and Chemistry Buildings. Other students with signs and placards immediately left the buildings complaining that no official notice had been given interpreting inside picket signs as obstruction. Around noon, Chancellor Fleming in consideration of the students' charge that the policy had not been officially communicated (although notices had been distributed) to all students as a University regulation, lifted the ban on signs inside buildings, but the three students who had been arrested were not released. The arrests hardened the students' determination to obstruct Dow interviews the next day, and they reaffirmed that purpose in an evening meeting on the 21st. The following day in the Engineering Building about 25 members of the Committee for Direct Action, yet another *ad hoc* "organization," blocked the office being used by the Dow representative. Then, according to the Engineering Placement Director, they forced their way into the Placement Office, "obstructed" and "interfered" with the work of that office. The Placement Director asked for assistance from the campus police, who followed previously announced procedure. The students refused to leave, and eleven were arrested and bodily removed without resistance. Other protesters outside the building then blocked the police vehicle and six persons were arrested for that offense.

Meanwhile, the SDS group, hearing of the arrests, staged a mass sit-in in the corridor of Bascom Hall, outside the office of Dean of Student Affairs Joseph F. Kauffman. At that time, Chancellor Fleming and Dean Kauffman were conferring with the President of the Wisconsin Student Association and some spokesmen for the protesters. The obstructionist group voted to keep the Chancellor and the Dean blocked in until charges against the seventeen arrested were dropped. Fleming negotiated a compromise by promising to hold a mass meeting at 8:00 P.M. and the protesters dispersed. At the meeting, Fleming announced that he had personally posted bond of more than $1,200 for the eleven who could not meet bond on their disorderly conduct charges.

The next day the Chancellor called a special faculty meeting to discuss the recent events and the enforcement of University regulations. He indicated to the faculty that enforcement "might, on occasion, require not only campus and city police, but possibly additional forces." [4] The faculty, by a divided vote, reaffirmed their intention of enforcing the regulation. They also, however, voted to reconsider the University's policy of permitting all *bona fide* employers to recruit on campus. As before, faculty action suggested a possibility that the protesters had achieved partial success. However, reaction from the campus generally was critical; *The Daily Cardinal* declared that the protesters had "defeated their cause by their actions . . . and lost the respect of elements which could have aided their victory." [5] Perhaps it would be fair to say that they had also been defeated by the Chancellor, whose flexibility and generous gestures had prevented escalation of the conflict and attracted considerable sympathy for the Administration's point of view.

The announced visit of the CIA in April, 1967, gave the war foes another opportunity to register dissent and the Administration and the activists joined in planning a peaceful protest. Extensive preparations were made by the Dean of Student Affairs and his staff in conferring with student leaders, including protest leaders, discussing and securing agreement on guidelines, and providing public address facilities near the entrance of the building where CIA interviews were scheduled. The interviews were carried out successfully while an all-day program of anti-war speeches took place outside. The demonstration was so peaceful that militant students later described it as "Administration-managed" and without effect. There was no further loss of campus support for the anti-war group, however, and the moderate protest may have gained them friends.

A different kind of demonstration occurred in May, 1967, in a city street which borders the University. Ordinary traffic on the street is restricted to one-way travel west, but one side of the street is reserved for buses to travel east. The one-way lane had caused much student irritation earlier, and the serious injury of a coed by a bus in the spring of 1967 provoked action. With the announcement by a professor that a group had organized to demonstrate against the "special privilege" given by the city to the bus company, a great number of students and spectators, estimated at nearly 2,000, gathered in the bus lane to obstruct traffic. Several hundred students began walking west, duly encountering a bus, and lying down before it. City police cleared the bus lane by dispersing the crowd, arresting approximately 35 demonstrators, and jailing 13 of them for disorderly conduct. University officials responded to requests that the students be disciplined with the statement that the University does not take action against students for off-campus behavior unless the action threatens the welfare of the institution or unless the conduct of such students indicates a continuing danger to persons or property or the educational process. In the bus lane case, according to University policy, the jurisdiction was clearly that of civil authorities.

The bus lane case was the last protest which Chancellor Fleming had to handle before his move to Michigan. Its outcome preserved intact his record of not subjecting any protester to University disciplinary proceedings. The Legislature, city officials, the more conservative citizenry and some elements within the University academic community, including some Regents, Alumni Association leaders, and a few faculty, had expressed increasing concern throughout the year at what seemed to them a dangerously lax policy. On the other hand, Fleming had maintained his support among the faculty and his good relations with the students, even with the activists. The protest activities had brought about some desired changes in policy and had won the support of some of the faculty members. The campus police had been in action once, but only after the clearest warnings had been given; the status of academic freedom and the right of open dissent had never been more secure at Madison. What may have been overlooked, however, was a more specific enunciation by the faculty endorsing the protection of the rights of others endangered by the unlimited protest activities.

Phase Two: Violent Confrontation

The 1967–68 year began with predictions for increased activism from every militant group among the 33,000 students. A special summer "board" of the Wisconsin Student Association (WSA) had completed a bill proposing to University authorities that "matters of solely student concern" be governed completely by students and their organizations. The Teaching Assistants Association, which grew out of their *ad hoc* committee to oppose the University's draft policy in May, 1966, announced a membership drive and a campaign to demand a collective bargaining agreement with the University. The SDS issued a new handbook charging that the University existed for only one purpose: "The training of its students in skills and attitudes that will make them useful to the government and to the large corporation." [6]

The appointment of a new Chancellor, William H. Sewell, Vilas Professor of Sociology, who had served the University for over twenty years and who had publicly indicated his opposition to the Vietnam war, may have made the anti-war leaders more confident in their planning. At the first faculty meeting of the year, however, Chancellor Sewell described the policy of the institution as guaranteeing free speech and the right of unobstructive protests, and announced that it was his intention to enforce that policy.

The first week of classes set the tone for the semester. A small group of activists attempted to disrupt ROTC orientation by "infiltrating" the sessions and shouting questions such as "Do we get any more money for killing Vietnamese civilians?" During the same week, the trial began for two of the protesters arrested for disorderly conduct in the previous February Dow affair. Robert Cohen, a teaching assistant, and Robert Zwicker, an undergraduate, argued during a trial which lasted more than two days that the University had no authority to make a rule prohibiting signs in buildings, and that the rule was never officially promulgated. Both were convicted; Cohen was sentenced to 14 days in jail and Zwicker was fined $100, but without money, he, too, was sentenced to jail. The bearded Cohen and mustachioed Zwicker were given a week by the Sheriff to volunteer for shaves and haircuts; both refused and at the Sheriff's orders deputies shaved Cohen's beard without his permission. Student protesters frequently picketed the jail during their term. Both Cohen and Zwicker were allowed to attend classes during the day, however, and Cohen continued to teach his assigned class.

The coming return of Dow's representatives further unified militants with groups normally less radical in style. The SDS and the Committee to End the War in Vietnam were joined by the United Campus Action student political party, the Concerned Black People, the Concerned Law Students, the Young Democrats, and the Wisconsin Draft Resistance Union (WDRU), all of whom voted to demonstrate against Dow's presence on the Wisconsin campus. Members of these various groups organized a steering committee known as the Anti-Dow Coordinating Committee.

On October 11, when anti-Dow leaders discussed means to be employed in the protest, there were several vague references to physical force. The Young Socialist Alliance representative analyzed the weakness of peaceful demonstration tactics and advocated a more effective attack on power structure. Zwicker, during one of his hours out of jail, and Wilfred Sorrell, a Concerned Black People's member, spoke against the use of peaceful demonstrations, arguing that they failed to accomplish any concrete change. Eventually, a resolution was introduced which provided for a peaceful protest on October 17 and for blockading of interviews on October 18. A mimeographed sheet enunciated a theme which was to be associated with the march on Washington of October 19: "We must move from protest to resistance. Before, we talked, now we must act. We must stop what we oppose." [7]

Apprised of these developments by the student newspaper, Student Affairs personnel, and handouts, administrative officials attempted to persuade the militants to keep their protest peaceful and to convince them that the University's regulations would be enforced. Guidelines for protest were prepared for each building in which Dow representatives would interview and the Dean of Student Affairs and his staff attempted to discuss the guidelines with potential protesters. The protest groups and their representatives, however, were not interested.

On October 11, Dean Kauffman issued a public statement which was liberally distributed in dormitories, on campus, and to the press which announced that the University planned to enforce regulations and that any student who "obstructs or otherwise disrupts the operations of the University or organizations accorded the use of University facilities" would be subject to University discipline "including disciplinary probation, suspension or expulsion, whether or not arrests are made." [8] Protest leaders responded to Kauffman's statement with charges of "threat," and "intimidation." Their attorney filed suit in Federal District Court to ask for a restraining order against the University. The Student Senate condemned the Dean's announcement, and the Concerned Law Students asked him to retract it. Kauffman took the position that he had no authority to do other than announce and enforce the policy. Communication between the Administration and militant spokesmen was severed almost completely.

President Harrington told questioners on the Board of Regents that policy would be enforced. Chancellor Sewell and his staff, including the Director of Protection and Security, Ralph Hanson, met with the Mayor and the Police Chief of Madison to discuss needs the University might have for assistance from local police. Dean Kauffman or Chancellor Sewell would authorize use of these forces. Guidelines for demonstrators were developed, arrangements were made to employ off-duty Madison police during the interviews, and enforcement and arrest plans were made. These plans called for the physical arrest and carrying away of obstructors who, it was assumed, would become limp.

The Dow interviews could hardly have been scheduled at a time more calculated to produce trouble. They came on the heels of the trials of Cohen and Zwicker, the forcible shaving of Cohen's beard and impending trials for other Dow demonstrators arrested in February, 1967. The SDS and the WDRU began the year by focusing on the University's involvement in the War, accusing it of providing research, manpower and facilities for war-related recruitment. Ferment over student demands for control over matters of "solely student concern" was at a peak on the campus. In nearby Milwaukee, daily demonstrations in favor of open housing were being led by

Father Groppi. Furthermore, the week that Dow was scheduled to appear had been designated Vietnam Week by the major anti-war organizations throughout the United States. During that week, student groups were to "educate" the United States by a variety of methods on the immorality of the War; the week was to end with a mass march on the Pentagon.

Nevertheless, Dow representatives came on October 17 as scheduled by the University Placement Office. Chief Hanson arranged for ten off-duty Madison police to report that day and twenty to report on October 18, the day of the announced obstruction. Dean Kauffman had asked deans of schools where interviews were to be held to have several senior professors on hand to assist in persuading students to abide by the guidelines, and to act as witnesses if necessary. Interviews on the first day were held at the Commerce Building and approximately 200 persons picketed the entrance to the building chanting such slogans as "Hey, Hey, L.B.J., How Many Kids Have You Killed Today?", and "Hell No, We Won't Go!" There was no obstruction that day, but at a noon rally, it was promised for the morrow.

October 18 began with a small number of demonstrators picketing at the entrance of the Commerce Building. About 11:00 A.M., over 100 protesters walked into the building and blocked the door of the office in which the Dow representative was located. About as many demonstrators continued to picket outside the building. Although campus police were present in the corridor, no effort was made to arrest the obstructors. By noon the corridor was obstructed also. Officials from the Office of the Dean of Student Affairs, including an associate dean, made repeated unsuccessful efforts to persuade the obstructors to remove themselves. Deciding not to arrest the persons immediately blocking the Dow interview office door because of the crowd's obvious hostility, Chief Hanson stated that warrants would be issued later, and via "walkie-talkie" communicated the state of affairs to the Chancellor and Dean Kauffman. Hanson's recommendation that additional police be requested from the city to keep order was approved and he telephoned Chief Emery to request every available man to come to the Commerce Building.

Uniformed city police arrived on the scene a few at a time, some in private automobiles. Many of them donned riot helmets and brandished riot sticks in full view of the growing crowd outside the Commerce Building, causing considerable excitement. The obstruc-

tors inside began to prepare for violence, warning the women to remove jewelry and glasses, to pull their knees up and cover the backs
of their heads with coats; a few of the protesters left the building.
Hanson proceeded to declare the assembly unlawful while the riot
police assembled in formation across the street.

At this point, several leaders of the protest asked for a deal with
the Administration, and four of them were then escorted to the
Chancellor and Dean Kauffman. Evan Stark, who acted as spokesman, told the Chancellor that if he would sign a statement asking
Dow interviewers to leave the campus and not return, the four students present would try to get the demonstrators to leave the building, but that they could give no guarantee of their success. Chancellor Sewell replied that he could not assent to the agreement because it was his responsibility to enforce University policy. The
four students left without another word, and returned to the Commerce Building to announce that the meeting had brought no results.

Madison Police Chief Emery, Chief Hanson, Chancellor Sewell,
and Dean Kauffman discussed the situation and agreed that arrests
would be necessary. Returning to the Commerce Building, Chief
Hanson again announced with a loudspeaker that the assembly was
unlawful and the participants must leave or be arrested. He then
rejoined the group of nearly 30 Madison police and proceeded to
lead them into the building. Chief Hanson stated later that he did
not tell the police what the specific objectives of the force would be,
nor did the ten to fourteen campus officers inside the building know
the intentions of the riot force. Chief Hanson said he planned to
direct the actions of the men once inside the building. But as the
police entered with Hanson leading them, they were pushed backwards through the entrance. At that point, the Chief lost control over
his own forces.

The riot police, for whom the experience of being thrown out of
a building was a novel one, forced their way back in, using force to
meet force in efforts to regain control. One officer was hit in the face
with a brick in the first few seconds of the melee, suffering a broken
nose. Police used their night sticks freely on the resisting protesters,
and as officers emerged from the building dragging those they intended to arrest, the crowd outside, now estimated at 2,000, became
menacing. Police were attacked with stones, bricks, bottles, shoes,
and even with their own night-sticks—for the outnumbered force lost
a considerable amount of its own equipment. The police van was

effectively blocked, then disabled. It became impossible for the police to make arrests. The Commerce Building was cleared in about 12 minutes, but the crowd outside proved harder to handle. Tear gas was used, but failed to disperse those subjected to it. Only when the County Sheriff's Department had supplied reinforcements did incidents taper off, and the crowd disperse. About 50 students had been injured, including many with lacerations and tear gas burns; about 20 police were also injured, three suffering serious or permanent damage.

The campus was barely clear of tear gas when the political reactions began to develop. A group of teaching assistants called for a "strike" to begin on October 20, during which only campus issues would be discussed in class. Protest leaders organized a mass rally for the evening, an event which attracted an estimated 5,000 students and almost 200 sympathetic faculty. At the rally, it was voted to strike the whole campus, beginning immediately. The student government initially issued a statement placing responsibility for the "tragedy and chaos that occurred on the University campus" upon "the demonstrators who persist in obstructing Dow Chemical." [9] However, after the rally they changed direction, and voted to join the strike. *The Daily Cardinal* declared in favor of the walk-out as a vote of "no confidence" in the Administration, while the Student Rights Party, one of the few which had opposed the Dow demonstration, voted to censure the Administration. The official voices of student opinion thus became solidified into almost unanimous condemnation of the Administration's handling of events.

A special faculty meeting was announced for the following evening. Various groups critical of the Administration began caucusing almost as soon as the violence was over. Between 150 and 200 faculty attended the mass protest rally, and many indicated some sympathy with its aims. The special meeting, attended by about half the 2,200 faculty, was the largest ever held, and closed circuit television had to be used after it was necessary to locate about 100 members in a room apart from the main auditorium. The University Committee proposed a resolution deploring the violence that occurred on the campus but commending the Chancellor's enforcement of University regulations. Several unsuccessful efforts were made by many faculty members to separate the two statements; resolutions declaring that police would never be called to the campus again and giving amnesty to the students involved in the demonstration were also defeated. After the faculty had debated the Chancellor's action for several hours, he stood to remind his colleagues that he had merely carried out policy they had determined and that none of them "had guts enough" to admit it.[10] The University Committee's position was finally adopted after parliamentary maneuvering of nearly six hours and by a faculty vote of 681–378. It was further resolved that the meeting would be continued on the following Monday to consider proposals for preventing a repetition of the violence.

The strike which had been called received some support the first day but fizzled on Friday, the day following the faculty meeting. Part of the reason for the failure was the militant leaders' preoccupation with two other demonstrations, a protest march to the local police headquarters or the State Capitol on Saturday, and the nationally sponsored demonstration march against the Pentagon that weekend. Several activists and their leaders left Madison on Friday to journey to Washington for the Pentagon march while others remained to lead a coat-and-tie orderly protest march on the State Capitol. The protesters taped a list of grievances to a Capitol door and thereby avoided direct confrontation with any official. Realizing that disunity and many separate activities had caused the strike to fail, the Teaching Assistants Association voted on Sunday, October 22, to end the strike whichever came earlier: (1) when the students ended the strike (already, most had ended it), or (2) at 4:30 P.M. on Monday, October 23, when the faculty meeting was to reconvene.

The October 23 faculty meeting was held in a spirit of reconciliation and compromise. The minority who lost in its efforts to change the University's policy of inviting all *bona fide* employers to interview on campus agreed to a motion proposed by the University Committee calling for the creation of a special student-faculty committee to study and recommend means of response to obstruction. The Mermin Committee (named after its chairman, Law Professor Samuel Mermin) was delayed in beginning work by a disagreement with the WSA about the method of selecting student members. It began its work in December, 1967, composed of seven students and eight faculty members including the chairman.

Opinion off-campus split along fairly predictable liberal and conservative lines. The Wisconsin Civil Liberties Union issued a statement indicating that it might press the Madison Fire and Police Commission for public hearings on the conduct of the police. The Attorney-General, Democrat Bronson LaFollette, decried the "police brutality" and called for a special committee to make a "full, fair, and objective analysis of the incident." The balance of indignation, however, as measured by mail and press content, appeared to lie with the conservatives.

The Republican-dominated State Legislature made the campus conflict its first major business of the session. The Assembly passed a resolution by a vote of 94 to 5 on the evening of the fracas, demanding that the Regents of both the University of Wisconsin and the State University System "re-evaluate administrative policies of excessive permissiveness in handling student demonstrators." The Senate was unwilling to wait for the Regents, however, and created an investigative committee of its own headed by the Lieutenant-Governor to inquire into the October 18 affair to determine if additional legislation were needed.

Many anti-University bills were introduced as a direct result of the violence. One proposal would have reduced the institution's budget. Another would have limited the enrollment of non-resident freshmen, for many legislators insisted that the majority of protesters were from out of state. Another bill would have added a number of legislators to the Board of Regents. Other measures would have restricted dissent on the campus. Fortunately, only three bills were sent to the Governor. The three included a new definition of unlawful assembly, and a stiffening of penalties for attempted assault and battery on policemen and firemen and for defiling the flag.

Many groups awaited University action in disciplining the students charged for their part in the riot. The illegal strike by several teaching assistants and some teachers complicated the Administration's problems of discipline. Not only was the substance of the issue at stake but disciplinary procedure was in question. In two departments, one TA in each was relieved of his teaching duties because of participation in the strike. Sixteen students who were known by University officials to be leaders in the Anti-Dow Committee and who were involved and identified in the Dow obstruction were suspended pending hearings by the Committee on Student Conduct and Appeals, but they were permitted to continue to attend classes. Special focus was directed to the case of Robert Cohen, a Teaching Assistant in the Department of Philosophy, who had been the subject of much publicity in previous demonstrations and who had a long record of protest activity on campus and in the city. The University found itself without a faculty-approved policy establishing procedure for dismissal of teaching assistants. Despite conferences involving the Chancellor, the Dean of the College of Letters and Science, and the Chairman of the Department of Philosophy, it was not clear which procedure should be followed. Meanwhile, external pressures for Cohen's dismissal were growing, and President Harrington, responsible for the multi-unit University of Wisconsin system, announced on November 15 that Cohen had been fired as a TA. He announced also that Evan Stark had been fired as a research assistant and had disappeared from the campus. Madison Chancellor Sewell took issue with the procedure for dismissing Cohen and publicly objected.

The Cohen issue as well as many others growing out of the affair were taken up by the University Board of Regents at its November meeting. With a fairly clear understanding that the measure would fail before its introduction, the Regents barely rejected (by a vote of 4 to 3) a proposal that everyone (professors and teaching assistants) who did not hold their classes during the strike period be summarily dismissed. But in deference to the Chancellor's position that no person, specifically Cohen, should be dismissed without due process, the Board agreed to a special Regent hearing for Cohen to protect his rights. In the meantime, appropriate faculty committees began to consider a grievance and dismissal procedure for teaching assistants. The need for a satisfactory procedure became more imperative as the Teaching Assistants Association demanded to be recognized as the sole bargaining and negotiating agent for all TA's with particular relevance to the Cohen case.

Discipline proceedings for the sixteen students suspended by the University began in late November after unsuccessful efforts by the protesters to have the University regulations declared unconstitutional. The state also charged and eventually convicted seven persons with disorderly conduct, some of whom were included in the sixteen suspended by the University. Hearings for the sixteen, charged with "misconduct" and "disrupting the campus," were punctuated by other student activists hissing, ringing bells, and waving dead birds and other distracting objects. Three of the students charged, including Cohen, abruptly discharged their attorneys during the proceedings, denounced the hearing committee as being in collusion with the Administration and walked out of the hearings. They were promptly and officially suspended. Six of the remaining thirteen dropped out of school and eventually the suspension for the other seven was lifted.

The violent confrontation had seriously factionalized the University, had involved physical injury to protesters and policemen alike, and had brought severe censure upon the institution from a variety of internal and external publics. The University's regulations had been tested and approved by the courts and the student left had discovered that the institution would resort to force to enforce a policy of equal rights. But the cost was considered high by Chancellor Sewell and a modified approach was to proceed from that judgment.

Phase Three: Avoiding Confrontation

Shortly after the October 18 Dow confrontation, student militants announced that the CIA would be next when its representatives appeared on the campus on November 27–28. After communication with the Administration, the CIA canceled its interview appointments for late November as did the Air Force. Although the cancellation made their situation more tolerable for the moment, administrative officials did not request the agencies to cancel their appointments. In fact, the Administration feared that if the agencies against which protest activities were directed refused to come to the campus, the student militants would have achieved victory in their efforts to violate the rights of students who wished to be interviewed by the armed forces, Dow, and the CIA; and the University's efforts to protect the rights of all students would have been defeated. The Navy and Marines, unlike CIA and the Air Force, informed the University that representatives would appear on the campus as scheduled on November 20. The student protest leaders who had already formed an Ad Hoc Committee Against the CIA held a rally to boast of their victory over the Agency and counseled students to obstruct the Navy and Marines despite the injunction. There was little enthusiasm exhibited in the small rally, however, nor were there any discernible plans of strategy made by the students.

On the other hand, the Administration made extensive plans to insure overwhelming enforcement strength in a confrontation. The armed services representatives were to be located in a large athletic practice building located beside a field house, both of which were surrounded by open parking lots. Persons not having business in the area were directed by University officials to stay away. Pre-planning conferences had explored the procedure and possibility of calling on additional emergency forces such as the National Guard and a decision was made to house 200 sheriff's deputies from surrounding counties in the field house. Shortly after rumor of these extensive plans were circulated, the Ad Hoc Committee to Protest Army Recruitment announced that it would stage a "peaceful confrontation with the warmakers." It was announced that the Madison Chief of Police would be in charge of the security forces stationed outside the building: a mixture of city and campus policemen, and the deputies, a total of approximately 300 men. The interviews took place with no difficulty and only a very small token protest but at a cost of around $15,000 for law enforcement forces alone. But avoiding confrontation through superior strength worked.

In the meantime, other actions on the issues presented by the protesters were underway. Two important committees were studying possible institutional changes to bring peace to the troubled campus. The Crow Committee, an all-faculty committee, had been at work since the late summer holding open hearings and studying the "role of the student in the governance of the University" in order to make recommendations to the faculty. Even before the committee undertook its deliberations, however, students held 94 voting seats and 9 non-voting seats on 17 of the campus committee areas. The Mermin Committee, the faculty-student committee, devoted its attention to modes of University response to obstruction, and secondarily, the University's policy of permitting all *bona fide* employers to recruit on campus.

While the Mermin Committee was studying the question of obstruction, the Chancellor postponed the second semester scheduled employment interviews of Dow, the Navy, and the Marine Corps. He explained that the interviews would be delayed until the committee made its report to the faculty and until the faculty had acted upon it. This action brought severe criticism from the Board of Regents and a petition from more than one thousand students (most of whom were enrolled in Engineering) requesting that the interviews be held.

Responding to pressures to make a report as quickly as possible, the Mermin Committee made a partial report to the faculty in March, 1968. The committee was seriously divided and presented minority and majority reports on continuing interviews, but the faculty majority once more reaffirmed the University's "neutrality" and its open placement policy for all *bona fide* employers. Following the action of the faculty, the Administration approved interviews for the Dow Chemical Company for March 30 and for the Navy and Marine Corps for April 11.

In making preparations for the appearance of Dow, the Chancellor requested the Company to provide sufficient representatives to complete the interviews in one day, and to hold an open forum with the students. The firm agreed to both requests. The Administration also carefully selected the date for the interviews, seeking every means to avoid physical confrontation with protesters. The date scheduled for the Dow Company was a Saturday, three days before the Wisconsin Primary and a Madison referendum on the Vietnam war. A large proportion of the student Left was involved and therefore sensitive to any adverse publicity they and their causes would receive from another obstruction. The date chosen for the Navy and Marines was the last day of classes preceding the spring recess. Furthermore, the Dow interviews were scheduled in the athletic practice building and plans included an "adequate" number (150 or more) of policemen waiting in the field house next to the practice building. Again, statements of University policy on obstruction were issued in the campus and public press. Although it was later rejected by the Regents, an interim discipline procedure was devised and approved by the faculty in view of the fact that the old procedure was considered deficient. The placement interviews both for Dow and the armed services (held in the Engineering Building without a large contingent of policemen) were completed without serious protest. Two persons who aspired to "civil disobedience" were obliged by the police and charged with disorderly conduct when they, each alone and separately, threw themselves prostrate before the entrance doors to the practice building.

The absence of significant protest when interviews were resumed was partly attributable to political developments on the national and international scene. The McCarthy and Kennedy campaigns for the Democratic presidential nomination, the withdrawal of President Johnson from that race, and renewed efforts for peace negotiations with North Vietnam removed frustrations and, at the same time, afforded an outlet within the larger society for activist students. Resurgence of civil rights activities including the Poor People's March also helped to redirect the energies of the activists.

There were several campus developments in the spring which, in addition to the national developments described above, brought about a thaw in the confrontation politics between student activists and the University. The activist leadership of the three previous years disappeared from the campus during December and January and new leaders were slow in appearing. In the spring student elections, the students were asked to vote on the University policy of permitting any *bona fide* employer the use of University facilities for employment interview purposes. A substantial majority approved the policy, and the controversy over placement was reduced somewhat.

Still another factor in the restoration of acceptable relations between students and the University was the willingness of the faculty to take positive steps towards more meaningful student participation in governing certain aspects of University life. As outgrowths of the Crow and Mermin Committee reports, the faculty proceeded to take steps contingent upon Regent approval to reduce the practice of *in loco parentis*. The faculty approved the abolition of dormitory curfew hours for women and ended the requirement that freshmen and sophomores must live in supervised housing. Further, they approved a general revision of the discipline system of the University by eliminating the penalty of expulsion for non-academic conduct, limiting discipline for non-academic offenses, restricting suspension to a maximum of two years, and establishing a Committee on Student Conduct Hearings consisting of five faculty and four students to replace the former discipline committee.

The Regents approved the policy which allows freshmen and sophomores to live in non-supervised housing but with the provision that written approval from parents would be required. The governing board demurred on the new discipline limitations and reorganization and took the faculty action under study.

The resurgence of involvement in behalf of black students which swept the country after the assassination of Martin Luther King also affected the direction of student activism at Wisconsin in late April and May, 1968. White activists from SDS, campus political parties, and anti-war groups joined the efforts of the organization of black students known as Concerned Black People to improve the University's programs for the disadvantaged. They demanded that the University divest itself of its Chase Manhattan Bank stock because of the bank's investments in the Republic of South Africa, establish a program to provide leave and salary for professors engaged in civil rights activities, increase curriculum offers in Afro-American history, life, and culture, employ a black educator as associate director of the program for the disadvantaged, and increase these programs for the disadvantaged by providing more dollars, counseling, and recipients.

These demands were presented to the Regents by white and black student spokesmen in May, with the crucial demand focusing on University holdings of Chase Manhattan Bank stock. Although the Regents considered the student demands, they declined to dispose of the stock. The protesters responded by holding a sit-in in the Administration Building where the Wisconsin sit-ins had started two years earlier. Although they entered the building after closing hours and the campus police chief was present during the sit-in, there was no effort to remove the protesters or to identify them for later discipline. Near midnight the group voted to leave the building and to meet again the following day to make plans for further protest action against the University. Around 1:00 A.M. the same night, an arsonist threw a fire bomb into the records storage room of the College of Letters and Science, causing extensive damage. Although some critics associate the act with the protest, the University and its police officials have separated the arson from the protest and have no evidence to connect the two.

The following weekend the black student leaders met with the Vice Chancellors of the Madison campus (in the Chancellor's absence) to agree on means of strengthening programs for the disadvantaged and to assure the black students that added curriculum offerings in Afro-American history, life, and culture were already planned for the fall. The only demand that the Vice Chancellors could not meet was the sale of the Chase Manhattan Bank stock since it was owned by the Board of Regents of the University of Wisconsin. The overtures satisfied the black students and despite the desire of a few white militants to provoke further confrontation, they withdrew their support and the protest group dissolved in disunity.

As the year came to a close Chancellor Sewell announced that he was resigning his administrative post to return to teaching and research. He expressed disappointment that he had to spend so much time handling campus crises, particularly those growing out of confrontation tactics, instead of working on educational improvements.

The militant student protesters achieved a questionable "victory" in contributing to the resignation of the capable scholar-administrator who was uniquely sensitive to the substantive issues raised by their protests while courageously committed to maintaining the traditions of freedom within agreed-upon regulations.

Although it is impossible to give any generally acceptable answer to questions about whether a particular administrative decision was the best one, it is possible to analyze the styles of administrative response as in the Wisconsin case and to suggest the implications of each. In such an analysis, one must bear in mind both immediate and long-range effects. In phase one, for example, the immediate gain of avoiding direct confrontation over the draft protest by flexible, liberal response to student demands has to be weighed against the long-term effect of poor public relations in the external community as well as the resulting militants' view that confrontation tactics were effective. The first major confrontation over Dow indicated the flexible, "tolerant" response could still be made but with more difficulty. Regulations and opinion had reduced the range of alternatives open to the Administration. Thus, Fleming's decision to post bail for the arrested protesters was a personal rather than an institutional decision. As the faculty hardened its position, the militants raised the level of protest activities, in each case going just beyond guidelines which had been liberalized during a previous protest.

Whether the gradually increasing toleration of protest activity could have been continued with Fleming's leadership is a moot question. It is clear, however, that the second style of administrative response, unwavering enforcement of University regulations, had more catastrophic immediate effects. The decision to authorize police to clear the Commerce Building succeeded in clearing the building, enforcing rules, and punishing leaders of the militant mob. Anyone who planned to flaunt the official rules would, henceforth, know that the University was capable of employing superior force to restore order; it is too early to say whether this deterrent effect will last. However, confidence in the University was badly shaken. Student organizations turned almost unanimously against the Administration, and showed corresponding sympathy for protest activities. Student opinion in general appeared critical of both the activists and the administrators. The faculty, while voting to support the Chancellor's decision, was badly split. The reputation of the University as a haven of academic freedom can hardly have been strengthened by the pictures of violence which appeared in the press across the country; some impact on the recruitment of new faculty and new students is to be expected, though it may not be easily measurable. The standing of the University with the people of Wisconsin has presumably suffered, since almost all reactions to the affair were strongly critical, either of "police brutality" or of "excessive permissiveness."

Most of the participants in the Commerce Building affair would probably tend, with benefit of hindsight, to wish that they had done other than they did at some point. In indulging such hypothetical speculations, however, there is no reliable way of knowing what results would have been produced by alternative courses of action. What can be said with considerable confidence and hindsight, however, is that it would have been better for almost all concerned if the battle at the Commerce Building had never occurred. Nobody with any real interest in higher education could suppose that kind of bloodshed to be appropriate to a college campus.

This was clear to Chancellor Sewell and he determined that such confrontation would be avoided if at all possible and that where implementation of University policy created high possibility of confrontation, tactics of time and place and superior force would be employed. Accompanying this tactic were sincere efforts by the Administration to examine substantive issues presented by the protests as promptly as possible through means acceptable to faculty and students. This type of response explains in great measure the more tolerable level of protest during the second semester.

In each administrative style, previous confrontations influenced decisions made both by administrators and militants. National trends and developments also affected the tactics and response of both. Response to militant protest, like other administrative decisions, is made within limitations and alternatives imposed not only by the conditions of the protest but by past courses of action. In highly emotional situations, and particularly in institutions where students and faculty are deeply committed to ideas of freedom and dissent, response to forcible confrontation by students is highly unlikely to produce entirely favorable immediate or long-term results. This was the dilemma faced by both Wisconsin chancellors in their attempts to protect the freedom of dissent and at the same time keep the institution open and free for others.

NOTES *

[1] "A Report on the Anti-Dow Protests on the Madison Campus of the University of Wisconsin on October 17–18, 1967," a mimeographed internal report, p. 6, quoting David Sellery, *Ferment at Wisconsin.*

[2] *Ibid.,* p. 7.

[3] *Ibid.*

[4] University of Wisconsin (Madison Campus) Faculty Document 122, March 6, 1967, p. 1.

[5] *The Daily Cardinal,* February 24, 1967.

[6] *The Daily Cardinal,* October 3, 1967.

[7] Mimeographed handbill in author's possession.

[8] Mimeographed statement in author's possession.

[9] The Madison *Capital Times,* October 19, 1967; *The Daily Cardinal,* October 19, 1967.

[10] The Madison *Capital Times,* October 20, 1967.

* This study was made as a participant-observer during the year 1967–68, from personal participation in administrative staff meetings, faculty meetings, and related conferences. Sources other than citations and participation included an extensive collection of handbills, newspaper clippings, and other general internal reports on the subject.

3

SAN FRANCISCO STATE:
THE TECHNOLOGY OF CONFRONTATIONISM

by Ralph M. Goldman*

THE OPEN SOCIETY—insofar as it actually is open and fulfills its claims—is a standing invitation to trouble. Its liberties, tolerance, and constraints upon powerful minorities invite attack, license, and violence by the aggrieved, short-tempered, and politically unskilled. Its ideological commitment to compromise and law invite tests of its physical strength and its willingness to assume risks. The open society is likely to be misused as much as it is used; in many circumstances, it operates as an imperfect mechanism—not equally or immediately open to all its members. If the open society has a chronic disability, however, it is its difficulty in recognizing and adjusting quickly to the new technologies of its assailants.

"Confrontationism" is such a new technology. It has been equipped by the great mechanical revolution in modern communications. Senator Joe McCarthy gave confrontationism its first major test run

* Dr. Ralph M. Goldman, Professor of Political Science at San Francisco State College, is the author of *The Democratic Party in American Politics,* co-author of *Politics of National Party Conventions,* and co-editor of the five-volume *Presidential Nominating Politics in 1952.* He is currently pursuing research in the field of international conflict and arms control. At the College, he has served as Director of the Institute for Research on International Behavior and as Associate Dean for Faculty Research. A version of this chapter appeared in *Dissent,* May, 1968, and is used here by permission.

in America. It worked so well that those incomparable technologists, the United States Army, finally stole the patent rights at the Army-McCarthy hearings. Today, confrontationism is being practiced on the nation's campuses, where the open society is most open and often most vulnerable. A case study in contemporary confrontationism, in particularly complex form, may be drawn from events at San Francisco State College—where a Hyde Park-type speaker's platform, the first on any American campus, sits in mid-campus; where there are more radicals and hippies per classroom than at most other colleges; where the faculty senate was the first in the nation to seat student representatives as voting members; and where the concept of a student-run experimental college within the regular college had its birth. More than most American colleges (and in many ways more than the rest of the society of which it is inescapably a part), San Francisco State has been a proudly open campus. There is consequently a special poignancy in hearing the pickets shout: "Shut it down!"

Confrontationism is a strategy with a distinctive set of technological attributes: *Instant Majoritarianism, Instant Equality,* and *Instant Replay.*

Instant Majoritarianism requires the presence of an adamant minority that suddenly wishes to be perceived as the majority. This minority often has the appearance and the idiom of revolutionaries. Instant Majoritarianism seems to be a by-product of our patent-medicine culture, wherein small pills are sold as quick cures for large illnesses.

Instant Equality elevates minorities in another way. The compression chamber for Instant Equality is the television screen and the newspaper headline, neither of which has room for more than two parties to any fight. Thus each party, by definition, is half the story, half the conflict, and equally as important as the other. The economics of screen space and newspaper paragraphs is such that third, fourth, and other parties are necessarily shunted off-stage. In this way, confrontationism simplifies conflict into "good guys" vs. "bad guys," and, regardless of complexities, compels the audience into dichotomous choices. A pitched battle with the cops is always productive of Instant Equality.

The third attribute of confrontationism is *Instant Replay.* A well-timed confrontation, usually at midday when sunlight is good, is assured a place on all evening television newscasts as well as in the breakfast editions of local newspapers. Instant Replay provides the prompt publicity necessary to confrontationism. Instant Replay also fixes the picture of "what happened" as though it all happened at the place of greatest movement, controversy, or violence. Action is an essential ingredient of good TV camera work, even if the cameraman has to provoke the action. Instant Replay reports "the action" before further information can arrive to provide a context for the action. This technological attribute challenges the tactical ingenuity of the cops, the Establishment, and competing minorities, each eager to transmit its own "action." Above all, Instant Replay pushes back the thin line between appearances and reality, further confounding the Silent Majority that watches the tube at home or glances at newspapers over breakfast.

San Francisco State, one of the largest of the 18 operating colleges in the California State College System, serves more than 18,500 students. The College has a faculty of 900 regular (i.e., voting) and 550 part-time (i.e., nonvoting) members—a faculty body of 1,450 in all. The operating budget of the College, appropriated by the California legislature, is roughly $20 million a year. The faculty, by attracting sponsored educational and research projects, has added between $4 million and $5 million to this thin budgetary soup. Nearly 60 academic departments offer a full array of bachelor's and master's degrees, teaching credentials, and other certificates. One department —Special Education—offers a doctorate jointly with the University of California; several departments, with international reputations, have some faculty more qualified than their counterparts at the University for doctoral instruction. These 60 departments of the College are distributed among 6 schools, headed by deans whose administrative and clerical staffs are laughably tiny.

San Francisco State is one of the leading urban colleges in the nation, despite the shadows cast over it by Berkeley and Stanford. Distinguished faculty are attracted to it by life in the San Francisco Bay Area and by a student culture that is, according to David Riesman, among the half-dozen or so most distinctive in the country. Very little else could attract or hold such faculty, for the teaching load is still an anachronistic 12 hours (nearly double the load of comparable institutions), the salary scale fluctuates around B according to ratings by the AAUP (American Association of University Professors), and research support, sabbaticals, stenographic help, administrative services, and other normal tools of academia are almost non-existent. The proportion of doctoral degrees among the newly hired faculty has dropped sharply in recent years, leading to a disproportionate number of part-time faculty (whose role in faculty affairs is a hidden dimension in the current crisis).

The 18 campuses of the California State College System serve over 200,000 students with a corps of more than 9,000 full-time faculty. This is the largest system of public higher education in the Western Hemisphere, established under a "Master Plan for Higher Education" by the Donahoe Act of 1960. Under this Plan the University (now with nine campuses around the state) was to specialize, as it always had, in professional training and "the research function." The colleges, many of them still state normal schools, were grouped together under a new board of trustees to function primarily as "teaching institutions." The two-year junior colleges—now numbering more than 80—constitute a third component of higher education. A principal architect of the Plan was Glenn S. Dumke, then President of San Francisco State College (1957–61) and now Chancellor of the entire California State College System.

Most students at San Francisco State—sometimes referred to as the Silent Majority—are older, married, parents, career-oriented, and employed at a full- or part-time job. All but 800 of them live off campus and fit their studies into a tight daily schedule. This Busy Majority tends to be liberal in outlook, too preoccupied to become campus activists, and unable financially to afford loss of course credits or school time. The current agony of most of this Busy Majority— black, white, and brown—is indeed something to behold, if only those who report the news would behold it.

The reader is asked to remember these descriptive details, for nearly all are grist for the confrontation mill.

Ron Moscowitz, a long-time education reporter for the San Francisco *Chronicle,* wrote on December 2, 1968: "How does a prestigious college like San Francisco State get in the almost helpless mess that the campus finds itself . . . ?" For some answers, he suggests, "one must go all the way back to the late 1950's, when the Master Plan . . . was adopted." Under that Plan, the University bested the colleges in caliber of students to be admitted, dollar support per student, faculty salaries, experienced administrators, budget and curriculum flexibility, to mention but a few of the discriminatory arrangements.

In the eight years since Dumke left campus to become Chancellor of the California State College System, San Francisco State College has had five presidents and a heavy turnover of administrators. In September, 1966, the College welcomed a new President, John H. Summerskill, former Vice President for Student Affairs at Cornell. His credentials seemed excellent: youthful, liberal, sensitive to the aspirations of minority students, and willing to spend hours on end in discussion with the student leadership.

Problems came upon Summerskill from the very beginning. His inaugural ceremonies on May 2, 1967, were enlivened by an unprecedented "picket-in" by the Students for a Democratic Society (SDS); the "demand" had to do with the issuance of student class rankings to draft boards. Two other confrontations developed later: one grew out of the invasion of the campus newspaper office, on November 6, by a group of Black Student Union (BSU) members—among them Black Panther leader George A. Murray—during which the paper's editor was assaulted and property was damaged; another resulted from the publication of alleged obscenities in one of the campus papers, *Open Process*. On December 6, 1967, BSU and MAPS (Movement Against Political Suspensions, an *ad hoc* student group) conducted a well-televised demonstration to protest the suspensions of George Murray and others. This demonstration led to rioting, including an attempt to burn down the college book store. President Summerskill adopted tactics designed to avoid a police-student confrontation. Since the campus is state property, city police, according to local understandings, usually come onto it on the invitation of the state official in charge, in this case, Summerskill. Summerskill did not call in the police, who were nonetheless on standby along neighboring streets. He simply closed the campus for the day. Property damage was light, and the militants were denied their confrontation.

The faculty and San Francisco community leaders promptly applauded Summerskill's restraint. The 21 Trustees of the State College System, several of whom were appointees of Governor Ronald Reagan, thought otherwise. In a televised meeting of the board, the Trustees submitted Summerskill to a humiliating interrogation. Faculty representatives at the meeting were similarly treated. On February 22, 1968, Summerskill tendered his resignation, effective in September.

Meanwhile, Summerskill had been working with a committee of deans to design a program of Black Studies. He also invited various student groups to prepare innovative curriculum proposals, which he subsequently transmitted as a grant solicitation to the Carnegie

Foundation. On February 9, 1968, he appointed Dr. Nathan Hare, a sociologist who had recently lost his job at Howard University because of his militance, to help design a Black Studies curriculum. By April 16, Hare submitted a formal proposal for a Department of Black Studies to be established by September, 1968. As these activities went on, Summerskill also took steps to recruit additional Negro faculty and administrators.

During the year another student group had come to the fore: the Third World Liberation Front, a loose coalition of black-, brown-, and red-skinned radicals. Third World leadership tends to be predominantly Mexican-American or Latin-American; one of its faculty sponsors has been Dr. Juan Martinez, a temporary instructor in history. On May 21, 1968, TWLF, BSU, and SDS staged a demonstration demanding the retention of Martinez (whose one-year appointment was terminating), the inauguration of a Black Studies program, the special admission of 400 minority students with less-than-admission-standard school records, and the termination of the College's contract with the Air Force ROTC.

The demonstration quickly became a violent confrontation. Personal assault and property damage were incurred more systematically than in December. President Summerskill called in the San Francisco police. Television cameras rolled as militants and police pushed each other on a parking lot next to the Administration building. In the midst of the ensuing marathon negotiations between militants and administrators, Summerskill departed—to the surprise of nearly all who were involved—for Ethiopia on a long-arranged consulting mission for the Ford Foundation. Chancellor Dumke issued a public notice of his dismissal almost immediately thereafter.

The faculty's presidential recruitment committee, weary of looking for leadership from off-campus, proposed three names, a usual number to be nominated, to the Chancellor and Trustees. All were on-campus faculty; one—Robert R. Smith—had a distinguished administrative record as former Dean of the College's outstanding School of Education. In February, 1964, Smith had created a state-wide furor with a letter of resignation that blasted Chancellor Dumke and the 21 Trustees for failure to seek adequate fiscal and popular support for their sector of the state's higher education. He was then, and still was in 1968, widely supported by faculty at San Francisco State and other campuses. In effect, the faculty recruiting committee gave the Trustees little choice.

The summer months were hectic. Work on the Black Studies curriculum was pressed forward, and in September President Smith created a Department of Black Studies, with Hare as Acting Chairman. The Trustees were given the College's formal proposal for a B.A. degree in Black Studies. Applications for special admission students were processed. Martinez was retained in an administrative post. New black administrators were recruited, including Dr. Joseph White as Dean of Undergraduate Studies, who was made responsible for administrative supervision of the new Department of Black Studies. In his initial address to the faculty, President Smith outlined elaborate plans for experiment and change. He looked forward to a good academic year. He did not reckon with the confrontationists.

Fall at San Francisco State turned out to be a continuing TV special. Only a skeleton of events will be reviewed here. How things appeared on campus often had more to do with struggles in arenas distant from the College. George Murray, the Black Panther Minister of Education, was also a part-time graduate student and part-time instructor at the College. He was to teach English as a "second language" to a class made up mainly of ghetto students. Another prominent Black Panther, Eldridge Cleaver, it should be noted, was scheduled to teach Social Analysis 139X across the Bay at Berkeley. Cleaver was also on the California ballot at this time as a nominee for President. Running for United States Senator was an outspoken conservative Republican, California Superintendent of Public Instruction Max Rafferty. Like Governor Reagan, Rafferty made much of campus unrest. In this setting, on September 26, six weeks before Election Day, the Trustees "suggested" to President Smith that he "reassign" Murray to nonteaching duties. Smith, with remarkable understatement, observed that Trustees' intervention in a faculty personnel matter without explicit charges was "most unusual." He declined to comply.

On October 9, Presidential candidate Cleaver spoke from the College's speaker's platform, treating the crowd to a generous flow of four-letter expletives. In the roster of names mentioned for condemnation or praise he never referred to his fellow-Panther, George Murray. On October 18 two bomblike contraptions were found on campus: one at the Admissions office, and the other at the door of the Political Science Chairman.[1] The special admission program had

[1] See John H. Bunzel, "Black Studies at San Francisco State," *The Public Interest,* 12 (Fall, 1968), pp. 22–38.

fallen somewhat short of the authorized 400 students, and the Political Science Chairman had been publicly critical of Hare's approach to Black Studies. On October 24, the Board of Trustees met in regular session at Fresno State College. Nearby, Murray delivered a speech to assembled students about killing the "white oppressors." At the Trustees' meeting, San Francisco State officials were presenting the case for a Black Studies Department, which was then authorized. On October 28, Murray, back in San Francisco, called for a strike of black and brown students on November 6, the day after Election Day. He urged striking students to carry guns onto campus, but it was not clear when or for what purpose. Later, Murray explained that it was "to protect themselves from the racist administrators." The next day Mayor Alioto asked his district attorney to look into "such exhortations to violence" to determine if a clear-and-present danger of violence existed or if a felony had been or was about to be committed. On Halloween Eve, Chancellor Dumke, citing Section 43522 of Title V of the California Administrative Code, directed President Smith to "suspend George Murray temporarily as a member of the faculty and as a student" on grounds of misconduct. Smith's response, in a public statement, was in part as follows: "The action of the Chancellor is unprecedented. He acted contrary to strong representations by community leaders . . . and against recommendations my staff and I made. We have an investigation in progress and necessary action would have been taken at the appropriate time."

Smith called for a confrontation of his own, inviting the Chairman of the Board of Trustees, the Chancellor, and their General Counsel to meet with him the next day, November 1, in San Francisco. They never showed up. Meanwhile, Smith notified Murray of his suspension. On November 4 the Black Student Union leadership, in the company of Dr. Hare and Dean White, held a press conference to issue Ten Demands and the formal strike call.

The Ten Demands, in brief, called for (1) immediate transfer of all Black Studies courses into the Black Studies Department, with full pay for their instructors, (2) a full professorship for Dr. Hare, (3) creation of an autonomous Black Studies Department, (4) filling of all unused admissions in the special admissions program, (5) admission of all black applicants into the College, regardless of number, (6) 20 teaching positions for the Black Studies Department, (7) dismissal of the Student Financial Aid officer to be replaced by a black person, (8) no disciplinary action against the strikers, (9) prohibition of Trustee dissolution of any Black Studies programs on or off campus, (10) reinstatement of George Murray. To these ten demands were added five more from the Third World Liberation Front: (1) creation of an autonomous School of Ethnic Studies; (2) 50 teaching positions for this school, including the 20 for Black Studies; (3) reinstatement of Murray; and (4) and (5) reiterating BSU Demands 4 and 5 so as to encompass "all non-white" students.

These demands, said the BSU and TWLF leaders, were "not negotiable." These leaders were indeed correct, in more ways than one. First, some of the "demands" were already in effect: a Black Studies Department as autonomous as any on campus; over 11 faculty positions (although not as many as 20) offered to Black Studies on an interim basis until regular positions could be funded the following year. Second, other demands required breaches of long-standing faculty and student due process: promotion of Hare outside normal promotion procedures; automatic reinstatement of Murray; dismissal of the Student Financial Aid officer without formal charges; admission of all non-white applicants, in effect, according to a racial criterion; blanket amnesty for strikers regardless of their acts. A third group of "non-negotiable" demands were those impossible for the College to implement: Trustees could not be "prohibited" from dissolving an academic program; unused special admissions "slots" could not be filled without appropriate applicants in sufficient numbers (student recruitment has been only partially successful). Non-negotiation, in fact, brought programs in being and those in process of development to a halt for the remainder of the academic year.

On November 6 the BSU strike began with a noon rally attended by an estimated 2,000 students. As the rally proceeded, student squads went into regularly scheduled classes to ask students to join them; some asked the instructor for permission. As reports of a typewriter thrown out of a window, several small fires, and disrupted classes reached President Smith, he called upon the San Francisco police to restore order. By 2:00 P.M., he closed the campus for the rest of the day.

During the next two days, confrontationists came from every direction. Some black militants made guerrilla-type raids into various offices and classrooms. A small explosion and several fires occurred around campus. Some forty faculty members, responding to the hiring-firing due process implications of Murray's suspension, issued their own strike call if Murray was not restored to faculty status by November 12.

On November 12, a formal meeting of the full faculty (attended, however, by only a minority) began a week of nearly continuous general meetings in lieu of teaching classes, while black militants marched in and out of classes that were being taught. The Police Department's Tactical Squad appeared and disappeared, taking photos and making occasional arrests. The first serious violence between police and students occurred on November 13, whereupon President Smith ordered the campus shut down. In the days that followed, several attempts to reopen classes brought violence and the Tactical Squad back onto campus. Finally, administrators, leaders of the faculty senate, and BSU-TWLF student leaders agreed to conduct a continuing, all-day debate on television. The performance ran true to confrontationist form, with student militants condemning the "white oppressors," and walking out on the proceedings during the second day.

President Smith was obviously not without his own confrontationist motivations. While the televised debates were going on, Smith departed for a meeting with the Trustees in Los Angeles. Encountering Trustee resistance to his own proposals and Trustee directives he could not agree to carry out, Smith announced his resignation from the College's presidency on November 26. With the Trustees' meeting still in session, Chancellor Dumke appointed Dr. S. I. Hayakawa, the renowned semanticist, whose name had been associated with the College for years, as Interim Acting President. This was to be Hayakawa's first experience of college administration.

The new president had the Thanksgiving holiday as a respite. But at 8:00 A.M., Monday, December 2, as students and militants returned to campus, Acting President Hayakawa, decked out in the tam-o-shanter that has become his campaign symbol, strode over to a striker's sound truck and wrestled for control of the equipment. Student strike leaders were suspended that same day, and for the next two weeks violence, police, and regular TV coverage kept the Busy Majority completely distracted. The local chapter of the American Federation of Teachers called for a strike on December 16, but Hayakawa suddenly announced the beginning of the Christmas vacation a week early, on December 16. When classes resumed on January 6, little had changed but the dramatis personae had grown remarkably, including a citizens' committee appointed by Mayor

Alioto, the San Francisco Area Labor Council, professional arbitrators, and others.

An Ecology of Confrontations

Norton Long of the University of Illinois has described local urban politics as "an ecology of games." At San Francisco State, one could call the criss-crossing lines of battle "an ecology of confrontations." The best way to cut through the confusion is to deal with one set of confrontationists at a time, and only with the major ones at that.

Blacks vs. Negroes. The difference between these two terms is a difference between aspiring new militant leaders and established older moderates, the difference between the Black Panther Party and the NAACP, each of which has its own internal factional version of the militant-moderate debate over tactics. "Militancy" sometimes becomes a euphemism for violence or the threat thereof. Some black leaders who advocate militancy because "it works" are clearly seeking leadership of the ghettos, just as the Jewish gangs of New York, the Irish gangs of Boston, and the Italian gangs of Chicago did before them.

At San Francisco State, the militant-moderate struggle has manifested itself in a number of ways: Minister of Information Cleaver's "put down" of the Minister of Education Murray; the incessant tactical debates within the Black Student Union; the prominence of Jerry Varnado, a BSU spokesman who quotes regularly from Che Guevara and whose television appeals are to "the beautiful black people out there"; the presence of black nonstudents during the more violent confrontations.

Above all, the tactic of confrontation "worked." The sustained television and press coverage has put Varnado, Murray, and other student militants on a par with the Governor, the Mayor, and the College's numerous presidents. Most significantly, the student militants have brought running to their side older Negro leaders who cannot afford to be bypassed. Dr. Carlton Goodlett—physician, publisher, and often considered "dean" of San Francisco's Negro leaders —joined the demonstrations, submitted to arrest, and was released on bail quickly enough to appear for interviews on TV. San Francisco's only black legislator, State Assemblyman Willie Brown— seriously threatened in his last election campaign by a black militant on the ballot—joined Goodlett. In the light of Instant Majoritarianism, the actions of Goodlett and Brown were far more significant than the unexciting pronouncements of a committee of Negro ministers who condemned violence and urged moderation.

On February 21, 1969, Acting President Hayakawa appointed a Select Committee, headed by Economics Professor Curt Aller, a man of substantial reputation in the labor-management relations field. Hayakawa authorized the Select Committee "to meet with student representatives and to come to agreement on substantive issues raised by the fifteen demands. . . ." On February 24, the Select Committee established contact with the TWLF-BSU leaders, who presented a set of three written "Preconditions for Peace Talks." One called for the participation of George Murray, then in jail. The Sheriff's Office was prevailed upon to allow for this arrangement. The second related to the problems of disciplinary procedures for striking students. This led to seven "recommendations" to Acting President Hayakawa regarding disciplinary matters arising out of the strike. The third precondition had to do with the handling of substantive issues, that is, the fifteen demands. The Select Committee favored dividing these into two categories: those which the College would implement on its own account, and those which the College and President Hayakawa would support as recommendations to the Chancellor and Trustees.

The exchanges between the Select Committee and TWLF-BSU continued until a "settlement" was announced on March 20. President Hayakawa acknowledged with thanks the fruit of their "arduous labors" in a statement issued on March 21. He welcomed the seven recommendations on disciplinary issues, but indicated that he would view them entirely as recommendations. He promised to respond on these issues on April 11, that is, after the Spring recess, in order to give the TWLF-BSU leaders an "opportunity to demonstrate their leadership in establishing peaceful conditions on campus." Hayakawa then proceeded to the substantive issues by reviewing College plans for the Black Studies Department and the School of Ethnic Studies, noting that George Murray's contract had already expired and that Nathan Hare's would expire in June, and reiterating his plans for carrying the College's educational services to all parts of the San Francisco community in an "Operation Outreach." Thus, the "nonnegotiable issues" had been "negotiated."

On April 13 and 14, Hayakawa announced the departure of police from campus, with the hope that there would be no need for them to return. He indicated that he would *not* review the disciplinary cases of student demonstrators acquitted by or receiving probation from campus disciplinary panels. But he did retain the prerogative of reviewing every case in which the panels recommend suspension or expulsion. Thus far, he reported, very few of the 500 disciplinary cases had been processed, and only ten involved recommendations for expulsion. This suggested "a high degree of compassion" on the part of the disciplinary panels, to which he was not adverse.

Even as Hayakawa spoke, "the action" had moved elsewhere— Stanford, Harvard, and back to Berkeley and Columbia. There were no "victory" statements from the TWLF-BSU leaders. In fact, the San Francisco State strike "settlement" seemed almost unnoticed and irrelevant. The victory seemed to be elsewhere: in the ghetto and on other campuses.

AFT vs. Other Faculty Organizations. Faculty in California higher education have an unusual number of organizations seeking to represent them. There is the conservative, strictly bread-and-butter, more than 100,000 civil-servant strong California State Employees Association (CSEA), which has a special section for college faculty. The California Teachers Association, of mainly elementary and secondary school teachers, has a relatively small California College and University Faculty Association (CCUFA). The American Association of University Professors (AAUP), strong at the University, has only recently begun to emerge on College campuses. Perhaps the largest and most active faculty interest group in recent years has been the Association of California's State College Professors (ACSCP). ACSCP's most vigorous challenger has been the American Federation of Teachers (AFT).

AFT Local 1352 at San Francisco State is particularly confrontationist in approach. For several years its 60–100 members have frequently thrown up a picket line or talked strike. It has had a large representation in the College's Academic Senate. But last year AFT Local 1352 had a hard time on campus. National AFT organizers, after failing to get it to soft-pedal Vietnam, the draft, and other nonunion issues, decided to let this local go its own way. And when the Academic Senate asked the faculty which organization should serve as its bargaining agent, AFT lost out by a small margin to ACSCP.

During the mid-December demonstrations, the AFT decided to piggy-back onto the student strike. It inaugurated a vigorous membership drive, and within a month claimed 400 members and the support of 60–80 percent of the faculty. On January 3, its president,

Gary Hawkins, announced to faculty members not belonging to AFT: "Violating our picket line will be interpreted to mean that you have chosen to be with the Trustees and against us. . . . You will not have the luxury of nice distinctions or Byzantine excuses." Many of the non-AFT faculty, with years of commitment to unionism and liberal causes, found themselves called "fink" and "scab" as they did what they never dreamed they would some day do, that is, cross a picket line.

The non-AFT faculty's problem vis-à-vis the AFT was semantic as well as practical. Was Local 1352 really a "union"? Did it not function more like a political group? The strike had not been called in a unionlike way, that is, before rather than after formal negotiating efforts had been initiated. Further, the ACSCP was the faculty's chosen bargaining agent. In fact, it was readily determined from payroll figures (union dues are deducted from pay checks) that the AFT had only 163 members among the 900 regular faculty and 66 members among the 550 part-time faculty—hardly the claimed 400. Finally, the roster of AFT demands, which included support for the student demands, changed from week to week.

Then the question arose whether the AFT strike was really a "strike." The ACSCP, on January 13, announced the results of a secret mail-ballot of the entire faculty on whether or not they supported the AFT strike. Of the 900 regular faculty, 80 percent cast ballots; voting against the strike: 464, or 64 percent. Of the 551 part-time faculty, 68 percent responded; 212, or 57 percent, opposed the strike. At the same time, many of the "strikers" kept leaving the picket lines to teach their classes—usually off-campus—or attend to normal committee, research, or other campus duties. The San Francisco Labor Council which, after much stalling, endorsed the strike, had some difficulties in convincing other unions that the College strike was real.

Meanwhile, state officials, particularly Governor Reagan and Chancellor Dumke, became adamant about terminating the services of faculty absent from classes. The state's personnel statutes prescribed that an absence "whether voluntary or unvoluntary" [2] of any faculty member from normal duties for five consecutive days shall be considered as having resigned. Reagan, whose winding past includes the presidency of an actor's union, issued a "you-can't-have-your-cake-

[2] Education Code, Vol. II (Section 24311).

and-eat-it" challenge, recalling that workers really on strike usually really withhold services and really lose their salaries.

The "crunch" for the ill-prepared and poorly supported strike came in mid-February as the College approached the start of Spring Semester classes. Unprecedented time-reporting procedures had been established to determine which faculty were present and which absent from their classes or other duties. The procedures resulted in some of the striking faculty losing pay. Neither a "strike fund" nor alternate arrangements for strikers' income had been worked out. Within this context, a letter from Trustee Louis Heilbron and Acting President Hayakawa, dated February 16, 1969, to George Johns, Secretary-Treasurer of the San Francisco Labor Council, became the basis for a "settlement." Heilbron was spokesman for an *ad hoc* "Regional Committee" of several Trustees living in the Bay Area but without formal negotiating status because California law prohibits the Trustees from engaging in labor negotiations. Johns represented the Labor Council's interest in the AFT strike.

The Heilbron-Hayakawa letter included nine provisions. One provision reviewed the statute requirements for relations between Trustees and faculty organizations. Another reiterated the College's formal commitment to creation of a Black Studies Department and a School of Ethnic Studies. Six provisions dealt with grievance procedures, amnesty, and other faculty employment issues arising out of the strike itself. A ninth declared that faculty assigned a reduced teaching load during 1969 would not be docked if such assignment "was made in accordance with College procedure and the staffing formula." This last provision was the only non-strike-related issue and referred to combined ACSCP-AFT efforts during the preceding year to have academic departments voluntarily reduce their teaching loads from 12 hours to 9 hours. Such reductions involve some subtle—and usually unpublicized—juggling of workload and staffing formula within departments. Despite the anachronism of a 12-hour load, the publicity attending this provision probably inhibited rather than promoted efforts to engage in such juggling. Who, after all, likes to be noticed with his hand in the cookie jar?

Needless to say, Local 1352 claimed a major "victory" as well as credit for the pacification of the campus. These claims were promptly challenged by other faculty organizations. What remains to be seen is the long-run consequence of the strike for the future of unionism in higher education.

Faculties vs. Trustees. The acrimony between the faculties of the State Colleges and the Trustees is everywhere evident. The electric response to Smith's resignation as Dean of Education in 1964 was the first faculty protest against second-class status in California higher education. But the 1964 confrontation was old-fashioned: petitions, speeches, a resignation, action at the legislature, and no TV.

Then, in 1965, the Trustees voted to correct an administrative error in faculty-salary budgeting by arbitrarily reducing salaries of all full and associate professors by 1.8 percent. An *ad hoc* organization, Faculties for the Defense of Education, sprang up on the campuses, again demonstrating the degree of faculty hostility, and receiving only Trustee scorn. By spring, 1968, the California State College Academic Senate expressed its profound antipathy to both the Trustees and Chancellor Dumke by voting "no confidence" in Dumke and urging him to resign. The Senate's action was supported in February, 1969, by a system-wide faculty vote of 3,743 to 2,227, with over 65 percent of the 9,148 eligible faculty participating. Nothing came of the request, a lesson in its own limitations that should not have been lost on the faculties.

At San Francisco State, few events have united the faculty more quickly than some high-handed action by the Trustees or the Chancellor. Faculty endorsement of President Summerskill was unanimous, for example, after the December 6, 1967, rioting, even as the Trustees humiliated him. The faculty supported, by a 2–1 vote, President Smith's agreement to have a continuing convocation; within the week he was compelled to resign because of Trustee intransigence. Conversely, President Hayakawa, acting in concert with Chancellor-Trustee tactics, is a source of wide-spread nervousness even among his closest faculty friends.

The only confrontationists among the faculty organizations are the AFT leaders, and they have acted accordingly. Will the faculties ever come to appreciate that under the present statutes and organization governing the State College System, they can only be losers in confrontations with the Trustees? Will the faculties find the skills needed to tackle the large tasks of designing and promoting new legislation for their self-governance and accountability? Unfortunately, confrontationism requires less homework than do drafting legislative bills and educating busy legislators.

Democrats vs. Republicans. The partisan confrontation was explicit in October and November, 1968. Republican candidate Rafferty was for law-and-order on the campuses, for "cleaning out" radical professors and hippie students. Democratic candidate Cranston was for organizational reform in higher education and expanded educational opportunities for all.

Less clear at that time were the makings of a confrontation in 1970, when Governor Reagan would run for re-election and San Francisco's Mayor Alioto would be his likeliest Democratic opponent. On the issues of law-and-order and campus unrest, which are bound to be prominent in the 1970 campaign, neither man could politically afford to appear weak or undecided. In this confrontation, Reagan has several built-in advantages over Alioto. Reagan can dramatically speak of "using bayonets" to keep the colleges open, but it is Alioto's police force that has the day-to-day dirty job. Reagan can safely refuse to negotiate with the militants and the strikers, whereas Alioto, immediately at the tangled scene, has little choice but to seek an avenue toward negotiation, difficult as confrontationism makes this. Every one of Reagan's "tough" comments—as governor—on the crisis generates statewide television coverage; Alioto the moderator has trouble getting balanced San Francisco coverage. The longer the crisis lasts, the fresher will be its tumultuous recollections for Reagan's law-and-order campaign in 1970; for Alioto, divisions among such fellow-Democrats as anti-Trustee Robert R. Smith and pro-Trustee Hayakawa can only be reflected in the 1970 balloting.

Liberals vs. Conservatives. For liberals, education is a civilizing force in human development. Education inhibits prejudice and brute passion. Hence, the schools must make their classrooms available to everyone, at whatever financial cost to society, and in these classrooms, the students' views and concerns are to be taken raw, to be milled and refined by the insights of academic disciplines and by the tests of reason and evidence. Even this oversimplified summary of a liberal view of education makes it easier to understand why liberals are committed to tuition-free higher education, continuing curriculum innovation, active community involvement by both students and teachers, open admissions to all who wish to enroll, and ever-increasing appropriations to support the educational enterprise. As liberal a faculty as that of San Francisco State would be untrue to its basic educational ideology if it did not interpret many of the student and faculty strike demands as worthy of support.

Conservatives, on the other hand, tend toward an elitist conception of education. Some students are simply better and smarter than others, and the social investment in them should vary accordingly. This conception has been embedded in the hierarchical character of higher education in California: the University has the best students and gets the most resources, the colleges rating second best, and the junior colleges even less. Another conservative proposition is that education is costly, hence, should be made available only to the loyal, the obedient, and the grateful. Troublesome students and colleges must be cut back in funds and other resources, particularly those as troublesome as San Francisco State. At his January 14 press conference and again on April 9, Governor Reagan was explicit about the "preponderance" of the liberal political viewpoint on college and university faculties; he argued that a better representation of other viewpoints needs to be achieved. State Superintendent of Public Instruction Max Rafferty is also succinct: the solution for SF State is "less students and less faculty." If SF State and other liberal colleges were half their present size, such reductions would penalize the "trouble-makers" and cut off the supply of "radical-liberal" citizens (who become voters) at the source. These views make the educational conservatives like Reagan and Rafferty eager and provocative confrontationists; the worse the crisis, the more quickly will faculty and students depart from the campus. Why struggle with cut-backs of college resources in budget-writing sessions when campus crises will do the job with less effort?

On the California campuses this confrontation is nothing less than a struggle for the minds and attitudes of the next generation of citizens. The stakes are therefore higher than the 1970 election or the survival of SF State. Poor judgment and little skill are disastrous in such a contest, as the liberal faculties have learned and will undoubtedly continue to learn. In fact, armies as small as the educational liberals' need extraordinary judgment in matches against larger forces.

In California, the liberals run the immediate risk of losing their basic idiom, either by letting it tumble out of their hands or by having it stolen right out from under their typewriter ribbons by the conservative confrontationists. To illustrate the first prospect, consider the action of the SF State Academic Senate in establishing a special committee made up of only the black members of the full-time faculty to create in turn a special personnel committee to determine the retention and promotion of Dr. Nathan Hare, the Black Studies Department Chairman. The Senate's Ad Hoc Committee on the campus crisis, composed—just as is the Senate—of liberals of long standing, enunciated the rationalization as follows:

Any attempt to make the Black Studies Department comply with the process by which a typical department achieves its agent's autonomy [in making academic appointments in the name of the College] is hopeless. Not because [that Department] hasn't a legitimate program with standards, but because we are white and they are black, and because this is no time for whites to say to blacks: "You must convince us of your standards before you proceed. . . ."

These are liberal professors instituting a segregationist dichotomy between white and black as the basis for a return to separate-but-equal arrangements in education. These are liberals arguing for the principle that a judgment about professional competence should be (we recognize that it too often is) made on the basis of race.

The second prospect—of having the liberal idiom stolen by the conservatives—is just as insidious. The most conservative members of the Board of Trustees, for example, have raised the obvious liberal questions about nondiscrimination in hiring practices of the Black Studies Department. Another example is Reagan's objection to limiting instruction to any single philosophy or ideology. His "trust and faith" lies "in the students' ability to hear varying points of view and to make . . . an intelligent decision." This is liberal vocabulary, but without liberal intent; e.g., Reagan's campaign to deny Eldridge Cleaver at the University and George Murray at the College status as temporary instructors.

In short, confrontationism, by rendering the liberals self-contradictory or speechless, has afforded the conservative confrontationists an opportunity to co-opt the language of liberalism as part of their campaign to undermine liberalism. Even the ordinarily vocal Max Rafferty has taken a back-seat on the higher education issue in recent months lest his hard-line get in the way of Reagan and the Trustees.

In many respects, confrontation is an ancient political tactic, in which leaders of a coalition isolate a common enemy against whom they may remain united, or flush an elusive adversary out into the open, or test a specific issue or degree of strength, etc. Traditional confrontations have been potent weapons of dissent in open societies. Since the thirties trade unionists and civil libertarians have been the most persistent and successful users of traditional confrontation. These are precisely the people presently most confused and distraught about contemporary confrontationism; witness the ambivalence of campus liberals—whether at SF State, Berkeley, or Columbia—union liberals, and civil-rights liberals. Does the confusion arise out of the impulse to withhold teaching services at a time when more and better instruction is needed as a civilizing instrument? or out of the crossing of a picket line in a non-strike called by a nonbargaining agent? or out of the separationist demands of militant Negroes whose "integration" into the grand opportunities of American life has been one's goal for decades? Have all these values gone topsy-turvy?

Contemporary confrontationism is a greater and more insidious threat to the open society than mere confusion of values and slogans. The dangers of this threat are inherent in the technological characteristics of confrontationism—that is, Instant Majoritarianism, Instant Equality, and Instant Replay.

Instant Majoritarianism. "Power" is often more in the eyes of the viewer than in the resources of the "powerful." Majority rule is a normal basis of power in the United States, except for those stubborn minorities who know how to filibuster in the U.S. Senate, etc. "Powerfulness," therefore, is being so perceived by others, usually on the basis of something real and observable such as many guns, much money, many words, or most votes.

Confrontationism, on the other hand, employs appearances and illusion rather than observable realities in order to elicit perceptions of "powerfulness": the Black Panther who shouts "kill, kill" (instead of teaching the English language, which he does so well), the Mexican-American student with his four-letter expletives (instead of the poetry he writes so well), the distortion on the face of the faculty member who shouts "scab" and "fink" at some long-beloved colleague, the crowding of small numbers of demonstrators into narrow parking lots and street corners to be filmed as a "mob," the planting of stink bombs that might yet become real bombs, the starting of small skirmishes to bring out platoons of police. Ordinary people, even at an off-beat college, view these manifestations as fearsome and, knowingly or not, easily attribute "power" to those who employ such appearances and tactics. In this way, we have seen, the powerful come to be perceived as weak or vacillating, and the minority to be as "powerful" as a majority. In other words, this is Instant Majoritarianism.

The danger of Instant Majoritarianism lies in the persistence of illusion untied to a negotiating and legislative process. Only in fairy tales does the mirror respond to the princess, and even there, odds are she was talking to herself. With the inadvertent aid of television and other mass media, Instant Majoritarianism threatens to make "due process" and the more traditional modes of petition and dissent not obsolete but irrelevant in America.

Instant Equality. George Orwell saw the danger of this characteristic of confrontationism when he wrote the slogans of the Party: WAR IS PEACE. FREEDOM IS SLAVERY. IGNORANCE IS STRENGTH. The danger lies in compressing a many-sided problem into a two-sided one and in equating the two elements in every dichotomy. The cost of unraveling some dichotomies into the complexities they really are can become oppressive if not overwhelming. Consider the cost of destroying the deceitful notion of SEPARATE BUT EQUAL. Consider the cost of demonstrating that the conflict in Vietnam is between more parties than the United States and North Vietnam. The danger is more than semantic. These particular false dichotomies were embedded in elaborate principles; significant segregationist and military behaviors were the consequence of each.

The ease and cheapness of achieving Instant Equality through the technology of confrontationism is too attractive to ignore. To get the cameras and the press onto the scene requires little more than phone calls reporting an imminent inflammatory pronouncement, or a rumor of plans for violence. This process gets to the point where tactical inventiveness is the order of the day for all sides; e.g., President Hayakawa's lone attack upon the strikers' sound truck—very photogenic! Here again, appearances—televised and headlined—are a danger to reality, but an even greater danger to reason. For, if war equals peace, why worry about either?

Instant Replay. In this technological attribute lies the very difficult problem of professionalism in American journalism. The current reportorial style of badgering rather than interviewing a public figure illustrates the problem. A logical line of questioning can usually cut to the truth of a newsworthy situation with greater precision than the meat-ax of a reporter's insult. But logical questioning is taken to be a bore, both on TV and in the headline that must be distilled from the event. Speed, brevity, and action demand that the interview become a confrontation. How else will the coverage compete with other exciting news for the evening broadcasts?

The traditional journalistic problem is to tell what is new and significant in an understandable and interesting manner. This dull professional dictum is quickly translated by the unprofessional into "Tell what is last-minute and violent or controversial, and do so in one-syllable words, breathlessly; the expert analyses can come later." The danger of Instant Replay is of the dimension of the McCarthy Era in American history. Instant Replay may define the components of an event in a pattern impossible to undo by subsequent reportage. Its description of violence may open the floodgates to otherwise inhibited violence elsewhere. Its unrepresentativeness and exaggerations may disrupt a firmly established public consensus. Its incomplete facts may become permanent public illusions.

At San Francisco State College, the day, the academic year, and perhaps the entire generation will continue to submit to the initiatives of the principal practitioners of confrontationism on both sides. More grave than our local problem is the question whether American society will be able to hear and attend to the legitimate, the burning problems of its students, teachers, Negroes, Mexican-Americans, and other dissidents, if it continues to be distracted by the tactics of confrontationism.

4

COLORADO: SOUNDS
OF STUDENT PROTEST DEFTLY MUTED

*by Billy Mac Jones**

MORE AND MORE in recent times, students have allowed peaceful and legitimate expressions of grievances and dissent to escalate into violence and obstruction. When this happens, university authorities have a choice of responses. They can react without plan, playing each move by ear, doing whatever seems best at the time. Or they can have a plan but, when the chips are down, can modify or abandon it in the face of demands from the protesters. Or they can commit themselves in advance to a course of action, and follow it as coolly and exactly as they are able. It is this writer's conviction that the third alternative offers the best prospects of protecting both order and liberty, two prerequisites of any center of learning. Events during 1967–68 at the University of Colorado illustrated how this could be done.

A growing, restive ferment among highly vocal student groups had been evident on campus at least since 1966. At first this was directionless, but it became increasingly critical of "administrative paternalism and outmoded societal mores." Unrest reached a peak in the

* Billy M. Jones, President, Southwest Texas College, San Marcos, Texas, was an American Council on Education Academic Administration Fellow at the University of Colorado in 1967–68. While at Colorado, Dr. Jones was in the office of the Vice President for Student Affairs for much of the year.

spring elections of 1967 when certain students sought to harness and ride the crest of student restiveness into campus leadership. Expressions of "student power" and "student rights" became overworked clichés, as they were on campuses throughout the nation, and their most vehement articulation came from the fiery campaign waged by the Talmey-Danish ticket.

Paul Talmey, a graduate student, campaigned for the presidency of the Associated Students of the University of Colorado (ASUC) as an outspoken critic of the administration, and pledged in his forty-point program to force a change in alleged *in loco parentis* policies. He asserted he would actively seek the resignation of certain student personnel officers, principally that of the Vice President for Student Affairs, who he claimed represented the Establishment rather than student concerns and problems. The other half of the ticket, Paul Danish, a bright part-time student of eight years or so, echoed his running mate's acrimony. He had attained some national prominence as a spokesman for some student groups; his position paper delivered at the annual meeting of the American Council on Education in October, 1967, stirred a lively controversy with at least one prominent authority on higher education. Danish and Talmey were elected by a bare majority of the *voting* students in an election in which approximately 70 percent of the student body did not participate. But the failure of the majority of students to participate seemed inconsequential and even added strength to the vocal minority.

Signs of restlessness were increasingly articulated by a hypercritical editorial policy adopted by the campus newspaper, the *Colorado Daily*. Hardly a day passed without an editorial broadside at some phase of the University's policy or its policy makers. Moreover, a disproportionate share of national news releases, chosen for their obvious protest content, slanted the *Daily*'s posture. With the spring appointment of Susie Schmidt as editor, the position of the paper crystallized even more behind student activist sentiment. In an effort to insulate the *Daily* from University control and action, Schmidt announced that it would seek to "go it alone," to pay its own way through advertising rather than seeking the support from student fees previously allocated by the University. The paper was to become a "spokesman for the student, not an organ of the administration."

A shift in campus sentiment toward national student organizations also occurred. Though once rejected by Student Senate vote, membership in the National Student Association now found several student and faculty advocates. An Association of Black Collegians was recognized by the University. The Students for a Democratic Society, after an abortive attempt to start a campus chapter in the spring of 1967, established a unit in the fall semester. While most professors remained conveniently or professionally aloof from the situation, some gave support and encouragement to protesting students, in some instances out of an honest conviction that their protests were legitimate.

Dr. Clark Bouton, Assistant Professor of Political Science, became faculty sponsor of SDS. That Bouton's views were in harmony with certain SDS principles was not widely known, but in some respects his acceptance of the sponsorship was not surprising. One of two principals in what was unquestionably one of the most heated issues on campus during the 1966–67 year, Bouton had emerged victorious in July, 1967, from a disputed tenure controversy with considerable faculty and student sympathy. Three of an elected, six-member Board of Regents had voted to withhold tenure from Bouton because, among other reasons, he had no scholarly publications to his credit. However, University President Joseph Smiley, following the unanimous recommendations of his administrative structure, broke a 3–3 tie in Bouton's favor. Smiley's action was roundly applauded by many student and faculty spokesmen, and the *Colorado Daily*. Perhaps resentment arising from the dispute, or a sincere conviction as to the legitimacy of student protests, or both, produced a fateful association between the professor and the organization. They were to be the catalysts for much campus unrest.

The success of the militant Talmey-Danish campaign and the publicity given both to the growing unrest among segments of the student body may have encouraged certain national organizations to designate the University of Colorado in 1967–68 as one of several target campuses for student power confrontations. If so, those who made the selection miscalculated. The administration was not deaf or calloused to student concerns as many critics claimed. Responses had already been made to some of the "demands" of the previous year. Funds were made available to the Associated Students for the recruitment of a "student's professor," a sort of academic gadfly, whose selection and assigned duties would be the sole responsibility of the student government. Regular bus transportation from blocks-away Williams Village, a student residence-hall complex, was initiated and expanded. Medical assistance and professional psychiatric advisement programs were extended with guarantees of confidentiality to the student with special problems. Moreover, a comprehensive review of student conduct codes and discipline was undertaken, first through an ad hoc committee and later by the Faculty Senate Committee on Student Affairs. Such administrative actions had calmed the militancy of many earlier protesters, a fact overlooked by those who might seek to organize student protests for extra-campus motives.

The doors were opened to 16,800 students at the University in September, 1967. With Schmidt at her typewriter and Talmey on the podium, student protesters rallied almost every week day in the University Memorial Center to inflame opinion and preach damnation upon the provincialism of Colorado's student environment. Lectures on civil disobedience, panels on drug use, and teach- or bitch-ins on any subject related to student rights or unrest were standard fare. Student curiosity filled Macky Auditorium to overflowing for the scheduled appearance of Dr. Timothy Leary, national figurehead for drug use, on September 22. Those who looked like Leary supporters cheered consistently. Others either verbally challenged his philosophy or departed early from indifference. If there was to be an early exposure of the general level of student attitudes, Leary unwittingly had provided the first opportunity to assess its character. The general and recognizable tenor of majority student opinion was moderate, if not conservative.

Persuaded, however, that the campus was ripe for protest, and encouraged by whatever else kindled their enthusiasm, SDS members held regular meetings throughout September and early October. They also manned an information booth in the loggia, dispensing anti-draft literature, "pill" information, etc. Only the scant few who participated in their open meetings or who listened seriously to their boasts knew that they planned other types of action.

On Wednesday, October 19, shortly after noon, Air Force recruiters were greeted by a group of some twenty demonstrators who promptly seated themselves in front of the recruiting booth. Among them was Dr. Bouton, who took his place on the loggia floor, and cheered when a prepared statement was read condemning the war in Vietnam and objecting to the presence of military recruiters on campus. Some passers-by applauded the SDS action; more, however, regarded it as childish bluster. A few even insisted that the administration ought to "throw the bums out" for insulting both the University and the armed forces. Both the recruiters and demonstrators remained until no purpose was served by extending the vigil. Only a few students had braved the crowded conditions at the booth to discuss possible service careers. Success? Unquestionably the SDS membership thought so.

Thus encouraged, the same group publicly staged a mock trial of General Lewis B. Hershey two days later. The General was condemned for draft discrimination, and hanged in effigy. This trial, said Bruce Goldberg, Chairman of the local chapter of SDS, "was part of the series of national anti-draft rallies."

Meeting over the weekend, SDS drafted a memorandum to President Smiley and the Regents demanding an open hearing "concerning the presence of military organizations on our campus." Asserting opposition to "governmental use of the military to implement a foreign policy" which causes the "oppression of millions of human beings," the memorandum concluded that to permit military organizations to use University facilities was to give tacit consent to such policies. Unless an open hearing on the matter was scheduled before 8:00 A.M. on the following Thursday, the memo threatened, "a demonstration will be staged on the ROTC drill field at 12:45 P.M. on that day." This threat was never carried out, not because the group lacked determination but because subsequent involvements completely overshadowed its importance.

These weekend discussions also produced a determination to confront CIA recruiters, whose scheduled interviews were to be held during the earlier part of the coming week. Such rumblings reached Vice President for Student Affairs Glenn Barnett early Sunday afternoon, and he alerted Miss Helen Carpenter, Director of Placement Services, in whose offices the interviews were to take place. She was advised that in the event of trouble she should contact Barnett immediately, and that a course of action had already been decided upon in the event disruptive demonstrations took place.

Nothing occurred until Monday afternoon, October 23, when a group of students, led apparently by John Buttny, Co-chairman of SDS, arrived at the Placement office and demanded to see the CIA recruiter, Jack Hanson. Hanson appeared, was handed a prepared statement, and was told to leave the campus. When he refused and was supported in his decision by Miss Carpenter, Buttny then telephoned Vice President Barnett and found that he also would not ask the recruiter to leave.

The students left in a huff, but returned with double force the next morning, equipped with guitars and a record player. Though technically they did not physically block the Placement office, their singing and yelling were greatly disturbing, as were their attempts to crash certain interview rooms from rear doors. University officials moved in and out of the area, warning students not to interfere with the operations of the Placement Service, and attempting to help soften the matter as much as possible. Another day had passed without an overly disturbing confrontation.

But the twenty-five to thirty demonstrators were back before opening hours on Wednesday, October 25, for the third straight day, this time with a plan to block the Placement office. Previous non-intervention by the administration may have produced some false feelings of security; additionally, some of the impetus was undoubtedly supplied by urgings from the national and regional SDS. Further encouragement was gained from faculty sponsor Clark Bouton, whose Tuesday evening speech on "Civil Disobedience and the Liberal Hang-Up" drew from his modest audience many SDS cheers when he made such pronouncements as "The key to the future lies in the opposition of the present." Bouton later disclaimed the charge that his speech, though sponsored by the SDS, was in effect giving license to their behavior. Nevertheless, when the Wednesday confrontation began, he was present (only as an adviser, he explained) and remained throughout the demonstration (because according to Bouton he wished to prevent violence toward and possible injuries to the protesters). One witness alleged that he reinforced a demonstrator's refusal to allow an employee the right to enter the Placement facilities.

The demonstrators expected and actually sought an early arrest by civil authorities. They asserted that they were not demonstrating against the University or the Placement Service—that if they could be assured that the CIA man would not come on campus, or would isolate himself so that they could demonstrate against him alone, they would leave. Without such assurances they were determined to stay. And stay they did, but not without generating intense emotions of anger among other students whose scheduled appointments represented the hopes of four years or more of schooling, appointments they could not now keep. University officials, exercising remarkable calmness and restraint, made efforts to encourage the demonstrators to end their obstruction, but without much success.

Simple ground rules had already been established. President Smiley had delegated discretionary authority over such matters to Dr. Glenn

Barnett, Vice President for Student Affairs. Barnett would decide when University policy had been violated and would then engage only the University staff in dealing with the matter until or unless outside aid became absolutely essential to the maintenance of order. Since order never became a serious issue, civil authorities did not become involved.

Barnett's actions were deliberate but considerate. Dean of Men James Quigley was sent to confront the demonstrators with the seriousness of their behavior, and Richard Stratton, Chief of the Security Division, was asked to stand by in case anti-demonstrators clashed with the protesters. Barnett called in appropriate members of the administration to advise him, but the decision was his. All concurred with him in deciding to allow the demonstrators to remain until normal closing time for the Placement Service, after which it was assumed that they would disperse voluntarily. Only the matters of keeping order, and of salving the annoyed feelings of the entrapped Placement personnel, caused much concern for the balance of the day.

As the mood of those who opposed the demonstration became more angry, Dean Quigley had to take steps to prevent a melee from starting between the two groups. One burly anti-demonstrator was heard to say to an officer: "Say the word and I'll personally throw every goddamned one of them out!" That he could have done so certainly was not doubted by the demonstrators. "Now you've blown it! Really blown it!" complained a protester to Quigley. "All we wanted was to be arrested and taken down and charged in city courts. Now see what you've done? We're likely to get hurt." Some danger of a brawl existed, but Quigley and campus security officers were successful in preventing it.

No arrest came, for the University's plan of action did not call for it. (Bouton later bitterly assailed the city police chief in his downtown office for not doing his duty in this regard.) After 4:00 P.M. the students left the Placement premises amid chatter as to whether their protest had succeeded and concern as to what action the University would take. By class time the next morning they knew the answer to the latter query: Dean Quigley as instructed presented each with a letter of specific charges of violations and ordered all to appear before the University Discipline Committee.

Moving against the organization was more difficult, however, for in almost an immediate about-face, the involved students denied that SDS had sponsored their actions, and asserted instead that they were a group of students acting collectively as the Ad Hoc Committee Against the CIA. Few people, if any, were credulous enough to believe the attempted ruse, but all legal proceedings which followed made reference to the group as the Ad Hoc Committee. No action was attempted against the organization.

In this, as they were to do in all matters relating to the case, University authorities worked closely with and followed the advice of Resident Legal Counsel John Holloway in making certain that the students' constitutional rights to due process and to legal counsel were not abridged. For their determination to afford every possible consideration to the accused, University officials ultimately received high commendation from the federal judge who heard the last appeal.

With what to some observers seemed like interminable delays, the disciplinary machinery began to turn. On November 9, the University Discipline Committee (UDC) heard the case and announced on November 15 that it had voted unanimously to suspend ten, and place on probation twelve of the students. Technically eight of the twelve students receiving lesser penalties were also suspended but immediately readmitted on probation. Of the suspended, eight were graduate students, most if not all of whom were affiliated with SDS. Upon being advised that an appeal against the suspensions could be made to the Administrative Council, the ten promptly voted to do so.

The suspensions touched off a new wave of protests. Paul Talmey, ASUC President, called the action vicious and singularly cruel because it in effect fined the eight graduate students $33,000 in fellowships and teaching salaries. He called for a protest rally and for the resignation of Graduate Dean E. James Archer, as the man responsible. Petitions were circulated among students and faculty, condemning the UDC action, and two hundred students marched, chanted, and sang on the front lawn of President Smiley's home in a late evening protest. Another group of thirty-odd students began a twenty-four hour vigil outside Regent Hall (administrative office building) complete with tent, bed rolls, field cooking stove, etc. For approximately three weeks this gathering slept by night in sub-freezing weather and withstood snow by day to pass out leaflets demanding "justice to the ten." Townsmen as well as faculty responded with food and encouragement; one church group later even served Thanksgiving dinner to the students. And finally, still trying to harness campus dissent, Talmey staged another protest rally outside Regent Hall on Friday, November 17, at which four hundred students gathered to hear faculty and students speak against the suspensions.

Talmey called for and got, on Tuesday, November 21, a "UDC Teach-In-Bitch-In" at which William Briggs (Dean of the College of Arts and Sciences) and E. James Archer (Graduate Dean), both UDC members, spoke in an attempt to explain the reasons for the disciplinary action. Archer apparently received much verbal criticism and abuse for his stand, just as he had from the day when the suspensions were announced. Feeling the pressure acutely, he submitted his resignation as Graduate Dean the following morning. The administration's solid front was thus broken and new hope was generated among supporters of the suspended students. A petition requesting a mitigation of the punishment was signed by 347 faculty members. Needless to say, the *Colorado Daily* found all such events newsworthy, and vitriolic editorials were standard fare for its readers.

A sub-committee of the Administrative Council heard the first appeal on December 13. This group sustained the earlier UDC decision with one exception; one of the two undergraduate students had his suspension reduced to probation after it was revealed that his record warranted additional consideration.

And then there were nine, for whom final appeal within University discipline structure was to the Board of Regents. For this appeal, which the Regents agreed to hear at their regular monthly meeting on January 13, 1968, the suspended students obtained the services of Walter C. Brauer III, an attorney representing the ACLU. Held in the simulated court room in the Law School building, the hearing bore only a faint resemblance to a trial. A faculty member presented a petition, urging the Regents to lessen the penalties and therewith to unite a divided faculty. One Regent then introduced a motion to reduce the sentence, but it failed to pass. After hearing arguments by counsel for the students and by Holloway for the University, the Regents deliberated for an hour in private. In a final show of deep concern, the students were asked, through their attorney, "if they were granted probation, would they promise not to engage in such conduct in the future and would they admit they were wrong?" Brauer reported that the students could give no such assurances and would never admit they were wrong. The vote was then, without dissent, to suspend the students.

"My God! Unanimous?" one of the students exclaimed disbeliev-

ingly. "Bastards!" another exclaimed in the defiant tone which has
become a characteristic of contemporary student attitudes. Still another threw a nickel on the table while others flung their identification cards at the table around which the Regents sat. That nine were
ultimately suspended was the result of at least two lines of thought:
past conduct on the part of some precluded further consideration;
and, graduate students are adults who can be expected to accept
some of the responsibility for respecting the general policies of the
University—especially when those very policies are misused to justify
selfish ends.

With the help of the American Civil Liberties Union, the case of
Buttny vs. Smiley (John Buttny and others versus University President Joseph Smiley and the Board of Regents) was quickly lodged
in Denver's federal district court. A hearing on the students' request
for a temporary injunction to restrain the University from its action
against them was set for late January, 1968. The students claimed
that their constitutional rights had been abridged.

The last appeal in federal district court was anticlimactic; the ham-
mer, in a sense, had already fallen on the nine suspended students.
All that remained was for the Honorable Alfred A. Arraj, judge of
the Denver Federal District Court, to review the handling of the case,
to find that he had no alternative but to concur with previous decisions, and thus to deny the students' request for an injunction against
the University. Arraj's ruling, delivered on February 2, 1968, provided legal opinions on several significant points of controversy:

1) The University has the power to formulate and enforce rules
of student conduct which are appropriate and necessary to the
maintenance of order;
2) Inherent in this power is the responsibility to afford everyone
freedom of movement on campus and within physical facilities;
3) A student does not surrender civil rights upon enrollment, nor
does he then acquire a right to immunity or special treatment or
the right to violate the constitutional rights of others.

He also found that the plaintiffs freely admitted and openly boasted
that their activity was civil disobedience, that they knew they were
in violation of University regulations, and that they fully expected
to be arrested and tried in civil courts as a means of pointing up their
intense opposition to the CIA. But their "interference with one of the

normal activities of the University" was much more than that which is fairly understood to be embraced within the term "political activity."

For the nine students, only three of whom were from Colorado, their participation in the CIA demonstration meant the loss of a semester's work as well as the balance of attendant monetary considerations, official citations of the incident on their permanent records, and suspension for one full semester. They could, however, petition for readmission in June, 1968, and also for removal of the disciplinary citation after three years have passed. Some in fact left for outside employment; others remained in the University community and attempted to continue in classwork even without hopes of receiving credit. When students reported these irregularities, regulations forbidding such attendance were promptly invoked, to the embarrassment of a few sympathetic professors.

For a Fulbright engineering student from Turkey, dismissal meant the loss of his student visa and ultimate deportation. The story was exploited by Russia's Tass News Agency, when under a dateline of March 8, 1968, *Izvestia* published an interview with Oguzcan Ozaltin, headlined: "For Refusal to Become a Spy." The article continued:

For his refusal to become an agent of the Central Intelligence Agency, Turkish engineer Oguzcan Ozaltin, who was studying at the University of Colorado, was deported from the United States.
Upon returning to his own country, Ozaltin told journalists at the airport: "The University of Colorado had a bureau which offers employment to graduates. One day a representative of the CIA appeared at the bureau and offered some graduates, including me, the opportunity to become an agent of this espionage organization.
"We took part in a protest. As punishment for this, nine persons, I among them, were dismissed from the university. After this, I was ordered to leave the United States within thirty days."

What of Bouton? The Board of Regents subsequently voted to have him appear with his attorney before them, to determine if action was warranted against him, but they did so only after he had refused earlier to appear before the Faculty Senate Committee on Privileges and Tenure as ordered by the Regents. The Regents decided after the hearing not to take any action against Bouton. But the serious question of the responsibility, even liability, of faculty sponsors for the actions of their advisees remains to be answered.

University administrators, the Board of Regents, and the legislature of Colorado have labored hard to create an atmosphere of responsible freedom at UC. Indeed no truer reflection of this attitude can be found than in the treatment accorded the CIA demonstrators. Responsible groups on campus, any campus for that matter, believe strongly that the University is not an appropriate place for acts of civil disobedience. It is instead the proper place for the freest expression of ideas, with the widest latitude for research and the dissemination of new findings, and with an absolute minimum (if any is at all needed) of censorship of any type.

It was this that SDS failed to understand. For one group to demand the restriction from campus of any other group, idea, or area of research is but to invite retribution on itself. The principle of noncensorship is as democratic and as worthy of defense as the constitutional right on which the protesters staged their demonstration: the right to dissent against matters which violate conscience. In a logical way, the two end up guaranteeing the same thing—freedom of expression. Throughout its plan to counter any possible disruptive action, University officials respected both principles. As long as dissent remained peaceful and unrestraining, no basis existed for interfering; once its nature became obstructive and the attitude of the participants unrelenting, no other course was left but to move with dispatch to remove the violators, and restore the normal operation of University functions.

Student unrest and protest are far from dead. An observer needs only to attend such functions as the recent lecture by Dick Gregory to feel the deep concern many students have for some of society's seemingly insoluble problems. Yet the same observer must be careful, at least at the University of Colorado, not to misunderstand the concern. An informed and sophisticated student body attends UC, approximately 40 percent of whom matriculate from outside the state of Colorado at high tuition rates. It is a bright group, made so by rigid entrance requirements, and is fun-loving and tolerant possibly because of its intellectual, affluent and cosmopolitan make-up. But it is also a sober, serious-minded lot with definite though multifarious career aspirations which sees the University as a cooperative, noninterfering, and censuring vehicle for the attainment of all reasonable educational objectives.

Student disenchantment with editorial policies of the *Daily* occasioned a referendum in which students by a margin of over 2–1 voted to establish a second campus newspaper. And as if to further blight the future of the *Daily*'s independence, it was subsequently announced that Schmidt's go-it-alone policy was failing, and that the newspaper faced an approximate $10,000 deficit for the year. Pat McGraw, newly appointed editor, announced that it would follow different policies in the year ahead.

The election of a moderate as the new ASUC President in 1968 did not signal a new era for the University of Colorado but rather a return to the mature rationale of a continuing one. There will be more student unrest, periodic militancy, and protests, and perhaps even renewed confrontations by the Students for a Democratic Society who have retained their recognized standing and University-assigned office, though they have lost much of their former leadership. Some legitimacy does indeed rest with the attempt to reconstitute outmoded conditions and to abrogate traditional attitudes and policies, for students and society as a whole seemingly wake up in a new world with each new decade.

These are the frustrating pains of inevitable progress. Rational minds and patient hearts must respond to the inherent challenge. For at least one period in the history of one institution, officials were determined to preserve the philosophy needed to sustain the only mundane vehicle equipped to transport mankind from one era to another—the university as a center for the advancement of learning.

5

PRINCETON: RADICAL ORGANIZING AND THE IDA CAMPAIGN

*by Jerry Hoffman**

PRINCETON UNIVERSITY is in many ways the archetype of the successful conservative university. Long known as a breeding-ground for the well-educated Southern gentleman, it has retained a strong residual flavor of both its "upper-class South" and "gentlemanly" heritages. Princeton students are almost uniformly the product of upper-middle and upper-class backgrounds. Almost half the present student body graduated from expensive preparatory schools (down from 60 percent a few decades ago). A very recent change in admissions procedures will produce future graduation classes "as much as" 4 percent black, but only five years ago, black students were so rare that the campus police tended to stop and question them; Princeton's first two hundred years saw an almost unbelievable total of three black graduates.

The gentlemanly tradition at Princeton carries beyond the bour-

* Jerome R. Hoffman graduated from Princeton University in 1968. He has been involved in radical activity since his senior year in high school. As a freshman at Princeton he helped organize SDS at the University, and was involved with numerous controversies and confrontations during his four years there. He expects to be equally active at Columbia, where he is now doing graduate work in English and Comparative Literature. Mr. Hoffman believes that "America, despite its strong reactionary tendencies and deeply ingrained anti-Communism, can be revolutionized."

geois, generally apathetic student body and into the university's official rhetoric. A student may be expelled for "conduct unbecoming a gentleman," and an elaborate honor system demands that each student "pledge his honor as a gentleman" that he has not cheated on his exams. Similarly, student cafeteria workers, as well as the black waiters in the mansion-like eating-clubs, are expected to refer to those students whom they serve as "gentlemen," as in "would you gentlemen like any more coffee?"

Princeton students generally lead two lives simultaneously: they do spend hours in the library when exams and papers are due; on the other hand, they avoid intellectuality of any type in their social lives. One eating-club boasts that upon entering its doors, one can be sure of leaving entirely the unpleasant world, not only of lectures, but also of thought. The prestigious faculty doesn't so much compete for attention as it accepts a share of it; after all, students must attend classes and do a good deal of work in order to get a degree. Princeton men are in a sense compensated for their efforts (as well as for the absence of women on a cloistered campus 50 miles from New York City, where the use of cars was forbidden until 1967) not only by their Princeton diplomas but by the country-club atmosphere of rolling lawns, tall trees and expensive tennis courts.

Other features of Princeton's traditionalism may be briefly mentioned: a fiercely chauvinistic alumni body which "boasts" numerous bank presidents, corporate executives, and an extraordinary number of major politicians, as proud of "Old Nassau's" football team as it is of its own Princetonian contribution "in the nation's service"; a Presbyterian heritage that has seen each Princeton President be a minister or the son of a minister, and that enforced a compulsory chapel rule for freshmen as late as 1964; a "bicker" process which makes social judgments of applicants to clubs and sets up an informal but pervasive social hierarchy on campus; and a political conservatism that had Princeton students voting overwhelmingly in a campus poll for Dwight Eisenhower over alumnus Adlai Stevenson.

It is this last trait, of course, that is most immediately relevant to a discussion of campus politics, though it would be foolish to claim that each of the aforementioned elements is not basically related to the others. And while in 1968 Eugene McCarthy's liberalism became the favorite of a plurality of the campus, the politics of the average Princeton student remains tied to a Republican background and a general feeling of apathy.

But we are going ahead of ourselves. For the Princeton of 1968 was very different, not only from the Princeton of 1956, but also from that of 1967. The specific changes are too numerous to list; for more important than these is the serious and broad transformation in campus attitudes throughout 1967–68, of which the various official "reforms" were only the outward manifestations and by-products. Much of this larger metamorphosis can be traced to the activities of the campus chapter of the Students for a Democratic Society (SDS). Founded in 1965, when the Young Republicans dominated whatever there was of campus politics, SDS could then muster only negligible support. A first meeting drew 12 interested students, and a slightly larger organizational meeting brought more hecklers than sympathizers. For about a year SDS faced tremendous hostility on campus, and distributors of leaflets could be sure of encountering not only anger and scorn, but barely repressed violence. This gradually changed to less serious, "good-humored" mockery and eventually to indifference, a reaction characteristic of the average Princetonian at the beginning of the fall semester of 1967. SDS at that time could still claim only 10 to 15 active members, compared to several hundred at places like Harvard and Columbia. Yet by the end of the school year in June, 1968, SDS had a campus mailing list of over 300, was able to call a demonstration that brought together more than 1,000 students, and saw one of its more active members elected student body president. It successfully challenged several of Princeton's most basic traditions and attitudes, and the reaction of students opposed to it again turned towards severe hostility and open violence (one leafleteer had a gun drawn on him, another had her hair set on fire, and several others were chased through dormitories).

What SDS was faced with, then, at the end of the 1966–67 school year was a conservative and apathetic student body which felt little sympathy for non-conformity and even less for political activism. The organization itself was rather weak, with small membership and practically no tactical experience. Past campaigns against Dow Chemical Company and military recruiters had gone largely unnoticed on the campus. So when several SDS members discovered the University's official connection with the Institute for Defense Analyses, and set off to do detailed summer research about both IDA and its ties with Princeton, there was little reason for much optimism.

IDA is, briefly, a research corporation associated with twelve "sponsoring" universities, which does scientific research for the Defense Department. In its official catalogue, IDA asserts that its goal is to find scientific talent which could be converted from purely academic concerns into working "in the national interest." Princeton was connected with IDA in three primary ways: it was a sponsoring institution; Princeton's President Robert F. Goheen sat on the IDA's Board of Directors; and the Communications Research Division (CRD) of IDA, which specialize in highly classified work, was located in a building adjoining the campus, owned by the University, and built for this purpose. IDA scientists report on, among other things, the feasibility and advisability of various counterinsurgency techniques and materials to be used both at home and abroad, and typical projects deal with chemical and biological warfare, tactical nuclear weapons' use, and various "glues," "nets," and other devices for "riot control."

In its campaign against Princeton's affiliation with IDA, SDS presented a number of arguments. A case was made for the university as a bastion of learning, separated from political conflicts, a fortress of institutional neutrality; faculty, it was argued, had the right to undertake whatever professional tasks they, as individuals, chose—even if this meant designing bombs for an imperialist war—but the institution should never become a tool of governmental policy. Princeton's sponsorship of IDA was shown to endanger such institutional purity. The secret research done at the CRD, we insisted, violated the policy of free and open scholarship to which Princeton was officially committed. Furthermore, it was pointed out that the Trustees —a small group of absentee rulers—had involved Princeton in the sponsorship of IDA, and that they alone had the authority to maintain or dissolve this connection. Such power on such an issue was plainly and objectionably undemocratic. Such arguments were based on "liberal" principles, and were instrumental in gathering substantial support from the faculty.

Many SDS members still consider some of these arguments to be at least partially valid. They do not, however, consider such a concept as university purity particularly important, and their objection to IDA and its repressive research would persist if the connection with Princeton disappeared—just as SDS presently opposes Lockheed Aircraft's bombers, Dow Chemical's napalm, and all of the many other corporate interests involved in the Vietnam War, as well as numerous other exploitative situations at home and abroad.

What might be called SDS's "radical" opposition to IDA can be summarized as follows. First, research that is done for the benefit of imperialistic and repressive forces is unjustified under any conditions, and it must be opposed regardless of whether it is considered valuable by one man or by an entire institution. Second, no university can possibly take a "neutral" stand on any issue, for just as the "neutrality" of Columbia's faculty in fact supported that group which held power (i.e., Kirk's administration), inaction under any circumstances is to the benefit of existing power structures. It is precisely because a university can have very real political effectiveness *as an institution* that it must be always willing to act decisively on political matters of importance (even when that means challenging the status quo). It was therefore important that Princeton should dissociate itself from the work done at IDA, for this would in effect be a condemnation of the purposes and policies served by IDA.

Discontent with the liberal arguments was present in SDS, though not fully formulated, even at the beginning of the year. It became truly powerful, however, as SDS speakers began to realize real contradictions in the arguments they presented. The avoidance of such contradictions was one of the important things that Princeton radicals themselves learned from the IDA campaign. While "liberal" arguments are sometimes valuable as organizing tools, they should never be employed when they are contrary to a radical analysis.

When the 1967–68 school year began in September, IDA was only one of several tentative SDS projects. An intensive leafleting campaign, which presented a general radical critique of the university, reached both incoming freshmen and returning upper classmen, and President Goheen's year-opening speech "cautioning" against too much student activism began to be more relevant to Princeton itself. While the year's first SDS meeting drew fewer than twenty people, each of them was seriously working to reach others, especially those who had appeared as interested sympathizers at an open house during the first week of school. By the beginning of October, forty students came to an SDS meeting, and committees were formed to discuss separate and specific topics. IDA was still only one of five such topics equally important and pressing. It was, however, the only one which might precipitate an immediate campaign, since the other four issues needed further long-term organizing and research.

SDS began its IDA campaign cautiously, distributing leaflets around the campus. Two open letters to Mr. Goheen were printed in *The Daily Princetonian*, along with his responses. It was at this point that it first became obvious that the IDA issue might become central and all-consuming in terms of time and activity. As is often the case, events influenced SDS's response as much as they were the result of SDS's planning. The campaign gathered momentum much more quickly than anyone expected, but SDS, while somewhat surprised, was well-prepared.

Throughout the campaign, SDS worked according to the principles of participatory democracy. Small groups met almost continuously to discuss strategy and tactical plans, which they then presented before full chapter meetings. Each participant at a meeting could speak at length, presenting any idea or plan he chose, and everyone had one vote. Despite the great length of such meetings and the inability of any few people to enforce a rigid plan or policy, decisions were made on time, and actions were prepared and executed. The loss in efficiency was far from crippling, and the gain in terms of mutual involvement was crucial.

SDS next asked to meet with the University's Board of Trustees with the intention, not of arguing its opposition to IDA, but of calling for an open full-university meeting to discuss and decide upon future policy. A university dean had admitted that the Trustees would in fact discuss IDA at their next meeting, and SDS claimed that the entire university community, and not just the Trustees, had the right to decide upon such a question. The Trustees, whose official power in the university is complete, and whose meetings are closed and unreported, replied to SDS that it was "not their custom" to allow outsiders into their meetings. And "custom," as has been noted, is very significant in Princeton affairs.

The campaign began to attract attention when about fifty SDS members requested that an SDS member be allowed to address the Trustees, and called for an open meeting. The marchers were met at Nassau Hall's closely guarded doors by two deans and two security officers, who reiterated the administration's position that the Trustees' meeting was closed; the demonstrators delivered a short written protest statement, and left.

It should be noted here that SDS fully expected to be refused entrance to the Trustee meeting. The refusal on the part of the Trustees in a sense gave sanction to more militant action. This should not be misinterpreted as a sinister method of justifying an unprovoked sit-in. We honestly wished to address the Trustees, and would have been pleased if allowed inside. Furthermore, the march was a legitimate test of the possibility of successful use of that type of approach. When SDS left Nassau Hall it knew that a sit-in was not only "sanctioned" but necessary.

The sit-in at IDA came (coincidentally) on the Monday following the October 21 march on the Pentagon, where thousands of students found themselves face to face with a very violent enemy which called itself law and order. People whose commitment had previously been mainly theoretical came to a quick and firm understanding of the task they faced if American society itself was to be changed, and the Washington confrontation led most of them to further and deeper involvement. The slogan "from dissent to resistance" became a national byword as students recognized just how ineffective their forceless protests had been, and how very forceful their continued resistance would have to be. So when Princeton students obstructed the entrance to the IDA building, they were taking an action they knew to be unavoidable if their opposition was to be meaningful. When their action proved to be as potent as soon became evident, they learned the vital lesson that the "Establishment," of which Princeton's IDA is but one form, could be opposed, and successfully, at least on a limited scale.

On October 23 at 7:00 A.M., some seventy students sat down in front of the doorway of the CRD building. While officials inside had been aware of the possibility of such an action, and signaled employees outside not to enter, several IDA scientists and other personnel did try to force their way in. They were unsuccessful, as the demonstrators linked arms in order to prevent passage. By about 9:30 A.M., with no new arrival of personnel, it was apparent that the IDA administration was waiting to find out how long we would stay. An SDS policy statement read earlier in the morning had called the demonstration a symbolic show of determination, and added that repeated and intensified attempts would be made to close the CRD building if satisfactory response was not forthcoming from the university administration. The IDA officials waited to see if SDS would leave, and allow the building to be at least temporarily reopened. The loss of half a day's work was clearly not a matter of great concern to them. President Goheen appeared and reiterated his stance that since IDA was not a part of Princeton, the university would have no official response to the demonstration. At the same time, he made what was to become a much-quoted comment saying, "This isn't Princeton." The remark betrays Goheen's certainty of the incongruity between

Princeton's gentlemanly traditions and serious radical activity; while it would have been entirely accurate at any earlier time, the sit-in itself made it as anachronistic as the ironic "Even Princeton" sign that had been SDS's slogan at a march on Washington a year before.

As the morning continued without further response from either IDA or the university administration, SDS was faced with an important decision. Some people thought that after having successfully closed the building for a day, we should leave and claim our victory. Others argued that the effect of the sit-in would only be significant if it forced a serious response—either of concessions or of arrest—from IDA or the university. Just as the lack of previous response had led us to choose to sit-in despite the possibility of arrest, so the feeling that only the shock of such arrest would be of ultimate value led us to stay. A vote was taken on the IDA steps, and a majority committed us to staying as a group. None of those who felt that leaving would have been a superior tactic would have thought of leaving while the others remained. The decision was made clearly within the hearing of IDA officials; thirty-one demonstrators were arrested two hours later. Many of the other demonstrators were away at class, and still others were at lunch. The long period of waiting had led us to expect that the police might not be called until much later.

The fact that the administration only responded to student concern after thirty-one people had been arrested was a source of anger, as well as of somewhat naïve shock, to many faculty members. Furthermore, as a result of the sit-in and the degree of seriousness it revealed, the campus community took a sudden strong interest in IDA; many professors admitted that previously they had been hardly aware of its existence. Goheen responded to informal faculty pressure later in the week by calling for an open meeting where he would "explain" university policy on IDA, and answer questions. After further pressure, this time directly from SDS, he agreed to change the format to allow for the presentation of prepared speeches from the floor. SDS members presented three such speeches at the meeting, each dealing with a different aspect of the issue.

At this well-attended (about 500) meeting, Goheen announced that he would appoint a faculty committee to study the Princeton-IDA relationship. This committee soon held its own open meeting at which SDS spokesmen again testified. It then moved into closed session and deliberated over a three-month period before issuing the "Kelley Report" whereby a majority of the committee called for the restructuring of IDA so as to end its institutional ties with the twelve sponsoring universities; if IDA failed to follow this advice, Princeton should unilaterally withdraw from the organization. The full faculty then voted overwhelmingly to adopt the Kelley Report.

SDS conducted a number of other activities during the remainder of the year, but none of which involved quite so much time and effort or received so much publicity as their campaign against IDA. This campaign, coming near the beginning of the 1967–68 academic year, set the tone for much of what followed; it will therefore be useful to analyze what it accomplished.

First, and most directly, SDS action initiated a process which will almost certainly lead to the ultimate withdrawal of Princeton from IDA. Further, activities at Princeton were echoed on other campuses: at the University of Chicago, the faculty has recommended withdrawal from IDA, and at Columbia, IDA sponsorship became an issue in the major confrontation of the Spring, 1968. IDA itself has already prepared one restructuring proposal, and is likely to have to develop others.

Second, the relationships between faculty, administration and Trustees at Princeton have been affected by the IDA debate. It is not the faculty which has traditionally held power in Princeton, just as it is certainly not the students. Each group had made a commitment on this particular issue, but each had then to refer its decision to another, separate, ruling body—the Trustees—who alone could *implement* university policy. Just as the Trustees had decided to join IDA in 1962 despite a decision (recommendation) to the contrary by the university's faculty-dominated Research Board, they now voted on Goheen's prompting to accept an IDA-sponsored "restructuring-plan," prepared secretly by IDA directors including Goheen, Columbia's Grayson Kirk, and MIT's James Killian, without even referring to the Kelley Committee (or the faculty) for its opinion. Though the administration sought to keep this decision unpublicized, it became obvious that it had made a show of its own pretensions to democracy. The faculty, in a completely unprecedented response, voiced unofficial anger and official dissatisfaction both with the new plan and with the behind-the-scenes maneuvering. A student protest which had IDA as one of its several concerns combined with a new faculty vote to bring Goheen to abandon his previous decision, and open further negotiations that will almost certainly lead to complete disaffiliation from IDA.

It should be noted here that SDS's real influence in this subsequent faculty protest was more indirect than direct. It was not so much the mass rally that affected the faculty, but rather the weight of the IDA issue, in relation to a student-opened discussion of power in the university. Faculty decisions have been subtly countermanded in the past, with impunity. But with IDA, students had made a strong commitment, and had demanded that commitment not be taken lightly. The faculty had appeared as a go-between for the students and the administration, and had taken very seriously Goheen's referral of the "decision" to them. Thus, with relation to this very public issue, where students were claiming that only the Trustees control the university, when their decision was so glibly flaunted by Goheen, the faculty, for perhaps the first time in its history at Princeton, decided to assert itself.

With regard to the Trustees, some recent research by students at Princeton, Harvard, Berkeley, Columbia and elsewhere is highly relevant. Preliminary compilations clearly suggest the interlocking nature of institutional power as related to large universities. Numerous studies have shown that the same men who hold industrial power also wield political, and often military power. (Eisenhower's "military-industrial complex" has become rather overworked after infinite citation.) Trustees and alumni officers of universities are also industrial magnates and political officials, and the policies of the universities with regard to such things as defense research, allocation of grants, and investments in South Africa, correlate very closely to the policies of the corporations and of the government. To some extent, then, SDS actions initiated a break-up of corporate power over the University.

A third consequence of the IDA campaign has already been touched upon: the greatly increased power and standing of SDS on the Princeton campus. When SDS speakers and faculty supporters made specific demands such as the establishment of a draft counseling service, and general demands for broad changes in the power structure of the university, Mr. Goheen again appeared and, while nominally taking issue with what had been said, promptly made numerous concessions to a group of SDS negotiators. The full breadth of those concessions cannot yet be determined; compared with their past impotence, however, student negotiators, with the threat of student militancy behind them, now seem to carry some real degree of power into these meetings.

SDS clearly became the major student political force at Princeton, but this is not to say that it felt no limitations of its strength. When SDS led a 1,000-student rally on May 2, it decided to demonstrate rather than sit-in. Though we might have taken over as many buildings as did our Columbia counterparts, we specifically chose not to do so because given the attitude at Princeton in contrast to that at Columbia, such an action would have alienated a majority of the campus. The non-obstructive demonstration, on the other hand, brought unprecedented support. The SDS's real power, however, made the threat of a sit-in, which was expected by much of the campus, very potent.

Because SDS is radical and militant, it must not be expected that it will always employ militant tactics. At the time of the October march on Washington some New Leftists began to misapply the slogan "from dissent to resistance." While the phrase was coined to show disaffection with ineffective activity and the willingness to use force actively when only such a method would bring response, it did not mean to establish a political dichotomy on the basis of tactics. Those who claimed that "liberals picketed while radicals obstructed" were wrong. Perhaps some liberals always would have been unwilling to sit-in, and perhaps radicals often went beyond picketing, but any political distinction, such as that between a liberal and a radical, must have a political, and not a tactical, basis. A liberal may be someone who desires to reform our society, while a radical faces the necessity of basically changing it. This has nothing to do with sitting-in or marching, for tactics is never an end in itself, and if a radical can best win converts or bring on "The Revolution" by signing a petition, he will, of course, do so. When a Dow recruiter came to the campus, we chose not to obstruct the building where he was to interview (as had been done at Harvard), but instead to form a token picket line. The bases for this decision were manifold, involving both an analysis of Dow's relative political insignificance in terms of the entire "war-machine" and various tactical concerns. Our feeling was that such a picket would be more effective in attracting popular support, while no less valuable in this case as a medium for expressing our views.

SDS, however, never knowingly sacrificed politics for effect. We will not exchange long-range goals for immediate power or popularity, as bourgeois political parties do. It might be very easy to win the support of vast numbers of people if we were to propound only that friendliness is virtuous. But if we are to build a base of supporters it must be a base which supports our ideological position, and not our love of our mothers. We build a base to accomplish political changes, just as we sit-in, or picket, or lecture to build the type of mass support that will make such changes attainable. This brings us to the following dialectical position. We could call for mother-love and virtue, and become very popular; but this would be meaningless. If we are to be effective and to serve the ideological goals we support, we must unite both "correct" (i.e., radical) politics, and public appeal. We must, in effect, build a base, and have it composed of radicals.

A fourth, and most important, effect of SDS's campaign was the development of a base for radical action. The New Left sees America today as an oppressive society whose generally imperialistic and racist policies at home and abroad are pursued by a small class of men who dominate its powerful institutions. In order to oppose that Establishment and counter its intolerable actions, basic changes in the control of power, as opposed to nominal reforms implemented patronizingly by the "ruling class," must be enacted. After watching the old left in America spend many years failing to achieve real social progress through electoral politics and cooperation with corporate reformists, the New Left has seen the need to act independently in creating a mass of people whose united actions could basically alter American society. If we are to stop the war, or combat poverty, we must not merely participate in marches, or vote for hardly distinguishable candidates (all chosen by, from, and for the Establishment). We must convince the public of the need for change, and organize that public into a coherent force. "Base-building," then, is the primary role of the "radical educator." We can then make the following schematization: the ideology of the New Left is that America must be radically changed if we are to achieve a healthy society; its strategy is to educate a mass of Americans and organize them into an effective force; and its tactics vary as the situation demands, so as to be able to serve the ideological (and strategic) ends. "Victory" in a campaign, then, can not be measured by simple analysis of the official response to any demand or demands; it is a function of the political effectiveness of such a campaign in terms of that public to whom the campaign was directed.

In light of this discussion, we can now see that the goal of the Princeton SDS in the IDA campaign was only partially the removal of IDA from campus. By choosing an issue which was directly comprehensible to its entire public—in this case, the university community—SDS was able to strengthen its political impact upon that public. By making the tactical decision to sit-in and be arrested, it shocked an otherwise apathetic community into a realization of the seriousness of its intent. By achieving a tactical "victory" (i.e., the unprecedented open meeting, the faculty committee, and the administration's eventual concessions) it proved to those people who had been pessimistic to the point of inaction that organization could bring political effectiveness. It created an awareness, both among those who participated and those who didn't, that those who now hold power are not indestructible, that they are subject to successful challenge by people who are sincere enough and committed enough to use "any means necessary." Actions like the sit-in led, for the first time in Princeton certainly, to an awakened and interested public that actually read leaflets and found itself learning things about not only IDA and Princeton, but also about the structure of American society and the nature and concentration of power within it.

Perhaps the most obvious result of SDS activities, in terms of base-building and increasing strength, was the election in April of an active SDS member, Peter Kaminsky, as student body president. He did not run as an SDS candidate, and SDS intentionally avoided any involvement in the election campaign. But constant early attempts by his opponent to "red-bait" Kaminsky proved highly unpopular, and were drastically reduced by the time of the election, which Kaminsky won handily. Far from reducing his SDS affiliations once in office, he led the SDS-sponsored mass rally on May 2.

Fifth, and finally, the IDA demonstration accomplished a great deal in terms of what is fashionably described in the New Left as "praxis." That is, the people who organized and ran the entire campaign learned a great deal from it. When a second campaign was initiated in the spring, many mistakes were still made, for the relation of tactics to strategy and ideology was still unclear to many of us. Many other mistakes were not repeated, however, and the general thrust of our actions reflected a far greater awareness of political ends. Most important, there will be even fewer errors and much greater clarity next time. And there will be more people with that understanding of what a campaign should do, and how to do it.

6

HOWARD: THE EVOLUTION OF
A BLACK STUDENT REVOLT

by Lawrence B. de Graaf*

IN THE EVOLUTION of campus protest, Negro colleges have played a paradoxical role. Their sit-ins at the end of the Eisenhower Era first revealed the potential of direct student protest. But these demonstrations were aimed at discrimination outside the campus, and they left Negro colleges largely unchanged until the late 1960's. The dramatic occupation of the Administration Building at Howard University in March, 1968, ended this era of internal calm, led to a series of demonstrations on other Negro campuses, and laid their peculiar institutional problems before a public audience. The development of this movement from 1964 to 1968 paralleled the change in Negro thought from integration to nationalism and thus provides a microcosm of the successive frustration and the generational and ideological frictions which made the voice of the militant nationalist the most conspicuous one in the black population. Yet, beneath the militant rhetoric, this protest was both nonviolent in nature and disillusioning to many in its results, affording material for reflection to both opponents and proponents of contemporary student movements.

* Dr. Lawrence Brooks de Graaf is Professor of History at California State College, Fullerton. He is a specialist in recent U.S. and Negro History and has served on several civil rights and community relations organizations. This chapter stemmed from his experiences as Visiting Lecturer at Howard University in 1968.

The events which culminated in the occupation of the Administration Building had three basic roots: the outdated institutional structure and policies of Howard, black nationalist ideology, and the atmosphere of frustration that evolved from repeated failures to secure campus reforms. The first two roots may be traced to the peculiar dual mission which Howard University, like most Negro colleges, had undertaken. From its founding in 1867, Howard had been dedicated to the task of providing educational opportunities to freedmen and their descendants who came from "underprivileged backgrounds." [1] Yet, it was designed along the lines of white colleges, imitating their curricular emphasis and striving to match their academic standards. Faced with this contradiction in purpose, Howard clearly emphasized the latter goal. Aside from its graduate programs in African Studies, there was little in the Howard curriculum or organization to meet the peculiar educational needs or desires of Negroes.[2]

Howard was not entirely successful in its efforts to emulate the better white universities. David Riesman and Christopher Jencks bluntly described Negro colleges as "an ill-financed, ill-staffed caricature of white higher education . . . near the end of the academic procession in terms of student attitudes, faculty competence, and intellectual ferment." [3] While Howard merited such criticism less than most Negro colleges, it had been forced to compromise academic standards in the face of the educational backgrounds of many black applicants. A survey in 1966 found that many students scored below 300 on SCAT placement tests compared to a minimum level of 400 at many white colleges, and that many students who were admitted subsequently dropped out. Howard's Graduate School had similar low standards.[4] But, up to 1968, most studies recommended that Howard resolve this problem by raising its standards. Creation of a separate division of compensatory education was the only suggestion directed toward accommodating a broader stratum of Negro society.[5]

This historic orientation of Howard was galling to black nationalists, for it implied that Negro culture was "inferior," an obstacle to learning rather than an area of education in itself. As if to support this implication, the college placed little emphasis on Negro-American curricula. Professor Sterling Brown was for years alone in including Negro writers in literature courses; the History Department had only one course in American Negro History. Furthermore, aside from a few educational experiments in ghetto schools, the college had made few efforts to study or actively participate in the black community around it. In its 1967 *Report* the Office of Higher Education criticized the Department of Sociology and Anthropology for lacking a research focus "relevant to the resources and opportunities for local, national and international service which exist at Howard. . . ." [6] Through the early 1960's, Howard remained aloof from the civil rights movement, hosting numerous speakers but never formally taking a stand as an institution. This rejection of black culture, together with the middle-class nature of most students and faculty bred an ironic situation in which the leading Negro university was afraid of its own environment. Most faculty and administration lived several miles north of the campus, and coeds were afraid to venture into the community dressed as Howard students.

The administration was not disposed to change the basic direction of the university. Negro college presidents had long played the role of intermediary between a hostile white community and their colleges and had thus developed an "Uncle Tom" image in their relations with the white community while exercising almost unlimited power over students and faculty in order to carry out their trust to white benefactors.[7] Dr. James M. Nabrit, Jr., prominent civil rights lawyer who had been at the university since 1938 and who became president in 1960, could not escape from this heritage. He had his own version of "white benefactors" to heed in the form of the Southern-dominated District of Columbia Committee of the House, which appropriated over half of the university's budget. He retained arbitrary power of dismissal over students and faculty and held views on Negro protest that became increasingly at odds with student activism. He defended off-campus nonviolent demonstrations as a "moral cause," but disapproved of them for campus reforms. His response to nonviolent demonstrations in 1965 was characteristic of his views through 1968: "Freedom is not a license to lawlessness and anarchy. Such a climate undermines the very foundation of freedom. . . . I will not sit by and see the University become a place of lawlessness and disorder." [8]

The faculty at Howard was in a poor position to mediate between such views and the rising tide of student militancy. It was sharply dichotomized by race, rank, age and attitude. The older, overwhelmingly Negro, senior and tenured faculty generally shared Nabrit's views. They were survivors of an era when Howard was the pinnacle of employment for a black Ph.D., and they retained the opinion that it was the finest college a Negro could attend. Hence, students should consider it an honor to be at Howard rather than question the relevance of their learning to contemporary race problems.[9] Arrayed against such "chitterling education" was a second faction, composed largely of young, white, junior, untenured faculty who seemed to have little respect for the traditions of Howard. Some of them remained on probation as long as ten years and could not vote in faculty meetings. In 1967 the Office of Higher Education noted widespread discontent among these instructors and recommended that their teaching loads and salaries be improved in order to build a potential graduate faculty.[10] Ethnically different, untenured and powerless, they not only frequently sympathized with student demands but made their own grievances a factor of contention in student protests after 1964.

Some writers have traced the wave of Negro student protests in 1968 to a "black cultural revolution," [11] but neither "black awareness" nor disaffection with middle-class values was very evident among Howard students until 1966–67, several years after black student unions had begun on Northern campuses. This was partly due to the lack of a need for racial unity comparable to that of Negro students on white campuses, but it was predominantly due to the apathy of most Howard students. Middle class in origin, steeped in Greek organizational activities, they had long showed little interest in student protest. Even the older faculty chided them for their lack of imagination, and campus observers were struck by their indifference to racial consciousness and by the dominance of middle-class aspirations. A paternalistic administration contributed to this atmosphere by strictly regulating campus groups, while denying Howard students the rights which many white institutions had recognized for decades.[12]

Neither the fragmented student government nor the civil rights movement affected this air of conservatism. The Non-Violent Action Group (NAG) conducted sit-ins in Maryland and Northern Virginia, picketed construction at Howard to protest job discrimination, and staged sporadic protests in the D.C. ghetto. But it received only token response from students and administration. In the summer of 1964, Howard had only 20 students in the Mississippi Summer Project, and one activist lamented: "The vast majority of the students are wrapped in the all-consuming desire to become bourgeois . . . thereby forgetting about the larger percentage of Negroes living in poverty and degradation. We do not know our culture, our history, our struggle for dignity that are intertwined in American civilization." [13] How such an apathetic student body evolved into a black student revolt is not evident from either the nation-wide move to black power or Howard's institutional weaknesses. It must be sought in the chain of events from 1964 to 1968 in which a few small movements for reform evolved into a student occupation of the campus.

The year 1964 saw both the beginning of ghetto riots in Northern cities and the surfacing of student protest at Berkeley. There is little evidence that either development influenced students at Howard, but some mild protests did erupt that year over a series of grievances concerning campus policies. The refusal of the dean of students to approve a speaker program unless a university official "co-moderated" it was criticized by the campus paper, *The Hilltop*, as "a blatant and unnecessary act of censorship." [14] The paper subsequently broadened its field, charging that Howard students lacked the rights of students elsewhere and that they had to resort to "crafty, under-handed, and at times malicious" tactics to circumvent administration obstacles. It criticized compulsory ROTC and stringent regulations on the hours and dress of women students (including a ban on slacks) and demanded more political organizations on campus and relaxation of attendance regulations.[15] In April, 1965, the student protest gained a *cause célèbre* when two popular professors, Amy Kleppner and Daniel Crabb, were demoted to lecturers. *The Hilltop* charged that their demotion was motivated by "the desire to rid the faculty of critics, dissenters and potential trouble makers," an impression which the administration would reinforce in the next three years.[16]

Administration efforts to bring about reform became themselves a source of student discontent. In the fall of 1964 several "reform committees," generally consisting of two students and a larger number of faculty and administrators, were set up. Student representatives complained that they were without power and were limited to "protesting or concurring with previously made decisions." [17] Seeking a more effective vehicle, student organizations in February formed the Students for Academic Freedom (SAF). They demanded greater participation in setting admission standards, financial policies affecting students, and new curricular programs. Late in April an SAF demonstration attracted 500 students, one of the earliest and largest gatherings to protest institutional conditions at Howard. Even marching on the Administration Building was discussed. The protest was short-lived, however, for neither the student press nor the vast majority of the student body was willing to support it in the face of strong administration criticisms.

In a statement endorsed by the Board of Trustees, President Nabrit denounced all who had participated in the demonstrations as "Greeks bearing gifts—they do not care about the Negro people—they do not love Howard—they do not believe in civil rights for anyone—they feed on disorder . . . they must be fought in every arena and they must not be permitted to prevail." He concluded by warning: "Those who disregard orderly procedure and policies have no place at Howard. Those who would remain at Howard and enjoy its benefits . . . must observe its rules and regulations." [18] This remarkable statement ended the SAF protest, but the attitude it revealed held ominous consequences for future student-administration relations. Nabrit had shifted the focus from the legitimacy of student grievances to the manner in which they were sought and proscribed nonviolent demonstrations as tantamount to anarchy. This attitude and the dismissal of several demonstrators planted the oft-repeated idea that peaceful protest for reforms was simply an invitation to expulsion.[19] His remarks also did little to impress upon faculty and administrators the need for revising college policies. The following academic year would be marked by apathy at all levels and a lack of student protest or institutional reform. It proved to be an illusory calm.

The academic year 1966–67, Howard's centennial, was marked by the most turbulent demonstrations in the recent history of the college. The tone of protest came to include demands for black power as well as the more familiar reforms of student power. By the summer of 1967 the spirit of student-administration cooperation that had characterized the previous year had been replaced by a loss of confidence in the will of faculty and administration to change, and a growing minority of the once-apathetic student body felt it must resort to direct action to improve conditions. Many of the seeds that would grow into the sit-ins of 1968 were firmly planted in the preceding year.

The earliest demonstrations were the outgrowth of one of the oldest student grievances: the lack of a written code of campus rules and of student representation in the judiciary process. Howard's administration retained an arbitrary authority to dismiss students without stated cause:

Attendance at Howard University is a privilege, in order to protect its standards of scholarship and character, the University reserves the right, and the student concedes to the University the right, to deny admissions

Students perceived this policy as a vehicle for campus of critics of college policies, and they made the inclusion students in the disciplinary process a prime target of reform. In principle, the administration agreed with them, having suggested a joint student-faculty judiciary council as early as 1961. But efforts to work out the details were inconclusive, and when, in the fall of 1966, the issue of campus discipline was revived, there was no student representation in the judiciary system.[21]

The initial challenge to these policies came from a group of Law School students led by JeRoyd Greene and Arthur Goldberg, the latter a veteran of the Berkeley Free Speech Movement and one of the few links between campus protest and events at Howard. In late November their protest was expanded into a coalition of student groups, the Student Rights Organization (SRO), and their grievances extended to include a lack of black awareness, the end of compulsory ROTC, and liberalized curfew hours.[22] A series of demonstrations in November brought about meetings between elected student leaders and administrators to draft an interim judiciary policy. Both the resultant proposal and a plan proposed in March, 1967, by President Nabrit's office granted the principle of student representation but left the judicial bodies predominantly composed of administrators and faculty. The campus press denounced these proposals for granting students "practically no authority to hear cases."[23] The Student Assembly rejected these plans, leaving the judiciary issue in limbo when dramatic events in March caused the administration to undertake immediate disciplinary action.

While most student leaders grew frustrated over institutional reform, black power ideology made its first noticeable impact on Howard activists. By the fall of 1966, national events had made it impossible for a Negro college to ignore such thinking. SNCC and CORE converted to all-black organizations, and Stokely Carmichael's Black Panther Party in Alabama inspired the rise of black power committees on several campuses, including Howard. Spokesmen for this position assumed an influence out of proportion to their number in the Howard student body. The editorship of *The Hilltop* passed largely into the hands of a "black awareness" group, and from the start of the fall semester virtually every issue stressed black conscious-

ness and criticized Howard for its lack of racial pr...
of white rather than black ideas and standards.[24] Militant spokesmen
like Carmichael, Floyd McKissick and Nathan Hare made numerous
campus speeches, and a vague sentiment of "black awareness" grew.
Developments on campus, in turn, directed much of this sentiment
against the Howard administration.

The first such development occurred in September, 1966, when
President Nabrit announced that he hoped to raise the admission
standards and bring greater racial mixture to the student body. Blacks
who failed to meet admission standards might be admitted to a year
of remedial work. In retrospect this announcement cast Nabrit in a
tragedian role. For, while it represented the thinking of academicians
writing on Negro colleges and the recommendations of the Office of
Higher Education, to many moderate students it was a slap at the
concept of racial pride and supported the militant charge that the
administration was composed of "Uncle Toms." [25]

The culmination of black power activities was the formation in
February, 1967, of the Black Power Committee by a group of
students and Professor Hare. This committee's "Black Power Manifesto" called for "the overthrow of the Negro college" and its replace-
ment by "a militant black university which will counteract the
white-washing black students now receive in 'Negro' and white
institutions." It suggested that the name of Howard University be
changed to Nat Turner or Garvey University and that the college
emphasize "subjects more pertinent to the present and future demands
of the black struggle in America and the world." [26] But here it ended.
The manifesto was almost entirely aimed at campus reform and made
little reference either to a race war throughout the nation or to a
revolution in the "third world." This, plus the limited student following of the committee through the spring of 1967 indicates that apathy
or moderation still dominated Howard students and that further
provocation would be needed to change sentiments of "black awareness" into large-scale protest.[27]

In March, 1967, the appearance of General Lewis Hershey to
speak on campus provided such a catalyst. Both the SRO and the
Black Power Committee turned out to heckle Hershey, but the black
power group also wanted to prevent him from speaking. When
Hershey stepped forward someone yelled "America is a black man's
true battleground" and some forty students ran to the stage and
forced him away. He refused to return to the podium, and the pro-

gram was cancelled.[28] Initial reaction to this incident was hostile to the black power students. Congressmen on the District of Columbia Committee pressured the administration to discipline the demonstrators and sympathetic faculty. Letters to *The Hilltop* protested making Howard "a haven of black power in a center of race controversy" and criticized the students for denying Hershey the right to speak, while student leaders apologized for the disruption.[29] Under the illusion that they were speaking for most of the college community, the administration announced early in April that students who disrupted General Hershey's speech would face hearings to determine whether they should be dismissed.

This order raised the still unsettled issue of college rules and disciplinary procedure, and prevailing student attitudes quickly changed. SRO leaders were angered that the committee hearing the arrested students was composed solely of senior faculty. Both they and black power students were upset that Robin Gregory, the first non-Greek, afro-hair-wearing girl to be elected homecoming queen, was among those being tried. On the 19th of April over four hundred students demonstrated against the proceedings, condemning the trial as a "kangaroo court." [30] Unrest reached a climax on April 26 when a group of students forced its way into Locke Hall to break up the trial of Robin Gregory. This demonstration was defended as a "legal protest against student intimidation," and one writer insisted, "You cannot fight quietly . . . you cannot deal with injustice lightly." [31] The goals of the fall reform movement were being merged with the militants' tactics.

The response of the Faculty Senate, the administration, and outside groups to these events completed the confrontation. After the Hershey incident, Nabrit issued a statement which the Senate amplified into guidelines on "academic freedom of speech and freedom of ideas." They provided that expressions of protest should be confined to specified areas and to orderly picketing which would not interfere with any programmed activities, that certain specific times would be set aside for rallies, and that Howard could not permit activities characterized by racism or bigotry.[32] These guidelines conflicted with both SRO's position of disrupting judicial proceedings until it obtained fair representation in the system, and the Black Power Committee's goal of greater race awareness and a black university.

Student leaders who sought reform through negotiation could point to little save frustration by the Spring of 1967. "University reform" committees had fallen into disrepute for their domination by older faculty and for their infrequent meetings. One student observed:

The present system of University-wide committees serves often to delay rather than to speed solutions to such problems as compulsory ROTC, dormitory regulations, and library hours. The idea is to promise one group of students that a particular problem is being attended to and refer it to a committee to arbitrate until the given group of students graduate.[33]

These frustrations became particularly acute after the Senate issued its guidelines on campus protest. Student writers charged that the faculty had betrayed the long hours of student-administration committee work. A joint student-faculty "steering committee" was set up after the April demonstrations to work out a better judiciary, but it did not come up with a plan until the summer.[34] In the meantime students, having lost faith in conventional committee procedures, turned again to direct action.

On May 10 hundreds of undergraduates boycotted classes. They demanded the dropping of charges against the Hershey demonstrators, the ending of senior comprehensives and compulsory ROTC, that no faculty member be dismissed or denied promotion because of activism, and repeal of the "guidelines" on student protest.[35] Black power militants and student rights activists joined in support of these demands, a further reflection on the moderate nature of "black power" at Howard. The faculty disciplinary committee, which had been meeting behind closed doors during the boycott, attempted to work out greater representation in the judiciary procedures. However, it refused either to end the disciplinary hearings of Hershey demonstrators or to make the committee a forum for considering other demands.[36] Robin Gregory was cleared, but neither the issues of a student judiciary nor the dismissal of demonstrating students or faculty who criticized the administration had been settled. When students returned in the fall they found that both of these issues had been resolved in a way antithetical to the demands of the spring protest.

During the summer of 1967 some 20 students and 6 professors, including Nathan Hare, received letters of dismissal from the president. All of the students had been active in the demonstrations of the spring of 1967; more had been sent warnings but were never dismissed. Only two of the professors, Doctors Hare and Lowe, appeared to have been very active in student demonstrations. All, however, were members of the Faculty Forum, the leading faculty group to criticize administration practices. The result was to accentuate the cynical attitude on the part of students and young, particularly white, faculty toward the administration and the likely results of frank criticism.[37]

Suspicions built by these events were compounded by other decisions on the part of Nabrit. It had been widely believed that the president, already past 65, would retire in 1967. Instead, he returned in the fall and announced that he might remain as president for four more years. He further upset student leaders by setting aside the draft judiciary system which had been painfully worked out by the student-faculty committee and replacing it with a "blue book" which gave a board, with a majority of faculty and administrators, most of the actual power.[38] By the fall of 1967 the unresolved issues between students and administration had developed to the point that the former no longer had faith that any compromise settlement would be carried out and the latter felt that students were incapable of confining their demands within reasonable or realizable bounds.

Students vividly demonstrated their feelings by marching out of the ceremonies on Opening Day in protest over the "blue book" and dismissals of the previous summer.[39] Their elected leaders used this angry mood to propose their boldest set of reforms. Barbara Penn and Ewart Brown declared both the "blue book" and the Faculty Senate statement of the previous spring "null and void." In their place they insisted on the adoption of a judiciary system similar to the one which had been worked out the previous May. The student leaders informed Nabrit that they had "decided to assume the responsibility for student conduct and discipline" and that for the president to dismiss a student under college rules which they had rejected would be a "clear challenge to student government." [40] The Annual Student Leadership Conference broadened these demands to include abolition of senior comprehensives, better support of the athletic program, changes in class hours and semester breaks as well as black awareness proposals that Howard become closer to the people and needs of the Washington ghetto.[41] This would be the last major effort that moderate activists would make to secure such time-honored reforms by conferences with the administration and with only passing reference to black awareness or basic changes in the nature or aim of the university.

On the judiciary issue and compulsory ROTC administrators made sincere efforts to meet student demands, but the manner in which these issues were handled heightened student frustration with conventional techniques and increased the attractiveness of direct action. On the judiciary issue, the student-faculty steering committee of May was reactivated and considered a proposal which made the student-dominated committee the body of original and stronger jurisdiction. However, the administration refused to surrender its right to circumvent this system in an emergency, and debate continued until the end of January at which time the faculty of the various schools rejected the judiciary proposals. When the spring semester began, Howard still had no judiciary system which met the approval of both students and faculty.[42]

Compulsory ROTC was an anathema to male students which many other colleges had terminated and which student leaders at Howard had protested against since 1965. A student referendum in October, 1967, showed 90 percent of those voting opposed it, but neither this vote nor accompanying resolutions from student government changed this policy until the militant freshman class took the question into its own hands.[43] On November 7 they disrupted a Freshman Assembly with cries of "ROTC no" and "Hell, no, we won't go." Many walked out of the assembly, and for the next two days drills of ROTC were broken up. The protest climaxed on the 9th with a sit-in in President Nabrit's office. In the face of such a protest, Nabrit accepted the mediation of Ewart Brown, and agreed to end the compulsory nature of ROTC immediately.[44] This was a significant concession to student demands, but the circumstances of this victory only reinforced the view that if students were to get anything changed at Howard "you have to stop things suddenly, you can't plan."[45]

While attempts at reform through the existing system continued, "black awareness" continued to have strong intellectual influence but limited organized support. Several such groups had formed during the spring and summer of 1967, and in the early fall they merged into a coalition named *Ujamma*, Swahili for "togetherness." The most radical of the black nationalist students founded a United Black People's Party.[46] These groups still did not attract any substantial percentage of the student body as members, and the UBPP came into disrepute in January, 1968, when both of its leaders were arrested on charges of having thrown bombs into the homes of

President Nabrit and Dean Frank Snowden. *Ujamma* became a significant nucleus for black awareness criticisms of the administration, but it was in ideology more than in campus organization that race consciousness made its greatest impact.

Student leaders made frequent reference to this attitude during the fall semester. Ewart Brown observed in his opening remarks in September that "Black leadership must be developed in a black university. This is the kind of leadership the movement needs now. We need leaders who can infiltrate the system and not be Uncle Toms." [47] The SRO platform in the fall combined insistence on student control of non-academic activities with calls for the "coming together of black people to achieve their liberation by any means necessary" and a greater emphasis on black studies and a closer relationship between Howard and the surrounding community.[48] Such suggestions that the causes of black awareness at Howard and black liberation in the nation were one and the same became increasingly attractive when campus issues remained unresolved through the winter of 1967–68.

It is only in the light of this evolution of frustrated reform and black awareness that the sequence of events culminating in the occupation of the Administration Building can be fully understood. Student leaders vowed to "get things straight in '68" and to "bring Howard into the twentieth century," yet they felt there was little hope of doing this through negotiation. Many students and faculty shared this mood, mocking certain conditions yet expressing the fear that anyone who criticized them risked dismissal. Such a situation seemed to await only one incident—akin to General Hershey's appearance the previous spring—to transform unrest into open student revolt.

This event was to come from an unexpected quarter: South Carolina State College at Orangeburg. A group of students there had begun demonstrations against segregation in bowling alleys and other public facilities. Rallies were held at which prominent SNCC leaders appeared. On the night of February 8, state highway patrolmen went to the campus and fired into a group of students. Three blacks were killed and thirty more wounded. Police allegations that they shot after being fired upon were not borne out by investigation, and the incident quickly became known as "the Orangeburg Massacre." [49] Disillusionment with white society and emphasis on black nationalism were intensified by this incident. Yet the most significant response of black students was aimed neither at South Carolina nor at white society in general. Rather, the incident became a focal point for discontent among Howard students.

On the morning of February 16, nearly 500 students staged a demonstration as an expression of sympathy for Orangeburg students that developed into an attack on Howard authorities for their failure to provide leadership for the black community. Onlookers received a mimeographed publication from *Ujamma* entitled "Spear and Shield" which laid down the reasoning that would characterize the spring protest.

> Black youth of today have learned that to be just like a white man requires a synthetic identity and to hate one's true self. . . . The black leader of today must direct himself to a new breed of leaders—leaders who take pride in their true identity and who instill similar pride in others.
>
> Unfortunately Howard University . . . is desperately trying to remain an imitation white school turning out imitation white people.

The letter went on to demand a new series of reforms largely aimed at creating a "black university." These included the resignation of Nabrit, Vice-President Wormley and Dean Snowden, more courses in Afro-American history and related subjects, reinstatement of Howard professors dismissed for political activism, a student judiciary committee and greater student control over budgetary matters, and making Howard more relevant to the black community. The paper gave the president until February 29, three weeks after the Orangeburg Massacre, to respond to these demands.[50]

To underscore their demands some *Ujamma* members took down the flag on the upper campus, explaining that "the flag flies over the land of the free and the home of the brave—Howard is a contemporary plantation." The flag and the list of demands were taken to Nabrit's office. Another group of students went to the girl's dormitory, ripped up a section of iron spikes that had been put on the top of the wall to discourage students from sitting there, and brought this and the flag to the office of Dean Snowden.[51]

To administrators and senior faculty the "Orangeburg Ultimatum" and the accompanying actions were reprehensible. Dean Snowden denounced "the irresponsible student behavior on February 16" and proposed that "the faculty consider means for restoring an atmosphere proper for the conduct of our educational activities." [52] An *ad hoc* committee was established to study such means. Both the thinking and recommendations of this body were typical of administration and senior faculty reactions to student protest since 1964. It was "deeply disturbed by the breakdown of orderly procedures . . ." and particularly noted the threats to disrupt the Freshmen Assemblies which led to their termination on February 20. These conditions, along with the Orangeburg Ultimatum made "increasingly difficult the process of education at Howard. . . . Some of the student demands attack the principles upon which our University was founded, and cause us to fear that the University itself may not survive." The committee recommended the formation of a committee of forty-eight drawn equally from administrators, trustees, faculty and students and hoped that public hearings by this committee would "dispel previous irritations. . . ." [53]

Such gestures and assurances might have placated unrest earlier, but they were clearly at odds with the mood of student leaders by 1968. There is little evidence that they had considered what they would regard as a satisfactory response to the Orangeburg Ultimatum. But in light of the atmosphere of black awareness and the frustrations of judiciary reform, none of the leaders could regard another committee of which they constituted a minority to be an adequate response. It but remained for the militants to demonstrate this on the day after the ultimatum deadline.

Charter Day, March 1, the anniversary of the founding of Howard, was an auspicious occasion for confrontation. To older faculty, the convocation was a reminder of Howard's proud past; to black nationalists it was a reminder of past evils and present inadequacies. Sensing the tension of the audience, the opening speaker appealed for mutual understanding between students and faculty, and ceremonies proceeded without interruption until President Nabrit took the podium to present awards to distinguished alumni. Two groups of students marched down the side aisles while others passed out mimeographed sheets entitled "Definition of a Black University." Following the second presentation students leaped on the stage, surrounded Nabrit, and after a brief exchange of words the president adjourned the convocation. Administrators and most faculty walked out and student militants took over to read the "Definition." [54]

This document essentially repeated the Orangeburg Ultimatum both in its criticisms and its combination of two aspects of student protest. One side reiterated the black power rhetoric that Howard was "a plantation that perpetuates the subservience of African people in America." It charged that the administration had "failed to make itself relevant to the struggle of black people for liberation and to the aspirations of its students to be a dynamic part of this struggle." [55] The other side of the "Definition" was a series of institutional reforms similar to those which student leaders had sought through negotiation. This two-sided nature of student demands, combining the transformation of Howard into a black university and reforms within the existing structure, was characteristic of the entire spring protest movement.

Initially, most students disassociated themselves from the disruption, regarding it as the work of a minority of black militants. Letters to *The Hilltop* generally agreed that conditions at Howard warranted protest but that the tactics of disruption lacked "finesse and cool." [56] But these attitudes changed rapidly on March 19 when the administration sent letters to thirty-nine students involved in the disruption ordering them to appear before a judiciary board to determine whether they should be expelled. These letters revived the issues of a student-controlled judiciary and defining campus rules. Denouncing the faculty-dominated hearings as a "kangaroo court," student leaders held a rally on behalf of the indicted demonstrators that drew a crowd of over 1,000, probably the largest rally ever held on the Howard campus. After a series of speeches calling for black awareness and student unity, Ewart Brown shouted, "Let's sit in at the A-Building." Behind a group of student leaders and *Ujamma* militants several hundred students followed into the building, sitting along the aisles of the main floor, and occupying the president's office. Shortly thereafter the administrators left and announced that the campus would be closed for the day. Student leaders replied that they would remain in the building until the charges against the thirty-nine demonstrators were withdrawn. Many coeds brought pillows, blankets and suitcases from their dormitories, and by evening a food crew had arranged for supper, student marshals were screening all persons entering and leaving the building, several announcements had been made to the press and the Howard sit-in was running as a well-organized affair.

The decision to stage a sit-in had apparently been reached only two days before the rally, and its leaders began with few long-range plans. On Wednesday, March 20, they were still uncertain of the extent of students' support and whether the normal functions of the university would be disturbed.[57] Shortly after noon, however, classes were suspended, and later in the afternoon an administration order arrived closing the campus until students evacuated the building. This order gave students until Friday to vacate the A-Building and left the threat that thereafter troops or police might be called in. Except for the Schools of Law and Medicine, which defied this order, all parts of the campus were closed, leaving the sit-inners in complete control of the A-Building in what one reporter called a "joyous coup." [58]

This order probably solidified student support for the sit-in more than any other action, for it closed dormitories as well as classrooms. Since a large percentage of the students at Howard were from out of town, many who had previously ignored the sit-in now became active participants out of exigency. Between 2,500 and 3,000 students remained on campus through the week. The number actually in the A-Building increased to approximately 1,000 by that evening and remained quite constant for the duration of the occupation. Another 1,000 circulated in front of the building, periodically singing or criticizing the administration. Many of these returned to the dormitories at night where they announced they had no intention of leaving by Friday and in one dormitory formed a "defense committee" to assure themselves against being locked out.[59] From beginning to end the sit-in was in the hands of a steering committee of student leaders. Students took over and ran the university switchboard, and some faculty were invited to offer their classes in the A-Building, since campus guards had locked all classroom buildings. Guest speakers and musicians maintained a continuous atmosphere of black awareness and cultural pride.[60] Throughout the week student support for the sit-in never visibly declined, but beneath this unity a crucial debate went on: what was the aim of the sit-in?

The dominant views of students and their leaders on this question vacillated throughout the sit-in. On the second day, Ewart Brown stated that the protesters would "consider" withdrawing from the Administration Building if charges against the demonstrators were dropped.[61] But the following day student leaders released to the press a sixteen-point set of demands which concluded: "This is not a movement based on dismissals of students or closing a university, therefore such concessions are not dealing with the root causes of our protest." The statement called for the "immediate resignation" of Nabrit, "faculty control over academic affairs and student control

over student affairs," a "black-oriented curriculum," a "black awareness institute," a new judiciary system and disciplinary code enforced
mainly by students, amnesty for sit-inners, and a reopening of the
campus by the weekend.[62] This militant stance also dominated the
songs, chants, taped speeches and live lectures heard by the students.
From this, some observers concluded that "The five day occupation
was . . . similar to the liberation of land as developed under revolutionary circumstances in the third world," and anticipated a sweeping
change in the orientation of Howard after the sit-in.[63]

However much the rhetoric of the sit-in echoed cries for a "black
university," however, it is difficult to conclude that that was the
ultimate objective of a majority of its participants. They shared a
disenchantment with seeking reform through regular channels and a
resentment against the Nabrit administration. Most students, however,
had more limited objectives than the sixteen demands. Some simply
wanted to stop the trial of Charter Day demonstrators. Others denied
they sought black power but criticized Howard officials for not giving
them more racial pride and for treating them like children. These
comments were especially common among Northern students who had
elected to attend Howard in hopes of experiencing racial leadership.
These motives were combined with an aura of fear for their status
at the university. A flyer passed out Tuesday asked, "Have *You*
Checked Your Mailbox Lately?" It urged readers to join the sit-in
to prevent the administration from "purging" all activists from the
campus. While the sit-in lasted this uncertainty over goals was an
asset. It concealed differences among leaders and it led outside groups
as disparate as the Medical School students and the Black United
Front of Carmichael to support it. But when student leaders negotiated a settlement it could not help but be disillusioning to some
students and observers.

In response to this display of student power, the administration
seemed incapable of either dislodging the students or of acting on
their demands. President Nabrit was away from the campus throughout the sit-in. His absence on the 19th deprived the initial march of
a person with whom to negotiate and may have been a reason the
students adopted a prolonged occupation of the A-Building.[64] For
several days no one could report his whereabouts. Press speculations
ranged from Switzerland to Puerto Rico, while campus rumors
claimed that he was "hiding" in a DC hotel.[65] Such reports, and
his eventual appearance in a local hotel, created the impression of

the administration shutting down the campus and running away from its students. A poster asked, "What's the difference between President Nabrit and Santa Claus? There is a Santa Claus." Vice-President Wormley was ill, leaving leadership of the college to the university's Secretary and Treasurer. Neither made public appearances or even informed the faculty of their role, leaving their location and motives a mystery.

Secrecy and divided efforts plagued the few efforts the administrators made to settle the sit-in. A committee of them remained in almost continuous session until the end of the sit-in, and it was this body which made the decision to close the campus.[66] On the third day of the sit-in five administrators met secretly with a group of student leaders. They refused to accept the sixteen demands, but discussed the question of a court injunction and use of troops. They subsequently claimed they told students they would not seek an injunction, but this was not made public, and a student contention that they received an ultimatum to vacate the A-Building by 5:00 P.M. Friday received wide circulation.[67] Anticipation of forceful eviction helped keep many students near the A-Building and led to a community rally there at the ultimatum hour. Instead of police, the committee of administrators appeared Friday afternoon for a second meeting which would eventually end the sit-in. But any image of willingness to compromise this might have gained was destroyed the next day when President Nabrit reappeared and stated that he would not deal with the students' demands and would seek an injunction against them.[68]

The crucial party in working out the settlement was the Trustees of Howard University. In earlier campus disputes they had supported the Nabrit administration, and on this occasion the board's president publicly condemned the sit-inners as "anarchists who have taken over the campus" and vowed that Howard would reopen "for people who want to receive a college education, not for students who want to sit in at the Administration Building." [69] A majority of the Trustees shared his views, but five, headed by Dr. Kenneth Clark, threatened to resign if the Trustees requested an injunction. They won approval for negotiations, and Clark and three others arrived at the A-Building Friday evening and entered into talks with the student steering committee. They offered four concessions: student control of a judiciary that would try the Charter Day demonstrators, promise of changes to make Howard "more attuned to the times and the mood of its people," a student-faculty board to work on student complaints, and amnesty for the sit-inners.[70] Students, in turn, would agree to vacate the A-Building and resume classes.

Early Saturday morning students were called together to meet the four Trustees and committee of administrators and to hear their compromise offer. In the ensuing discussion the student leadership was "really split down the line" as a vehement argument ensued between those who favored acceptance and those who saw it as a "sell-out" of the sixteen demands. Several outside speakers, especially former professor Nathan Hare, urged the students to reject the Trustees' offer on the grounds that it did not meet most specific points of their demands, retained President Nabrit, and left further reform up to Trustees and student-faculty committees.[71] But most students accepted the arguments of the Steering Committee that the concessions won would be a means of gaining other demands and that committees would function differently at Howard now that students were assured of membership on them and had demonstrated the pressure they could apply if committees evaded campus issues.[72] They voted to accept the compromise and end the sit-in. The discipline which distinguished this demonstration from many others added a final flourish as student crews mopped all floors they had occupied and left the A-Building in virtually the same condition it was in when they had entered.

Events in the remaining weeks of the spring semester suggested two different conclusions concerning the significance of the Howard protest. Initially, it seemed to be the vanguard of a spreading black student revolution. Influenced by the extensive television and press coverage of the Howard sit-in, students at several other Negro colleges occupied campus buildings or boycotted classes and issued lists of demands. Morgan and Bowit State Colleges, Maryland, Cheyney State College, Pennsylvania, Fisk University, Tennessee, Tougaloo College, Alabama, and Virginia Union and Bowie State, Maryland, were among the campuses affected. Yet, none of these demonstrations lasted as long or received comparable publicity to Howard's, and each turned out to have unique grievances and demands. Ninety Howard students traveled to near-by Bowie State only to find that their black power songs were unwelcome in a student body that was 45 percent white. The Bowie protest against administrative ineptitude and sub-standard physical conditions was one in which black students stressed unity with whites rather than cultural uniqueness.[73] After this rebuff the campus press was virtually devoid of mention of a spreading black student revolution.

The sit-in also left its impact on the administration and tenured faculty of Howard. Shortly after reopening the campus, President Nabrit called upon the faculty to take leadership in a "reassessment, re-evaluation, and re-examination of Howard." [74] This attitude resulted in several immediate reforms. The thirty-nine Charter Day demonstrators were given a hearing before a court of students and law professors which dismissed the charges against them on the grounds that there was no judicial system in effect which students and faculty had agreed on when the charges were made.[75] The Faculty Senate approved a permanent judiciary system guaranteeing all students a hearing before a student-dominated board. They were to receive copies of university regulations so they could no longer be expelled without knowing the rules they had violated. To implement the remaining points of the settlement a faculty-student committee was established to study existing programs and suggested changes in black studies courses, compensatory education, an Afro-American Institute, and university involvement in the community.[76]

To the more militant activists, however, the settlement and subsequent developments suggested a revolution betrayed rather than spreading. Even as demonstrations spread to other campuses they were mocking the idea that the sit-in had been a victory for the students and accused the Steering Committee of "the biggest sell-out in the history of the new black student left." [77] In the weeks that followed, proponents of swift and sweeping changes suffered several rebuffs. They lost a chance to negotiate further demands with sympathetic parties when a meeting of Liberal Arts School faculty on March 28 rejected a resolution calling for reforms of "structural weakness in the organization of the University" by "greater faculty participation." Instead the meeting voted to reconstitute a Board of Trustees committee which was dominated by older, tenured faculty. Subsequent meetings with student representatives conspicuously excluded their militant wing and dropped the call for transforming Howard into a "black university." [78] While an "Afro-American orientation" to Howard's curriculum was announced on April 4, specific courses had to go through a bureaucratic maze, and by the end of the semester most proposed courses had not been processed. The joint student-faculty committee studying new programs simply recommended in late May that the university assess what was being done in Afro-American courses, community involvement, and other of the sixteen demands and offered neither specific proposals nor any sense of urgency for change.[79] Not even the election of a militant activist as Student Assembly president could change the view of many sit-inners that their protest had gained nothing save the dropping of charges against Charter Day demonstrators.[80]

Their disillusionment with the aftermath of the sit-in reveals that although the militants had disrupted Charter Day and largely organized the sit-in they had lost the leadership of student protest when it was settled and could not bring pressure for more radical or rapid changes in the weeks that followed. Several factors seem responsible for this development. First, it is questionable whether proponents of immediate radical change ever clearly dominated the thinking of the campus. Not only did many sit-inners have limited goals, but they had criticized the administration for closing the campus. When it was reopened most students had a greater interest in returning to classwork than in assuring that Howard was transformed into a black university. The second factor was quite unexpected, however. Less than two weeks after the settlement, a sniper's bullet in Memphis unleashed a chain reaction of black wrath which would divert the attention and energies of *Ujamma* from the question of campus reform. Nowhere was this reaction more immediate or intense than in Washington. By Thursday night crowds of black youths had rampaged beyond control. On Friday the university was closed in mourning, and thousands of angry blacks held rallies. As major shopping centers were looted and burned, leaving many families without food, leaders of the Steering Committee formed the Howard University Relief Force and did yeoman work as a center of food distribution. This riot deprived Howard students of all but three days of classes between April 4 and 22, by which time they were even more concerned with studies and less with campus reform. Visits to Columbia University to support black students there and participation in the Poor Peoples' Campaign absorbed the energies of many activists through May.[81] It was thus as much by chance and their own dissipation of activities as by conservative design that the militants who had set the pace of campus protest early in the spring failed to reshape the university after the sit-in.

In retrospect, the Howard sit-in stands out as an example of the changing mood of black Americans and an indication of the limitations of that transformation. In four years the dominant attitude at Howard changed from one of preoccupation with white middle-class values and indifference to the "Negro Revolt" and the role of the university in it to a rejection of such values and to direct action to make Howard more relevant to blacks in their quest for identity and power. But this trend should not be overemphasized. Through the fall of 1967 student protests were largely an indigenous response to campus conditions, and institutional reform remained the prime motive of most of those participating in the sit-in. Nor does the ascendancy of militant attitudes fit any broad stereotype of campus activists or theory of nation-wide causation. Howard's militants had no connection with Students for a Democratic Society or any "white-dominated" radical group, and there is little evidence that black militants from outside the campus played any significant role in changing student attitudes and actions.

This evolution is also significant for the insights it contains for both critics and proponents of contemporary student movements. It was the procrastination of the administration and senior faculty towards granting modest campus reforms that was most responsible for creating the impression that protest through negotiation was futile and that only direct action would bring about substantial change. Through such action students brought attention to many conditions at Negro colleges which were outdated or paternalistic compared to white institutions and to new areas of curricular emphasis in which Negro colleges might make a more significant contribution to their historic purpose of race advancement. Reforming these conditions in response to demonstrations did not tear down the fabric of law and order. Rather, it held the promise of making Howard a more viable institution.

Yet the very evolution of the nature of student protest had brought in its wake some ominous consequences. By the fall of 1968 the movement had created a strong atmosphere of race awareness which, frustrated in its quest for a black university, has shown signs of turning against white instructors regardless of their abilities or previous sympathy with student protests and of creating deep schisms among students. Whether the momentum for change built up by the sit-in completes the task of reforming Howard's shortcomings or produces an atmosphere of factionalism and harassment may well determine the ultimate significance of the sit-in of March, 1968.

NOTES

[1] United States Office of Education, Bureau of Higher Education, *Report of Survey of Howard University, College of Liberal Arts,* May 2–3, 1966, p. 2.

[2] *Ibid.,* p. 1; United States Office of Education, Bureau of Higher Education, *Report of Survey of Howard University, The Graduate School,* June 26–27, 1967, p. 3.

[3] David Riesman and Christopher Jencks, *The Academic Revolution* (Garden City, N.Y.: Doubleday & Company, Inc., 1968), pp. 425, 428.

[4] *Report . . . College of Liberal Arts,* p. 2; *see also* the detailed discussion of this problem in Riesman and Jencks, *op. cit.,* pp. 428–31; *Report . . . Graduate School,* p. 49.

[5] *Report . . . College of Liberal Arts,* p. 3; L. Richard Meeth, "The Transition of the Predominantly Negro College," *Journal of Negro Education,* Fall, 1966, pp. 500–501.

[6] *Report . . . Graduate School,* p. 31; *Yearbook* of the *Journal of Negro Education,* Fall, 1966, which is edited by the Department of Education at Howard, was devoted to higher education for Negro Americans but contained no mention of the growing trend of black awareness or of the need to make the university more "relevant" to the black community. These topics are also largely missing from the reports on Howard by the Office of Education.

[7] Earl J. McGrath, *Predominantly Negro Colleges and Universities in Transition* (New York: Columbia University Teachers College, 1965), p. 124; Riesman and Jencks, *op. cit.,* pp. 421–22.

[8] James M. Nabrit, Jr., "Critical Summary and Evaluation," *Yearbook* of the *Journal of Negro Education,* Fall, 1963, p. 514; Nabrit, letter in *The Hilltop,* May 1, 1965.

[9] Susan Jacoby, "In Search of Black Identity," *Saturday Review of Literature,* April 20, 1961, pp. 61–62.

[10] *Report . . . Graduate School,* pp. 45, 48.

[11] Lerone Bennett, Jr., "Confrontation on the Campus," *Ebony,* May, 1968, p. 27.

[12] *The Hilltop,* October 23, 1964, p. 7; *see especially* article by Ronald Ross, February 19, 1965, p. 5; Carol Joffe, "Student Conservatism at Howard," April 9, 1965, p. 2.

[13] *Ibid.,* October 23, 1964, p. 5.

[14] *Ibid.,* December 4, 1964, p. 2.

[15] *Ibid.,* January 17, 1965; April 26, 1965.

[16] *Ibid.,* April 26, 1965; April 9, 1965.

[17] *Ibid.,* November 13, 1964.

[18] Quoted in *ibid.,* May 1, 1965, pp. 1–2.

[19] Interview with Brenda Adams, June 12, 1968.

[20] Quoted in *The Hilltop,* January 15, 1965, p. 2.

[21] *Ibid.,* November 6, 1964; May 1, 1965; November 18, 1966.

[22] *Ibid.,* November 1, 1966, p. 1; December 2, 1966, p. 4.

[23] *Ibid.*, March 10, 1967, p. 2.

[24] *Ibid.*, December 2, 1966, p. 5; September 14, 1966, p. 2; October 14, 1966, p. 2.

[25] McGrath, *op. cit.*, p. 4; Leroy B. Allen (President of Cheyney College), "The Possibilities of Integration for Public Colleges Founded for Negroes," *Journal of Negro Education*, Fall, 1966, p. 453.

[26] Nathan Hare, "Final Reflections on a 'Negro' College: A Case Study," *Negro Digest*, March, 1968, p. 45.

[27] *See* Nathan Hare, "Legacy of Paternalism," *Saturday Review of Literature*, July 20, 1968, for an interpretation of black power at Howard having essentially institutional rather than revolutionary demands.

[28] *The Hilltop*, April 7, 1966, p. 1.

[29] *Ibid.*, April 14, 1967, p. 2.

[30] *Ibid.*, April 21, 1967, p. 1.

[31] *Ibid.*, April 28, 1967, p. 1.

[32] *Ibid.*, May 5, 1967, pp. 1–3.

[33] *Ibid.*, May 7, 1967, p. 2.

[34] *Ibid.;* interview with Dr. Harold Lewis, June 21, 1968.

[35] *The Hilltop*, May 12, 1967, p. 1.

[36] *Ibid.*, May 19, 1967, p. 1.

[37] Both students and faculty endeavored to overturn these dismissals by legal means. Professors in the case of *Hare et al. v. Howard* lost a ruling in a lower court, but four students won a case during the summer which ordered the university to reinstate them. Hare, "Final Reflections on a 'Negro' College," p. 47; interview with Brenda Adams; *The Hilltop*, September 15, 1967, p. 3. JeRoyd Greene subsequently received a scholarship to Yale Law School and did not exercise his legally won right to return to Howard.

[38] *The Hilltop*, September 16, 1967, p. 4.

[39] *Ibid.*, September 15, 1964, p. 4.

[40] *Ibid.*, September 29, 1967, p. 6.

[41] *Ibid.*, October 5, 1967, pp. 4–5.

[42] *Ibid.*, November 3, 1967, p. 8; December 8, 1967, pp. 1, 4; February 16, 1968, pp. 1, 11.

[43] *Ibid.*, October 26, 1967, p. 2.

[44] *Ibid.*, November 10, 1967, p. 9.

[45] Interview with Brenda Adams.

[46] *The Hilltop*, November 3, 1967, p. 4.

[47] *Ibid.*, September 15, 1967, p. 2.

[48] *Ibid.*, September 29, 1967, p. 4.

[49] Jack Bass and Paul Clancey, "The Militant Mood in Negro Colleges," *Reporter*, May 16, 1968, pp. 21–22.

[50] *The Hilltop*, February 23, 1968, p. 1; "Spear and Shield," Vol. 1, No. 2.

[51] *The Hilltop*, February 23, 1968, p. 1.

[52] "Minutes of the College of Liberal Arts," February 19, 1968.

[53] Memorandum from the Committee of the Faculty of the College of Liberal Arts to Dr. James Nabrit on Challenges and Responses to Howard University Community, February 27, 1968; Minutes of a Call Meeting of the Faculty of

the College of Liberal Arts, February 27, 1968; Minutes of the Faculty of the College of Liberal Arts, February 29, 1968.

[54] *The Hilltop,* March 8, 1968, p. 2.

[55] "Definition of a Black University," p. 1.

[56] *The Hilltop,* March 8, 1967, pp. 4, 7.

[57] *Ibid.,* March 22, 1968, and personal observations; interview with Ewart Brown, June, 1968.

[58] *Washington Post,* March 21, 1968, pp. 1, 8.

[59] *Ibid.,* March 21, 1968.

[60] *The Hilltop,* March 29, 1968, pp. 2–3.

[61] *Washington Post,* March 21, 1968, p. 8.

[62] *The Hilltop,* March 22, 1968, pp. 1, 2, 4.

[63] Courtland Cox, Marvin Halloway, Charlie Cobb, "Open Forum," *The Hilltop,* March 29, 1968, p. 5.

[64] *The Hilltop,* March 22, 1968, p. 2.

[65] Television news broadcast, March 19, 20, 1968; *Washington Post,* March 21, 1968.

[66] Remarks by Dean Frank M. Snowden, Jr., to meeting of faculty of College of Liberal Arts, March 28, 1968.

[67] *Ibid.; Washington Post,* March 22, 1968; interview with Ewart Brown; *The Hilltop,* March 29, 1968, p. 2.

[68] *The Hilltop,* March 29, 1968, p. 2.

[69] *Washington Post,* March 21, 1968.

[70] *The Hilltop,* March 29, 1968, p. 2.

[71] Interview with Brenda Adams; *The Hilltop,* March 29, 1968, pp. 2, 4; April 5, 1968, p. 7.

[72] Interview with Ewart Brown; *The Hilltop,* March 29, 1968.

[73] *The Hilltop,* March 29, 1968, p. 1.

[74] *Ibid.,* April 5, 1968, p. 1.

[75] Minutes of a Call Meeting of the Faculty of the College of Liberal Arts, March 28, 1968; interview with Ewart Brown.

[76] *The Hilltop,* May 3, 1968, p. 8; April 26, 1968, p. 1; Memorandum from Stanton Wormley to Academic Deans, May 6, 1968; Report of the Faculty-Student Committee on Means of Implementing and Recommending Objectives "D" and "E," May 23, 1968.

[77] *The Hilltop,* April 5, 1968, p. 7.

[78] Minutes of Meeting . . . March 28, 1968; Resolution . . . of the Faculty at an *Ad Hoc* Meeting Held on March 25, 1968; Resolution Adopted by a Committee of the Faculty and Heads of Departments, Appointed March 23, 1968; *The Hilltop,* April 26, 1968, p. 5; Minutes of a Call Meeting of the Faculty of Liberal Arts, April 4, 1968.

[79] *The Hilltop,* April 26, 1968, p. 1; Memorandum from Stanton Wormley to Academic Deans, May 6, 1968; Report of the Faculty-Student Committee on Means of Implementing and Recommending Objectives "D" and "E," May 23, 1968.

[80] Interview with Brenda Adams; *The Hilltop,* May 17, 1968, p. 1.

[81] *The Hilltop,* May 3, 1968, p. 1.

7

OHIO STATE: FREE SPEECH AND STUDENT POWER

*by James S. Turner**

"As LONG AS I'm a member of the Board of Trustees no Communist, fellow traveler, Fascist, or Nazi is going to have an invitation to speak here." [1] This statement by Brig. Gen. Carlton Dargusch, Chairman of the Board of Trustees, sounded the beginning and set the tone for a decade and a half of struggle to allow free speech at Ohio State University. From 1951 to 1965 there were three major confrontations over free speech at Ohio State. In the first encounter students took almost no part, in the second they played a supporting role, and in the third they assumed the leadership. By succeeding where the others had failed, they showed that student power can be an effective force for university improvement.

When the Ohio Agricultural and Mechanical College opened its doors in September of 1873, it had a student body of twenty-four. The only Ohio School established under provisions of the Morrill (land-grant college) Act, it began operation on a farm two miles north of Columbus. In 1878 its name was changed to The Ohio State

* James S. Turner is a 1969 Ohio State Law School graduate. After earning his bachelor's degree in political science at The Ohio State University, he served in the United States Navy. Since leaving the service, he has been working with several activist organizations in campus and off-campus educational, social, and political issues. Presently he is a Consultant to the Center for the Study of Responsible Law, Washington, D.C., Ralph Nader, Chairman of the Board.

University. While the university has grown in size and scope in the past 95 years, it has never quite outgrown its origins.

Over half of its 2,790 acres, now located near the center of Columbus, are devoted to research and teaching in agriculture. Nearly 90 percent of its more than 40,000 students are Ohioans, and the University is proud of its service in providing the state with engineers, doctors, nurses, veterinarians and other professionals. In addition Ohio State is the nation's sixth largest grantor of Ph.D.'s and seventh largest grantor of baccalaureate and master's degrees. But the University often seems proudest of all of possessing one of the most powerful and respected athletic empires in the nation.

Ohio State University also entertains an enjoyable and profitable relationship with the military. It produces almost as many career officers as West Point. The biggest spectacle in the academic year is the May Day parade of about 6,000 ROTC Cadets and Midshipmen around the center of the campus. Novice G. Fawcett, president of the University since 1955, has received one of the highest civilian decorations given by the Army for his support. The largest private contribution to the University (about 7 million dollars) was received in 1953 from a retired Army colonel.

This grant was jeopardized by the panty raids and other antics which were a prominent feature of student life at that time. The University was driven to hire a former FBI agent as Assistant Dean of Men. Student government confined itself to the running of beauty contests (at least three a year), dances and various other social functions. Two fraternity-based "parties" competed for office. During one election, one was accused of stuffing the ballot box and the other of stealing and burning the ballots. The election results were supposedly determined in a secret meeting with deans. When, years later, student politics started to turn toward political issues a major charge leveled by the party in control was that their opponents could not run social affairs as well as they did.

Ohio State, then, had most of the characteristics associated with a conservative university when the free speech debate began. It was governed throughout the period of the controversy by a conservative Board of Trustees, led by John W. Bricker, formerly Governor and U.S. Senator, and a leading figure in reactionary politics. Contributing further to its conservative posture is its location in a city whose "political spectrum begins on the left with moderate Republicanism, and moves rightward towards absolute darkness." [2]

The free speech confrontation began in the summer of 1951. The University's College of Education, following all prescribed rules, had invited Harold O. Rugg, professor emeritus of Education at Columbia University's Teacher College, to address a traditional summer conference. Two of the three Columbus newspapers (the *Dispatch,* vehicle of a prominent Columbus family, and the *Journal,* starting place of William Dean Howells and owned by the same family) attacked the meeting by asking, "Why Rugg, of all persons?" The Columbia professor was labeled a socialist, left-wing propagandist unfit to address Ohio students. Letters to the editors of these two papers poured in asking for an investigation of the University. Governor Lausche, sensitive to the pressure, asked the Board to investigate. The result was a pair of unanimous Board motions which condemned the invitation to Rugg as "not in accord with the traditions and objectives of The Ohio State University," [3] and a ruling that all proposed speakers' names be presented to the president's office "for clearance ten days prior to extension of the actual invitation." It was this pair of motions, passed in September of 1951, that became known as the Ohio State gag-rule.

Early in the following month Ohio State President Howard L. Bevis invoked the new rule, denying a request from the campus chapter of the Fellowship of Reconciliation to allow Cecil Henshaw, a pacifist and former Quaker college president, to speak. Bevis also announced that the Board had further instructed him to review "for clearance prior to issuance . . . all questionnaires prepared by an individual employed by the University in a department or College thereof." [4]

The president and the Board came under immediate attack. The Ohio Education Association, the Executive Board of the Ohio CIO, the Franklin County Council of Churches and the Catholic Diocese of Columbus condemned the President's veto. The faculty of the College of Education, the local chapter of the American Association of University Professors, the Conference of the Teaching Staff, and the Faculty Council urged the Board to reconsider its vote establishing the restrictions. Newspapers around the state, including the Columbus *Citizen,* joined the attack.

In response to this pressure (identified as "misunderstanding" by the Board), the Trustees softened their position. While unanimously reaffirming the gag-rule motions they gave the president the option of suspending the ten-day screening requirement at his discretion, and they agreed to meet with a committee of the Faculty Council to discuss the gag-rule. It was at this point that *The New York Times* and the national AAUP voiced their opposition to and criticism of the Board's position. The *Times* ran four articles and a critical editorial while the AAUP called on its local members to work for freedom at the University. In addition the Student Senate conducted a poll among students that showed 2,986 against the Board's position and 637 for it. The University Religious Council joined the majority in its condemnation of the speakers rule.

On December 10 the Board adopted a policy statement which had been worked out in two meetings with the faculty committee designated to carry out the discussions promised by the Board. The statement asserted that inviting proper speakers "is now and has always been primarily a faculty responsibility subject to University administrative procedures." [5] To carry out this responsibility, the Board announced that a committee of the faculty would meet regularly with the Board. According to the Alumni Magazine, "The only issue which had separated the two groups [faculty and Trustees] from the beginning was the question as to how the screening of the speakers should be done and by whom." [6] At the same time the Faculty Council unanimously stated that "it finds itself in essential agreement with the Board's policy with respect to the responsibility of the faculty for the selection of speakers." [7] Even the AAUP chapter seemed satisfied. The Board had said that the faculty was in charge of speaker determination, and as far as the faculty at The Ohio State University was concerned, the battle was over and they had won.

Lost somewhere in the compromise was the warning of *The New York Times* editorial: "What is at stake in Ohio is something greater than a quarrel between Administration and Faculty. The principle involved here goes to the heart of a University's existence and affects every University in America; it is the spirit of free inquiry." [8] What the faculty had won in its battle was the right to exclude subversives. If it did well at this it would be in charge. If it failed it was still up to the president to take the final necessary "action." A key section of the policy read:

If a faculty member proposes to have someone speak on the campus or under University auspices and there exists a doubt as measured by generally accepted standards as to whether the proposed action would be in the best and overall interest of the University . . . the faculty member concerned shall consult with his colleagues and cause the matter to be referred through his appropriate department chairman and dean to the President's office for advice and action.[9]

Nowhere in the discussion of the issues was there mention of any role for students in determining which speakers they would be allowed to hear, or how they would keep alive *their* spirit of free inquiry.

In April of 1956 the national AAUP censured The Ohio State University, partly as a result of the December 10, 1951, policy statement worked out by faculty representatives and the Board of Trustees. It was the feeling of the AAUP's investigating committee and the position of the organization that as long as the president of Ohio State had the right to take final "action" on any controversial speaker, the standards for academic freedom had not been met. A second ground for censure was the existence of a university rule requiring every faculty member to sign a non-Communist loyalty oath. The final ground for censure was the suspension and subsequent dismissal of a tenured professor for asserting his rights under the Fifth Amendment to the House Committee on Un-American Activities.

While there was some discussion of these problems before the censure, it is quite clear that the AAUP action accelerated activity for reform. The Faculty Advisory Committee (FAC), created by the Board in 1951, had acquired permanent and standing status in 1954; now it entered into intensive discussions with the Board, with a view to getting the censure lifted. After two years of negotiations, FAC recommendations, which appeared to be sweeping changes, were approved by the Board on September 1, 1958. The loyalty oath was deleted from the rules; invocation of the Fifth Amendment was no longer to be grounds for dismissal, and the word "action" was removed from the powers of the president under the speakers rule. As a result of these changes, the memorandum of the local AAUP seeking Ohio State's removal from the censured list was unequivocal concerning the speakers rule: "In short, for the power of the President to act, there has been substituted the duty of the faculty member to consult." [10] When their report was presented to the national AAUP, the University was removed from its list of censured institutions.

This outcome was hailed not only as a triumph of the faculty and a vindication of free speech, but as a tribute to all segments of the University. Prof. Robert M. Estrich, who has been a prominent defender of free speech on the campus, put it this way: "More important to me than any other aspect of the entire problem is a spirit among the faculty, administration, and Board of Trustees that when problems arise which are of concern to the faculty, there ought to be free and careful study, and that they ought to be worked out among the three." [11] For the students, the campus newspaper, the *Lantern,* commented in a similar vein: "The issue of the pro and con of the AAUP censure is hardly the point now. The point is that the university faculty, administration and the Board of Trustees have clarified presently confused rulings and set up clear, workable procedures which are not part of the University Rules. Such co-operation and spirit deserves commendation—ours included." [12]

In December, 1959, just eight months after the censure was lifted, Hubert H. Humphrey, then a candidate for the presidential nomination, was invited to speak at Ohio State by the president of the Young Democrats Club. The Senator accepted, the meeting was announced, and the speakers rule was on the front pages again. The administration felt that since Humphrey was a presidential candidate there was "doubt as measured by generally accepted standards" that his visit would be in the best interest of the university, and asked for a review of the invitation. The meaning of "best interest" was interpreted in light of a July 7, 1950, Board ruling banning the holding of meetings organized in the interest of political candidates "whether addressed by the candidates themselves or by others in their behalf." [13]

For suggesting that the policy be invoked against Humphrey the University came under immediate unpleasant pressure. Since the invitation had been made publicly there was widespread interest in the outcome of the conflict. A delegation of Ohio State Young Democrats and campus reporters attended a major Democratic fund raising dinner in Washington four days before the scheduled speech, and found the controversy of interest to many of the guests. Much of what was said about the issue both publicly and privately found its way into the campus newspaper. Finally, Dean of Student Relations William S. Guthrie announced the University's decision. "Because the Young Democrats Club had invited its speaker, made arrangements for a meeting place, and announced the meeting in the *Lantern,* I advised the Club president and adviser that I would not interfere with their plans although in my opinion they chose an interpretation of policy regarding a candidate's appearance on campus with which I disagree." [14] Humphrey spoke. But the unlikely head-line "Humphrey Welcome If He Avoids Politics" [15] captured the atmosphere of the university as the 1960's began.

In the Spring of 1961 William Mandel, an outspoken critic of the House Committee on Un-American Activities, was invited to speak on the campus by Henry St. Onge, a member of the English teaching staff. Mandel was banned. But once again a showdown on the issue of free speech was narrowly avoided. Because St. Onge was an assistant instructor, he was not entitled to invite speakers under the rule. When a student group (Students for Liberal Action) tried to extend the invitation in its own name, it was held by the Faculty Advisory Committee that the faculty adviser to a student organization had to desire to invite the speakers his group invited. SLA's adviser did not want to invite Mandel and so to him fell the responsibility for not allowing the speech. The administration thus avoided responsi-bility for limiting whom the students heard.

After the controversy, the FAC said the speakers rule "does not take any account of the customary relationships between student organizations and their faculty advisers." [16] One year later, in April, 1962, the Faculty Council adopted an FAC recommendation whereby a faculty adviser did not have to agree with the views of a speaker invited at the request of the organization he advised. Once again the Faculty Council was satisfied that finally the problem of guest speakers had been solved.

However, on April 25, 1962, a matter of days after the adoption of the new rule, the president banned Phillip Luce (an alumnus of the University), Clark Foreman (Director of the Emergency Civil Liberties Committee) and Burton White (a Berkeley student) all of whom intended to speak out against the House Committee on Un-American Activities. The three had been invited by the new adviser of SLA in accordance with the provisions of the new rule. One hour before the announced meeting was to begin the president of the University ordered campus police to close and lock the doors of the Law School building, where the meeting was to be held, and banned all student meetings in the building for the day.

For the first time in the free speech controversy student reaction was immediate and strong. Standing outside the building where they had come to hear the speakers, various student leaders deplored the action to the press. The President of the Student Body called the action "unfortunate." The president of the Young Democrat Club said the action "impedes academic freedom," and the spokesman for SLA "regretted" it. Leaders of these three organizations joined to coordinate the protest and the next day 75 students met in *ad hoc* committee to raise money and plan a rally. The *Lantern*, the Student Senate, the Ohio State Civil Liberties Committee, the Young Democrats and about half a dozen *ad hoc* groups issued mimeographed newspapers on the incident which deplored, attacked, or regretted the president's action. For the first time there was deep, active and organized student concern.

But it was the outraged members of the faculty who led the protest. The Faculty Council and the Faculty Advisory Committee had spent twelve years drafting and modifying the speakers rule and just a few days earlier it had eliminated what it thought was the last flaw. It had been the assumption of the Faculty Council, the AAUP local, and the national AAUP that authorization for the kind of action taken by the president had been deleted from the rule. The faculty protesters argued that the president had misread and under-mined the years of work that had gone into perfecting the rule. Many of these faculty members, already dissatisfied with the general atmosphere of the University, began to organize to express their concern. Dr. Eric Solomon described their activities:

There was no formal organization; we simply invited [faculty] people worried about academic freedom who would bring their friends, and we exchanged horror stories. These little meetings had . . . rather important consequences, however. . . . In the Spring of 1962, we had a nucleus; we were ready to respond instantly . . . to the encroachments upon our sense of academic freedom.[17]

The overall strategy plan was laid out by the faculty leaders. Dr. Solomon and others who were considered to be "faculty friends" of the students urged their younger associates to leave the issue in their hands. The arguments they gave were convincing. These faculty members thought that they would be able to muster sufficient votes in the Faculty Council to censure the president's action. Since it seemed that demonstrations might jeopardize that effort, the student coordinating committee contented itself with raising money, organizing an off-campus rally, and publishing a mimeographed newssheet called

"Free Speech." Although such activities were aimed at supporting the faculty, Trustee Bricker commented that "it is my personal feeling that the students who are trying to run the university rather than get an education had better move on." [18]

When the crucial faculty meeting was held on May 14, 1962, events did not go as Dr. Solomon and his allies had anticipated. While a majority of the teaching faculty of the Arts and Sciences, Law, Education, Engineering and other academic fields were ready to censure the president's action, they found themselves outvoted. Not only did large numbers of medical doctors with minimal teaching responsibilities appear to claim their places on the faculty, but almost 800 agricultural extension workers and county agents were, it developed, also entitled to vote. Rather than censure, a vote of confidence in the President's handling of the Luce affair was passed, 1,036 to 509.

Then it was the students' turn. Over the summer and in early fall of 1962 faculty leaders informally told students to plan their own strategy. Many faculty members were planning to leave and most others felt that there was little more that they could do. So on November 21, 1962, SLA president Niki Schwartz asked permission to invite Frank Wilkinson, a critic of HUAC, to the campus. After much communication, the president asked SLA to have Wilkinson sign a loyalty oath in order to remove "grave doubt" that his appearance was in the best interests of the University. When SLA refused to comply, permission for Wilkinson to speak was denied by the president. In response to the denial, a suit was filed in Federal District Court against the university by Niki Schwartz, one other SLA member, and Wilkinson, asking that the rule be declared unconstitutional. A law suit had been first suggested publicly outside the law building the day of the Luce lock-out by the vice president of SLA, but was quickly forgotten in the faculty strategy of containing the issue within the university framework. Now the case was in the courts and would remain there for the next two years.

With Wilkinson banned and the case in the court the *Lantern* added to the controversy by running a story with a five column banner headline reading, "Academic Atmosphere Called Unsatisfactory by 15 Resigning Ohio State Faculty Members." [19] The president responded immediately by saying: "The story in the student newspaper created the erroneous impression that the 15 individuals interviewed had chosen to accept other positions primarily because of the current discussion concerning guest speakers." [20] He went on to say that the people leaving had cited other reasons as well; that 27 other persons were leaving and had not been interviewed; and that the number of resignations was fewer than it had been in the 1959–60 academic year. The *Lantern* then obtained the names of the other resigning professors, interviewed them, and found that half of them cited the troubled atmosphere at Ohio State as one of their reasons for leaving. In addition the paper discovered more professors had resigned than in 1959–60. After completing its investigation and reporting its results the *Lantern* left little doubt that the atmosphere was troubled.

The next step in the battle was taken by Senator Bricker, who had been defeated for reelection in 1958 and was trying for his party's nomination for his old Senate seat. Certainly with his knowledge and perhaps by his instigation, the Ohio State speakers rule was introduced as a bill in the State Legislature on March 25, 1963, by Columbus Representative Chalmers P. Whylie (Republican). The public reason Whylie gave for introducing the bill was to prevent people like Luce from speaking at other state universities in Ohio. Later he privately told Niki Schwartz that the real reason for the bill was to defeat the law suit.[21] One newspaper captured the attitude of much of the state when it said, "The heat cannot be turned off Ohio State by turning it on sister universities. Ohio State will be no less a laughingstock in the academic community if the other tax supported campuses are made the butt of Mr. Bricker's joke." [22]

Students led the opposition to the Whylie bill (House Bill 880) in the Ohio House of Representatives. "Prominent representatives of the Student Senate as well as a number of individual students representing other campus organizations testified against it and brought with them verified petitions signed by more than 3,700 Ohio State students in 'respectful opposition' to the bill." [23] The final number of signatures exceeded 6,000. The students were not alone in their opposition to the Whylie bill, being joined by Congressman Taft (opposing Bricker for the Senate) and a number of important newspapers throughout the state. Nevertheless, when Governor Rhodes finally moved to emasculate the bill, his action must be seen as a tribute to student strategy and political potential.

The next step was taken by SLA. The group had waited one year for the law suit to be determined. The Attorney General of Ohio had said that "A change now in the rules can only confuse things." [24] The Board told the Faculty Advisory Committee that "discussions of the speakers rule should be held in abeyance pending the outcome of the law suit." [25] So SLA decided to take the initiative. It asked permission to have Ann Braden, another HUAC critic, speak. Negotiations with the administration produced an agreement that the Board would consider the rule at its meeting if the request to have Braden speak were withdrawn. SLA agreed. But the Board did not discuss the rule.

SLA then moved towards a confrontation with the Administration. They asked permission to invite Russ Nixon, a critic of HUAC, Editor of the *National Guardian*, and often identified as "a Communist" to speak on the campus in the expectation that it would be refused. At the same time SLA set up a "Free Speech Front" to broaden their base of support, and planned mass protest rallies. The administration, in a remarkable reversal of previous policy, raised no objection to the Nixon invitation. Confrontation, however, was only postponed. At an April rally attended by 1,500 people, SLA leaders gave the Administration an ultimatum, demanding that the gag-rule be changed within three weeks, and invited Herbert Aptheker to speak at the end of that time. The administration responded six days later by announcing a ban on Aptheker.

The following day, April 21, a second rally attracted 2,000 sympathetic listeners. During his speech to the crowd Jeffrey Schwartz, brother of the first plaintiff in the still pending law suit, urged all who wished to participate in direct action to join him in a planning meeting. At the meeting it was decided to picket the administration building the next day.

About four hundred and fifty students effected a moving picket line around the administration building the next day at noon. Bright blue and white buttons saying "Free Speech Now" appeared. Schwartz and Gary Bower, who had also been a leader of the student protest during the Luce lock-out, entered the administration building for talks with the vice president. The talks, however, failed to produce significant results. After a vote was taken, two hundred and seventy of the four hundred and fifty students entered the building for Ohio State's first sit-in. Once inside, the students voted to end the sit-in at closing time but to be back in one week if the Board had not agreed to discuss the speakers rule at its next meeting. The Board refused and the students were back, this time for an all-night stay.

Between the two sit-ins, nine faculty members joined the public fray by seeking to invite Aptheker themselves. Their request was denied after the second sit-in and the base of dissatisfaction broadened. The *Lantern*, calling the second sit-in "another successful move by the Free Speech Front," [26] was only one of a number of newspapers and groups impressed by the Front's activities. On May 6 the traditional May Day ROTC parade was joined by an FSF sponsored teach-in. Finally, on May 8, the morning of the Trustees meeting, approximately 100 faculty members picketed outside the administration building where the Board was gathering. Four hundred and twenty-eight faculty members had petitioned the president to have the rule discussed by the Board at this meeting. The president recommended against the discussion, and the Board agreed. On May 14, in response to a lack of action by the Board, FSF announced that it would "bring Aptheker to the OSU campus within a week." [27]

Exactly a week later Herbert Aptheker was on the Ohio State campus. A crowd of between 2,500 and 3,000 had come to hear. But Aptheker did not speak. Instead, he sat silently on the stage while faculty members read excerpts from his books to the huge audience. The books were from the Ohio State University Library.

Herbert Aptheker's non-speech received nationwide coverage. *Time* magazine carried a photograph, and commented on "the futility of the ban." [28] The Cleveland *Press* said that "The trustees of Ohio State University can blame themselves for the campus ruckus caused by the appearance of Herbert Aptheker. . . ." [29] A motion was introduced into the Ohio House of Representatives, commending the orderly way in which the students had gone about protesting the rule. The Columbus *Dispatch* sadly acknowledged the strategic triumph of the free speech forces: "So grim is the temper of events that a return to the madcap frolics of panty raids, or other steam-venting student activity would be welcomed as a return to comfortable normality." [30]

At the July meeting of the Board of Trustees, President Fawcett noted that the issue was now placed in a new conceptual framework: "In recent controversies on this matter, I have noted that disagreement has centered more on the *right* of students to *hear* extremists express their view than on the *right* of the extremists to speak." [31] The president further noted that "according to the best estimates I have seen, as many as 75 percent of our students feel strongly that a change in our speakers rule is essential." There was in fact nothing new about this opposition—a poll of November, 1951, had shown only 22 percent of the students supporting the rule. What was new was that the students had now organized to express their opposition, thus forcing the administration to recognize its existence. President Fawcett recommended to the Board that the gag-rule be abandoned, and the substitute preferred by FSM be adopted in its stead.

The Board rejected the President's proposal. Senator Bricker insisted that "There will be no Communists, Nazis, Fascists or other subversives, or their supporters, teaching or speaking at Ohio State while I am on the Board if I can prevent it," [32] thus demonstrating that nothing which had happened since 1951 had made any impression upon him. Though it was summer and school was out, FSF managed to get 300 students and faculty to march to the Ohio State House. Once there, they were addressed by several legislators including the Democratic leader of the Senate who said his resolution supporting FSF and attacking the rule would pass "only if people like you press and press, otherwise it will die in committee." [33] At this time FSF announced that definite arrangements had been made to bring Aptheker back, this time to speak, in the fall quarter, whether the rule was changed or not. Quoting from a Toledo *Blade* editorial the Front said that the Board had "ruled out reason and invited rebellion. It is our hope that a Berkeley can be avoided at OSU in the fall, but only one thing will do that: A Board of Trustees brought back to their senses; the end of anti-intellectualism, Brickerism, and the end of the Speakers' Rule." [34]

FSF continued its pressure through the rest of the summer. Petitions against the rule and for an Aptheker speaking appearance were circulated throughout the state. Plans were laid for student-faculty strike if disciplinary action were taken against students because of the free speech fight. On August 12 a former Ohio Supreme Court Judge and a State Legislator addressed an FSF sponsored teach-in. Finally the September Board meeting came. The president raised the issue. And the Board passed the new rule. The combined efforts of the Governor (repeating the role he played in defeating the Whylie bill) and the president, by keeping negative votes away from the meeting and convincing a new Board member to vote "aye," carried the day. Fifteen years of controversy were ended.

On October 18, 1965, Herbert Aptheker spoke to 384 people. On November 28 Frank Wilkinson spoke to 250 people. Dennis Knepley, leader of FSF, announced, "Wilkinson's appearance will signal the end of the free speech controversy at Ohio State." [35] The law suit, still pending at the time, became moot and was dismissed. Since then there have been no speakers banned at Ohio State. The student drive for free speech succeeded where earlier efforts had failed.

The history of the removal of the gag-rule at Ohio State illustrates the contrast between faculty and student tactics in pursuit of a common goal. Faculty opponents of the gag-rule labored for twelve years, behind the scenes and out of the limelight, to get the rule changed. Teachers have a commitment, both intellectual and material, to the institution they serve which induces them to try to put it in the best possible light. They have a further professional bias towards the use of reason rather than pressure, and a sometimes naïve faith that they are dealing with people who can be swayed by logical argument. Thus when the AAUP censure was removed in 1959, Professor Meno Lovenstein, head of the local chapter, dismissed the whole censure as "a misunderstanding," [36] while Professor Robert Estrich remarked that "With such intelligent consideration, an educational institution can solve any new problem." [37] Professors much prefer consensus to conflict; even when the students had taken the leadership in the last, successful phase of the struggle, their faculty supporters persisted in working to prevent "a direct confrontation between the administration and the students." [38]

The faculty, as members in good standing of the academic community, prefer to see college problems resolved on the campus, without interference or external pressures. They are loath to adopt tactics which are outright political, or designed to gain popular off-campus support for their position. Possessing considerable status and a measure of power within the academic system, they tend to work within the system, not to oppose it. Unfortunately for them, their power, when tested by an attempt to exercise it on a crucial and controversial issue, often turns out to be hollow and illusory, as Ohio State faculty discovered more than once during the free speech controversy.

The faculty through its elected representatives on the Faculty Council and the Faculty Advisory Committee had on three different occasions expressed its belief that academic freedom in relation to guest speakers was adequately protected. Each time subsequent events proved them wrong. At each stage in the rule's development the faculty made a clear stand against the gag-rule. But at each of these stages the concession they received in writing never became actual in fact. With each succeeding controversy the administration was always able to overcome the last concession.

The students started from what appeared to be a considerably weaker position than the faculty. They had no tradition of organized concern for academic freedom, no regular voice in the higher councils of the University, no national association of status and experience comparable to that of the AAUP to support them. Jeffrey H. Schwartz, an Ohio State protest leader from 1962 to 1965 and a spokesman and organizer of FSF, has described the task facing the students: "The position of students in relation to the university is analogous to the position of many groups in the larger society which are excluded either in fact or by law from the decision-making process under which they live. . . . Our problem may be stated as follows: how can groups and individuals who have little or no power to influence the outcome of the decision-making process organize maximally effective . . . protest movements?" [39] "Organize" became the key word. The problem was to find, develop and use the tools that would organize the widespread dissatisfaction with the rule in such a way as to make clear to the administration that it could no longer impose its will on the people whom it was hired to serve.

In this task the students were free of the academic reticence that inhibited faculty members. The students were less anxious to protect the institution they attended, to confine their discontents to the proper channels, or to avoid unfavorable publicity. This lack of reticence gave them a freedom of action that the Ohio State faculty had denied itself. It allowed them to attack the speakers rule in court, to focus large amounts of unfavorable publicity on the University and finally to enlist the support of political leaders in their cause—all actions expressly rejected by faculty strategists in early phases of the same struggle.

The students, either by choice or by chance, had been very shrewd at playing the political realities. At no point did they violate any University rule. Still they were able to mount massive demonstrations that focused widespread ridicule on the gag-rule. "This was the main function of the demonstrations at OSU, to call attention to the controversy outside the confines of the university and thus to widen the arena of power in which the conflict was being waged." [40] The student leaders believed that "To obtain desired results a protest group must use the currency of politics. . . ." [41] The student campaigns in the free speech fight were successful largely because of the inherent weakness and stupidity of the gag-rule. The students succeeded because they were able to bring the indefensible rule to the attention of the courts, the general public and the politicians of Ohio. Jeff Schwartz' conclusion is that "the FSF demonstrations were a necessary, although probably not sufficient, condition for a rule change, given the situation at Ohio State in 1965." [42] In reaching their goal the students became a credit to themselves and their university and improved Ohio State's general appearance to the outside world. Student power was vindicated at Ohio State.

NOTES

[1] *The New York Times,* October 26, 1951.

[2] *New Republic,* May 25, 1968.

[3] Minutes of the Board of Trustees of The Ohio State University, September 4, 1951, pp. 76–77.

[4] The meaning and origin of this provision is obscure and is important only because its announcement later in the controversy spurred faculty protest. The entire provision was almost immediately forgotten and appears never to have been put into effect.

[5] Minutes of the Board of Trustees of The Ohio State University, December 10, 1951, p. 208.

[6] "Speakers Screening Rule Agreement Is Reached," *The Ohio State University Monthly,* XLIII (December 15, 1961), p. 6.

[7] "Faculty Approves Ruling," *The Ohio State University Monthly,* XLIII (January, 1952), p. 9.

[8] *The New York Times,* October 30, 1951.

[9] Minutes of the Board of Trustees of The Ohio State University, December 10, 1951, p. 208.

[10] Application of The Ohio State University Chapter of the American Association of University Professors for Removal of The Ohio State University from the List of Censured Administrations, November 20, 1958, p. 14.

[11] *The Ohio State Daily Lantern* (hereafter *Lantern*), April 30, 1959.

[12] *Ibid.*

[13] *Ibid.,* January 25, 1960.

[14] *Ibid.*

[15] *Ibid.,* January 22, 1960.

[16] "Faculty Advisory Committee Statement," *The Ohio State University Monthly,* LIII (May, 1961), p. 8.

[17] Eric Solomon, "Free Speech at Ohio State," *Atlantic Monthly,* CCVI (November, 1965), pp. 119–24.

[18] Columbus *Dispatch,* April 27, 1962.

[19] Len Downie, "Lantern Interviews Stir Controversy," *The Ohio State University Monthly,* LIV (July, 1963), pp. 12–13.

[20] *Ibid.*

[21] Jeffrey H. Schwartz, "The Speakers' Rule Controversy at Ohio State," Master's Thesis in the Faculty of Political Science, Columbia University, 1967, p. 45. This thesis is the only thorough treatment of Free Speech at Ohio State. The fact that its author was one of the major leaders and architects of student protest at Ohio State from 1961 to 1965 and that his brother was similarly occupied from 1958 to 1963 gives the paper an authenticity hard to duplicate. In addition it was conceived and executed in the same spirit that marked the Schwartz led demonstrations, namely, "We are sitting-in to build a great university not to tear down a bad one." This thesis is important reading for any person interested in the potential and meaning of student power.

[22] Toledo *Blade,* May 8, 1963, reprinted in the Akron *Beacon Journal, Lantern* and *The Ohio State University Monthly.*

[23] "House Bill 100: Students Spearhead Opposition Against Its Passage," *The Ohio State University Monthly,* LIV (June, 1963), p. 15.

[24] Letter of Ohio Attorney General William Saxbe to Chairman of the Board Thomas F. Patton, October 17, 1963. Contained in the Faculty Advisory Committee Report to the Faculty Council, February 11, 1964 (in the files of the Secretary of the Faculty Council), cited in Schwartz, *op. cit.,* p. 48.

[25] Report of Board Chairman Patton to the FAC on November 22, 1963.

[26] *Lantern,* April 30, 1965.

[27] *Ibid.,* May 10, 1965.

[28] *Time,* June 11, 1965, p. 77.

[29] *Lantern,* May 25, 1965, quoting the Cleveland *Press.*

[30] Columbus *Dispatch,* May 23, 1965; reprinted *The Ohio State University Monthly,* LVI (June, 1965), p. 23.

[31] Novice G. Fawcett, Recommendations to the Board of Trustees at their July 8, 1965, meeting; reprinted *The Ohio State University Monthly,* LVII (September, 1965), p. 5.

[32] John W. Bricker, Statement read at the July 8, 1965, meeting of the Board of Trustees, *ibid.*

[33] Columbus *Dispatch,* July 16, 1965.

[34] Schwartz, *op. cit.,* p. 71.

[35] *Lantern,* November 19, 1965.

[36] *Lantern,* April 30, 1959.

[37] *Ibid.*

[38] Interview with Roland J. Stanger (a senior faculty member who aided FSF) conducted on May 31, 1968, based on a memo prepared by Professor Stanger on May 24, 1964.

[39] Schwartz, *op. cit.,* p. 47.

[40] *Ibid.,* p. 108.

[41] *Ibid.,* p. 107.

[42] *Ibid.,* p. 109.

FOUR

New Patterns of Power

1

FACULTY MEDIATION
IN CAMPUS CONFLICT

by William R. Morgan*

THIS CHAPTER explores the role which faculty have played and can play in episodes of student protest, and especially their performance and potential as mediators. The issues, magnitude and intensity of protests vary tremendously, as does the course of their development, so eventually it seemed wise to narrow the focus of inquiry to a limited class of protests—those against war-related recruiting on campus. However, this decision can be justified only in terms of some more general considerations relating to faculty roles and concerns.

First, faculty are more concerned with protests if the issue is national in scope, such as civil rights or the Vietnam war, than they are with such strictly on-campus issues as dormitory regulations, food service, publications censorship, and student political rights and freedoms. James F. Volkwein, for example, surveyed 78 senior colleges and universities, which together accounted for 430 organized

* William R. Morgan is a doctoral candidate in the Department of Sociology at the University of Chicago. This chapter describes part of his thesis research which was supported primarily by a grant (MH 14305) and by a predoctoral fellowship from the National Institute of Mental Health, Public Health Service. The author expresses his gratitude to his thesis committee, Professors Richard Flacks (Chairman) and Fred L. Strodtbeck of the University of Chicago and Jack Sawyer of Northwestern University, for their assistance, but especially to his wife Barbara for her moral support.

protest incidents during 1966–67, and found that some faculty participated in 71% of the protests over off-campus issues, but in only 38% of the protests dealing with on-campus issues.[1] It may be that faculty perceived on-campus issues as, for the most part, trivial or as matters for students and administrators to work out between themselves, and in which the faculty had no real interest. Certainly when the issue was faculty retention, faculty tended to get involved. Or it may be that the style of protest works to restrain faculty. To take an extreme example, when on some campuses students resort to throwing food in the cafeteria in order to get their food service improved, faculty prefer to stay out of range. In contrast, faculty frequently view peace demonstrations which involve orderly rallies, marches, and vigils as dignified bearings of moral witness fully appropriate to an academic setting.

Second, of the various issues which concern student activists, probably none attracts more faculty sympathy than that of peace in Vietnam. Prestigeful faculty signatures have appeared on many full-page newspaper ads opposing the war, and many faculty have participated in teach-ins, draft counseling, and demonstrations. Press coverage of faculty dissent has sometimes given an exaggerated impression of united and collective faculty opposition to the war. However, David J. Armor's 1966 survey of a random sample of professors from 17 Boston-area colleges found that 15% called for immediate withdrawal of troops, while 46% believed bombing in the North should be stopped,[2] and 66% of faculty respondents in this study believed the United States should not have become militarily involved in Vietnam. By contrast, 36% of the general public and 31% of college graduates thought this, according to a national Gallup poll cited by Armor which was taken during the same time period as his study. Of the faculty surveyed, 38% reported having signed one or more anti-war petitions, the mildest type of protest activity, and 23% said they had written one or more public letters, such as to the editor. A much smaller proportion of faculty, 10%, said they had participated in demonstrations and teach-ins on the war.

A national poll of social psychologists, taken one year later in 1967, revealed increased dissent, although of a moderate nature.[3] Of 1,771 respondents, only 16% called for immediate withdrawal of troops, but 76% chose among three forms of gradual military withdrawal, with only 4% favoring the current military policy. Social psychologists may or may not represent faculty opinion in general;

various studies have indicated that social science and humanities faculty tend to be farther left politically than those who teach natural sciences, business, or engineering. Considered together, however, the two surveys indicate that faculty as a whole have been dovish, but that only a small proportion have been radical dissenters.

Opposition to the war in Vietnam, however, does not necessarily imply opposition to on-campus recruitment by the armed forces or war-related industries. Initially it seems probable that most faculty favored an open-campus recruitment policy, such as that upheld by virtually all administrators. Yet when the students accused the universities of complicity in the war effort because of their cooperation with such recruitment, there was at least a basis for sympathy on the part of faculty. We decided, therefore, to survey those campuses which had experienced some protest against recruitment policies, in an attempt to assess the role of the faculty in a situation which would tend to exert conflicting pulls of loyalty upon them.

The Survey

Questionnaires were designed to elicit information about the sources, development, magnitude, and after-effects of protests against recruiting policies. In May of 1968 questionnaires were sent to all schools known to have had recruiter demonstrations during the previous Fall. Schools which had recruiter demonstrations during October–December, 1967, were identified through newspaper articles selected by two news-clipping agencies.[4] Any schools with demonstrations in the Fall, but which were known also to have had sizable recruiter demonstrations during the previous year, were excluded, as were any schools where demonstrations did not occur until after December. This made it possible to assess the impact of the demonstrations and the development of conflict over a constant time period, roughly that of one academic year. The final sample to which questionnaires were sent included 76 schools, and 75 of them returned at least one questionnaire.

At the same time, a general questionnaire on demonstrations and student affairs was sent to 89 schools believed not to have a recruiter demonstration. The schools selected for this questionnaire were matched with the set of demonstration schools by region, type of control, size, and academic quality, institutional variables commonly reported to be associated with the incidence of demonstrations. Unexpectedly, of the 83 matched schools which returned at least one questionnaire, there were 31 that reported having recruiter demonstrations during the Fall. These 31 schools were added to the 75 previously identified, to give a sample of 106 schools which had experienced recruiter-related protests.

Although the questionnaire called mostly for factual information, some judgment and selective recall were involved in the responses, and so an effort was made to get a variety of viewpoints on the demonstrations. At least one administrator, one faculty member, and two students from each school were mailed a questionnaire, each being told that others at their school were receiving the same form. Whenever possible persons identified in the newspaper articles as prominent participants in the demonstrations or their aftermath were selected. If no specific names were available questionnaires were sent to the Dean of Students or similar office, to a social science faculty member identified in his school catalogue or professional directory interest listing as someone likely to be concerned with student affairs, and to students affiliated with the campus newspaper or student government.

A total of 96 administrators, 62 faculty, and 117 students responded, for a total of 275 questionnaires from the set of 106 schools. Preliminary analysis of response agreement within each school indicated that in general it was high, with disagreements occurring randomly among the respondents. What significant differences there were amongst the respondent types will be considered elsewhere. Information for each school was pooled, usually by averaging responses on each item, or in the case of certain open-ended questions by selecting the response giving the maximum amount of information.

At 76% of the colleges studied, students consulted with one or more members of the faculty prior to the demonstration, expressing their objections to having war-related recruiters on campus. Given the social tendency to talk to people with attitudes similar to one's own, as well as the reputed importance to student activists of the moral support of liberal faculty, these conversations were presumably held with sympathetic faculty.[5] Such professors would not have been hard to find. According to estimates of the informants, an average of 17% of the faculty at each school sympathized with student objections to recruiting policy prior to the demonstration, and 5%

were said to have openly supported students on this issue—by signing petitions, letters in the campus newspaper, etc.

Such preliminary faculty involvement probably helped to resolve the doubts of some students not yet fully committed to protest, while having little impact on administrators. Hardly any informants reported any significant predemonstration action by administrators which could be construed as being receptive to the student position against recruiting. This initial indifference came in spite of students reportedly having expressed their objections to recruiting prior to the demonstration through an average of four out of the seven available communication channels asked about in the questionnaire—campus newspaper editorials, meetings reported in the campus newspaper, student government resolutions, petitions, leaflets, conversations with administrators, and conversations with faculty.

In fact, the net effect of this predemonstration communication seems to have been to polarize the positions of the two sides. The more students tried to communicate, probably the more convinced they became that allowing on-campus recruiting for an illegal war was wrong, and the more occasions there were for the administration to appear intransigent. The amount of communication correlated positively with the occurrence later of organized civil disobedience at the demonstrations. Organized civil disobedience was defined as the refusal to obey administrative or police directives by more than ten demonstrators. In most cases the disobedience took the form of sit-ins which blocked access to the recruiters. When communication was low (0–2 channels used), civil disobedience occurred in 12% of the demonstrations, whereas when there was a medium (3–4) or high (5–7) amount of communication, the incidence of civil disobedience was 36% and 43% respectively. This correlation may mean only that extensive communication prior to the demonstration is part of the general climate of protest associated with civil disobedience, but it also seems to suggest that the "persuasive appeal" forms of communication available to students are inadequate.

When administrators did respond to these student objections, they confined themselves to affirming existing recruiting policy and warning against interference during the impending recruiting visits. The reasons they usually gave were three. First, they stated that a ban on a particular set of recruiters would be a violation of the free speech policy of keeping the campus open to all outsiders. Second, they said that such a ban would infringe on the rights of those students wishing to see the recruiters. Finally, they set forth the norm that the use of coercion by students was an unacceptable means of influence on campus. Administrators did cooperate in planning for the demonstrations at several schools, more to prevent disruption than out of sympathy for the student position. At only 5% of the colleges was the demonstration specifically forbidden, though administrators were aware of student plans to hold a demonstration at 83% of the schools studied.

Some faculty members participated in the demonstrations at 80% of the colleges. Over all 106 schools the average number of faculty demonstrators was seven, compared with an average of 170 student demonstrators. The average ratio of one faculty to every 23 student demonstrators is not too unlike the comparable ratio in the classrooms. There is no evidence, however, that faculty took a leadership role in the demonstrations in any way resembling their position in the classroom. Some faculty wished merely to express publicly their objections to the war, and carried home-made placards indicating this intention. Other faculty were objecting to the presence of recruiters, but sometimes on grounds other than their direct connection with the war. For example, the CIA was odious to faculty at some schools because of reports that scientists doing research abroad had been requested to do CIA intelligence work at the same time. Still other faculty wanted less to stop recruiting than to suggest alternative courses for potential recruits. This was most likely to happen at demonstrations against armed service recruiters, and to involve faculty having some connection with the draft resistance effort.

Regardless of their motives, however, the presence of a few faculty in the picket lines certainly must have increased the legitimacy of the demonstration for many doubtful observers, and even for some student demonstrators. For members of the campus community—administrators, faculty, and students—seeing an admired colleague or teacher participating made it much harder to reject the validity of the demonstration. The general public, to whom faculty activists are known mainly from the safe distance allowed by the television news show, could either dismiss these few faculty as "oddballs," or could accuse them of being the real instigators of the apparent troubles. It is only when the faculty acted as a body with respect to the demonstration that those outside the campus were likely to take serious notice.

The occurrence of organized civil disobedience at the demonstration had an overwhelming effect on the likelihood of the issues in the conflict between activists and administration being taken up by the faculty and student body as a whole. As Table 1 indicates, the question of whether or not to restrict war-related recruiting was evaluated by faculty councils and student governments about twice as often at schools where the demonstration had involved civil disobedience. Similarly, the emergent issue of the propriety of the administration's efforts to control the demonstrators arose much more frequently in both bodies, but particularly in student government, when there was civil disobedience.

The reasons for this broadened participation are apparent from the concomitant events associated with civil disobedience. (Table 1) First, the interruption of normal campus activities—classes, lectures, appointments, and so on—meant that more students and faculty were directing their attention, whether voluntarily or not, to the protest. They were much more likely to take a serious look at the demonstrators, some by direct observation, others through second-hand reports. Such legitimizing features of the protest, a prominent one being faculty participation, were now likely to be considered in evaluating the confrontation and its issues. The most important legitimizing feature, though, was the fact that the demonstrators were attempting to take action on a general position which many observers strongly agreed with, namely that the Vietnam war should be stopped.

The administration position, being for the most part identified with the recruiters and the status quo, garnered little sympathy. Although most faculty and students disapproved of the students' use of direct action tactics, the administration's efforts to control the demonstrators were even less well received. Since faculty originally tended to share the administrators' concern about minimizing disorder, many became doubly concerned when it was apparent that the administration's efforts had in fact contributed to the disorder. As Table 1 indicates, when civil disobedience occurred most administrations took various coercive measures in an effort to control the demonstration. The table shows also that at some demonstrations control measures were taken even without the stimulus of civil disobedience. Table 2 indicates in more detail the kinds of controls which were used (the

TABLE 1

IMPACT OF ORGANIZED CIVIL DISOBEDIENCE
AND ASSOCIATED EVENTS

	Disobedience Occurred	
Proportion of schools where the following took place:	YES (n = 33)	NO (n = 70)
Associated Events		
Overall disruption—campus activities interrupted to some extent.	94%	39%
Faculty participants, five or more.	52%	30%
Personal violence, one or more incidents.	45%	10%
Coercive controls used by administration at demonstration.	88%	27%
Disciplinary action begun by administration.	70%	6%
Faculty Council Response		
Resolution on administration control measures passed.	39%	14%
Resolution on recruiting policy passed.	55%	25%
Student Body Response		
Resolution on administration control measures passed by student government.	64%	9%
Resolution on recruiting policy passed by student government.	52%	30%
Referendum on recruiting policy held.	46%	16%

top four actions were the ones reported as coercive controls in Table 1), and their reported effect. The more severe the control measure, the more likely it was to backfire and aggravate the protest, making the demonstration larger or more immediately disruptive, and sometimes leading to a new demonstration directed against the control tactics used.[6]

Consequently many faculty were disillusioned by their administration's control response. They could not change what had already been done at the demonstration, but they could address themselves to the question of appropriate discipline, and many did this.

Also associated with the occurrence of civil disobedience were incidents of personal violence, defined here as hostile physical contact between a demonstrator and a policeman or administrator. In

TABLE 2

AGGRAVATING EFFECT OF ADMINISTRATION CONTROL MEASURES
ON THE DEMONSTRATIONS

Severity of Measure:		Frequency of Control Measure n = 102	Frequency of Effect: Protest Expanded
High	Some demonstrators were arrested.	11%	73% (11)
	Used police.	16%	50% (16)
Medium	Took demonstrators' names for later disciplinary action.	32%	31% (33)
	Warned demonstrators to quit or face discipline.	39%	23% (40)
Low	Promised action on demonstration issues afterwards.	14%	7% (14)
	No confrontation.	66%	2% (67)

the heat of the confrontation tempers become frayed, and isolated encounters of this sort sometimes occur. Who assaulted whom tends to be an ambiguous question at best, each side usually blaming the other. Violence of a more organized nature occurred in those instances where police took action to remove the demonstrators from the scene. This form of violence evoked a negative attitude toward the administration from most students and many faculty, and this is shown in part by the relatively large proportion of protests which expanded when arrest action was taken. (Table 2)

Faculty as Mediators

The faculty have some tendencies to take a position between those of the students and the administration, and are to this extent equipped to serve a mediating role. Mediation is never easy, however, particularly when the conflict has reached the polarized stage usually characteristic of civil disobedience confrontations.

Effective mediation depends entirely upon the degree of *confidence* and *trust* which unions and employers repose in mediators. The mediator is a bridge between the parties. His *strict impartiality* and his *freedom from coercion,* intimidation, or influence *from any source,* together with his wide experience in industrial relations situations, earn him confidence, and a position as an advisor which makes him of great value to the disputants. He is not necessarily wiser or more able than the representatives of the parties, but his *middle position* gives him the advantage of objectivity which they frequently do not possess. . . . In short, it is essential to the effective performance of the mediator's duty, that his institutional and personal relationships be such that neither side will have its suspicions aroused, however unjustly, that he is answerable to another with a suspected partisan stake in the dispute.[7]

The above passage is in reference to federal labor-management mediators, who presumably act as disinterested outsiders. By comparison, faculty are very much insiders to student-administration conflicts, and frequently are highly interested in the outcome. Their institutional and personal relationships make them susceptible to influence from both sides, but especially from administrators, so that the necessary attainment of impartial judgment, equal confidence and independent action is difficult. On the institutional level, the faculty's overriding interest in maintaining the order of the university gives most of them a far greater allegiance to the authority exercised by the administration than to the demands sought by the demonstrators. On a personal level, frequent ties of friendship as well as concerns about promotions, salary, and the funding of research help to affirm this faculty-administration allegiance.[8]

The difficulties of mediation are illustrated in the efforts of an *ad hoc* group of approximately 200 concerned Columbia faculty (referred to as the AHFG) to mediate between the students and Administration during the Spring 1968 building occupations.[9] The initial resolution they passed on terms for a just settlement clearly reflected partiality to the Administration. The resolution condemned the actions of the demonstrators, with no comment on the past behavior of the Administration, and further called for the establishment of a tripartite (administration-faculty-student) disciplinary board, thus rejecting the student demand for amnesty. The most meaningful concession sought from the Administration was a call for the temporary suspension of work on the new gym, one of the two issues which sparked the revolt. Their actions could hardly be considered independent either, since the meeting at which the settlement resolution was passed was briefly chaired by President Kirk himself. In consequence, it is not too surprising that the student demonstrators were suspicious of the AHFG's proposals, and in the end angrily rejected them as a "sell-out" position. When President Kirk soon afterwards called for an unprecedented Joint Faculties meeting, the AHFG had an opportunity to create broadened support for a new compromise position and thus bring greater pressure on both sides. A fair compromise collectively recommended by ˙e faculty as a whole would have been hard for either side to deny. The AHFG did formulate and pass by a huge majority such a proposal among themselves, but then they failed to bring it to a vote at the Joint Faculties meeting. This resolution would have called for the application of uniform penalties, somewhat in between the students' demand for total amnesty and the administration's plans for graded individual punishments. In contrast, the resolution which the combined faculty finally did pass flatly rejected the student position and gave President Kirk an implicit mandate to call in the police to clear the buildings.

At other schools, conflicts have arisen where the bonds between the faculty and the administration and the students were nearly equalized, allowing the faculty to mediate more effectively. The faculty in these cases achieved a high degree of impartiality, even without the traditional mediator's outsider perspective, by becoming equally committed to the competing interests of the students and administration, and equally sympathetic to the two parties separate from their interests. In addition, an important factor in their efforts was that these faculty groups for the most part acted through the official faculty councils of their schools, and thus were able to assume an independent authority position some distance from both sides. This degree of independence worked to prevent either side from interpreting and then rejecting the faculty proposal as merely a weak, equivocal posture biased by prior sympathy with the other side.

Data on the faculty's performance as mediator was obtained by a number of items in the survey. One prominent kind of mediating activity was the resolution weighing the administration's handling of the demonstration, a type of action implying that the administration's ability and equanimity had already been called into question, either by the faculty themselves or by others, usually students. The more controversial, active forms of control, as already shown, were employed at a relatively small proportion of schools, and consequently the need to pass judgment on the administration was limited to a correspondingly low number of schools. Overall, faculty resolutions on the administration were passed at about one-fourth of all the schools, and under half the schools where civil disobedience occurred. These resolutions, considered in terms of answers to whether or not the administration acted appropriately, took two distinct forms. First were those which straightforwardly approved or praised the administration's handling of the demonstration, frequently accompanied by a statement condemning the demonstrators. Only one-fourth of the resolutions took this form. The second, predominant form reflected a position of dissent from the administration, usually expressed in a positive, student-oriented manner. Specifically, they contained recommendations of leniency in the upcoming disciplinary decisions on the demonstrators, or provisions to establish a study committee on demonstration policy. Sometimes these resolutions expressed approval or disapproval of the administration as well, but this was a secondary emphasis in the formal statement.

The faculty call for moderate discipline contained in these resolutions undoubtedly arose in part out of sympathy with the moral concerns of the demonstrators, and in part out of a political awareness of general student opposition to harsh discipline, but, as is being stressed here, also out of feeling that the administration had mishandled the demonstration. These faculty were not simply intervening on behalf of their students, excusing their use of direct action tactics out of sympathy with their concerns. On the contrary, an important idea implicit in their resolutions was that the administration, because of their control actions, bore part of the responsibility for the disruption which occurred, so that severe disciplinary action against the students would be unfair.

This sentiment for moderation in the disciplining of the demonstrators was reflected on the whole in the administration's final dispensation of the cases. Whereas school disciplinary action was taken after 25% of the demonstrations, only one student was finally expelled and 76 suspended, these actions being confined to eight schools. In the remaining instances students were either placed on probation, given suspended suspensions (equivalent to probation), or officially warned or admonished, and some had their cases dismissed.

With respect to recruiting policy, a popular compromise endorsed by faculties was to remove the special privileges previously given to military recruiters, and sometimes to all public sector recruiters, of being allowed to set up tables in areas of high student density—the union, the cafeteria, the halls of class buildings, and so on.[10] Military recruiters would no longer enjoy the privilege of high visibility, but would instead have to share with all other recruiters the placement center or other more remote locations. Students could garner some satisfaction from knowing that military recruiting capability on campus had been reduced, even if not eliminated. Administrators could expect that the more remote, less populated recruiting locations would discourage the development of large disruptive protests against the recruiters.

This plan to diminish recruiter activity was, in fact, the most frequent resolution passed by the faculty councils. At the 36 schools in the study where faculty took formal action on recruiting policy, 12 passed resolutions of this type. At four schools such a proposal was defeated by a close margin, and at six schools a resolution to establish a committee to study this and alternative new proposals was passed. For the rest, at five schools faculty passed resolutions to ban military recruiters, four temporarily and one permanently, whereas at only nine schools did faculty pass resolutions straightforwardly reaffirming the existing open campus recruiting policy.

Students also took collective action on recruiting policy in the demonstration aftermath, as already shown in Table 1. At a few schools, usually highly selective, small, private institutions, students worked intensively on joint committees with faculty, developing the recruiting policy proposal on which the faculty council later voted. In most cases, however, students simply voted on the protesters' demands and submitted the results directly to the administration. This occurred with student referenda at 26 schools and student government resolutions at 37 schools. Only five (19%) of the referenda and 20 (54%) of the resolutions favored restricting war-related recruiting.

A comparison in Table 3 of the relative effect of faculty and student proposals on the final recruiting policy adopted by the administration suggests the weight of faculty opinion in settling the issue.

TABLE 3

Outcome of Deliberations:	Faculty Council Resolution	Student Govt. Resolution	Student Referendum
	(Proportion of schools adopting recruiting restrictions)		
Against new restrictions.	0% (9)	35% (17)	43% (21)
No vote taken.	33% (69)	33% (63)	39% (74)
Support new restrictions.	74% (27)	70% (20)	60% (5)
	(105)	(100)	(100)

In this table comparisons are made using the three-fold division of action against, or action for recruiting restrictions (including here for faculty the four narrow defeats of restriction proposals), and no action at all. The case for faculty predominance from this table is mainly that when faculty opposed recruiting restrictions the administration concurred in all instances, whereas when students opposed restrictions their administration still implemented restrictions in nearly half of the instances. Support by faculty and students for recruiting restrictions was equally likely to result in the administration's implementation of restrictions. The moderate form of the administration's restrictions, however, resembled more closely the faculty proposals than the student recommendations, the latter for the most part being restatements of the protesters' original demands.

Administrators implemented restrictions at 44 of the schools in the study. At 32 of the schools the restrictions simply involved the withdrawal of special privileges from military recruiters, usually moving them to more remote locations. At nine schools either some or all recruiters were temporarily banned until a new recruiting policy, usually like the above, could be agreed upon. Finally, at one school all recruiting and placement services were dropped permanently. It is an interesting aside that these restrictions, which primarily affected military recruiters, took place nearly equally often at schools where the reason for the initial demonstration was a recruiting visit from Dow Chemical Company.

Probably at very few schools did administrators consider these changes to be of much importance in meeting the protesters' concerns about reducing complicity in the war effort. Their main expectation was that disruptive recruiting protests could less easily take place. Similarly, few protesters heralded these changes as a major victory for their cause. In Washington, however, where individual events are more likely to be viewed as an aggregate whole, there is some evidence that these changes may have been a serious concern, particularly for those worried about the growing anti-war sentiments at the time. In May the Pentagon released a list of 22 schools which had placed bans on military recruiters (only four of these schools were included in the present study).[11] Following this, the Senate added in June to its National Aeronautics and Space Administration appropriations bill a provision denying grants (NASA had given $100 million in grants to universities the previous year) to schools which bar military recruiters. In sponsoring the bill, Sen. Carl T. Curtis (R.-Neb.) stated that "institutions have an obligation, patriotic in nature, and in the interests of our country to cooperate with programs of the U. S. Government."[12] In the light of this statement, those administrators who had earlier dismissed student charges of complicity with the war effort might be well-advised to take more seriously the political ramifications of their ties with the federal government.

Patterns of Influence in the Academy

To summarize briefly, this study has shown how student activists, indirectly through the faculty, have brought their values to bear on an institutional policy change. Faculty served as mediators, making proposals which usually took into account both student anti-war sentiment and administration concern over disruptive demonstrations. An analogy was made with the outside mediator in labor-management disputes, and then it was shown how the natural bonds of most faculty with administrators made this position of impartial mediator difficult to assume. It was argued that the special circumstances surrounding recruiting protests, namely, sympathy with the demonstrators' aims and concern over the administration's apparent mishandling of the demonstrations, helped to override these bonds and make mediation possible.[13]

The suggestion here that university influence relations bear some resemblance to labor-management bargaining patterns is not a popular view in the academy. The prevailing norm is that true universities, as centers for "the life of the mind," implement change only after reasoned persuasion, rational discourse, and the like. In response to student protests, there is a firm denial that coercion has any proper role in university dialogue. As student protests continue to occur, however, there is an increasing recognition of the current unreality of this norm. In fact, some commentators have argued that reasoned persuasion in universities has never been an accurate label for the prevailing influence relations. This argument states that using the myth of civility to describe these relations is a control technique of the powerful, that "the denial of the relevance of power is a position most widely held by those who have the power—senior professors and deans." [14] Bargaining between and among faculty and administrators is seen as the normal course of events. These faculty and administration conflicts are softened, however, by a general agreement to conduct them within the system of committees and meetings by which most major colleges and universities govern themselves. Based upon this recognition, the question of student participation in this committee machinery is no longer a yes or no proposition, but rather one of how this student participation can be most meaningful to all concerned.

The conception of reason and coercion as separate entities incompatible with one another in the academic world is symptomatic of the polarizing tendencies of the current era of student protests. Clearly the findings presented in this chapter confirm that student coercion has bred faculty and administration reasoning. The particular form of faculty crisis mediation described, however, is beset with structural difficulties, so that in normal circumstances faculty have no incentive to bargain for distinct student values and interests. If it is granted that the growing numbers of student activists do have deeply held values on which they are willing to act, and that the implementation of their values can be of benefit to colleges and universities, then it is evident that forms for meaningful, direct student participation in institutional governance will have to be found before rancorous confrontations will decrease.

NOTES

[1] James Fredericks Volkwein, "Research Summary: Relationship of College Student Protest and Participation in Policy Making to Institutional Characteristics." Summary of his Ph.D. thesis for the Department of Sociology, Cornell University, 1968.

[2] David J. Armor, Joseph B. Giacquinta, R. Gordon McIntosh, and Diana E. H. Russell, "Professors' Attitudes Toward the Vietnam War," *Public Opinion Quarterly,* 2 (1967), pp. 159–75.

[3] Philip Brickman, Peter Archibald, and Phillip Shaver, "SPSSI Vietnam Survey," reported in the Newsletter of the Society for the Psychological Study of Social Issues, July, 1968.

[4] Miss Mary Lou Frampton of the National Student Press Association and Mr. Phil Semas of the National Student Press Association kindly made available these clippings to me.

[5] Edward E. Sampson, "Student Activism and the Decade of Protest," *Journal of Social Issues* (July, 1967), p. 15; Kenneth Keniston, "The Sources of Student Dissent," *ibid.,* p. 125.

[6] For each of the six possible control actions the informants said was used, they indicated whether the demonstration soon ended, became smaller, proceeded unaffected, became larger or more disruptive, or resulted in a later protest demonstration. Answers in the last two categories comprised the "protest expanded" effect reported in Table 2. Avoidance of direct confrontation appears to have been the least aggravating response, although this effect is mitigated somewhat by the tendency to use this procedure at initially mild demonstrations. Still, in the eight instances where this procedure was followed when there was initial civil disobedience, the protest subsequently expanded in only one case.

[7] *First Annual Report, Federal Mediation and Conciliation Service* (1949), pp. 3, 4, quoted in Karl Braun, *Labor Disputes and Their Settlement* (Baltimore, Johns Hopkins Press, 1955), pp. 89–90.

[8] For a formal argument on faculty and administration ties, see Troy Duster, "Student Interests, Student Power, and the Swedish Experience," *American Behavioral Scientist,* June, 1968, pp. 21–28.

[9] Comments on Columbia are based on critiques by former AHFG members F. W. Dupee in the *New York Review,* September 26, 1968, and Marvin Harris in the *Nation,* June 10, 1968.

[10] An explicit, student-oriented rationale for this compromise plan was that, as a result of a Fall directive from the Selective Service Director, the possibility, however remote, existed that a student could lose his deferment and be drafted because of participation in an illegal recruiter demonstration. Selective bans on military recruiters only were ruled out because of freedom of speech principles, but restricting access to military recruiters in order to diminish both the students' opportunity and need for illegal protests would be an appropriate safeguard of the students.

[11] Reported in *Science,* June 21, 1968, p. 1320.

[12] *Science, loc. cit.,* and *College and University Business,* August, 1968, p. 39.

[13] Although the primary intent of the survey was to assess the behavioral dynamics of protests, a related source of variation, the institutional context of the protests, was also examined. The demonstrations altogether took place in a very diverse set of institutions, but those which involved civil disobedience took place more frequently at schools of high educational quality, and secondarily, at schools of high enrollment. As argued by others who have reported similar results, these schools are more likely to have an active population of student radicals and a progressive, independent faculty—hence student civil disobedience followed by faculty mediation occurred more frequently at them.

[14] Amitai Etzioni, "Confessions of a Professor Caught in a Revolution," *New York Times Magazine,* September 15, 1968. Martin Trow, "Conceptions of the University: The Case of Berkeley," *American Behavioral Scientist,* June, 1968.

2

THE TRUSTEES AND PROTEST

by Julian Foster

·

THE GOVERNING BOARDS of American colleges and universities have been a traditional target of radical criticism. Thorstein Veblen attacked them in his *Higher Learning in America*,[1] and Hubert Beck provided supporting data for the Veblen position in his *Men Who Control Our Universities*.[2] This study, undertaken in the late thirties, has recently been replicated by Troy Duster.[3] The general thrust of these and other works of the same genre has been that trustees are rich, reactionary and remote from higher education, and that they tend to impose their ideals and ways of thought upon the institutions over which they preside. They have been pictured as threats to academic freedom and to liberal education itself, and it has been charged that they are anxious to force colleges and universities to serve the interests of the relatively small segment of society from which they are drawn, which may most easily (if imprecisely) be described as "The Establishment." Certainly few boards have maintained close contact with either faculty or students, and arrangements for regular consultations with these groups are rare indeed.

Those who have written to defend the functioning of the boards tend to contribute to the polarization between trustees on the one hand, faculty and students on the other. Beardsley Ruml's and Donald H. Morrison's *Memo to a College Trustee*[4] combines a plea for increased board control over the curriculum with a slashing attack on the performance of faculty in this area. Gerald P. Burns[5] has offered similar strictures on faculty government, insisting that decision-making in higher education should be reserved almost entirely to administrators and governing boards. Raymond M. Hughes[6] took a similar position. None of these writers gives serious attention to the question of whether students should participate in policy-making, but it seems evident that the arguments they offer against faculty power would apply even more forcefully to the students.

Most governing boards hold closed meetings, to which access even of directly interested parties is severely restricted. At some public institutions, meetings are open to the press, but in such instances, there is usually reason to think that some policy-making goes on informally and out of the limelight. Arguments can be offered in favor of closed sessions: members of the boards may feel more free to speak their minds, and be less subject to external pressures. But one effect has probably been to make trustees into a shadowy presence, poorly understood and often unappreciated by those whom their decisions may affect. On the campus itself, it is often only the president who really knows what the trustees' views are, what they have done, and why they have done it. The temptation for a harassed president to use the board as a buffer, subtly blaming unpopular decisions on it, or implying that while he might well make some concession, the board undoubtedly will not, is considerable. The sweeping legal authority which boards possess tends to mislead others into attributing great powers to them, even though in practice most boards generally confine themselves to the giving of advice and the ratification of administrative decisions. When in addition, such groups cloak themselves in secrecy, do little to dispel the notion of their immense power, and become most prominent when their decisions are most unpopular, it is clear that they will inevitably become a subject of controversy and some resentment.

To the student activist with a leftist or Marxist ideology, the governing board combines characteristics of all he most dislikes: wealth, privilege, authority, tradition and the *status quo*. The occupations of board members often provide an easy and tangible means of demonstrating the linkage between the university and the "military-industrial complex." Spokesmen amongst the trustees frequently praise such old-fashioned virtues as chastity, patriotism, obedience to legitimate authority, and other ideals which are anathema to many protesters.

When student protest develops, the immediate targets may be administrators or administrative policies, but at least an undercurrent of hostility to the governing board is usually present. In prolonged and violent protests, as at the University of California, San Francisco State College and Columbia University, the governing board usually becomes a major subject of attack; proposals for curbing or abolishing such boards are not infrequent.

Some student activist groups have carried out sporadic research on trustees, often designed primarily to confirm their darkest suspicions. However, very little reliable data about governing boards has so far been available. The stereotype has developed easily, and has been supported by a few conspicuous instances. In 1968, however, the first large-scale and comprehensive study of trustees was carried out by Educational Testing Service.[7] Questionnaires were sent to 10,036 trustees of 536 colleges and universities of all types from junior colleges and technical schools to major public and private universities. Usable responses were received from 5,180 board members, or 52.5% of the total sample. The questionnaire attempted to establish biographical data, determine attitudes and values on matters of higher education, and obtain a picture of the activities undertaken by trustees. The results allow comparison of the stereotype with the reality. The findings are reported more completely elsewhere.[8] The concern here is with those aspects of trustee lives and opinions which are relevant to student protest, and which illuminate the role which trustees are likely to play in the ensuing conflict.

Activists and others allege that trustees are members of "The Establishment," meaning generally that they are rich, and work at occupations enjoying high social status. Data on total family income before taxes tend to confirm this, with 69.3% reporting annual incomes of $20,000 or more, while only 8.0% had less than $10,000, as the majority of the American population does. Sixteen percent reported incomes in excess of $100,000. When data for 30 private universities selected for their academic prestige were isolated, 42.7% of the trustees of these institutions fell into this extremely wealthy category while only 4.9% reported incomes under $20,000. Major student protests were also considerably more frequent at these institutions, so there is some indication that the boards which most often confront protest are also those which have the richest members.

Trustees were asked to select from 31 categories the one which best described their primary occupation or, if retired, their former occupation. The largest group (38.8%) were executives or administrators of manufacturing, merchandising, banking, investment or insurance firms, or of non-profit foundations and organizations. Various professions constituted a further 33.4% of the sample, and another 10.7%, almost all on the boards of church-related institutions, were in the clergy. Few occupations at the lower end of the social scale were included; 6 trustees (0.1%) were labor union officials, and 1.2% identified themselves as "non-executive members" of firms. One does not know the occupations of the 6.7% who chose the inevitable "Other" category, or the 0.7% who did not reply, but it seems evident that trustee occupations are those enjoying considerable prestige in American society. Questions about memberships on other kinds of boards showed that 20.2% had served on the board of a corporation whose shares were traded on a stock exchange during the previous five years, while 90.4% had served on boards of various civic organizations.

A further controversial point, which is raised by student protest in a particularly acute form, concerns the extent to which trustees have direct knowledge of and experience with higher education. Occupational data revealed that 6.4% were administrators in colleges or universities, 3.6% were faculty members, and 3.3% were teachers in primary or secondary schools. Most had, of course, been students although 8.0% had not attended college, and a further 18.1% had not acquired a baccalaureate or higher degree. Data on age, however, indicated that such experience was somewhat remote in time: only 5.2% were under forty, while 72.9% were fifty or over. Asked how much time they devoted to the various aspects of their work as trustees, the median reply was between five and six hours per month. It appears that in many ways, trustees are "outsiders" within the academic community.

Responses to another set of questions demonstrated that few trustees had tried to improve their understanding of the matters before them by general reading. Given a list of fifteen important works on higher education,[9] 834 trustees admitted that they had "never heard" of *any* of the books, while only one of the books (*Memo to a College Trustee*) had been "read completely" by more than 10% of the trustees. A comparable question showed that board members pay no more attention to periodicals dealing with higher education than they do to books. The symposium most likely to give insights into the contemporary campus culture, Sanford's *The American College*, had been read, completely or partially, by 10.6% of the respondents. The only radical book on the list, Goodman's *Community of Scholars*, was the least familiar to trustees, with only 1.4% declaring that they had read it through. It is thus evident that trustees have, by and large, rejected the opportunity for a deeper understanding of protesters and protest issues which is presented by scholarly reading.

Black protest has recently assumed increasing significance, both at Negro colleges, and at other institutions by associations of black students. A major theme, sometimes referred to as Black Power, has been that members of other races should not make decisions for blacks; the corollary is that non-blacks cannot fully understand the problems which blacks face, nor undertake to solve them. In this connection, the racial distribution of trustees is of interest. Only 1.3% of all trustees in the sample indicated that they were Negro, while a further 0.3% identified themselves as other than Negro or Caucasian. Of the 68 Negro trustees, 52 were on the boards of predominantly black institutions, but were outnumbered there; 57.7% of the members of such boards were Caucasians. The remaining 16 black trustees were divided among the 518 white institutions in the sample; protesters concerned with racial issues on such campuses are thus very likely to face boards devoid of Negro representation.

The data suggest that trustees may not be so overwhelmingly conservative as has sometimes been supposed. Asked "Which of the following best describes your political ideology or leaning?" 20.8% identified as conservatives, 15.4% as liberals, while 60.9% preferred the label "moderate." Party preferences leant more markedly to the right: 58.2% Republicans, 33.3% Democrats. Another question asked trustees to indicate similarity or dissimilarity between their own views and those of eighteen political figures. Nelson Rockefeller proved the most acceptable (67.5%) with Richard Nixon (62.4%) in second place. Ronald Reagan, not generally regarded as a champion of higher education and certainly an outspoken critic of student protest, was thought similar to themselves by 47.4%, substantially ahead of both Barry Goldwater (38.0%) and Lyndon Johnson (36.7%). William F. Buckley, Jr. was thought similar by 24.8%, but figures further to the right, such as George Wallace (8.8%), Robert Welch (5.3%) and Ayn Rand (5.1%), commanded comparatively little enthusiasm. Trustees for the most part reject right-wing extremism in favor of a centrist position.

However, many causes of student protest, including draft resistance, opposition to Dow Chemical and other war-related recruiters, and black militancy are not likely to commend themselves in any way to those who identify with centrist politicians, any more than those politicians can command the respect of student activists. The more "respectable" leaders with whom young people have tended to identify were considered by trustees to have views surprisingly similar to their own: Eugene McCarthy (52.8%), William Fulbright (46.3%) and Martin Luther King (39.1%).[10] This suggests that trustees may have some sympathy with both opposition to the war in Vietnam and with non-violent civil rights activity. Robert Kennedy's views, however, rated as similar to those of only 32.3% of trustees, and figures further to the left were rejected more strongly: Norman Thomas (16.7%) and Benjamin Spock (12.0%). There was one solitary trustee who found the views of H. Rap Brown "very similar to mine," while 1.1% thought them more similar than not to their own. It thus appears that while a fairly large proportion of trustees can respond to figures who command enthusiasm on the campuses, only a few can identify to any extent with those, like Spock and Brown, who could best be described as militant. Yet the existence of this minority, however small, would probably come as a surprise to many student activists.

The attitudes of trustees to a number of issues in higher education was assessed in a number of statements to which the responses "Strongly agree," "Agree," "Unable to say," "Disagree," or "Strongly disagree" were invited. Responses to some statements relevant to student protest and student concerns are reported in Table 1. It is evident that trustees feel strongly that the student enjoys his status as a matter of privilege, not of right (Item 1), which view presumably may serve as a basis for belief that the institution can withdraw this privilege for reasons which it judges sufficient. It is further clear that militant protest activities constitute such a reason in the minds of most trustees (Item 4), who thus take a considerably tougher stand on this matter than most administrators or faculty have been prepared to do. Trustees do, however, endorse a degree of academic freedom for students; the fact that a slim majority oppose administrative control over the contents of the student paper may surprise some activists (Item 2). Views on student rights to hear whatever speakers they may choose are somewhat less liberal (Item 3). Trustees also lean towards the view that colleges and universities may

TABLE 1

Statements:	Trustee Responses (%):				
	Strongly Agree	Agree	Unable to Say	Disagree	Strongly Disagree
1. "Attendance at this institution is a privilege, not a right."	53.5	38.1	1.5	4.5	1.1
2. "The administration should exercise control over the contents of the student newspaper."	5.5	34.3	6.6	41.3	10.1
3. "All campus speakers should be subject to some official screening process."	14.6	54.5	3.8	20.1	5.4
4. "Students who actively disrupt the functioning of a college by demonstrating, sitting-in or otherwise refusing to obey the rules should be expelled or suspended."	37.9	42.9	6.8	8.9	2.3
5. "Students involved in civil disobedience off the campus should be subject to discipline by the college as well as by the local authorities."	14.7	33.9	11.0	31.8	7.0
6. "The grading system now in use needs to be modified."	3.9	23.5	41.0	28.4	1.2
7. "A coeducational institution provides a better educational setting than a college for only men or women." *	14.5	49.5	12.9	19.5	2.5
8. "Fraternities and/or sororities (or similar social clubs) provide an important and positive influence for undergraduates." *	5.3	39.2	18.0	30.1	6.3
9. "The institution should be actively engaged in solving contemporary social problems."	13.0	49.8	8.2	23.3	3.8
10. "There should be opportunities for higher education available to anyone who seeks education beyond secondary school." *	31.3	53.6	2.7	9.9	1.5
11. "Colleges should admit socially disadvantaged students who appear to have potential, even when such students do not meet normal entrance requirements."	10.7	55.6	10.4	19.5	2.6

* Statements marked thus were asked in general terms; others were asked in relation to the trustee's own institution.

389

properly punish students for off-campus civil disobedience (Item 5), a proposition which is hotly denied by all activists.

Student activists have campaigned for educational reform, in some cases setting up experimental colleges and courses. Standard grading procedures are almost always absent from such ventures. Item 6 suggests that trustees have not made up their minds on this particular reform; certainly there is little of the strong attachment to present grading practices which some would expect. A further aim of activists at some institutions has been the breaking down of rules barring the opposite sex from admission, and everything in the new left philosophy and life-style leans towards an easy mixing of the sexes with equal rights for women. Most trustees appear to accept this goal (Item 7), though about one-fifth still prefer the sexual segregation which now seems to be a vanishing pattern. Activists are seldom members of fraternities or sororities, organizations which have been frequently accused of discrimination, both racial and social. Only a small minority of trustees appear strongly devoted to the fraternal system (Item 8), but more look upon it favorably than appear to be critical. On these issues, admittedly but a small sample of those educational reforms espoused by activist movements, there appears at least to be no polarization between activists and trustees.

A primary tenet of many activist movements has been that the universities are not doing enough to resolve pressing social problems. About a quarter of the trustees, however, believe that this is not the business of universities (Item 9), while only an eighth of them are firmly committed to a policy of forceful social concern. Admissions policies which tend to exclude the disadvantaged have been another activist target, particularly for black students. A substantial majority of trustees take the view that there should be higher educational opportunities for all, even when criteria of ability are excluded (Item 10), and an only slightly less substantial number favor the waiving of rigid admissions criteria (Item 11) which is probably a prerequisite if any great number of graduates from ghetto highschools are to attend college. On the social philosophy of the university, then, there is a considerable gap between activist and trustee views, but at least on one practical kind of application of this philosophy, the differences are of far smaller magnitude.

Activist movements almost always contain some element of the demand for "Student Power." College presidents may grant, negotiate or resist such demands, but in the latter case it is quite common for them to pass on some of the onus to their governing boards, and sometimes to insist that, logically and necessarily, it is these boards which must have authority within the institution. Boards of trustees come into clearest confrontation with activists over this issue of student power. But while boards commonly possess a vast share or a monopoly of the legal authority to make institutional policy, it has long been clear that they cannot and do not exercise this authority in many areas. Delegation of authority to the president and administration for the day-to-day operation of the institution is universal, and delegation of authority to the faculty over purely academic matters is extremely common. The concept of a student sharing of power, however, is comparatively new, and much more controversial.

Trustee attitudes on the proper distribution of power within colleges and universities were revealed by a series of questions asking them where they believed major authority over various matters should be located: with trustees themselves, the administration, the faculty, the students and/or "other." The results indicate that there is no important topic on which a majority of trustees feel the students should have a major share of authority. However, a substantial minority of trustees (from 25 to 44%) believes that students should play a major role in establishing rules regarding student housing, creation or elimination of local chapters of fraternities and/or sororities, in dealing with students caught cheating, in determining the nature and scope of the athletic program, in formulating institutional policy on student protests and in choosing a commencement speaker. Many of these have become protest issues. Fifteen percent of the trustees would give students a say in adding or deleting specific courses, but there is a clear consensus (97% or more) among board members that students should not be involved in adding or deleting degree programs, appointing the college president or the academic dean, determining tuition or fees, dealing with a professor accused of immoral conduct with students, tenure decisions on faculty members, decisions regarding general admissions standards and criteria, policies regarding faculty leaves and sabbaticals, and the granting of honorary degrees. Many of these issues, too, have become the focus of student protest, with ethnic studies programs and the admission of disadvantaged students being especially important. It is of interest that almost all trustees reject the student claim that they are entitled to play a major role in such matters.

Activists have demanded total student control over matters perceived as affecting primarily the students. It was striking to find that most trustees are not prepared to let students exercise sole authority in *any* of the areas listed. Between 2 and 3% of the trustees were ready to turn over to students choice of a commencement speaker, creation or elimination of fraternities/sororities, and dealing with cheaters. There were no other significant concessions.

Trustees, then, are remote from most students in their social circumstances, and do qualify for "Elite" and "Establishment" labels so frequently pinned on them by their critics. In their beliefs, both about campus matters and the larger society, trustees may be less conservative than some have supposed, but their attitudes approach those of activists only on incidental matters; there are virtually no trustees whose posture resembles that of any facet of the new left. On the basic issue of student power, only a minority of trustees are willing to see students participate in important ways in making any of the policies which will affect them, and virtually none appear ready to hand over policy areas to the students without subjecting them to major checks.

The gulf between the backgrounds, attitudes and beliefs of trustees and those of student activists is thus a very large one. To the extent that confrontations occur between these two groups, prospects for agreement or even mutual understanding appear small. In light of these data, it seems that administrators may play more of a mediating role between activists and trustees than perhaps either side is aware of. It may also be suggested that faculty in most institutions are likely to have more in common with student activists than with trustees. It would be interesting to get responses to the same questions from faculty, administrative and student groups; this writer's impression is that such a study might show the trustees to be relatively isolated from the other three groups.

NOTES

[1] Thorstein Veblen, *Higher Learning in America* (New York, Sagamore Press, 1957).

[2] Hubert Beck, *Men Who Control Our Universities* (New York, King's Crown Press, 1947).

[3] Troy Duster, "The Aims of Higher Learning and the Control of Universities," unpublished paper, Berkeley: University of California, 1966.

[4] Beardsley Ruml and Donald H. Morrison, *Memo to a College Trustee* (New York, McGraw-Hill Book Co., 1959), p. 7, and *passim.*

[5] Gerald P. Burns, *Trustees in Higher Education* (New York, Independent College Funds of America, 1966), p. 146 and *passim.*

[6] Raymond M. Hughes, *Manual for College Trustees* (Ames, Iowa, Iowa State College Press, 1943).

[7] Educational Testing Service joined with Morton Rauh, Vice President for Finance at Antioch College, to carry out the study. The American Association for Higher Education and the Association of Governing Boards of Universities and Colleges also sponsored the study.

[8] Rodney T. Hartnett, *College and University Trustees, Their Backgrounds, Roles and Educational Attitudes* (Princeton, N.J., Educational Testing Service, 1969).

[9] AAHE, *Faculty Participation in Academic Governance;* Brubacher and Rudy, *Higher Education in Transition;* Corson, *The Governance of Colleges and Universities;* Dodds, *The Academic President: Educator or Caretaker?;* Goodman, *The Community of Scholars;* Hofstadter and Metzger, *Development of Academic Freedom in the United States;* Kerr, *The Uses of the University;* McGrath, *The Predominantly Negro Colleges and Universities in Transition;* Millett, *The Academic Community;* Pattillo and Mackenzie, *Church-Sponsored Higher Education;* Perkins, *The University in Transition;* Rauh, *College and University Trusteeship;* Rudolph, *The American College and University;* Ruml and Morrison, *Memo to a College Trustee;* Sanford, *The American College.*

[10] Martin Luther King was shot during the period when the questionnaires were being completed; all were received before the murder of Senator Robert Kennedy.

3

ON DEMONSTRATION

by Ed Schwartz*

Now THAT a healthy number of colleges across the country have demonstrated, are demonstrating, or will demonstrate, it is time to outline a few guidelines by which uprisings can proceed. As a veteran of both guerrilla and conventional warfare with the Oberlin College administration, I can assure neophytes in the profession that the game theory of campus combat is not as easy as it looks from the press reports. One must consider items ranging from student body support to public relations. Issues might even be a factor. First, four general rules.

RULE ONE: Decide whether yours is a reform movement or a revolution. Reform movements aim at implementing change in a specific area of college policy, e.g., social rules, faculty tenure, cafeteria food. Once demands have been met, protest ceases. Revolutionary movements aim at implementing basic changes within

* Edward Schwartz, a graduate of Oberlin College where he was an activist student leader, was President of the United States National Student Association during 1967–68. Advancing the concept of "Student Power" during his term of office, Mr. Schwartz appeared frequently on various campuses and at national educational conferences to articulate his concern for an increased role for students in structuring and governing higher education. This chapter was written originally in 1965, three years prior to most of the major university disruptions. Mr. Schwartz is presently attending the Florence Heller School of Social Welfare at Brandeis University.

the university, e.g., resignation of the president, abolition of the board of trustees, elimination of classes.

Reform movements are candid as to goals, swift in execution, and receptive towards negotiations. Revolutionary movements are secretive as to goals, gradual in escalation, and receptive towards riot. Your decision between the two will reflect various considerations: the degree to which you despise the administration; the degree to which your student body shares your sentiment; or the degree to which your student body can be encouraged to share your sentiment.

Admittedly, a movement which begins with limited goals can reach revolutionary proportions if the powers-that-be act stupidly in dealing with its participants. Similarly, a projected revolution can collapse if administration acceptance of subsidiary demands stifles the enthusiasm of its followers. While the latter development is more disappointing than the former, both should be foreseen. This leads us into our second point.

RULE TWO: Know thine enemy. If you are fighting for reform, at least discover which individuals or committees exercise authority over the question. How silly it is to fight a college president for a social rules change determined by the faculty. All he has to do is say, "Well, I'm just one among many on this issue," and then where will you be?

By the same token, if you are interested in revolution, determine who should be ousted. For example, your college president may be an impossible man. He might be supported, however, by an atrocious board of regents or trustees which would appoint somebody worse to take his place. This may be advantageous in the long run if you think you can sustain the battle, but an equally plausible alternative is to aim at issues for which you would fight irrespective of particular personalities.

RULE THREE: Know thy campus. "To know" in this rule means to possess an understanding of the main grievances of the student body. In crisis situations, temperament can be ascertained easily, but the normal lull is less indicative. It is clear that a reform movement protesting policies to which the campus is indifferent has as much chance of success as the antifluoridation fighters. The same principle applies to revolutionaries. The American Revolution may have been fought around the Declaration of Independence, but there was that business with the tea to get things moving. And remember, the anger of a student body subsides around examination periods.

RULE FOUR: Know thine allies. "Allies" refers to anyone in the faculty or administration who agrees with you. Without question, the Public Relations Quotient of a student demonstration multiplies twofold if the angels of academia back it. In some instances, desire for such support may influence your initial choice of aims and actions, depending on what you expect to accomplish. The main problem, of course, is to determine whether Professor X is a friend throughout, or whether his good graces are contingent upon long-term approach. You may decide to forego his friendship. If you do, at least evaluate your reasons carefully. A disenchanted ally can be a vengeful enemy.

In certain cases, allies may be found off campus. Most universities have some unenrolled students who are attached to the campus atmosphere but not subject to its discipline. These will usually be available for picketing or a mass rally. More important, some protests will be supported by community leaders, especially leaders of ethnic minorities. These are worth their weight in gold, PRwise. But to attract them, the issue will have to be national in scope. They will not be concerned with the dress code or the dormitory hours. They will often be more interested in revolution than reform.

Reform movements are less exciting than revolutions. Even so, the effective implementation of university reform is an art unto itself, demanding a degree of political sophistication as refined as that of the revolutionary. An understanding of the temperament of the student body, a sensitivity to the personality of administrators, an effective utilization of communications media, and an awareness of the importance of timing are all necessary. These, however, are only the prerequisites. Specific points must be considered.

Any successful reform movement must rely on campus consensus. This does not mean that everyone will work actively in the effort. It does mean that you cannot afford to alienate a large segment of the student body. Administrative resistance will be strengthened if it has the backing of any significant number of students. College presidents and deans like to believe that the students are satisfied with the status quo, and uninterested in reforms. Any tangible evidence may serve to verify these suspicions. If the reformers do not plan carefully, such suspicions could be justified.

Consequently, the coordinating committee of any demonstration group should include as many from the campus Establishment as possible. Student government representatives, fraternity leaders, newspaper editors, judicial board members, and political spokesmen all qualify. Admittedly, the initial coordinating committee must not be too large; anything more than 12 or 13 becomes cumbersome, but the greater the scope of representation within that number, the better the chance of success. Too many movements collapse because student leaders work at cross purposes. Sometimes convictions necessitate clashes, but these should be avoided if at all possible.

The first task of such a coordinating group is to decide the area of protest and to find a specific solution. Careful consideration should be accorded to the number of people who would be willing to demonstrate on a given question. The precise goals of the movement should be formulated with considerable care. Generally it is best to work out whatever solution is really the most desirable from the student standpoint, and to aim at that. Pessimism about whether it is "acceptable" should not be allowed to get in the way. If compromises must be made, let the administration or the faculty propose them. The movement will then be free to press for further reforms later, without revising its goals.

Once the goals and general strategy of the movement have been determined, a mass meeting is usually the next step. If the issues were chosen carefully and a sufficient number of campus notables assembled in support, a substantial turnout should be assured. The leadership should use the meeting to explain their plans, opening the floor for questions, and being ready to make minor changes to win additional support. The gathering should also be used for organizational purposes: there are signs to be made, petitions to be circulated, fact sheets to be written, subsequent meetings to be addressed. The original organizers cannot take on all these responsibilities if they hope to keep up with their class work, and in any case, many people become more attached to a movement once they have done some work for it. Involvement breeds identification.

The vital principle in developing a movement is momentum. If you pull out all the stops the first day, you will be left without an encore. The initial steps should be forceful, but moderated. The proposal should receive the support of the student government, the campus editor, and any other influential groups. Sometimes an ad in the school paper, signed by as many notables as you can muster, is impressive. Assign students to talk to as many members of the faculty as they can; if the campus is too large for this to be effective on a random basis, at least contact the more influential faculty spokesmen. At no time is flamboyant language helpful.

Demonstrations should follow the principle of momentum. Enunciation of demands should precede action on behalf of them. The first demonstration should be something mild: a march, perhaps. If you begin with an enormous crowd, be careful that subsequent efforts are not substantially smaller; this will make it appear that support is being dissipated. If you cannot get unanimous agreement on a particular tactic, at least try to ensure that the opposition is silent. Timing is the key—knowing when the campus is ripe, and when it isn't. If you are too far ahead of your student body, or too far behind it, you can only fail.

A word about the radical alternative. On most campuses, there will be a group that refuses to accept a leisurely pace for anything. While they can be annoying, they can also be useful. Nothing is more effective in dealing with an administrator than saying, "We're the responsible group. If you don't do something now, the extremists will take over." In fact, in some situations it might be wise to quietly encourage an extreme threat, providing that you keep your approval hidden from those with whom you must deal. If the hotheads threaten to disrupt your gains, try to stop them, but don't try too hard. Most of the time, their support isn't worth the publicity you accord in fighting them.

None of these is a sure-fire technique to achieve reform. Sometimes nothing will work. Tactics other than these may be more suited to particular situations. These, however, should prove effective in most circumstances. If they consistently fail, then you might wish to consider revolution.

It is doubtful that there are more than five schools in the country at present where more than a tiny minority of students are ready for a revolution geared to basic changes within the university. This is understandable. Revolutions are justifiable only after everything else has failed—all attempts at working through the channels, at petitioning the administration, and at demonstrating for reform. They must be based on a cumulative list of grievances and frustrations, usually covering a span of many years, which have left the student body no alternative other than a major thrust to eliminate the president, to achieve equal representation on the board of trustees, or to reorganize radically the committee structure to increase student influence. Even in such an environment, however, revolutions demand careful planning. The core of a revolutionary planning group should be small, unrepresentative, and cognizant of the movement's major objectives.

While momentum is desirable in reform movements, it is essential to revolutions. In general, the goal is to create a dialectical situation, in which the administration is forced to reject seemingly "reasonable" requests for change in such a manner as to alienate the entire campus. The initial moves should be mild—perhaps more so than those of a reform group—but the life-span is longer and the termination violent. The aim is to avoid negotiation, because the implicit goals are non-negotiable; but the movement must seek to appear receptive at every stage. The image of impetuous administrators thwarting a thoughtful student body must be created. This image is necessary both in gaining campus support and in maintaining good relations with the press. Indeed, if the situation is such that revolution is essential, the "image" is probably reality.

Thus, some issue should be found which the campus would generally favor, but which is certain to be rejected vehemently. The president should become angry, make inflammatory statements about the student body. Ideally, he should threaten expulsion. Even on frustrated campuses, students must be weaned gradually into revolutionary fervor. If your first proposal is not acceptable to many students, the administration's reactions will outweigh their reservations. A slur on the character of any student group within reasonable bounds of respectability is an indirect slap at the entire campus. That should be made clear.

In developing the movement, you must insure either that your requests are impossible to achieve or that indignation against the administration per se renders them inconsequential. Negotiation should be out of the question. Ideally, the administration should take this position; but if you can make the president or regents appear unreasonable, at least you'll have sufficient grounds to argue it yourself. "How can we bargain with someone who has called us . . . ?" is a respectable position if an astounding epithet can be substituted for the ellipsis. Here again, if the administration is as tactless as many are, the insults will come. The important point is that as soon as you reach the conference table, you have no further basis on which to act. Your biggest problem is to strike a balance between respectability and intransigence. This is what makes revolution so difficult.

In general, demonstrations should start small and grow, but there is a case for something dramatic in the beginning, like a sit-in, which would threaten the academic existence of the participants. Be careful, however. If the first move appears too inflammatory, the students may feel that the administration's response is justified. If you can get a few campus "respectables," or even invulnerables like honors students and Woodrow Wilson winners, you have a much better chance of success. If you're going to play martyr, at least be sure that the campus will recognize you as such. College degrees are still important no matter how faulty the educational system may be.

These are the elements of the planned revolution: gradual escalation, non-negotiable tactics, administration fury, and campus response. Sometimes a movement for reform can unintentionally produce the same results, but that depends on the savoir-faire of the college president. Conversely, projected rebellion can be lost in the maze of committees if any of its intermediary steps are thwarted with tact.

In concluding, I offer one final word of advice: if you are going to plan a movement, whether it be for reform or for fundamental change, make sure that you are intellectually and morally justified in doing so. Demonstrations take time and threaten the reputation of the university. If a campus situation is serious, these liabilities should be borne; if you are just looking for an excuse to let off steam, you deserve to be stopped. As much "fun" as demonstrations may be, they are still a tactic used to implement a worthy objective. If there is no such purpose, you hurt not only your own student body, but the legitimate causes of campus groups across the country. If recent constructive movements degenerate into frivolity, the ultimate victim will be higher education itself. Zeal can never be an excuse for irresponsibility. The stakes are simply too high.

4

STUDENT PROTEST:
AIMS AND STRATEGIES

by Julian Foster

STUDENTS HAVE always had the preferences, needs and convictions to which institutions of higher education could not or would not cater. Mere dissatisfaction with the *status quo* does not constitute protest. Students in America, as in the rest of the world, have frequently during the course of history defied authority; but mere defiance, however violent, does not qualify as protest. Students, particularly American students, have long been organized in quasi-political fashion; student governments have as often as not been the creation of administrators as much as of students themselves. Such governments have been concerned with student desires in one way or another, but have not regularly struggled with higher authority. Their operations cannot therefore be called protest in any general way. Yet protest implies each of these elements—unsatisfied desires, a willingness to go outside normal channels, and a degree of purposive organization.

Student protest is, by definition, an attempt to influence the course of ongoing events. It must be distinguished from the more traditional campus disruption by its purposive character, the fact that those involved agree in some measure on a common aim. Campus explosions may reflect underlying discontents, much as the looting and burning in some ghettos certainly is related to the discontents of the inhabitants, but unless the goals of the effort have been clarified, such happenings are excluded by definition from this book. Protest for our purposes involves a purposive attempt to exert influence.

Those who have power do not "protest" in this sense. One does not hear of presidents or trustees protesting; rather, they act. If faculty can be said to protest, it is a sign that they have failed to attain the normal degree of influence over the decisions which affect them. If student protest seems to occur almost everywhere, one logical prerequisite of this is that students lack power almost everywhere. Until very recently, the institution which placed students on key committees or listened seriously to their proposals was exceptional; nor are there now any institutions at which students can realistically be said to have a great share of legitimate authority. "Protest," then, serves as a general label for the ways in which a group which is devoid of legal authority or regular means for influencing events can seek to do so.

Students wish to protest a great variety of matters—some of them campus affairs like dormitory rules, censorship and curriculum, but others of national scope. The university itself appears to be a logical target for protest in the first kind of cases, since it has the power to remedy the alleged grievance. But the war in Vietnam, which Peterson found to be the most prevalent single cause of protest in 1968,* could hardly be thought to be the responsibility of the universities. Racial discrimination, which has occasioned some of the most violent activism, is probably less prevalent in the campus community than in almost any other area of American life. Yet protest seems, regardless of the issue concerned, to involve conflict between students and university authorities. It may be useful to ask why this is so.

An inspection of the variety of approaches by which students have attempted to influence the great national issues of the sixties reveals a pattern. In the early part of the decade, many activists from Northern states visited the South to do battle with local authorities there. Freedom rides were designed to influence opinion by turning the spotlight on the arbitrariness and brutality of Southern law, while Negro registration drives opened the way to direct power through the electoral process. The students who visited the South engaged in conflict, and saw their efforts bring considerable victories. Blacks have now, by and large, taken over the attack on Southern segrega-

* See Part I, Chapter 4.

tion. White students in the North have engaged in sporadic attacks on the amorphous forms of discrimination to be found in their local communities, but this has never assumed the proportions of a mass movement. The enemy is less easily recognized, and when found he tends to fade away rather than to stand his ground, inviting confrontation and strife.

Sen. Eugene McCarthy's presidential campaign was another off-campus activity which enrolled college students in massive numbers. The McCarthy forces did electoral battle in the primaries from New Hampshire to California, always with some prospect of success, and with occasional and much acclaimed victories. When the *realpolitik* of the Democratic Party caught up with the crusaders at the national convention, the McCarthy forces did not go down to defeat easily. No one knows the extent of overlapping membership between the earnest canvassers who kept "Clean for Gene" and the demonstrators who fought in the streets and parks of Chicago. But both activities had in common that they tended to make converts for the cause by a process of conflict with authority—first with "the Establishment" as personified by President Johnson, later with Mayor Daley's police.

Other off-campus activities have been less successful in attracting student support. Occasional blocking of troop trains, burning of draft cards and the picketing of draft centers and military installations have been carried out by students and by those allies who have worked with them on the campuses. The March on the Pentagon in 1967 seemed a logical mode of expressing criticism of U.S. military policies, and Resurrection City was planned to confront Congress and President directly with some facts about poverty and race. Yet more and more of these approaches to the logical pressure points, the places in the system where solutions could be forged, seem to have lost their power to command student enthusiasm. Martin Luther King's March on Washington had only marginal student participation, and it is some time since there have been conspicuous numbers of students involved in a protest of this kind. Large (though unknown) numbers of students continue to tackle social problems through quieter methods of community action—tutoring, organizing self-help projects, etc.—but such approaches are not directed primarily at opinion formation or at reform of established policies and institutions.

The instances cited so far seem to support the following generalization: *When students are to be effective in influencing opinion or in reforming policies, they engage in some kind of public conflict*

with authority, a conflict in which a measure of victory is possible.
The presence of conflict makes student activities newsworthy, which
they would not otherwise be, thus providing an audience. The role
of underdog is an appealing one, fraught with overtones of courage,
conviction and possible martyrdom. The potential of victory may be
necessary if the struggle is to seem genuine and to continue to engage
the participants.

These considerations may explain the course which recent campus
protests have followed. The brief history of the teach-in movement
is illuminating. These marathons, which contained elements of information giving, revivalism and endurance test, originally seemed a
promising way of dramatizing opposition to the Vietnam War. In the
earlier teach-ins there were elements of conflict with speakers differing and debating with one another; the organizers were always doves,
but the hawks and the State Department were represented. When
Britain's first teach-in was held at Oxford, State flew Henry Cabot
Lodge over for the event; his lack of success with a hostile audience
illustrated a belatedly recognized fact—that the role of villain had
been assigned to him by the predominantly radical audience. When
one of the last major teach-ins was held in 1967 at the California
State College at Fullerton, efforts were made to obtain pro-War and
middle of the road speakers, but such invitations were no longer being
accepted. The program eventually consisted of 17 vehement critics
of the War and one agricultural economist who was willing to say
that the pacification program was not all bad. The result was inevitably dull and repetitive, with the arrival of an American Nazi
picket-line the major excitement of the day. The days preceding,
however, had been ones of considerable drama on the campus, for
it had been a question of whether the college's president, who considered that the teach-in organizers had failed to keep their agreement with him, would cancel the event. This question engaged the
campus community and the local press in a way which the event itself signally failed to do.

It is not difficult to see why this should be so. The conventional
operations of those who would present their views to an audience—
lectures, rallies, local organizing of a non-partisan kind, and so on—
are not particularly well fitted for their purpose, for they lack drama.
The news media will not cover them, the uncommitted and uncon-
vinced will remain remote. If, however, there is an element of real
conflict introduced, interest is aroused. Prohibitionist tracts were dull,

but prohibitionists breaking up saloons were news. Rational pleas for votes for women fell largely on deaf ears, but when suffragettes began to disrupt public events, everybody at least knew about it. Student petitions, picketings and minor illegalities are of little interest—unless they bring those students into conflict with authority. The most available authority is the university administration, and furthermore, it is the right kind of authority for the purpose in that it contains elements of weakness, points where pressure may be effective, so that the outcome of the conflict is unsure, and some measure of victory probable.

If protest activities are understood in theatrical terms, it is clear that the administration has a role to play. This role can be assigned by the student activists because it is they who possess the initiative; they can protest or not, be moderate or aggressive, and have a fair notion of the kind of response they will elicit. The administration's attitude tends to be passive, for on the whole they would like nothing better than for the whole thing to subside; if they are not careful, their passivity will make them manipulable.

Casting the college administration as the villain demands no ingenuity when the cause of protest is restrictive dormitory rules, censorship of speakers or an irrelevant curriculum. When the focus is on racism or Vietnam, however, more ingenuity may be needed if the target of protest is to seem appropriate. The logic then is the logic of symbolization—that if X can be perceived as symbolizing Y, then by attacking X one can attack Y. Vietnam is thousands of miles away, and Washington, where Vietnam policies are made, is distant from most campuses. Dow Chemical, however, is fleetingly present in the person of its harassed recruitment officers, and since Dow makes napalm, Dow can function as a stand-in for the whole Vietnamese involvement. To point out that most of Dow's production is non-military, or that other firms make more war weapons, or that if Dow did not make napalm, someone else would is irrelevant once Dow has been chosen as a symbol and recognized as such by all involved.

Dow recruiters, however, while they may serve as occasions of anti-war protest, are somehow inadequate as personifications of the war machine, and it is difficult to stage a satisfactory conflict with them. The focus thus naturally turns to the Administration which allows the Dow man on campus; the logic of symbolism finds no difficulty in forging the tenuous chain of guilt from Vietnam to army weapons to Dow Chemical to company recruiters to those who permit such recruiters on campus, and the Administration finds (usually with a mixture of irritation and amazement) that it somehow has come to carry the whole burden of American involvement in Asia on its shoulders.

When the target is racism, the protests may take on a little more substance, for it is a rare institution which avoids any taint of discrimination and which neither employs nor enrolls prejudiced people. Fraternities and sororities have been traditional bastions of prejudice; it was a shot fired from a fraternity in the general direction of a black student which set off a sit-in at Dartmouth, and other institutions have had similar experiences. Athletic staff seem less sensitive than most to racial awareness, and they who have to deal most directly with black students; the behavior of coaches became a central issue at San Jose State and Oregon State University. Demands for a curriculum more relevant to black needs and interests, especially for black studies programs are clearly important, as are admissions policies for disadvantaged students. Yet there are many instances when the causes espoused by black students and their white allies seem curiously ritualistic.

Courses in Swahili, for example, seem unlikely to draw much enrollment, but are considered essential by some black militants. The demand for more black faculty members may be substantial, but when the BSU at San Francisco State made the promotion of Dr. Nathan Hare from Associate to full Professor one of their "non-negotiable" demands, it would seem that Dr. Hare must have assumed a symbolic role. Black students at Princeton got into their first confrontation with President Goheen over the question of how extensive the University's observance of the death of Martin Luther King should be. An altercation between a part-time volunteer coach and a black athlete at San Fernando Valley State College led to a massive sit-in and temporary imprisonment of acting President Blomgren. At Howard University, the causes espoused by students sitting in the administration building were real and of long standing, but the occasion was the killing of three black students by police at Orangeburg, South Carolina. In such instances, it appears that the real target, whether it is the racism of white society in general or the perpetrators of particular acts against black people, is out of reach, and so the college administration is selected as a stand-in for the guilty parties.

Similar considerations apply to other non-campus issues. Thus the natural desire to protest South Africa's racial policies may seem to have no immediate outlet, since virtually everyone on the campus is likely to disapprove of them. But wait—there are American firms which do business in South Africa, and either the university may own stock in such firms, or it may have trustees who do so. Chase Manhattan Bank thus becomes a stand-in for the South African regime, and any argument about the nature and effects of the bank's South African involvement—whether, for example, it may improve the lives of South African blacks, or provide a lever by which apartheid policies may be softened and undermined—becomes irrelevant. Perhaps one of the reasons that protest against Communist actions and regimes is so rare on the campuses may be that it is virtually impossible to locate any local authority who can by any conceivable stretch of logic be held responsible for them.

Student demands thus appear to range from the real to the symbolic—real in the sense of being based on immediately felt needs, symbolic in that whatever is demanded stands in place of what is actually felt or desired. It is not always easy to disentangle the two; a demand for the ending of rules governing dormitory visitation, for example, may stem from a real irritation at regulations which disrupt social life, or it may involve an obsolete and unenforced rule which must be abolished "as a matter of principle." In the latter case, the abolition may serve to symbolize the recognition of student maturity.

However, it is important for administrators to make this distinction if they are to frame an intelligent response to student activism. If the protest is directed towards a change which the activists desire for its own sake, then enacting the change may well halt the protest, and negotiating a compromise concerning it is likely to be feasible. If, however, the cause of protest is symbolic, then it is more likely that a concession will merely serve to switch the focus to some other symbolic cause. Those who oppose Dow recruiting privileges or university sponsorship of the Institute of Defense Analyses or who select a ritual hero for promotion or a ritual villain for dismissal may not be terribly interested in whether their immediate and apparent aims are achieved. Just as such goals are often more symbolic than real, so the institution's response may have to be a matter of style; the activists may be placated or enraged, given popular status or deprived of support more by the way the institution responds to them than by any actions it may take on the matter at hand. Quiet negotiation of such matters is, from the protesters' standpoint, quite unsatisfactory, since it would mute the movement whose essential purpose is the stimulation of opinion. Nor is the granting of half a symbol likely to earn the university much gratitude. The institution should assess the intentions of the activists and the spirit behind their demands, for only by doing so will it be able to estimate which actions on its own part are likely to bring about whatever outcomes it seeks.

Strategies of Protest

Since by definition, "protest" excludes the use of normal channels of decision-making, the problems of protest strategy may be seen as essentially ones of attaining power in the absence of formal authority. Two basic strategic alternatives are available. The first is the strategy of persuasion; lacking authority themselves, the student activists can seek to influence the minds and behavior of those who possess the authority either by direct approaches or by the enrollment of strong allies who can bring pressure to bear on the decision-making process. The second strategy is that of coercion. Students practicing this mode seek to control the actions of decision-makers by means of imposing sanctions for undesired actions, or even more directly by taking decisions themselves and forcibly excluding all other options. Although there have been protest actions which fell somewhere between these categories, or which possess elements of both, in most situations coercion is quite unpersuasive. Viewed thus, student protests can be divided into two reasonably clear and separate categories.

There are many styles of persuasion, but the rubric of protest includes only those which involve a measure of defiance, a set of overt actions aimed against authority. Protest of this kind should be seen as an essentially theatrical occasion. The intended audience may include the administration—normally participants in the performance—fellow students, faculty, the trustees, the local community, legislators and other political leaders, or the public at large. It is obviously essential to reach the intended audience if there is to be any impact. If the protest is aimed at the campus community, the college newspaper may be a sufficient medium of communication, and a substantial proportion of the audience may even witness the protest events themselves. If a wider impact is sought, the protesters should naturally take steps to see that press representatives and television crews are on hand. Normally, such preparations are made simply enough, a few phone calls with a suggestion of dramatic events to come being sufficient to attract the news media. It may be, as some assert, that many protesters have an element of exhibitionism in their make-up and deliberately court publicity for this reason; but it should also be realized that it is the publicity which confers much of the significance on their demonstrations.

If the news coverage is to be live, rather than *ex post facto*, there has to be prior notice. Spontaneous demonstrations, or events which are intended to be minor and unexpectedly or uncontrollably escalate, will lose some of their potential impact because of the lack of coverage. Thus the mass arrest of demonstrators against Dow at Indiana University represented some degree of failure on the part of protest leaders, for they had intended to mount a major effort against a visit by Dean Rusk a few days later, a project for which they could have expected national coverage. A major problem for protest strategists is that group decisions are often taken democratically and under emotional pressure (as the Indiana one was), rather than with a full assessment of the strategic options available.

Any dramatization of a cause at least raises the matter in the minds of the audience. Some protesters seem to assume that any attention is better than none, and that the virtue of their cause will speak for itself without any effort at making it persuasive. Others feel that the problem is to attract an audience, and then convince them by strength of argument. Marches, picket lines, mass rallies, guerrilla theater and the rest thus assume the old-fashioned role of the barker; they are merely publicity gimmicks to pull the crowds, who will then hopefully be swayed by traditional means. More effective forms of protest, however, integrate action and argument into a dramatic form not unlike the morality play, in which the audience is able to distinguish the good from the bad characters without the pedestrian requirement of weighing logical arguments.

To be persuasive, the protesters must project an image of some virtue; no easy task in a society which tends to value the conformist above the unconventional and the mature above the callow, and to have hierarchical expectations according to which students should learn passively from those who know more than they. One attack on this stereotype is frontal, by demonstrating a grasp of facts and a capacity for analysis comparable to those on which the faculty pride themselves. If students pleading for a relaxation of *in loco parentis* practices can convincingly show that they are concerned more with the educational values of self-determination than they are with the simpler pleasures of having sex or liquor or pot in the dormitories, they are likely to gain powerful allies within the academic community. One of the more immediately successful SDS projects was the attack on university participation in the Institute of Defense Analyses; a factor in this success was the carefully researched and reasoned position papers which the organization was, on this occasion, able to offer. Student demands will generally be more appealing and so more successful if they are supported with the kind of solid preparation which is expected of reform proposals in the non-student world.

An important addition or alternative, however, is commitment. To some extent, arduous preparation indicates commitment, but a willingness to take risks or undergo suffering may carry more immediate conviction. Participation in community projects has been a major activity of SDS, but it has not been well publicized, for it lacks the drama inherent in conflict. The invasion of the South by Northern white liberal students during the earlier part of the sixties showed commitment more impressively, because of the risks they ran from the Southern authorities. Risk-taking behavior on Northern campuses tends to be less notable, simply because the risks are smaller; yet willingness to confront the police, to be physically assaulted, arrested and tried, experiences which most middle class administrators and faculty would find highly repugnant, provides evidence that activist concerns are not trivial and that activists are prepared to make a significant investment in them. When activists undergo deliberate physical suffering, as when Berkeley student president Charles Palmer undertook a hunger-strike in support of minority demands or when University of Colorado students camped out in winter weather on campus, they are providing unanswerable proof of their seriousness.

The image projected by the activists, however, may be less important to the success of the protest than the behavior of the administration. Little is expected of student groups, whereas institutions have a reputation to maintain. Activists can therefore score an important moral victory if they can plausibly depict the institution as irrational, a failure by its own professions of intellectual integrity.

Strategies for imputing intellectual cowardice to the opposition are nothing new in American politics. During the election of 1924, Burton K. Wheeler, running for Vice-President on the Progressive ticket, conducted a series of debates with "Silent Cal" Coolidge by the simple expedient of appearing on the platform with an empty chair beside him, to which he addressed telling questions which received, of course, no reply. A variant on this was developed by Ohio State students, when they had Herbert Aptheker, banned as a speaker, sit silently on the platform while faculty members read from his works. The student paper at Troy State University (Alabama) replaced a censored editorial attack on George Wallace with a large blank space and the word "Censored," instead of with the piece on raising dogs which the administration had recommended as a suitable alternative, thus drawing expulsion from the College for the editor, and sparking a legal case which he eventually won.

The pro-censorship position is an uncongenial one for an institution, particularly if that institution is going to attempt to apply its rules consistently. All the protester has to do is select the most ridiculous available instance, and give the non-event maximum publicity.

The institution is in a particularly vulnerable position when a faculty personnel case is at issue. Denial of tenure to a popular young professor has occasioned a number of protests. The faculty member is free to give his side of the story, which usually involves assertions that he is being replaced because of radical political activities or because of his criticism of the university's established powers and policies. These assertions, suitably embellished, can be passed on to the students, as when one faculty speaker at U.C., Irvine, told a rally that the History Department consisted of "fifteen brilliant young men and five old goats." Senior faculty and administrators might then like to tell their side of the case, but because of the confidentiality of the personnel process and possibilities of grievance procedures and other legal action, they hesitate to do so. Thus one of the minor issues at San Francisco State concerned the non-retention of Dr. Patrick Gleason for 1969–70; Gleason told several newspapers that he was being removed because of his radicalism in college politics, even though the department chairman and others responsible for the decision against him were themselves radicals. In such a situation, the institution is virtually unable to defend itself, save by simply denying the allegations: a weak and unconvincing response at best.

The protesters' position is strongest when the institutional forces show no real interest in communicating, or make a mockery of the consultative process. On December 11, 1968, the governing Board of the College of San Mateo altered the rules of the College Readiness Program, a program for disadvantaged and minority students largely run by students themselves, so that a group of American Indians and another of orientals, whose entry had been planned for, could not attend. The Board gave no notice of the proposed change even to Bob Hoover, the program's black Director; the Board Chairman commented that this "was the type of decision that students shouldn't have anything to do with anyway." * On the following day a student visited the office of the President and apparently struck him; he was joined by twenty more protesting his arrest, and chairs were thrown through the president's window. The following day, a rally led to violence, with injuries to twelve and about $8,000 in damage. More than 400 police restored order and subsequently controlled access to the campus. The Board showed how much it had learned by inviting students to meet with it on the decision to require all non-students to get visitors' passes before being allowed on campus. The students who appeared all spoke against the new regulation, and several asked questions. The trustees refused to reply to the questions, waited for the students to finish, and then passed the proposal without further debate. Such procedures play into the hands of activists.

A more rational administrative style may, by shrewd tactics, be made to appear less open than in fact it is. Thus at Princeton, SDS demanded an audience with the trustees to discuss war-related research; the trustees responded that it was never the practice to have non-members of the Board address general trustee meetings, but that SDS spokesmen were invited to meet with the appropriate committee. This offer SDS refused, and a group of radicals showed up peacefully enough outside the full trustee meeting, to be met with by the Dean of Students standing, George Wallace style, in the door. A photograph in the *Princetonian* captured the encounter, and the willingness of a trustee committee to meet with SDS was forgotten.

An alternative or supplemental strategy for the protester intent on discrediting the administration is to make the latter appear not only irrational, but also intolerant, bullying or inept. In many immediately theatrical ways, the protesters appear to be the underdogs. They are poor (actually most of them are middle class and prosperous, but they seldom look it) where the administrators are solidly affluent (they may actually be underpaid, but they tend to emulate the appearance of the business executive). The students have no authority;

* Los Angeles *Times* (February 16, 1969), p. 21a.

the administrators control the institution (or rather, in face of protest they pretend to do so). The administrators inhabit what is often the university's most imposing building, while the activists can only claim the grass and the asphalt as their territory.

The simplest way to make the institution appear repressive is to defy one of its rules. The institution can then either initiate disciplinary proceedings, which are usually ponderous and slow, or it can ignore the violation, thus appearing weak and lacking in consistency. The protesters have a choice of rules, and naturally tend to pick those which offer them their best opportunities; in many instances, the existence of the rules is the cause of the protest, permitting protest aim and action to be combined. Thus a ban on demonstrations and political activities in a certain area or of a certain kind may take the form of precisely those banned activities. Protests against dress codes may take the form of mass wearing of the prohibited dress. Protests against rules banning dormitory visitation may involve the massive mobilization of visitors, or a "sleep-in"—a strategy widely discussed and appreciated for its pleasurable effectiveness but seldom implemented. The administration in such cases must choose either to overlook violations of its own rules, or to punish large numbers of violators. The first course will give protesters a chance to claim that violation of the rules has been officially approved, while showing the administration weak and confused. The second involves the ever unpleasant spectacle of an institution exacting penalties from persons who have sacrificed themselves for a cause.

Martyrdom is thus a desideratum of protesters, particularly if the martyrdom is both spectacular and relatively painless. No one likes to see a man punished for his ideals, and this is a value held particularly strongly in the academic community. If the activist is hardly a Socrates, and even if he is being punished for his actions rather than his beliefs, the sympathy of the community is likely to be with him, and the proportion of students hostile to the administration will increase in consequence. There are few things better suited to the stirring of protest—as events at Berkeley, Columbia, Colorado, San Francisco State, Wisconsin and elsewhere have abundantly demonstrated. A demand for amnesty is likely to be among the first advanced by any group which has deliberately broken the rules. Such demands should be recognized as something more than the natural desire of violators to escape punishment, for they are an integral part of the theater of protest.

Expulsion is sometimes called "academic capital punishment," but it is almost unheard of at some of those institutions which have undergone the most violent protests. Despite such dramatic descriptions, most colleges and universities tend to be kindly to the point of ineffectuality when it comes to disciplining students, with few penalties at their disposal and a great reluctance to impose them. Something more dramatic is likely to suit the protesters' purposes better; physical violence, preferably on camera, is ideal.

Violent opposition can come from counter-protesters, but generally police are a more reliable and impressive source. The sight of them in action on campus is guaranteed to win some support for the activists; the problem is to get them there without behaving in ways which will lose more than their presence will gain. The violence at Berkeley in early 1969, with students attacking non-strikers, using rocks and bombs and disrupting classes and a mysterious fire gutting Wheeler Hall, was so extreme that little criticism was heard when Governor Reagan declared a state of emergency and moved the Highway Patrol to the campus. When, however, comparatively undestructive demonstrations in favor of the People's Park later the same year brought forth massive police retaliation, including the dropping of tear gas from a helicopter and the fatal shooting of one protester, criticism of the forces of "law and order" was far more widespread.

When Oberlin students blockaded a naval recruiter in his car, college authorities and police apparently tried to avoid making arrests by using tear gas in an attempt to break up the crowd. The attempt failed, the activists received credit for their toughness in withstanding the attack, and forces of law and order had neatly linked themselves with violence, repression and gas warfare. When they resigned themselves to making arrests, the students marched peacefully to the station, only to be disappointed; they were not booked. At Madison, police called to clear the Commerce Building were given both insufficient instructions and insufficient equipment; both sides suffered considerable casualties in the melee that followed. At San Francisco State, the city's Tactical Squad came on campus with padded uniforms, helmets, plastic face-masks and other accoutrements of creatures from outer space; the fact that they did in fact generally avoid the casual violence which has occurred in other confrontations tended to be obscured by the image they projected. New York's Finest gave a preview of happenings at Chicago when they rousted the Columbia students with a maximum of unnecessary violence and bloodshed.

At Harvard, SDS was initially able to make little impact, but when a sit-in produced mass arrests, President Pusey was divided from his faculty, support for protest among moderate students grew immensely, and the situation improved greatly from the radical perspective. Whatever the considerations that led to calling in the police in these and other cases, it is evident that their entry upon the scene was almost inevitably a moral victory for the protesters. Just as capital punishment stirs more controversy than the murder which preceded it, so the violence of the protesters tends to be obscured by the counter-violence of the police.

While attracting retaliation is perhaps the most productive aim of violent tactics, some other possible gains may be noted. One kind of violence which may pay unexpected dividends is extremely unattractive *per se:* personal threats. Bullets have been rolled under doors at San Francisco State, homes bombed (or bombings attempted) there, at the College of San Mateo and at Howard, and telephone threats and warnings have become relatively commonplace. At Howard, the effect was that when students staged a generally non-violent sit-in, the president disappeared for a week, apparently to a Washington hotel. At San Francisco State, President Summerskill, after some months of extraordinary pressure, one evening gave in to all the demands currently made upon him, and the next morning flew to Ethiopia, one of the more unusual ways of resigning from office. At San Fernando Valley State College, the aggressive tactics of the BSU, which had included physical detention of the President and other administrators for several hours, and later (it was widely assumed) burning the President's office, had lost support for their cause on the campus. Their position was rapidly restored, however, when a rally at which acting President Oviatt was to speak was cancelled, a state of emergency declared on campus, and several hundred people who had come to attend the rally were hauled away by the police while offering no resistance. Oviatt was impressed with an anonymous death threat, but his forceful reaction put his administration into an irretrievably false position, generated a sympathy for the protest which had seemed inconceivable a few days previously, and inevitably led the college to a compromise settlement with the black leaders.

Violence on the part of either protesters or authorities normally represents a moral defeat. It is for this reason that coercive tactics are usually incompatible with persuasive ones. On a public level, the institution which yields to threats must do so in spite of the tactics used, not because of them. Whether it yields at all will depend on the personalities of the administrators, and the relationship of the coercive threat to the scale of the demand.

Obstructive or violent means can be used to prevent the college or university carrying out some disliked practice. ROTC has been a popular target of protest activities. ROTC buildings have been burned at Stanford and Wisconsin and drills have been disrupted at San Jose College, Columbia and elsewhere. These tactics can prevent operations temporarily, but are likely to lose sympathy. The moderate approach which persuades faculty that ROTC courses are not respectable—a conclusion recently reached by the Harvard faculty—is more likely to be productive. Recruiters are another prime target of obstruction, and sometimes of violence, as when the Dow recruiter at Harvard was held prisoner for seven hours, but again there is little evidence that such opposition prevents recruitment from continuing, and the dangers of building up sympathy for the lonely victims are considerable. The same considerations apply to disruption of visiting speakers. It is relatively easy for activists to prevent a man from being heard; Lewis Hershey and James Reston have been shouted down, cabinet officers of the Johnson regime were driven to abandon campus appearances, and even Edward Kennedy, with his considerable appeal to college students, was heckled fiercely at Madison. But any satisfactions felt by the protesters at such "victories" must be mainly psychological, for disapproval and resentment of their actions will be widespread.

Use of coercive tactics to prevent the institution acting are thus of dubious value; as a means to getting it to undertake some positive program, they are generally disastrous. One possible outcome was shown at San Fernando Valley State, where a group of BSU members took over the Administration Building, holding Acting President Paul Blomgren and his staff prisoners for several hours. There was much threatening language, some roughing up of deans and, according to some, threats with switchblade knives. Faced with a list of demands, Blomgren agreed to them all. The black students left the building, and the next day were arrested; Blomgren announced that he had signed under duress, and regarded the agreement as invalid. Coercion may thus force temporary concessions, but it can seldom be sustained.

In Western society aggression and anger are not generally admired, and white radicals who display such behavior seldom find it wins converts. Black aggression and black anger, however, are perceived by an increasing number of whites, particularly by those liberals commonly found in positions of academic power, as justifiable and even praiseworthy. Blacks were submissive for so long that an assertion of black pride seems appropriate; they were dealt with so shabbily by the white power structure that resentment appears as a reaction long overdue. It is hard to see colleges and universities as having recently been in the forefront of racism, just as it seems unfair to charge that white liberals who have been fighting for years for civil rights bills are racists. Yet white liberal guilt is such that black reproaches now tend to be accepted without much question. A pattern of white submission to black anger, first set in a large and public way at the Conference for a New Politics in August, 1967, can make rage and aggressiveness an appealing posture for a black activist.

Thus an impromptu and somewhat hostile rally by black students at midnight outside President Goheen's home convinced him that Princeton classes should be cancelled after the murder of Martin Luther King. When sociology instructor Harry Edwards charged the college with a variety of sins in its race relations, San Jose State College President Clark hastened to call for a full investigation, even though little had been heard on the issue previously. That Edwards's demands were backed by a threat to destroy the football stadium did nothing to weaken their moral force; for too many whites, such a self-sufficient and domineering attitude makes a welcome change from the "Uncle-Tomism" which was for so long the characteristic black stance. Most whites are uncomfortably aware of past racial sins of omission and commission committed by themselves or their institutions; further, they are ready to admit that they have been slow to see black viewpoints and perhaps are even unable to judge their own records by black standards. Charges of institutional racism therefore catch most administrators and faculty where they are most sensitive, and as often as not, elicit some admission of guilt which is sincere even when it is least specific. Black anger is thus persuasive in part because it assumes the guise of justified retribution.

In the racial context, white authorities are thus often ready to do what all protesters want them to do, which is to cast themselves in the role of villain. Activists by and large proclaim an unshakable conviction in their own virtue, and seek to show that those whom

they are active against have done wrong. If the protest issue is one
on which the administration does indeed feel guilty and insecure,
therefore, half the battle is won. It is extremely difficult for a college
administration to defend a policy in which it does not itself believe;
if it tries to do so, it will almost inevitably find itself mired in eva-
sions and hypocrisies, playing the villain's role assigned to it with
ultimate conviction.

*   *   *

We have here tried to delineate some rational strategies for protest, to indicate some relationships between means and ends. Yet
politics is not an exclusively rational basis, and mass politics tends
to be less rational than most other kinds. Pride, anger, obstinacy and,
above all, failure to comprehend the aims, motives and standards of
others can lead to miscalculations or to no calculation at all. What
seems surprising is that so much protest activity *is* explicable in
Machiavellian terms, even while its rhetoric may be more reminiscent
of Wagnerian opera. It is perhaps because an underlying rational
pattern is so often followed that student activism has been relatively
successful in bringing about change.

5

THE DYNAMICS OF INSTITUTIONAL RESPONSE

by Julian Foster and Durward Long

FEW INSTITUTIONS want protest. There is a certain academic distinction about student unrest—all the best places seem to have it—and there may well be satisfactions in knowing that the students have some serious concerns and a proclivity for doing something about them. But since protest, for reasons given in the previous chapter, almost inevitably develops into a clash between students and campus authorities, it represents a deterioration of relationships which is unacceptable *per se*. If the administrators happen to share the students' concerns for racial justice and peace, they may be happy that students have become enthusiastic over such matters, but this satisfaction is not likely to survive the discovery that they themselves are going to be held guilty of racism or war-mongering. Personal relationships may survive even quite violent protests, but the roles assigned by the logic of the drama are those of antagonists, and no amount of administrative subterfuge or self-delusion can disguise this.

The institution, therefore, finds itself engaged in a contest which it did not invite, and which often it has attempted to stave off. The protesters will inevitably have some goals, and so will know the stakes for which they are playing. The institution, by contrast, may be thoroughly confused, not knowing what its goals are, and responding from hour to hour to stimuli from its opposition. The students are in the game to win; the administration may be in it with only the hope that it will at some time be over.

Yet it may be that there are implicit institutional goals, which may not be recognized by harassed administrators at the time they are confronted with protest simply because no one asks the relevant questions. If a rational strategy is to be developed, an aim must be posited; if institutions do not know what they are trying to do, they will be thrown back on individual reflexes, outworn and unsuitable precedents, unenunciated standards of right and wrong. Three institutional goals in protest situations will be suggested here; they are hypothetical, in the sense that many institutions may not have acknowledged such goals, yet useful if it is correct that such goals would be acknowledged if they were formulated, or that they can serve to explain actual institutional behavior.

The first such goal is that institutions do not want to modify or change their policies by procedures other than those to which they have become accustomed. Colleges and universities tend to develop rules of operation which are not unlike the constitutions of political systems. These constitutions distribute power among administration, faculty, trustees and (sometimes) students, and it seems safe to say that while occasionally there may be agreement on shifting the balance of power in one direction or another, such shifts must be made in accordance with the system (a constitutional amendment rather than a *coup d'état*) if they are to be acceptable. Administrators or others thus may be willing to yield power; but we assume they are unwilling to have it taken from them. A protest aimed at increasing student control over their own lives may be acceptable to the institution if it can be dealt with through the usual channels, but it is assumed here that it will be unacceptable if the intention is to take power rather than to request it.

Further, most colleges and universities have adopted decision-making processes characterized by rational deliberation and consensus-building. In such models, issues arise, study committees are appointed to find facts and make recommendations, and the available options are then discussed at some length before one is chosen. The eventual outcome is often a compromise between conflicting interests and opinions, and it is generally the hope that even those who dislike it will have been drawn towards accepting it as legitimate if not desirable. Student protest naturally tends to disrupt this mechanism, in that it tends to place a low value on lengthy or thoughtful deliberation ("needless delays"), while the more aggressive protesters also tend to disdain compromises ("cop-outs"). Protest which involves subjecting traditional decision-making bodies to external political pressures or to the threat of retaliation for wrong decisions naturally violates the model of rational and objective deliberation.

If, however, the protest feeds new input into the decision-making process without having any tendency to destroy it, there is no cause for institutional resistance. In some cases, the outcome may simply be that the college or university reassesses its position; few would object to a protest if this were the aim. Protest activities may change the picture which decision-makers have of their environment. They may become conscious of the social costs of physical expansion which requires the destruction of neighboring dwellings, or they may have their attention directed to the implications of classified research contracts. Most likely, the protest will recast institutional perceptions of those who engaged in protest; if the institution has some pretensions to democracy, in the sense that it tries to take account of the interests and desires of its members, then the revelation that a certain segment of the constituency feels strongly on some point will itself be a new input.

A second institutional goal is to enforce such regulations and observe such procedures as it has itself set up. This is generally true of any rule-making institution. There may be a case for altering the rules, but until this is done, the institutional focus must be on enforcement.

A third goal is the avoidance of precisely those things which the protesters promise it: embarrassment and/or violence. Both are hurtful *per se*; if they were not, they would not form the essence of protest strategies.

Underlying these goals is a particular kind of institutional self-concept. Colleges and universities have pictured themselves as conflict-avoiding systems, in the sense that it is hard to imagine administrators or faculty members who would prefer permanent conflict to consensus, or see it as better than a necessary evil. If a different kind of model were adopted, it is not easy to foretell what the consequences might be. If, for example, a university were to see itself primarily as a democratic system, geared to doing whatever its citizens demanded of it, would conflict then be dysfunctional? Lipset has observed that "democracy requires institutions which sustain legitimacy and consensus," [1] and there are convincing arguments to be made for the position that democracy might not survive if all issues were removed from contention. But at present, those in charge of colleges and universities would appear to subscribe overwhelmingly to a consensus model. Since student protest is a violation of consensus, it seems appropriate to hypothesize that while it may be ready to grant legitimate demands and take into account new inputs, the underlying institutional goal must be to render student protest properly submissive; that is to say, to exterminate it as protest.

Given this goal, some evaluation of alternative administrative strategies may be attempted. Three basic options are available. The first is persuasion; activists may be met on their own ground by an administration which is also willing to play to the same audience, and to attempt to substitute its own scenario for that conceived by the protesters. If this counter-strategy is successful, the protesters will fail because their chosen audience will regard *them* as the villains and the administrators as heroes; the protest will thereupon build opposition, not support, and will eventually collapse. The second option is restriction. The administration may seek to crush the protest by direct means: injunctions, threats, physical force, and penalties. If the protest is of the persuasive type, such an administrative response is likely to play into the protesters' hands, but if the activists are employing coercion themselves, the loss of face inherent in wielding repressive authority will be far less. The third option is concession: to destroy the protest by yielding as much as is necessary of what it demands. A concession strategy presupposes that the activists are demanding something which it is within the institution's power to bestow; if the activist goal is revolution rather than reform, concession will merely lead to further demands.

However, the college or university which proposes to frame a rational strategy in face of protest must engage in some prior planning. Quantitative data on this and all other matters dealt with here is—unless otherwise stated—drawn from the Protest Survey described in Part I, Chapter 5. Most institutions indicated that discussions had been initiated prior to the climactic event of the protest, but 14 percent stated that no such discussions had taken place. Planning, if it is to be functional, implies some foreknowledge of what may be expected to occur. While 304 institutions reported that

---

[1] Seymour Martin Lipset, *Political Man* (Garden City, N.Y., Doubleday & Co., 1960), p. 403.

they had some definite knowledge that protest was to occur, 94 had to rely on "vague rumors" and 96 others admitted that they were taken totally unawares. Protest was not infrequently triggered by a decision or announcement of the administration itself; in 90 such instances, the possibilities of protest ensuing were fully considered, 58 institutions gave this "some consideration," but in 68 cases the administrator completing the questionnaire indicated that no attention was given to this aspect of the situation. There thus appears to be quite a wide gap of understanding on many campuses. Successful strategies in face of activism are not easily discovered at any time; operating with incomplete data can only increase the difficulties.

Persuasive Strategies

Few administrators have been particularly imaginative in their efforts at persuasion. The typical method involves the issuing of formal statements through the press, couched in official and restrained language and appealing to norms which are patently unrelated to the protesters. Those institutions which reported protest activity also reported the issuance of resolutions or "official statements" by various elements in the college community, as indicated in Table 1; probably there were many more instances in which the President or some other official commented on the action in a less formal manner. It appears that while all concerned tended to take a critical view

TABLE 1

THE CAMPUS COMMUNITY COMMENTS ON PROTEST

	Statement or Resolution by:			
Topic:	Trustees	Adminis-tration	Faculty	Student Govern-ment
On protest *tactics:*				
a critical statement	12	26	8	8
an approving statement	4	6	5	6
On the *substantive issue* involved:				
supportive of protesters	7	28	27	51
opposed to protesters	13	26	14	13

of activist tactics, the most widespread reaction was support for the protesters' substantive goals by faculty and student governments. It seems doubtful that the administration will gain much by securing condemnation of tactics accompanied by endorsement of protest goals for it is on the matter of substance that action may have to be taken. The institution which tries to take the position that although the aims of a protest may be valid, the protest movement should be defeated because it has not pursued its goals in a proper manner may well have difficulty persuading its publics that it is not hung up on procedural trivialities. It is sometimes easy to forget that democracy is essentially a way of reaching decisions.

A few administrations have shown greater public relations sense in the way they have presented their side of the issue. A message may come across far more forcefully if it is accompanied by a display of physical courage. President Robert Clark of San Jose State went out alone to speak to what appeared to many in his administration to be a hostile and threatening student mob; he was successful in substantially de-fusing protest sentiment. This is a high risk technique, however, and not all administrators are equipped for such a confrontation. At San Francisco State, President Robert Smith put on his own theater when he summoned the entire campus into continuous convocation. He demonstrated impeccable cool in face of such epithets as "racist pig" tossed at him by fellow panelists, and might perhaps have resolved the crisis on the campus had not his Trustees made demands upon him which led to his resignation. His successor, President Hayakawa, also demonstrated considerable public relations style, climbing on a protester's sound-truck to disconnect the public address system, distributing tam o'shanters and blue armbands to sympathizers, and unleashing unconventionally direct blasts at any and all critics. He was not able to get cooperation for his scheme to equip the Tac Squad with garlands of flowers, symbolizing love, but did appear himself at several press conferences thus ornamented. Few university presidents have found more ways of dramatizing their point of view; it was perhaps his misfortune that the content of his message reflected less creative imagination.

In many circumstances, defense may be the best form of attack. If the activists have developed a script which requires the administration to assume the villain's role, all the administration need do to defeat the protest is to fail to perform as expected. One strategy for this revolves around "guidelines." The activists intend to put on a demonstration for the purpose of denouncing the administration; they want the drama of a confrontation. A possible administrative response may be to offer cooperation in the enterprise. "You want to hold a rally? Certainly, where would you like it? Can we lend you some public address equipment? You are planning a sit-in? How about the corridors of the Ad Building? If you must take over an Office there is the Placement Center; you could be assured of safety there." And so on. If the protest leader is naïve enough to fall in with such plans, he is in danger of finding himself with an occasion from which all possibilities of drama have been drained, and which succeeds mainly in demonstrating the good faith and tolerance of the college administration.

The formulation of guidelines for protest does not, of course, necessarily imply Machiavellian motivations on the part of the administration. Eighty-three percent of schools encountering violent or obstructive protests did develop such guidelines before the event, as did 61 percent of the institutions experiencing physical but non-obstructive protest, and 48 percent of those where protest was confined within diplomatic channels. If something is to happen, it is a natural administrative reflex to try to arrange that it happen in a controlled, orderly, safe and convenient way. Yet the student activists who cooperate with such endeavors may be giving up their most effective weapons by so doing. Having chosen to precipitate a conflict, they are, by agreeing to draw up and follow guidelines, deliberately minimizing the scale of that conflict and robbing it of the spontaneous action which is likely to give it maximum impact.

Activists frequently insist that they want to debate the issues, particularly when no one seems willing to debate with them. Where they have been refused debate, activists have generally been able to capitalize on the refusal; not only do the counter-arguments go unheard, but it is usually possible to attribute devious motives to the opposition. Dow Chemical's policy of discouraging their representatives from discussing issues relating to the manufacture and use of napalm provided demonstrators with an opportunity to demand free and open debate, and be denied it, thus strengthening the rationalization that by trying to ban such recruiters from the campus they were not interfering with free speech. The occasions when the Dow man did enter into discussion usually proved anti-climactic; they were most satisfactory to the demonstrators when he attempted to confine himself to stating his personal opinions and avoiding comment on company policy, thus presenting a spectacle of open and idealistic students in confrontation with an opponent who was afraid to speak too much of the truth.

Some of the dangers and difficulties of debating with activists were illustrated at Princeton when President Goheen decided to hold an open forum in response to the arrest of SDS members in front of a building leased to the Institute of Defense Analyses. Goheen found himself playing three roles: chairman of the meeting (at Princeton, the President is always in the chair at any meeting he attends); resource person, since he knew more about the University's affiliation with IDA than anyone else, being a member of IDA's board; and spokesman for the University–IDA link. That he managed to carry off all three roles without the potential conflicts becoming too obvious may be tributed both to his skill and to the general conservatism of the Princeton milieu. Later developments, however, which included first a faculty committee report recommending the severance of ties with IDA and then a faculty rejection of a compromise proposed by Goheen, produced a situation where in retrospect it seems that the President was dealt a defeat by SDS, an interpretation which would have been less plausible had he not been induced to take so public a stand in response to the initial radical challenge.

This illustrates a major dilemma faced by administrators who are willing to take up the radical challenge to debate. The radicals know what their task is: to demonstrate that some administrative rule or practice is wrong and should be changed. The administration's goals are less clear, being primarily defensive. The issue has been selected by their critics, who are likely to have chosen some topic on which the institution is indeed vulnerable. If the administration mounts a wholehearted defense of their past performance, rebutting the radical critique, they will in effect be endorsing the status quo, and even putting their own prestige behind its maintenance. If they admit—what may well be their own opinion—that changes are in order, they may seem to be conceding that the radicals have the greater wisdom; further, it will take an expert debater to ensure that in the course of public discussion, the administration neither commits itself to reforms which it has not thought through or which may be rejected by faculty or trustees, nor projects a picture of itself as conscious that things are bad but yet unclear as to what can be done about it.

A further difficulty for the administration side in a debate with activists is that where the activist can say whatever he likes and can be, in a most literal sense, irresponsible, the administrator is part of a coherent organization. The administrator has power, and therefore little excuse for not attempting to implement whatever he may advocate; the activist, by contrast, can recommend wildly problematical solutions, secure in the knowledge that no one will be asking *him* to make them work. The administrator has the prestige of office, and whatever he says will therefore be taken as being said on behalf of the institution, even though such an intent may be disclaimed; the activist, on the other hand, may be a member of no formal organization, but even if he holds an office in one, the amorphous structure of radical groups generally precludes any attempt at holding the group responsible for one of the utterances of its "spokesmen." The administrator is a member of a team, and so tends to be restrained in airing any internal differences within the administration; subordinates such as deans are in a particularly difficult position if they are appointed to speak for the administration, yet disagree strongly with the president on the issue. In such a situation, frankness may be almost impossible; student audiences may not always grasp all sides of the issue, but they are particularly alert to persons over thirty who tell less than the whole truth.

Faculty members, it may be noted, suffer from these various disadvantages to a far lesser extent than administrators. Circumstances will vary, as will the willingness of faculty to become involved; but it would appear at least that administrators should consider the possibility of having a faculty member represent the opponents of protest. If this is not feasible, an alternative precaution is for the administration to be very clear about what it is likely to do before appearing on a platform with its critics. If it is going to stand pat, it can mount the most ringing possible defense of the *status quo*; if it is going to move toward reforms, it can steal some of the radicals' thunder; if it is uncertain as to its future course of action, it had better stay quiet or resort to empty rhetoric.

Restrictive Strategies

Another general strategy available to the administration is to restrict or inhibit the protesters. This may include the prevention of certain actions which might endanger life or property and the normal functioning of the institution, and setting up conditions which will make it possible to punish the violators. Choice among these may be made in light of the weight given to enforcement of institutional regulations against other factors such as danger to life and/or probability of injury. None of these restrictive strategies is likely to commend itself to the academic community, which is by nature open, tolerant and permissive; yet some degree of restriction may be inevitable if the activists intend to block, obstruct or in any way to coerce others, and the alternatives may then be viewed as lying between restriction by the protesters or by the institution.

Prevention of protest is difficult, owing to the wide variety of alternatives open to protesters. One approach is to set severe penalties for certain types of protest, and to make sure that these are well publicized. Apparently undeterred by considerations of due process, the President of Notre Dame announced that any protesters who violated the institution's authority by sitting-in or otherwise obstructing would be given fifteen minutes to get out. If they did not do so, they would be suspended. If they did not then move, they would be expelled five minutes later. At the time of writing, nothing has occurred which would incur this retribution, but it should be noted that the national publicity given to Father Hesburgh's announcement leaves him very little room for second thoughts; having made such a pledge, the administrator who failed to keep it would lose all credibility. Thus an administrator may tie his own hands, but in doing so he also makes it clear to protesters that he has no options and that they can therefore be sure what to expect. Such a policy might be called one of Massive Retaliation, to stress its resembance to the foreign policy of the United States under John Foster Dulles; Dulles, however, was less specific than Father Hesburgh about what would trigger such retaliation. Such policies do not appear popular on American campuses. Only forty-four institutions gave students specific warnings about penalties they might incur if they protested, while 105 more issued warnings of more general kinds. These warnings applied most often to disruptive, violent or obstructive behavior.

The fact that campuses which issued such warnings subsequently had more violent and disruptive protests than campuses which did not is not, of itself, proof that such warnings are ineffective, for it may be that they are issued only when a serious protest is virtually under way. However, the data in Table 2 give some tentative

TABLE 2

LEVEL OF PROTEST AND PRIOR WARNINGS TO STUDENTS

Level of subsequent protest:	Students were given specific warnings n = 44	Students were given general warnings n = 105	Students were not warned n = 93
Violent	7%	7%	5%
Obstructive	13%	26%	7%
Physical	39%	45%	32%
Diplomatic	42%	22%	55%

indications that warning students of penalties "in general terms" may be the least effective strategy, that it is better to make the warnings very specific or else not to make them at all.

Another preventive measure is the injunction. Seeking to obtain court injunctions against certain illegal acts may be pursued as a course of prevention which may be less risky than other alternatives. However, issuance of clear warnings that violators will be prosecuted is almost certain to cause activists to accuse the institution of intimidation and prior censorship, and so may actually widen their base of support while giving questionable additional basis for disciplinary action after the violation.

Less direct variants of preventive strategy may often be more effective, unless the situation has already escalated beyond repair. The administration controls the timing of events such as the coming of recruiters, the issuing of new rules, the imposition of penalties. Unpopular actions which may stir protest are less likely to do so if they coincide with examinations, vacations, or with times when activists are otherwise committed. President Hayakawa did more to restore peace at San Francisco State by moving the 1968 Christmas vacation forward one week than he had managed to achieve by extensive use of police; had he not done this, the strike would have been reinforced by an unknown number of highschool students whose vacation began a week earlier, and the likelihood that considerable violence would have occurred appears to have been very great. Physical positioning can also be important; if happenings which activists may regard as "provocative" are staged prominently at the center of the campus, the challenge may be regarded as irresistible.

The use of tact whenever possible may serve to prevent protest; activists tend to respond quickly to anything which offends them, and the administrator who wants a quiet life is well advised to discuss, explain and even placate when his institution undertakes something which he knows will be unpopular in certain quarters.

Finally, there are directly physical forms of prevention. The following stratagems were either planned for or used by the number of institutions indicated:

	Planned	Used
Certain buildings locked or closed.	36	21
Certain open areas cleared or closed off.	32	22
Students physically removed from certain places.	79	17
Students passively resisting arrest pulled away.	45	9
Students actively resisting arrest overpowered.	39	13
Other such actions.	13	9
No such actions.	224	271

It should be remembered that only institutions which actually experienced protest during 1967–68 were responding to this question.

The most direct kind of prevention is that provided by the presence of police. If police in superior force are already positioned on the scene and have established a cleared perimeter for protection of those persons or buildings under attack, the task of defending and holding is far less precarious, although provocative to the protesters, than clearing persons or building controlled by large numbers of protesters. The calling in of off-campus police usually reflects a concern with protection of property, of the rights of non-protesters and, in extreme cases, of life and limb. Further attractions of the police presence are that it may undermine the confidence of all but the most ferocious activists, and that it can lay the necessary foundation for later punishment of protesters by the courts. During 1967–68, thirty-eight institutions reported summoning local or city police, while four turned to the state police for help. In twenty-one instances, the police were brought on in a primarily preventive-protective role, before the protest reached its climax. Many more institutions made some plans for use of police; fifty-six invited representatives of off-campus police forces to participate in their planning for protest, and one hundred thirteen authorized a campus official to summon police aid should need arise.

There are also powerful disincentives to calling police: their presence is inflammatory, expensive, and a tacit admission that the institution can no longer handle its own affairs; further, police intervention runs flatly counter to academic traditions, and is likely to leave a residue of bitterness which will be difficult to overcome. The appearance and utilization of armed forces are not generally viewed by the academic community as a protective action but rather as an intimidating or punitive measure. Unless it is justified by flagrantly destructive or coercive conduct from the protesters, such an action will inevitably create much sympathy for them. If students are injured, whatever the circumstances, the charge of "police brutality" is almost certain to emerge as a new issue. Some administrators and many faculty committees prefer to permit obstructors to occupy campus property for long periods of time, rather than have them forcibly expelled; this was the policy at Brandeis and Chicago, while at Stanford the hands-off policy of the administration appeared as a moral victory when it was carried out at the same time that massive force was being employed at Harvard. The summoning of police to deal with disruption will appeal to many, but on the whole it seems more likely to be approved by those less directly involved in higher education. President Pusey at Harvard lost status with students and was rebuked by the faculty for his forceful action, while retaining the support of the trustees and alumni and being praised by a substantial segment of the public. President Pitzer of Stanford tended to grow in stature on campus, but was threatened with the presence of the army, interested in safeguarding classified documents in the occupied building, and was criticized for his softness by Governor Reagan.

The use of off-campus law enforcement, summoned to disperse or arrest a protest group, even under prearranged conditions, includes the certainty that the University becomes *accountable* for the outcome of the exercise of that force, although it may very well not be specifically *responsible* for the acts of the force. Of those institutions which made specific plans for the involvement of police, eighty-six reported the existence of precise contingency plans for various eventualities, but thirty-two indicated that "The police were to be given a relatively free hand to use their own judgment." Yet there seems little reason to expect most officers to be sensitive to the subtleties of the academic situation, and every reason to expect that they will approach the student obstructor as they would any other lawbreaker or disorderly person. Given a building to clear, the police will use as little or as much violence as they see fit. If the officers are indifferently disciplined or conservatively led, they may decide to deal out some physical punishment to protesters on the spot, as happened in the streets of Chicago and on the campus of Columbia. Where protests led to injury, the most common sufferers were "students resisting arrest or dispersion" (eleven campuses) and "police attempting to restore order" (nine campuses).

In carrying out their duties, the police may or may not decide to make arrests, and will not necessarily be guided by institutional wishes in this. Once arrests have been made, the college or university cannot decide what charges will be brought. Thus when black students occupied the administration building at San Fernando for an afternoon, detaining acting-President Blomgren and many of the staff inside while they made their demands, the President called police shortly after his release; it is doubtful, however, that he antic-ipated that the students would be charged with a variety of felonious crimes, including one (kidnapping) which is a capital offense. It is safe to say that while the institution which calls the police must be concerned with the reactions of multiple audiences to its doing so, the police will not usually share this concern, or take it into account when choosing their own course of action.

Control of police becomes particularly difficult in certain circum-stances. Police may be invited to resolve a situation, yet given no precise instructions, nor any indications of what they should do if certain contingencies develop. Police may, for example, plan to make arrests, but they may do so on the expectation that those to be arrested will go along peacefully, and have little to guide them when they meet resistance. There is much to be said for placing police under the command of a college official. Local police forces are usually willing to do this, at least in theory, but if the college official is reluctant to authorize arrests when protesters violate law or do property damage, he may find his power to command to be tenuous. Disruptive scenes on the campus often possess an element of the game about them, but if the police cannot be made to see this, any light-hearted elements in the situation will soon disappear.

Before the police are called, it is important that the reasons for calling them and the tasks to be assigned to them be carefully defined and analyzed. At Indiana, the police were called during a relatively peaceful occupation of the Placement Office, while at San Fernando

Valley State, they were used to remove more than two hundred participants in an entirely peaceful rally. If it is assumed that in such cases the police involvement was due to something other than administrative error, the most plausible explanation of institutional motives is that the authorities wished to punish the protesters for the usual reasons—deterrence, retribution or reform. At Wisconsin, Berkeley and San Francisco State, however, the police function was different, since it was to keep the campus operational. In such situations, the immediate aim is only to get the protesters to stop whatever they are currently doing, not to punish them. The San Francisco Tac Squad has had more practice in this exercise than any other force, and seems to have achieved mastery of the form; they can converge on an illegal rally or picket line in such a way as to put it to flight, yet always leaving an avenue of escape. Violence and arrests are thus avoided, and direct protester-police contact minimized.

There is one other repressive resource which may be available to the institution: the counter-protester. Students opposed to protest but not to physical combat (reputedly they tend to be physical education majors, hence the generic term "jocks") can be subtly mobilized or restrained by the administration, since they are basically responsive to its authority. At Iowa, counter-protesters were allowed to menace and manhandle peace pickets for several hours while campus police stood by. At Columbia, counter-protesters encircled occupied buildings to prevent food from being brought in. They were frustrated in this by the simple expedient of throwing the food into the windows over their heads; nevertheless, it seems possible that they might eventually have routed the sit-in, had the police not been called to do the job, and it seems probable that had President Kirk wanted them to desist in their efforts, he could have persuaded them to retire from the field. The most overt attempt at using counter-protesters occurred at San Francisco State when President Hayakawa called upon those who supported his hard line policy to wear blue armbands. The armbands, never popular, disappeared within a few days, but not before an anonymous armband wearer had been photographed while apparently attempting to brain a lady picketer with a length of lead pipe. Whether or not this exhibit was genuine, the administration which does not restrain its "jocks" will be held accountable for whatever they may do, although its control over them is uncertain at best.

One most successful strategy dependent on the counter-protester may, however, be mentioned. Counter-protesters may sometimes be effective in stopping a demonstration, as when twenty-five to thirty students at California Polytechnic, Pomona, attempted to seal off the Marine Corps' recruitment table, only to be disbanded by a considerably larger force of their student opponents. At another somewhat rustic California campus, a tiny contingent of pickets were so threatened by the resentful majority that they had to be rescued by the campus police; for a cop-hating leftist, such an experience can be traumatic. Generally, however, a jock-based strategy is likely to be effective only on campuses so conservative that protest presents no real problem.

Once the height of a demonstration has been passed, the question of visiting retribution on the offenders naturally arises. According to a report of the National Student Association, based on 2,000 newspaper clippings, there were 221 major demonstrations at 101 colleges and universities during the first six months of 1969. The report stated that 38,911 students (or 2.6 percent of the students enrolled in the colleges studied) participated in the 221 protests. Less than 2 percent of those involved appear to have been punished. A total of 417 were arrested, while 174 were expelled, 119 were suspended and 34 were placed on disciplinary probation. Of those expelled, 50 were reinstated pending hearings, and of those suspended, 59 were to be reinstated once apologies were made. Findings of the Protest Survey also indicated that punishment was seldom inflicted; of the 515 institutions reporting the incidence of protest, 27 also reported the bringing of civil charges, while 58 indicated that on-campus penalties had been inflicted. Only 15 percent of the colleges and universities reporting protest also reported some punitive action against *any* student. It thus appears that the average protester is in little danger of facing institutional or legal reprisals.

One popular "solution" for protest is the speedy and severe punishment of all concerned. Those who oppose this often ground their objections on concepts of academic freedom and due process, and a general revulsion against punishing a man for acting on his beliefs. However, the hard-line policy is occasionally employed. At the University of Denver, for example, an attempted occupation of the administration building was dealt with by on-the-spot expulsions, with apparent success. But it may be doubted whether this technique is generally applicable; four prerequisites for success may be suggested. First, the institution should be private, so that attendance is clearly more a privilege than a right. Private school penalties are less likely to be reviewed by the courts; further, if suspension or expulsion will involve the sacrifice of a status for which considerable fees have been paid, the penalties may be more of a deterrent. Second, the student population should be somewhat conservative, and so unlikely to sympathize too much with the martyred activists. Third, the faculty should either be similarly conservative, or else so subdued that it will not mount an effective challenge to the administrative decree. Fourth, the campus should preferably be largely residential, rather than commuter; expellees who are forced to leave a dormitory will probably leave town, whereas expelled commuting students at such places as Berkeley, San Francisco State, and San Fernando Valley State and Columbia are still available for demonstrations, and likely to be considerably more disruptive in them than they were when they had status to lose. These conditions may suggest why the hard-line repressive strategy has seldom been attempted at many of the most protest-prone schools.

If the institution considers the possibilities of punishing protesters, it should first reexamine its disciplinary procedures. These mechanisms were seldom designed with massive violations or defiant defendants in mind; often they belong to a more paternalistic age. Characteristically, it was assumed that accused students would be few in number, contrite or fearful in demeanor, and ready to accept justice from those in duly constituted authority over them. Instead, a protest is likely to involve a large number of violators convinced of the rectitude of their conduct, contemptuous of the proceedings in which the university seeks to enmesh them, and armed with either some courtroom abilities or an attorney who knows more about constitutional rights and protections than anyone on the judicial panel is likely to do. Disciplinary hearings in such circumstances can be extraordinarily slow and time-consuming for those who conduct them. If they are held in secret, charges of injustice which the protesters are likely to bring anyway will receive *prima facie* support, but if they are open, there is little guarantee that the audience will behave: disruption of disciplinary hearings has taken place on a number of campuses. In either case, the holding of hearings tend to produce martyrs, and to serve as fertile source of additional protest activities. Even when the hearings are ended, the penalties awarded may not solve the problem. The institution has few choices available to it other than probation (too mild to be much of a deterrent) and either suspension or dismissal, which may be thought too severe and which, if dispensed on a massive scale, could leave the institution seriously short of students. Penalties in between these tend to be non-existent or slightly ludicrous, as when Barnard College punished a co-ed for sharing an apartment with her boy friend by banning her from the student cafeteria and other such fringes of institutional life. All too often, the institution may go through the long process of holding hearings on violators, with all the fuel this is likely to provide the cause of protest, only to impose negligible punishments on those involved.

A further difficulty arises when the question of who should be penalized has to be faced. The most frequent choice of victims was "Those who took part in a particular action" (e.g. failing to move by a certain time, resisting arrest, etc.)—such a group was penalized by forty-seven institutions. Fourteen others reported punishing all those who took part in the protest, while twelve penalized "Those known to have been leaders, organizers or inciters of protest." It is not evident which of these selections meets any abstract standard of justice, but it is certain that whatever the approach used in inflicting institutional discipline, there will be many who will be convinced that justice was not meted out equably. This sentiment will be strengthened to the extent that an obvious element of the arbitrary entered in; asked to indicate how violators were identified, sixty colleges and universities reported that "Only protesters recognized by officials were identified"—more than the number selecting any other response. Further support will be given to those charging institutional injustice if any protester is punished both by the civil courts and by the institution; twenty-five campuses reported one or more such instances of "double jeopardy."

In the aftermath of a protest, the application of disciplinary measures against those involved in the protest is second only to the use of police as an explosive issue. Almost immediately after the demonstration the militant students generally question the "legitimacy" and justice of the disciplinary process. In many cases, the student left has instituted legal action to prohibit institutions from enforcing "vague and indefinite" regulations or rules which are considered in violation of civil liberties as provided in the United States Constitution. Their efforts have produced re-examination of codes of student conduct and a host of legal cases, some of which define more clearly than ever before the relationship of student rights to educational institutions' authority. Brown, Columbia, New York University, Illinois and Wisconsin are examples of institutions which modified their disciplinary processes in post-demonstration crises.

Given these difficulties, the college or university which takes the view that individual protesters are just like any other individual delinquents and should be dealt with by the same procedures will have to be lucky if it is not to play into the protesters' hands. It is seldom good strategy to apply a method designed for one kind of problem to another and totally different kind. At San Francisco State, efforts at disciplining George Murray, a graduate student and part-time faculty member who was involved in a raid on the student paper, disintegrated in complete confusion when the President decided that the panel which had originally heard the case and handed down a penalty was not, after all, the appropriate one. At Howard, imposition of penalties merely stimulated further violations, until eventually the protest reached such dimensions that the administration was forced to reverse itself. The cry for amnesty is always a fairly persuasive one, calculated to broaden the support for protest, and the desire for it is naturally very personal to the protesters. Once it is recognized that discipline or amnesty are themselves factors in the political situation, it becomes clear that treatment of offenders must be determined in part at least by political considerations if it is to serve the institution's goals. This truth is one which few administrators would care to admit in public.

Concession Strategies

The third available option for the institution is concession. This is, superficially at least, the simplest response: the students want something, the administration gives it to them, and all is sweetness and light once more. If by some strange coincidence all sides can agree on the wisdom of a proposed change, protest becomes unnecessary; but major protests develop and focus on precisely those concessions that have been resisted, for it is the resistance which builds up the pressure.

The college or university which contemplates giving the protesters part at least of what they want generally has three kinds of cost to calculate, three *prima facie* restraints. The first is the cost in terms of the intrinsic change contemplated; money that may have to be diverted from other projects, students diverted from a sound and orthodox course into what may be a disastrous experiment, faculty members of dubious standing retained at the expense of obtaining superior replacements, and so on. If the institution is reluctant to make the change save under pressure, it is likely that it views the proposal as a retrograde step.

The second kind of cost is in support of anti-protesters; by pleasing the activist, the university may be alienating trustees and potential donors, putting additional burdens or restraints on the faculty, increasing the difficulty of administration, outraging the state legislature and public, or even discouraging the non-protesting students. Many college presidents have found themselves caught in such a squeeze; before the development of student protest, students were an interest group which could be generally and conveniently ignored, but now their views may carry weight comparable to those of the faculty or the trustees in the mind of the purely pragmatic administrator.

The third and most imponderable cost is the possible impact of the concession on the course of protest itself. A version of the Domino Theory is widely held, according to which each appeasement of the activists merely encourages them to further demands, each pressed with additional fervor in light of the evidence that the administration is "soft." Whether or not the Domino Theory describes any particular reality can only be assessed by persons acquainted with campus in question: persons who are sensitive to the mood of the student body as a whole, who know its leaders individually, and who are aware of extent of support stirred by various possible demands. Anyone who is generally of the opinion that activists are troublemakers who seize upon the first issue that occurs to them as an excuse for disorder will naturally be a Domino Theorist. Anyone who believes that activist leaders are essentially moderate and practical persons who mean what they say will reject the Theory as cynical defeatism. Neither will be right more than a part of the time.

It is evident that American colleges and universities are making considerable use of concession strategy. Of the 399 institutions which reported that some planning was undertaken *before* the protest reached its climax, 275 stated that this planning was partially or (in 134 cases) principally concerned with meeting the issues raised by the students and satisfying some of their requests. During this pre-protest period, 198 institutions reported that discussions were held between the administration and the protest leaders, while 287 administrations dealt with student government officials on the protest matter. At the height of the protest 54 percent of responding institutions reported that they took the initiative in negotiating the substantive issues with the students.

This process of negotiation was not mere maneuver, as Table 3 indicates.

TABLE 3

ACTION TAKEN ON THE SUBSTANTIVE PROTEST ISSUE

	Before the protest	During the protest	After the protest
Appointed a study group or committee.	96	29	79
Changed policy somewhat as urged by protesters.	32	27	102
Changed policy substantially as urged by protesters.	14	10	33
Other major changes were made.	11	6	22
No changes in policy were made.	135	140	160

While a pattern of concession was by no means uniform, it is apparent that institutions were ready to restudy their positions on the issues raised, and that a considerable number of them did make partial concessions on these issues. A few plainly conducted battlefield diplomacy by making concessions during the protest. It is of interest that more study groups were appointed before the protest than after; establishment of such groups may be seen as a prudent stratagem, but it appears that it is not a particularly effective one. The fact that a total of 218 policy changes were reported clearly indicates that concession strategies are popular, and protest an effective instrument for bringing about change.

Where persuasive and repressive strategies focus largely on the uncommitted parts of the campus community, concessions are aimed directly at changing the posture of the activists. In employing them, communication is vital; the negotiator who does not know what may be in the minds of his opponents is at a tremendous disadvantage. In this connection, it is interesting to note that during 1968–69, one of the commonest concessions was the establishment of Black or

Ethnic Studies programs in response to the call of black militants. Yet the minds of such militants are surely remote from those of the white middle-class academic administrators and faculty who make the concessions. Whether or not minority studies are academically justified, there must be considerable question whether they truly represent something that black militants want. It may be that black hostility towards society at large runs far deeper than that of other militants, and that these programs are purely symbolic of a much larger concern which will be barely touched by the concession made. Yet even if these experiments do turn out to be unrelated to the real roots of black alienation, it is conceivable that willingness to adopt them may in turn serve as a ritual but nonetheless convincing gesture of appeasement.

Concession strategies are likely to create strains within the institution. To many, the idea of yielding to pressure is repugnant. At meetings of the Princeton faculty during 1968, a long process of making concessions to student demands was punctuated by explanations that no concessions were being made, but things were being changed because it was right to do so; such reassurances were received with loud applause, and the process of conceding then resumed. Presidents who have made a career out of trimming their sails to the alumni or the governing board may have great difficulty in perceiving students as an equally deserving (because equally powerful) pressure group. Student militants are seldom distinguished for their good manners, and often lack the normal prerequisite of a good negotiator: an ability to be liked by his opponents. These inhibitions to sound negotiation will be reinforced if the school is held in the spotlight of publicity during its period of confrontation. When the television camera appears, student militants compete for greater exposure with ever more extreme and uncompromising statements, while administrators tend to become models of dignity and toughness under the magic eye of the public.

Nor is the university an organization suited to negotiation, for power tends to be dispersed within it. The dean of students may be able to make commitments for the president, but it may be impossible to promise curriculum change however willing he may be to see it, if this requires faculty approval. Negotiation is generally easier if power is centralized; student protest tends to hit those institutions at which it is most dispersed.

Further dispersal of power to include students within the regular decision-making structures of colleges and universities has been widely recommended as an antidote or a preventive measure for protest. Most protests are implicitly concerned with student power, so there would seem to be logic in hoping that to grant some power voluntarily would convert activists to use of established channels of policy-making. Whether with this motive or not, it is very clear that colleges and universities all over the country have been moving rapidly towards inclusion of students in policy-making positions, to the point where such arrangements are becoming universal. The number of institutions placing students on committees and holding open forums on policy or some equivalent has come close to doubling since the Berkeley outbreak in late 1964. Of those institutions which

TABLE 4

THE MOVE TO INVOLVE STUDENTS IN
INSTITUTIONAL POLICY-MAKING

Date Instituted:	n = 1244	Students sit on committees	Forums on institutional policy, etc.
1964 or earlier		50%	41%
1965–67		30%	27%
1967–68		10%	9%
Planned for 1968–69		3%	5%
No such arrangements		6%	18%

now have students on committees, 33 percent stated that they were included on "most or all major committees," while 72 percent reported that such arrangements had been expanded during 1967–68. Of those which held policy forums or the equivalent prior to 1967–68, forty-seven percent estimated that such mechanisms saw more use in 1967–68 than they had previously. It is difficult to avoid the inference that many of these reforms have been inspired by student protest and the desire to avoid it.

Whether such hopes are based on any sound foundation is less easy to see. In Table 5, the association between incidence and level of protest on the one hand, and a variety of indicators of student power on the other is shown. As can be seen, amount and levels of protest tend to be associated with more institutionalized student power, not less. Three kinds of causal explanations seem possible. One is that colleges and universities have yielded power to students when those students showed signs of activism, and not before. Another is that involving students in policy-making and giving them a measure of power and freedom whets their appetites for more, and that institu-

TABLE 5

INSTITUTIONALIZED STUDENT POWER AND LEVELS OF PROTEST

		Level of Violent	Protest: Obstructive	Physical	Diplomatic	None
Have students traditionally	yes	1%	5%	16%	23%	56%
played an important role in	no	2%	3%	14%	24%	57%
framing institutional policy?						
Students on most committees.		3%	5%	20%	26%	46%
Students on some committees.		1%	4%	13%	24%	58%
Students not on committees.		0	0	2%	12%	86%
Are there periodic forums	yes	1%	4%	14%	26%	54%
on institutional policy?	no	1%	3%	11%	15%	69%
Is there	Virtually none	3%	9%	25%	25%	38%
faculty or	Some	0.5%	3%	13%	28%	56%
administrative	General					
supervision of	sup'n	2%	2%	8%	17%	71%
the student	Specific					
paper?	sup'n	1%	2%	4%	20%	73%

tional concessions thus have the reverse effect of that presumably intended. A third explanation, which may be better than either of the other two, is that student power and student protest are not directly causally connected, but that both are the product of similar factors, such as institutional status, caliber of students and size of enrollment. All that it seems safe to conclude here is that while there may be excellent reasons for involving students in institutional affairs, there is no quantitative evidence that to do so will lessen the chances of subsequent protest.

The Impact of Protest on Colleges and Universities

While it may still be too early to assess the overall impact of student protest on colleges and universities in America, the Protest Survey indicates that administrators tend to be optimistic. Asked to check any of the following nine consequences of protest, the selections of the 535 institutions who experienced protest were as follows:

The protest and its handling enhanced the standing of the institution with many people.	150
Most students have become less sympathetic to protest activities.	143
The treatment of the protest by the press and other media tended to hurt the institution.	68
The protest has worsened relations between the institution and the local community.	47
Most students have become more likely to support protests.	39
Relationships between Administration and Faculty have deteriorated somewhat.	37
The State Legislature has become less supportive, more critical of the institution.	24
Relationships between the Administration and the students have deteriorated somewhat.	22
The institution has become less attractive to potential faculty members.	8

More than half the institutions did not indicate that any of these effects applied to them. It is thus apparent that only a small minority of administrators feel that protest has hurt their institutions or relationships within them, while a substantial number are confident that their handling of protest paid dividends in student support and community respect.

Comparisons of the aftermath at those schools which punished the protesters and those which did not reveals no clear pattern; despite the general impression that the public wants a tough line pursued with activists, the punitive institutions and the non-punitive ones give rather similar estimates of the impact of their policies on faculty, students and public. Only forty-seven (of 535) indicated that they felt the demonstration worsened relations between the institution and the local community. This seems to run contrary to common sense and the "facts" as presented by the press and it could very well indicate a perception-gap concerning the effects of campus protests on the larger community, especially political and legislative bodies. Scenes of anarchy and chaos may deter not only continued financial support by private donors and legislatures but also promising students. It is reported, for example, that Columbia suffered a dramatic drop in applications for admission as a result of the May, 1968, affair; trouble with the institution's fund-raising campaign is also expected.

Conditions in Wisconsin exemplify one possible aftermath of violent protest. More than twenty bills were introduced in February, 1969, as means to combat campus protest. Included among these were measures to eliminate faculty tenure; to require a non-resident's fee at least five times the resident tuition; to render ineligible for admission to the University and the State Universities and for employment by state agencies any person convicted of treason, sabotage, display of seditious flag or emblem, and desecration or improper use of the flag; to make ineligible for state loans, scholarships, and tuition remissions any students who broke college regulations; to reduce out-of-state enrollments; to require the expulsion of students and dismissal of faculty members who participate in disruptive demonstrations, and the discipline of faculty members who "honor, aid or abet students in strikes, demonstrations, and riots," and to authorize the governor to take over such disrupted campuses by proclaiming a state of emergency. Others proposed to limit the enrollments of state institutions and to require the Madison campus to reduce its 34,000 to 30,000; to prohibit faculty and administration personnel from recruiting out-of-state students (except for athletics); and to bar any person convicted of a felony or of a misdemeanor stemming from student turmoil to attend a state institution of higher learning for two years and six months respectively. Another bill proposed to permit campus authorities to declare the campus off-limits to persons other than students, faculty, and staff personnel. The use of sound-amplifying equipment on campus without permission was proposed as a misdemeanor. Some of these have become law.

For a public institution there is always the possibility that obstructive demonstrations will create majority legislative support to investigate not only the protest but also other areas of university activity about which there had been only minimal minority concern previously. At Wisconsin, one legislator suggested that the pending budget of the University of Wisconsin be delayed until its President was fired. Partly as a result of the legislative hue and cry, two investigative committees were authorized to look into the obstructive demonstrations and to examine the structure and administration of all of higher education in the state. This has more significance when related to the legislature's resolution of praise to the State University System for expelling ninety-one Oshkosh blacks for a destructive demonstration. Still other legislative proposals suggested adding legislation watchdogs to the UW Board of Regents or the creation of a legislative liaison committee with the Regents.

Many measures proposed for Wisconsin also appeared in the California legislature, while Governor Reagan and other conservative politicians made as much political capital as possible out of the situation, and San Francisco State President Hayakawa found himself in a position to launch a political career because he had acquired a tough reputation. According to the Field Poll, 72 percent of Californians in 1969 favored expulsion for students defying authorities, compared with 66 percent in 1967. Thirty-eight percent strongly opposed student participation in college rule-making where only 19 percent had done so two years earlier; during the same period, support for the right of a professor in a state supported institution to speak and teach as he sees fit declined from 32 percent to 23 percent.

Other states where punitive legislation was proposed included Colorado, Iowa, Kansas, Maryland, Michigan, Missouri, New York, North Carolina, Rhode Island, Tennessee, Texas and Utah. President Nixon has denounced protest and congratulated counter-protesters, and Congress has debated action against them. Whatever those in academia may think, it is difficult to avoid the conclusion that protest has hurt higher education in the eyes of politicians and the public.

Although there may be considerable difference of opinion concerning the effect of protest on groups outside institutions of higher learning, it is clear that protest has effected significant change within colleges and universities. These changes may be grouped in the following general areas: (1) student participation in the governance of higher education; (2) abandonment of the *in loco parentis* philosophy in higher education; (3) more explicit codes of student conduct and behavior; (4) re-evaluation of the due process system for students as evaluated by American law; (5) provision for more student involvement in the educational and political process; (6) reconsideration of traditional content, methods, structures, and evaluations of collegiate instruction and (7) continued politicization of academic and professional disciplines. Not all of these changes are improvements; nor are all institutions subject to the same rate and method of implementation. Institutions have responded both in bureaucratic "adjustments" and in basic attitudinal changes concerning the role of the student and the external relationship of the institution to the larger society. But whatever the outcome of these institutional responses, higher education will never be the same as before the massive use of the protest tactic.

The tactic holds an awesome mixture of promise and threat. By its use, such stalwart mainstays of academia as the one-way mass lecture, the vested-interest departmental structures and governance methods, and even the graduate school and its nineteenth century elitist approaches, are feeling the tremors of change. Curricula that are developed for interests and needs other than those of students are being questioned, self-protecting non-evaluative approaches to teaching by departmental powers are less and less secure, and decision-making without the involvement of students and their needs is less common. On the other hand, political stance is becoming more important in academic disciplines and teaching than balanced inquiry and judgments, while freedom of inquiry and speech is often attacked if such inquiry and speech does not lead to the "truth" of the radical left. Legitimacy is endangered by a new definition of self-proclaimed morality, and long and hard fought victories for public support of massive higher education are being reversed. Over and above these effects is the more critical one of feeding an increasingly violent society more violence.

The crucial question in this setting is whether desirable changes in collegiate institutions can be brought about by tactics other than disruption and violence. When these changes are effected by sustained student concern applied in legitimate and non-disruptive ways, they are not as likely to produce the undesirable side-effects which are now so evident. The most severe indictment of higher education is that faculty members and administrators have been so unreceptive to change that reform must be pressed by the students they are to serve in ways of their own choosing. It remains to be seen whether administrators and faculty can regain their leadership roles.

6

SOCIAL EXCHANGE THEORY
AND THE UNIVERSITY

*by Daniel Kornstein and Peter Weissenberg**

THE PRESENT ERA of student protest in America, which began with the Berkeley demonstrations of 1964 and reached its most violent point so far at Columbia four years later, has been more described than analyzed. Numerous causal hypotheses have been advanced, but few attempts have been made at developing a conceptual framework within which protest can be understood. Social exchange theory offers one possible interpretive structure. We shall here attempt to apply it to student protest in general, and to events at Columbia University in particular.

The process of exchange had gone on for many centuries before a formalized theory was developed.[1] The basic tenets of social exchange theory were set down by George Homans[2] and Peter Blau.[3] As an explanation of interpersonal and group behavior, social exchange differs from purely economic exchange in that the latter includes some sort of contractual agreement that specifies what is to be exchanged. Social exchange implies an unspecified obligation on the part of the recipient to return a gift or favor of equal or almost equal value. The donor expects that his gift will be returned, though

* Daniel Kornstein is a Graduate Assistant and Dr. Peter Weissenberg is an Assistant Professor of Management Science in the Department of Business Enterprise and Accounting at the State University of New York at Binghamton.

he may not know exactly how or when. The "when" is significant; an obligation must not be returned too quickly or too slowly. The receiver will reciprocate voluntarily because he may want to discharge the obligation, or because he may want social approval. Satisfactions from exchange depend on the expectations of the individuals as well as the actual reward.[4] If there is no reciprocity, there may not be any future exchange, or there will be unequal exchange. It is unequal exchange that gives rise to power among individuals and in groups.

In their discussions of exchange theory both Homans and Blau used the concept of profit. Each exchange transaction has a certain cost(s) and reward(s) associated with it. The exchanges that are the most profitable (rewards less costs) are the ones that people enter into. Thus profit is a decision criterion by which individuals evaluate exchange relationships.

For this analysis the most significant aspect of exchange theory is Blau's power schema. Basically, power results from unequal exchange; there is an imbalance of obligations incurred in social transactions. If an individual can control the supply of scarce resources, he will have power over those who demand this resource. By supplying scarce resources, the supplier may obligate others to him unless certain alternatives are available. Blau described the four alternatives to compliance that may be open to individuals. At the same time he enumerated the requirements that powerholders must meet if they are to retain power.

The first alternative is to receive benefits, but to provide inducements to the supplier. This alternative implies that the recipient also has control over some strategic resource. The requirement for power in this instance is for the powerholder to remain indifferent to these inducements.

The second alternative is to obtain the resource from another supplier. Consequently the requirement for power is to control all the strategic resources. If this alternative is to be open, there must be a competitive rather than a monopolistic market.

The third alternative (and one that is increasing in popularity) is to take the resource by force. This requires physical coercion, but nonetheless it is one way of securing independence. Those who have power or the scarce resource retain it by law and order. In any social system there have to be rules if the society is to function.

The final alternative to compliance is to do without. Individuals can often survive if they modify their needs or aspirations. If a group of people (not just one individual) can form a new value structure that negates the worth of the resources, they will remain independent. If those in power wish to stay in power they must perpetuate the current system of values.

Before attempting to apply social exchange theory to student protest, it may be helpful to consider the institutional structure of universities. In a general sense, the university is a work organization; it performs certain tasks in order to accomplish a set of goals. The traditional structure of the university is characterized by formal lines of authority, with the administration as the main source of power. The university, however, is a professional organization, and the line-staff relationship is usually different in professional organizations. The professionals should have the line authority because they perform the major tasks of the university.

Administrators offer advice about the economic and organizational implications of the various activities planned by the professionals. The final decision is, functionally speaking, in the hands of the various professionals and their decision-making bodies.[5]

Although the university is a professional organization, the line authority has rested with the administration at the more traditionally structured schools like Columbia.

A basic goal of the student power movement is to place severe limits on the power of the administration, and in some instances to limit the power of the faculty. Students want a greater say in policy making and in decision-making; they want to make the social rules and regulations. The more radical groups such as the SDS want students to determine the goals of the university. The conflict thus centers about the role of the student in the university. Is he a client or a member of the academic community? If the relationship is of the client-professional type, then the students would be expected to adhere to the rules and regulations. However, many students today feel that they should be full members of the community, and should therefore have a voice in the decision-making process.

Columbia University offers instruction to over 20,000 students in two major undergraduate colleges (one for men and one for women) and several professional and graduate schools in which the majority of students are registered. A privately controlled, non-sectarian, co-educational institution, originally founded as King's College approximately 200 years ago, Columbia is a relatively wealthy university located very close to the heart of the large black and Puerto Rican ghetto area of the largest city in America. The university has been controlled by a Board of Trustees dominated by rich, prominent, powerful whites and has not been notably sensitive to ghetto concerns. Suffering from a poor quality of student life, faculty detachment, outdated and unresponsive organizational structure, and a unique geographical setting which intensifies strains of black-white community relations, Columbia exploded in the events of April, 1968.[6]

The immediate setting for the explosion was a demonstration by the Columbia SDS on Tuesday, April 23, at the Sundial, a campus rallying point for demonstrators, to demand that Columbia sever its association with the Institute for Defense Analyses, that students (primarily the SDS leadership) who had demonstrated against IDA on March 23 in disobedience to President Grayson Kirk's ban on indoor demonstrations be given public hearings "with full rights of due process," and that there would be no discipline upon "those who opposed Columbia's unjust policies." The SDS demonstration was joined by the Black Students Afro-American Society, a relatively small and previously politically weak group, protesting the construction of a new gymnasium in Morningside Park, the only open space available to the nearby ghetto inhabitants. The two protests became one as the crowd of demonstrators moved toward nearby Low Library, to be detoured by a line of counter-demonstrators, then on to the excavation site of the proposed gym where they were discouraged by police. Returning to the Sundial, the dissident students responded to their leaders' exhortations to take a hostage in retaliation for the arrest of one of their group at the gym site by occupying Hamilton Hall, a classroom building in which the administrative offices of Columbia College are also located. The demonstrators, including SAS and SDS members, then attempted to force Dean Coleman to negotiate the issues, but he refused to do so under duress. He was subsequently trapped with two other officials in his office for twenty-six hours during which the black students expelled the white militants from Hamilton Hall early Wednesday morning, April 24. The SDS group proceeded to occupy Low Library, in which President Kirk's office is located, while other Negro groups from Harlem joined in support of the blacks in Hamilton Hall.

Counter-demonstrators organized to confront those holding the buildings. On the evening of the 24th, School of Architecture students took over Avery Hall and on the 25th, another classroom building, Fayerweather Hall, was occupied by students not ordinarily part of the SDS group. Thus by Thursday afternoon, April 25, student groups controlled four major buildings on the Columbia campus. A fifth, Mathematics, was soon added. The original student demands were more strongly worded and lengthened to include demands that the ban on indoor demonstrations and the probation sentence on the March 23 IDA demonstrators be rescinded, and that full amnesty be granted to all involved in the present protest.

The administration refused to accede to the demands and the students refused to leave the captured buildings. The university did agree to a temporary halt in the construction of the new gymnasium but the building remained occupied. Negotiation by the Ad Hoc Faculty Group during the week of April 23–29 deterred the administration from bringing in the police; [7] on April 29, the police were called, and removed the demonstrators from the five occupied buildings. The fact-finding Cox Commission reported that 696 persons were arrested and more than one hundred were injured in the process.[8] Another clash with police erupted the following day when students demonstrated at the entrance to the university. Alleged "police brutality" caused many people not associated with the university to support the students. Further confrontations occurred on May 22–23 when Hamilton Hall was seized again by SDS leader Mark Rudd and his supporters, producing a chaotic melee when the police cleared the building and the campus.[9] Most spring semester classes at Columbia had eventually to be abandoned.

During the summer Dr. Grayson Kirk, President of the University, resigned in an explicit attempt to restore some unity to the campus. Fall registration was disrupted by SDS, demanding the reinstatement of those not permitted to register because of their participation in the April–May takeovers. The Fall demonstrations were generally unsuccessful, but the peace established on the campus was an uneasy and uncertain one.

The events of 1968 have brought about considerable changes in the structure of the university. Previously, major policies were made by the administration, working closely with the Board of Trustees; both students and faculty appeared to acquiesce in this situation. General faculty meetings were never held, the absence of a big enough room being given as a sufficient reason for this. Yet the student demonstrations, although they have split the faculty into numerous factions, have notably increased its power. It was a committee of twelve professors, appointed on April 30, which began to lay plans for long range peace at Columbia. By the end of the summer, many of their recommendations had already been adopted.[10]

Blau defined power as follows:

The ability of persons or groups to impose their will on others despite resistance through deterrence either in the form of withholding regularly supplied rewards or in the form of punishment, inasmuch as the former as well as the latter constitute, in effect, a negative sanction.[11]

Several implications of this definition should be noted. The concept of power denotes a recurrent ability of individuals or groups to impose their will on others. Influencing *one* particular decision is not power over others; power has to be a continuous process. A second implication is that power has an element of voluntarism. An individual can choose the "punishment" instead of compliance. This, says Blau, distinguishes power from physical coercion where the individual has no choice. Power is inherently asymmetrical. The source of power is onesided dependence, and interdependence indicates a lack of power. The direct source of power is the ability to control needed resources. The major resource which the university controls, and which has given it power over the students, is the ability to grant degrees which certify that the student has received an appropriate education.

Students come to the university on their own volition ostensibly to learn and to take advantage of the university's resources. So, if the students elect to go to college, they must "exchange" something in return for their education. Tuition and fees are exchanged, in part, for the cost of the education, but something else also is exchanged in the process. Under the traditional structure, the exchange was that the students complied with university rules and policies. The university (administration and board of trustees) controlled the scarce resources, thus creating an imbalance of exchange, and so, power for the university. Until recently, this imbalance went unchallenged. The student power movement now argues that the principal goal of the university should be to serve the students, and that the university is, or should be, a democratic community. The students are, in effect, calling for a major reorganization of the university system and goal structure. One must examine the alternatives available to them to see whether or not their demands are likely to be met.

One alternative that is open to the students is to obtain the resource or service from another source. During the riots at Columbia, strike leaders were setting up "free university" classes while the campus was in a turmoil. Many radical students feel that a free university that serves the students is the only viable structure for learning. At present, however, the free university faces many difficulties. It lacks the basic resources to conduct organized research. It is doubtful that business and professional organizations will recognize the free university as legitimate higher education. More fundamentally, it lacks the attraction for the most important resource, a wide variety and sufficient supply of competent professors. In the short-run at least, the free university is not a relevant alternative for most students. If in the long run it proves to be one, then the traditionally structured universities will no longer have a monopoly over a scarce resource and their power over students will decline.

A second alternative would be to simply do without the resource. Students could lessen their demands for education, and new ideologies regarding the value of education could arise. But this alternative seems irrelevant. Society ascribes a high value to advanced education, and without it the individual's chances for success are severely reduced. For the most part, students attend college to better their lives, and there is a low probability that the value of education will decline. Since the current values regarding education are being perpetuated, the powerholders in the university can maintain their power because they control this resource. Pressure on the students, however, to obtain some control of the processes of acquiring an education, which is in essence the scarce resource that they cannot do without, comes from their perception that the costs involved in continuing to submit to the power of the university in exchange for the granting of the degree are too high under present conditions.

Another alternative that Blau described was to obtain the resource by force. The action by the Columbia students was at first an attempt to force their demands upon the university. However, student coercion encountered resistance from the university officials, and after some hesitation, the police were called in; rebellious violence was met with legitimized violence. Blau's model implies that the forces of law and order will generally operate to protect the powerholder against coercive attempts.

The fourth alternative that may be open to the students is to supply other inducements to the powerholders in the university. This implies that the students have control over some strategic resource. If the university is to maintain power it will have to remain indifferent to the student inducements. Before the student power movement, the university could remain indifferent to the student demands because the only scarce resource was education. However, the Berkeley demonstrations and, to an even greater extent, the Columbia disorders, illustrated that the students had suddenly developed the realization that they could withhold from the university a resource which had been available to them in the past, but which they had not been completely aware of: the obedience or orderliness which the university needed in order to maintain the educational process. The result of withholding this resource from the university, of course, was the violent protest itself. The recognition of this ability to withhold a previously unrecognized resource, "orderliness or obedience," is perhaps the most significant effect of the riots at Columbia. The students have developed a negative resource that changed the imbalance of exchange.

Thus the students can threaten protest and the university can threaten sanctions. This situation is what Prof. William F. Whyte terms "negative exchange." Instead of the usual form of exchange that Blau described where positive values are exchanged, negative reciprocity is an exchange of more or less equal negative values. This situation tends to be unstable, and the normal functions of those involved cannot be carried on.[12]

Social exchange theory may also illuminate the new circumstances in which the faculty find themselves. The faculty are essentially a professional body with a commitment to a discipline. The university needs them to carry on its business, and so long as the supply of faculty tends to be equal to or greater than the demand for their services, the faculty does not control a scarce resource. However, a number of factors have been in operation since World War II which have altered this situation. The expansion in enrollment has meant a correspondingly greater demand for qualified professors, and at the same time the rising level of such qualification in the shape of an increased insistence on possession of the doctorate has tended to restrict supply. Faculty have become increasingly attached to their disciplines, necessarily at the cost of loyalty to the particular institution that employs them. Further, opportunities for employment outside academia are on the increase. Faculty have become "cosmopolitans" in Gouldner's sense of the word.[13] They have a resource to exchange with the university, and the latter's power over them has been correspondingly reduced.

This new independence can enable them to function as a strong countervailing force to the administration. At Cornell, for example, they have acted as a separate but powerful body, restraining the administration from responding to student demands in coercive fashion while quieting the students by pressing for certain changes in the university's policy. Blau has suggested that there may be another exchange relationship between faculty and students.[14] A faculty member may seek approval or status from the students, and will therefore attempt to provide services to them. This could encourage the faculty member to ally himself with student movements. If such motives are to be operative, it is implied that the administration no longer has power over a faculty member—a condition which the institution of tenure has done much to bring about.

The crisis at Columbia was thus one in which two of the participant groups came to a fuller realization of resources available to them, and of their consequent power position. Whether both faculty and students will be able to maintain their position of increased influence at Columbia and elsewhere remains to be seen; this may depend largely on whether their new resources continue to be so readily available. It is not at present clear whether the expansion in faculty or student power may not bring about a corresponding reduction for the other. We have here attempted to apply the descriptive power of social exchange theory. Our future task will be to see if the model can predict, and to devise the appropriate means for making the necessary empirical tests.

NOTES

[1] M. Mauss, *The Gift* (Glencoe, The Free Press, 1954).

[2] George C. Homans, *Social Behavior: Its Elementary Forms* (New York, Harcourt, Brace and World, Inc., 1961).

[3] Peter M. Blau, *Exchange and Power in Social Life* (New York, John Wiley & Sons, Inc., 1964).

[4] *Ibid.,* p. 143.

[5] Amitai Etzioni, *Modern Organizations* (Englewood Cliffs, N.J., Prentice-Hall, Inc., 1964), p. 81.

[6] Cox Commission, *Crisis at Columbia,* Report of the Fact-Finding Commission Appointed to Investigate the Disturbance at Columbia University in April and May, 1968 (New York: Vintage Books, 1968), pp. 30–53; see also Jerry L. Avorn, Robert Friedman, and members of the staff of the *Columbia Daily Spectator, Up Against the Ivy Wall* (New York, Atheneum, 1968), pp. 1–27.

[7] Cox Commission, *op. cit.,* pp. 99–140.

[8] *Ibid.,* p. 142; see also "Rebellion at Columbia," in *The New Republic,* May 16, 1968.

[9] Cox Commission, *op. cit.,* pp. 180–82; Avorn *et al., op. cit.,* pp. 253–76; *The New York Times,* May 19, 1968, p. 1.

[10] *The New York Times,* May 1, 1968, p. 43c; September 16, 1968, pp. 1, 50.

[11] Blau, *op. cit.,* p. 117.

[12] William Foote Whyte, "Toward a Transactional Theory of Social Relations," unpublished manuscript, 1968.

[13] Alvin W. Gouldner, "Cosmopolitans and Locals," *Administrative Science Quarterly,* Vol. 2, No. 3 (December, 1957), pp. 282–292.

[14] Letter to the authors.

FIVE

Perspectives on Protest

1

BLACK PROTEST

by Durward Long

IT WAS NOT until 1968–69 that protest by black students came to overshadow other kinds of campus activism in its frequency and intensity. The level and style of black protest has made several sharp changes of direction during the sixties. It would be rash indeed to predict what comes next, but it seems safe to assume at least that the present cannot be understood without some historical perspective.

In January, 1960, four students at North Carolina Agricultural and Technical College, a predominantly black institution, were discussing segregation and what could be done about it. They decided that talk should lead to action, sat at a local "whites only" drugstore lunch counter and were refused service, were told to leave and refused, and were arrested for trespassing. It could soon be seen that this quiet action had come at a moment when many Southern blacks were ready to begin defying the segregationist laws, patterns and institutions under which they had lived for so long. Eight days later, 25 students from Winston-Salem Teachers College were arrested after a similar sit-in. Between February 8 and 12, further sit-ins at segregated facilities were staged by students throughout North Carolina; from North Carolina College, Fayetteville Teachers College, Johnson C. Smith University, Barber-Scotia College, Elizabeth City Teachers College, Kittrell College, Shaw University, Friendship

Junior College, Clinton Junior College, St. Augustine College and William Penn High School in High Point. The sit-in movement spread rapidly to Virginia, where students from Hampton Institute, Virginia State University, Virginia State College and Norcom High School in Portsmouth became involved, and to Tennessee, where Fisk University proved to have many potential black militants. In the deep South, Alabama was the first state affected, with Alabama State College students undertaking a sit-in in Montgomery on February 25, while others at Tuskegee Institute boycotted classes and staged a march. Black-white relations in the South had entered a new phase, and it was black students from segregated institutions who had brought this about.

Two other kinds of events occurred early in 1960 which helped shape the struggle for racial justice. In March and April, widespread disorders occurred in South Africa; the police dealt with a crowd of protesting blacks at Sharpeville by opening fire upon them, killing fifty-six. The brutal consequences of segregation could hardly have been better dramatized. In California, college students initiated the kind of demonstrations which have now become so familiar, protesting the execution of Caryl Chessman and later besieging the House Committee on Un-American Activities in San Francisco; the possibilities of direct student action were being explored. When a conference at Raleigh drew these various threads together and established the Student Non-Violent Coordinating Committee (SNCC), the stage was set for the next few years; student activists had discovered the weapons with which institutional racism could be fought in America.

The next four years saw an intensive struggle for civil rights in the South. In 1961, the Congress on Racial Equality (CORE) organized freedom rides to protest segregated transportation, while SNCC ran voter registration campaigns in such unpromising areas as Pike County, Mississippi. Students in the North organized pickets around chain stores whose segregationist policies were the subject of Southern protest. Many white students spent summers in the South, and not a few encountered institutionalized violence, tolerated and sometimes perpetrated by the police. More than a thousand were arrested for demonstrating in Albany, Georgia, during the summer of 1962. Several civil rights workers were killed in the more backward parts of the South. Demonstrations eventually reached massive proportions with the bus boycott organized in Montgomery and the march from Selma to Montgomery, both organized by Martin Luther King.

At least three characteristics differentiated black student efforts during this period from the pattern which was to develop in the later sixties. The first was the target: Southern social and governmental institutions and the mores of Southern society generally, and not the administrations of universities or any agency widely respected outside the South. Secondly, the participants were black and white, working together. Organizations such as SNCC, CORE and NAACP encouraged white membership, and often had whites in leadership positions, and the missionary spirit of Northern college students temporarily in the South was generally seen as a sign of hope on the part of the vastly larger number of Southern blacks. Thirdly, the style was non-violent. Influenced by the Christian pacifism of Martin Luther King, the civil rights workers employed marches, pickets, boycotts and sit-ins to dramatize racial injustice and stir the conscience of the public. When arrested, they submitted, when attacked, they seldom retaliated; their strategy was one of moral superiority, with its attendant costs in suffering and occasional martyrdom. These characteristics placed the protesters squarely within the main-stream American tradition, and earned them considerable admiration. There was, in the early sixties, none of the all-embracing hostility towards the "establishment," whether in universities or the federal government, which was to be expressed later; nothing which could be termed "inverted racism" had yet appeared, nor had the civil rights movement linked itself with other radical thrusts directed at American foreign policy, urban problems or campus reform.

This situation began to change in 1964. At the Democratic National Convention that year, the Mississippi Freedom Democratic Party delegation attempted to dislodge the "regular" delegation from the state; an unfavorable compromise offer was refused, and the delegation was not seated. At the election which followed, black candidates captured very few offices in the South; when Julian Bond was elected to the Georgia legislature the following year, the victory was snatched away by the entrenched powers, who refused to seat him because of his views on Vietnam. Such developments contributed to an increasing distrust of the normal political channels as viable means to reform. Meanwhile, direct action at Berkeley illuminated the potential of other methods.

In 1965, another ingredient was added. For a few days, the Watts district of Los Angeles was effectively out of control, as blacks rioted, burned and looted. Disorders of varying proportions have occurred in the ghettos of almost every major city in the United States during years since. Nothing had previously demonstrated the depth and nihilism of black alienation, or had pitted the black poor and the white power structure in such flat opposition. Instead of falling in with the goals and strategies of white liberal idealists and intellectuals, the blacks had performed an existential act—irrational, violent, aimed at no coherent or constructive purpose, yet vividly expressive of an attitude almost incomprehensible to most whites.

The ghetto uprisings posed a crucial problem for black leadership, for to condemn them was to condemn a substantial portion of black America, yet to do anything else would break with the liberal tradition and the white liberal allies amongst whom most black leaders had functioned until that time. Out of this conflict grew the slogan "Black Power." [1] As conveniently ambiguous yet emotionally satisfying as most successful slogans, Black Power has come to be advocated by black political leaders of widely differing perspectives. In May, 1966, Adam Clayton Powell spoke of "black power" to achieve God-given rights. Almost simultaneously, participants in the Memphis to Jackson march were chanting: "We want black power, we want black power." A position paper by the members of the Atlanta Project of the Student Non-Violent Coordinating Committee submitted to SNCC in 1966 carried the theme, "If we are to proceed to true liberation, we must cut ourselves from white people. . . ." [2] SNCC leader Stokely Carmichael announced his views on Black Power in a lecture by that title at the University of California at Berkeley on November 19, 1966,[3] and in 1967 he published a book of the same title, co-authored with Roosevelt University political science professor Charles V. Hamilton.

During the latter half of the sixties, the pendulum has gradually swung towards the more militant black position. Faith in democratic processes has been eroded by the successive murders of leaders in whom many blacks could trust: John F. Kennedy, Malcolm X, Martin Luther King and Robert F. Kennedy. It has been further damaged by the slowness of change; fifteen years after *Brown vs. Board of Education*, most black children still attend segregated and inferior schools, and after numerous civil rights bills have been enacted, many blacks find themselves as poor and underprivileged as ever. The discovery that anger can produce more action than suffering and pleading has been a powerful lesson. After 1966, established organizations like SNCC passed into the hands of anarchic leaders like

H. Rap Brown, while para-military organizations on the boundary lines of legality suddenly flourished. The Black Panthers have become the most prominent of the latter, with Eldridge Cleaver, now on the run, and Huey P. Newton, in jail for shooting an Oakland policeman, their most charismatic leaders.

In view of such developments on the national scene, it is hardly surprising that black protest has become increasingly militant in recent years, until it has overshadowed all other kinds of protest in 1968–69. Yet the willingness of black students to employ force or the threat of violence on campus reflects the rather sudden change and the acceptance of the concept by college blacks in 1967. Black students on predominantly white campuses prior to 1966 were typically from middle-class families which had traditionally occupied leadership positions in the black community. These students generally saw no conflict between themselves and the predominantly white institution in which they were enrolled or with the middle-class aspirations of other students. Somewhat protected by their environment from the worst excesses of racism, any discrimination which they did encounter was generally considered as inevitable and historical, to be overcome and eventually changed by following Booker T. Washington's exhortation to acquire skills with which to contribute to the larger society. Such students were quite resistant to the notion of Black Power and, in fact, black student leaders at the National Student Congress of 1966 rejected the concept when it was offered by their more militant white brothers. They had not yet come to understand or accept the implications of "institutional racism."

By the fall of 1967, however, the stance of black students on white campuses was a different one. It was obvious that they, too, advocated the use of Black Power to gain their objectives. The radical change in SNCC was reflected in the militant position of black students. The "Black is Beautiful" sentiment for a separate identity had won the support of large numbers of black students all over the nation, among those attending predominantly black institutions as well as those on white campuses. After a summer of aggressive racial demands which erupted into riots in several instances, participating students could hardly be expected to eschew the same methods of force on college campuses. The change in attitude was forcefully demonstrated in the action and organization of black delegates attending the 1967 National Student Congress. They maintained solidarity in forcing the white delegates to endorse a resolution calling for the liberation of race "by any means necessary." During the same summer, a Black Power conference of over 1,000 blacks assembled in July, and the Conference for a New Politics in Chicago in August set the stage for black humiliation of "whitey" and the tone of black separatism.

This dramatic about face may be explained in part by the large increases in enrollments of blacks from other than middle-class homes, which was stimulated by several provisions of the Higher Education Act of 1965, by other federal legislation, and by intensive efforts by colleges to recruit disadvantaged blacks. Between 1965 and 1968 many institutions developed several types of programs for the disadvantaged which, in the early period at least, emphasized expanding educational opportunities for Negroes. These first programs generally focused on assistance to "developing" institutions (the common euphemism for predominantly black colleges) and the exchange of students from those institutions with students from the white institutions. By the spring of 1967, these programs had evolved to emphasize the recruitment of black students for enrollment in predominantly white institutions. In many places, admissions standards were lowered for culturally disadvantaged students. Programs for the disadvantaged were more and more designed primarily to bring more blacks to the white campus, and more and more of them were recruited from the inner cities. Wherever they came from, they were very conscious of Black Power and often adopted quite a different value system than that of students of their color prior to 1965.

But the change was also due in part to the rapidly increasing intellectual base to the Black Power movement which gave it more dynamism and helped to increase its unity. The writings of Eldridge Cleaver,[4] Kenneth Clark,[5] Stokely Carmichael, and Franz Fanon[6] gave blacks an ideological structure. The passionate loyalty of a new breed of young Negro intellectuals to promoting black identity gave the movement additional energy. Carmichael and Hamilton called attention to the fact that "The black intellectual is coming home." Carmichael discerned that "one of the most promising developments . . . is the new mood among black college students. . . ." He, like many college administrators later, found the agitation on campuses to have "less of a moral and more of a political orientation." [7]

Indeed, many of the middle-class blacks were beginning to adopt the Black Power mode. As late as 1967 a study of the middle-class Negro reported that his attitude towards the poor black resembled that of the middle-class white towards the poor of his race. Another study, a year previously, indicated that poorer urban Negroes especially despised the black bourgeoisie for their imitation of whites, what was sometimes "Hi-Fi Uncle Tomism." Black Power aspired to remove these attitudinal barriers and to unite all blacks, the middle class and the poverty stricken.[8]

The new posture brought about shifts in campus life. The goal of integration, long the aim of black and white liberals, was suddenly replaced with an insistence on black pride and its concomitant, black separatism. All-Negro fraternities and sororities revived at some institutions. As if by national design, black student organizations sprang up across the country. They went by a variety of names: Afro-American Student Union (Berkeley, Northwestern), African and American Society (Harvard), Association of Black Collegians (Cornell, Princeton, St. Louis University), Association of Black Students (Wayne State), Black Law Students Union (Yale), Concerned Black People (Wisconsin, Madison), Negro Alliance for Progress (University of Texas), Students Afro-American Society (Columbia), United Black Students (Ohio State) and Black Students' Union (California universities and colleges). For purposes of political base-building, some black students merged with Third World Liberation Fronts and other groups which could encompass Mexican Americans and less numerous ethnic minorities. African and West Indian Negroes were also enrolled as allies, and African dress, hairstyles and traditions began to be adopted by black Americans. To what extent there was central direction or coordination of the new movement it is difficult to say, but certainly some black leaders have implied the existence of unity, while the disciplined character of some of the black campus protests suggests a greater degree of cohesion than is manifested by many white militant groups.

One of the less militant groups, the National Student Association, also renewed its concern with racial protest in the fall of 1968, sponsoring with Notre Dame University a national conference of 290 students from 84 campuses to discuss "institutional racism" and to formulate plans to attack discriminatory policies. Suggestions discussed by the conference included pressuring accrediting agencies to demand more relevant and effective courses for black education, developing definitions for "racial malfeasance" to cut off federal funds, and the dissemination of information about racist practices and protests. The conference agreed to reassemble in the spring to discuss tactics.[9] This renewal of concern by the NSA may very well stem from the increasing tendency for black students to go it alone with their own local organizations and, in many cases, black rejection of the leadership of NSA affiliates. To assist the NSA in its program of involvement with black students the Ford Foundation awarded the student organization a $7,260 grant in 1968, which was used for research and to prepare a preliminary report of the black student in higher education, focusing primarily on the predominantly Negro colleges.

Largely as a result of the successes of the independent black student protests and a persuasion that SNCC is no longer student-oriented, black students met at the end of the 1967–68 year to form a new organization. The founding conference, attracting 78 delegates from 37 colleges in 19 states, met at Shaw University to establish the Congress for the Unity of Black Students or CUBS. Designed to pressure colleges and universities to establish Afro-American courses and other changes, CUBS plans also to recruit more black students and encourage them to attend college. Among the speakers who appeared before the conference were Georgia black legislator Julian Bond, Los Angeles militant Ron Karenga, poet LeRoi Jones, and Shaw University President James E. Cheek. While varying degrees of militancy were expressed by the speakers, all were united as to the need for determined action in the white community.[10] The conference demonstrated clearly that pressures by Negro students on American colleges and universities are just beginning if CUBS succeeds.

According to the Protest Survey* more than 10 percent of the climactic protests of 1967–68 were concerned with racial issues. Only three of these 52 race-related protests occurred at predominantly black institutions; opposition to *in loco parentis* policies was the commonest cause for activists on black campuses at is was on white ones. The most noticeable contrast between protest issues on predominantly black and other campuses was that none of the black institutions cited recruitment or the war in Vietnam or the draft as the occasions of their strongest protest of the year, whereas these issues were raised in some of the most dramatic confrontations at non-black colleges and universities.

In 1967–68, racial issues accounted for 8 percent of the climactic protests in four-year colleges, 11 percent in junior colleges, and 14

---

* See Part I, Chapter 5 for a fuller account of this survey.

percent of that experienced by universities. A comparable survey for 1968–69 will, it is anticipated, show a greater concentration of the racial action in universities and junior colleges. Universities tend to be larger than the other categories, and therefore to have a sufficient black enrollment to provide a nucleus for organization; junior colleges tend to have less protest overall, and it is therefore easier for black activists to outshine other kinds. California junior colleges have been especially lively during 1968–69, with black students confronting local governing boards and insisting that the community based nature of such institutions requires them to meet black needs. Black protest in California filtered further down the educational ladder, to the high schools and junior high schools. Carver Junior High School in Los Angeles erupted at the same time as various largely Negro junior colleges in the city were experiencing some violent protest. High school students confronted the city school board, demanding that they, and not the board, choose the new principal; a white principal was in fact replaced with a black, though not with the man of the BSU's choice. Black high school students have also become active in New York, Louisiana, and elsewhere. Further, both high school and college students have received some strong support from the black community; 24 percent of institutions experiencing race-related protest reported the involvement of non-students, as contrasted with only 12 percent being involved with protests of other kinds. It is thus apparent that black protest is less a specifically collegiate activity than are other kinds, and correspondingly more of a community project.

Black institutions clearly experienced a higher percentage of protests, and more significantly, a higher proportion of violent and obstructive protests than did white institutions. (See Table 1.) It is also clear that the data indicate that racial issues (wherever they occurred) prompted violent and obstructive demonstrations in higher proportion than other issues combined. Faculty members were much more significant as leaders in protests on black campuses than at white institutions. Generally, however, faculty support overall was less in incidents involving racial issues.

Black protest has also tended sometimes to seem more organized than other kinds. It appears that the leadership of black students' organizations on different campuses keeps in closer touch than does the leadership of multi-campus white organizations, and some militants evidently rather enjoy giving the impression that the "black movement" is a highly cohesive and conspiratorial entity from which whites are excluded. While more than one-fourth of the black institutions with protest reported that no organizations were involved in the demonstration, only 15 percent of the white colleges found no organizations involved. Of the organizations reported by black institutions, 11 percent were national groups and 11 percent were local *ad hoc* organizations, both about twice the percentage of similar types fielding protest on white campuses. Conversely, white institutions reported that nearly 8 percent of the organizations on their campuses were "leftist" groups as compared to 3 percent at black colleges. White campuses related that more permanent local groups were involved in their protests in a proportion twice that in black institutions. The group on white campuses most often reported is the Students for a Democratic Society while black national groups (SNCC, CORE, Afro-American groups) were mentioned most frequently by respondents from black colleges.

TABLE 1

BLACK PROTESTS TEND TO BE MORE VIOLENT

Intensity of Protest:	Black Institutions n = 35	Other Institutions n = 1217	Racial Issues n = 52	Other Issues n = 450
Violent	12	1	10	2
Obstructive	9	4	11	9
Physical but Non-Obstructive	18	14	39	33
Diplomatic	21	24	40	56
No Protest	40	57		
	100%	100%	100%	100%

Black protest has presented somewhat contradictory faces. On many occasions it appears violent; yet often the black students seem more disciplined and purposeful than the white radicals who may be allied with them. At Columbia, for example, the blacks occupied Hamilton Hall in conjunction with the SDS group, but shortly afterwards asked the latter to leave, the grounds given being that the whites were less desperate and less totally committed than the blacks. When the police came, however, the blacks yielded up their building in an orderly fashion, without property damage or the pointless and bloody struggles which characterized the clearance of Low Library.

An examination of data relating to violations by the protest activity, the use of physical force and/or police, and discipline produces interesting contrasts between black and other issues and white and black colleges. Dissent at the latter involved infraction of civil law and university regulations more frequently than at white institutions. As one might expect, discipline was also applied more frequently at black institutions. A somewhat surprising conclusion emerges from the data on the use of police and force to confirm that off-campus police were called in a significantly higher percentage of cases of protest on black campuses and protests about racial issues than other single issues. The use of tear gas and mace was a companion to injuries in a much higher proportion of incidents on black campuses than their counterparts. Arrests and injuries were also more frequent when racial protests were at issue. These data clearly indicate that even in 1967–68 racial protests (either racial by issue or racial by setting and participants) evoked a greater physical response and the use of force than did other kinds of protests. It is not possible to determine by the data whether this occurred because of the fact or the stereotyped fear of a tendency of violence and destruction to accompany black protest. The data demonstrate that racial issues on all campuses evoked the highest percentage of sit-ins and detention of officials and that a higher percentage of protest activities at black institutions involved the detention of college officials, strike or boycott of classes and disruptions and strikes. The pattern of "force and threat" in black protests which prompted the use of physical and police force in 1967–68 came to be almost standard in 1968–69, breeding escalation both in the tactics of protesters and the forces of repression.

Survey data on resolutions and statements made by trustees, administrators, faculty, and student government in response to protest on black and white campuses show an interesting contrast. No group of trustees of any black institution experiencing protest issued a supportive statement while several boards of white institutions supported the substance of the protest issue and a few endorsed the protesters' tactics. Conversely, administrations at 21 percent of the black institutions endorsed the substance of protest as compared to 5 percent of the white colleges. Action by the faculty also differed at black institutions, where not one faculty reported a resolution in favor of the protesters' tactics or their demands. This represents a contrast with white colleges in which the faculty supported the protesters' demands in at least 6 percent of the demonstrations. Reflecting the weak state of student government on black campuses the data reported that in only one case did student government of a black college take a position. In that one case it supported the protesters as contrasted to more than fifty similar resolutions of support on white campuses.

Winning support for the substantive issue of their demonstrations is fundamental to the movement. Support for their tactics in achieving substantive agreement is relatively unimportant. In this light it is interesting to examine the reactions of groups, trustees, administration, faculty and student government, to the protests over racial issues. Questionnaire data report that in only one protest was the substance of the issue opposed by a resolution or statement and then by a student government organization. Furthermore, there were twice as many statements supporting the substance of the issues as critical of the tactics. Where criticism occurred, it generally came from the trustees and administration and in only two cases did faculty groups oppose the protest and then only the tactics. This is consistent in extreme of course to the change of policy indicated earlier in this chapter.

The protesters' success in achieving their specific objectives can be known only to themselves. In some cases their goals are not in clear view. But in terms of action taken on the substantive issues which formed the subject of protest, data from our questionnaire may be helpful. As Table 2 indicates, 24 institutions (47.3 percent) experiencing racial protest made the typical collegiate response in appointing a study group or committee to examine the issue at question, 19 (37 percent) changed institutional policy *somewhat* in the direction of the protesters and 9 (18 percent) changed policy *substantially* toward positions urged by protesters. In short, more than half (55 percent) of all respondent institutions experiencing protest on racial issues responded positively to the wishes of the activists. There was less positive response on other issues.

The picture is similar for protests on black campuses. Seventy-three percent of this group reported change in the direction of the protesters while only 36 percent of the white institutions responded similarly. A higher percentage of black institutions also adopted new rules or policies both to limit or prevent protests and to broaden the right to protest. While more black campuses strengthened security forces in response to protest, a higher percentage also revised disciplinary procedures to guarantee due process. It is clear that a greater proportion of black institutions responded than did their white counterparts; it may be that there was a greater need for revised rules and procedures on black campuses.

The picture conveyed by the data is clear in some aspects, namely, that the protests had considerable effect upon moving the institutions to make changes of policy. Whether these changes on the part of the institutions emanated from the rational conviction reached by deliberation that such changes were educationally and "morally" correct or whether the academic community simply "caved in" to moralistic demands shall be left to critics and friends.

TABLE 2
PROTEST PRODUCES CHANGES
(In Percentages)

Actions on Substantive Issues:	Black Institutions	Other Institutions	Racial Issues	Other Issues
Appointed committee or study group.	58	36	47	34
Changed institutional policy in the direction desired by protesters somewhat.	41	26	37	24
Changed institutional policy in the direction desired by protesters substantially.	32	10	18	10
No information or no change in policy.	27	64	45	66

Race-related protests were more concentrated in terms of time: 80 percent of them occurred during April and May, 1968, compared to 32 percent of other kinds of protest during those months. These months, of course, had special significance for blacks; Howard, the leading black university, had ceased functioning because of a student strike in March, and Martin Luther King was killed in early April, an event which triggered riots in many ghetto districts.

TABLE 3*

MONTH PROTESTS OCCURRED, 1967–68

	Black Institutions	Other Institutions	Racial Issues	Other Issues
September	0	3	0	2
October	1	35	0	35
November	1	38	4	33
December	1	25	2	23
January	0	15	1	13
February	1	36	0	38
March	5	46	1	45
April	3	97	22	74
May	2	105	19	84

* The figures on issues and institutions do not form identical totals because some institutions did not identify the issue of their protest.

Perhaps one of the most interesting and somewhat surprising answers from the Survey deals with the respondents' evaluation of the general effect of the protest on campus and on the college or university standing in the larger community. Only one respondent from the black institutions stated that the protest had made students more likely to support protest activity while 18 reported that students were less sympathetic to protest. In addition to this somewhat surprising evaluation was the indication that 11 black institutions felt the protest improved relations among campus groups. The latter is even more surprising when taking into consideration that respondents volunteered that evaluation under the unstructured category of "other" on the questionnaire. Also puzzling is the data that only 4 of the 51 black institutions perceived the protest as worsening relations with the local community but 19 reported that "the protest and its handling enhanced the standing of the institution with many people." Nearly 50 percent of the black institutions (or twice as many as white ones) perceived the protest as enhancing its standing in this way. Forty percent of the protests on black campuses came as sudden developments as contrasted to 16 percent of those at white institutions, but 14 percent of the latter were the outcome of a fairly protracted series of student complaints. Respondents from black institutions reported that 29 percent of the protests on their campuses were "triggered" by an outside event as contrasted to only 9 percent of the episodes on white campuses. The activities of students caused more outbreaks at black colleges than at white ones and administrative acts prompted more protest responses in white institutions than black ones.

In 1968–69, the sit-in tactic was stepped up and periods of "liberation" were more protracted. There was also an escalation in physical confrontation, destruction of property, and conditions threatening violence. Black protests disrupted campuses all across the country. At Berkeley, police routed a racially mixed group protesting cancellation of a course by Eldridge Cleaver, and found that considerable property damage had been done. Wisconsin State University at Oshkosh expelled ninety black students after a destructive occupation of the Administration Building. At the University of California at Santa Barbara, sitters-in occupied the computer center, where the most expensive and sensitive of university property is located, a tactic adopted on various other campuses. In January, 1969, a black sit-in at Swarthmore came to a tragic end when President Courtney Smith died of a heart attack while waiting for a faculty committee's report on the black demands. Shortly after the announcement of Dr. Smith's fatal seizure, the blacks left the building they had controlled for nearly a week. At Brandeis during the same period, black students held control of Ford Hall in which the telephone switchboard and the computer installation for the campus were located. The demonstrators left the building after eleven days with amnesty in doubt and with the rejection of their demands for an autonomous, black-controlled black studies program. Black and Puerto Rican students at CCNY occupied President Buell Gallagher's office for four hours to win a variety of demands. On Valentine's Day, 1969, black students at the University of Illinois staged a three-hour occupation of the Administration Building, leaving peacefully after having cleaned up the place. A week later, students at Wesleyan marked the anniversary of the assassination of Malcolm X by taking over a classroom building.

An increasingly violent and destructive trend seems to be affecting black protests. At Beloit College, forty blacks burned the president in effigy when presenting their demands, and firebombs later exploded in the college's infirmary and in two dormitories. In May, 1968, while the Columbia disruption was at its height, various officials and secretaries at Ohio State University were held captive for a day by students allegedly armed with knives, gasoline bombs and fire hoses. The following academic year saw violence at San Mateo College, where a new president, less sympathetic than his predecessor to programs for the culturally disadvantaged, got hit in the face, and various other injuries and considerable property damage occurred. At Napa Junior College, two buildings burned shortly after some black militant leaders were suspended. At San Fernando Valley State College, blacks frog-marched the head coach to the Administration Building, which they occupied, holding the president and others captive for several hours. At Roosevelt University, about a hundred black and white students forced their way into the office of President Rolf A. Weil and attempted to force him to sign a statement giving amnesty to students disciplined for previous demonstrations for more black studies. While in the office, they attacked reporters, ripped telephones from the walls, pulled fire alarms, and turned on fire hoses. At the University of Wisconsin (Madison), militant blacks disrupted traffic, some classes, and rambled through the Memorial Library, confusing card catalogs, book shelving, blowing pepper into the study rooms and ventilating system, and chanting, "Oshkosh, hey," and "Sock it to me black power." At San Francisco State, a strike led by black and Third World students became the occasion of almost routine violence as bombs detonated regularly on the campus. At San Francisco, San Mateo College and Howard University, the bombings were extended to the homes of faculty perceived as unsympathetic. Physical confrontation of black and white students at Ferris State College in Michigan amidst cries of "White Power" underscored another volatile prospect.

The escalation of defensive tactics in 1969 brought National Guardsmen to the campuses of the University of Wisconsin at Madison and Duke University in Durham, North Carolina. At Madison the protesters shifted their tactic from a sit-in on campus to a "hit and run" technique in which large numbers of demonstrators moved from intersection to intersection in the city streets blocking traffic until easily dispersed by local policemen. A further step in the escalation of tactics of offense occurred in April, 1969, when a portion of nearly a hundred blacks visibly armed themselves during a sit-in in the Cornell Student Union to extract agreement to their demands, including civil and campus amnesty.

For all their violence of style, however, black protests have often focused on attainable goals; whites may engage in symbolic attacks on the War in Vietnam via Dow Chemical's recruiter, but blacks tend to be interested in tangible gains. The contrast between style and intent was well illustrated at San Jose State College, where sociology instructor Harry Edwards, later to earn fame for his efforts at organizing Olympic athletes, launched a sudden frontal assault on the administration. On September 14, 1967, he made a speech in which he declared that discrimination in San Jose was worse than in Mississippi; he then put forth various demands, and gave the College an ultimatum: "grant them or make significant advancement toward them" or the blacks would disrupt the football game the following weekend by burning the stadium.

Edwards' flamboyant style can easily give the impression of a wild-eyed revolutionary, intent not on reform but on disorder, and violence and power for their own sakes. Yet his actual demands were of a different kind: that no "closed door sessions" be held concerning Negro grievances; assurance that Negro and white athletes would be treated equally; notice to fraternities and sororities that equal treatment must be given to Negro rushees; and the establishment of a program to bring the proportion of Negro and other minority group students at San Jose up to their percentage of the general population. Each of these "demands" was in fact something to which the College could readily agree, and on each of them progress could be and was made. President Clark eventually called off the football game when Edwards explained that he could no longer control the situation, but only after the "demands" had been met and groundwork for a less erratic cooperation laid for the future.[11] The same kind of practicality marked some of the angry outbreaks following the murder of Martin Luther King. The Northwestern Afro-American Student Union, for example, presented demands which included (1) a statement by university officials deploring white racism, (2) assurance that Negroes would compose 10 to 12 percent of each freshman class, with at least half of the number from urban ghettos, (3) an increase in financial aid, (4) establishment of a black student housing unit, (5) new courses in Negro history, literature, and art, and a voice in approving professors to teach them, (6) black students' approval of personnel employed to counsel them, (7) a facility for social and recreational uses by blacks, and (8) Northwestern's desegregation of all its real estate holdings. The administration and trustees agreed to many of the demands which the institutional leadership felt obliged to meet as a matter of moral conscience.[12]

The Protest Survey indicated that race-related protests tended to involve composite lists of demands, rather than a single issue; 20

campuses reported unrest of this kind. Demands for black curriculum or black faculty were the most popular single race-related issue (8 cases), while allegedly racist athletic policies sparked four protests. Ten others fell into the "miscellaneous" category, while in eight instances, black demands were joined with others unconnected to race.

The educational problems faced by blacks are reflections of their larger difficulties in American society. There are still comparatively few black students enrolled in institutions of higher education. It has been estimated that approximately 8 percent of disadvantaged high school graduates, most of whom are Negro, attend college as compared to more than 50 percent of all high school graduates. Probably less than 1 percent of the youth in Harlem enroll in college,[13] and it has been estimated that only 1 percent of the Negro high school graduates in New York City want to go to college, as compared to 50 percent of the white graduates.[14]

No national statistics on the numbers of blacks enrolled in higher education are available because many institutions do not collect data on race, believing that to do so might give grounds for charges of institutional racism. What figures there are, however, suggest that despite conscious efforts at increasing the number of black students in higher education, little had been achieved by the close of the 1967–68 academic year. Berkeley, with 28,000 students, enrolled only 400 to 500 blacks; Harvard had about 200 blacks among its 15,000. Wisconsin's (Madison) 33,000 included about 300, Northwestern had 124 in its 9,000 total, Cornell registered 200 blacks of 14,000 students, the University of Texas' 29,000 included 250 blacks. Columbia admitted only 36 black freshmen in 1967. Institutions with more than 1 percent of students who are black are relatively rare.

The exceptions to this low percentage are dramatic ones. Merritt College, a two-year junior college at Oakland, California, has been transformed from 10 percent black five years ago to 40 percent black in 1968–69. It has a black president, a militant Soul Students Advisory Council which organized the Black Panthers in 1966, and an Afro-American Studies Department which graduated five persons with the Associate Arts degree in 1968. Merritt is also the *alma mater* of Black Panther leaders Huey P. Newton and Bobby Seale. Specializing in preparation of blacks for semi-professional jobs or four-year colleges, Merritt's Associate Arts degrees are recognized by California's Board of Education as temporary teaching qualifications if the teacher works simultaneously on a baccalaureate degree. The institution is establishing challenging patterns for other collegiate institutions, both in its programs for blacks and the physical confrontations and acts of vandalism which have accompanied them. Although no formerly predominantly white institution experienced the same dramatic increase in the numbers of black students, several colleges more than doubled their percentages by 1968 as compared to the previous year.

Predominantly black institutions in the southern and border states still enroll more than half the black students in college, and there are heavy concentrations of blacks on a few northern campuses, particularly inner city public junior colleges. Short of money, and located in areas where a racially conservative white establishment hold traditional power, few predominantly black colleges have attracted well-qualified faculty, have adequate facilities, or can provide good quality education.

One solution is to press for the admission of a greater number of black students to predominantly white colleges; admissions policies have been the targets of a number of black protests. Despite the nearly revolutionary results of recent programs, admission of lower income and black students still constitute a major problem in higher education. Results of these programs were indicated in an analysis of enrollment for the fall of 1968, which showed a dramatic increase of students from low-income families between 1966–68. In fact, the percentage of freshmen from low-income families increased from 7.5 percent in 1966 to 10.8 percent in 1968.[15] However, since most black children, whether in the rural south or the inner cities of the north, have attended inferior high schools which did little to provide the intellectual stimulation which many white children acquire at home before they even attend school, merely to admit them to college does not solve the problem. Special efforts have also to be made to keep them in college if they are to succeed. Nor is merely a gradual enlargement of the small black minority which attends college necessarily seen by blacks as desirable. Too often in the past, college-educated blacks have alienated themselves from others of their race, moving into typically white middle class housing and jobs, and assuming many white middle class attitudes. For white society to co-opt 10 percent instead of 5 percent of blacks naturally is not perceived by the black majority as a solution to their problems.

Black studies, which became almost invariably a major item in the demands of protesting blacks in 1968 and 1969, was seen as a possible answer to these manifold problems. It also became easily the most successful protest project of any advanced by militants. In the spring and summer of 1968 colleges and universities throughout the country adopted the concept of black studies with almost unbelievable universality. Harvard announced a full year's course in the "Afro-American Experience," headed by a faculty of four in fields of history (American and Latin American), poverty studies, African and American Negro studies, followed by a committee report in 1969 recommending a degree program in American Negro Studies.[16] But Yale's student-faculty committee preceded Harvard by a half year by its recommendation of an interdisciplinary undergraduate major in Afro-American studies in the early summer of 1968. Dartmouth, Williams, and Boston University announced enrichment of the curriculum with black history, Afro-American studies, including African languages, poverty studies, and black sociology and other courses now being styled black studies.[17] At Cornell an advisory committee of eight black students and nine faculty members organized an Afro-American studies program to begin in the fall of 1969.[18] The University of North Carolina at Chapel Hill announced that its students can specialize in African and Afro-American studies. Smaller institutions grappled with the high costs of instituting such studies, and although Atlanta University, a predominantly Negro institution, announced in late 1968 the formation of a Center for African and African-American Studies to assist in the new curriculum development, beginning in January, 1969,[19] it is questionable whether such a center will give any order to the rapid change.

Whatever the roots of the rapid compliance with protest demands, it is already evident that such compliance does not necessarily solve all problems. Berkeley began a program in the fall of 1968 by offering four courses in Black Studies taught by black instructors but was soon thereafter presented with demands for a completely autonomous black student college. Before the Black Studies program was underway a month at Harvard one of the teachers, Prof. Frank Friedel, was denounced by a black coed in his Negro history lecture as knowing nothing about Negro history. In the second half of the course, Harvard blacks forced Friedel to give up direction of the course and the reorganization of another in urban studies, drawing protests from more than a hundred faculty members. At the University of Illinois,

Prof. Robert McColley, another white teaching Negro history, had his classes disrupted by blacks at the beginning of the year on the grounds of his color.[20] Wisconsin (Madison) began a "concentration" of black studies in 1968 only to be pressured by protest in early 1969 to create a department of Afro-American Studies for 1970.

Of doctorates granted between 1964 and 1967, only 0.78 percent went to blacks; the proportion in previous years was probably even lower. In 1968, a Ford Foundation Survey showed that only 1.72 percent of graduate students in the arts and sciences were black.[21] As a reflection of the small numbers of blacks represented in the professions a recent conference on "The Negro in Medicine" reported that blacks constituted only 2.2 percent of the physicians in America in 1968.[22] Nor is there much evidence that what black academics there are want to abandon their traditional fields and engage in black studies. The demand that all instructors of black students be black is thus totally impractical, unless traditional qualifications are to be completely abandoned. Further, such a demand raises questions about the purpose of the program. If it is to be therapeutic, to meet the "need at this stage for black identity, self-awareness and togetherness," [23] as Roy Innis has advocated, a real conflict with established academic values looms. As the historian C. Vann Woodward has pointed out, while there is a legitimate need for Negro history, "the fulfillment of the need will not be instant, the learning of the history painless, or the content of it exclusively or predominantly glorious." [24]

Not to be overlooked in the process are the Negro institutions which have been trying to upgrade their faculties over a long and agonizing period, and which are now being raped by white institutions scrambling for black faculty to teach the special programs. It might make better sense for the black students to be sent from small white institutions to the predominantly black ones for a year or more of study in Afro-American Studies than for the smaller white institutions to try to maintain a weak black studies program. The present direction of the black movement seems destined to destroy the strength of the old Negro colleges when the philosophy of separatism underscores their need and value more than ever.

The admission of students from culturally disadvantaged backgrounds to institutions with high academic standards naturally creates some problems of survival. Ethnic studies departments may play a role in this process. According to John Roche, analyzing the black students' aims at Brandeis, the creation of a black studies program, completely operated and taught by blacks, is now a defense against being admitted to institutions and academic programs for which they have insufficient preparation. In this setting, black studies appear to be a refuge, an island to which to retreat.[25] Many black studies proposals include provisions for extensive counselling and other forms of compensatory education. The need for such precautions is clear if students poorly prepared for college are to succeed.

It is not entirely clear how ethnic studies prepare a student to earn a living, unless he intends to be a social worker or minority community leader. Sir Arthur Lewis, a black economist at Princeton, has examined this dilemma, and recommends as follows:

Let the clever young black go to a university to study engineering, medicine, chemistry, economics, law, agriculture and other subjects which are going to be of value to him and his people. And let the clever whites go to college to read black novels, to learn Swahili, and to record the exploits of the Negro heroes of the past: they are the ones to whom this will come as an eye-opener.[26]

If the new courses were merely electives, such a critique would not carry much weight; however, a major point in black students' demands on many campuses has been that there should be not only a major but an autonomous department administering and teaching it, and sometimes an entirely separate and all-encompassing program for black students in the program. Such proposals naturally smack of racial separatism, and it is ironic that when Antioch, Northwestern and other institutions have tried to meet this black demand, they have found themselves in violation of the Civil Rights Act, prompting the U. S. Office of Education to issue warnings to other institutions. This call for instant independence raises what are perhaps the most pessimistic suspicions about the new programs—that they may turn into centers of militant indoctrination, or even bases for militant social action. Defending the demand for autonomy, a position paper given at a Black Power Conference at Merritt College asserted:

Whitey will immediately block anything meaningful out of a system that he controls, and we know it. . . . If you think black studies is inde-

pendent, ask yourself what happens when the department desires to pur-
chase guns, mortars and tanks and begins to teach urban guerilla warfare
tactics to its students.

Beset with such friends and enemies, adopted with a minimum of
planning and discussion, and under extraordinary pressures, it will
not be surprising if the ethnic studies programs fail to come up to
expectations. It may be that in a few years they will be as dead as
the programs of Armenian Studies which were liberally endowed at
a time when the social conscience was driving many Americans to do
something about another persecuted people. Yet it is clear that where
for years American academics acknowledged that blacks had been
poorly treated, it was not until black student protest erupted that they
began constructive action to right the balance. Whether present remedies, adopted almost frantically and in great variety, will succeed
remains to be seen; but even if they do not, they may be replaced
by something more effective. There is surely also a possibility that
out of all the rapid change and experimentation which has been
brought about largely by black protest, new vistas, methods and goals
for the education will emerge, to the benefit of all.

NOTES

[1] Stokely Carmichael and Charles V. Hamilton articulated the concept in a
very persuasive manner in their 1967 publication *Black Power: The Politics
of Liberation in America* (New York: Vintage Books, 1967). *See also* Fred
Powledge, *Black Power White Resistance* (Cleveland and New York: The
World Publishing Company, 1967), and Floyd B. Barbour, *The Black Power
Revolt* (Boston: Extending Horizons Books, 1968). For a monograph on the
aspects of the development of SNCC, *see* Howard Zinn, *SNCC: The New
Abolitionists* (Boston: Beacon Press, 1964).

[2] The paper is included in Joanne Grant (ed.), *Black Protest* (New York:
Fawcett World Library, 1968), pp. 452–456.

[3] *Ibid.,* pp. 459–465.

[4] *See* Eldridge Cleaver, "My Father and Stokely Carmichael," *Ramparts,*
April, 1967.

[5] *See* Kenneth B. Clark, *Dark Ghetto* (New York: Harper and Row, 1965).

[6] *See* Franz Fanon, *The Wretched of the Earth* (New York: Grove Press,
1968), and *Black Skin: White Masks* (New York: Grove Press, 1967).

[7] Carmichael and Hamilton, *op. cit.,* p. 184.

[8] Eli Ginsberg, *The Middle Class Negro in the White Man's World* (New
York: Columbia University Press, 1967), and John F. Craft, Inc., "A Report

of the Attitudes of Negroes in Various Cities," prepared for the U.S. Senate Subcommittee on Executive Reorganization, 1966, pp. 18–20.

[9] *The Chronicle of Higher Education,* December 9, 1968.

[10] *Ibid.,* May 6, 1968.

[11] From a case study of the incident by Dr. Albert Watrel, now President of Slippery Rock State University, manuscript in editors' possession.

[12] Information concerning the Northwestern protest was derived from a wide variety of newspaper coverage, interviews with student observers, and statements from the institution's administration. Particularly valuable is St. Louis *Post-Dispatch,* September 5, 1968, Chicago *Sun-Times,* May 5, 1968, and a printed "Letter from Northwestern," to Alumni which included a statement of the Board of Trustees of Northwestern University and a description of the protest events.

[13] *Report of the National Advisory Commission on Civil Disorders* (New York: Bantam Books, 1968), p. 452.

[14] *The New York Times,* January 12, 1969.

[15] From an analysis by Joseph Froomkin, assistant commissioner for program planning and evaluation of the United States Office of Education, as reported in *The Chronicle of Higher Education,* March 10, 1969.

[16] *The New York Times,* January 22, 1969.

[17] *Ibid.,* June 23, 1968; *The Chronicle of Higher Education,* December 23, 1968.

[18] National Association of State Universities and Land-Grant Colleges, Circular Letter No. 33, October 30, 1968, p. 11.

[19] *The Chronicle of Higher Education,* December 23, 1968.

[20] *The Los Angeles Times,* January 2, 1969.

[21] Fred E. Crossland, "Graduate Education and Black Americans," mimeographed paper, Office of Special Projects, Division of Education and Research, New York, The Ford Foundation, November 25, 1968.

[22] Lee Cogan, *Negroes for Medicine* (Baltimore: The Johns Hopkins University Press, 1968), p. 3.

[23] *The New York Times,* January 22, 1969; also American Council on Education, "Higher Education and National Affairs," January 17 and January 24 issues. See also the opposing statements of Wilkins and Hare in *Newsweek,* February 10, 1969, pp. 56–57.

[24] C. Vann Woodward, "The Hidden Sources of Negro History," *Saturday Review,* January 18, 1969, p. 18.

[25] Madison *Capital Times,* January 22, 1969.

[26] Quoted in the *Princeton Alumni Weekly,* March 18, 1969, p. 15.

2

PROTEST AND THE CATHOLIC COLLEGES

*by Robert Hassenger**

IF ONE WERE interested, prior to 1967, in finding a real live specimen of the species *Studens activus,* he would not be likely to have begun his search on a Catholic college campus. With the great majority of American collegians, the students in Catholic colleges and universities were a relatively contented sort. Or, if that is not strictly accurate, the kinds of things bugging them were such that they were not manifested in easily discernible forms. By the spring of 1967, students in at least the leading Catholic colleges and universities began to bestir themselves in sufficient quantities to cause people to take notice. This chapter is a set of notes on some of the reasons this occurred.

Data from the Protest Survey, which is described more fully in Part I, Chapter 5, were made available to the present author. Of the 196 Catholic schools responding, 14 were universities, 140 liberal arts colleges, 23 junior colleges, 11 were theologates, and 8 were teachers colleges. Fifty-four were men's colleges, 95 were women's colleges, and 47 were coeducational. Seventy-six were in the Northeast, 75 in the Midwest, 20 in the South, and 25 in the West.

* Dr. Robert Hassenger is Director of the Office of Educational Research at the University of Notre Dame, where he also teaches in the Sociology Department. In 1967 he edited *The Shape of Catholic Higher Education* (University of Chicago Press).

The great majority of respondents from all types of schools indicated that there was no obvious sign of student activism on their campuses prior to 1967–68, and Catholic schools did not differ from others here. Forty-three percent of the public institutions reported student protests had occurred in 1967–68, 47 percent of the Catholic colleges and universities, 41 percent of the Protestant schools, and 32 percent of the Fundamentalist institutions. It was the type of protest that most distinguished the various kinds of schools.

The protests on most Catholic campuses were not very dramatic. Twenty-five percent involved peaceful picketing and marching, 5 percent a "strike" or boycott of classes, and 4 percent sit-ins which prevented normal use of buildings. There was virtually no physical obstruction of buildings or events, and in 56 percent of the protests, there was not even picketing or marching. What most often occurred were primarily "verbal" forms of protest, such as open forums, student meetings, petitions, deputation calls on the president, and the like. In four-fifths of the demonstrations no violations of any sort occurred, and in the remainder, all were apparently violations only of university regulations or guidelines for protest, and not of civil law. The average number of participants reported was only about 50, and only in about 5 percent of the demonstrations were there more than 100. In only 1 percent of the cases did expulsion or suspension result for the participants.

Most Catholic colleges and universities were founded to fulfill the dual purpose of preparing a largely immigrant population to swim in the mainstream of the culture, and to provide them a set of spiritual waterwings, that they would not lose their faith there. For example, as the Nineteenth Century was about to dawn, the nation's first Catholic college, Georgetown, described its mission thus:

Persuaded that irreligion and immorality in a youth portend the most fatal evils to subsequent periods of life, and threaten even to disturb the peace, and corrupt the manners of society at large; the directors of this Institution openly profess that they have nothing so much at heart as to implant virtue and destroy in their pupils the seeds of vice—Happy in the attainment of this sublime object, they would consider their success in this alone, as an ample reward for their incessant endeavours.[1]

With such moral educational goals in mind it is not surprising to find that student life at Georgetown was most carefully regulated: this discipline, the college catalogue stated.

has in view the safeguarding of those hours of study so necessary to prepare for attendance at the various College exercises, which is required to
produce that intellectual and moral training which it is Georgetown's aim
to impart. . . .[2]

Nor was Georgetown atypical in its concern. At post-Civil War Notre
Dame, the catalogue indicated that attendance at religious services
required, and not only tobacco as well as liquor banned, but

No book, periodical or newspaper shall be introduced into the College,
without being previously examined and approved by the Director of
Studies. Objectionable books found in the possession of Students will be
withheld from them until their departure from the University.[3]

The Catholic institutions of higher learning had no monopoly on
such paternalism, of course; the colonial colleges were founded with
such ends in view, and similar educational styles prevailed in many
places until well into the Twentieth Century.[4] But the college- and
university-changing phenomena, which Jencks and Riesman have
called "the academic revolution," and the winds of social change
which transformed both individuals and institutions such as the family
and the church, had worked a vast reduction in the levels of paternalism on most American campuses by the end of the Eisenhower era
in 1960. Even at that late date, however, the Catholic colleges and
universities had undergone only modest changes in their regulation
of student life. When this writer was graduated from Notre Dame in
1959, students were still required to make three "morning checks"
each week, to sign in by a specified hour each night, and forbidden
to leave the city on the weekend of a major social event which he
was known to be attending. Further, the electricity was turned off—
not just the lights, the *electricity*—at midnight or shortly thereafter,
in all but the senior halls, since underclassmen presumably did not
themselves know when to retire. Floor prefects were expected to
enforce quiet after this time. This benighted practice was discon-
tinued in 1960–61.

In one of the largest Catholic universities in 1967, male students
could not wear t-shirts, jeans, sweat-shirts, or shorts; women's regulations were even more strict, and included a limitation of the places
where they could smoke. In this school's manual, it states that "if it
appears from the record that a student is not meeting the prescribed
requirements, either scholastically or otherwise, he may be placed on

probation or he may be requested to withdraw from the University." Students could be dismissed for "conduct or attitudes which, in its estimation, are not in conformity with its objectives and standards, or for any other reason for which it deems such action advisable. The University is the sole judge in the disposition of all cases involving disciplinary action of any kind. Every student, by the very fact of his registration at the University, recognizes this right." Or, as the president of a very famous Catholic university once put it, "If you don't like it here, you can go somewhere else!"

The latest available evidence indicates that Catholic schools are only slowly transforming this climate of order and docility which characterized so many of them as late as the mid-1960's.[5] Nor is this surprising. In a time when half of the Catholics were "either immigrants or the children of immigrants," as Greeley characterized the Catholic adult population in 1968,[6] most of the students from working and lower-middle class families coming to college were seeking visas to suburbia. During such a time, which lasted into the late 1950's at even the Georgetowns and Notre Dames, and still is found at the large urban institutions such as St. John's on Long Island and the University of Dayton, business and engineering programs were the staple of the Catholic colleges and universities, along with the theology and philosophy which a largely minority group felt necessary in a society which was not without hostility. But increasingly, Catholic students are today much more likely to look like other third-generation Americans, and will be less interested both in vocational curricula and in religious traditions meant at least in part to distinguish Catholics from other ethno-religious groups.

So far, however, there is little conspicuous dissent on the Catholic campuses. Students at Catholic colleges are becoming involved in the governance of their institutions, but as yet they are less involved than students elsewhere. Of the 196 Catholic colleges, 88 percent stated that students were represented on at least some university committees, 14 percent indicating that students sat on "most or all major committees" (compared to 32 percent in the major Protestant colleges, 76 percent in the Fundamentalist Protestant schools, 37 percent in the public institutions, and 26 percent in the private secular schools).[7] Although students had been represented on such committees at about half of the American colleges and universities by 1967, only 27 percent of the Catholic schools provided student representation at that time, and almost half of these did not do so until 1967–68. At a third of the Catholic schools, neither faculty nor students has been very influential in setting policies, a much higher proportion of disenfranchised than was found for any of the other types of college and university. More than a third of the Catholic college respondents said that only rarely had student governments in their schools made requests or demands related to institutional policies, prior to 1967–68.[8]

Only about a fourth of the Catholic colleges had newspapers which made frequent critical assessments of institutional policies, compared to a third of the newspapers in both types of Protestant colleges and in public institutions, and more than two-fifths of those in private secular schools. But, although student editors in church-related colleges were much less likely than those in public and private schools to be completely free from attempts to bring influence to bear on their papers, there was very little direct supervision reported by respondents on either the Protestant or Catholic campuses.[9]

In light of this climate, it is hardly surprising to discover that the major focus of protest on Catholic campuses in 1967–68 was on-campus issues. On matters of curricular change, student membership on university committees and other matters of educational policy the religiously affiliated schools were the most active, with 34 percent of the Catholic college demonstrations focusing on such matters, 22 percent of those at schools with ties to major Protestant denominations, and 15 percent at the Fundamentalist schools (compared to 19 percent and 16 percent, respectively, of the public and private institutions' protests). And in the area of student life (such as dorm regulations and visiting hours, dress, food, censorship and the like), 56 percent of the Protestant colleges with student demonstrations reported they were about aspects of student life, as were 42 percent of those at Fundamentalist institutions, more than a third at both the private (36 percent) and Catholic (35 percent) colleges and universities, and 22 percent of those at public institutions. Two-thirds of the protests on Catholic campuses were concerned, then, either educational policies and practices, or matters of student life. About half of the demonstrations at private secular colleges and universities were about such matters, and two-fifths of the protests at public institutions.

By contrast, only 10 of the 82 (12 percent) Catholic schools which had some kind of student protest reported these took the form of opposition to the war, the draft, armed services or Dow Chemical recruiting, and the like, compared to a third of the demonstrations at private colleges, 28 percent of those at public colleges, and 10 percent at the two types of Protestant schools. In one other area, concern for issues which can be grouped under the heading "black power," only 5 percent of either the Catholic or Protestant schools with protests indicated they were about the numbers of Negroes admitted, the opportunities to study the history and culture of the Afro-Americans and the like. Fourteen percent of the demonstrations on public campuses were about such matters, and 9 percent of those in the private secular schools.

Yet such issues as peace and civil rights can be expected to be at the core of an increasing amount of student activism on the Catholic campus. By 1968, when 22 percent of the Harvard seniors planned to leave the country or go to jail if their applications for draft deferments were turned down,[10] protests against Dow and ROTC were beginning to draw large numbers at Fordham and Notre Dame. The present writer assumes that this is the pattern which will be found on at least the major Catholic campuses in the years immediately ahead.

An example of protest in a formerly quiet setting occurred at New Haven's Albertus Magnus College when, in the Fall of 1967, students demanded jurisdiction over the areas of dress, social life (curfews, hotels, liquor, etc.), smoking, campus absences, library hours and the like, and found that the College administration unilaterally disbanded the "Cooperative Council"—which was as close as these young ladies had come to student government—invoking a 1927 clause giving the administration complete control over the "relation of the College with the outside world." (Such language speaks volumes for the way many Catholic women's colleges have viewed their educational missions.) But the administration found itself faced with a "girlcott" of classes, plus considerable embarrassing publicity from the Yale and New Haven papers, *The New York Times*, and *The National Catholic Reporter*, and were forced to back down. More such confrontations—with similar outcomes—can be expected to occur in the months immediately ahead.

Certainly students are more sophisticated about how to bring off a successful protest. At Albertus Magnus, students had easy access to friends, lawyers, and even meeting places at Yale, to professors, sympathetic alumnae, and the media. There was a dramatic quality to students from a school whose image was that of a sleepy Catholic women's college standing up for their rights, which the media delighted in. Students got great coverage for the "happy day" parade they held celebrating the feast of the College's patron saint, during the "girlcott" of classes. They were shown as responsible, happy, ungrudging students who were only asking the administrators to be treated as adults. After such coverage, the outcome of the protest was never in doubt: the students obtained the demanded concessions. The success of the Albertus students was due in part to tough-minded leadership. One of the principal leaders has well caught the kind of thinking Catholic college administrators are going to be seeing more of:

It is harder to have a "rebellion" in a girls' school because females tend to be more obedient to authority and timid. However, if girls are aroused and organized, a *successful* revolution is much easier. For example, there was one time when a college guard was going to call in the dogs to move us. We had a newspaper photographer with us. Could you imagine the bad publicity if the paper appeared with pictures of dogs sent on girls! College administrators cannot use *physical* pressure [her emphasis]. Girls also do not face threat of expulsion followed by the Draft or losing their college degree and therefore a chance for a successful career to support a family, two pressures men are faced with.[11]

The new attitude was obvious in the triumphal tour of liberal theologian Hans Kung, who spoke on numerous Catholic campuses in 1966. It was also manifested in the student support of Charles Curran, at Catholic University. In this case, the issue was ostensibly one of due process: a man had been fired without a hearing, even though he had been recommended for promotion by both his department colleagues and the academic senate. But underneath the surface was the whole question of the magisterium. As a "Pontifical" university, Catholic University has been considered something of an "official" church institution. It was *The* Catholic University of America. (The whole matter of both the meaning and advisability of "pontifical" status is today open: at best, it seems to be a kind of seal of approval; at worst, it seems to unnecessarily restrict an institution, both academically and administratively.) In the Curran case, a committee of bishops from the episcopally dominated board of trustees decided to dismiss the mildly controversial young theologian, and the entire board rubber-stamped this decision with little or no discussion. These bishops, archbishops and cardinals were shockingly unfamiliar with the American academic process, having received their entire educations in seminaries and the closed Catholic universities of the early twentieth century. And they were simply not used to giving reasons for their decisions: most certainly did not in their dioceses. As one of them put it, when asked about the firing, "You don't have to give reasons." But faculty and students voted almost unanimously to boycott their classes until Father Curran was reinstated, and the board of trustees was forced to reverse its decision, with Curran receiving both a promotion and tenure.

The "magisterium" or "teaching authority" of the church has traditionally been held to inhere in the bishops who, considered spiritual descendents of the original twelve apostles, supposedly inherited more than ordinary providential assistance in their decisions. In practice an individual bishop often felt he could speak "for the church," and did not hesitate to extend this authority to the Catholic college located in his diocese. But all this has changed, in large part because new conceptions of what it means to be a Catholic or Christian have stripped the "official church" of its great weapon: excommunication. Many Catholics feel as Protestants do today that it is their church as much as the bishops', and would scoff at the suggestion that they could be "thrown out" of it.

Further, some hold that, whatever "magisterium" might mean, it inheres in the whole church, developing through time, and not in a given group at a particular moment in history. This is the only way, say they, to account for the evolution of doctrine, and the clear changes that have occurred over the years. And even this kind of "magisterium" would have only an indirect influence on a church member, speaking to the consciences of members of the academic community the same way it might speak to those in political life.[12]

Through the mid-1960's, with the Catholic college or university to some extent identified with the institutional church, and at the same time attracting those Catholics who, because of age, ability, and needs for group solidarity, were most likely to join in a revolt against established ways, the campus became the locus for much of the protest occurring within American Catholicism, with the same dynamics at work in a Fordham or Boston College as in the SNCC or Black Panther groups at Oberlin or Columbia. However, the generation which has moved through high school after the Vatican Council seems to have fewer hang-ups about the church, and are now beginning to involve themselves in the kinds of protest the other contributors to this volume have described.

Most of the protests have been of a "liberal" variety, with students asserting the primacy of conscience over the dictums of church authority. Thus, one saw such headlines as "Students' Action Helps Fr. Riga Keep His Job";[13] or "Students Defy Boston College, Hold Lecture on Birth Control." [14] But there was at least one manifestation of a quite different kind of protest. Again, the emphasis was on individual expression; but the content was what most observers would have to term "conservative." I refer to the "Pentecostal Movement," whose members support such beliefs as believing that God will guide one in opening the Bible at random, to find a passage which addresses itself to one's pressing concern at that time. The social scientist observing such groups in action cannot help but point to a variety of social and psychological considerations. In my own observances of the forty or fifty students comprising Notre Dame's pentecostal group in 1967, I was struck, first, by the concentration on certain psychosomatic symptoms, as individuals gave public testimony to the effects of their "baptism of the spirit," having had the hands of several laid on them, accompanied by prayer that they would "receive the holy spirit." Many stated that a deep inner peace followed, often after a considerable period of time during which they had felt themselves agitated, but this was exemplified primarily by the loss of such symptoms as cold and clammy hands, "uneasy stomach," "nervousness," and the like. Some even got up and talked about their symptoms at the time ("my knees are shaking"), the very things they would have been concerned to disguise previously, but for which they could expect to receive understanding from the group.

Another phenomenon to be noticed is the place of sublimated sexuality in the group. One sensed that many of the participants had been extremely rigid about their own bodies, and had experienced very little physical contact with members of either their own or the other sex. The "love" for each other that group members professed— often accompanied by a touch on the arm or face—was a way of working former conflicts through. They were also enabled to verbalize their own sensitivity, which had been taboo—particularly for the males—in their own backgrounds. And some who would have been unable to enter a deep emotional relationship with a single other could spread their emotional need around, diffusing it among several, thus avoiding the risk of rejection a commitment to one other would imply.

The importance of the group as an identity-conferring device was also apparent. One of the interesting things about the development of the movement was that many of the members had participated over the preceding year or two in "study weekends" or "marathon retreats," where they first began to develop new styles of religious behavior. Then some were prayed over by visitors from another campus, and received the "gift of tongues." One had the real sense that it was very important for those who had previously shared something with these initiates to attain the same "gift."

As Erik Erikson[15] and others have pointed out, identity for the late adolescent involves a synthesis of both identification with and rebellion against parents and the past they represent. When the struggle of an individual for identity coincides with that of a cultural or even a subcultural segment, such as the changing American Catholic church, the individual can work out his problems by simultaneously acting against his parents and for an existing group he must, "for its own sake," help reform. Erikson terms this the "unique intersection of life history with history," and suggests it is especially likely when social change has made adults unsure of their past, its values and norms: sensing themselves that things need changing, those who might defend the past cannot really commit themselves to doing so.

Solomon and Fishman[16] have given youth movements, in which members see themselves acting on behalf of ideals and for others (who may not know what is "good" for them), the label "pro-social," and observe that

commitment to a "cause" and a group allows one to identify with universals and values beyond the self. This identification provides security, a sense of being and meaning, and an ego-expansion in which secondary omnipotence is not a small factor. Through his fidelity the member strengthens the movement and is in turn strengthened as he becomes an integral part of something much larger than the self.[17]

Berger also describes the kind of escape a surrender of the self can provide, and how this lends itself to some forms of religious expression: "The 'I am nothing—He is everything' now becomes enhanced by the empirical unavailability of the other to whom the masochistic surrender is made." [18]

Submersion in such a group can be a substitute (and an adjustive one) for the emotional dependency of childhood. Group cohesiveness is increased by a sense of persecution from outsiders,[19] which may lead to feelings of invulnerability. "When ritualized or dramatized it illuminates the moral lagging of others and, by way of example and implied shame, urges the members on to greater effort." [20] Such groups—whether pentecostal Catholics or SNCC—provide opportunities to try on new roles and behavior, to have close personal contact without risk.[21] Involvement may be quite casual at first, such as the student described by Sampson, who first become associated with the Free Speech Movement because he recognized an old friend in the crowd, and as he looked around, he "knew they were the kind of people he had been looking for." [22] When these people become his, he is likely to react as did the Berkeley student who, when asked if he had been arrested in the Sproul Hall sit-in, replied: "No, I wasn't. I kept trying to get in so I could be arrested, but they locked us out. I really wanted to take part." It is for such reasons of group solidarity that there was a considerable drop in psychiatric referrals during the 1964 Berkeley demonstrations.[23]

That many involved in such a movement have only the scantiest notion of what the real issues are;[24] that there is a strong dose of romanticism, with an apparent belief that students can overcome the banalities of their parents' lives or of the middle-class world generally; that there is a kind of arrogant superiority conferred on one who participates in such a movement;[25] all these can be readily granted. But they do not lessen the attractiveness of involvement in an identity-conferring campus group.[26]

Where the predisposition for generation and support of student protests is available, Catholic college administrators are going to have their hands full heading these off or cooling them out. Although I have suggested that student activism on the Catholic campus will increasingly resemble the varieties found in other American colleges and universities, it is also certain that some brouhahas will arise because of the avowedly religious commitments of the Catholic institutions. While few people pretend to know the exact nature of the "Catholic university," in the late 1960's, the revised Notre Dame Statutes specify that the intellectual life of the University "should at all times be enlivened and sustained by a devotion to the twin disciplines of theology and philosophy," which are "viewed as being central to the University's existence and function." Similar language is used by the University President, in his Introduction to the new Notre Dame faculty manual, revised during the 1965–67 academic years. In the section on academic freedom in the manual, the faculty member is reminded of his responsibility not to "maintain a position contrary to the basic aims of this Institution as outlined in the Introduction." In a later section defining criteria for dismissal from the University, one matter is "continual serious disrespect or disregard for the Catholic character of this institution." Presumably students will also be expected to take a school's "Catholic character" into account, however difficult such a thing is to operationalize. Catholic colleges and universities will undoubtedly be able to enforce more stringent regulations than state institutions. St. John's University in New York recently won a suit brought against it by students who had been expelled for marrying in a civil ceremony, and in 1957 the Massachusetts State Court upheld Brandeis' right to dismiss students even without a hearing. Today, students would almost certainly be given a hearing.[27] Due process may be required, but—as private institutions—it will still be possible for Catholic schools to enforce legally any kind of reasonable regulations they choose to establish.

Whether they will be well advised to create rules and make demands at variance with the norm for other institutions of higher learning in America is less clear. While there is presently something of a backlash mood among the middle majority, against activist students they perceive as "dirty, long-haired beatniks," it is unlikely that the private universities and colleges, already faced with considerable competition by the mushrooming public educational enterprise, will find it easy to enforce regulations which seem to the new student generation less wrong than meaningless. If they do, it will be difficult to disagree with Jencks and Riesman that such attempts have "little more chance of success than a colonial administration confronted with a determined guerilla movement . . . the occupying powers may win all the battles while gradually losing the war." [28] The student activist will then be able to say to the Catholic college president or dean of students—citing that most unlikely of sources, Edmund Burke—"The question, my dear sir, is not whether you have the right to make us miserable, but whether it is not in your interest to make us happy."

NOTES

[1] From the Archives of Georgetown University, cited in an unpublished paper, "The Tradition of Autonomy in the Catholic University?" by Msgr. John Tracy Ellis, presented at a meeting sponsored by the International Federation of Catholic Universities, July 20–23, 1967.

[2] *Ibid.*

[3] *Ibid.*

[4] Frederick Rudolph, *The American College and University: A History* (New York, Random House, 1962).

[5] *See* Robert Hassenger and Robert Weiss, S.J., "The Catholic College Climate," *School Review,* 74 (Winter, 1966), pp. 419–445.

[6] Andrew M. Greeley, *The Changing Catholic College* (Chicago, Aldine Publishing Co., 1967), p. 23.

[7] In the complete sample, students were more likely to serve on most major committees at all-male schools than at women's or coed institutions, at colleges (and even two-year colleges) than at universities, and at the more selective institutions.

[8] Such demands were the established mode of operation at more than two-thirds of the entire sample of men's colleges, 61 percent of the women's schools, and 56 percent of the coed institutions. The more selective and the larger the school, the more routine were these periodic demands.

[9] Only in 2-year colleges and at the least selective schools was such control at all common.

[10] *The New York Times,* January 15, 1968.

[11] Correspondence with the writer from Mrs. Deborah Hawkins Johnson, June 29, 1968.

[12] For a fuller discussion of the decline of the magisterium, see James Colianni (ed.), *The Catholic Left* (New York, Chilton Books, 1967).

[13] *National Catholic Reporter,* May 10, 1967.

[14] *Ibid.,* April 26, 1968.

[15] Erik Erikson, "Identity and the Life Cycle," in G. S. Klein (ed.), *Psychological Issues,* No. 1 (New York, International Universities Press, 1959); *Childhood and Society* (New York, Norton, 1950); *Young Man Luther* (New York, Norton, 1958); and *Identity: Youth and Crisis* (New York, Norton, 1968).

[16] J. Solomon and F. Fishman, "Youth and Social Action: An Introduction," in the number of the *Journal of Social Issues* entitled "Youth and Social Action," 20 (October, 1964), pp. 1–27.

[17] *Ibid.,* p. 16.

[18] Peter Berger, *The Sacred Canopy: Elements of a Sociological Theory of Religion* (New York, Doubleday, 1968), p. 155.

[19] In their discussion of the "Five Factors Crucial to the Growth and Spread of a Modern Religious Movement" (the pentecostals), Luther P. Gerlach and Virginia H. Hine note that opposition from the larger society serves "to intensify commitment, unify the local group, and provide a basis for identification between groups"; *Journal for the Scientific Study of Religion,* 7 (Spring, 1968), p. 37.

[20] Solomon and Fishman, *op. cit.,* p. 17.

[21] Because "the movement" comes first. Several students in the Notre Dame group told how they had "been tempted by the devil" to "do things" to girls from the group to which they had become attached, but that they could confess these longings to the girls, ask for their help, and they would pray together until desire passed.

[22] Edward Sampson, "Student Activism and the Decade of Protest," in Samp-

son (ed.), "Stirrings Out of Apathy: Student Activism and the Decade of Protest," *Journal of Social Issues,* 23 (July, 1967), pp. 1–33.

[23] Calvin Trillin, "Letter from Berkeley," *The New Yorker,* 41 (March 13, 1965), pp. 57–102.

[24] Glazer has pointed out the inconsistency of the radical students who insist that the "university make no judgment as to the legality or illegality of their actions and that it leave it to the civil arm alone to determine whether they have broken the law," but when CIA or Dow Chemical recruiters come to the campus the students "insist that the university must make a judgment as to the morality of the activities it permits on the campus." Nathan Glazer, " 'Student Power' in Berkeley," *The Public Interest,* No. 13 (Fall, 1968), p. 8.

[25] As J. Solomon and F. Fishman put it, "Purity is juxtaposed to corruption and hypocrisy in all spheres—social, political, personal, and sexual. The cultural norms of the movement are built around these concerns"; *op. cit.,* p. 17.

[26] As Lipset has recently put it, "Thus, as in the case of workers and employees in a bureaucratized industry, a sort of student syndicalism would seem to be emerging which seeks to regain symbolically for students as a group the influence which they have lost individually." Seymour M. Lipset, "The Activists: A Profile," *The Public Interest,* No. 13 (Fall, 1968), p. 43.

[27] The U. S. Court of Appeals required reinstatement of six state university students dismissed without a hearing, in 1961, and this ruling was upheld in a federal district court, in 1963.

[28] Christopher Jencks and David Riesman, *The Academic Revolution* (Garden City, N.Y., Doubleday, 1969), p. 59.

3

STUDENT GOVERNMENT:
SANDBOX OR SOAPBOX?

by Robert H. Shaffer*

A CASUAL observer need only pick up a popular magazine or news-paper to see that questions of student government, student power, and student relations are currently of great interest to the public as well as to educators. No educational conference or publication is complete today without some spokesman attempting to interpret the student movement or to suggest appropriate institutional responses to it. Unfortunately, much of this discussion stems from the wrong motive: a vain hope for a magical formula to prevent riots and demonstrations. The reason for discussion should be the realization that the present structure of higher education is missing an important foundation stone—that of student involvement in the ongoing proc-esses of policy formulation and decision making. Current trends in student life have driven home the point that the vitality of higher education is weakened because of this lack of student participation. Higher education, once regarded as the hope of the world, is suddenly beset with doubts and self-criticism because of flaws revealed not

* Dr. Shaffer, on the staff of Indiana University since 1941, served as Dean of Students of that institution from 1955 to 1968. Long active in various student personnel associations and youth organizations, he served as adviser to the National Student Association for nine years. Presently, he is teaching at Indiana University as a Professor in the Schools of Business and Education.

only in its structure, but in its heart and mind. A student activist made the point in a speech to the National Association of Manufacturers when he said, "The most fruitful thing I can say to you about the student rebel is that you are just not getting the message." [1] The message is now being received loud and clear. Students, student input, and student support are of fundamental importance to all of higher education.

Traditionally student government has been seen as a laboratory in which students could learn the problems and processes of democracy as a preparation for leadership in society. While this view has been held for many years, and still is on many campuses, it has many flaws. Participation in student government is viewed by many students today as restricted and meaningless, partly because they reject the view of college as mere preparation for life and see it as living. The alert student wishes to stretch out beyond the limits imposed upon a typical laboratory and to exercise responsible citizenship, self-direction, and autonomy immediately. Furthermore, the laboratory view of student government implies that the university is responsible for all activities in the laboratory and is thus liable for what is said and done in the name of student government—a position no longer tenable in view of present-day developments in student life.

This traditional view of student government was characterized by Samuel D. Gould, when serving as Chancellor of the University of California at Santa Barbara, as exemplifying "a disregard for the democratic process that must shake the faith of students who observe or are subject to them." [2] Gould suggested some of the attractions of this limiting view from the administrative standpoint:

It is, of course, the better part of discretion to put the student leaders out to pasture in some remote corner of the institutional ranch where, with adequate fencing, they can graze peacefully and wax fat and docile. They will then always be properly diffident, will be grateful for any little attentions tendered them, and will never ask embarrassing or challenging questions. They will graduate with the same sheeplike acceptance of directions that they brought with them as freshmen. They will also make no contribution to their own growth or that of the campus except to advance the state of atrophy in themselves and in their institution.[3]

Such a view of its functions may explain why established student governments have rarely led protests or demonstrations. In fact, the traditional student government structure is often the initial point of attack by student power advocates. The activist usually equates student government with a company union if he thinks of it at all. Unfortunately, the operations of student governments on many campuses have been so innocuous and so reflective of the establishment that even the non-activist has been tempted to classify them as non-representative, or even as anti-student. Those involved in student government can become equally frustrated. In a confrontation with the administration of the University of Indiana, the Student Senate of that institution eventually adopted a resolution which was to be sent as a letter to the University's Board of Trustees, and which stated:

We intend this to be very last piece of campus mail to be brushed aside. If you choose to close legitimate channels to the students, our constituents will be forced to use less legitimate ones. The name of the game, gentlemen, . . . is called "Pressure." . . . We fully intend to organize ourselves into a pressure group if that is all that matters to you.[4]

A possible effect of ignoring such pleas is suggested by Carl Davidson of the Students for a Democratic Society. Writing as a theoretician of the militant organization, he urges the creation of a Campus Freedom Democratic Party (CFDP) to take over student government with the main goal "to develop a radical consciousness among *all* the students, in the *real* struggle yet to come against the administration." The strategy to accomplish the objective is

a year-round electoral campaign for the purpose of educating students about their system; building mass memberships in dormitory and living area "precincts"; constantly harassing and disrupting the meetings of the existing student government (for instance, showing up *en masse* at a meeting and singing the jingle of the now defunct "Mickey Mouse Club"); and, finally, winning a majority of seats in student government elections. As long as CFDP has a minority of the seats, those seats should be used as soapboxes to expose the existing body as a parody of the idea of government.[5]

He went on to urge further that student government push through a list of demands which would include a time-limit for the administration to reply. If granted, the students would promptly celebrate the victory of their revolution; if refused, the CFDP would abolish student government and set up a student government in exile. In

Davidson's proposal, an alternative to the Campus Freedom Democratic Party concept would be a Free Student Union as a counter-institution to the existing student government which would encourage non-participation and engage in campus agitation, mass violations of existing rules, "non-violently seizing IBM cards," disrupting oversize classes, and "non-violently attempting to occupy and liberate the student newspaper and radio station."

The approach to reform by Davidson and the observations by President Gould should surprise no one familiar with student government on most college campuses. It has had to fight for status and leadership with militant groups as well as with the establishment representatives. In its insecurity it has often retreated to insignificant and superficial activities which brought a minimum of pain and considerable rewards of a transient sort. If it is to be enabled to contribute its potentially valuable services of facilitating institutional response to the current student movement, it must be strengthened against blackmail and threat from all sources. It must be brought into the inner rooms of policy formulation and decision making in an effective manner as a worthy partner with other segments of the institution. The epithet "sandbox government" must be rendered obsolete by making student government representative of student needs, demands, and problems as well as a valuable channel for effective contribution to the institutional response processes.

It is irrelevant for critics of student government to point out that the value of student input is weakened by lack of knowledge, continuity, time, or experience, observations which are all true. Certainly it is not philosophically sound to dismiss student efforts by saying they have no clear programs or goals, criticism which is often valid. Nor is it adequate to lash out at the cumbersome, inefficient mechanics of many student governments, a tempting response by harassed administrators or amused faculty members. Student response to these points is embarrassing and to the point: "Your house is not in order either, and you have more knowledge, more time, more experience, and more resources. Don't cast stones!" The fact is that a disturbingly large number of students are uneasy about the higher educational establishment. They may not be able to articulate its problems or offer solutions but their feelings cannot be dismissed. Student government offers a way to educate them about and involve them in the inner workings of academia and the values of its traditions and institutions.

Even the term "student government" is a misnomer which reduces the expectations of students, faculty and administrators alike. If students are only to manage their own affairs "as students," such activities will have little to do with the educational vitality of the institution. The goal of student governance should be the effective involvement of students in the policy formulation and decision-making processes of the institution. Perceived in this way, the range of experiences available to students is limited only by the competence, vision and creativity of the students, faculty and administration.

This broader concept eliminates the question "In what areas do students have complete autonomy and sole legal authority?" Radical student spokesmen are prone to demand this kind of independence. Yet they should realize that not only is legal authority likely only to be delegated to them, and therefore to exist at the discretion of the governing board, but also that if they had total control over certain areas, these areas would inevitably be ones marginal to the vital enterprises of the institution. Just as faculty associations such as the AAUP have abandoned the call for total self-government by faculty over a limited area, so students should realize that they can enjoy most involvement and responsibility and contribute most constructively by working with other segments of the academic community on the maximum variety of problems.

There is little doubt that the student movement has made a lasting impact on collegial governance through its tendency to demand and negotiate instead of confer and converse. In fact, a true dialogue has a very low priority in the activists' repertory: bargaining from raw power has a high rating. By focusing their reform demands on relatively superficial but extremely irritating regulations and procedures, the student movement has gained enough power through numbers, faculty support, and societal tolerance to question the traditional mechanics used by academia for resolving its difficulties. In fact, unless the institutional response meets their demands in part, activists on many campuses feel strong enough to challenge basic structures such as faculty councils and boards of trustees. Many observers feel therefore that there is a real threat to the academic world in the tendency to take so-called rights through mass action and raw power. The Boston Tea Party, the American Revolution, Gandhi's Satyagraha or Soul Force movement and Che Guevara's guerrilla warfare philosophy are somehow all wrapped into a holy war against real or fancied wrongs at old *Siwash* and the multiversity alike.

In the tactics of the militants, the recording device has become a symbol of the new approach to the interaction of student, faculty, and administration on many campuses. "Get it down so we can show the rank and file what we are up against!" is a cry which restricts conversation, limits analysis of alternatives, and embarrasses anyone who thinks expansively. Recorded discussions taken at meetings in which the participants themselves were serious and sincere in their efforts to resolve difficulties suddenly become hilarious examples of the intransigence, hypocrisy, and even dishonesty of the administration when played before a student senate or mass meeting. Isolated comments or statements taken out of context suddenly become rallying cries for the revolution. Buell Gallagher has termed this approach eristic, aiming at victory rather than truth, as opposed to the heuristic which seeks the truth.[6] In turn, students charge administrations and faculties with playing the same game on a more sophisticated level. Students interpret the ambiguity, delays, lack of direction, and overlap of authority evidenced by the typical institutional committee structure as barriers deliberately erected to handicap student participation.

If militancy and confrontation are not to replace reasoned discussion, student government must be strengthened. But it is perhaps unfortunate that this need should be at its most urgent in a period when student governments are beginning to face considerable problems in communicating with their constituents, and so in maintaining wide support. Increasing enrollments have resulted in much larger budgets, more complex organizations, and the need to recruit many more workers. Each of these developments brings with it problems of management, administration, and organization. Large budgets require bookkeeping and controls. Personnel must be trained and supervised. Since most student government officers are volunteers, they need to be constantly encouraged, stimulated, and rewarded with recognition and a feeling of achievement. Consequently, the personality cult is disappearing and giving way to the organization. This change often means that the nominal president is not the real head of the organization operating student government, creating a close analogy between current bureaucratic problems of student government and the Federal government. All too often student governments, because of their bureaucracy and administrative structure, have to adopt the techniques of investigating committees, the exposé game, and exaggerated publicity to maintain the attention of the public and give feelings of achievement and satisfaction to workers. Since on many campuses it is impossible for student government personnel to maintain a personal contact with their constituents, the propaganda sheet and even the "big lie" have become useful techniques. In view of the fact that the student power concept has given student governments a great impetus, it is important that institutional facilities be utilized to assist student governments in being the best operating organizations possible.

A view of student government which is currently gaining adherents sees it as merely one facet of student political activity, and further believes that this activity should have as its goal the achievement of social and economic change in American soci 'y as a whole. Students have played an increasingly large political role in the United States during the past few years. Civil rights activities on a local level expanded with the movement of numerous Northern white liberal students into the South during the period of the freedom rides; more recently, the campaigns of Senators McCarthy and Kennedy were powered largely by collegiate volunteers, and the withdrawal of President Johnson was credited by some to the implacable hostility with which a large segment of the college generation viewed him. Student governments organized lobbies to legislative bodies to work for larger university budgets and to defeat bills they considered undesirable. The mass media, public interest in the campus, and politicians themselves added support to the activities. Thus the trend is firmly established. There are no longer any separation of off-campus and on-campus controversial issues, whether the topic is peace in Vietnam, admission of Red China to the U. N., or the nomination of a Presidential candidate.

Thus it is clear that a process of transformation in student government is under way. Much depends upon whether this process can be successfully completed. It is clear that the concept of student participation in policy making is gaining wide acceptance. More and more colleges and universities are placing student representatives on committees where their presence would have occasioned much surprise and displeasure only a few years ago. Another index of this change in attitude is afforded by an examination of the literature on the administration of higher education. For example, John J. Corson's *Governance of Colleges and Universities*, published in 1960, and generally considered one of the most outstanding books on its subject, does not discuss student government in any way. It does not have the word "student" listed in the index and dismisses the role to be played by students in a note in the appendix in commenting on selected readings by saying, "Two studies, written in rather crusading terms, deal with the role to be played by students." [7] It is unlikely any book on the governance of colleges and universities would be written today without discussing the input which students must and do make.

However, it is not yet clear that all the implications of this new student involvement have been explored. Activists are already complaining that student seats on influential committees, sought so eagerly such a short time ago, are mere "tokenism," and in fact it may be that such student representation is much less significant than either its proponents or its critics originally thought. The new mechanisms of student involvement have yet to prove themselves. Similarly, the fact that students, faculty and administrators may join in hoping for a more meaningful and effective student government does not of itself guarantee that this will come about.

The new situation places an especially heavy load on the student government adviser—the administrator or faculty member who meets with the student legislators. Students reject the advisory relationship but accept a communication channel or a facilitating agent to assist them in carrying out their objectives. On smaller campuses where a faculty member frequently serves as student government adviser, he is being asked to define his role so that it is clear that he is not present as a watchdog or censor, but rather as a colleague or coach who will assist student government in pressing its views or demands upon the institution. In this new role the adviser is also seen as a "resource person" who is available to give the student government leaders information or assistance in carrying out their activities. Some students are demanding that the adviser, whether he is a faculty member or a dean of students staff member, act as an advocate on their behalf in supporting their demands, securing a hearing for their appeals and pronouncements, and in general serving as their agent rather than the institution's agent.

Whether this and other necessary adjustments can be made remains to be seen. It is unfortunate that it took the impetus provided by some disillusioned young radicals to secure genuine consideration of university reform. The motive of containing protest, and of channeling student activism into non-violent modes is a compelling one for many administrators; yet concern with defusing the militants should not be the only or even the prime motive for change. The challenge to the educator today is to prevent his own cynicism, prejudices and limitations and the inflexibility and complacency of his institution from inhibiting and handicapping the new generation in going about the business of seeking a relevant higher education.

NOTES

[1] Jeff Greenfield, as reported in *Moderator,* I (February, 1966), p. 56.

[2] Quoted in Gordon Klopf, *College Student Government* (New York, Harper & Brothers, 1960), p. 7.

[3] *Ibid.,* p. 8.

[4] "Enough is Enough," resolution of the Indiana University Summer Student Senate, Indiana University, July 25, 1968.

[5] Carl Davidson, "Towards Student Syndicalism," *New Left Notes,* September 9, 1966.

[6] Buell Gallagher, "Student Unrest," in Esther Lloyd Jones and Herman A. Estrin (eds.), *The American Student and his College* (Boston, Houghton Mifflin, 1967), pp. 291–298.

[7] John J. Corson, *Governance of Colleges and Universities* (New York, McGraw Hill, 1960), p. 197.

4

STUDENT POWER AND
IN LOCO PARENTIS

by Stanford Cazier*

FOR YEARS colleges and universities have asserted or assumed that one of their prerogatives is the sanctioning of certain types of student conduct. Some institutions have adopted a common law approach to student discipline, while others have established guidelines, albeit minimal in many instances, for the regular handling of misconduct cases. But regardless of the approach, the process has been administrative in character, with the colleges and universities imposing rules of conduct as they would establish a curriculum—on the grounds that they know what is best for the students. However adequate these discipline programs may have been in the more tranquil atmosphere of intramural affairs, the rapid politicization of much of student activity in recent years, including protest against "rationalizations" of higher education, has led many institutions to a serious review of their regulation of student conduct, particularly conduct which is currently termed "political" in nature or which may lead to the disruption of a university's operations. Few schools have anticipated the necessity for any substantial revision in student discipline procedures; they have been brought to this realization by specific

* Dr. Cazier, an American Council on Education Academic Administration Fellow at New York University in 1967–68, is Associate Professor of History and Assistant to the President, Utah State University.

instances of student protest. The most common agency of reappraisal is a joint committee of faculty and students. Examples of this pattern of response are readily available.

In the spring of 1965, following almost an entire semester of student protest, the Academic Senate of the University of California, Berkeley Division, created a Select Committee to study Education at Berkeley. The focus on curricular shortcomings as a cause of student unrest was reflected in the resultant Muscatine Report, which did not deal with disciplinary matters. However, after a student strike in December 1966, the Academic Senate established another student-faculty commission charged, among other things, with considering the "fairness of disciplinary procedures and methods of reviewing the content of rules. . . ." The commission's report "The Culture of the University: Governance and Education" called attention to the "preoccupation with controversies over rules" at Berkeley:

The content, enactment, and enforcement of rules regulating student conduct have posed something of a puzzle on this campus in recent years. Although the rules have been the storm center of recurring crises, the chief protagonists have repeatedly depreciated their significance. The administration has lamented the controversy over rules as a diversion from the problems of education, while student activists have deplored the tendency of regulatory disputes abruptly to steer the pattern of student protest off its intended course. (p. 57)

In the fall of 1966, after students at Brown University protested the use of "academic punishments for social offenses," President Ray L. Heffner appointed an Advisory Committee on Student Conduct (Magrath Committee) to, among other assignments, "examine the relationship between student conduct and the proper atmosphere of a university." In January 1967, one month after students at New York University had staged a sit-in and a boycott of classes in opposition to a tuition increase, the University Senate established a student-faculty commission (McKay Commission) to study and recommend ways to increase student participation in University affairs—including the structuring of student discipline.

Cornell University established a student-faculty-administration commission (Sindler Commission) in the spring of 1967 to review "the purposes, bases, and scope of University regulation of student misconduct." The need was apparent, as the commission reported: ". . . like most universities, Cornell has not operated by a deliberate, internally consistent set of principles and policies designed to guide its regulation of student conduct. . . . Hence, . . . Cornell was not well prepared this past academic year to respond to the multiple conflicts that emerged." The Magrath Committee and the McKay and Sindler Commissions issued reports in 1967, calling for major revisions in the regulation of student conduct at their respective institutions.

The University of Wisconsin, which has experienced as much student unrest as any institution, has had a corresponding wealth of committee responses. A thorough, two-year study of the problem of student misconduct at Wisconsin had been reported in detail in the summer of 1965 by the Committee on Noncurricular Life of Students (Remington Committee). While the Crow Committee was addressing itself to this mandate in the fall of 1967, students protesting on-campus recruitment by the Dow Chemical Company had a violent confrontation with the Madison police, and a second ad hoc committee was established On Mode of Response to Obstruction, Interview Policy, and Related Matters (Mermin Committee). The Crow Committee gave a broad interpretation to the parameters of student conduct identified as subject to University regulation by the Remington Report, and the Mermin Committee split, eight to six, over the correctness of this interpretation. The implications of this divergence will be developed below.

During 1966–67 student unrest and dissent at the University of Colorado prompted the Regents to call for an examination of a statement on Discipline Procedures and Structure adopted in 1960. Accordingly a student-faculty-administration committee conducted a thorough review and submitted a report at the end of the academic year, recommending revision in policy. Before this report was referred to the Regents, however, a new wave of protest was sparked by the suspension and probation of several students who had obstructed CIA recruitment in October 1967. Responding to this, the University Senate authorized its Student Affairs Committee to conduct a study of discipline policy and procedure. Submitting its report to the Senate, the Committee commented that it had "had the special benefit of considerable unrest and student agitation for change as accompaniment to its deliberations. These factors have no doubt influenced the character of its response."

Other comparable reports include one at the University of Kentucky, "Non-Academic Relationships Between Students and the University," the work of the Commission on Open Expression and Demonstration on Campus at the University of Pennsylvania, special efforts of members of the Faculty Senate at the University of Massachusetts, "Student Residence Open House Policy Recommendation" and "Picketing and Other Forms of Demonstration on the University Campus," and a variety of committee reports of the Commission on Student Life at Oakland University. Numerous other institutions have conducted less formal examinations of student discipline.

Other colleges and universities have moved more directly to the task of revising discipline procedures or of recasting them in an entirely new format. The Universities of Oregon and Washington provide excellent examples of these options. In its Student Conduct Program, the University of Oregon has produced a model which has been widely emulated, particularly following its publication in the *California Law Review* in 1966. The flexibility in the amending process is one of its most attractive features. At the University of Washington, the Faculty Committee on Student Affairs prepared a draft of new regulations which is admirable for its clarity and economy of exposition and for its procedural guarantees. In restructuring student discipline, many schools display less effort and imagination than Oregon, Washington, and the other institutions making substantial reviews, but few are immune from the climate of student protest.

Approximately twenty commission and committee reports and forty codes and drafts of codes were examined for this study, and from them a number of generalizations and possible trends may be inferred:

Rationale

Colleges and universities, especially those which are residential, have traditionally acted *in loco parentis*. In the past this principle has granted to universities rather arbitrary power in regulating student behavior, and until recently the courts have backed them in the exercise of surrogate authority. Such a concept was more meaningful in a society in which parents did indeed govern their children's lives with a firm hand, setting standards, formulating rules, and punishing transgressions. The role of surrogate parent is one which many universities are now attempting to repudiate—at least publicly. When Dean William Buckler said at a recent New York University Founder's Day address that "the American college should shed, and shed quickly, the uniform of the policeman and frock of the priest," he probably assumed that his counsel included the doffing of mother's apron as well. The Crow Committee at Wisconsin stated that "we advocate practically complete withdrawal by the University from its *in loco parentis* activities." Last fall the Sindler Commission reported: "We explicitly reject the 'service facility' and 'in loco parentis' views of a university as unsuitable for Cornell's needs." There is, perhaps, something repugnant to both faculty and student sensibilities in the notion of an institutional parent imposing its own moral standards on those who attend it.

But if universities are sincere in their current rejection of *in loco parentis*, they are not always thorough. The Sindler Commission, for example, advocated that

> When University officials apprehend a student for activity in violation of both the Code and the law, we recommend that all but very serious breaches of the law be handled internally within the Cornell jurisdiction. . . . We recommend that student possession, use, or sale of marijuana be treated as a Code offense. . . . We recommend that the University seek to assume full responsibility in handling the student marijuana problem, and in the context of the Code rather than law enforcement.

A residuum of paternalism also remains from the Magrath Committee's efforts to seek substitutes for *in loco parentis* at Brown University:

> In our view, the concept of "in loco parentis"—if indeed it can be dignified by calling it a concept—is essentially irrelevant to the problems confronting Brown University. For reasons that we have already noted, a university community such as Brown, which includes young people in various stages of developing maturity, must have a certain number of basic student conduct regulations. It must also express its legitimate concern through counselling and education.

The concept of *in loco parentis* may be both unclear and emotionally unsatisfactory, but unless universities are prepared—as most are not —to abandon all efforts to regulate the non-academic lives of students, some form of paternalism is inevitable.

No generally recognized principle has emerged to take the place of *in loco parentis*. The Senate Committee on Student Affairs at the University of Colorado sought refuge in the principle of *ex contractu*:

The relationship of the University with the student . . . is in the essential nature of a contract involving a set of rights and obligations, reflecting both the purposes of the University and those of the students in attendance. . . . The University, therefore, exercises its authority over students in terms of the mutual interests of both parties and in terms of their contract with each other.

A model code prepared by a Law School seminar at New York University during spring semester, 1968, advances the *fiduciary concept* as being a more appropriate identification of the relationship between the University and the student. The concept was suggested by Warren Seavey in the *Harvard Law Review* and is borrowed from the law of trusts:

A fiduciary is one whose function it is to act for the benefit of another as to matters relevant to the relations between them. Since schools exist primarily for the education of their students, it is obvious that professors and administrators act in a fiduciary capacity with reference to the students. One of the duties of the fiduciary is to make full disclosure of all relevant facts in any transaction between them. . . . The dismissal of a student comes within this rule.*

The general tendency now is to justify the institution's regulation of student lives in terms of its fundamental purposes. Most of the codes, drafts, and committee and commission reports include a statement of general philosophy, principle, or policy under which a code is defended. Invariably this involves a proclamation of the purposes, functions, or interests of the college or university, which are identified as being the purveying of knowledge, the advancement of knowledge, and service to society where knowledge applies. Not infrequently, however, reference is also made to the development of students. The reader is then cautioned that these ends can be met only in a properly conditioned atmosphere. The creation and maintenance of this atmosphere becomes the responsibility of all members of the academic community. By implication, a breach of that responsibility is properly subject to university discipline:

* Warren Seavey, "Dismissal of Students: Due Process," *Harvard Law Review,* LXX (November 3, 1957), 1406.

The University is maintained by society for the accomplishment of certain special purposes, namely, the provision of programs of instruction in higher education, the advancement of knowledge through scholarship and research, and the provision of related community services. Like any other social institution having its own special purposes, the University must maintain conditions conducive to the effective performance of its functions. Consequently, it has special expectations regarding the conduct of the various participants in the academic community. Student conduct which distracts from or interferes with the accomplishments of University purposes is not acceptable. (University of Washington, Draft)

We feel that a code necessary for community living and orderly procedure has been established. This statement allows for maximum individual freedom while providing a workable framework for the accomplishment of the social and academic purposes of the College as a whole. (Scripps College)

If they do not state it directly, many of the rationalists assume that students need guidance through regulation, since, while they are approaching maturity, they are not mature.
Implicit:
The University is dedicated not only to the learning and the advancement of knowledge but also to the development of ethically sensitive and responsible persons. It seeks to achieve these goals through a sound educational program and policies governing student conduct that encourages independence and maturity. (University of Oregon)

Explicit:
The concept of adolescence is a valid one. . . . Most people, however, grow toward maturity, and we believe that the wisest response to this process of maturation and adult socialization is a structure in which negative student conduct rules are gradually and significantly diminished. (Magrath Committee Report)

Almost without exception, institutions insist that they will take cognizance only of that behavior which adversely affects their *purposes*, *functions*, or *interests*, and the most recent committee efforts have been at pains to achieve consensus on the denotation of these terms.

There shall be no regulation unless there is a demonstrable need for it which is reasonably related to the basic purposes and necessities of the

University as stipulated herein. (Academic Freedom for Students at Michigan State University)

The whole process of discipline is meaningful only when it is relevant to the generic functions and purposes of the University. Because of its primary function as an educational institution the University will only engage in actions or processes for which it is designed and which are vital to its basic concerns. (SCSA Report on Discipline Procedures and Policy, University of Colorado)

A student enrolling in the University assumes an obligation to conduct himself in a manner compatible with the University's function as an educational institution. (University of California Policies Relating to Students . . . , February 19, 1968)

Only where the institution's interests as an academic community are distinct and clearly involved should the special authority of the institution be asserted. (Joint Statement)

Those code formulations which also attempt the delineation of the purposes, functions, or interests of the university *agree* that behavior which causes impairment of the intellectual atmosphere, the educational process, or the achievement of personal educational objectives is actionable by the university, but they *disagree* as to the proper role of the university when its ancillary functions are adversely affected by student action—action which may even cause physical injury to members of the university community and damage to university property:

The University may apply sanctions or take other appropriate action only when student conduct directly and significantly interferes with the University's (a) primary educational responsibility of ensuring the opportunity of all members of the University community to attain their educational objectives, or (b) subsidiary responsibilities of protecting the health and safety of persons in the University community, maintaining and protecting property, keeping records, providing living accommodations and other services, and sponsoring non-classroom activities such as lectures, concerts, athletic events, and social functions. (University of Oregon)

The University may apply sanctions or take other appropriate action only when student conduct has an adverse effect on distinct University interests, namely: (a) The opportunity of all members of the University community to attain their educational objectives, (b) The generation and maintenance of an intellectual and educational atmosphere throughout the University community, (c) The protection of health, safety, welfare and property of all members of the University community and of the University itself. (Sindler Commission Report)

Disagreement on these issues is pronounced at the University of Wisconsin. The Remington Report had identified three areas as being properly subject to university discipline:

1. Student conduct which is indicative of a continuing threat to the personal safety of members of the University Community.
2. Student conduct which seriously damages University property.
3. Student conduct which is unduly disruptive of the educational process.

The Crow Committee had no difficulty accepting areas one and two of the Remington Report, but felt that the lack of precision in the terms "disruptive" and "educational process" required a closer examination and possible restatement of area three. The result was a recommendation of sanctions for "intentional conduct" which "clearly and seriously obstructs or impairs a significant University function or process."

A minority (6 members) of the Mermin Committee, reporting two months after the Crow Committee, agreed with the broadened, if more precise, restatement of area three by the Crow Committee. However, the majority (8 members) was critical of the Crow Committee for being too solicitous of the "interests of the institution to the point of neglecting the interests of the student involved" and for the enlargement of the "scope of academic discipline to cover all political activity on the campus which is obstructive." Further, the majority found this action to be "regressive and repressive" and suggested that "the University should be concerned, in the application of academic sanctions, *only* with its academic relationship with its students." (Emphasis added.)

There is some irony in this very important report in that the protagonists cite some of the same studies in support of their recommendations. Irrespective of these recommendations, the minority appears to have been more judicious in the use of these studies, particularly the Remington Report, the Joint Statement on Rights and

Freedoms of Students, and the Report of the Study Commission on University Governance (Berkeley, 1968).

The expressed sensitivity of the majority of the Mermin Committee for the "interests of the student" is symptomatic of the shift away from the idea that the university always knows what is best for students to the new concept that students have rights as well as responsibilities. That is, current code formulations are admitting that the university's interests may come into conflict with the interests of its students, or with freedoms which students ought to have.

Older rules of student conduct have usually placed emphasis on students' responsibilities while remaining silent on their rights. At best this is a negative conception of the role of students in the collegiate community. In order to correct this conception, representatives of a number of national educational organizations met in the fall of 1966 to draft a "Joint Statement on the Rights and Freedom of Students." During 1967, several of these national associations, beginning with the National Students Association and the American Association of University Professors, endorsed the Joint Statement.

Either following this lead or coming at the issue concurrently, a number of institutions are now prefacing new codes with a "bill of rights" for students. In 1967, Michigan State University issued a document entitled, "Academic Freedom for Students . . . ," prepared by the Faculty Committee on Student Affairs. In seeking an "operational definition" of academic freedom for students, the Committee identified the rights as well as the duties of students "in regard to conduct, academic pursuits, the keeping of records, and publications." Early in 1968 the Student Government Association of Emory University completed a draft of a new student constitution containing a Bill of Rights. At the University of Iowa a proposed amendment would add a "Student Bill of Rights and Freedoms" to the student constitution. And the declaration and defense of student rights contained in the New York University Law School model code covers 18 pages. While the declaration generally subscribes to the rights enumerated in the Joint Statement, it makes a much more extensive elaboration of the rights of protest and privacy rights.

Codes and Substantive Due Process

The general thrust of these changes in fundamental theory is clearly in the direction of greater student freedom. Faced with student protest, the universities have rethought their position on control of the non-academic lives of students, and in consequence have been moving towards a relaxation of rules and controls.

Parietal rules, a favorite concern of protesters, have been relaxed at many institutions. At New York University it was decided to place decisions on hours in the hands of the student residents. Within a week of the biggest protest rally ever held on the Princeton campus, the Trustees approved extension of the hours during which women visitors could be entertained in the dormitories—a concession which was rejected by student leaders, who insisted that their concern was not with particular hours, but with the general principle of self-determination for students. Other liberalizations which have followed protests have included the abolition of dress requirements on several campuses, the abandonment of efforts to determine what speakers could be invited to appear on campus (Ohio State University), and the granting of broader political rights (Berkeley). Some idea of the enlarged scope of student freedom may be gained from the "Rights and Freedoms" enumerated in the Joint Statement:

    I. Freedom of Access to Higher Education
    II. In the Classroom
        A. Protection of Freedom of Expression
        B. Protection Against Improper Academic Evaluation
        C. Protection Against Improper Disclosure
    III. (Confidentiality of) Student Records
    IV. Student Affairs
        A. Freedom of Association
        B. Freedom of Inquiry and Expression
        C. Student Participation in Institutional Government
        D. Student Publications
    V. Off-Campus Freedom of Students
    VI. Procedural Standards in Disciplinary Proceedings

More generally, a frequent complaint of students, particularly in the last few years, has been that substantive code provisions may be so vague that they cannot tell when conduct becomes misconduct. Examination of some codes illustrates the force of this complaint. Thus the first regulation at Princeton reads:

All students are expected to conduct themselves in a manner becoming scholars and gentlemen. The University reserves the right at any time to suspend or dismiss a student for . . . unsatisfactory conduct, or for any other appropriate reason determined solely in the University's judgment.

While in Washington Square College of New York University a student can face suspension or expulsion for "Conduct tending to bring the name of the College into disrepute."

The general demand for precision of language in the proscription of certain types of conduct has led many of the discipline review commissions to call for greater specificity as a partial guarantee of substantive due process:

Such minimum rules as are formulated ought to be stated as explicitly as possible, though we recognize that effective rules cannot be over-elaborated and addressed to every conceivable nuance that might exist in a particular situation. We are opposed to vague rules such as those contained in phrases that make students liable for "ungentlemanly conduct," "conduct unbecoming to a student" or "conduct against the best interests of the institution." (Magrath Committee Report)

Offenses permitting application of University discipline should be inferrable without strain from one or more of the three categories of "University interests" and should be stated in specific language to the exclusion of catchall phrases. (Sindler Commission Report)

Every regulation shall be brief, clear and specific as possible. (Academic Freedom for Students at Michigan State University)

Pursuant to the Magrath Committee Report, President Ray L. Heffner addressed a letter to all Brown University students in the fall of 1967, wherein he outlined "as explicitly as possible" the standards of conduct expected at Brown.

The Joint Statement provides additional endorsement of this trend: "The institution has an obligation to clarify those standards of behavior which it considers essential to its educational mission and its community life. . . . Offenses should be as clearly defined as possible." In February 1968, the University of California amended its "Policies Relating to Students" to bring them into accord with the Joint Statement. Commenting on the new definition of conduct, President Charles J. Hitch said that he and the chancellors of the nine campuses hoped to "define more precisely the meaning of standards of conduct" and that the amendment was "a clarification rather than a change of University policy." The new standards of conduct proscribe the following categories of misconduct:

a. Dishonesty, such as cheating, plagiarism, or knowingly furnishing false information to the University;
b. Forgery, alteration, or misuse of University documents, records, or identification;
c. Obstruction or disruption of teaching, research, administration, disciplinary procedures, or other University activities, including its public service functions, or of other authorized activities on University premises;
d. Physical abuse of any person on University-owned or -controlled property or at University-sponsored or -supervised functions, or conduct which threatens or endangers the health or safety of any such person;
e. Theft or damage to property of the University or of a member of the University community or campus visitor;
f. Unauthorized entry to or use of University facilities;
g. Violation of University policies or of campus regulations, including campus regulations concerning the registration of student organizations, the use of University facilities, or the time, place, and manner of public expression;
h. Use, possession, or distribution of narcotic or dangerous drugs, such as marijuana and lysergic acid diethylamide (LSD), except as expressly permitted by law;
i. Violation of rules governing residence in University-owned or -controlled property;
j. Disorderly conduct or lewd, indecent, or obscene conduct or expression on University-owned or -controlled property or at University-sponsored or -supervised functions;
k. Failure to comply with directions of University officials acting in the performance of their duties; or
l. Conduct which adversely affects the student's suitability as a member of the academic community.

A paradox thus appears. The immediate impact of protest is in the direction of an abandonment of rules, but the demand for specificity leads to a proliferation of them. Whether a definition such as that enunciated at the University of California represents the proper balance between the demand for specificity and rules which are "over-elaborated and addressed to every conceivable nuance" remains to be seen.

The codes are enforced by a list of sanctions which are assigned to the possible offenses. Traditionally, academic sanctions have ranged from letters of reprimand to expulsion (defined at the University of California as being "permanent termination of student status without possibility of readmission to any campus of the University"). However, in an atmosphere of growing deference to both substantive and procedural due process, recent code recommendations counsel the imposition of penalties only under the principles of reasonableness and commensuration. Further, the most recent drafts and reports would not only reserve dismissal or suspension for serious misconduct, they would also reject expulsion as a mode of academic sanction:

Suspension and dismissal is a severe sanction, and it should be relied upon only as a final resort in cases where there is a serious or persistent violation of the written student conduct rules. Students should not be suspended temporarily within a given semester. (Magrath Committee Report)

The draft of new regulations at the University of Washington lists dismissal as the most severe penalty the University may impose, and a dismissed student may, upon written petition, be readmitted to the University.

If the members of the Mermin Committee at the University of Wisconsin could not agree on some important issues, they were unified in rejecting expulsion as being inappropriate discipline in a university community:

We have come to the unanimous conclusion that no argument justifies the employment of this academic equivalent of banishment, and we recommend that the University relinquish this power.

Two months previous the Crow Committee Report had included expulsion, without comment, as a possible University penalty. The Mermin Committee would also limit a sanction of suspension to a maximum of three years.

Beyond the question of the severity of penalties, the majority of the Mermin Committee concluded that sanction policy was characterized by confusion and was in need of close scrutiny, if not reform, suggesting the desirability not merely of alternative penalties but alternatives to penalties:

The limited variety of sanctions available make it difficult to deal with situations in which a slap on the wrist (probation) is ineffective and banishment (expulsion) is inappropriate and overly harsh. The increasing importance of higher education and the trend toward much freer access to it render even temporary banishment less desirable. When harsh sanctions are available to the University, there will in times of crisis be strong pressures, both from within and without, to employ them. On occasion, this indeed puts the University into the position of acting as an agent of social control for the larger community. . . . We think it far more constructive to formulate basic principles that may serve to delineate that mode of response which is proper to a University. (Mermin Committee Report)

Codes, Civil Law, and Double Jeopardy

A major demand of many activists has been that the universities cease to perform a police function, and instead confine themselves to such rules and rule-enforcement as is directly related to their central academic purpose. As has been shown, there is some university thinking in sympathy with this demand. A logical consequence of such a policy would be that the university should not duplicate enforcement of such civil laws as may affect its students or govern their behavior either on or off campus, if such laws are irrelevant to the *academic* enterprise. Many universities already lean toward the position that they will at least seek to avoid duplicating the work of the courts:

Ordinarily, the University will not impose further sanctions after law enforcement agencies or the courts have disposed of a case. (University of Oregon, emphasis added)

Students who violate the law may incur penalties prescribed by authorities, but institutional authority should never be used merely to duplicate the function of general laws. (Joint Statement)

Student conduct subject to University discipline . . . may also simultaneously be violations of the law. This is irrelevant to establishing the boundaries of University discipline . . . but is relevant to whether the University will choose to exercise its jurisdiction. (Sindler Commission Report)

However, the student argument that the university cannot impose some additional penalty for an offense which has already been punished by the courts is generally rejected, with the proviso that a review of the civil action should precede the imposition of any additional penalty:

The University will review the circumstances leading to the arrest of a student or his conviction by a court of law. If the action is the result of conduct deemed improper and prejudicial to the interests of the University community, and counseling is considered inadequate for the offense, the matter will be referred to an appropriate university judicial body or officer. (Florida State University)

The notion that such a policy involves a breach of the constitutional principle of "no double jeopardy" is generally denied:

Off-campus misconduct, legal or illegal, and whether or not tested in the courts, may raise questions concerning the suitability of a student to be a member of the University community. Furthermore misconduct on the campus may be judged not only by the aforegoing standards of legality and suitability as a student, but by its disruptiveness in the normal functioning of the institution. . . . Under these conditions, action may be taken both by civil authorities and by the University without constituting double jeopardy. (University of California, Irvine, Draft)

"Double jeopardy," which is proscribed by the U. S. Constitution, protects a person from being tried twice for the same offense. It is not considered the same offense, and hence, the protection does not apply, when the person's action constitutes several offenses tried by one jurisdiction or separate offenses against different jurisdictions for which he is tried by those jurisdictions. Technically, then, the responsibility of students to the University and the civil society, wherein the same misconduct could be punishable by both, occasions no double jeopardy. (Sindler Commission Report)

The issue has been argued by two faculty committees responding to student protest at the University of Wisconsin. The Crow Committee held that

As a general rule, the University should not apply its disciplinary powers in instances where the matter has been taken up by normal civil law processes; but in serious cases in the three categories above specified, the University should be free to impose discipline.

A minority of the Mermin Committee subscribed to this position, but the majority would severely limit the imposition of university authority where civil authority had taken action against student conduct. The majority recommended that

> If some particular behavior is prosecuted in a criminal court, the University shall normally accept the court's judgment as full disposition [and] . . . that in those rare instances in which an individual is liable to the imposition of both University sanctions and those of another authority for some particular behavior, University policy be that he not be forced to contest simultaneously both sets of charges.

The majority position was that students are *both* citizens and members of the academic community and that the rights and burdens they enjoy as citizens are not diminished by virtue of university attendance:

> Some may argue that students have responsibilities beyond those of other citizens, and that these responsibilities include obeying the law more carefully than other citizens. Students indeed have responsibilities in addition to those of other citizens, but these relate to their academic performance, and not to their public behavior. . . . To provide special protections for students involved in illegal activity would be unjust. To add sanctions on top of those of the criminal law is equally unjust and would unnecessarily restrict the behavior of one group of citizens in our society.

The immediate implication of the Mermin Committee majority view was that the Chancellor erred when he insisted that student interruption of activities at the campus Placement Office in 1967 was a matter for University discipline. The Committee majority implied that, although this protest took place on the campus, it did not interfere with the University's essential "educational process," and therefore that if an infraction of law took place, it was the business of the police and not the University authorities. With the increasing politicization of students, this plainly means that police may become an ever more frequent presence on the campus—ironically, in the name of academic liberty. At stake appears to be the autonomy of the university. Whether or not the recommendations of the majority "invite external controls" is a key issue in the debate among the members of the Mermin Committee. And that debate should become public.

Code Administration and Procedural Due Process

Today there is as much concern for the requirements of "procedural due process" in the administration of codes of conduct as there is for "substantive due process" in code formulation. Surprisingly this concern has not produced a distinct separation between the legislative and judicial functions in student discipline. Some programs even call for a tight linkage, if not merger, of the agencies formulating, administering, and evaluating student discipline procedures:

The present Board of Review for Disciplinary Cases was unanimous in its view that there had to be a close tie between the makers and the enforcers of student conduct rules. (Magrath Committee Report)

The (Student Conduct) Committee shall consist of four faculty members and three student members (and) . . . is designated as the agency within the University which has primary responsibility for the student-conduct program. The Committee shall be responsible to the faculty and the President of the University for recommending policies relating to student conduct, for formulating or approving rules and enforcement procedures within the framework of existing policies, for disposing of such individual cases as may properly come before it, and for recommending to the President of the University changes in the administration of any aspect of the student-conduct program. (University of Oregon)

In defense of this practice, the recent code of the New York University School of Law suggests that the separation of powers found in the United States Government is a model which is "not inexorable . . . Accordingly, no compelling need should be felt to separate for all purposes the legislative, executive, and judicial aspects of the rule-making and enforcement procedures relating to student conduct in a university."

Regardless of the degree of separation between the functions of code formulation and enforcement, genuine provision is currently being made for student involvement in both. In preparing its report, the Magrath Committee at Brown University surveyed the discipline procedures at thirty-seven institutions:

First, virtually all of the responding deans (twenty-three of twenty-six) reported that students were part of a mechanism "primarily responsible for the formulation of student conduct regulations." . . . Second, a strong majority of the deans (19) report that students are formally and significantly involved in rendering decisions in the most serious disciplinary cases.

In addition, the most recent codes, drafts, and reports are almost unanimous in recommending significant student participation in code preparation and administration.

The safeguards or guarantees presently being built into discipline proceedings would seem to satisfy the requirements of procedural due process. At New York University an Interim Committee on Student Discipline based its procedural rules on those used for removing tenured faculty members—an action which should provide ample protection for students at most universities. The Joint Statement on Rights and Freedoms of Students outlines some hearing committee procedures which are suggested for "situations requiring a high degree of formality":

1. The hearing committee should include faculty members or students, or, if regularly included or requested by the accused, both faculty and student members. No member of the hearing committee who is otherwise interested in the particular case should sit in judgment during the proceeding.
2. The student should be informed, in writing, of the reasons for the proposed disciplinary action with sufficient particularity, and in sufficient time, to insure opportunity to prepare for the hearing.
3. The student appearing before the hearing committee should have the right to be assisted in his defense by an adviser of his choice.
4. The burden of proof should rest upon the officials bringing the charge.
5. The student should be given an opportunity to testify and to present evidence and witnesses. He should have an opportunity to hear and question adverse witnesses. In no case should the committee consider statements against him unless he has been advised of their content and of the names of those who made them, and unless he has been given an opportunity to rebut unfavorable inferences which might otherwise be drawn.
6. All matters upon which the decision may be based must be introduced into evidence at the proceedings before the Hearing Committee. The decision should be based solely upon such matters. Improperly acquired evidence should not be admitted.
7. In the absence of a transcript, there should be both a digest and a verbatim record, such as a tape recording, of the hearing.

8. The decision of the Hearing Committee should be final, subject only to the student's right of appeal to the President or ultimately to the governing board of the institution.

Current practice at many institutions subscribes, and sometimes adds, to these standards. Generally, options are available to the accused student as to the formality of a disciplinary hearing, as to the agency which will conduct the hearing, as to whether students will sit on the hearing committee, and as to appeal:

In all cases involving possible suspension or dismissal, the student shall have an option to appear before the dean or the Council. . . . Where the student elects to have his case decided by a dean or by the Council, he may request that the student members of the Council not sit in his case. . . . In all cases decided by a dean or by the Council there shall be a right of appeal to the President of the University. (Magrath Committee Report)

Consistent with the desire to let students enjoy the burdens as well as the benefits of citizenship, the Mermin Committee at Wisconsin was unanimous in denying them the option of a hearing before faculty members only:

We question the wisdom and justice of any proposal . . . which provides the opportunity for the defendant to choose the panel of judges to hear his case. We know of no reason to permit it in obstruction cases, nor have any reasons been supplied for permitting it in other cases.

Some code recommendations go beyond the Joint Statement guidelines in allowing students the option of professional counsel. In the University of Washington Draft the "student may be represented by counsel and/or accompanied by an adviser of his choice." In the New York University Law School Code a "student charged with misconduct also has the right to be represented by counsel or an adviser. He may be a member of the faculty or an individual from outside the college." A serious implication of inviting professional counsel is the threat of making the disciplinary proceedings adversary in character. The NYU code cautioned against this possibility by suggesting that the hearings be keyed "to do substantial justice" but not be "unduly restricted by the rules of procedure or evidence."

The threat of adversary proceedings is not confined to the presence of professional counsel, but is also a function of the formality and structure of the discipline process. In the Student Conduct Program of the University of Oregon reference is made to "a special assistant to the Student Conduct Program who will serve as a prosecutor for the Student Court and who shall be responsible to the Student Conduct Committee." In the Draft of New Regulations at the University of Washington an "Assistant Attorney General" will represent the University in hearings before the University Discipline Committee and "shall present the case on behalf of the initiating officer." And not infrequently codes refer to the accused and the person presenting the case in terms of "parties."

While the recent code of the NYU Law School denies the necessity for a categorical separation between code formulation and enforcement, it does counsel the separation of "the prosecutorial function from the fact-finding and judging function." The Mermin Committee of the University of Wisconsin agrees with this position and supports "the principle that at least as long as the administration plays a 'prosecutor' role its role as adjudicator should be minimized." A number of recent code formulations agree that this principle is served in part by having the members of hearing committees elected, rather than appointed by the administration.

Finally, not only do recent codes and drafts protect the right of the student to testify and present evidence in his own behalf, but many of them also recognize the student's right to remain silent, or as Academic Freedom for Students at Michigan State University states it, "the student shall be entitled to refuse to answer questions." And the Student Conduct Program of the University of Oregon outlines proceedings to cover varying contingencies, including the occasion when "a student may elect not to appear for a hearing." It is clear that the widespread reevaluations of student disciplinary philosophies, policies and procedures which has been described here has in large measure been prompted by student militancy.

If the committee reports, codes, and drafts of codes examined suggest a substantial liberalization in current student disciplinary procedures at a number of universities, it is well to remember that we have here a report of intent, rather than an evaluation of practice on any of these campuses. The extent to which these proposals will be implemented in practice still remains to be seen, but it is difficult to avoid the conclusion that student protest has sounded the death-knell of the *in loco parentis* relationship between colleges and universities and their students.

CODES, DRAFTS OF CODES, COMMITTEE AND COMMISSION REPORTS USED IN THIS STUDY

American Association of University Professors, et al.
"Joint Statement on Rights and Freedoms of Students," *AAUP Bulletin,* LIII (1967), p. 365.

Brown University
"Community and Partnership: Student Conduct at Brown," Report of the Advisory Committee on Student Conduct, *The Pembroke Record,* May 3, 1967.
Letter from Ray L. Heffner, President of Brown University, to All Students of Brown University, September 18, 1967, pursuant to the above Report.

University of California
"The Culture of the University: Governance and Education," Report of the Study Commission on University Governance, Berkeley, *The Daily Californian,* January 15, 1968.
Draft of Policies and Regulations, Irvine, August 3, 1967.
Handbook for Campus Organizations, Santa Barbara, 1967–68.
University of California Policies Relating to Students and Student Organizations, Use of University Facilities, and Non-Discrimination, July 1, 1966, and February 19, 1968.

University of Colorado
Report of the Senate Committee on Student Affairs on Discipline Procedure and Policy, January 12, 1968.

Cornell University
Report of the University Commission on the Interdependence of University Regulations and Local, State and Federal Law, *The Cornell Daily Sun,* October 4, 1967.

Drake University
Residence Hall Handbook, 1967–68.
Student Handbook, 1967–68.

Emory University
"The Emory View," A Handbook for Students, 1967–68.

Florida State University
"Pow Wow," A Student's Guide, 1967–68.

Indiana University
Regulations Affecting Student Life, 1967–68.

University of Iowa
Regulations Adopted February 9, 1968, by the State Board of Regents Relating to Disruptive Acts at Regent Institutions.

Student Bill of Rights and Freedoms (proposed constitutional amendment).

University of Kentucky

"Non-Academic Relationships Between Students and the University," Report and Recommendations of Committee on Student Affairs, as adopted by the Board of Trustees, May 2, 1967.

University of Maryland

General and Academic Regulations, 1967–68.

University of Massachusetts

"Proposed Policies Dealing with Picketing and Other Forms of Demonstration on the University Campus," Report of the Faculty Senate Ad Hoc Committee on Picketing, November 13, 1967.

"Student Residence Open House Policy Recommendation," Special Report of the Faculty Senate Committee on Student Affairs, December 14, 1967.

Student Handbook, 1967–68.

Michigan State University

"Academic Freedom for Students at Michigan State University," Report of the Faculty Committee on Student Affairs, 1967.

New York University

Draft of a Code of Student Conduct, Commission on Student Life, 1968.

"Policy and Procedures Regarding the Confidentiality of Student Records," Office of the Registrar, April 5, 1968.

Report of the Senate Commission on Student Participation, May, 1967.

Report of the Committee to Implement the Report of the Senate Commission on Student Participation, November 2, 1967.

Rules Regulating Student Discipline Proceedings in Matters Affecting More Than One School, adopted by the Senate Interim Committee on Discipline, February 23, 1968.

Statement of Policy on Student Conduct at New York University, approved by the Senate of New York University, February 29, 1968.

"Student Conduct and Discipline Proceedings in a University Setting," Proposed Codes with Commentary, New York University School of Law, May 31, 1968.

Student Discipline, Washington Square College, April 13, 1967.

Oakland University

Recommendations of the Committee on Student Expression, approved by the Commission on Student Life, April 6, 1967.

Report of the Commission on Student Life, May 11, 1967.

Recommended Additions to the Board of Trustees Policy on Student Records, September 20, 1967.

Student Handbook, 1967–68.

Oberlin College

Student Regulations, 1967–68.

Ohio State University

Versions of Student Constitution Compared, *The Ohio Lantern,* December 1, 1967.

Ohio University
    Information for Students, 1967–68.
    Student Records at Ohio University.

Oregon State University
    Beaver Code, A Student Handbook of Information, 1967–68.

University of Oregon
    Student Conduct Program, published as revised July 1, 1965, and July 1, 1967.

University of Pennsylvania
    Report of the Commission on Open Expression and Demonstration on Campus, April 22, 1968.

Princeton University
    "Gentleman's Agreement" Between the Members of the Upperclass Eating Clubs and Princeton University, 1967–68.
    "Students and the University," Faculty Advisory Committee on Policy, December 12, 1967.
    Recommended Alterations in the "Students and the University" by The Undergraduate Assembly, February 29, 1968.
    Undergraduate Regulations, 1967–68.

Rice University
    The Honor System, April 1960.
    Student Responsibility (catalog statement) 1967–68.

University of Rhode Island
    Student Handbook, 1967–68.

Scripps College
    The Guide to Student Life, 1967–68.

Utah State University
    General Rules of Conduct, 1967–68.

University of Washington
    Draft of New Regulations on Student Conduct and Discipline, November 20, 1967.

Wisconsin State University
    Recommended Statement on Students' Rights and Rules of Conduct at Wisconsin State Universities, Education Committee of the Board of Regents of State Universities, December 1, 1967.
    Resolution to Adopt By-Law (based on the above statement), January 18, 1968.

University of Wisconsin
    Report of the Non Curricular Life of Students Committee, August 12, 1965.
    Student Power Report, Wisconsin Student Association, Recommendations to the Faculty, October 12, 1967.
    Report of the Ad Hoc Committee on the Role of Students in the Government of the University, February 6, 1968.
    Report of Ad Hoc Committee on Mode of Response to Obstruction, Interview Policy, and Related Matters;

Part One: Placement Interview Policy, March 13, 1968;

Part Two: University Discipline as a Mode of Response to Obstruction, April 25, 1968.

Policies and guidelines for Student Life, Part Two of the Student Handbook, 1967–68.

5

STUDENT ACTIVISM, THE LAW, AND THE COURTS

*by William W. Van Alstyne**

THE CURRENT concern with the legal relationship of students and
educational institutions, particularly colleges and universities, emerges
from the sustained student pressures to secure an expansion of their
rights and privileges and the recent willingness of courts to re-examine
philosophical bases of the student-university relationship. In part,
the frequency of court cases and legal interpretations of student rights
is the logical result of the new mood of students which encourages
legal attacks upon traditional concepts of law. It is also partly a
result of the changing realities of the relationships of college-age
citizens with societal institutions. In these conditions, the adherents
of the legal doctrine of *in loco parentis*, justifying the institution's
right to act as surrogate parent, have declined in number as institutions have altered their approach. Some have suggested that the

* William W. Van Alstyne is Professor of Law at Duke University. One of the
foremost authorities on the application of civil law to student protest, his recent
contributions to the literature in this field have been outstanding. Most of this
chapter was published in a special issue of the *Denver Law Journal*. Permission
to reprint the article written by William W. Van Alstyne has been obtained
from the *Denver Law Journal*, University of Denver (Colorado Seminary),
College of Law. The article appeared in Volume 45, Issue Number 4 of the
Denver Law Journal. Copyright 1968 by the *Denver Law Journal*, University
of Denver (Colorado Seminary) College of Law.

doctrine of a fiduciary relationship—in which the student gives certain rights in trust to the institution in exchange for an educational experience—be substituted for the *in loco parentis* principle as more appropriate to today's society. While there is considerably more protection from arbitrariness in the fiduciary concept it still fails to make a clear distinction between the institution's authority over off-campus as contrasted with on-campus behavior.

In response to the pressures of student activism, many legal philosophers and college administrators have begun to develop an approach to student-institutional relationships which distinguishes between the student as a citizen and the student as a resident of the institution. This distinction virtually implies that useful legal distinctions can be drawn according to the capacity in which a student may act and the place within which the university presumes to assert its authority. Thus, it may be suggested, while the student remains as a resident within the campus he is subject to the plenary authority of the university which may appropriately restrict academic residency to those agreeable to its rules. Accordingly, on-campus conduct not in conformity with the rules may forfeit the student's residency. On the other hand, once the student moves away from the campus he acts as a private citizen bound only by laws applicable to citizens in general. Like other unattached citizens, however, he is no longer subject to any extraterritorial claims of the university whose jurisdiction is confined to its own precinct, the campus.

The resident/citizen distinction appears to be fair both to the student and the university. It releases the student off the campus from worry that he is less free than other citizens, and it releases the university from concern that it is less free than other property owners. If one readily accepts the campus relationship as one of the ownership and tenancy, moreover, the university's claim of plenary on-campus authority seems to be entirely reasonable and wholly straightforward. The essential core of property ownership consists of the power to exclude and the concomitant authority to expel those who seek to remain in defiance of the owner's rules or wishes. Where the property is placed in the hands of trustees who are given legal authority by the state or a private benefactor to promulgate rules for the general governance of the institution, it is utterly unremarkable that those who are admitted as academic residents should expect to abide by all campus rules which condition their residency. No significant legal problem would appear to arise so long as the rules are confined to the campus itself and so long as they offend no state law or public policy otherwise applicable to landholders and educational institutions in general. The university does not attempt to force anyone to attend, and, unlike the situation in secondary education, the student is not compelled by law to matriculate. As a free agent who voluntarily applies and may just as readily abandon the university whenever he feels like it, the student resident must reasonably expect to conform to the trustees' regulations while he is on university property.

If the residential relationship of the student is viewed as one of contract involving private agreements respecting access to and use of campus services and facilities, again we seem to reach the same result. Indeed, the free market contract model of comparison provides an answer to those who would criticize the fairness, and not merely the legality, of campus rules. Within the free market contract model diversity among colleges and their differing sets of rules is expectable and desirable. Competition of colleges offering different academic life styles maximizes consumer satisfaction by providing a broad range of alternatives to the differing preferences of the students. The success or failure of the college to attract and to hold students against the competition of colleges offering different academic life styles is itself the best and the only secure measure of the wisdom of its rules. Certainly this seems eminently sensible at least where the college formulates its rules only in terms of on-campus conduct and does not attempt to extort contractual concessions to rules affecting off-campus citizenship prerogatives of those who enroll with it. So long as the legal requisites of a contract are satisfied (e.g., contractual capacity, mutual assent, conscionability of specific terms), there would seem to be little basis for a lawyer to reproach the rules regime of any given college.[1] Were it not primarily for certain constitutional protections applicable to students as citizens, moreover, there would be little amiss were a college contractually to bind its students to fulfill any number of promises respecting their off-campus conduct as well.

In both respects—the property analogy and the contract analogy—the public as well as private universities would thus appear to possess plenary authority on campus. Similarly, when the state undertakes to establish a college, it may be seen to operate in the capacity of a proprietor who is subject to the usual rules of law respecting the use of his own property and not subject to constitutional norms which affect him only when he, acting in a governmental rather than a proprietary capacity, attempts to regulate private conduct removed from his property.

For all of its hoary tradition, however, the on-campus/off-campus distinction is unsound and the property or contract analogies are very insecure as a matter of law.[2] In contemplation of evolved constitutional law, all such models are subordinate to constitutional norms whenever the institution is so significantly aided by government that its rule-making authority partakes of governmental power.[3] The distinction between the State acting in a governmental capacity and the State acting in a proprietary capacity has been substantially abandoned.[4]

Issues of constitutional law to one side, however, the appropriateness of certain rules in an institution presuming to call itself "academic" would still be open to discussion; surely it is proper to suggest that truly academic institutions may be undermined and disserved by rules which inhibit either academic or non-academic freedom either on campus or off campus—rules which are, incidentally, wholly inessential to the orderly operation of a university. Under either of *these* models—the university as an academic institution and the university as an instrumentality of government subject to constitutional restriction on behalf of personal liberty—the one hundred percent on-campus/off-campus description of university jurisdiction will not stand up.

Specific illustrations of constitutional control of the publicly supported college as land holder, trustee, or contractual promisee are readily available. A property holder need not grant permission that his land or buildings be available to students or to anyone else as a place to hold meetings for discussing public issues, hearing guest speakers, or assembling to express some grievances (least of all against the property holder himself), whether or not such assemblies were orderly and whether or not such meetings did not conflict with anything else the property holder intended to do at the time. If he elected to lease the property to a group of persons, moreover, he could readily evict them in the event they breached a covenant not to hold such meetings.

If the property holder is placed in a position of power through an exercise of public largess, however (as through the expenditure of tax revenue in the operation of a college or university), his authority is hedged by constitutional restraints which protect "the freedom of speech, or of the press, or the right of the people peaceably to assemble and to petition the Government for a redress of grievances," and which forbid him to deny equal protection of such rights.[5] Accordingly, on-campus bans against guest speakers have been enjoined where the rule supporting the ban was so vague as to reserve *carte blanche* censorship to the administration[6] and where the university classified speakers as acceptable or unacceptable in terms of their political affiliations,[7] their unrelated conduct before congressional committees,[8] or their having been subject to an unadjudicated criminal charge—even one of murder or homosexual soliciting.[9] Where no physical disorder is imminent, whe   there is no substantial basis for supposing that the speaker will himself violate the law or incite others to a violation in the course of his remarks, where the facilities are otherwise available and other guest speakers are generally allowed on campus, the student residents interested in hearing a given speaker on campus may not be denied. Moreover, peaceful political expression or orderly and nondisruptive assemblies on campus by students meeting to express some felt grievance against the college itself is a protected form of expression.[10] Nor may the college mute criticism of itself by forbidding critical student comment in the campus newspaper.[11] In all of these respects, university government is subject to a substantial degree of constraint similar to that which limits the civil government from which it derives its powers. As a campus constituent of that university government, the student does not forfeit his freedom of speech and cannot be made to barter it away as a condition of being admitted or of remaining.[12]

Additional illustrations make the point that a student cannot be made to leave his rights as a citizen outside the college's doors. Unlike the situation respecting the private landlord who may contractually reserve a right to enter and inspect the premises at any time and for reasons satisfactory only to himself, however, it is exceedingly likely that the fourth amendment's interdiction of "unreasonable searches and seizures" restricts colleges receiving substantial public support from imposing such sweeping conditions upon a student's privacy in on-campus lodgings as those which may be reserved by contract to a private landlord. Random fishing expeditions without warrant and without an excusable emergency, resulting in the seizure of things subsequently introduced in a disciplinary hearing to provide a basis for expelling the student, are probably forbidden.[13] The fact that the premises, and the very rooms themselves, may be owned by the state does not displace the fourth amendment or eliminate a student-citizen's right to due process respecting the manner in which evidence used against him has been seized. The fourteenth amendment makes no broad distinction between "governmental" and "proprietary" state action, and a state university must continue to observe standards of constitutional fairness even when acting as a proprietor.[14]

Finally, norms of constitutional law have been applied with increasing frequency to the *procedure*, even more than to the substance, of college discipline.

In ordering the reinstatement of university students dismissed without hearing for alleged participation in off-campus demonstrations, a federal court of appeals observed in 1961:

The precise nature of the private interest involved in this case is the right to remain at a public institution of higher learning in which the plaintiffs were students in good standing. It requires no argument to demonstrate that education is vital and, indeed, basic to civilized society. Without sufficient education the plaintiffs would not be able to earn an adequate livelihood, to enjoy life to the fullest, or to fulfill as completely as possible the duties and responsibilities of good citizens.[15]

In view of the importance of the students' interest which was placed in jeopardy by the threat to dismiss them, the court required that such action must not be taken without the institutional observance of certain minimal procedural safeguards which would lessen the likelihood of errors and prejudice.

Succeeding cases have made clear that the degree of quasi-judicial formality in college disciplinary proceedings need only be proportioned to the gravity of the offense, and that no college need fear that every alleged infraction, no matter how minor the penalty, must be determined in a cumbersome and divisive adversary proceeding.[16] When the consequences attached to the alleged misconduct are very serious to the student's future, however, an increasing number of procedural requirements must correspondingly be observed. In the gravest cases (*e.g.*, those involving expulsion, long-term suspension, widely available recordation of offenses carrying a high degree of popular stigma), the college must probably proceed with at least as much care as is now required of a juvenile court—especially as so many of its students are not juveniles and not at all subject to the fading rationale of *in loco parentis*.

The jettisoning of *in loco parentis* was, it may be suggested, long overdue in any case. For one thing, the mean age of American college students is more than 21 years and there are, in fact, more students over the age of 30 than younger than the age of 18.[17] Even in Blackstone's time, the doctrine did not apply to persons over 21.[18] For another thing, it is unrealistic to assume that relatively impersonal and large-scale institutions can act in each case with the same degree of solicitous concern as a parent reflects in the intimacy of his own home. The parent is doubtless restrained in tempering discipline with love and concern which one expects of a father or mother while the institution cannot hope to reflect the same intense degree of emotional identification with those in attendance, no matter how well it may intend otherwise. The institution is also subject to different concerns—to keep its eye on reaction by the local press, disgruntlement among alumni, dissatisfaction among benefactors, and others whose practical influence combine to bring about an administrative perspective less loving and more divided than a mother has for her own son or daughter. It simply blinks at reality to treat the mother and the college as one and the same in drawing legal analogies, no matter how frequently one refers to his *alma mater* for other purposes. Finally, there is this also to be said: a parent's disciplinary authority does not extend to the power literally to expel a dependent minor from his own home, but to lesser penalties only. Yet, the typical sanction imposed by the alleged surrogate parent, a college, is the sanction of expulsion itself—with all of the serious consequences to the student's future already noted above. As the analogy of *in loco parentis* is several times false in fact, we need not be surprised or alarmed that it is now being discarded. Large scale collegiate operations, the heterogeneity of their student bodies, the varying ages of their students, the irreducible impersonality of their operation, and the grave consequences of their disciplinary proceedings, all support the heightened requirements of greater procedural fair play in their treatment of alleged violators of their rules.

The immediate, practical and constitutional result of these phenomena is this: colleges and universities may no longer enforce their rules through sanctions seriously jeopardizing a student's career in the absence of procedures which are fundamentally fair. The essential elements of fair procedure include (but may not be limited to) the following requirements:

1. Serious disciplinary action may not be taken in the absence of published rules which

　　a) are not "so vague that men of common intelligence must necessarily guess at its meaning and differ as to its application";[19] and

　　b) do not depend upon the unqualified discretion of a particular administrator for their application.[20]

2. Where the rules are reasonably clear and their application does not depend upon uncontrolled discretion, a student still may not be seriously disciplined (as by suspension) unless

　　a) the student charged with an infraction has been furnished with a written statement of the charge adequately in advance of a hearing to enable him to prepare (*e.g.*, 10 days);[21]

　　b) the student thus charged "shall be permitted to inspect in advance of such hearing any affidavits or exhibits which the college intends to submit at the hearing";[22]

　　c) the student is "permitted to have council present at the hearing to advise him";[23]

　　d) the student is "permitted to hear the evidence presented against him" or at least "the student should be given the names of the witnesses against him and an oral or written report on the facts to which each witness testifies";[24]

　　e) the student or his attorney may question at the hearing any witness who gives evidence against him;[25]

　　f) those who hear the case "shall determine the facts of each case solely on the evidence presented at the hearing";[26]

　　g) "The results and findings of the hearing should be presented in a report open to the student's inspection";[27]

　　h) "either side may, at its own expense, make a record of the events at the hearing." [28]

These procedural safeguards roughly parallel some of the standards required of criminal courts in their disposition of offenses punishable by fine or short-term imprisonment. The comparison is not fortuitous because it is now evident that expulsion or exclusion from college may, in the long run, disadvantage an individual at least as much as a single infraction of a criminal statute. There should be no surprise, therefore, that students are entitled at least to a similar degree of due process as a suspected pickpocket. Indeed, the requisites of due process still evolving from federal decisions are substantially less than standards already recommended by professional educational associations. The Association of American Colleges (representing administrations of nearly 900 colleges), the American Association of University Professors (representing about 86,000 full-time faculty at accredited institutions), the National Student Association, the National Association of Student Personnel Administrators, the National Association of Women Deans and Counsellors, and the American Association of Higher Education have recently approved a Joint Statement on Rights and Freedoms of Students which goes considerably beyond the requirements suggested in court decisions.[29]

Somewhat anticlimactically, however, it is necessary to note a few additional matters in rendering our treatment of student procedural due process with complete accuracy:

1. The federal cases involving procedural due process for students have been disposed of by courts below the level of the United States Supreme Court and thus their utterances on this subject are not necessarily the last word. Indeed, a number of federal courts disagree among themselves respecting the requisite degree of college due process.[30]

2. On the other hand, it is reasonable to expect that additional safeguards may be posed by the courts if it appears that complete fairness is still not being observed. For instance, it is foreseeable that random and unannounced searching of student rooms may be forbidden, that students may not be coerced into admissions of misdeeds, and that some greater degree of cross-sectional representation on hearing boards may eventually be required.[31]

3. A clear distinction will probably continue to be made, however, respecting campus offenses carrying such relatively insubstantial penalties (*e.g.*, social probation, minor fines, loss of auto privileges) that formal due process is not demanded and may well be dispensed within the interest of administrative convenience. A distinction will probably continue to be made as well in instances where students face the prospect of being dropped due to inadequate grades.[32]

4. Finally, disciplinary proceedings are different from counselling proceedings where the student does not stand in jeopardy of a penalty. So long as the counsellor is required to respect the confidentiality of his relationship and acts without power to impose punishment, no

reason exists to import an adversary or quasi-judicial procedure which would undermine the counsellor's essential functions.[33]

The ultimate legality of a college rule, then, clearly cannot be measured merely by the geography within which it has to operate. And it is well that this is so, for it also means, of course, that rules which are otherwise reasonable do not become unreasonable merely because they may sometimes circumscribe conduct which occurs outside the campus itself. The constitutional emphasis turns not upon distinctions between students as "citizens" and students as "residents"; it turns, rather, upon the larger reasonableness of each rule, and the parameters of "reasonableness" are several, not singular.

Dual Residency and Double Jeopardy

Despite what we have said earlier in this chapter, for certain significant purposes a student does reside in several communities at once and is made answerable for his conduct to the law of each community in turn. His dormitory may have rules affecting his conduct as a dormitory resident, his college has overlapping rules which affect him as a resident of the college, the city laws may overlap both college regulations and dormitory rules, and so on right on through some federal statutes. A single act of misconduct may accordingly subject a student to a multiplicity of trials and punishments, exactly to the extent that the laws of these several jurisdictions happen to overlap. Thus, a student who rifles the drawer of a roommate and steals a postal money order may

a) be tried by a dormitory council, and if found guilty of violating a rule forbidding theft in the dormitory, he may then be fined or expelled from the dormitory as otherwise provided by the dormitory rule;

b) be tried by the college judicial board, and if found guilty of violating a rule forbidding theft, he may then be fined, suspended, expelled, or otherwise disciplined as provided in the college rules;

c) be tried in the municipal court for theft, and if convicted he may then be fined or jailed (or both) pursuant to local ordinance;

d) be tried in the superior court for theft, and if convicted he may then be fined or jailed (or both) pursuant to state statute;

e) be tried in federal court for theft, and if convicted he may then be fined or jailed (or both) pursuant to federal statutes applicable to theft or postal money orders.

We accept this scheme of multiple trials and multiple punishments for a single offense, even while readily acknowledging that the individual has obviously been placed in personal jeopardy more than once for a single act.

We accept this arrangement of multiple trials and multiple punishments, that is, in spite of the constitutional provision that no person shall "be twice put in jeopardy . . . for the same offense." Our understanding is, rather, that there were five different offenses in this one event and the student was tried and punished once for each offense, even allowing that he performed but a single act and endured an accumulation of five trials and five punishments.[34] Since each community has a separate legislative capacity of its own over its own territory, the aggregation of trials and punishments results without constitutional objection because the student was, while living in one place, a resident of five communities with each overlapping all the lesser ones within it.

It may be that in the relation of parietal college rules and state laws, the spirit if not the technical form of double jeopardy is violated,[35] especially where the college has a purely duplicative rule that quite literally presumes to make an academic offense of anything forbidden by any local, state, or federal law. Assuming that a student drives too fast on the interstate highway, for instance, the hazards for which he is responsible by his conduct are already policed by the general speeding law he has violated; to the extent that the college would discourage speedy driving for the *very same* reasons, *e.g.*, to protect the lives and safety of others, it has no interests sufficiently different from those already reflected in the general speeding law so to warrant its piling on a separate prosecution and punishment. Indeed, where the reckless driving occurred away from campus, the college itself has no separate community interest of its own any more than the town has a proper basis for assuming criminal jurisdiction under municipal ordinances for reckless driving offenses occurring beyond municipal limits. Where the reckless driving occurs within campus precincts, moreover, still all appropriate college concerns may be adequately fulfilled in the treatment of the alleged offender in the course of his trial in the municipal court. Thus, application of a college rule applicable even to offenses committed on campus might appropriately await the determination of the municipal court proceedings.

What I mean to propose by this suggestion is a serious, three-step re-evaluation of the very great number of college rules which overlap local, state, and federal laws—rules, for instance, broadly punishing vandalism, theft, assault, drug use, and alcohol abuse. The first step requires a review of the college rules to determine whether they are, in their subject matter and scope of application, justified in terms of a clearly discernible college purpose not already composed in other laws applicable to the conduct in question, or whether, to the contrary, the college rule merely duplicates what may certainly be appropriate police interests, but interests already covered in general law. (In this connection, the locus of the offense may be important. Vandalism of the college library, for instance, specifically affecting college property, does a kind of damage distinct to the college itself apart from the shared community concern to deter criminal behavior.[36] Vandalism of a downtown shop does not directly injure the college, and the wrongfulness of the act as an offense to the community is readily punishable under existing local or state law.)

The second step is to determine whether the function of a college rule which has an *a priori* basis to protect the college itself ought nonetheless not be applied to a given infraction because an overlapping local or state law has already been applied in such a fashion that the functions of the college rule have themselves been discharged in the regular, off-campus proceeding. As to this second step, many colleges have operated in an utterly different fashion; where college rules and state laws have overlapped, a number of colleges have established working relations with the downtown police so that the alleged offender is released to the college and favored in this regard over non-students arrested under identical circumstances. This, of course, is the seemingly benevolent edge of *in loco parentis*, the college acting to favor its students, shielding them from responsibilities unequally borne by non-students less favored than they. (The benevolence may sometimes be only a "seeming" one, however, for the college, seeking to maintain the goodwill of the police, may in fact then discipline the student far more severely than would the court downtown—as by expelling him and terminating his educational career, rather than by imposing the fine or brief term in jail that he would have received downtown.) These arrangements seem to be so doubtful both in terms of their legal correctness and in terms of their educational wisdom, however, that they should now be reconsidered. They are legally doubtful to the extent that the police, by such arrangements, unequally favor those who are fortunate enough to be students. They are educationally doubtful, for some students may acquire an elitist notion of themselves, placing themselves above other citizens, while others may feel that they are made whipping boys within the college in order that the college may preserve its good standing with the town. On both accounts, the practice should be seriously reviewed.

This does not mean that the college should take *no* interest in its students involved with the courts: the fact that the student may be far from home, in need of counsel, and practically disadvantaged in comparison with a local resident may of course make it perfectly appropriate for the college to assist him in his difficulty—short of buying off the police by promising suitably stringent treatment of its own.

There is, however, a third step in this review. Some off-campus offenses, not themselves more detrimental to the college than to the larger community which polices them, may nonetheless raise appropriate questions for independent review within the college—questions respecting the continuing safety of the college itself. The crime of selling narcotics is sometimes committed by persons who are themselves addicted and who engage in proselytizing others to secure funds to meet their own needs, as well (in some cases at least) as to lessen their own feelings of guilt by providing themselves with reassurance that others will also use narcotics. A person tried and convicted in a regular court of law may, as a youthful first offender, be given a suspended sentence and then be released to return at once to college. Yet the college may need to satisfy itself that the young man's return to campus will not carry an unreasonable risk to other students, and the college might therefore wish to make an independent inquiry to determine the safety of allowing the student to remain on campus. In short, since the municipal court's exercise of judicial discretion in the treatment of a given offender need not have given special attention to distinct college interests, the commission by a student of certain types of crimes may make it appropriate that the college review the circumstances to determine whether separate protective measures of its own would be warranted.

The shift in emphasis, however, is both real and important. Colleges would no longer undertake to duplicate general law by taking their own pound of flesh through expelling every student convicted of a criminal offense, nor would they seek to undermine the accountability of their residents to regular law by providing them an academic sanctuary for offenses committed in the larger community. They would, rather, leave the policing of municipal concerns to the municipal authorities, assisting their students only to insure their fair and equal treatment in the regular courts, and utilizing such information as they otherwise receive about criminal law violations only to determine whether, in the nature of the student's conduct and the delay or result reached in the regular courts, there is some substantial need of the college requiring separate action by the college to secure its own safety.

Crime and Punishment

> My object all sublime
> I shall achieve in time
> To let the punishment fit the crime
> The punishment fit the crime. . . .

We have known for a long time that the sanctions employed by our regular criminal law—usually fine or jail—are frequently unimaginative and unduly inflexible. Yet, our general scheme of sanctions in our colleges is less imaginative by far as it traditionally has tended indiscriminately to employ an academic death penalty as the preferred sanction for offenses which may have little or nothing in common with each other or with academic fitness. The "death penalty" in this sense is, of course, expulsion. Its necessary effect is to terminate the individual's academic status, even though the offense to which the sanction is tied represents neither academic failure nor academic misconduct on the student's part.

If the student had failed to perform minimally acceptable academic work, or if he has violated fundamental standards respecting the integrity of *that* work (as by plagiarism or cheating), it may not be inappropriate for the college to reconsider his fitness as a scholar. If his misbehavior is more essentially in the abuse of some privilege he entertains as a resident or citizen on campus, however, surely it may be better to fashion deterrent or corrective sanctions which adequately respond to that variety of misconduct but which do not terminate his academic status.[37]

The suggestion for a more discriminating treatment of disciplinary sanctions, reserving the academic sanction only for academic offenses except in the extraordinary case of residential misbehavior which is so repeated that its repetition finally requires removal of the student, can be readily expanded. The student determined to have violated a rule respecting drinking in the dormitories may surely be adequately rebuked and others adequately deterred by the temporary suspension of significant social privileges. One might even be so enlightened as to suggest some counselling—even to require it if drinking appears to be a regular problem for the student. Whatever his offense to the rules and mores of the dormitory, however, it is difficult to see the wisdom of suspending him with its necessary effect of withdrawing educational opportunities.

Even in the aggravated "residential" case, *e.g.,* the case of a student chronically raucous in a dormitory, the offense is more accurately to others in the dormitory and it may, at most, be more responsive to evict him merely from that facility than to evict him from the classrooms as well, where he has committed no offense. To be sure, the student may endure a degree of hardship in finding lodgings elsewhere—but not so much as though the university gave him no opportunity to try as by expelling him.

The first level of concern with the new dimensions of student power is a careful examination of institutional conditions which may actually provoke protest. Careful, systematic, and joint student-administrative-faculty review of basic institutional practices, policies, and structures, and immediate attention to any matters which have been the subject of persistent rumor or complaint are steps which should be considered for their own merits as well as for the defusing of radical movements. In this process of examination, efforts should be taken to revitalize the established means to express grievances and effect recommendations and to revitalize faculty participation. As important is the development of clear and defensible rules of substance and procedure by which the institution functions, not only in its disciplinary machinery but in the normal process of operation. Urgent attention to long neglected problems, improved communication to identify problems, to dispel rumor, and to benefit from student and faculty reactions and increased sharing of non-trivial responsibility of faculty are minimal steps easily within the capacity of most universities to pursue at once.

The second level of concern is with the crisis that occurs in spite of one's best efforts to alleviate grievances and provide orderly means of change. The management of such crises becomes a matter of strategy with the institution as well as the protesters, of course, but fairness and creditability are themselves the most critical elements of a strategy determined to minimize the conflict. Beyond fairness and creditability, however, the institution must examine the many options and priorities open to it in its initial response and in the immediate and long term aftermath as discussed in the chapter "The Dynamics of Institutional Responses" in this volume.

The aftermath may itself fall into three parts. The first of these is the follow through with respect to alleged rules violations and infractions of law to determine the appropriate treatment of each participant and the conditions under which he may resume his academic career. The second is to review the subject of the crisis itself, both in terms of the possible merit of the grievance it sought to dramatize and what it may indicate in terms of a larger structural inadequacy that gave rise to such disorderly action. And the third is to review the institution's overall situation in light of stresses or weaknesses uncovered in the confrontation which has just transpired. The last is doubtless as important as anything else, if an unfortunate history is not to repeat itself.

Despite precautions for avoiding an extra-legal conflict of students and the institution and the most attentive analysis of the after-effects, it is clear that activists will continue to press their case in the courts. The resulting judicial interpretations of the rights of students and of institutions of higher learning and the enactment of new laws promise to create a new specialty in American law and to make ours a vitally important time in this development. In the process, institutional responses to assure impartial justice, in substance and procedure, will redound to the strengthening of higher education and to the benefit of the larger society.

NOTES

[1] While there may be some merit still remaining in treating the legal student-college relation as one of contract (*e.g.*, where in fact the student could select any of several different kinds of colleges and where the rules or general conditions of each are well known to him in advance), this view needs far greater judicial supervision than it has received thus far. Typical student cases involving private colleges have manifested a shocking indifference to a number of considerations which have tempered the law of contracts even in more commercial fields such as insurance and sales. *See, e.g.,* University of Miami v. Militana, 184 So. 2d 701 (Dist. Ct. App. Fla. 1966); Stetson Univ. v. Hunt, 88 Fla. 510, 102 So. 637 (1925); Gott v. Berea College, 156 Ky. 376, 161 S. W. 204 (1913); Carr v. St. John's Univ., 17 App. Div. 2d 632, 231 N.Y.S.

2d 410 (1962); Anthony v. Syracuse Univ., 224 App. Div. 487, 231 N.Y.S. 435 (1928); Barker v. Trustees of Bryn Mawr College, 278 Pa. 121, 122 A. 220 (1923).

[2] *See* note 1 *supra.*

[3] Green v. Howard Univ., 271 F. Supp. 609 (D.C. Cir. 1967); Commonwealth v. Brown, 270 F. Supp. 782 (E.D. Pa. 1967), *aff'd,* 392 F. 2d 120 (3d Cir. 1968), *cert. denied,* 391 U.S. 921 (1968); Guillory v. Administrators of Tulane Univ., 203 F. Supp. 855 (E. D. La. 1962), *vacated in part,* 212 F. Supp. 674 (E.D. La. 1962). *Compare* University of Miami v. Militana, 184 So. 2d 701 (Dist. Ct. App. Fla. 1966), *with* Parsons College v. North Cent. Ass'n., 271 F. Supp. 65 (N.D. Ill. 1967). *See also* Burton v. Wilmington Parking Authority, 365 U.S. 715, 722 (1961) (privately operated restaurant under arm's-length lease with public parking authority subject to equal protection clause: "Only by sifting facts and weighing circumstances can the non-obvious involvement of the State in private conduct be attributed its true significance."); American Communications Ass'n v. Douds, 339 U.S. 382, 401 (1950) ("When authority derives in part from Government's thumb on the scales, the exercise of that power by private persons becomes closely akin, in some respects, to its exercise by Government itself."); Marsh v. Alabama, 326 U.S. 501, 505 (1946) (Privately owned company town subject to fourteenth amendment. "We do not agree that the corporation's property interests settle the question. . . . The more an owner, for his advantage, opens up his property for use by the public in general, the more do his rights become circumscribed by the statutory and constitutional rights of those who use it."); Eaton v. Grubb, 329 F. 2d 710 (4th Cir. 1964) (private hospital receiving federal aid and performing "public function" subject to fourteenth amendment). *See generally* A. Miller, *Racial Discrimination and Private Education* (1957); Dorsen, "Racial Discrimination in 'Private' Schools," 9 *William and Mary Law Review* 39 (1967); Van Alstyne and Karst, "State Action" 14 Stanford Law Review 3, 28–36 (1961); Note, "Private Government on the Campus—Judicial Review of University Expulsions," 72 *Yale Law Journal* 1362 (1963).

[4] *See, e.g.,* Brown v. Louisiana, 383 U.S. 131 (1966); Lamount v. Postmaster General, 381 U.S. 301 (1965); Cox v. Louisiana, 379 U.S. 536 (1965); Sherbert v. Verner, 374 U.S. 398, 404 (1963) ("It is too late in the day to doubt that the liberties of religion and expression may be infringed by the denial of or placing of conditions upon a benefit or privilege."); Wieman v. Updegraff, 344 U.S. 183 (1952); Frost & Frost Trucking Co. v. Railroad Comm'n, 271 U.S. 583, 593–94 (1926) Knight v. State Bd. of Educ., 200 F. Supp. 174 (M.D. Tenn. 1961). For discussion of this subject see Hale, "Unconstitutional Conditions and Constitutional Rights," 35 *Columbia Law Review* 321 (1935); Linde, "Constitutional Rights in the Public Sector: Justice Douglas on Liberty in the Welfare State," 40 *Washington Law Review* 10 (1965); O'Neil, "Unconstitutional Conditions: Welfare Benefits with Strings Attached," 54 *California Law Review* 443 (1966); Reich, "The New Property," 73 *Yale Law Journal* 733 (1964); Van Alstyne, "The Demise of the Right-Privilege Distinction in Constitutional Law," 81 *Harvard Law Review* 1439 (1968); Note, "Unconstitutional Conditions," 73 *Harvard Law Review* 1595 (1960).

[5] *See* authorities cited notes 3, 4 *supra.* Once it is clear that the property

owner's operation is sufficiently pervaded with governmental presence as to make the Constitution apply, it is appropriate to suggest that one can no more rely on the right-privilege distinction than can the government itself.

[6] Dickson v. Sitterson, 280 F. Supp. 486 (M.D.N.C. 1968) ("known member of the Communist Party," "known to advocate the overthrow of government" held void for vagueness). The current speaker regulation in force at the University of Mississippi is probably vulnerable on the same basis (see Note, "Mississippi's Campus Speaker Ban: Constitutional Considerations and the Academic Freedom of Students," 39 *Mississippi Law Journal* 488 (1967)), as is the Louisiana Statute (see 42 *Tulane Law Review* 394 (1968)). An anti-demonstration rule in South Carolina was also recently held void for vagueness, prior restraint, and inadequate standards, in Hammond v. South Carolina State College, 272 F. Supp. 947 (D.S.C. 1967). It is clear that special first amendment concerns require a degree of clarity, precision, standards, and specificity in this area considerably in excess of what may be demanded of other types of rules as a matter of due process. *See, e.g.,* Keyishian v. Board of Regents, 385 U.S. 589 (1966) (and cases cited therein); Ashton v. Kentucky, 384 U.S. 195 (1966). For other discussions of constitutional limitations on speaker control see Pollitt, "Campus Censorship: Statute Barring Speakers from State Educational Institutions," 42 *North Carolina Law Review* 179 (1963); Van Alstyne, "Political Speakers at State Universities: Some Constitutional Considerations," 111 *University of Pennsylvania Law Review* 328 (1963).

[7] Danskin v. San Diego Unified School Dist., 28 Cal. 2d 536, 171 P. 2d 885 (1946); Buckley v. Meng, 35 Misc. 2d 467, 230 N.Y.S. 2d 924 (Sup. Ct. 1962). *See also* United States v. Robel, 389 U.S. 258 (1967); DeJonge v. Oregon, 299 U.S. 353 (1937).

[8] Dickson v. Sitterson, 280 F. Supp. 486 (M.D.N.C. 1968) (special regulation of any speaker having utilized his privilege against self-incrimination before a state or federal investigating committee held invalid as an unconstitutional condition upon the use of the privilege).

[9] Student Liberal Fed'n. v. Louisiana State Univ., Civil No. 68-300 (E.D. La., Feb. 13, 1968); Stacy v. Williams, Civil No. WC 6725 (N.D. Miss., June 30, 1967) (involving a temporary restraining order to enable the speaker to appear, but evidently on the basis that his contract antedated the speaker's rule rather than on a free speech or equal protection basis).

[10] Hammond v. South Carolina State College, 272 F. Supp. 947 (D.S.C. 1967). *See* Burnside v. Byars, 363 F. 2d 744 (5th Cir. 1966) (classroom wearing of "Freedom" buttons protected by first amendment). *See also* Brown v. Louisiana, 383 U.S. 131 (1966); Cox v. Louisiana, 379 U.S. 559 (1965); Edwards v. South Carolina, 372 U.S. 229 (1963); West Virginia Bd. of Educ. v. Barnette, 319 U.S. 624 (1943); Tinker v. Des Moines Independent Community School Dist., 383 F. 2d 988 (8th Cir. 1967), *cert. granted,* 390 U.S. 942 (1968).

But distractingly raucous demonstrations or other modes of expression which directly disrupt or obstruct authorized activities on campus may appropriately be punished. Blackwell v. Issaquena County Bd. of Educ., 363 F. 2d 749 (5th Cir. 1966); Barker v. Hardway, 283 F. Supp. 288 (S.D. W. Va. 1968); Zanders v. Louisiana State Bd. of Educ., 281 F. Supp. 747 (W.D. La. 1968); Buttny v.

Smiley, 281 F. Supp. 280 (D. Colo. 1968); Jones v. Board of Educ., 279 F. Supp. 190 (M.D. Tenn. 1968); Goldberg v. Regents of Univ. of Cal., 248 Cal. App. 2d 867, 57 Cal. Rptr. 463 (1967); *in re* Bacon, 240 Cal. App. 2d 34, 49 Cal. Rptr. 322 (1966). And certain facilities may probably be closed altogether to demonstrations, without regard to whether the demonstration would have been orderly. *See* Cameron v. Johnson, 390 U.S. 611 (1968); Adderley v. Florida, 385 U.S. 39 (1966); Cox v. Louisiana, 379 U.S. 559 (1965).

[11] *See* Dickey v. Alabama State Bd. of Educ., 273 F. Supp. 613 (M.D. Ala. 1967), *final decision postponed on appeal,* 394 F. 2d 490 (5th Cir. 1968). *See also* Pickering v. Board of Educ., 391 U.S. 563 (1968), holding that a teacher may not be fired because of partially false statements critical of the trustees which appeared in a letter to the editor published in a regular newspaper and which concerned an issue of general public interest.

[12] *See* authorities cited note 4 *supra. See also* West Virginia Bd. of Educ. v. Barnette, 319 U.S. 624 (1943); Dickey v. Alabama State Bd. of Educ., 273 F. Supp. 613, 618 (M.D. Ala. 1967) ("A state cannot force a college student to forfeit his constitutionally protected right of freedom of expression as a condition to his attending a state-supported institution.").

[13] People v. Overton, 51 Misc. 2d 140, 273 N.Y.S. 2d 143 (1966) (fourth amendment's ban against unreasonable search extends to student's school locker, and vice principal may not grant consent to police search); Moore v. Student Affairs Comm. of Troy State Univ., 284 F. Supp. 725 (M.D. Ala. 1968) (fourth amendment applied to student's on-campus room, search upheld on "reasonable" cause, dicta imply that fishing expedition search would taint evidence seized pursuant thereto). *See also* Camara v. Municipal Ct., 387 U.S. 523 (1967) (housing code regulation providing for warrantless administrative searches struck down); Parrish v. Civil Serv. Comm'n., 66 Cal. 2d 260, 425 P. 2d 233, 57 Cal. Rptr. 623 (1967) (welfare payments cannot be conditioned on consent to submit to warrantless searches). *See generally* Note, "The Fourth Amendment and Housing Inspections," 77 *Yale Law Journal* 521 (1968).

[14] *See* Van Alstyne, "The Demise of the Right-Privilege Distinction in Constitutional Law, 81 *Harvard Law Review* 1439, 1458–64 (1968).

[15] Dixon v. Alabama State Bd., of Educ. 294 F. 2d 150, 157 (5th Cir.), *cert. denied,* 368 U.S. 930 (1961). *See also* Knight v. State Bd. of Educ., 200 F. Supp. 174 (M.D. Tenn. 1961).

[16] *Compare* Cafeteria & Restaurant Workers Local 473 v. McElroy, 367 U.S. 886 (1961), *with* Greene v. McElroy, 360 U.S. 474 (1959). *See also in re* Gault, 387 U.S. 1 (1967); Hannah v. Larche, 363 U.S. 420 (1959); Joint Anti-Fascist Refugee Comm. v. McGrath, 341 U.S. 123 (1951).

[17] U.S. Bureau of the Census, Dep't of Commerce, Current Population Reports, Series P-20, No. 110, Population Characteristics 12 (1961).

[18] W. Blackstone, *Commentaries* *453.

[19] Dickson v. Sitterson, 280 F. Supp. 486, 498 (M.D.N.C. 1968). *See also* Hammond v. South Carolina State College, 272 F. Supp. 947 (D.S.C. 1967); Buckley v. Meng, 35 Misc. 2d 467, 230 N.Y.S. 2d 924 (Sup. Ct. 1962); Soglin v. Kauffman, Opinion and Order No. 67-C-141 (W.D. Wis., Dec. 11, 1967) (General "misconduct" rule as applied to demonstrations acknowledged to raise grave first amendment question, although temporary restraining order with-

held pending fuller hearing. "The constitutional requirement of reasonable specificity and narrowness in rule-making in the First Amendment area has not as yet been suspended in non-university society.").

At the same time, a number of recent federal decisions have not demanded even ordinary clarity in rules, and some have upheld student suspensions based merely on a wholly undefined "inherent power." *See, e.g.,* Dunmar v. Ailes, 348 F. 2d 51 (D.C. Cir. 1965); Barker v. Hardway, 283 F. Supp. 228 (S.D. W. Va., 1968); Zanders v. Louisiana State Bd. of Educ., 281 F. Supp. 747 (W.D. La. 1968); Buttny v. Smiley, 281 F. Supp. 280 (D. Colo. 1968); Jones v. State Bd. of Educ., 279 F. Supp. 190 (M.D. Tenn. 1968); Goldberg v. Regents of Univ. of Cal., 248 Cal. App. 2d 867, 57 Cal. Rptr. 463 (1967); Morris v. Nowotny, 323 S.W. 2d 301 (Tex. Civ. App. 1959).

Vagueness and ambulatory administrative discretion as well as lack of notice of rules are constitutionally vicious, even aside from whether or not an individual had reason to suppose that he might subsequently be punished for his proposed conduct. The general problem is very well reviewed in Amsterdam, "The Void for Vagueness Doctrine," 109 *University of Pennsylvania Law Review* 67 (1960); Collings, "Unconstitutional Uncertainty—An Appraisal," 40 *Cornell Law Quarterly* 195 (1955).

[20] Applied in Hammond v. South Carolina State College, 272 F. Supp. 947 (D.S.C. 1967). *See also* cases cited note 23 *supra.*

As a practical guide, colleges should be most clear and confined, and provide for the least general administrative discretion with respect to rules applied to first amendment interests (i.e., speech, assembly, petitioning, or association). Vague, overly broad, or standardless rules in this area are regarded as unconstitutional per se due to their chilling effect on these preferred freedoms. *See, e.g.,* Zwickler v. Koota, 389 U.S. 241 (1967); Keyishian v. Board of Regents, 385 U.S. 589, 603–04, 608–10 (1966); Elfbrandt v. Russell, 378 U.S. 127 (1964); Dickson v. Sitterson, 280 F. Supp. 486 (M.D.N.C. 1968). Specificity and notice of the rules may also be demanded under circumstances where the rule requires those subject to it to take some affirmative act, or to avoid conduct which they might reasonably suppose not to be wrongful. *See, e.g.,* Lambert v. California, 355 U.S. 225 (1957). That is, the more peculiar the rule in terms of the ordinary expectations of those bound by it, the more necessary are clarity and notice. For the rest, greater flexibility is doubtless constitutionally permissible. *Compare* Lanzetta v. New Jersey, 306 U.S. 451 (1939), *and* Connally v. General Construction Co., 269 U.S. 385 (1926), *with* Nash v. United States, 229 U.S. 373 (1913), *and* United States v. Petrillo, 332 U.S. 1 (1946). A recent attempt to provide a reasonably clear list of basic regulations at the University of California is described in 17 *American Council on Education Bulletin* No. 8 (1968).

[21] Esteban v. Central Mo. State College, 277 F. Supp. 649 (W.D. Mo. 1967); Schiff v. Hannah, 282 F. Supp. 381 (W.D. Mich. 1966) (en banc); Woody v. Burns, 188 So. 2d 56 (Fla. Ct. App. 1960). *But see* Jones v. Board of Educ., 279 F. Supp. 190 (M.D. Tenn. 1968) (Upholding expulsions based on two days' notice); Due v. Florida A. & M. Univ., 233 F. Supp. 396 (N.D. Fla. 1963), (required only that changes be read to students at the beginning of the disciplinary hearing).

[22] Esteban v. Central Mo. State College, 277 F. Supp. 649, 651 (W.D. Mo. 1967).

[23] *Id. See also* Moore v. Student Affairs Comm. of Troy State Univ., 284 F. Supp. 725 (M.D. Ala. 1968); Goldwyn v. Allen, 281 N.Y.S. 2d 899 (Sup. Ct. 1967); Madera v. Board of Educ., 267 F. Supp. 356 (S.D.N.Y. 1967), *rev'd,* 386 F. 2d 788 (2d Cir. 1967) (on grounds that the hearing was not essentially disciplinary or penal, but more in the nature of counselling to determine the appropriate school in which petitioner should be located), *cert. denied,* 390 U.S. 1028 (1968). *But see* Wasson v. Trowbridge, 382 F. 2d 807 (1967) (Merchant Marine Academy); Dunmars v. Ailes, 348 F. 2d 51 (D.C. Cir. 1965) (military academy); Barker v. Hardway, 283 F. Supp. 228 (S.D.W. Va. 1968) (suspension upheld, notwithstanding refusal to permit students to be represented by counsel). *See* Buttny v. Smiley, 281 F. Supp. 280 (D. Colo. 1968) (counsel permitted); Jones v. State Bd. of Educ., 279 F. Supp. 190 (M.D. Tenn. 1968) (counsel permitted); Goldberg v. Regents of Univ. of Cal. 248 Cal. App. 2d 867, 57 Cal. Rptr. 463 (1967) (counsel permitted—entire hearing procedure unusually comprehensive).

[24] Esteban v. Central Mo. State College, 277 F. Supp. 649, 651 (W.D. Mo. 1967). *See* Dixon v. Alabama State Bd. of Educ., 294 F. 2d 150 (5th Cir.), *cert. denied,* 368 U.S. 930 (1961); Knight v. State Bd. of Educ., 200 F. Supp. 174 (M.D. Tenn. 1961). *See also* Moore v. Student Affairs Comm. of Troy State Univ., 284 F. Supp. 725 (M.D. Ala. 1968); Schiff v. Hannah, 282 F. Supp. 381 (W.D. Mich. 1966).

[25] Dixon v. Alabama State Bd. of Educ., 294 F. 2d 150 (5th Cir.), *cert. denied,* 368 U.S. 930 (1961) indicated that cross-examination may not be required: "This is not to imply that a full dress hearing, with the right to cross-examine witnesses, is required." Esteban v. Central Mo. State College, 277 F. Supp. 649 (W.D. Mo. 1967) held that a student, but not his counsel, has the right to cross-examine. Yet, in most recent cases, disciplinary boards permitted cross-examination by student or counsel. *See, e.g.,* Moore v. Student Affairs Comm. of Troy State Univ., 284 F. Supp. 725 (M.D. Ala. 1968); Zanders v. Louisiana State Bd. of Educ., 281 F. Supp. 747 (W.D. La. 1968); Buttny v. Smiley, 281 F. Supp. 280 (D. Colo. 1968); Jones v. Board of Educ., 279 F. Supp. 190 (M.D. Tenn. 1968); Dickey v. Alabama State Bd. of Educ., 273 F. Supp. 613 (M.D. Ala. 1967); Goldberg v. Regents of Univ. of Cal., 248 Cal. App. 2d 867, 57 Cal. Rptr. 463 (1967). There appears to be little reason to forbid so customary a function of counsel, reserving to the hearing board substantial discretion to limit counsel's participation to avoid unreasonable delay, harassment, or simple grandstanding. None of the cases suggest that formal rules of evidence need be observed nor is any such requirement suggested by customary practice in adjudicative administrative hearings.

[26] Esteban v. Central Mo. State College, 277 F. Supp. 649, 652 (W.D. Mo. 1967). *But see* Jones v. Board of Educ., 279 F. Supp. 190, 200 (M.D. Tenn. 1968), which heavily qualifies this view and, notwithstanding its cautionary language, accepts what is both a questionable and unnecessary practice. "There is no violation of procedural due process when a member of a disciplinary body at a university sits on a case after he has shared with other members information concerning the facts of a particular incident. . . . This limited combina-

tion by a school administrative body of prosecutorial and adjudicatory functions is not fundamentally unfair in the absence of a showing of other circumstances, such as malice or personal interest in the outcome of a case." It would appear that there may implicitly exist a "personal interest" in the outcome under such circumstances, as well as an unfair disadvantage to the student in not knowing what alleged information may thus be privately circulated within the hearing board.

[27] Dixon v. Alabama State Bd. of Educ., 294 F. 2d 150, 159 (5th Cir.), cert. denied, 368 U.S. 930 (1961); Esteban v. Central Mo. State College, 277 F. Supp. 649 (W.D. Mo. 1967); Woody v. Burns, 188 So. 2d 56 (Fla. Ct. App. 1960).

[28] Esteban v. Central Mo. State College, 277 F. Supp. 649, 652 (W.D. Mo. 1967). The better practice in terms of fairness and economy, at many institutions, is to have a simple tape recording of the entire proceedings from which a typed transcript can be prepared if necessary. In addition to the cases previously cited, for illustrations of the varying degree of procedural due process required by other courts see Woods v. Wright, 334 F. 2d 369 (5th Cir. 1964), and the marginal due process held to be sufficient in Wright v. Texas Southern Univ., 277 F. Supp. 110 (S.D. Tex. 1967), aff'd, 392 F. 2d 728 (5th Cir. 1968); Wasson v. Trowbridge, 382 F. 2d 807 (2d Cir. 1967); Due v. Florida A. & M. Univ., 233 F. Supp. 396 (N.D. Fla. 1963). Essentially no procedural due process was required in Greene v. Howard Univ., 271 F. Supp. 609 (D. D.C. 1967), on the theory that the university was private and not subject to the fifth or fourteenth amendments. The case is almost surely in error; even before hearing an appeal on the merits, the court of appeals ordered temporary reinstatement of the students. Civil No. 1949–67 (D.C. Cir., Sept. 8, 1967).

[29] Joint Statement on Rights and Freedom of Students, 53 A.A.U.P. Bull. 365, 368 (1967). See also A.C.L.U. Academic Freedom and Civil Liberties of Students in Colleges and Universities (rev. ed. 1965) (this is an earlier ACLU statement to which the Joint Statement is indebted). Comprehensive reports on student rights and freedoms have also recently been completed at the University of California, Michigan State University, Cornell University, Brown University, University of Wisconsin, and Swarthmore College.

[30] See notes 21–28 supra.

[31] On the particular point of random searches see text accompanying note 13 supra.

[32] See, e.g., Connelly v. University of Vt., 244 F. Supp. 156 (D. Vt. 1965). Compare Woody v. Burns, 188 So. 2d 56 (Fla. Ct. App. 1966).

[33] See, e.g., Madera v. Board of Educ., 386 F. 2d 778 (2d Cir. 1967); Cosme v. Board of Educ., 50 Misc. 2d 344, 270 N.Y.S. 2d 231 (Sup. Ct. 1966).

[34] Overlapping and consecutive state and federal prosecutions have been upheld by the Supreme Court; see, e.g., Abbate v. United States, 359 U.S. 187 (1959); Bartkus v. Illinois, 359 U.S. 121 (1959); United States v. Lanza, 260 U.S. 377 (1922). Overlapping and consecutive state and municipal prosecutions have also been upheld by a number of state supreme and inferior federal courts. See, e.g., Louisiana ex rel. Ladd v. Middlebrooks, 270 F. Supp. 295 (E.D. La. 1967); State v. Tucker, 137 Wash. 162, 242 P. 363 (1926).

[35] I think double prosecutions for the same offense are so contrary to the

spirit of our free country that they violate even the prevailing view of the Fourteenth Amendment. . . . Looked at from the standpoint of the individual who is being prosecuted, this notion (of multiple sovereignty) is too subtle for me to grasp. If double punishment is what is feared, it hurts no less for two "sovereigns" to inflict it than for one. If danger to the innocent is emphasized, that danger is surely no less when the power of State and Federal Governments is brought to bear on one man in two trials, than when one of these "Sovereigns" proceeds alone. Bartkus v. Illinois, 359 U.S. 121, 150–51, 155 (1959) (Black, J., dissenting).

[36] Arguably, however, the damage "distinct" to the college is civil rather than criminal, since the criminal aspect is already fully reflected in the general criminal law which makes vandalism a punishable offense. Thus, the college might appropriately confine itself to seeking compensation in the same manner as anyone else, through a common law tort action. Even when the criminal mischief is against the college's own property, therefore, it as arguable that the college should not necessarily utilize its own quasi-criminal processes to duplicate those already brought to bear by the muncipal or state court.

[37] The point is further developed in University of Kentucky, Report of the Senate Advisory Committee on Student Affairs 5 (December 9, 1966) (mimeographed): "In formulating the recommendations which follow, the Committee first identified five separate areas of student-university contract: 1) the student as a scholar, 2) the student as a tenant, 3) the student as a member of a student organization, 4) the student as an employee, and 5) the student as a customer for goods and services. Only in the first of these areas can the University appropriately apply its distinctive disciplinary punishments (such as suspensions and expulsion). . . ." *See also* Goldman, "The University and The Liberty of Its Students—A Fiduciary Theory," 54 *Kentucky Law Journal* 643 (1966).

6

THE CLIMATE OF PROTEST

by E. Joseph Shoben, Jr.

REBELLION IS no novelty on the American campus. Princeton alone had six revolts between 1800 and 1830; and in the nineteenth century, students resorted to more or less violent forms of protest on at least one occasion in each of nearly a hundred colleges and universities as different as Harvard and Georgia, South Carolina and Hobart, Williams and the City College of New York. But in their massiveness, in the widespread nature of their effects, and in their twin focus on the character of the educational experience and on sociopolitical matters like the war in Vietnam and the agonies of race relations, the student rebellions from Berkeley in 1964, through Columbia in 1968, and into the uneasy autumn of that year are at least partially discontinuous with their predecessors. It is beyond debate that academic weather all across the country has become fearfully stormy, and there is a real need to examine some of the conditions affecting the climate of protest in our institutions of higher learning.

Students: New and Numerous

If we turn first to the students themselves—those whose rebellions have forced an unwilling reappraisal of the estate of American higher education at a time of its greatest affluence and apparent success—

we cannot help being impressed first of all by their sheer numbers. Enrollments in the fall of 1968 in the approximately 2,400 colleges and universities of America were well in excess of seven million young people, and virtually half of last June's high school graduates are now part of a college campus of some kind or another. Viewed in the light of history, these figures are not only staggering in their absolute magnitudes; they imply an unprecedented diversity of student bodies. The heterogeneity of American life itself is reflected in the heterogeneity of its collegial institutions, defining a complexity of needs to be met and backgrounds to be dealt with for which there are simply no historical guides. In addition, this diversity permits young men and women to cross more easily than ever before the boundaries of social class and cultural experience, to explore both their differences and their common concerns, and to form new coalitions of political purpose as well as friendship.

Two forms of perspective highlight the significance of these observations. One is the contrast provided by enrollment data for 1900, when only a fraction more than 4 per cent of the nation's far fewer high school graduates went on to college. For a change to our present circumstances to take place during the lifetime of a man just reaching the retirement years marks an authentic revolution in social policy. Similarly, it suggests a radical shift in the distribution of information and technical skills, if not in wisdom, over the population, especially the population of young people.

The other source of perspective derives from setting observations of college youth in the more general context of contemporary youth culture. We are familiar, for instance, with the fact that almost half our total population is under 25 years of age. Although the exact meanings of that fact are not entirely clear, it represents a change in our numerical center of gravity that is novel, and there may be considerable significance in the implication that 50 per cent of our people have no direct memory of the Second World War and therefore have not built into their emotionally undergirded values a direct appreciation of the reasons for which it was fought. Unless there are unlikely alterations in our rate of natural increase, a slight majority of Americans may be under 21 in 1972, the next presidential election year; they will almost surely exceed 45 per cent. If we assume no change in the legal requirements for voting or in the voting behavior of various age groups, we must still cope with the likelihood that the median age of those casting ballots may be only a little more than

26. In any case, one can hardly escape the conclusion that, on the basis of numbers alone, youth is becoming an intensely potent force in American life.

Moreover, as their numbers have grown, the proportions of youth on college campuses have gone up even more dramatically, and the opportunities for interaction and organization that college-going provides have given students a kind of corporate identity that is tacitly acknowledged in a variety of ways. The Selective Service System deals with them on special grounds; Madison Avenue's advertising companies mark them as a central important and distinctive "target public"; they are vigorously courted politically, witness the campaign strategies of the late Sen. Robert F. Kennedy; and their mores are recognized as sharply different from those of older generations whether that recognition entails positive acceptance, neutral tolerance, or hostile outrage. National student organizations have proved that they enjoy a high degree of viability, and student leaders have been able to establish and to maintain loose networks of individuals and groups which support and reinforce one another in the mutual pursuit of several kinds of goals.

College and the Dissident Impulse

When numbers of significant size become colored by a sense of group solidarity, a potential for power and influence results. It is hardly surprising, therefore, that students have begun to press for a greater share in the making of those political, social and educational decisions that they perceive as affecting their welfare and their destiny. It is even less surprising that the university campus should prove a prime locus for their efforts. The university is where they are—in critically impressive masses; and the university is the basic source of the felt commonalities and corporate identity that nourish their self-confidence, their sense of strength, and their belief in their own sufficient unity.

Nevertheless, surprise may be quite an appropriate reaction to an inference suggested by these reflections: The rebellions that have rent the academic fabric for the past four or five years are in significant degree a straightforward product of rapidly and enormously increased college attendance. Strongly abetted by the mass media, the new technologies of communication, and the mobility and relatively easy access to travel that young people now enjoy, college-going itself has given students in a fundamental fashion their contacts with each other, their opportunity to organize themselves, and at least a good deal of the knowledge and many of the ideals on the basis of which their corporate activities are rationalized. Thus, the emergence of students as an influential bloc, both in the academy and in society generally, rests significantly on (a) a national policy that has steadily and rapidly enlarged the accessibility of higher education and on (b) various components, both formal and informal, of the college experience itself.

We know, for example, that at least the leaders among activist students come from liberal and well-educated homes. It seems quite probable that the parents of these young people were themselves responsive to college faculties who were highly skeptical of traditional values and often sharply critical of the Protestant ethos in American culture. Such an intellectual influence has operated simultaneously, of course, with increasingly more permissive patterns of child rearing. Indeed, the ideas of liberal intellectuals have defined the rationale for these more comfortable socialization practices, and it is hardly an accident that a pediatrician of the eminence of Dr. Benjamin Spock has been intimately and prominently connected with protests against the war in Vietnam. For many of those who are now leaders of student rebellions, then, it seems likely—to argue only the minimum case—that academic officials and governmental representatives (such a policemen) are among the first adults whom they have met who do not at least pretend to pay a comparable attention to the ideas and anxieties of youth that they give to those of elders. In short, the critical disposition, the value placed on self-determination, and the tendency "to think otherwise" that are typical of dissenting student leaders may well originate in precisely the democratic commitments and the heritage of intellectual skepticism for which our colleges have most proudly stood. If, from one point of view, we may have erred in the kind of educational experience we have developed for American youth over the past half-century, from another angle of regard, we may have made our most serious mistakes by permitting too long a hiatus to lie between our stimulation of youthful concerns and of youth's participatory impulses and our creation of the social forms that would facilitate their employment in culturally contributory ways. In any case, it is difficult to escape the strong implication that today's unruly student scene is partially a product of the colleges' own influence—a natural outgrowth of the characteristic stance of our institutions of higher learning and our national educational policies designed out of a compound of good will and social necessity.

Sociolegal Considerations

For in addition to numbers, the dynamics of corporate identity, and the consequences of mass college-going, students have been shaped in their attitudes and their fundamental conceptions, whether implicit or explicit, by a culturally determined change in the nature of their relationship to their colleges and universities. It may be well to remind ourselves here that young people in the United States have attended college under basically (which is not a synonym for "exclusively") two conditions. The older pattern is that of a third-party beneficiary contract. That is, an agreement was entered into between an institution and a student's parents for the benefit of the latter's child. Because the youngster was not himself a party to the contract, and because he was essentially *sent* to college in order to enjoy the special assets of an elite, he was presumed to have little or nothing to say about the processes by which his benefits were to accrue to him. So long as the circumstances of American life made this arrangement viable, it provided an authentic basis for *in loco parentis* as an operating policy and for a conception of the academic community as including scholars and the university's other official personnel but not, except in the most mythological sense, the student body.

With the passage in 1862 of the Morrill Act, which signalized a change in American society in the direction of democratization and an increased emphasis on technology, a new pattern of student-institution relationships emerged to join the first. College became a primary avenue of social mobility. There was still an implied contract, but the parties were the institution and the student himself rather than his parents, and the terms held that the youngster's opportunity for wealth and status would be materially increased by his successfully discharging the obligations laid on him by the university during the period of his attendance. The symbol of his success, of course, was his degree; but the nature of his obligations, while not unreasonable or entirely arbitrary, was completely in the hands of the institution. Although his power of choice was somewhat enlarged, the student still, if he wanted an improved socioeconomic position, had to leap whatever hurdles the college required and to conform to whatever rules it elected to enforce. Again, the arrangement worked effectively —and for a very large proportion of contemporary students, it continues to work effectively—so long as upward social mobility was a central motivant and so long as the evidence was persuasive that college-going did indeed lead to a higher rung on the ladder of income and status.

But as our society has become progressively more technologized and technical, the almost insatiable need for highly trained manpower, linked to a credentialing function assigned to colleges and universities, has sharply if subtly redefined the circumstances under which students come to our halls of learning. Some but proportionately very few of today's undergraduates are "sent" to college; a very large number continue to come in search of occupational and professional upgrading and to attain a status in advance of that occupied by their families. But a significant proportion of them attend college because they are wooed, pressed, invited, and all but bullied into doing so. In so technologized and managerial a world, any society that is to survive must extend the education of its young citizens; and although the humane virtues in our expanding access to higher education are incontestable, that expansion of access is also a reflection of societal necessity. It is no longer a contract, therefore, that lies at the heart of the student-institution relationship, but a matter of what Sir Henry Maine would have called status—the special status of a young man or woman in a society that, for its own protection and wellbeing, must see to it that he or she is adequately trained. Thus, the process of college-going has been transformed from either a personal privilege or a device for the improvement of personal status to a *societal* benefit. As a result, students are no longer constrained from having a good deal to say about the nature of their educational experience: If I am to attend college in large part for the good of my society, then my democratic heritage, which has always legitimized my criticism of my social experience, also legitimizes my criticism of my educational experience; because society has never had the right to take advantage of me unreasonably, the university, if it is to be so directly a mechanism of society, has no right to impose unreasonable demands upon me in the course of my acquiring the training which is externally demanded.

This alteration in the student-institution relationship, although it has not been formally defined or tested in the courts, amounts to a fundamental change in the sociolegal foundations of higher education. As such, it interacts with the factors we have considered previously to determine the atmosphere of discontent and rebellion on the nation's campuses, and it raises questions about the qualifications of youth to engage in the active criticism of an institution as basic to modern life as is the university.

Changes in Adolescent Growth

These questions obviously have no sure answers, but the quest for reasonable responses to them leads to at least two major and relevant observations. One bears on the changing biology of youth; the other has to do with the comparative ranges of information commanded by the generations.

Studies of adolescent growth have consistently indicated that the mean age of girls at menarche has declined on an average of six months per decade since 1880. When one remembers the dramatic suddenness with which interests, attitudes, and behavior alter at the onset of menstruation, it is clear that this increasingly early attainment of biological maturity is a matter of some consequence. The data for boys, although the criterion of pubescence is far less clear, are similar, suggesting a progressively earlier entry into physiological adulthood. How to account for these phenomena defines a puzzle for physicians and students of human development; improvements in diet, in prenatal and general medical care, and in public health standards probably explain some but not all of the variance in these changes. Whatever their explanation, however, the facts seem to be clear, and they make it plain that incoming college freshmen now have about three years' longer experience of biological adulthood than did their counterparts in 1900. It seems highly probable, therefore, that institutions that still operate educational programs based in significant degree on the structures, rules, and conceptions of that earlier day will be sufficiently out of phase with the needs and characteristics of this virtually new breed of student to warrant at least a serious reexamination of their functions and procedures.

Similarly, it is clearly—even embarrassingly—demonstrable that present-day youth know more than preceding generations at a comparable age. Scores on the same standardized achievement tests given twenty-one years apart in the same school system, for example, have shown differences of almost a full standard deviation in favor of the current crop of youngsters. If they are no wiser or more insightful than were their parents and grandparents, contemporary young people possess a larger store of sheer information as a result of improved schools, a generally elevated level of literacy and comprehension, and the influences of mass media, particularly television but including such other resources as newsweeklies and both the popular and the so-called "underground" press. Nor can one discount here the greatly increased opportunities for travel and for discourse with others that young people now enjoy; and, again, mass collegegoing itself explains a measure of the greater knowledge available to those now in their late teens and early twenties.

Maturing earlier and knowing more than their forebears at the same age, adolescents today represent an extreme case of the typical problem posed by adolescence in civilized cultures: Adults in physiology and information, they can find few roles available that challenge their talents, meet their needs for responsibility, and permit them to occupy respected and meaningful niches in the larger society. There are few frustrations so severe as an unbridgeable gap between readiness for full participation in the life of the community and access to appropriate forms of participation. Following the old formula, frustration of this level of intensity increases the probability of either hostility and aggression or primitivation and regression, the childish insistence on one's own way and the refusal to consider compromises that characterize more than the young when under duress of this variety. In any event, the dynamics of adolescent growth are not irrelevant to the climate of rebellion in our halls of higher learning, and they suggest some of the reasons why students press so urgently for "power" and a more determinative part in the governance of the university and for full membership in a bona fide academic community. If the educational endeavor is again to be conducted in our colleges with both effectiveness and tranquillity, it seems quite likely that these factors will have to be more fully understood and accommodated within our institutional frameworks.

Ideologies in Conflict

But there is still another element—perhaps a fundamental one— that must be seriously considered in our efforts to understand the current climate of protest. What may be at issue is a confrontation between two quite different ways of viewing the world, between two quite different forms of basic faith. One is the broad *essentialist* orientation, which has been dominant in Western thought for centuries; the other is the *existentialist* conception of life, which has emerged relatively recently as an articulate challenge to the older *Weltanschauung.*

The essentialist stance is generally rooted in what is enduring, universal, formal, and rational in the universe and in human experience. Although their ranks include both idealists and naturalists, essentialists conceive of human nature as basically constant. For them, variations in conduct and culture are basically changes rung by history and circumstance or recurrent themes, not indicators of genuine novelty or true emergents in the social world. Valuing continuity, they look upon tradition as close to the fountainhead of wisdom and insight; and because of the same prizing of continuity, essentialists celebrate foresight as primary among the virtues of man and regard highly those persons who are oriented to the future, who are mindful of the rainy tomorrow which must be guarded against, and who control their impulses in the light of their possible consequences. It follows that not only are predetermined, rationally chosen goals important and desirable, but so are rational and, where possible, standardized procedures for attaining those aims. In turn, these desiderata define the groundwork for the development of comprehensive systems, intellectual as well as technological; and this option in favor of the systematic, the rational, and the standardized reinforces the notion that feelings, emotions, and the irrationalities of experience, although they can be enjoyed sparingly and through such formalized expressions as art, must, at bottom, be curbed and controlled as threatening to what is best in human potentialities—the reasoned attainment of effective and efficient techniques for reaching rationally elected objectives.

The existentialists, on the other hand, argue that the formal, systematic vision of the essentialists leads inevitably to depersonalization, to anomie and the curtailment of individuality, and to governmental arrangements and cultural patterns that ultimately are unavoidably authoritarian. For the existentialist, vitality is a fundamental value, and vitality is found in an endless quest for *meaning,* a search that can only be conducted among the concrete and undeniable realities of personal experience. If Plato embodies in many respects the essentialist mode *par excellence,* his depiction of Socrates remains almost a prototype of the existentialist style. The Socratic spur to question basic assumptions, to find in reflections on intimate experience the valid bases for the beliefs on which men must act, and to prize the dogged, persistent *process* of inquiry beyond the acquisition of knowledge itself is close to the core of both existentialist thoughtways and existentialist motives. In Buber, Camus, and Sartre, the elaboration of those thoughtways and motives elevates the irrational and affective side of man to a plane equal in value to his rational aspects. In their view, continuity with the past is much less important than the relevance of ideas, of artifacts and institutions, of social forces, and of even other people to immediate and personal needs. Indeed, both the past and the future are experientially compressed into present memories and present expectancies: What is, is *now,* and that *now* is an insistent demand that can be examined and controlled but that cannot be gainsaid or ignored. Thus, the existentialist advocates an education that centers around sensed problems, that affords room for the development of the emotions as well as the intellect, and that enables the individual man to engage himself socially and politically without losing his identity to them. In human relations, existentialists accept the concept of responsibility but find its authority not, like the essentialists, in rules or imposed obligations deriving from inherited traditions, but in mutual concern and caring. Similarly, knowing the way in which manners and formalized interpersonal styles can deteriorate into lies and manipulations, they opt for authenticity, for "telling it like it is," and for spiritual and emotional directness in the dealings of men with men. Ethically, tolerance of ambiguity is a higher virtue than foresight; commitment in spite of uncertainty ranks above prudence, and participatory involvement commands a more favorable evaluation than fitting oneself into predetermined structures.

In this too rapid contrasting of two philosophies in conflict, the aim is neither to suggest that they have no regions of congruence nor to present one as superior to the other. Neither is it to imply that essentialism is the exclusive intellectual property of the elderly and existentialism the only ideology of the young. Rather, the purpose is to indicate something of the profound differences in assumption and stance that characterize the proponents of each, to measure in some rough fashion the breadth of the chasm across which they must talk, and to argue that this controversy has particular significance for the university because essentialists are overwhelmingly the masters there, and existentialists are just as overwhelming, despite their frequent inarticulateness about such matters, dominant among activist students and their faculty supporters. That ideas have consequences is a proposition from which few members of the academy would dissent; the consequences of these very different ideas entail a clash of genuine severity.

To essentialists, existentialist radicalism can too easily couple ignorance with impatience, a combination that is always threatening to civilized ways of life; and it is clear that anxieties on this score are justified by the incivility, the violence, and the unproductive outcomes of more than one campus disruption both in the United States and abroad. Similarly, the essentialist is likely to be offended by the existentialist's disregard of the amenities of negotiation and by his lack of faith, often expressed in vulgarities, in order, evolution, and compromise. Most of all, the essentialist mode in its liberal forms is alarmed by the existentialists' willingness to play fast and loose with the ethic of civil liberties, to restrict the free thought and speech of others, and to flaunt the restraints of valid laws when their moral conscience allegedly gives them leave to do so. On the other hand, existentialists find little that is persuasive, when their passion for peace and justice is aroused by such issues as the war in Vietnam or the plight of the American Negro, in the essentialist logic of gradualism or the essentialist sense of the wisdom of compromise in a fundamentally imperfect world. Nor do they find the traditions of civility compelling when those traditions, politicized, have been bound up with colonialism, racism, the suppression of the emotions, and formalist sterility in art and education. To them, essentialist ideas have too frequently been the justifications for the state's demanding loyalty in time of war, the school's insisting on a discipline aimed, in the name of "forming character," at social compliance, and the community's enforcing rules of personal conduct that invade privacy and unnecessarily constrain sexual variety.

Thus, a philosophical dimension of major importance is added to the rift on the campus. Ideological differences, sometimes only implicit but seriously determinative, make productive conversation as hard for one side as for the other. Because the passionate, existential style of student leaders occasionally takes on ugly forms, represents an unfamiliar source of power in our institutions, and is both distracting and evocative of anxiety, it leads administrators and faculty leaders to react with distaste and defensiveness. Pressed into the role of adversary, they are sorely tempted to resist all recommendations for change on the ground that virtually any concession would represent a kind of academic Munich, and they are more likely to perceive all activists as cut indiscriminately from the same nihilistic, conspiratorial cloth. Under these circumstances, it is only a short step to policies of deterrence through restrictive regulations, espionage systems, and strong punishments; on the other side, impulses to violence and destructive disruption become easier to rationalize and more appealing as the only way in which persons of integrity can win a responsive ear.

Two points are noteworthy in this context. First, the philosophical conflict is congruent at many points to the social psychological conditions previously outlined here that account for campus demonstrations and confrontations on the basis of the dynamics of frustration and aggression. Indeed, this collision of opposed ideas represents in part an intellectualized translation of very similar if not the same factors. Second, the philosophical schism in the academy is a reflection in a dark glass of other conflicts in modern culture. Existentialism is, to a significant degree, a response to the breakneck rate of social change, which leaves the individual man swallowed in a vortex of powerlessness; it is a proclamation of personhood in the face of an increasing dominance by technology and technique that intensifies the developmental problems of identity and makes difficult a sure sense of self; it is a celebration of intimacy in human relations and the trustworthiness of feelings in personal experience at a time when interpersonal affairs are perceived as increasingly manipulative and the affects trampled under a chilly rationalism. Most of all, it is a romantic reaction against an overweening and growing emphasis on reason and control unchecked by a shared sense of what is good and lovely in life's immediacies. Once again, the battle lines within the university are microcosmic reproductions of kinds of warfare in the world at large, and it seems improbable that the atmosphere of antagonism in the academy can be transmuted into productive forms without reference to problems in the surrounding society and the encompassing culture.

The Decline of Liberal Education

By its traditions, the concept by which the university has attempted to engage students with the affairs of the larger community is that of liberal education. One need not yearn nostalgically for halcyon days that never were to defend the thesis that undergraduates are currently hard put to find a consistently liberating experience in their college attendance. If the essence of a liberal education is hard to pin down with finality, its core lies somewhere in a fusion of three processes. One is the identification of the values to which a man may both properly and critically commit himself; a second is the development of at least rudimentary ways of thinking seriously about the major problems of one's society; and the third is the enlargement of one's capacity to enjoy the exercise of one's own imagination and intellect. A liberal education, then, frees the individual from the parochialisms of his own time and culture; it cultivates those habits of informed self-scrutiny which are the basis of the examined life, and it makes more probable the experience of joy by strengthening the response to both art and nature as well as by disciplining the artistic and scientific impulses. Its goal is understanding more than information; and its method is systematic observation and wide reading, subjected to open but critical reflection. Its product is ideas, moral as well as intellectual; and if only some of those ideas are likely to be truly novel, a high proportion of them are likely to be personally relevant and meaningful, to roll back the horizons of his own potentiality in some developing youngster, and to create useful bridges between what he studies, what he experiences outside the academy, and his changing visions of the kind of life he wants to lead.

At the moment, it is fair to say that the student revolt is based in part on the frustration of a desire for just such a liberating experience. For most activist students, there is little goodness of fit between what they are required to study and the kinds of lives they dream of as worthy of free men. The gap between their apprehension of the campus and their apprehension of the world beyond its precincts makes college, for them, a gross and even an immoral irrelevance; and the collegial emphasis on the acquisition of facts and formal skills, on prerequisites demanded by "the logic of the disciplines," and on examinations and grading gives rise more to the image of a goose being stuffed for the table than of a man being freed to live an examined life.

The death of liberal education is probably a consequence of the relatively new vitality of the graduate school, and the vitality of the graduate school is a concomitant of society's voracious need for increasingly specialized and technically skilled manpower. If one accepts inevitability in the growth of graduate training, however, one need not accept inevitability in the way in which graduate concerns have permeated not only the entire university but the independent college. Undergraduate studies are oriented more and more toward graduate admissions standards. A larger and larger share of undergraduate tuition is plowed into the support of graduate enterprises. As soon as they can be reasonably well identified, the most academically able undergraduates are recruited to post-baccalaureate training in the professions and the standard disciplines. And at an increasing rate, professorial status and monetary rewards are dependent on graduate involvements; if a faculty member is neither teaching graduate students nor sending a sizable proportion of his undergraduates on to graduate training, then he is viewed as low on the totem poles of his disciplinary tribe and as probably of doubtful competence.

With the graduate school in control of the *rites de passage* through which one must travel *en route* to a professorial post, the lowered availability of a liberal education in the United States becomes understandable. The graduate school may turn out finely trained specialists, well grounded in the niceties of research and well equipped to perform technical services in the advancement of their disciplines. It does not by design turn out men of liberal scholarship, deeply concerned with helping students to find liberation in the adventures of their college years. Liberal education is in decline because there are too few teachers to provide the conditions for it and to represent, sensitively and wisely, its purposes and its values.

One result has been the establishment in scores of universities of "counter-institutions," the so-called Free Universities in which the usual academic conventions and constraints can be ignored in the quest for more meaningful lines of study. Whatever one's judgment about these enterprises may be, they bear touching witness to the way in which the university, stressing graduate training and formal research at the expense of virtually all its other functions, has impoverished the educational experience for its undergraduates. Although the majority of students have willingly bent with this trend, satisfying themselves with training for careers and the bread and circuses still available to the reasonably affluent in a campus environment, the activists are not without warrant when they charge that the temples of intellect are not the homes of vigorous discussion of the things that matter most. Those genuinely concerned with the character of the good life and the lineaments of the good society in the contemporary world must turn to each other, to the amateur, or to the cynical professorial showman on the academic stage, who excites his charges rather than assists in their education. There is little to surprise in these students' electing the first of these options; but their doing so defines an adversary relationship between themselves and the college, and the lines are thus drawn tight with respect to specifically educational issues.

Is There an Academic Community?

If the climate of protest is enhanced by the decline of liberal education, it is made still more rainy and uncertain by operating conceptions of the academic community. When students press for a larger role in the governance of our institutions, for a major hand in formulating the rules under which they must live on campus, and for a more influential voice in the determination of collegial policy, they are seeking full membership in a community from which they feel excluded. It is not necessary to impugn anyone's intentions to suggest that their feelings match reality reasonably well and to ask if the exclusion which they perceive is at all justified.

The ruling conception of *communitas* within the academy is that of an organization of scholars sharing intellectual interests. When the rhetoric is stripped away from this highly positive idea, the current communitarian situation emerges as decidedly fractionated. The primary and dominant intellectual interests of the university's scholars are the technical research concerns of highly specialized faculty members. The department, therefore, and not the institution as a whole, becomes a *de facto* organizational unity within which the only approximations to community can be consistently found. Even within departments, a kind of civilized anarchy obtains inside the house of intellect. In psychology, for example, investigators of the neurophysiological bases of behavior and investigators of the dynamics of child development speak such different languages that they rarely find ground for mutual discourse. In chemistry, biochemists and petroleum chemists seldom share in any mutually facilitative fashion the intellectual interests of greatest concern to each. In departments of literature, Renaissance scholars and experts in structural linguistics seldom seek each other's company for academic purposes, and historians preoccupied with the Civil War live in contented mutual isolation from historians whose focus is on modern Asia.

There are, of course, many exceptions to this state of affairs, but two general points are central and, in the main, undeniable. First, what sense of community one finds on the contemporary campus is essentially a faculty property. It is the professors—certainly not the students and particularly not the undergraduate students—who in a loosely organized way enjoy sets of shared intellectual interests. Because of the pressures of specialization, growing out of the explosion of knowledge and the societal requirements for research as a means of supporting and expanding our enormous technological enterprise, the extent to which these sets of intellectual interests are shared is remarkably small. It is only a slight exaggeration to say that the modern university is much less a community of scholars than it is a common institutional roof over the heads of individual research men, each doing what he significantly calls his "own work." Second, what binds the faculty together most effectively is less any community of scholarship than concerns about conditions of work within the college or university. Salaries, teaching loads, the availability of research facilities, office and laboratory space, secretarial support, and comparable matters are likely to be the objects of genuinely *common* professorial interest. Of profound importance and wholly proper objects of faculty concern, these topics suggest a very different meaning from the traditional one in the phrase "community of scholars," and it implies that students are, indeed, excluded from that community simply because they cannot be expected to share a professor's objectives and passions in these areas. There is even a hint here that students, except as graduate apprentices and a form of relatively inexpensive academic labor, are something of a nuisance—a notion that is given some weight by the wryly good humored comments by all of us associated with institutions of higher learning about how pleasant the university is during the Christmas holidays, when students are not around to distract us from our real concerns, or about how fine a place a university would be if one didn't have to deal with students.

When, on the other hand, students are insistent about their membership in the academic community and their right to a part in its governance, the typical response is that they are unfit for such a role because they are transient, *i.e.,* they are enrolled for only four years. In many ways, this contention is less than persuasive. For one thing, criteria of duration are not applied to faculty members or administrative officers as a basis for their exercising a voice or a vote in university councils. Neither an assistant professor nor a dean must reside in an institution for more than four years or sign a letter of intent to do so in order to enjoy these attributes of membership. For another, it is at least possible to argue that students maintain a *longer* relationship with their universities than does any other academic constituency. Students become alumni. As alumni, they become legislators, trustees, members of corporation boards, and elements of the general public to which our institutions of higher education must increasingly look for support and understanding. The extent to which they are likely to supply that support and understanding is dependent in some significant measure on the nature of their experience as undergraduates. If the experience was a favorable one in which they learned something about the complexities of operating a great university or an independent college, then the probability is increased of their reacting in helpful ways. If the experience was one of frustration or one perceived as formalized hurdle-leaping, then that probability declines. The lack of public comprehension, even among college graduates, of such issues as academic freedom, the values of scholarship that has no immediate "practical" application, and the role of the university as a social critic is a source of genuine trouble for the academy now. Such troubles will be markedly compounded when today's activists move into positions of public influence, carrying with them the bitterness and the rage for reform that many of them have developed.

True enough, including students in the academic community would require expenditures of time and imagination on the processes by which they can be responsibly inducted, made aware of the problems and complexities that must be faced, and helped to shape constructive roles for themselves. True enough, the introduction of student influences into the patterns of university government would entail decisions not to the taste of many faculty members and administrators now in power, and it would result in changes that may not be either foreseeable or entirely consonant with present practices. But change is king in our era, and change is inherent in complex institutions that take democratic values and procedures seriously. Further, as universities become more and more dependent on informed public support, they may find few effective alternatives to educating their students, who become their numerous alumni and their largest constituency, in the intricacies of collegial purpose and the hazards of institutional operation. In any event, if the dynamics of the youth culture, which we considered earlier, are at all correct as sketched, the immediate cost in discontent and violence of continuing to exclude students from the academic community may be prohibitive, just as the longe-range expense in a disinterested or somewhat vindictive public may prove damaging beyond all expectation. What seems clearly needed, of course, is an overhauling of the basic conception of the academic community and a more inclusive definition of its plural values, its distinctive human concerns, and its qualifications for meaningful membership.

The Curriculum and the Future

As it stands, that community is open to serious charges of neglect in its educational responsibilities. We have seen how the objectives and methods of liberal learning have languished in the face of the graduate school's growing hegemony, but the problem has an even more fundamental form. The tempo and radical character of social change challenges one of the oldest assumptions of the academic world. For centuries, it has been taken for granted that the mastery of one's culture is the hallmark of the educated man, that familiarity with the past is the groundwork for an effective coping with the issues of the present and the uncertainties of the future. When the rate of change was slower, that faith was well placed, and the transmission of the culture was indeed an appropriate and sufficient educational objective. If the curriculum suitably served that aim, then it was fully justified.

As we approach the twenty-first century, however, the massiveness and intimacy of the processes of change—the forces of the great cultural discontinuity through which we are living—raise root questions. Is it still true that yesterday's experience is the best preparation for today's life and tomorrow's problems? However necessary the knowledge of our fathers may be, is it sufficient for the world of our children or our children's children? Whatever the civilizing effects may be— and they are large and invaluable—of familiarity with our traditions, are those traditions adequate guides to humane decisions in our special time in history? The mere fact that such questions can be seriously asked implies, at a minimum, that our curricular assumptions have grown gray at the edges and that our faith in the bases of curriculum construction is vulnerable to the winds of change that blow all through our contemporary culture.

One of the conditions of student protest is that classroom experience rests too completely on what is perceived as anachronistic assumptions, on an insufficiently examined belief that the transmission of the culture provides an adequate *modern* education. Virtually the only modification in this belief that has been reflected in curricular revision has stemmed from the influence of the graduate school and the forces making for academic specialization. What seems to be relatively novel in the pattern of course offerings in our colleges and universities is its organization according to the internal logic of the departmentalized disciplines. Thus, undergraduate sociology and physics are typically developed along lines of graduated complexity as essentially independent domains of knowledge. This approach is certainly defensible and appropriate in relation to the goal of creating specialized scholars, well prepared for graduate work. It may be less suitable as a way of making knowledge personally meaningful to students attempting to grapple humanely and effectively with themselves and their society. And from legitimate educational points of view, one is at something of a loss to find other bases of the curriculum than the transmission of the culture and the unfolding of disciplinary logic; a curricular foundation distinctively relevant to our era is apparently yet to be invented.

But the issue cuts still deeper. If the characteristics of contemporary society and contemporary culture challenge the sufficiency of tradition and continuity as the fundament of a modern education, they also make questionable the age-old tenet that it is the business of the old to instruct the young. Given the criticisms of their heritage that youth (and not youth alone) have given voice to, and given the pace and ubiquitousness of cultural change, is it not possible that the academic community can better be conceived as a community of learning rather than of teaching and more usefully be thought of as the locus of a mutual and widespread quest for wisdom and meaning than as the site of young people's instruction by older people? That kind of instruction is sure to continue because of the special aptitudes and insights of elders and because there remains incontestable viability in both the transmission of the past's legacy and the exploration of the inner logic of the disciplines. But it need not be a matter of right or of an unexamined but conventional function of older persons in relation to college-age youth.

Thus we are led toward a third conception of the curriculum as a vehicle for stimulating and maintaining the vigorous and serious debate of significant ideas. The marks of educational growth become the acquisition of progressively more disciplined habits of reflection on one's experience, the development of more logical ways of considering problems and more persistent tendencies to examine basic assumptions, and an increasing respect for both knowledge and other points of view in the consideration of serious issues. It is well to remember here that the processes of debate, when internalized, are simply the processes that we call thought, that in the formation of beliefs, especially those beliefs on the basis of which men act, there are always affective components that are linked to interpersonal considerations of some kind, and that the formation of beliefs through debate exposes one's own implicit assumptions to examination as well as entailing the identification and criticism of the unspoken bases of the positions taken by others. If, therefore, Platonic notions of the pursuit of Truth as the primary function of the university are vitiated in some small degree by this conception of a modern education, the ideal of the examined life is not. Without impairing other academic goals, it refocuses academic energies on the realm of normative judgment and the problem of how all of us, not just the young, can acquire more skill and greater insight in dealing with those questions of morality, politics, and spiritual growth which, like the Queries of the Quakers, may have no definitive answers but about which it is humanly fatal to stop thinking.

In his *Point Counter Point,* Aldous Huxley forty years ago made one of his protagonists argue that barbarism consists in an imbalance of the inherent qualities of humanity—that there could be barbarians of the emotions and of the spirit as well as of the intellect, and that all were equally threatening to the tissues of civilized life. The point applies to the present situation in the college curriculum. There are too many factors now at work that at least permit to run unchecked a disposition to emotional and spiritual barbarism while the intellect alone is being cultivated. In that direction lie antiquarianism and the brutalities of technological creativity unrestrained by humane values and normative commitments of a generous and humanly concerned sort.

The Nihilistic Cadre

Such concerns, interacting with the war in Vietnam, the grave issue of racial injustice, and other serious rents in our social fabric, provide a backdrop for that extremely small but influential cadre of students who are essentially nihilistic in outlook, anarchistic in ideology, and convinced that the American "system," because of its corruption, must be destroyed as a prerequisite to the building of something more humane, generous, and decently productive. What that "something" may be is not necessarily their responsibility to define; their self-appointed job is simply that of tearing down the diseased structure to make way for the better day which others will design. It is true, in general, that this tiny faction within our student population has almost as little intrinsic appeal to peers as to the official personnel of our colleges and universities. Nevertheless, those who compose it have nerve; they have studied with care the guerrilla methods of such revolutionaries as Mao Tse-tung, Che Guevara, Ho Chi Minh, and others; and often through committed and dangerous participation in civil rights drives through the South, they have acquired a genuine skill in the tactics of disruption and have reflected seriously on this experience and its applicability with suitable modifications to the academy as "the enemy." As they interpret history and their own backgrounds, they regard the appeals of reason and the processes of dialogue as obstructionist devices, employed by the Establishment to prevent action and to dissipate the energies of those who would remake the world. Essentially unimportant by themselves, the nihilists gain significant power when they can make common cause with other student groups, all of them more numerous than their own.

Such coalitions have tended to form, for the most part, under one or more of four primary conditions. One is when a persuasive case—sometimes more apparent than accurate, sometimes based in unfortunate fact—can be made that administrative leaders or faculty bodies have been unresponsive to student expressions of concern. Responsiveness in this context does not necessarily mean wishy-washyness or a tendency to accept student recommendations simply because they are made; it does imply a willingness to listen, really to hear what is said, and either to entertain and act upon the possibility of changes in directions resembling those advocated or to reject the request on the basis of explicitly given reasons. Firm but well and fully explained refusals, given publicly, seem better calculated on the whole to inhibit the joining of student resources than does official silence, a failure to understand the communications of students, or verbal acceptance with no subsequent modifications in policy or procedure. These latter administrative reactions are often perceived as subtle forms of violence and evoke an anger similar to that elicited by a literal blow.

A second condition for the formation of coalitions seems to be fulfilled when students become convinced that they are inappropriately excluded from participating in the making of decisions which affect their personal conduct, their off-campus behavior as citizens, or the expression of their political or moral opinions. The regulations finally adopted seem far less important than the *process* of student participation in the generation of rules and policies. The implications here, of course, are that student involvement must be widely understood and appreciated, that it must be meaningful rather than *pro forma,* and that it must be continuous.

The third condition seems to rest on demonstrations that the college or university has been guilty of some actual "injustice." Contracts to conduct classified war-related research, official initiative in bringing a government spokesman to the campus to discuss the war in Vietnam, the admission of too few Negro students, and a number of other familiar matters can fall under this heading. Although one can argue that such charges are often unfair or neglectful of the complexity of the issues involved, such arguments are essentially beside the point in the present context. Universities that would minimize the perils of disruptive tactics would do well to remember that any policies touching on the issues associated with Vietnam or on race relations must either be carefully rationalized and explained, involve the participation of students in their formation, be explicitly balanced by some clearly offsetting factor, or be reduced in their touchiness by some combination of these possibilities. This observation does *not* imply that the authority for institutional decisions must be given over to students; it does mean that the nihilistic element has a greater opportunity to develop supportive constituencies if decisions of these kinds are not given legitimacy through adequate discussion and involvement.

Finally, anarchist tacticians gain a great deal of support among their peers when one or more of their number achieves some form of martyrdom. Suspension or expulsion from the institution on less than clearly justifiable grounds, arrests (particularly under conditions in which physical force is used) by the police, and disciplinary actions that have the appearance of arbitrariness are all dangerous in this respect. Other students, having at best only minor sympathy for the style or objectives of the nihilist, can be rallied around him readily if they can be induced to believe that he has been wronged in the sense outlined here.

A Taxonomy and Its Strategic Implications

What is the nature of these other campus groups whom anarchists can rally to their support, thereby gaining the strength they otherwise, in their extremely small numbers, lack? Given the diversity and rapidly changing composition of contemporary enrollments, a taxonomy of students is very difficult to devise, not least because it probably would go rapidly out of date. Nevertheless, there are some points that can be made, at least in general terms, with reasonable assurance. We know, for instance, that the great majority of students are conventionally motivated, not usually concerned in socially conscious ways about the searing issues of the day, reasonably respectful of traditional authority, and essentially privatistic in their values and outlook. Right-wing extremists among students, although hardly non-existent, are small in numbers, not particularly vocal, and incapable of commanding much of a following. Conservatives, like those represented by the Young Americans for Freedom, enjoy a greater numerical strength even though they are still a small minority; they tend to be quiet in their style, and they have a disposition to work through regular channels. Nevertheless, it is noteworthy that they share with their peers on the Left an interest in student power, and they have worked hard on some campuses for a higher degree of involvement by students in the decision-making processes of the institution. There is a large group of liberal students, eager to reform the "system" but to keep its basic structure intact and its fundamental procedures in working order; and there is a smaller but growing body of radicals, marked by an activist style, an emphasis on welfare values, and a willingness to form alliances with any like-minded group on particular issues.

Because the radicals will cooperate with virtually anyone on an issue-by-issue basis, because they believe that "anti-communism is an insufficient basis for policy," they can easily be perceived on some occasions as either in the employ of communists or the dupes of some communist-like conspiracy. As is the case with nihilists, however, it is extremely difficult to find any evidence to support a conspiratorial theory of student unrest. Even in the case of SNCC and other Black Power groups, there is little to suggest a mastermind at work or some central direction to a tightly organized and disciplined scheme to overthrow the Establishment on a grand scale.

Instead, what seems to be the case is a loose network of individuals and groups, maintained by extensive round-robin correspondence and the shoestring publication of such newspapers as *New Left Notes, Liberator,* and the *Guardian,* all based on a common discontent with some of the seamier aspects of American life, especially with our foreign policies and our manifold forms of racial injustice. If one reads their literature and bothers to talk at length and to develop relationships of reasonable trust with their representatives, one finds that the leaders of SDS, the United Christian Movement, and some of the Negro groups are remarkably frank about their goals, their plans, and the means by which they hope to achieve the reforms and institutional transformations that they seek.

The central point is that, apart from the nihilists, the devices of discussion and dialogue and the processes of gradual change, provided that they are not too slow, are as congenial, with some exceptions, to radical student leaders as they are to liberals among the student ranks and on the faculties and administrative staffs of colleges and universities. So long as the radicals have an appropriate basis for believing that they are in meaningful and honest communication with influential professors and responsive administrative officers, they are unlikely to be successfully captured by the nihilists. Their willingness to form alliances with any likeminded group with respect to particular issues, however, means that they have no intrinsic objection to joining forces with anarchists; and whenever the conditions are fulfilled for the formation of such a coalition, the radicals, bringing a fair proportion of liberal students along with them, will rally under the banner of anarchistic champions. When such *ententes* are consummated, then particular institutions are likely to have some uneasy (or far worse) days.*

Selecting the Sites of Rebellion

As we ponder these reflections, it is well to remember our new problems of sheer scale and something about the backgrounds of experi-

---

* Negro student groups, like the Afro-American Students League or the Black Student Union, are in general far more precise in their objectives and disciplined in their style than their white radical counterparts; and although they can command a great deal of support from white students, they typically prefer to press their causes on their own. Despite several exceptions, their demands on colleges and universities have rarely challenged "the System"; rather, they have aimed at establishing a special place for themselves in it, and if their separatism often raises serious problems with respect to traditional ideas of civil rights and an integrated society, their background and their fight for ethnic pride frequently make their requirements surprisingly reasonable.

ence that a small but significant minority of students infuse into the college scene. With between seven and eight million young people enrolled, if we assume that the percentage of disappointed and disenchanted college youth reaches no more than 5 per cent—a quite conservative estimate—we find that they will still number between 350,-000 and 400,000. The meaning of these impressive figures becomes clearer if we simply distribute them over our nearly 2,400 institutions; on the average, such a procedure puts something like 145 to 165 potential sources of rebellion on every campus. Before examining the implications of their *not* being distributed in such a regular fashion, a parenthetical reminder may be in order: Our *quantitative* growth in higher education may have been so great as to produce genuine *qualitative* changes; and these changes are sometimes difficult to grasp and to evaluate most usefully in relation to those alterations that may be called for in our institutional policies and in the address of colleges and universities to their administration of student affairs.

It appears that a process of self-selection operates to produce a clustering of rebellious activists on a relatively small proportion of campuses although data to substantiate such a hypothesis are not yet available. There are significant indications, however, that the institutions where activists are visibly influential are colleges and universities known for at least a degree of liberalism and the additional characteristics of less restrictive parietal rules, traditions of vigorous support of academic freedom and sources of outspoken student and faculty criticisms of the nation's political, social, and economic life. A preliminary report of data now being collected by the American Council on Education indicates that freshmen's personal values and political views compare favorably with the institutional characteristics of the college they enter; more significantly the preliminary report strongly suggests that entering freshmen of institutions having considerable protest have political and social views which are identified with student dissent.

It is suggested that perceptive, bright youngsters in whom the rebellious impulse is active move, in the main, toward those institutions in which the opportunity for rebellion appears largest. If one thoughtfully calls the role—Berkeley, Columbia, Wisconsin, Iowa, Duke, Swarthmore, Michigan, Oberlin, and so on down a long list—one finds a high proportion of universities and colleges in which the probability is high that (a) the institutions will be profoundly reluctant to muzzle expressions of critical dissent despite offenses against the usual canons of taste, (b) some small but influential segment of the faculty will legitimize student protest of several kinds, (c) there is a relatively large body of students (and a much smaller one of professors) who, although unlikely to initiate demonstrations or confrontations, have sympathies that can readily be engaged with respect to certain key issues, and (d) there is a tradition of at least some minimum of student autonomy in such enterprises as the editing of the college newspaper, the operating of political organizations on campus, the bringing of guest speakers to the university community, etc. Given such a base from which to move, clever rebels can readily find a cause, capitalizing on some of the sources of frustration that have been previously outlined here as a way of building up adherents. In short, activist students tend to choose the more liberal institutions for the straightforward reason that they are more permissive toward critical spirits. Thus, there is no more surprise in the concentration of protest on more "open" campuses than there is in the French Revolution's occurring in France rather than eighteenth-century Bulgaria. The conditions of revolt—freer play for the dissenting voice, a larger body of people sympathetically informed about perceived injustices or frustrations, a modicum of support within the power structure, some reasonable probability of reinforcing successes, etc.—are better fulfilled there, and a significant proportion of contemporary young people are well aware of it.

Past the Point of No Return

At least two conclusions seem hard to avoid. One is that the phenomena of student activism are likely to remain as a long-term influence in the affairs of higher education; the other is that the varieties of social control that could once be comfortably exercised in our colleges and universities have probably lost their validity. Increased numbers and a sharply increased diversity of students, the dynamics of corporate solidarity among them, changes in the sociolegal bases of their relationship to their institutions, and alterations in adolescent growth patterns in the directions of more advanced maturity and increased knowledge are all trends quite improbable of reversal, and they all are strong determinants of the disruptive winds blowing through college corridors. In consequence, there is real danger in the still detectable tendency to look upon student unrest as we have experienced it on the road from Berkeley past Columbia as a kind of variant on old-style youthful high-jinks, rather more virulent but belonging essentially to the same category as panty raids or installing a cow in the chapel bell tower. It seems far more probable that we have turned a real and abrupt corner so far as the fundamental characteristics of students and their relationships to the university are concerned, and educational policies and practices will have to take account of that turning for a long time to come.

The point is italicized by reference to the old complex of rules and sanctions by which order has historically been maintained in the American academy. The utility of these instruments of control was closely bound up with the relatively homogeneous aspirations and conventional values of a relatively homogeneous student body. Fulfilling the obligations of membership in an elitist family or coming massively from ambitious and upwardly mobile middle-class homes, youngsters were willing, for the most part, to strive more uncomplainingly for the credential signified by the baccalaureate degree and to accept an essentially deferential role in relation to their elders as part of the *rites de passage* of winning a more or less favored and well remunerated place for themselves in the adult world. Under today's circumstances, the old deterrents to disruption are far less persuasive for far larger proportions (and therefore for gigantically increased absolute numbers) of students. A large segment of the Negro student population, for instance, feels that, with little to lose, considerable risks can be invested in the assertion of grievances, needs, and rights. A highly significant although hard-to-determine portion of other students, born to reasonable affluence and reliably backed—at least financially and in moments of personal crisis—by their parents, find little ground for surrendering their autonomy, for inhibiting the expression of their most serious concerns, or for conforming to what they perceive as irrelevant academic demands and the neglect of grave threats to our civilization simply for a degree that would serve as their ticket to a job with General Motors or the federal government. In addition, there is some strong evidence that large numbers of youth enroll in college with idealistic and even romantic expectancies of intellectual stimulation and an opportunity to win an effective and meaningful grasp on what they regard as the planet's major problems. When these expectancies are disappointed without the provision of acceptable outlets for sublimated fulfillment, the result is once again frustration and the increased probability of hostility and aggression that frustration breeds.

In any event, the climate of protest on the American campus is likely to be more marked by thunder and lightning if our colleges and universities fail to respond more rapidly and more extensively to the changed and changing character of their basic clientele, to the philosophical, political, and moral questions that students now seriously propound, and to the educational issues that they and our disjunctive time give rise to. The fundamental conditions of that climate are profound; and whatever its rights and wrongs, its phenomena are not evanescent. In coping constructively with them, we may extensively remodel our houses of higher learning so that they may remain true to their ancient functions of nourishing the values of civilization and fusing the power of cultivated intellect with the freed aspirations of the human spirit.

INDEX